MY LEBANESE ANCESTORS

THE HISTORY OF
BCHAALEH AND SALIMA,
LEBANON

This book contains the history of these two villages. It portrays some of their ancient and modern families including some of those who moved away. The book reports some actual, written, original documents along with background information which has been handed down by earlier generations in their oral traditions. All these reveal the true history of these families. It also passes on this heritage to their descendants who now live throughout the world from Egypt to Brazil, Australia to the United States of America and many places in between.

By Father Stephen Bachaalany

Translation Team Leader Paul Knieser

1947

Original Edition Printed by
FADIL AND DZHAMIL -AD-DAURA.
First English Translation Edition
Translation Team Led by Paul Knieser
Olean, New York   USA
2004

© Paul Knieser, All Rights Reserved
Olean, NY USA 2006
Orlando, FL 2017
Third Edition Revised
Translation Editorial Team:
Sarah E. Knieser, Nigel Knieser
Abe Knieser, Sarah (Missy) Knieser
Ruby Knieser, and John (Jack) Knieser

Publisher: tradition, Hamburg, Germany

Dedication:

As the team leader, I find it necessary to acknowledge each of the following:

First and foremost: to my wife, Sarah, without whom this translation would not have been completed. Her support in so many ways was essential. She brought the fullness of life when she entered my world.

And, To my children, whom I love so dearly, may they appreciate the lives of so many people who have anonymously contributed to their lives!

Now, and, hopefully, forever, at least a few of those ancestors, along with our children, will have names and recognition as their lives continue to live down through the ages:

Paul, Jr., Nigel, Abraham, Sarah (Missy), Ruby, and Jack (John).

Copyright © 2017 Paul Knieser

Editor: Paul Knieser

Translation Team Leader: Paul Knieser

Publisher: tredition, Hamburg, Germany

ISBN
Paperback: 978-3-7323-8862-2
Hardcover: 978-3-7323-8863-9
eBook: 978-3-7323-8864-6

Printed on demand in many countries

All rights reserved. No part of this publication may be reproduced, distributed, or transmitted in any form or by any means, including photocopying, recording, or other electronic or mechanical methods, without the prior written permission of the publisher, except in the case of brief quotations embodied in critical reviews and certain other noncommercial uses permitted by copyright law. For permission requests, write to the publisher.

CONTENTS

	Page
Contents	5
Introduction to the English Edition	11
Preface	15

Section 1: Bchaaleh And Its Families

Chapter 1:	Its History	17
Chapter 2:	The History Of The Lebanese Families	23
Chapter 3:	The Bshe'lani (Bachaalany) Families	27

Section 2: Abu Rezk Bachaalany

Chapter 1:	The Situation At His Time	35
Chapter 2:	The Story Of Abu Rezk	37
Chapter 3:	The Sons Of Abu Rezk	41
Chapter 4:	Prince Younes And His Martyrdom	45
Chapter 5:	Tripoli And Its Ties With Younes.	51
Chapter 6:	King Of France And Bachaalany Family	57
Chapter 7:	From France To Lebanon	61
Chapter 8:	From Kisrawan To Salima	63

Section 3: Salima And Its History

Chapter 1:	Its Description, History And Vestiges	65
Chapter 2:	The Church Of Saint John The Baptist	73
Chapter 3:	The Church Of Our Lady Of Deliverance	81
Chapter 4:	The Church And Monastery Of Saint Peter	85
Chapter 5:	The Church Of Saint Anthony	101

Chapter 6:	The Church Of Saint Elias	105
Chapter 7:	The Church Of The Lady Of The Castle And Our Lady Of Lourdes	107
Chapter 8:	Assembly Hall Of The Druzes	109
Chapter 9:	Schools Of The Capuchin Fathers	111
Chapter 10:	Public And Private Schools	125
Chapter 11:	Brotherhoods And Associations	129
Chapter 12:	Manners, Traditions And Social Conditions	135
Chapter 13:	Courageous, Famous And Down-To-Earth	153
Chapter 14:	About The Immigrants And The Expatriates	159
Chapter 15:	Spiritual And Scientific Leaders	163
Chapter 16:	Facts, Events and Tales	181

Section Four: History Of The Families Of Salima   193

Chapter 1:	The House of Abi Al Lam'	195
Chapter 2:	The House Of The Bachaalany	211

Abou Youssef; Neama; Abou 'Oql;
Abou 'Oun Al Abbssy; Abou Attallah;
Al Qassouf; Karam; Nassrallah Al Mazmouk
Al Erian; Nohra Soyad; Ghatas Aboud;
Al Zaghloul; Wahba; Bou Heriz; Atia;
Bou Saber; Al Karargy; Al Shamrawy;
Metri Al Sayeg

Chapter 3:	Zein House	303
Chapter 4:	The Asmar House	311
Chapter 5:	The Nakouzy House	313

Al Khoury; Aba Safi; Aba Tarbea;

Abou Eissa; Moussa Daher;
Abou Mhaya Saad Ghayad; Abdel Hay;
Kenaan Abou Nasar Hanna Bin Tanious;
Al Hadany; Sahyoun; Al Honoud;
Al Shahrouny; Eishy; Abou Saqr.

Chapter 6: The Anton House   327

Chapter 7: The Maronite Families And Count Tarazi   333

Chapter 8: The Kassab House   337

Chapter 9: The Khawaja House   341

Al Hada; Bshour; El Tafkagy; Bou Mikhail

Chapter 10: The S'eid House   351

Chapter 11: The Masry House   355
The Families Who Joined The Al Masry
Folks In The Past; The Families Who
Joined The Al Masry Folks Recently;
Mohamed House; Al Siqly House.

Chapter 12: The Expatriates From Salima   363

The Expatriate Citizens Of Salima;
List Of The Expatriates From
Salima In Brazil - The Year Of
Their Migration And Death

Section Five: Families Emerging From Bchaaleh   375

Chapter 1: The Moubarak House   377

Moubarak House In Baqatouta;
In Baqaata; In Kafrteya,
Al Sheyah And Beskinta .
Moubarak House In Rashmeya;
In Al Nadra & Egypt;
In Bdadoun & Al Betroun

7

Chapter 2:   The Khoury House   387

Chapter 3:   The Saad House   391

Chapter 4:   The Habqouq House   395

Chapter 5:   The Harfoush House   397

Chapter 6:   The Abi Rashed House   399

Chapter 7:   The Gibran House   401

Chapter 8:   The Qash'amy And Abi Nakd House   403

Chapter 9:   The Abi Eissa And Meshleb House   405

Chapter 10:   The Jabour, Mel'eb And Shahwan House   407

Section Six: Present Families Of Bchaaleh   **409**

Abou Rezk, Al Shediak & Abou Marq House; Maroune House; Shedid House; Abou Mansour House; Nassar House; Al Eishy House; Wahba House; Abou Olwan House; Alk Hany House; Al Helew House; Mehana House; Faisal Al Shediak House; Abou Barakat House; Al Geagea Al Shalfoun House; Areef House; Saqr House; Father Boutros House; Fares Ibrahim House; Dagher House

Annex   **431**

-- Story Of Prince Younes The Maronite (From The Original   French)   431

-- D.O.M Stephanus Pertus (From The Original Latin)   435

-- List Of The Attached Pictures   437
    (A photo of Anthony Bachaalany has been added for this edition.)

-- Main Events Of The Author's Life And The Publication Of This Book   439

-- The People Who Helped And Cooperated   439

-- The History Of The Maronite Families   440

-- An Added Personal Letter About Salima's Fate.
    (An addition to the Original Arabic Edition.)   440

-- Photographs   443

--A Sample Genealogy   456

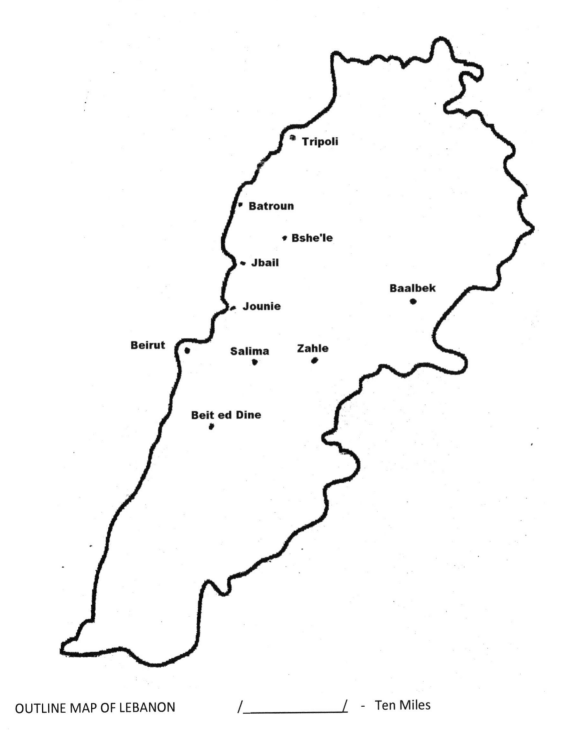

OUTLINE MAP OF LEBANON /_____/ - Ten Miles

10

INTRODUCTION TO THE ENGLISH EDITION

I must begin the Introduction to this Third Edition with an explanation for the difference in its subtitle and other spelling differences from the previous editions. When I was working on the original translation manuscripts before 2004 there was an international attempt to adopt a universal spelling for place names throughout the world. At that time it appeared that "Bshe'le" was going to be the accepted standard. Even today, in 2017, there are some internet places that still use that spelling. However, since 2004, with the dominance of internet giants like Google and Wikipedia and others, the spellings that they have selected for places have become the standards. In many cases, Google and others will also point out the various spellings in use. So in keeping with this trend I have used the Google spelling for Bchaaleh as the standard. Many Lebanese relatives of mine seem to like this change. Also, for the main group of people from Bchaaleh, who are the basis for most of the book, we have changed their spelling from Beshelany to Bachaalany. Those who still carry the Bachaalany name today are in the majority with that spelling. However, bear in mind that there are still many who use their special adopted spelling which ranges from Bishallany, used by Anthony Bishallany, the first Lebanese immigrant to the US, to those using Machaalany and dozens of Bachaalany variations.

Now, on to other thoughts about my many decades of work on this history.

Very simply, working on this translation has been a delightful journey of adventure. I have met ancestors and distant relations who lived hundreds of years ago. Now, over the years, I am able to introduce them to my children and hundreds of thousands, if not millions, of other descendants.

I have worked on this over a span of more than thirty years. However, the intensive effort to complete the translation has occurred over the last few years. I have spent thousands of dollars to bring this to a conclusion. I refuse to even think about the number of hours I have devoted to this.

Lest some one think, for a moment, that I am some skilled translator fluent in Arabic and other languages, I wish to set the record straight immediately. Others far more knowledgeable than I have done the real work. I have been the one privleged to polish this final version. Translators from Lebanon to Egypt to Russia have all been involved in this version. As the final editor, I must take the ultimate responsibility for the version you now read in print. I am hopeful that it is totally without error. Should some reader doubt the truth of the translation or have some question relating to the content, please, contact me. I am hoping that there will be a future edition that will be even better than this one; perhaps, with color illustrations of the places and people mentioned so often in the book.

The story of this translation is, in itself, a tale almost too strange to be believed. So many incidents and developments from my life have come together in this project. Yet, as those events occurred, it was impossible to see the role that they would come to play in making this book a reality.

Let me cite a couple of examples. On a trip to Lebanon in 1968, I visited Salima in an effort to contact any distant relatives. The first person I encountered was an old man in the town square. We asked if he knew of any relatives in town of Nejm Knieser, who had left in 1895. We explained that I was his grandson. The old man slowly pulled out his tattered wallet and produced a very old newspaper clipping. To my surprise, it was the obituary of my grandfather from the Olean Times Herald of 1922. The old man explained that he had grown up with my grandfather. After Nejm emigrated to the United States, he used to send money and magazines, etc. to him. Someone in Olean had sent him the obituary and he had carried it with him ever since! He then led us to the house of Michel Bechaalaney, a distant cousin, and our story of this unfolding quest in geneology became much more serious.

The Arabic names and words heard as a child began to make sense as this project developed. The broken English and improper grammar used by those immigrants was encountered again in many original texts of this book translated by Middle Easterners of today, and, they made sense!

From my earlier experiences of working in a library, a book bindery, writing and publishing a scuba diving magazine, not to mention 30 years of teaching history, all helped to make this task easier than it might have otherwise been.

And, even now, events occur which might be called coincidence, but which are so incredible that one must wonder if some invisible force is causing events to unfold. As an example, I can say that even though I wanted to get this latest edition in print, I was often side tracked with our family's move to Florida in 2016. However, our rented home as I write this, is owned by a Brazilian woman, Andrea, who lives in Belo Horizonte where some of the relatives in this book actually moved to and settled. Also her first name, Andrea, is the same as the name of one of my direct ancestors. And when our family first stayed at her house was the first time that I noticed that the first letter from our first four children, in their birth order, Nigel, Abraham, Sarah, and Ruby, spell the name of our family's earliest named ancestor, Nasr! And it was while staying in Florida in early 2017 that we encountered a publisher's offer that would get us back in print with maximum speed and minimal cost. And so it is that this latest edition came to be. All this while staying in the home we rent from the lovely Andrea Silveira Miranda Silva. I should also mention that she lives only two hours away from Oliveira where so many Lebanese from Salima settled that for a while they called it the Second Salima! There just seem to be so many invisible threads that connect us in this life, whether we realize it or not. To quote Andrea in one of her email's: "How life is interesting". She has even offered to go to Oliveira together if I can just get to Brazil. Time will tell!

Now, let me make a couple of points that will make it easier for the reader to comprehend the names and places discussed. I MUST EMPHASIZE THIS POINT: the names and places in this book have no single, accepted spelling. In so many languages there is one way to spell a word, and that is that. A letter out of place or substituted makes it a wrong word. In the style of Arabic used in this book, the vowels are, for the most part, left out. The understanding was that an intelligent reader would know what the word was. For the translators, this sometimes made the task extremely difficult. I personally spent hours trying to locate a single village by first trying to determine an acceptible spelling. For many names, especially of villages, I found French words that corresponded with the Arabic names. This task was complicated even more when discussing the names of individual people, families, "Houses", etc.. To give but one example, the name of the main family of the book, the Bachaalany family has many different spellings. Some of the various spellings of just this one family name include: Bachaalany, Bechaalany, Bishalaney, Beshalany, Bishallany, Bichalani, Bachaalany, and Bshe'lani. That is, by no means, a complete list. The name Knieser, I am told, has dozens of spelling variations.

Also, don't hesitate to use your computer and Google similarly spelled names. For example, the district of "Kisrawan" that is often mentioned here is currently spelled "Keseran" by the Lebanese and their postal division. It is spelled "Kesrouan" in Wikipedia, so you can see how confusion and research problems still exist. Salima, in the past, was often cited as belonging to the El Metn region but today is in the Baabda. Today Lebanon is divided into eight governates which are subdivided into 26 districts. The boundaries today are not what they often were in the past.

To further complicate things for the reader who has little or no acquaintance with specifics of the Arabic language or the use of names, some words have been left in for a bit of flavor for the way the language is actually used. For example, many men were referred to with the name Abu (or Abou, Abi), which means "a father". It probably best corresponds to an Englishman being referred to as "Sir". It isn't part of the persons name but it keeps showing up, sort of a casual reference showing respect. We also left in the word "Mar" meaning "Saint" in many lines since it was often coupled with an Arabic or Syriac Saint's name. "Bin" and "Al" are two other words sometimes left in. "Bin" means "the son of" and it very often appears in the series of names indicating an ongoing son to father to grandfather, etc. relationship, and, also, often giving the person's most recent name. "Bint" means "the daughter of". "Al" simply means "the" but was often used in the person's name to indicate with a bit of emphasis that the person belonged to that House (or clan, family). Thus, Tanious Bin Khatar Bin Boutros Abou Tarbeiz Al Nakouzy, as it appears in this book, should read Tanious the son of Khatar who was the son of Boutros from his father Tarbeiz, the Nakouzy (House). So in that one name you have at least five generations named! By the way, do not confuse the name Khoury which means Father as in priest. One must remember that married men in the Maronite Catholic Church are allowed to become ordained priest, an ancient practise that continues today, in Lebanon. So Khoury may simply point out that the person was a priest, or it could be the family's name that became established because some ancestor was a priest.

A very important rule to remember when reading the names in this book, especially if you are trying to locate a possible ancestor who might have spelled their name different, remember, PLEASE REMEMBER, pronouce the word. **Say it aloud, if necessary.** You may suddenly understand that the name is, in fact, the one you were looking for. As an example, the famous Lebanese born poet who became extremely popular in the United States was Khalil Gibran, sometimes called Gibran Khalil Gibran. In the first draft of this translation his name was spelled Jobran Khalil Jobran. In my first quick reading, I didn't recognize that this was, in fact, the famous author. But I kept saying it aloud and then it dawned on me. This was the case for many names. I knew people named Harris but their relatives in the book were spelled "Heriz".

To send me comments or questions about this book is to use the internet. You can reach me at the following email address: *pjxkebay@gmail.com.* I will do my best to be helpful if possible.

I have included a sample family tree for our most ancient known ancestors using my personal family. This is simply intended to be an example of how simply a tree can be made from the information in this book. I hope many readers will update their family tree and keep it with their copy of this book, allowing their descendants to see the connection to their more ancient ancestors in this book. This will personalize your copy by including the important names and pages that fit your family tree.

As an added item, for my Lebanese grandparents, Nejm and Anna Knieser, I analyzed their genetic dna as passed down from the male line and the female line. This was as a participant in the National Geographic's Genographic Project. The female line marker passed down to Anna is from an ancient ancestor who lived on the Lebanese coast 40,000 years ago. Nejm's male genetic trait comes from a man who probably lived in the Lebanon area 30,000 years ago. Both genetic indicators certainly seem to back up the oral traditions and claims in this book. It appears that our ancestors, indeed, have occupied the Lebanon area for tens of thousands of years!

Please note that the first recorded person for the Bachaalany group was a man named Nasr. We only know his name and the names of his two sons Rezk and Sa'b.

Throughout the book, Father Stephen Bachaalany continually refers to his multi-volume set <u>The History of the Maronite Families.</u> To this day, I still don't know if it was ever published. I suspect it was not. Also, I don't know the whereabouts of the many documents he cited in this book.

I ended the book with a letter I received many years ago from that special cousin I met decades ago in Salima. Sadly, the letter describes the destruction of much of Salima resulting from the invading Syrians. What a tragedy. Although there have been recent attempts to restore it, and the local Maronite Church has been reopened, there is still much repair work to be done. Many of Salima's earlier residents, our relatives, who lived there for centuries, have yet to return. Like so many places in the Middle East, Lebanon, is still a problem that has yet to find its solution. Now with the horrible destruction of the 2006 Israel-Hezbolah war in Lebanon, rebuilding will take many more years.

I would like to add one further item missing from the earlier editions. It was vaguely referred to by Father Bachaalaney when he talked about the old olive trees in Bchaaleh. Today you can read about them in Wikipedia and on their own web pages, The Sister Olive Trees, the Noah Trees. The trees, it seems, are much older than Father Bachaalany imagined. They may be 7000 years old! Since learning of them, I can only envision in my mind how many of our ancestors must have tended to those trees. How many consumed the olives, made oil, sat under them...even, as children, climbed them. It seems that our special family still occupies some special attributes that make us unique. Indeed, the places of our ancestors hold treasures for the whole world.

A special thanks must go to Mr. Al Beljaev of Vologda, Russia, who was my main contact for this translation. He was an acquaintance made through the eBay professionals services section. Without his assistance, this translation would not have been accomplished.

I also need to add a special thank you to Butch (Leon) Young of Olean, NY. For his time in proofreading, and, even more, for his shared enthusiasm in the search for ancestors. "Thank you, Butch!" Like all good people, Butch, you passed way too soon. I miss you.

Now to Father Bachaalany's history! Enjoy!   --Paul Knieser   --Kissimmee, Florida --March 30, 2017

PREFACE

I thank God for the interest which I have always had in the history of my family. I used to ask my late father and some other old men about the family's origins, importance, and the times of its dispersal throughout Lebanon and the world. This passion for the knowledge about my family increased as time went by. I developed my research techniques and increased my knowledge. I recorded everything I heard or read. I kept even the smallest detail. I wrote them all down. At first they were all disconnected since I knew nothing about the art of writing history or of recording stories.

Day after day, this love of history grew until it drove me to spend all of my time buying and reading history books, searching for documents and manuscripts, and, recording traditions and tales that had been told and retold down through the generations. After some time I had collected a large set of documents, texts, letters and manuscripts relating to the historical events of the past. This precious treasure was composed of true stories, proofs and testimonials, all revealing the social and religious conditions of our ancestors. At the same time, I also learned that tradition alone was not sufficient to write the accurate history of our people. Proofs, logical reasoning and true documents are necessary components of this task.

I have used these approaches to accomplish my scientific family research. I have used it to uncover the origins of the families, their different branches, and even filling in some missing links in the family chain, tying the families to their ancient roots. I was able to construct a complete lineage for many families, thus achieving a goal I had struggled to accomplish for a very long time. I have spent about fifty years working on this project.

It was only after I had gathered all this material, allowed my thoughts to ripen, checked on the validity of the material and my logic, that I decided to publish it. I was over seventy years old and feared that if I did not publish it now then it might be lost. I also wanted to avoid the criticism of future generations…the criticism that we level against out predecessors who allowed so much history to be lost because it was never recorded and published.

During the course of my research, I found documents about Youssef Beik Karam and the Lebanon situation. I wrote a chronicle of the events entitled: <u>Lebanon and Youssef Beik Karam</u>. It was published in 1925 and enthusiastically received, especially by the Lebanese emigrants.

When I had the chance I used to write articles for magazines and newspapers.

I also wrote a history of the Lama Princes (Omara' al-Lamay'een). I wrote a history of the Maronite Bishopic of Beirut. I also compiled a chronicle of the students of the Hikma College from 1875 to 1925. None of these have been published due to a lack of interest among our countrymen.

The work that I have completed which holds most of my research is a synthesis of all I have found and heard. It is <u>The History of the Maronite Families</u>. It is an encyclopedia like work where one can find the history and the origins of every Maronite family and its importance. The preface of that work is a summary of the history of the Lebanese Maronite community and an outline of the history of Lebanese families in general. That book will be printed in ten volumes, or, perhaps, summed up to take less space.

I decided to publish this history of my family first. I have been preparing it for a long time. It contains everything concerning the village of Bchaaleh, the land of my ancestors, and, Salima, the village to which my grandfathers migrated, and, where I was born. It includes the story of all of the families in these two towns whether old or new. This book is written in a modern, sophisticated style.

There are still many documents and information that I have been unable to include in this book. I am forced to be satisfied with a summary of these items or at least a reference to them in footnotes. I also want to apologize for publishing so little about some families. I had a difficult time finding material relating to them.

I hope this book will be a landmark to all my countrymen, and, especially, to the emigrants who have been among some of the most ardent supporters of our national resurgence. I hope, too, that it will be an example and incentive for our relatives and citizens to carry on such literary activities. In this way we can revive our national heritage and spread the history of our ancestors. A new generation can record their events and, at the same time, make immortal the memories of the old.

--Father Stephen Bachaalany
--Salima, Metn, Lebanon. August 15, 1947

BCHAALEH AND ITS FAMILIES

Section 1

ITS HISTORY

Chapter 1

Its History And Monuments. - Its Beauty. - Its Name. - Its Castle. - Its Monuments And Churches. - Our Lady. - Saint Stephan. – The Hermit (Al-Habees). - Saint Saba. - Saint Thomas. - Saint Sarkis. - Saint Risha. - Saint Doumit. - Religious Festivals. - Old Olive Trees. - From Its Stories. - Its People and Agriculture. - Its Industries. - The Immigrants.

Bchaaleh, to which all the Bachaalany (Bshe'lani or Bechelani, etc) families are related, is a beautiful town. It has high mountains, forests, a perfect location, pure water, fresh air, good soil and delicious fruits.

Its people were and always will be among the strongest, kindest, healthiest and the most brilliant. Heroes lived there. They took their mountains as a shelter and they left behind a castle, their customs, and their way of life.

Priests and hermits lived there too. They left many monuments…their monasteries and hermitages.

Bchaaleh produced many reputable and notable men of politics and science who made their impact on history. They include people like the Patriarch George Habquq (Habkouk) and Sheik Abu Rezk and his son Prince Younes.

Its name is most correctly written as Bchaaleh but some write it as Bshe'li. Also, I saw one of its old inhabitants write it as Bsho'le.

Most probably its name is an Aramaic Syriac name like the names of other places in Lebanon.

The "B" letter in its name signifies "the place" while the rest of the name signifies "Greatness and Highness".

Its name may be taken from "Beit Aile" which means "The House of God".

Some thought that it is Arabic, meaning "Flame of Fire" which in the old days used to signify the offering of sacrifices to the gods by burning, or as a way of announcing news through lighting fires as is still done today in Lebanon.

I don't agree with this latter explanation since the village was there long before the era of the Arabs.

The Crusaders called it "Betzaal", so some people thought that this village was a shrine of the God "Saturn". But it is most probable that the European Crusaders mistook this name as they did with so many other Middle Eastern names.

The most amazing thing in Bchaaleh is Qal'at al-Hesn, which is located on the northeastern side. It is a rocky hill that looks like a natural fortress. From a distance it looks like a mast.

Near it, there is the Monastery of St. James, a sanctuary of Lebanese monks.

If you stand in this castle, you can see a wonderful view: the sea and coasts from the west, the villages stretching till the regions of Cedar from the east, and wide plains from the north and south. There is only one path leading to this fortress which is the path from the direction of Bchaaleh, which was protected by the ancients so that no one could invade it unless he was able to pass through there.

One of Bchaaleh's monuments is the remains of a structure built in the Middle Ages on the remains of a castle built by the Phoenicians and destroyed later by Pompey, the Roman leader, when he conquered al-Sham (invading Damascus, the northern lands of the Arabian Peninsula) in 64 BC.

One of the wonders of this castle is a huge rock with a groove in the middle. It is like a mushroom surrounded by a man-made circular indentation which drains into a deep groove. Some said, that this rock was a Phoenician altar, where they offered their sacrifices to their gods.

To them, the rock was the symbol of the gods and the canal inscribed in the rock was for the passage of the blood of their sacrifices.

There is no mention of it in the Chronicles that I located.

The castle is about 350 meters long and 150 meters wide. Beneath it, there is a place known as The Midan (the arena, like a race course) which, I think, was used for horse racing, and beside it, cemeteries and sarcophagi where people have found money and rare documents. I saw there the remains of a tower with a sarcophagus beside it, which they say belonged to one of the greatest men of the castle. Inside the sarcophagus there is a great coffin covered with a truss. The coffin was lifted from its place for treasure hunting after the discovery of a small golden statue and old documents. It caused the spread of rumors about the presence of a buried treasure in the castle, which made the people of Bchaaleh start digging all over it.

I saw some of the money they found which consisted of Roman, Greek, and Phoenician coins. This shows that the area was controlled by the different governments of Tripoli, Rouad and other Phoenician kingdoms. This is the strongest evidence that proves how ancient Bchaaleh and its castle are.

Other evidence that proves the ancient existence of Bchaaleh is the presence of many churches and monasteries. These are signs of civilization and prosperity in agriculture. Wherever priests and monks built a church or a monastery, the place became inhabited with people who were prosperous through their knowledge and agricultural industry.

In Bchaaleh, there are nine religious sites: seven of them were most probably churches for the people who lived around them. The remains of their houses are still there today. The other two sites are large independent monasteries.

It is clear that our ancestors and monks were extremely active and industrious. Wherever they lived, they constructed marvels of architecture.

These nine religious sites were:

1, The Church of Our Lady-- It is an ancient small building built on a rock in the middle of Bchaaleh. The great Historian, El Douaihy mentioned it in his annals: "In 1626, the priest Youssef Habib (translated more literally as "Youssef, son of the priest Habib") demolished the church and turned it into a vault". This witty priest placed a stone with a faded writing on the top of the church's door. This writing is still there on the western side of the church's wall. The people kept it when they restored the church in the beginning of this century. This valuable faded writing cannot be read at all. It was most probably Syriac which was the language spoken and written by the Maronites until 1470.

Beside this church, to the north, is the grave of the priest Sama'an Toulaoui, from the Monks of Saint Anthony. He was also one of the students of the Maronite school in Rome.

He accompanied the Patriarch Estephan El-Douaihy to Rome (1659 AD) and was mentioned by Elias al-Chaziri in the poem that he wrote dedicated to the students of that school. The poem says:

> *"The priest Sama'an Thulany was a saint in the Monastery*
> *I want him to pray for me so that I can be saved from sins*
> *His grave is in Bchaaleh and still its walls are standing there*
> *In the Church of the Virgin, the Mother of kindness.*
> *He cures the sick. Pilgrims visit his grave. The aching sleep on it.*
> *Just one single day on it heals all illnesses*
> *God warned him of his death one day before;*
> *The priests of the village and the notables are witnesses of that.*
> *He was well known for his saintly demeanor and by his great humility.*
> *He kept his Order's rules faithfully: purity and chastity."*

We understand from these verses that the priest mentioned above, died in Bchaaleh and was buried near its church. He might have been either a monk in one of its two monasteries which were flourishing in those days, or, a hermit in the hermitage still known in Bchaaleh under the name of "al-Habees" (the Hermit). He was transferred after his death to the grave near Our Lady's Church mentioned above. We conclude from this that the priests in Bchaaleh were numerous. They still are today. There has always been a generous response to the calling of the priesthood.

2. The Church of Saint Stephen-- In the place of the present church, a small church once stood. In 1796 it was mentioned in a document of Gabriel al-Hani. This signifies that it is ancient. It is a beautiful, wide, well built church. It was restored in 1880 AD by a man from Choueir of the Ba'qalini (Ba'aklini) family. They were well known for their resoration skills. It has a beautiful hexagonal two-layered dome, with the most wonderful decorative drawings of the art of the late brothers: Michael, Tanous, Hanna and Khair Allah Doumit, who were among the most precise craftsmen in Bchaaleh. They built it like the Dome of the Church of Our Lady of Deliverence in Zahle.

This church has three altars and a picture of Saint Stephen, painted by the famous Italian painter Gosta (Juste). It also has luxurious furniture and elaborate decorations.

3. Saint Mama-- It is located in the lower part of the town. Its remains are only its wrecked walls and the picture of the Saint which is kept in the central parish church. It was painted by the painter Kanaan Dib from Dlebta in the middle of the last century. Also, beside the church there is a water well.

4. Al-Habees (The Hermit)-- It is a cave in a rock not far from the village known as al-Habees (The Hermit). It was most probably a home for some hermits. Perhaps the Priest Sama'an Toulaoui whom I mentioned above as being buried beside Our Lady's Church used to live in this hermitage. The people of Bchaaleh used to visit "The Hermit" whenever anyone became ill. They lit a candle inside the cave as is still the custom in Lebanon. There is mentioned in the writings of the Annals of El Douaihy the name of a hermit in the 16th century, from Bchaaleh, He was called the Priest, Hermit Sarkis, from the Habkouk family.

5. Saint Saba-- Nothing remains from this religious site but ruins. It is located far from the village..

6. The Monastery of Saint Thomas-- It is a thirty minute walk from Bchaaleh in the direction of Hadthoun. Only walls remain of it. It was an old Monastery. It has oak trees growing in the middle of it. Pilgrims come from many places to this shrine to be cured from ulcers and wounds.

7. The Monastery of Saint Sarkis (St. Serguis)-- This is a small sanctuary located to the west of the village. It fell into ruins but the family of the house of Sarkis Wahba (Wehbeh) from Bchaaleh restored it. It is the property of the family.

8. Saint Risha-- The people of Bchaaleh say that this was a nuns' convent. The walls still stand. The location of the building is very beautiful surrounded by tall oak trees.

9. The Monastery of Saint Doumit (Dumet)-- It is the largest and oldest religious site in Bchaaleh. It was built on the side of a hill overlooking the Mediterranean Sea. It is no wonder that the monks chose this site as a home. It is a beautiful location, surrounded by oak trees, fields and woods. All of this surely encouraged the monks to worship God and to pray to him night and day.

Only the church, a cave by its side, and a Byzantine-Syrian style flight of stairs which led from the church to the monastery, are still left from the whole building. Some sections of the walls still have some large pieces of columns, similar to those found in Jbeil (Byblos) and Batroun. Some restorations from the Middle Ages can be seen. On one of its columns to the right of the altar, there is a Greek inscription of the name of God. It is most probable that there was a fortress or a Christian church there. It was probably destroyed in the wars but was restored by the monks after the Maronite leaders brought peace to the mountains of Lebanon and made it a place of safety for Christian refugees.

The destruction of the monastery and the dispersion of its monks were probably due to the wars between Youssef Pasha Saifa and Prince Emir Fakhr al-Din (1621 AD) which led to the migration of many Maronites to Aleppo and Damascus in Syria. Religious leaders and monks were persecuted and there was an increase in banditry and famine in the country during the years of 1633 through 1638.

The Greek writing on the column in the worshipping place was probably the writing that Father Lamens, S.J. mentioned. He said he thought it to be the item searched for at Bchaaleh by the famous French traveler Renan who did not find it as he declared in his book.

This Greek writing was from the Roman era (64-635 AD). The church was restored in the later part of that period. Beside the monastery, there are very tall oak trees. They provided shade for the people when they gathered to celebrate the feast of Saint Doumit.

Also, there is a well filled with earth and a huge rock (part of the altar of the tabernacle) which some people said that a strong man from Bchaaleh once lifted with his bare hands.

Also there is a painting of Saint Doumit which was painted by Kanaan Dib from Dlebta.

The people still celebrate the feasts of these Saints today. They don't work on these days especially on the feast of Saint Doumit when they make a huge celebration on the 7th of August. The people of Bchaaleh and those of the neighboring villages attended this festival.

To each of these churches belong some plots of land that have been donated over the centuries by generous, wealthy and pious believers. Our ancestors were very religious and that is why so many churches and places of worship were built.

In Bchaaleh there are a few olive trees on the sides of its southern road. They most probably date back to the time of the Romans who conquered Lebanon in the early Christian era. They helped to improve agriculture in the area. These trees are very old and they still bear fruit today. (Editor's Note: These are the trees which today are known as the Sisters Trees or the Noah Olive Trees, actually 16 olive trees that some estimate to be up to 7000 years old. What a thought that these trees would have be witness to the lives of so many generations of our ancestors.)

It is said that there were many olive trees like this in Bchaaleh but most of them were destroyed during the long years of fighting between the Qais's (Kaissi or Qays) Party and the Yemen's (Yamani or Yaman) Party.

Most of the names of the places in Bchaaleh are Syriac in origin such as Mar Qafta, Bu'ran, 'Ain Mai Tuba, etc..

I found in the house of the deacon al-Shediaq (Shidiak), the Annals of the great historian El Douaihy written in Karchouni. It was owned by the priest Antoun, one of the deacon's grandfathers, who used to live in Tripoli and whose family originally came from Akkoura.

Bchaaleh in the time of the rule of the "Mutassarifiah" ("Mutasarrifiyya", according to Google's most accepted spelling) was a village that belonged to the Tnourine (Tannurin) district, the Batroun province. The number of electors in Bchaaleh was about 280 and the number of inhabitants was about 850. It lost a large number of its inhabitants in World War I. It is 1300 meters above sea level, with a fertile soil where most of our country's crops are planted. Although it has little water, its crops are much better than other lands where water is abundant because of the fertility of its soil. It has different kinds of fruits like apples, peaches, pears, figs and grapes. Its grapes are considered among the best in the country, and they are stored until December and sold in Tripoli and Batroun at the highest prices. Its wheat is no less than its grapes, due to the care given to it by its people. In the third place comes the olive crop. There are also oak trees, which are used as fuel for heating in the winter.

In spite of the fact that Bchaaleh is an agricultural village with some textile weaving, it has begun to adopt some of the latest industrial and modern arts. Thus, some local people have become skilled in construction, wood working and other skills. Others became good in trading. Still others became good in science.

But, in spite of all this, Bchaaleh is still by and large an agricultural village. Its women used to weave national textiles like bed sheets, and silk and cotton shirts. However these industries have become extinct today.

In the area of immigration, Bchaaleh has had a large share since many of its inhabitants migrated. Some moved to Egypt at the end of the last century. Then they migrated to America, Africa, and other places. They established an association in Los Angeles in the United States. This association has made very important contributions to the country.

I will speak about this subject later.

THE HISTORY OF THE LEBANESE FAMILIES

Chapter 2

The History Of The Lebanese Families. - The Changes In The Family Names. - The Loss Of Knowledge About Family Origins (Ancestry). - Lebanese Origins. - The History Of Lebanon. - Its People And Their Races. - The Maronites.

Before I speak about the history of the families of Bchaaleh, I would like to start with an introduction about the history of the Lebanese families and their origins. This is taken from my unabridged book: <u>The History of the Maronite Families,</u>

It's well known to people acquainted with the history of Lebanese families that it is full of ambiguity and misunderstandings. Many illusions and superstitions have been linked to the origins and descent of these families.

There are no trustworthy resources and one cannot rely on the oral traditions carried on from generation to generation.

Also, there are no general or special dates to refer to and no handwritten vestiges revealing the truth about the origin of each family. There are a few noble families whose stories have been recorded by historians. In rare cases there are some families who are mentioned in different reliable sources or who are mentioned in connection with some general dates.

The remaining references are just various sayings and personal manuscripts that are of no great use to the researcher unless he has a wide knowledge and the wits and the ability to distinguish between the genuine and the fake, the useful and the useless.

The most important reasons for explaining how so many Lebanese families' histories were lost is that disasters happened. The stories of how families were dispersed and relocated were often lost because of horrible wars and conflicts. These calamities hit eastern Lebanon in particular, especially the Maronites.

The last major disaster to occur was the departure of the Crusaders from Lebanon. The destruction of Kisrawan in the year 1307 forced its inhabitants to migrate to the north.

The Maronites inhabited the region between the Ibrahim (Abraham) River and Al-Bared River up to the time when the Ottoman Sultan Selim I seized Bilad al-Sham (the northern lands of the Arabian peninsula) in the beginning of the 16th century.

The Sultan brought security to Lebanon. He treated Lebanon's ruling princes kindly and Kisrawan again became full of Maronites and others in the reign of the Assaf princes.

The Maronites started to gradually migrate to the cities of Metn, Chouf, and Jezzine especially during the period of Fakhr al-Din.

These continuing migrations caused the weakening of the sense of family belonging. Also the loss of the origins of the Lebanese families occurred, thus many family names were mixed up.

23

Some families were named after the village they migrated to such as "al-Hasruni","al-Hadthuni", "al-Kafuri", " al-Tarabulsi", and "Ada".

Some were named after the name of the great grandfather who migrated to the village such as "Rezk", "Bakhus", "Estephan", and "'Oan".

Some were named after their profession, such as "al-Haddad" (The Blacksmith), "al-Sayegh" (The Jeweler), "al-Khayyat" (Tailor), "al-Farran" (Baker), "al-Ashei", "al-Shediaq", and "al-Khouri" (The Priest).

Some were named after an event or a characteristic related to their grand father such as "al-Baz", "Thib", "Ghanem", and "al-Shamali"

These new families' names were the reason for the loss of knowledge about many family origins in Lebanon.

The only thing that was left is what families inherited from their ancestors and the stories that people tell to one another. Many of these tales are doubtful or confusing due to the similarities between many family names and the surnames in many families.

For example: the names "Khuri", "Haddad", "Rezk", and "Karam" are names for many families who are totally unrelated to each other.

Thus, the researcher of the origins of the Lebanese should be accurate, patient, and have the ability to distinguish the contradictory stories.

One of the most difficult things for any historian to know is the truth about the origins of the Lebanese. There are so many unsubstantiated allegations and so many variations in the stories that are told.

This one claims that the Lebanese come from an Arabic origin; that one: Phoenician origin; others: of the Crusaders' blood or Greek blood, not to mention the Syrian Aramaic, Kurdish, Persian, and Ethiopian origins!

Thus, we must stay with the tried and true methods of the researcher, and, especially, the new researchers. They are able to add to the knowledge of the old historians due to the new views based on extrapolation and careful examination of monuments and manuscripts. The findings of these new researchers can be summarized as follows: Most of the areas of Lebanon were inhabited before the dawn of history. Lebanon was first mentioned 2800 years before Christ. In those ancient days the Babylonian ruler Sargon (Serjun) came (ca. 2450 B.C.), and other kings of Babel. And the Sumerians came to fish and to get wood and rocks for building their temples and palaces.

In the year 1200 BC, Tiglath, the Assyrian, mentioned that he hunted an elephant in Lebanon. Also, there were cuneiform inscriptions of the Assyrians and the Babylonians on the rocks of Nahr al-Kalb (the Dog River).

The clearest of these inscriptions were those of King Nebuchadnezzar, the Chaldean conqueror. Also, the ancient Egyptian, Thutmose (1500 BC) mentioned Lebanon and its fruits and wines in his hieroglyphic writings. And Ramses, the Egyptian Pharaoh, conquered Lebanon as is clear from the writings of Nahr al-Kalb (the Dog River) stone writings.

The inhabitants of Lebanon were Aramaic and Phoenician Canaanites.

It used to be held that the Phoenician history in Lebanon dated back to 2000 BC. Modern science has now proven that they were in Lebanon since 3000 BC or before. Their monuments and artifacts still exist in Byblos (Jbeil), Beit Mary, Tyre, and Sidon.

The Lebanese national museum has precious collections of these ancient historical treasures.

In the year 1500 BC, the Hittites came to Lebanon from the north, competing with the Phoenicians as mentioned in the Bible. The Bible also told about the beauty of Lebanon, its greatness, and its bountiful harvests of rice, fruits and wine. There are about 60 biblical references to these topics.

The Romans came to Lebanon in the year 64 BC. Their monuments show how great Lebanon became in their era and it prospered even more in the Byzantine era. And also, Christianity gradually entered Syria.

The Arabs conquered Lebanon in 632-640 A.D.and the people of Lebanon, at that time, spoke the Aramaic Syriac language.

After the Arab conquest, north Lebanon remained prosperous and autonomous with Syriac as the native language.

Even though many centuries have passed, Lebanon has preserved its Christian heritage right up to the present.

Lebanon was very difficult to conquer due to its rough terrain and the great strength of its people. The Arab Islamic invasion took place in the years between 632 and 640. The Muslims were unable to conquer the mountainous Northern Lebanon. The Maradites (Mardaites and Maradah), the Mountain Princes, kept plundering the coastal cities and other places occupied by the Arabs. So much so that the Umayyad rulers were compelled to befriend the Byzantine kings who in turn instructed the Maronites to stop attacking the Arab towns.

At that time, the strength of the Maronite nation was shining brilliantly!

No one denies that South Lebanon was conquered. It was held for a long time by the Arab tribes especially in Ma'an, Tannuh and Shehab. Many of the Christian families of the South are of Arab Ghassanite origin. The Ghassanites emigrated from Yemen in the early Christian era and mixed with the Syriacs in Huran. They adopted the Christian religion and the Syriac language. I think that this is the only Arabic origin of some Maronite families which is historically proven.

In conclusion, I shall repeat what I said in my other book History of the Maronite Families: Lebanese families descend from the Aramaic Phoenician races. All the invaders who entered into this land were assimilated and nothing or almost nothing remains from them except for a few legends. Thus, to write a detailed and accurate Lebanese history, one can only rely on serious documentation from the sixteenth century onward.

For many good reasons, it appears that Syrian cities remained Aramaic and Syriac in language and religion during the era of the Khalifs Rashedoun and the Umayyads.

Lebanon didn't adopt the Arabic language until the end of Umayyad era (661-750) and the Abassid (755-1258) era when the Arabic language started to gradually spread in Bilad al-Sham (the northern lands of the Arabian Peninsula). Thus, the Arabic language entered Lebanon to find the Syriac language struggling and trying to protect itself. This struggling continued for a long time, and the Lebanese continued to speak Syriac until the middle of the 17th century and into the 18th century.

In eastern Lebanon, there are still three villages who speak Syriac today. These are: Ma'lula, Nag'a and Gab'adin.

Although I stand strongly by what I previously said, namely, that the Lebanese are Aramaic in origin, I cannot deny that south Lebanon, such as Ma'an, Tanukh, and Shihab, was invaded by Arabic tribes (shortly after the conquest) and during the Crusades.

Also, I cannot deny that some Christians of the south come from Gassanid origin and that many Maronites of the north migrated to the south.

From the Christians, there are some who had Crusaders' blood and a little of Greek and Roman blood. But no matter what, the Arabic and Crusaders' blood was mixed together with the more dominant national blood. Today, these bloods have essentially disappeared almost without a trace.

The Gassanids left Yemen a few centuries after Christ and invaded "Houran". They converted to Christianity and spoke both the Syriac and the Arabic languages. They married with their Aramaic neighbors and, in the end, the Maronites didn't have any recognizable Arabian blood. I have spoken in detail about this subject in my book: The History of the Maronite Families.

Our summary, then, is this:

Researchers favor the view that the Lebanese families, especially the Maronites, came mostly from the Aramaic, Phoenician strain. Other groups who entered were assimilated. Those who took refuge in Lebanon seeking protection from its people or mountains, or those who entered it at times of war, ancient or new, have mixed with its people the same way as wine mixes with water. Nothing of the stories of their coming or mixing remains. There are only legends that can never be fully trusted by the historian.

I repeat, the stories of the nations who came to Lebanon with the old wars and invasions, and mixed with it's people, are unreliable.

For this reason you can see that any true researcher, when he gets back to the 15th or 16th century, loses all reliable resources. There is nothing to prove the verification of kinship, and thus the chain that was binding a family with its ancestors has been broken. The only thing that remains from those ancestors is their traditions.

Therefore, it is essentially true to say that we don't know for certain any stories about the families that migrated from Bchaaleh. We don't know even about those who remained there starting from the 16th century. There are only a few stories and I doubt the truthfulness of those. In this, we are like most Lebanese families who have no knowledge about their early history. I might add that if I didn't take the initiative of writing down and documenting the remaining stories, it would have all disappeared. Like so many other stories they would have faded to tall-tales and illusions.

No matter what, though, it appears that Bchaaleh was populated by Lebanese Maronites from Aramaic origins before the Ottoman invasion occurred and they remained in the village after the Ottoman invasion.

The families that belong to Bchaaleh are the descendants of those people.

THE BACHAALANY (BSHE'LANI) FAMILIES

Chapter 3

Classification Of The Bachaalany (Bshe'lani, Bishalany, or Bechalany, etc.) Families. - The Bachaalany Family That Migrated. - The Families Living In Bchaaleh. - The Slogan Of Banu Al-Bshe'lani (The Descendants Of Bachaalany). - Tales And Illusions. - Houran And Akkar. - Being Descendants Of Banu Ghassan. - Bshe'lani And Mesh'elani.

Now, let me move on to the search for the origins of the families of Bchaaleh.

The families belonging to the village of Bchaaleh consist of two main groups: a group that belongs to Bchaaleh in name and origin, and, a group that belongs to Bchaaleh in origin only.

The first main group is also divided into two sections:

First, is a section that maintained the family name Bachaalany from the time they left Bchaaleh village until now. They are the children of the Bachaalany who descended from Abu Rezk Bachaalany and his three sons: 1) Younes, 2) Abu Youssef Rezk , and 3) Abd Allah; and, the brother of Abu Rezk, Abu Sa'b..

This family left Bchaaleh going to Tripoli in the beginning of the 17th century. Then, after some time, they moved to Kisrawan, then to Salima of Metn and, then, on to other places.

Second, is the other section whose grandfathers were called Bachaalany for a period of time after they left Bchaaleh but then their sons and grandsons adopted other family names. These family names have branches and even other offshoots from these branches.

These include the house of Habquq who produced Girgis (George) Habquq Bachaalany, the famous archbishop of Akkoura and the Archbishop John Habquq Bachaalany and the Archbishop Abd Allah Habquq and many others famous leaders.

They are the same ones who inhabited Bikfaya and the Youth House of Waban and other places.

Some of them took new family names according to their new branches while others maintained the family name Habquq, the name of their great grandfather. Some of these still have the Habquq name today.

The second main group which belongs to Bchaaleh in origin only is divided into two sections: The first section consists of those whose great grandfather left Bchaaleh a long time ago going to different parts of Lebanon.

They became families, and each family took the name of their ancestor as a family name.

These families had new branches with new family names, but they know very well that they come originally from Bchaaleh. Their names are:

1- The House of Mubarak (in Kisrawan and Chouf), from them the House of al-Khuri (in Rechmaya) branched off, and also the house of al-Saad (in Ain Traz).

27

2- The House of Harfush in Bkasin.

3- The House of Abu Rashed in Niha and Wadi Shahrur.

4- The House of Abu Issa and Mashlab in Shurit.

5- The House of al-Kashma'i in Bikfaya and the House of Abu Nakad in al-Mohaidetha.

6- The House of Saad and Gobran in Boshrai.

These families probably left Bchaaleh after 1600. We make this judgment based on the stories that are told about each family.

Based on what we know of the migration route of most of the Christian families from northern Lebanon to the area beyond the Abraham (Ibrahim) River, these families went first to Kisrawan then to Metn and Chouf, and, then, further south after 1600 AD.

I said "most of the families" because some migrated from around 1500 AD, and, a few even sooner than that, going to Kisrawan then moving to the south.

If you refer to the <u>Annals</u> of El Douaihy, citing the migration movement of the Maronites, you will find the proof of this.

The second section which belongs to Bchaaleh in origin, but not in name are the families who live in Bchaaleh to-day, whether they are old or new. They are:

1- The House of Bu Shadid.

2- The House of Bu Mansur.

3- The House of Maron.

4- The House of Bu Rezk, al-Shediaq and Abu Mark.

5- The House of Nassar.

6- The House of al-Ashei.

7- The House of Wahba.

8- The House of Bu Elwan.

9- The House of Bhanna.

10- The House of Faisal or al-Shammas or al-Shediaq.

11- The House of Bu Daher or Arrif.

12- The House of Sakr al-Bagani or Tadros Tuggar.

13- The House of Ga'ga al-Shalfoun.

14- The House of Rezk al-Shabtini.

15- The House of al-Hani or al-Hamsh.

16- The House of al-Helw or al-Dasher.

17- The House of Bu Harb.

18- The House of al-Khuri Boutros.

All these families are of Bshe'lani origin because they have lived in Bchaaleh. Whether they left Bchaaleh or stayed there, they are still Bachaalany (Bshe'lani) by origin and by land.

The only family who kept Bachaalany as a family name is Banu (Descendants or Children of) Bachaalany who lived in the village of Salima in Metn region.

They maintained their family name and never wanted to change it. For good and for bad, whether they are near or far, they preferred the family name Bachaalany which is the best and noblest family name. Even recognizing that the famous Abu Rezk is their ancestral leader, master and source of their prosperity and pride as a family, they still didn't take his name but kept the family name. Even though they have tremendous pride in their great ancestor, Abu Rezk, still they maintained his family name, Bachaalany.

The blood relations between the different families that left Bchaaleh such a long time ago are hard to identify. With each family going its own way and the passage of so much time, it makes it difficult to discover and connect the exact blood relations.

Also there is no way to identify the blood relations between the families that left Bchaaleh and the families that stayed.

Some have claimed that the families who lived in Bchaaleh in the past come from one grandfather but this is not certain.

What is clear is that Sheik Abu Rezk Bachaalany must be related to the house of Abu Rezk and al-Shediaq. There are so many similar names in the lineage of both strains. And so many people of these families call one another by "my cousin". They know that in spite of being in different locations now, their grandfathers migrated from Bchaaleh alone or in groups in the 16th and 17th century. They know that the injustices and persecutions of those days drove their ancestors from Bchaaleh. These calamities, together with being blood related, united them and made them one.

All I have been able to do is to construct a general pedigree for all the branches. I hope and wait for the appearance of some documents that show the connections between the different branches.

The Origin of the Bachaalany (Bshe'lani)

There is no doubt that this family belongs to the village of Bchaaleh in Batroun region.

The famous knowledgeable historian, Patriarch Estephan El Douaihy, the Maronite from Ehden has briefly mentioned the stories of the great grandfather Sheik Abu Rezk Bachaalany, his sons and his brother Abu Sa'b. Unfortunately he said only that he was from the notables of the Maronites, as reported by Archbishop Youssef al-Debs. He didn't refer to his family origin because Abu Rezk was very famous and so well known at that time that it was unnecessary. Also, the matter of family origin was not an important issue at that time.

Because every person has some natural curiosity to know about his ancient origins, every one who was related to Bchaaleh village and Abu Rezk Bachaalany started to search for their history before the time of Abu Rezk. Sadly, there wasn't anything more to learn than what El Douaihy and others had mentioned.

A few years ago, some people claimed that the descendants of Bachaalany originated from the Gassanids who left from a village in Houran called Sha'el or Mesh'al more than 1500 years ago. They also claimed that they arrived in Lebanon and established a village naming it Bchaaleh after the name of their old village.

Out of ignorance this story has been transferred from one generation to the other as if it was true.

Knowledgeable people didn't believe this ridiculous, fabricated story until one day the late Sheik Melhem Nahra So-wayd, a member of the descendants of Bachaalany, wrote it down in a manuscript about the family. He wrote that very same story which did not rely on any documents or factual reference or even a trustworthy narrator!

Some of the poor and the illiterate almost believed it even though there are facts and documents that disprove it.

While I was searching for the truth, I was told that there was a manuscript owned by a Maronite priest in Jbeil called al-Khuri Youssef and known as al-Zanati.

This manuscript contained some chronicles and among them was the story of the families who migrated from Bchaaleh.

A friend of mine, the late Maron Sfeir, who used to go to these areas to trade and gather information, told me a story referring to the owner of a manuscript which goes as follows:

"The origin of the family of al-Khuri Saleh, the Sheiks (Counts) in Rechmaya is traced to the family of Mubarak who came to Bchaaleh from the village of Kafr Tabu from Akkar in the year 1300 AD. The name of the great grandfather was 'Sahyun (Zion)' who belonged to the tribe of Banu Ghassan, the kings of al-Sham (northern lands) for about 400 years until the religion of Islam appeared. Then they faded. Their origin was from al-Azd Banu Kahlan from Yemen.
They were pious brave Christians. Sahyun had a son in Bchaaleh called Rezk and Rezk had two sons: Younes and Mubarak. Younes had five sons, the elder was Rezk who was the great grandfather of Rezk family. Younes was martyred in Tripoli. From Mubarak, the well-known family branched, then came Shaheen who was the great grandfather of the house of al-Tawil.
From the offspring of Mubarak al-Khuri came Saleh who left Kisrawan for the town of Rechmaya in the year 1700 AD. One of al-Khuri Saleh's sons was al-Shediaq Gandur who had a son called Saad who had a boy called Gandur."

I don't know what the sources are from which the owner of the manuscript has taken this story. The story and the owner was also told by Father Estephan El Douaihy (also spelled Duwayhi or Douaihi) in his book, The Pearl Necklace of the History of Lebanon.

I tried to find out about any information concerning this manuscript and its owner who died many years ago. I contacted his relatives and found out that this priest used to tell many strange stories about the families and their history.

This priest used to receive information seekers and when they came to him, he would go to his room. After a while, he would come out and give them what they wanted to hear without letting them see the manuscript.

The heirs of the priest do the same thing, too!

Thus no knowledgeable person ever examined the manuscript to assess its historical value.

It seems that this priest fabricated the stories and that he used to tell them to the information seekers that came to him.

I learned from talking to people who received information from him that he is not trustworthy and his stories have no proof.

Some stories are really unbelievable since they were very ancient stories that contained strange facts. Indeed, I noticed that he made mistakes in telling well-known historical events that were mentioned by El Douaihy. Thus, if he made mistakes in telling recent events, then how can any one depend on him with respect to ancient matters?!!

How can we depend on a narrator who makes such mistakes on the one hand, and then, on the other hand, ignore the words of El Douaihy who is considered the best investigator and historian of all times?!!

Thus the presence of a blood relation between some Lebanese families whether Maronite or Melkite or Banu Ghassan (The Gassanids) is unproven because of the absence of any clear document or historical certificate that can be trusted.

And yet, there is a famous Lebanese Historian, George Zidan who implied there was a chance that this story could be possible according to what he had heard from some families who confirmed it.

My famous friend, the well-known researcher Issa Iskandar al-Ma'ruf, who spent all his life searching for the origins of families especially his own family, could not find any trustworthy witness or any true document to support the families' claims of being related to the Gassanids.

I have mentioned before that investigators and researchers came to the conclusion that the Lebanese families, especially the Maronite families, were from an Aramaic Phoenician origin. Also that the other ethnic groups who melted in were mostly Melkites, i.e. the Orthodox, and the Roman Catholics. There is only a very weak possibility that Maronite blood contains any Gassanid connection

El Douaihy and other trustworthy historians say that Abu Rezk and his relatives were from the notables of the Maronites.

The claim that the Bachaalany families came originally from Banu Ghassan leads us to research the meaning of the word "Bshe'lani". The Bachaalany family took this word as a family name and were very proud of it. It was considered to be their link between the past and present.

I mention the following to prove this fact:

1 These families belonged to the village of Bchaaleh. It was their home land, and it was such because Bchaaleh was the home land of their great ancestor Abu Rezk, his sons and grand sons and all their relatives.

All these families have preserved this family name inheriting it generation after generation till today.

Also, none of them were ignorant of the fact that they all belonged to the Bchaaleh village in the Batroun region.

Also, they keep their relations with the people of Bchaaleh even today. This is due to their strong sense of family identity. I stayed in Bchaaleh for 5 years (1893-1898) when I opened a school there to teach the youth of Bchaaleh.

2 Whether old or young, all members of the families that migrated from Bchaaleh in olden days and who dropped their family name "Bachaalany" know very well that they originated from Bchaaleh.

Banu Mubarak, al-Khuri and al-Saad confirmed this. Also, Banu Harfoush and Abu Rashed confirmed this. Again, this was confirmed by Banu Gobran, Banu Abu Nakd and Kasma'i and Banu Meshleb, Abu Issa and others.

Surely, all these families can not be wrong.

3 The famous Patriarch Estephan El Douaihy from Ehden who was the contemporary of Abu Rezk Bachaalany and his sons has mentioned their stories and the stories of the Archbishops who lived in Bchaaleh, as appears from his draft in Bkerke.

The same thing applies to the copies made from his <u>Annals</u> by his permission or made in his own times.

This word "Bchaaleh" appeared in the chronicles of the Shihab Prince Haidar, Sheik Tonus al-Shediaq, al-Hadthuni, al-Debs, Durian, Shebli and other historians.

4 In some Maronite monasteries, I have found about 50 old manuscripts and about 50 original documents which mention Girgis, Abd Allah, Yuhanna and Youssef Habquq al-Bshe'lani and the rest of the priests who came from that family. They are mentioned by their names and their signatures, written in their own handwriting or the handwriting of others and containing the words "Bachaalany" or "of Bchaaleh"

Their names and signatures were in the Arabic, Syriac and Karchouni languages.

Also, the Patriarch Boulos Mos'ad who was well known for knowing all about family origins and descedents, used to meet any one who came to him from Bchaaleh with the greeting: "Welcome to the descendants of Prince Younes bin Abu Rezk Bachaalany"

The archbishop Youssef al-Debs mentioned in his famous chronicle the stories of Abu Rezk and his sons and always connected them to the village of Bchaaleh in the Batroun region.

Youssef al-Debs was the first one to find out about the book of De La Roque's journey.

From this book, of which I have a published copy, al-Debs took all the stories about Prince Younes and his martyrdom.

5 I have in my possession hundreds of documents, letters and deeds from the middle of the 17th century up to today. They all mention the family name "the Bachaalany" ("al-Bshe'lani") the same way as we pronounce it and write it today. The oldest deed in my archives, which goes back to the end of the 17th century, contained the sentence: "Hatem Abd al-Karim Bachaalany from Salima has sold...".

Hatem Abd al-Karim Bachaalany is one of the great grandfathers of Karam Bachaalany.

The same can be said about all the other deeds in my possession.

6 We possess some of the still surviving belongings of Hanania Bachaalany. He was the Patriarch of Anthonean Monasticism in Rome (his relatives today are in the towns of Salima and Shamlan). He visited Europe and was honored from its kings and princes and they presented him with many gifts.

Among the manuscripts of the Saint Ash'eia Monastery in Rmana, there are many of his papers such as certificates from presidents in Latin that contained his name as: "The Patriarch Hanania Bachaalany, the High Priest of Anthonean Monasticism."

I will speak about him later on.

Towards the end of the 19th century, some illiterates in the town of Salima changed the name Bachaalany to Machaalany or Mesh'elani. The reason for this was that our co-citizens in Salima, and especially the Druze, thought that the first syllable Bshe' which in Arabic means "horrible" is an insult. They could not let that be. So they changed the B in al-Bachaalany to an M, making it Mashaalany. The wise did not go along with this and they kept their original name the way it was. They kept it the same in their letters, signatures, and conversations. They did this in their eagerness to preserve the true family name from distortion.

Another way the erroneous tradition grew was because of two men, both descendants of Bachaalany who left the town of Salima in the beginning of the last century. They went to the western part of Lebanon. The first, Gabur, left and went to Abeia, and the second, Hanna, contacted the Shihab Prince Haidar and lived in the town of Shamlan. They carried along with them the false name Machaalany. Both of them were illiterate. Their children and grandchildren carried the same false name as their parents did. Many writers and men of letters who descended from these two families continued to make the same mistake especially now that they were far away from the town of Salima, the center of the family.

Well, it happened that the late Sheik Melhem Nahra and his sons, the late Naguib, the late Youssef and the late Selim believed that fabricated story and they passed it along. They met and knew the grandsons of Hanna of Shamlan after they moved to Zahle. The grandsons were Ibrahim, Khalil, Naguib and Nasib. The Sheik and his sons thought that these were highly educated men who could not be wrong about using the name Machaalany. So it was that they agreed

32

with them. Thus, the false tradition got into the minds of some ignorant members of the Bachaalany family and it was perpetuated.

To justify his grave error, Sheik Melhem wrote a manuscript saying: "The origin of our family is Banu Ghassan. Fifteen hundred years ago our great grandfather Machaalany Ghassan used to live in Houran in a village called Masha'el or Sho'la or Mesh'al. After a long stay in that village, and after many squabbles and fights with other inhabitants, his offspring migrated to northern Lebanon. They built a village there in the Batroun region which they called Bchaaleh Therefore, our great grandfather Machaalany and Bachaalany are the same person....."

Sheik Melhem almost got away with this fabricated story. But it is not backed up by any fact or true story. It was almost believed by the ignorant and the poor.

Because of all this, my brother Sheik Habib Bachaalany confronted him and wrote a very critical article in a newspaper that he used to send to the immigrants abroad. In this article he showed the falseness of the story using logical evidence and historical facts.

I, also, tried to explain to Sheik Melhem and his sons how they were wrong. I tried to convince them that no one in the family, which has always preserved their great name, can approve of what he has written in the manuscript.

Thus, they must correct this grave mistake. They must return to the true course because this new family name of theirs distorts the clear historical facts and breaks the links between the old and the new generations. It splits the family of Bachaalany.

They excused themselves, however, saying that they were now known in Zahle and other places as Machaalany so they couldn't change their names.

We later learned a strange thing about Sheik "Melhem". He had a diary which is in his own hand writing which we found in the possession of his son-in-law, the late " Abu Aql al-Khuri". In it he wrote about Bachaalany events. This diary included historical events starting from the year 1860 up. Most of them talked about the Bachaalany family. They were mentioned tens of times as Bachaalany. There was not a mention of "Machaalany" or "al-Mesh'elani" in them. This diary is kept among my historical manuscripts with other letters of the Sheik signed under the name "Melhem Nohra Bachaalany".

He also mentioned in his diary a place in Kisrawan called Klud Bachaalany. There the family of Abu Rezk hid. Today the place belongs to the family of Kaisar al-Zughbi from Karnet Shahwan.

What is even stranger is that the Sheik used to be the president of the Saint George Association for the youth of the descendants of Bachaalany about the year 1870 in Salima. He chose the word "Manhar" as a slogan, which is an abbreviation from his name "Melhem Nohra". He wrote on the flag of the association this sentence " O, Christian Saint George, save your Manhar Bachaalany". This flag is still there today in the club house of the association. It should be mentioned and emphasized that Sheik "Melhem" and his father were famous and reached their lofty positions only because they belonged to the large honorable family of Bachaalany.

The weirdest thing of all this, is the Bachaalany heritage of Abdu Agha Nohra al-Arian. He is the uncle of Nohra Sowayd and the reason that the family of Sowayd belonged to the Bachaalany family. It was their grandfather who married Zahra, the sister of Abdu Agha which made Nohra a member of the Bachaalany family from his mother's side. These details are: from the deeds and records of the financial dealings between Abdu and the princes, the archbishops, and, others. Also referenced is the will of his wife. All of these had the name Abdu Nohra Bachaalany on them.

Add to all this, the fact that in the Church of Saint Michael in the town of al-Chiyah where he spent his last days, there is a shrine of Abd with his name Abd Bachaalany written on it.

Keeping in mind that the sons of this family are ignorant about there family names, could it possibly be that Nohra Sowayd knew the history of his family better than his uncle?!

If the family name Machaalany which was mentioned in the story had a document that supported it, it would have been safely kept in the village of Bchaaleh where the family belongs. And why would all the ancient manuscripts which belonged to the Maronite Archbishops, and all the records of the princes and rulers, where we find so many family names of the relatives… why would all of these say Bachaalany!! And they do say Bachaalany. I have these scripts.

Most of the names of the Maronite families, like other Lebanese families, are newly adopted. Since the old names keep getting replaced with new ones, and since it is only one, two or three centuries since these have occurred, digging deep and researching can trace back to the old names.

Therefore, the Bachaalany family could never have adopted the alleged name "Machaalany Ghassan" some 1500 years ago and yet have there be not a single incident, tradition, date, document or vestige that proves this to be true.

Bchaaleh village, which is an ancient village and one of the noblest home lands of the Maronites in Lebanon, preceded the era of the Arabs in Lebanon and was mentioned by the Crusaders as "Betzaal". This was distorted just like many other Middle Eastern names were distorted by the Westerners. Westerners simply could not pronouce the words correctly!!

Bchaaleh is an Aramaic Syriac word.

The Roman and Greek monuments in Bchaaleh signify how old this village is.

The allegations that its name comes from the names "Sha'la", "Sha'el", or "Mesh'al" are false.

All these pieces of evidence and logic clearly prove that the family name Bachaalany is the true family name, not Machaalany.

ABU REZK BACHAALANY

Section 2

THE SITUATION AT HIS TIME

Chapter 1

The Rule Of The Muqaddams After The Mardaites. – The Turkmans. – The Ma'ns. – The Ottoman Sultans. – The Independence And Political Parties. – Taxes And Injustice. – Immigration And Moving. – The Deterioration Of Policies. – The Families' Rise To Power. – The Martyrs Of The Maronites.

I mentioned earlier that most historians agree that the Maronites are of an Aramaic Phoenician origin and that they are among the original inhabitants of Lebanon.

I also said that the Maronite sect originated in the north of Syria in the fourth century and it gained strength in Lebanon in the seventh century. It flourished in the era of the Maradah. It has maintained its freedom and customs for a long time even though the times and the governments have changed greatly.

After the defeat of the Kisrawan territory, the Maronites were trapped in northern Lebanon. They formed a strong group headed by their spiritual leaders. They chose rulers from among the best men and they were known as the muqaddams.

The muqaddams took power after the Mardaites. Peace, prosperity and freedom prevailed in their era.

When the Muslims took power in Syria, their leaders were busy competing with each other for power. This kept them out of Lebanese and Maronite affairs.

The Turkman controlled the coasts of Kisrawan while the Tanukhs and the Ma'ns controlled the west and south.

When the Ottoman Sultan Selim I conquered Bilad Al-Sham and defeated the Mamluks, he called into his presence the Princes (the Emirs) of Lebanon. He approved of their rule and their customs, and imposed a light tax (Jizyah) on them.

Of the Turkmans, Prince Assaf was very famous and many people used to name their Turkman children after him.

The Turkmans were good at politics. They were fair and they rose in power and the towns prospered. Then their power faded and the Ma'ns took power.

From the Ma'ns, Prince Fakhr al-Din I was a great ruler and he applied a wise policy. The people loved him.

His gradson Fakhr al-Din II followed in the footsteps of his grandfather and he made his efforts to unite the Lebanese emirate.

35

He fought the Saifa family who had taken the property of the Assaf family. The Ma'ns were victorious and they took back their properties.

It is no secret that the Ottoman Sultans appeared at the beginning as just and fair rulers. Soon, however, they lost these good qualities.

The Sultans used to rely on their viziers and workers to carry out their policies. These workers were frequently unjust and unfair to their subjects.

The situation worsened and the towns were full of unrest, turmoil and civil wars. Envy and conspiracies prevailed due to the quest for power and money.

The free nature of the Lebanese and their inherited independence were the most important factors that kept them patient. They endured these calamities.

It was these characteristics which also kept them autonomous. The national rulers and princes kept their power as usual. The viziers did not interfere except for occasional power struggles.

In this way, it was easy for the Ottoman rulers to control the Lebanese rulers. These Ottomans took the side of the Lebanese ruler who paid more in taxes. He, in turn, imposed more taxes on his subjects to satisfy the greed of the workers. Soon the subjects became over burdened and exhausted.

This was one of the reasons that motivated the subjects to migrate from one place to another. They sought shelter from the overtaxation and injustice.

The deterioration of the Maronites in the north and the interference of the foreigners were the reasons why the noble families rose to power in Lebanon after the muqaddams.

These noble families made a very great impact on the history of Lebanon.

In their wisdom, these noble Lebanese families wanted to gain the favor of their Muslim rulers. In this way they could save their people from the oppression and injustices of their oppressive rulers. Often these rulers listened to slander and lies which led to the deaths of many members of the noble families.

Also, these Muslim rulers used to try to convert these families to their religion and, if they refused, they would kill them without any mercy.

The Patriarch Estephan El Douaihy, the great historian, has mentioned many incidents that showed the deceit of these rulers such as the killing of Abu Karam al-Hadthy and Kanaan al-Daher and others.

El Douaihy and other patriarchs were sickened by the course of events in the north and turned their attention to Kisrawan, Metn, and Chouf. They expended their energies to spread the Maronite religion in these places. In this way they would strengthen their position and be able to protect themselves from calamities.

The fairness of the Ma'n princes and their favorable attitude toward the Maronites helped in this situation.

The same is true for the Shihab princes in Chouf, the Lam'i in Metn, and the princes of Banu al-Khazen in Kisrawan.

This is how it was in seventeenth century Lebanon.

THE STORY OF ABU REZK

Chapter 2

His Fame. - His Origin And His Family Name. – His Up Bringing And Brilliance.   – His History In Tripoli. – He And The Rulers. – The Rise To Power Of Abu Rezk. – Envy And The Quest For Power. – The Forgiveness Granted By The Sultan. – Abu Rezk And The Patriarchate. – Assuming High Office. – His Greatness And Influence. – The Count (Sheik) Abu Sa'b, His Brother. – Disasters He Faced And His Martyrdom.

During those times, lived the great grandfather Sheik Abu Rezk, one of the Maronite greats. He was a very famous man. He is mentioned by the Patriarch Estephan El Douaihy in his famous book: The Annals.

The Patriarch Estephan El Douaihy did not talk about the origin or geneology of Sheik Abu Rezk because he was often brief in his writing and Abu Rezk was so famous that he needed no discussion.

I read in his Annals that sometimes he called him "Sheik Abu Rezk from Bchaaleh" and sometimes "Sheik Abu Rezk Bachaalany". This certainly meant that Abu Rezk belonged to that historical town and that he was born and raised there.

When he moved to the town of Tripoli and lived there, his fame was well known due his his brilliance in management and politics.

It was also mentioned in the Annals that the ruler of Tripoli, Hassan Pasha al-Arna'ut, appointed Sheik Abu Al Rezk as his deputy in charge of managing his properties. Then, in 1644, he appointed him to govern Gebbat Boshrai.

Patriarch Estephan El Douaihy then mentioned: *"In 1645, Sheik Abu Rezk governed al-Gebba and al-Zawya. And in the year 1646, he governed al-Daneya and Akkar together with al-Gebba and al-Zawya, and thus the Sheik lived in Tripoli and was like a brother to Hassan Pasha."*

Then he mentions: *"In 1647, Omar Pasha appointed Abu Sa'b, Abu Rezk's brother, to the Sheikdom of Gebbat Boshrai while Abu Rezk became the ruler of Akkar, al-Daneya, al-Gebba and Akkoura."*

Next he says: *"In 1650, al-Gebba was ruled by Sheik Abu Rezk from Bchaaleh who was a famous and prestigious man in Tripoli."*

When El Douaihy mentioned the death of the Patriarch Girgis Omaira of Ehden he said: *"On the 15th of August, 1644, he was succeeded by Youssef Boutros al-Akuri, from the town of Beit Halib, as the new Patriarch with the attention of Sheik Abu Rezk from Bchaaleh."*

Thus, it appears clearly how this great man, through his own efforts, managed to take charge of difficult situations. And this, in a time when power was in the hands of Turkish rulers. In a time when Muslims had all the influences in a city with a majority of Muslims...and this man, a Christian, who came down from the mountains!

So it is that El Douaihy wrote in his Annals, in the original written copies kept in the library of the Maronite Patriarchate and those in the Vatican Library in Rome...this excludes references to the printed copy where the pubilsher ignored some facts that were mentioned in the old original copies.

The two researchers, al-Debs and Durian, were excellent in telling the stories of Abu Rezk and his family.

Douaihy says that in the year 1644, Mohammed Pasha Arna'ut was ousted from his position as the ruler of Tripoli, and Hassan Pasha seized it. In the year 1649, Omar (Pasha)Bec ruled Tripoli and he returned Abu Rezk Bachaalany and Bin al-Sahyuni back to their positions. He also appointed Abu Sa'b Bachaalany, Abu Rezk's brother, as the Sheik of Gebbat Boshrai.

In the year 1651, Omar Pasha was ousted from his position as ruler of Tripoli and Hassan Pasha regained it and gave Sheik Abu Rezk Bachaalany his old position. Then Bin al-Sahyuni became more powerful than Abu Rezk and fired him and his followers. In the year 1652, Mohammed Pasha al-Arna'ut returned to rule Tripoli and deputized Abu Rezk in all his affairs including rule over the villages. Thus he was called "The Sheik of Sheiks".

All of this filled the Muslims with envy and they said: "We, Muslims, should not be followers to a Christian man."

Douaihy also says that on the first of April, 1653, Mohammed Pasha Al-Arna'ut arrested Sheik Abu Rezk. The reason was that some of Abu Rezk's enemies told lies. Abu Rezk had some Sheiks from Beit Hobaish and another large group of friends come to stay at his house. The reason was to do some shopping and celebrating for the wedding of one of their sons.

Wicked people told the Pasha about this and they made him believe that the reason for the visit was so that Sheik Abu Rezk and his children could flee to the lands of the Ma'ns. The Pasha ordered the arrest of Sheik Abu Rezk, his children and all his visitors, about 90 people altogether. Then these enemies ruined his house and stole his possessions.

After a few days, news arrived telling of the ousting of Pasha al-Arna'ut and his being replaced by Hassan Pasha.

Abu Rezk and all the prisoners were released from their imprisonment in Hamat. When Hassan Pasha was about to appoint Sheik Abu Rezk to be in charge of his affairs, a messenger from the Sublime Porte (al-Bab al'Ali) arrived asking for the head of Abu Rezk.

Hassan Pasha and Bin Sahyun advised him to save himself by convertng to Islam. He relunctantly did so and they gave the messenger 1000 piasters and he went back to Istanbul.

Abu Rezk went back to Tripoli with Hassan Pasha who appointed him to be in charge of Gabla and Lazekeia.

Before Abu Rezk's departure for Gabla and Lazekeia, he told his brother Abu Sa'b to take his children and head for the lands of the Ma'ns.

Hassan Pasha did not like this, which made Abu Rezk fear his reaction. To remove any doubt in the mind of Hassan Pasha, Abu Rezk married a woman of Moussa Pasha.

In 1650, the Sultan appointed Bashir Pasha.

At that time, troops were being gathered to fight the Ma'ns.

Bin Alam al-Din and Bin al-Sahyuni went to join the troops on their way to fight the Ma'n Prince Melhem. He had defeated them earlier in the 1650 Battle of Wadi al-Qarn. Meanwhile Bashir Pasha headed for Istanbul. When Bashir

Pasha arrived in Adana, some people told him that Abu Rezk was a supporter of the Ma'ns. They said that he had sent his children to them and that his brother Abu Sa'b was among the Ma'ns in that Battle of Wadi al-Qarn.

Because of this, the Pasha order the execution of Abu Rezk.

In the beginning of March, Abu Rezk was executed in Kounia, Turkey.

Bashir Pasha was killed while entering Istanbul. Mourad Pasha took his place.

So it was that Abu Rezk became a martyr for the sake of his religion and what was to become his country, Lebanon.

THE SONS OF ABU REZK

Chapter 3

Younes, Abd Allah and Abu Youssef. — The Elder Son Younes. —Leaving Tripoli.   — The Party Of Banu Qays And The Party Of Banu Yaman. — The Defeat Of Banu Qays. — The Ma'n Princes. — The Ma'n Prince Ahmad. — His Death And The End Of The Rule Of The Ma'ns. — Political Changes. —The Arrest Of Sheik Younes. — His Execution On The Stake.

The late Sheikh Abu Rezk, who was killed in 1654 in Kounia, had three sons: Younes (Jonas), Abd Allah and Abu Youssef (Joseph).

Sheik Younes, the oldest son, was the most knowledgeable, the most capable in politics, and, the strongest.

The loss of his father did not break him but instead, made him strong and desirous of following in the footsteps of his father.

The sons of Sheik Abu Rezk, especially Younes, because he was the oldest, must have received a good deal of education in science and literature, as was the custom of the noble families at that time.

At that time, Tripoli, the city to which their father migrated, was full of churches and monasteries.

It was then and still is the headquarters of the Maronite Archbishop of Tripoli. Many Maronites used to take refuge in Tripoli so as to be close to the northern cities. These cities were the stronghold of Christianity and many Maronites going back for many, many years.

These northern cities still have many noble Maronite families living in them today. There are also still many western religious communities represented in them, namely, the Capuchins, the Jesuits and the Lazarites. There are also many consulates for European countries.

The translators for the French consulate were from two noble families: Tarbeia al-Shadrawi and Karam of Ehden.

In their schools the missionaries used to teach religion and literature as well as European languages such as French and Italian. They also used to teach the Syriac and Arabic languages.

The reason they used to teach Arabic was so that they could perform their religious role in preaching, for discipline and teaching good manners.

This means that Sheik Abu Rezk most probably left the education of his sons in the hands of these missionaries. They would have received a good amount of education in science, languages and literature.

This is based on what was written about these three sons, especially Younes.

The family of Sheik Abu Rezk left Tripoli in the year 1653. With their uncle Sheik Abu Sa'b they went to the land of the Ma'n prince who was at that time, Prince Melhem. He died in the year 1658. He was the ruler of Chouf, Metn, and Kisrawan where the family stayed while waiting an opportune time to return to Tripoli.

At this time there was a longstanding hostility between factions which included clans and families. It involved Christians and Druze. It often transcended religious ties. The two groups were the "Qaysi" and the "Yamani". The Bachaalany family belong to the Qaysi party and they were involved in intense fighting. Their leader was killed for his affiliation. Victory was a fleeting prize. At one time it went to the Qaysi party and at another time to the Yamani.

Estephan El Douaihy who was a contemporary of those days tells of the defeat of the Qaysi in 1660. He mentions the disappearance of the Ma'n Prince Melhem. He tells of the power take over by Banu Alam al-Din the Yemenis. He records the torturing of the Qaysi at the hands of the Ottoman soldiers. He wrote of the ruler (Wali) of Sidon who tried to set up the two princes, Qorqomash and Ahmad. This led to the killing of Qorqomash while Ahmad only managed to escape by a miracle.

The Qaysi once again rose to power and Prince Ahmad came out of hiding to gain control of Metn, Chouf and Kisrawan.

In 1684, Prince Ahmad gained even more power and extended his control to Gebbet Boshrai.

He hunted down the Hammadis so they fled to Baalbak. When Prince Ahmad died on 15 September 1698 without leaving a son to succeed him, the Lebanese agreed on his nephew Prince Bashir Shihab I as a successor.

When the situation calmed down, the Bachaalany family returned to Tripoli. Sheikh Younes and his brothers maintained their patriotism and never waivered even with the change in policies and rulers.

Douaihy didn't mention anything about them during that period except for what I read in his Annals. He said that Sheik Younes was involved in the following situation. In 1686, the Pasha sent people to burn the villages and towns of the north because the Hamradis didn't pay their tax money to the government. A judge was sent to write a statement confirming their guilt with an order to send it the Sublime Porte in Istanbul.

Sheik Younes bin Abu Rezk intervened in the matter. He went to the judge trying to change the mind of the ruler by telling him that the people of al-Gebba are Christians (Dhimmies) and that they have paid three quarters of the total amount due. He said that they promised to pay the rest. Sheik Younes had an official request sent saying .that they should not be harmed.

In this record of al-Doualhi that is preserved at the Patriarchate there are written details of his financial dealings with others, the incomes and expenses of the Patriarchate along with other useful information. I read the accounts of Sheik Abu Youssef Rezk 'and Sheik Younes, the two sons of Abu Rezk Bachaalany.

From that record, I report the following:

"In the year 1687, from Sheik Youssef Abu Rezk, a deposit of 90 piasters at the time of drought; and also from the aforementioned, a deposit of 200 piasters, a silver watch and some ammunition. The 290 piasters were returned back to their owner in full.

In the year 1687, from Sheik Younes, 100 piasters with a receipt... In the Year 1688, from Sheik Abu Youssef Rezk 100 piasters with interest.

In the year 1691, from Sheik Abu Youssef Rezk, we received 115, he received 15, with 100 remaining.

Sheik Younes 50 and 50 came to him, 10 from the hoppers of his wife. And also 30 from his son 10 and from other notes, 25, and 5, and 10.

In the year 1690, from Sheik Rezk, we received 115. He received 15 through Girgis bin al-Qasbas. The remaining 100 taken to the coming second year with an interest of 18 piasters. Also, there are 10 piasters as a loan with 5 being the price of wholesale rice. From Sheik Rezk, 133 piasters. He received 5 through Youssef al-Entari, 78 paid to him in person, another 5 paid in June, 5 in Kannoubine, 5 through Abu Youssef of Itu, and 50 on August 5 paid through Antonius Zoaitar. 10 piasters were paid back from this ....

In the year 1691, from Abu Youssef Rezk there is 133 which he received through Hanna Tlag with 50 remaining.

I also read the following in a deed dated 1103 Hegira (Lunar): *"written by Younes bin Rezk, witnessed by Abd Allah in 1676 AD"* and *"the government money was paid through Sheik Younes".*

The enemies of the Bachaalany family in Tripoli continued to wait for an opportunity to destroy them. This chance came when Hussein Pasha became the ruler of Tripoli. In 1687, Hussein Pasha ordered the arrest of Sheik Younes, his brothers Abd Allah and Abu Youssef Rezk, and their children because of the case against their father Sheik Abu Rezk 33 years prior.

Most probably, these enemies of the Bachaalany family told the ruler that their father was a friend of the Ma'ns, the enemies of the country. They probably said that he sent his sons and his brother, Abu Sa'b, to support the Ma'ns in the struggle for Lebanon's independence.

El Douaihy wrote in his <u>Annals</u>:

"In the year 1687, Hussein Pasha took power in Tripoli. He then arrested Sheik Younes, his brothers Abd Allah, Rezk and their children because of the case against their father Abu Rezk Bachaalany. Younes had to convert to Islam to save his children. On the 29th of September they escaped in the dead of night with 20 people. They fled to Kisrawan to be under the protection of the Ma'ns and Sheik Abu Kunsuwa Fayad.".

Then Douaihy mentioned:

-"In the year 1693 Arslan Pasha was appointed the ruler of Tripoli
-In the year 1697 Arslan Pasha received the call to the Hajj (the Muslim Pilgrimage to Mecca). In his absence his brother Keblan Pasha took his place and arrested Sheik Younes, the son of Abu Rezk Bachaalany.
-On May 21, Younes was executed on the stake after being offered Islam. He refused the offer."

All of the painful incidents that occurred in these days had a major impact on the people, especially on the Patriarch Estephan El Douaihy. His heart was torn apart because of the persecution, the discrimination and the cruelty which his people suffered. It was so bad that he gathered other Maronites with him and they all left these northern lands. They went to Kisrawan, Metn, and Chouf.

The houses were destroyed, villages abandoned, and the fields were left fallow. The result was that the resources of the government were dramatically reduced. It became such a problem that the rulers of the northern regions entered into negotiations with the Patriarch. They wanted him to go back to Kannoubine. They wanted his followers to go back with him and return to their normal life.

These negotiations between the government of Tripoli and the Patriarch were conducted through Sheik Rezk (Youssef Rezk Bachaalany), the son of Abu Rezk Bachaalany. At that time he was also negotiating the release of his brother Younes who was imprisoned in the jail at the Tripoli castle.

In an archive in the Patriarchate, I found among the papers of El Douaihy two original messages: one from the ruler (Wali) of Tripoli and the other from the Katkhuda of the ruler (i.e. his adviser).

Both of them are addressed to El Douaihy through Sheik Youssef Rezk. They contain earnest appeals for the Patriarch to return to Kannoubine with his followers. They seek a return to their traditional lives.

I present them here:

(The Official Seal Of Arslan Mohammad, The Ruler of Tripoli)

To the pride of Christianity, Estephan, Patriarch of Kannoubine, may God bless him,

...and the other issue is that as soon as this message reaches you and you read it, you would become satisfied and your heart would become still. It has come to our knowledge that you have been subjected to an unjust act, but fear not, for you know how we have favored you since such a long time ago. And you know that we can never harm you or anyone else in any way. All we want is that you should think about the good things.

Sheik Youssef Rezk.has informed us about your situation. God willing, this blessed year will bring you nice things from us.

We hereby inform you that we have issued an official request to the immigrants of al-Gebba, asking for their forgiveness for any harm that has been done to them.

All we desire is that everything will return to normal and that, God willing, all they want will come true..." (1697).

And, the second item:

"From the Advisor to the Ruler of Tripoli, Hajj Islam,

Dearest Estephan, the Patriarch of Kannoubine, may God ...,

...and the second issue is that we inform you that an Official Request will reach you at the hands of the carrier of this message from His Highness Afandina (Our Chief), may God protect him.

The purpose is that you do as it says and become satisfied in all ways, and come back together with all the immigrants of al-Gebba (Gebbat Bcherri).

Of course, you know that from a long time ago. you have had a special place in Afandina's heart. And you know that he used to depend on you in all the matters of the Gebba and that it is not possible that you should leave your place.

The purpose is that as soon as you receive this message, we hope your only answer is that you will come back to al-Gebba.

We have also asked Sheik Youssef Rezk to try to convince you to return by telling you of your fulfillment, thus Afandina will likewise find fulfillment with you.

God willing, this blessed year will bring you fulfillment and satisfaction. This you can rely on."

--The Official Seal

--The Signature of the Advisor (From The Archives of Bkerke, Douaihy 10 & 21).

PRINCE YOUNES AND HIS MARTYRDOM

Chapter 4

His Family And Origin. -His Wide Properties. - His Manner And Influence. -The Reasons Behind The Complaints Against Him. - Being Arrested With His Family. - Being Forced To Convert To Islam. -His Escape To The Lands Of Kisrawan. -His Return Back To Christianity. - The Case Of Forced Conversion That He Filed. - The Verdict Of His False Conversion To Islam. - His Return To Tripoli And To His Position. - The Malicious Campaign Against Him Again. - His Arrest, The Promise Made To Him And The Threats. - His Steadfastness, Strength And Patience. - His Death On The Stake. - The Christian Hero. - The Confiscation Of His Properties And His Brothers' Properties. - His Brother Rezk's Travel To Europe. - The Assistance Of The King Of France To Him. - Ai-Douaihy's Pamphlet For The Christian Princes.

The Archbishop Youssef al-Debs published in this chronicle the story of Abu Rezk Bachaalany and his sons. He took his account from the <u>Annals</u> of El Douaihy.

The contemporary French world traveler De La Roque has translated what Archbishop al-Debs wrote about Younes Bin Rezk. He did so in the book about his journey to the East which he published after the King of France approved of its contents. I translated it from French.

Here is a translation of what De La Roque wrote:

"The Biography Of The Maronite Prince Younes Who Died For His Religion."

"Prince Younes comes from one of the noblest families in Mount Lebanon. He was a close relative and ally to the Prince of the Maronite sect and its leader. He owned many possessions and real estate at the foot of Mount Lebanon in Tripoli and Jbeil. The income from these was not less than 100,000 Liras.

He was handsome, intelligent and a very good politician. All these good qualities gained him the trust of the viziers of the Sublime Porte and many Syrian rulers. Their benefits from his experience in managerial work made his power almost equal to that of the actual rulers.

His wealth brought him the envy of others and although he was straight and clean, he was resented by some of the Muslims with high positions in that region. They resented him to the extent that they all agreed on getting rid of him.

What helped them reach their goal was the cruel and mean personality of the new ruler of Tripoli, Keblan Bin al-Matragi. The conspirators made complaints to the new ruler about Prince Younes' great wealth. The Governor believe the accusations and arrested Younes, his brother Prince Abu Youssef, their two wives and their children along with many of their relatives and followers. In all, there were more than fifty persons arrested.

Younes was then told that he had committed a serious crime and that his punishment would be his execution along with his whole family. He was informed that the only way out would be for him to convert to Islam. At first, he refused

45

bravely, not caring about the threats. Later, however, he thought about his family and what would happen to them. Because of that, he pretended to be a Muslim. However, he made a strict bargain that his family be allowed to remain Christian and that they be released from prison as soon as possible.

The ruler, seeing that it would be very detrimental to lose such a man, accepted this condition and gave his family the freedom of faith and work. Prince Younes was proud of what he did because he saved many lives from Islam. He saved his daughters and nieces from the greed of Muslim leaders who wanted these women to themselves.

Younes kept praising the ruler. For 40 days he did this so as to hide his real intentions. During these forty days, he managed to send his wife, children and relatives secretly to the high places of the mountains of Kisrawan where they found safety and security. Then after forty days he followed them.

The first business that he took care of was to go directly to the Maronite patriarch. On his knees he cried bitterly, confessing what he did out of weakness. He professed that he will always be a Christian. Then he renewed his faith. He then gained the reconciliation with the Church from the Patriarch after he consented to the penitence imposed on him. This made a strong impression on the Lebanese people who praised his deeds and strong faith.

After the Prince had pleased God and returned to his religion, he insisted on clearing his case before the people. Consequently he gathered all the evidence proving his forced conversion and sent it to the Court of the Sultan in Istanbul. It was delivered by some viziers who were close to him.

At this point, the Pasha was forced to defend himself relying on his friends and allies in Istanbul.

But since the case was a religious one, the Sultan turned it over to the Higher Mufti (Sheik of Islam).

After the Mufti examined the case thoroughly, he reached the conclusion that righteousness was on the side of Younes. Accordingly, the Mufti issued the verdict that the conversion of Younes was by force and thus a false conversion. Furthermore he ordered that Younes must not be treated as a Muslim who abandoned his religion joining the infidels (Christians).

This verdict astonished many people but it didn't clear Younes' conscience. He was feeling a very deep pain inside because of the hardships that he caused to the Christians of a city that contained a large Christian population. This feeling kept bothering him, so one day, he went back to Tripoli and there he showed his Christianity in public and in the presence of the ruler in a very strong act of courage.

But the Muslims weren't able to do anything to harm him.

Also, it was out of good luck, that the ruler was ousted and a new ruler took his place. This new ruler invited Younes to do some important work, appointing him the responsibility of taking care of the wide desert of Tripoli which at that time suffered from unrest.

And to make him feel totally secure, he obtained a high decree from the capital, Istanbul, proving the validity of the verdict of the Mufti. This gave permission to Younes and his family to stay and fulfill their religious duties, forbidding any attempt to harm them in any way in the future.

Thus the Prince stayed with his family in Tripoli for about 5 years in total security, taking care of his work in sincerity, until 1695. Then the ruler died. Now with some of his friends dead and others ousted, his enemies took advantage of the opportunity. To destroy him they filed a complaint against him with the new ruler accusing him of slandering Islam.

The new ruler ordered his arrest. He was constantly threatened. He was tortured. They tried to convince and trick him to abandon his faith. For two years they did this!

This ruler even promised to give him back his properties and to appoint him to an important position. He said he would recommend that he follow him in the government of Tripoli, but Younes was rock-steady. He proved how real a Christian he was and that this persecution was a blessing from God to wash away his previous sin with his spilled blood.

Finally the ruler resorted to other tactics. He tried in person to convince Younes to abandon Christianity but the response of Younes was that he would never exchange the pearl of his faith with the unworthy shell of Islam.

The ruler was furious and outraged by this last response of Younes so he promised him the ugliest fate.

The ruler treated Younes like an infidel dog and ordered his execution on the stake.

In those days, the verdicts of the rulers were final and irreversible. They had the authority in their hands to kill whoever they wanted and forgive whoever they wished.

Before carrying out his execution, the ruler sent a group of Younes' friends to convince him to yield. It was in vain. He was stronger and braver than ever.

They took him out of prison with a stake on his shoulder to a nearby hill. There he would be executed. Before they reached this place, they walked him around the city, with people in front and behind him taunting him with the worst insults.

For the last time the governor offered to forgive him and return his properties. It was no use.

The words of Younes proved that he was a brave Christian for he often used to say: "I am sure that God will take care of me and my family and properties".

And so it was that this Christian hero suffered tremendously and with great courage in front of the city. Its citizens witnessed his death on the stake. Right up to his last breath, he was thanking God and praying to Him, mentioning the Virgin Mary and the Holy Saints. He died on a Monday in May 1697.

His body remained on the stake for five consecutive days guarded by two groups of soldiers to prevent the Maronites from stealing it.

Many trustworthy eyewitnesses swore that on the first day of his martyrdom, they saw a crown of light over his head which frightened the soldiers and made them run away.

The soldiers claimed that it was fire from hell that came to burn the body of this infidel but time proved otherwise. The light kept appearing and the body remained safe. The guards were so terrified that they stayed away from the body.

Some of the Muslim dignitaries expressed to the Ruler their disapproval of leaving the body on the stake for fear that the people would rise up in revolution against them.

So one of the cousins of Younes was allowed to remove the body. He put it in a well not far from the Maronite grave yard. Then, after two days, he took it secretly to the Church of Saint John in Tripoli where it was buried behind the pulpit.

People wondered how a dead body could stay fresh during these eight days without any hint of foulness coming out of it.

After the death of Prince Younes, his brother Prince Abu Youssef, who suffered the agony of imprisonment like his brother, almost died in prison. Fortunately some of his friends intervened with the ruler. They managed to pursuade the prince to give up all his properties in return for his life and the lives of his family members.

After he was released from prison, he traveled to Europe asking the Christian Princes for help.

I did see him in Paris and got together with him for months, during which time he was a true example of patience.

The King has bestowed his favor on him writing about his situation to his ambassador in Istanbul and to his consuls in the East. The King also sent a letter full of condolences to the Patriarch of the Maronites.

As for me, I heard from him the full story of the life and death of Prince Younes which I summarized here. It is in complete agreement with what was written by the Patriarch of the Maronites and the King of France. It also agrees with the report submitted by the Consul of France in Tripoli which was approved by the French and Spanish priests in the Holy Lands."

Henry Mondrel, the English missionary, narrated in a book about his trip <u>From Aleppo to</u> <u>Jerusalem</u> that on the 8th of May 1697, the Consul of England took him to the citadel of Tripoli where the doomed Younes was imprisoned. He had been jailed because of his conversion to Islam and subsequent return to Christianity. He commented that Younes said he was facing death as atonement for his sin. Younes was executed two days after his travel with the English traders who were with him.

According to the words of this writer, the execution's date becomes the 12th or the 13th of May.

This is the translation of what Henry Mondrel said about his trip:

"Saturday on the 8th of May: After lunch, Mr. Hestence, the Consul of England, came to me to go and visit the citadel of Tripoli, which is built on a hill that looks over the city. It contains no weapons or ammunition and that makes it useful for nothing but to be a prison. When we visited it, we found a Maronite prisoner called Sheik Younes who abandoned his religion and converted to Islam then repented this since and suffered death as atonement for this sin. By the order of the Ruler of Tripoli, he was executed on the stake two days after we visited.

This punishment was chosen by the Muslims for the gravest criminals. It is inhuman and a barbaric act, which they perform as follows:

They take a stake of wood with a diameter like that of a thigh and about 9 feet in length. It has a sharp and tiny pointed edge. Then they force the criminal to carry it to the place of execution, similar to what the Romans used to do in the past when making a criminal carry his cross.

When they arrive at the location of the execution, they force the tip of the wooden stake through the bottom of this doomed man and keep pulling him from his legs till the stake comes out through his shoulder. Then they would hold it up right and fix it in the ground. The doomed man stays in this unfortunate state. Some of these doomed men would be left for an hour suffering the incredible pain. Then they jab them in the chest with a spear and thus end their doomed lives." (Mondrel, page 237).

De La Roque has reported that there was a pamphlet from the Patriarch Estephanos El Douaihy to the generous people of Europe carried by Abu Youssef Rezk and it is in Latin.

He reported also that there was the signature and the seal of the Patriarch in Syriac and Latin. In the middle of the seal there is a picture of the Virgin Mary with Little Jesus on her hand and around his head two crosses. The picture is beautiful and the seal is large.

This is the whole pamphlet that was translated at its time by al- Debs:

Signature in Syriac: *"The humble Estephan Boutros, the Patriarch of Antioch"*   The same is also in Latin.

"Greetings and God's blessings to every one who reads or hears this document.

Let it be known that our dear son, Abu Youssef Rezk, is a Maronite Catholic man of our subjects and of the notables of our dominion.   He is the brother of Sheik Younes who was forced by the Turks to abandon his religion by word but not in his heart.   He was forced to do so in order to save his little children.   However God helped him escape after forty days.   He escaped to Kisrawan where he confessed his sin and accepted his penitence.   He appealed his treatment to the Great Turkish Sultan and he was award a high decree.   The decree was based on a judge's verdict that his abandoning his religion was by force and thus invalid.   He then went to Tripoli and publicly displayed his Christianity for five years.   Hatred and malice grew in the hearts of some of the people in authority until they managed to have him thrown in prison.   They had him executed on the stake.   All during his torture he bravely showed his steadfast faith in Jesus Christ.

His brother Rezk (Youssef Rezk Nasr Bachaalany) was imprisoned too and lost an amount of money in the several thousands.   His properties were confiscated and sold including even his house and furniture.   He couldn't continue in his country or provide for his family, that is to say, his children and the children of his brother Younes.   They are fifteen in number and he was forced to borrow money to provide for them.   He doesn't have enough for them.   They came to us many times asking that we accompany this Sheik Rezk, the father and uncle of these children.   Armed with this document, thus, I have high hopes that the generous people who feel for the wounds of this man and his chaste mother would help them.   For their generosity we would pray that they gain the reward from our Great God, his glorification, and the praises to the One Who said in the Holy Bible: 'whatever you do to one of these little brothers of Mine, then to Me you do it..'   And I ask God to reward those who grant aid by giving them one hundred times their charity in both this life and the next.

Given in our Chair at Kannoubine, October 15, 1699. (Signature of the Patriarch attached with his seal).

Additional Signatures: Yousself al-Hasarati, Archibishop of Jbeil in Huqa; Yuhanna Habquq, Archbishop of Batroun in Qazzhia; Gabriel El Douaihy, Archibishop of Safd in Saint Sarkis, Ehden.

TRIPOLI AND ITS TIES WITH YOUNES

Chapter 5

Its Description In Younes' Times. – Its Rulers. – The Patriarch And The Archbishops. – The Relatives Of Younes And His Friends. – His Monuments In Tripoli. – Dramas And Poems About Younes. – A Comparison Of The Deaths of Younes And Abu Rezk.

Here I must tell you about the situation in the city of Tripoli at the time of the martyrdom of Sheik Younes. I must also mention the Rulers who governed this city, in succession, one after the other. I will tell of the stories and remnants that clarify what De La Roque, the French traveler, has said about this martyr.

I hope that my friend, Father Aghtanious Tanous, the Lebanese priest, will reveal much more of these stories and relics in his book <u>The Chronicle Of The Maronite Bishopric Of Tripoli.</u> Hopefully he will publish this book soon.

The following was mentioned in a book written in Latin <u>Some Eastern Cities</u> by two knowledgeable Maronites: Gabriel al-Sahyouni and Yuhanna al-Hasrouni (page 54):

"Tripoli is an ancient city whose name means 'the three cities'. In olden days it actually consisted of three cities.

It is situated about a mile away from the sea on two hills. Part of it rises gradually on some very beautiful hills while the other section consists of plains that extend in front of it.

From the direction of the sea, there is a wide land that adorns the city and constitutes a source of many benefits.

In this spot there are many olive trees and gardens of citron trees, pomegranate and sugar cane.

From the other side that looks on Lebanon, there are dense gardens of olive trees with delicious fruits. These gardens extend fifteen miles in length and eight miles in width.

These olives are the reason for the wealth of the people of the city.

In the middle of this spot, there is a sweet water river that divides it into two equal parts. This river originates from Lebanon and its water divides the gardens spreading its waters on both banks. After the river leaves the city, it waters the gardens beneath the city until it meets the salty seawater one-mile away.

There is also the water from a spring that comes out of the mountainside of Mount Lebanon and passes through the city. Its water runs in a canal until it reaches the port one-mile away. This provides life to the inhabitants.

Tripoli is known for its varied delicious fruits especially bananas. It also has an abundance of wine, oil, wheat and other grains.

Tripoli has no walls surrounding it but it has on the coast secure square shaped towers. On one of its hills, there is a secure citadel which the natives say was built by the Europeans. (This is the same citadel that was for a period of time the prison of Younes, as it was also the prison of Younes' father and his family and friends. The fortress still stands today.

What makes Tripoli a very important and wealthy city is that it is the center of trade. This is the place where many precious goods come by land and sea to be exported to other countries." (Refer to the book "the translation of El Douaihy" by Archbishop Shebli, page 49).

Father Philip, one of the Carmelite priests, said in the book about his travel to the East (1629-1640), published in the year 1652, page 68, which I translated as:

"The location of Tripoli is at the foot of Mount Lebanon with a wide plain that measures a six mile square. This area separates it from Mount Lebanon.

The plain is green on both sides, with various trees planted in it, especially mulberry trees that produce a large harvest of silk.

There is a river known as "the Sacred River" where several springs coming out of Lebanon meet. The river runs through the middle of the plain and the city. It runs for one and a half miles until it flows into the sea.

Guarding this port are seven towers with their canons. They protect the city from the attacks of the Buccaneers."

Various rulers came into power in Tripoli around this time. In 1686, Hussein Pasha ruled. He imprisoned Younes, his two brothers, and their children in 1687.

He was succeeded by Mohammad Pasha in 1691. Then came Ali Pasha al-Nakdi in 1692 who was ousted in 1693 and replaced by Arslan Pasha bin Ahmad Agha bin al-Matalji, the governor of al-Lazeqeia, who was originally from al-Lazeqeia.

Several years later, his brother Qablan Pasha, who was mentioned by the traveler Jean De La Roque (1661-December 8, 1745) in his book, took power. He ruled until the year 1695 when he arrested Younes and imprisoned him in the famous citadel. Younes ended up being executed on the stake 1697.

The previously mentioned Arslan Pasha returned to power in 1698.

At that time, the Maronite Patriarch was the famous Patriarch Estephan El Douaihy from Ehden (1670-1704). He is the one who wrote the detailed stories of Abu Rezk and the shorter stories of Younes.

It was written in the Annals that Younes was killed on May 21 whereas De La Roque and Henry Mondrel say that he was killed on the 12th or 13th of that month.

The head of the bishopric of Tripoli at that time was Archbishop Youssef Sham'oun al- Hasrouni who was the secretary of El Douaihy. El Douaihy promoted him to the Archbishopric of Tripoli in 14 July 1675. His name was Youssef Ne'ma bin Barbour al-Hasrouni, a student of Rome, who was known for his knowledge. He died in Kannoubine 1695.

It appears that the chair of the Bishopric then remained empty after him until 1698. This was due to the prejudice and the persecutions that existed. Then Ya'qub (Jacob) Awwad was promoted as the head of the Bishopric of Tripoli. He became the Patriarch in 1705 and faced huge persecutions. He died in 1733.

My friend, the historian, al-Kursaqf Boulos Qarali found a letter in Italian attached to a book. The book, found in Diman, was written in Syriac. It appeared from this letter that it was sent from the Franciscan Fathers in Tripoli to the Maronite Patriarchate and was about Younes Bachaalany and his brother Rezk.

The letter referred to the concern that these virtuous priests and missionaries had about the affairs of Younes. They wrote of his fulfillment of his religious duties in his last hours. They spoke of him in glowing terms.

I have never been able to read the whole content of this letter.

I found a court order dated 9 Rajab 1255 Hegira (1840) issued by the judge of Tripoli saying that the place known as the grave of Mar Yuhanna (Saint John) in this city, being claimed by Hanna Girgis Abu al-Hawa, is indeed owned by the Maronites

This was at the time of Philipus, the son of Isaac Tarbeia, fiduciary of the Monastery of Mar Yuhanna of the Maronites.

The text of this court order was given to me by my friend Father Aghtanious Tanous, taken from volume three of the registers of the Maronite Patriarchate, page 46. It is a good possibility that this Monastery and grave are the burial place of the Martyr Younes as mentioned by De La Roque.

One of the stories told in Tripoli is about a shrine called the shrine of Ha Abd Allah, saying that this shrine is the grave of Sheik Younes Bachaalany. This shrine is located at the southern entrance of the city in Mahallet al-Ram at the beginning of Aqabet al-Laouz. It is known to the Muslims as a grave of a Christian man.

Also, there is another place in this city in Mahallet al-Sagha. It is a shrine of the Catholic Church that is known as "Lady of Younes". It has an old picture of the Virgin in it. This shrine is a small temple visited by pious people (These are the words of my friend Monsieur Arsanious al-Fakhuri).

From the surviving papers that mention Younes Bachaalany is a French drama written by one of the Jesuit Fathers who named it "The Martyrdom of Prince Younes". It was performed by the students of their school in Ghazir before the school was moved to Beirut. The late Monsieur Boutros Arsanious Kour, the president of Mar Yuhanna Maron Kfarhi has relayed this information to me. He saw the performance of this play when he was one of the students of the school in Ghazir.

About 1910, my friend al-Khuri Yuhanna Habib Rahma, one of the Lebanese missionaries and the president of their school in Buenos Aires, wrote an Arabic drama about the martyrdom of Younes. It was a well recognized piece of literature and art. The drama was performed first in Jounieh, then in the school of the Benevolent Missionaries in Buenos Aires, Argentina. I have in my possession the original version of the drama in the handwriting of its author. I protect it as a precious treasure.

There is also a play of the same kind about the Martyrdom of Younes which was written by Father Yuhanna Khalifa, the Lebanese Priest from Hadthoun. He published it in 1937 and presented a copy of it to me.

Also, around 1893, my relative Sheik Youssef al-Khuri Hanna Bachaalany wrote a poetic drama about our grandfather Abu Rezk. It was performed by his students in Salima, then, later, by the students of the school that we opened in Bchaaleh that same year. It was performed on the eve of the Saint Doumit festival.

It was seen by visitors to the schools of the Jesuit Fathers in the entire Batroun region. Furthermore, many of the notables of Doma, the people of Bchaaleh and many others also saw it. All of them thoroughly enjoyed the play since the name of Abu Rezk is so commonly spoken there.

Also, my relative, the late Sheik Habib Shaiban Bachaalany wrote a long poem including in it the stories of Abu Rezk and his son Younes. The poem has many recollections of our ancestors. It also presents many lessons stressing our obligation to try to imitate our ancestors in all their virtues.

It starts with:

> *On the foundation of copying the grandfathers*

one builds the supports of honor
The glorious deeds of the grandfathers
brings back to life the feeling of pride in self and the new generation
O offspring of Bshe'lani
come yearning to the great history of your family.

And it ends with:

O hill of striving
greetings upon you from the children of the martyred hero.
In your arena the glory of Jesus shone atop the heads of bodies.
And your miracles took place so religion can kick the stubborn
In this place a deep faith shone in the living and the dead
O Bachaalany folks you will be blessed
if you follow in the footsteps of the grandfathers.

It is useful to compare the killing of Sheik Abu Rezk and the death of his son Younes. In this way we can see the similarities and differences in their situations and circumstances.

El Douaihy did mention the stories of the father and his son…some briefly and some in more detail. From his references one can see that this investigating historian has mentioned the stories of Abu Rezk in quotes taken from others. The reason for this is because when he returned from Rome after attending the Maronites school from 1641 to 1655, all the events of Abu Rezk were already finished. The stories of Younes and his brothers, however, were witnessed by El Douaihy himself. He was directly involved with them from the beginning to the end. Yet he mentioned these events only briefly for many reasons. The most important reason was his sensitive position with the Rulers of the Ottoman lands. Also, he could spread the word about what happened to Younes in ways that did not required the written word.

What is important, however, is that the Patriarch did mention that they killed Younes after they offered him Islam and he refused. El Douaihy mentioned the killing of Abu Rezk without any reference to him being offered Islam. This is why I think there is the difference.

The historian El Douaihy, so famous for his credibility and truthfulness, is simply telling the stories of both exactly as they happened. So he writes "Younes was killed after they offered him Islam and he refused." Because the whole incident of Younes occurred in the city of Tripoli in front of people, Christian and Muslim, there were many witnesses. Whereas the killing of Abu Rezk occurred in Kounia in the lands of the Turks, in a far away place. He was killed as a stranger in a place where he was not known. Thus El Douaihy can only mention the story as he heard it.

But the killing of Abu Rezk must have happened in 1654 in the same way as the killing of his son Younes in 1697, the killing of Abu Karam al-Hadthi in 1640 and the killing of Kan'aan al-Daher 1741… all killed exactly in the same manner: The accused is offered Islam and if he refuses then he is killed with no mercy. If he accepts then he is forgiven, no matter what his crime is. And thus the execution of Abu Rezk is the strongest evidence that they offered him Islam as usual. But he refused. So, they killed him.

This uncertainty about the killing of Abu Rezk is the reason why the honorable Patriarch did not include him among the "Martyrs of the Maronites" in the digest that he ordered to be published. My relative, the historian al-Khuri Ibrahim Harfoush was able to obtain a copy of this digest in 1937.

Among the names that are included in the digest are:

1- the Patriarch Gabriel from Hajoula 1296 or 1367.
2- Abu Karam Ya'qub bin Elias al-Ra'is al-Hadthy 1640.
3- Younes bin Abu Rezk al-Bshe'lani 1697.
4- Sheik Kan'aan al-Daher.

As for what Jean De La Roque said: "Younes was an ally and very close to the Prince of the Maronites and their President" and this can only be explained by what the late Sheik Farid al-Khazen said. Who is referred to as the Prince of the Maronites? It is Sheik Hesn al-Khazen, the eldest son of Abu Qonsowa bin Abu Naoufal al-Khazen. He was at this time the most prestigious Sheik of the Maronites and gained the position of consul of Beirut 1697 succeeding his father. He was known in France as the Prince of the Maronites. (Refer to The Traditions of France in Lebanon which was translated to Arabic by Father Abboud, page 175)

It is also written in this book on page 193 that Sheik Hesn wrote to a French Ministry that he is providing the expenses for three Maronite families that were forced to convert to Islam then converted back to the Catholic Religion. These families are the families of Younes, Abd Allah and Youssef Rezk, the sons of Abu Rezk. Most probably, Sheik Hesn was the husband of their sister or the sister of Hesn was the wife of Younes and died as recorded by Sheik Farid in Ghousta.

What I know is that after the disaster that befell them in Tripoli, my ancestors took refuge with the al-Khazan people, their relatives and allies. They lived there for a while before moving to Zouq al-Kharab and Haret al-Balana in Salima. Both of these two places were part of the district of al-Khazen in Kisrawan.

The first one is Hanna Bachaalany who is the son of Bu Mhanna. His testimony was included in the deed involving the Monastery of Kannoubine (1641) by Archibishop Girgis Habquq Bachaalany.

The second one is Ne'ma who is the son of Hanna Bachaalany. The third one is Abd Allah bin Abd al-Messeeh Bachaalany. Both of them were mentioned as witnesses in the deed of Tarbeia bin Ya'Qub Al-Torjoman to the Maronite Patriarchate in 1127 Hegira. There may have been other cousins there too.

Also famous in Tripoli was Sheik Tarbeia bin Hobaish bin Moussa bin Nassif. He was appointed as the ruler of Ghazir 1686. It is he who was assigned by Patriarch Youssefal-Akouri and his Archbishops to accompany Archbishop Michael Sa'ada, the Archbishop of Tripoli, with a recommendation to be carried to Europe. The Sheik was so famous that his prestige would make the religious mission easier to carry out. The Sheik's fame was as great in the West as it was in the East. (refer to The History Of The Notables by Sheik Tanous al-Shediaq, page 99 and the patriarchal magazine by its owner al-Khuri Boulos Qarali, year 6, part 6).

It is a good possibility that this Sheik is the one whose relatives came to Tripoli because of the marriage of his daughter. They were the ones who were the guests in the house of Sheik Abu Rezk. They were his friends, relatives and allies who were subjected with Abu Rezk to the injustice and imprisonment that I previously mentioned.

THE KING OF FRANCE

AND

THE BACHAALANY FAMILY

Chapter 6

French Documents About Younes. — The Travel Of His Brother Rezk To France. — His Meeting With The King And His Ministers. — The Grant Of The King To Him. — The Letter Of The King To The Ambassador In Istanbul. — To The Ministry Of Foreign Affairs. — About The Book Of The Christian Vestiges. — Father Godar. — Restelle Huber... etc.

It was out of good luck that I was able to obtain the French documents about the killing of Sheik Younes. The same applies to those documents pertaining to the travels of his brother, Youssef, to the capital of France, his meeting with its great King, Emperor Louis XIV, and the King's grant to him. This gift is considered great by the standards of those days and is regarded as a magnificent gesture of compassion from the royalty of France to the Maronites and the people of Lebanon.

I had known of the existence of these documents in the archives of the French government where they still exist today. I requested an opportunity to view these precious documents. The great Archbishop Boutros Shebli, the head of the Beirut Diocese (1908-1917) personally fetched them and gave them to me with his own hand.

The King of France, the Great Monarch, Louis XIV, is a famous historical figure. He died in 1715 at the age of seventy-seven after ruling for seventy-two years.

I present here the translations of these French documents:

<u>From The King To His Ambassador In Istanbul</u>

"August 10, 1701, concerning Sheik Abu Rezk, the Maronite Roman Catholic, whose properties have been confiscated by the Turks:

Outbound from Marly, August 10, 1701, to Mr. Friole:

Sheik Abu Rezk, the Maronite Roman Catholic, has shown me that he and his brother Younes are from the notables of their dominion. Their high rank, their wealth, their standing in the Catholic Church which they always preserved, brought on them the envy and hatred of the Muslim Turks. Younes was the victim of their revnge when they executed him on the stake. His brother was able to escape saving himself, his children and the children of his brother about 13 or 14 in number. This only after all his properties were confiscated and stolen.

The Antioch Patriarch has testified that all that has been said is true. He has asked me to place him under my protection emphasizing that he is one of the notables of the land and that it would be beneficial to the Catholic religion if he were to regain his previous status.

Thus, I direct this letter to you to tell you that it is my desire that you help him with your care and authority. I request that you use all your powers and under all circumstances possible, assist him so that he can fulfill all the just causes that he seeks and turn away all worries concerning his religion in the future, and thus..." (The Ministry of Foreign Affairs, Part 36, page 135.)

From The King To The Ministry Of Foreign Affairs

"On August 7, 1701, an order with the value of 300 Liras in an extraordinary way to Sheik Abu Youssef Rezk, the Maronite Roman Catholic.

Outbound from Versailles on August 7, 1701, to be preserved, pay by hand to Sheik Abu Youssef Rezk, the Maronite Roman Catholic, an amount of 300 Liras, issued to him in an extra ordinary way." (The Ministry of Foreign Affairs, volume 86, page 129)

From The Minister Of Foreign Affairs To The Ambassador

"On August 20, 1701, to Mr. De Friole, about Sheik Abu Youssef Rezk, the Maronite Roman.Catholic, outbound from Marilee on August 20, 1701.

You are looking at the letter of the King that I attached to this message. You are aware of the desire of His Majesty concerning the oppression suffered by Sheik Abu Youssef, so I add to this only that if they, in the East, want to force a retribution on him because of his travel to these countries, then you must use your position to prevent them from harming him with all that you can." (The Ministry of Foreign Affairs, part 36, pages 136, 137 and 138)

Also, I might add, Father Rebat al-Yasu'ey said in his book, The Christian Vestiges, part 2, book 2, page 371, translated from the French:

"And in my diary, the following instructions about the passports that were issued by the King in Versailles on August 3, 1701, section, treasury 7, section 68, page 140; passport issued to Don Youssef Misessle. On August 10, 1701, Foreign Affairs, correspondences with Turkey, Politics, section 33, page 138: passport issued to Sheik Abu Youssef Rezk who is heading to Istanbul. And in the same date, page 140, passport issued to Khuri Elias. ...and on November 2, 1702, page 230, passport issued to Francis al-Maroni from Aleppo." (The Christian Vestiges, volume 3, page 543).

It appears that Sheik Youssef Rezk was accompanied by the aforementioned al-Khuri Elias, the secretary of Patriarch El Douaihy. He is mentioned by De La Roque as going to the King of France carrying a letter from El Douaihy in Azaar in 1700 asking him to intercede with the Sublime Porte to prevent the assaults on the Maronites. He also carried the response of the King to El Douaihy from August 10, 1701. Since the passport of Abu Youssef Rezk and that of al-Khuri Elias are shown as issued on the same date, it seems very likely that they may have traveled together to Istanbul and then Lebanon.

Father Godar al-Yasu'ey said in his printed, illustrated, French book, The Virgin in Lebanon,, page 276, speaking about the oppression suffered by the Christians in the East:

"...such was the suffering of Prince Younes, one of the notables of the Maronites, in May 1697, who was offered by them to abandon his religion but he refused. They executed him on the stake and he died while making supplications to the Virgin Mary. His brother escaped to France seeking help from Louis XIV. The King wrote to Monsieur De

Friole, his Ambassador in Istanbul concerning the brother, Sheik Abu Youssef Rezk, who came seeking the protection of the King. Since Prince Younes was killed by the Muslims and his properties confiscated, the brother was forced to escape seeking protection, so answer his request."

(Refer to the book, <u>Voyage de Syrie et du Mont-Liban</u>, about the trip of Jean De La Roque, 10 August 1701 to Syria, Parisian Edition, 1722, page 276).

Monsieur Restelle Huber, the French Consul in Beirut, has written a book in French called <u>The Traditions</u>. He published it in 1918 then again in 1921. Al-Khuri Boulos Abboud translated it to Arabic and this is what came in the book as taken from original historical documents:

(Restelle Huber, the Arabic version, pages: 193, 209, 215 and 243):

"The Maronite family of Abu Rezk in Tripoli has suffered a great deal of pain and torture. This is proof of the barbarism of the perpetrators. These oppressors have tortured and caused excruciating pain to Sheik Younes Abu Rezk. He was the leader of his family. They tortured him in every way, forcing him to convert to Islam in exchange for the lives of his small children. Thus he abandoned his religion in word only, with an eye full of pain and a heart extremely depressesd. After a short period of time he repented his sin and returned back to his religion. He then went to Constantinople. Then he recklessly and arrogantly returned to Tripoli. The Turks caught him and silenced him but this time he openly showed his faith. While he was being tortured these villains confiscated his possessions and even wanted to take the possessions of his brother, Abu Youssef. So it was that Abu Youssef came to be in the position of being the sole provider of his children and those of Younes. There were fourteen children altogether. He found himself unable to provide so he traveled to France. (Refer to De La Roque's travel book, speaking about the Sheik, his trip to France, and calling him Prince Abu Youssef). In France he sought the generosity of King Louis XIV, carrying a document from the Patriarch and the Consul (the testimony of El Douaihy, dated 15 October, 1699, and the testimony of the French Consul in Tripoli, dated 20 October, 1699. Then there is the letter of the Patriarch to King Louis dated 9 August, 1700, the French Ministry of the Navy). Both of them have testified to the truth of his situation in order to move the heart of the King for him." (Arabic version of Restelle Huber, page 209.

Then, Huber said in another place:

"Count Boncher Tran wanted to ease the effect of the refusal on Sheik Hesn al-Khazen, the Consul of France in Beirut, so he gave him a gift of 1000 Liras to be delivered to him by the Consul Stal. The intent of this money is to be used by the Sheik to provide for three Maronite families that returned to the Catholic religion after being forced to abandon it. They were at the Sheik's residence for two years and he was providing for their expenses. Sheik Hesn made it clear to Stal that his financial situation did not allow him to continue providing for them and that he intended to send the three families to France. There, they would be safe from the enemies of their religion. The French Consul told him that this was not possible and that he had petitioned the King to generously supply him with his help. The money was nothing but this gift. The amount was given to him with a promise of repeating it. (Stal Magazine, January 5, 1705, and his letter to Boncher Tran, March 2, 1705, from the papers of the Ministry of Foreign Affairs; and, the letter of Boncher Tran to Stal, June 17, 1705, from the Ministry of the Navy, 7-73, page 127; Restelle Huber, <u>The French Traditions</u>, Arabic version, p. 193.)

Sheik Hesn died on November 26th, 1707.

Restelle Huber said that King Louis XIV was not able to fulfill the request of Patriarch El Douaihy. And then he said that the King didn't want to delay his help to Sheik Youssef Rezk because his circumstances touched his heart deeply.

As a result, the King granted Sheik Youssef Rezk 300 Golden Liras as an extraordinary grant. In addition to this, the King gave him a French passport and recommended him to the Ambassador. The Sheik traveled to Istanbul seeking help and justice. He also wrote to the Ambassador asking that he be saved from the evil of the Turks after he returned home. (The decision was dated August 7, 1701, by the Ministry of Foreign Affairs, and Boncher Tran to Friole, August 20, 1701, in the Ministry of Foreign Affairs, and Restelle Huber, the Arabic version, page 215.)

And Restelle Huber said:

"Sheik Hesn al-Khazen, the Consul of France, supplied protection in his house for many of the unfortunate Christians, saving them from the evil of the Turks. He gave them shelter until they might be granted forgiveness from the Pasha, or, until he might find another shelter for them. Thus it was that he protected five Maronites from the unfortunate family of Abu Rezk who were forced to convert to Islam with the sword over their necks. They ran away and escapted without any criticism directed toward the Consul." (Restelle Huber, Arabic Version, page 243. (Boular to Boncher Tran, July 12, 1707. from the Papers of the Ministry of Foreign Affairs, Tripoli.)

FROM FRANCE TO LEBANON

Chapter 7

The Companions Of Rezk In His Travels. – His Knowledge And Educational Background. – His Syriac Manuscripts. – The Failure Of His Mission To Istanbul. – Empty Promises. – The Increase In Oppression And Hardships. – Qlud Bachaalany.

I don't know the whole picture about what happened to my ancestor Abu Youssef Rezk in his travels to France and Istanbul. I don't know if he was alone or accompanied by someone. I do know that travel at that time was full of dangers and hardships.

I know that there were three people sent by Patriarch El Douaihy to conduct his sectarian business in Rome and France. They were: Yuhanna Marmaghoun, al-Shediaq Yuhanna al-Khuri Qeddisi (Geddisi), and, al-Khuri Elias Sham'oun al-Hasrouni. The latter most likely accompanied Abu Rezk in his travels since both of them obtained traveling tickets to Istanbul with the same date. (Refer to the book <u>His Friend And Lawyer</u> by the late al-Khuri Boutros Ghaleb, pages 258 and 280).

Some would wonder if Rezk knew a European language that would have helped him in his mission in Europe and Istanbul. Or, perhaps, his companion was translating to him since the three that I mentioned were able to speak European languages, but I can't confirm this. But I do know that the sons of Abu Rezk grew up in a house that valued education in Tripoli where missionaries were teaching European languages as I mentioned before. Accordingly, it is possible that they were highly educated. From the words of De La Roque, it appears that he spoke with Rezk and took from him the stories of his brother Younes and his family. De La Roque never mentioned that this occurred using a translator.

My researcher friend, Father Antonious Shebli, the Lebanese priest, mentioned in an article he wrote ("al-Mashreq" 24: 658) that he found among the manuscripts of the Monastery of Our Lady of Maifuq a book of Syriac grammar numbered 24. The book which is in the handwriting of our grandfather Rezk had at its end: "*This book is finished with the help of God, the King, the Giver, with the hands of the humble Youssef Rezk al-Bachaalany in 1730.*"

This manuscript has been transferred together with other manuscripts to the Monastery of al-Banat (The Monastery of the Girls) in Jbeil.

If this book is proved to be in the handwriting of Youssef Rezk bin Abu Rezk, and I know no one else carrying this name, then it is evidence of his vast knowledge and his work in science. I have yet to see the book to judge the degree of knowledge and education.

This manuscript shows me that Abu Youssef Rezk was still alive in 1730 and that he used to spend his time in writing and copying right up to his last days.

The knowledgeable Sheiks of the family say that he died in Salima. And they say that he is the ancestor of a family tree that is known as the branch of Abu Youssef. It is one of the branches of the Bachaalany people in Salima. This is according to the exact text of the lineage of the Bachaalany people as dictated to the late al-Khuri Yuhanna

Bachaalany (the priest, Father John Bachaalany). He was one of the knowledgeable people of that period. The dictation was given by Nejm Andrea, who was considered the head of the Bachaalany people and their elder at this time period.

It hurts me very much that the chain of stories of Youssef Rezk is incomplete. I don't know if he succeeded in his mission to Istanbul. I don't know if he received security for his life, the lives of his family, and their properties. I don't know if he at least received any compensation for the properties that were confiscated in Tripoli.

But the persecution of the clergy and the people in the north of Lebanon increased and the immigrants flooded out of these areas. They escaped from oppression and taxes. This makes me think that Abu Youssef did not succeed in his mission in the Capital of the Sultanate. Thus he probably returned home content with what he received from the generosity of the King of France.

From examining the stories about al-Khuri Elias, the accredited envoy of the Maronite Patriarch to Rome and France, I have come to these conclusions: Al-Khuri Elias was probably the companion of Rezk in Europe and Istanbul; the Sublime Porte did what he usually did with the recommendations of the Kings of Europe, and he answered through their Ambassadors with empty promises that frequently came to nothing.

I don't think that the recommendations carried by Rezk had any effect. They were empty promises that were useless. Especially, since the oppression of the Christians in the areas around Tripoli increased. (Refer to the Annals of El Douaihy and the book His Friend And His Lawyer).

Therefore, my ancestors, who were dispersed into the different areas of Kisrawan, came together after Rezk came back home. They inhabited Haret al-Balana and Zouq al-Kharab, of the villages of Kisrawan.

I can cite the exact period of time in which they lived in these areas. But I also know, from what was told to me by the grandfathers and fathers, that they started leaving these areas gradually. Whenever they were able to sell their real estate and homes they moved. This is because of their poverty and oppression. There was turmoil and turbulence, too, in the land because of the struggle between the Yamani party and the Qaysi party that worsened in Lebanon.

My late father told me, passing on what his father and Nejm Andrea told him, that our grandfathers spent part of their lives in the different areas of Kisrawan in a state of poverty and hardship. They were forced to abandon their houses in Tripoli where they lived a luxurious life. They left their wonderful homes and many properties seeking shelter in hidden far places away from civilization. "*They were like lost people in the wilderness, living in caves and cracks in the earth.*"

I pictured them in my mind like Bani Israel (the Israelites) in Babylon "along the rivers of Babylon we sat, there we hung our melody instrument and wept."

There remains a place that witnessed their ordeal. It is in Qarnet Shahouan and it is still known today under the name of one of these grandfathers, Qlud Bachaalany. It is a place far away from civilization, far from the possessions of the deceased al-Khuri Boulos al-Zoghbi and his brother the deceased father of Dr. Qaisar al-Zoghbi.

It appears that one of my grandfathers used to hide in that place and thus it was called after his name.

"Qlud" is the plural of "Qald" which is a slang word meaning a trough carved in a rock in the wilderness where rainwater collects providing a person water when needed.

FROM KISRAWAN TO SALIMA

Chapter 8

The Disasters That Befell the Bachaalany folks. - Their trips to the Strip (Qate'). - Their Relationship With The Ma'n House And The Qaysi Party. - Baret al-Balana And Zouq Al-Kharab. - Their Relationships With The Ma'n Princes. - Their Migration To Salima.

It appears from what I have already mentioned that Bachaalany folks migrated three times from Tripoli to Kisrawan and the Strip (Qate') of Kisrawan. The borders of the Strip of Kisrawan extend to the south to the river of Ja'mani. The Strip of Kisrawan was an area that belonged to Kisrawan in the days when the al-Khazen people were feudal lords. The first migration was in 1653 when Abu Rezk Bachaalany told his brother Sa'b, the day he went to Jable, to take his children and family to the lands of Ibn Ma'n. The second was after the death of Abu Rezk. Hussein Pasha caught and imprisoned the family in Tripoli, accusing them of the crimes of their father. But they excaped to Qate' Kisrawan on September 29, 1687. The third was in 1697 the day of the execution of Younes when they fled to Kisrawan and Qate' (the Strip). That was their last time in Tripoli.

Whoever follows the stories of this family from the very first days of Abu Rezk then after him his sons and grandsons will see that they were always members of the Qaysi Party. They were friends and allies to the Ma'ns, always siding with them and always helping them. No matter the circumstances, no matter where they were, they were always loyal to them. This too was their attitude towards the al-Khazen people that I mentioned before. The Ma'ns were considered the leaders of the Qaysi people.

This is the reason why the Bachaalany took refuge during the hard times with their friends, relatives and allies in Kisrawan and the lands of Ma'ns. There they could hide from their unjust rulers.

During that period, the Bachaalany used to visit the Ma'n Princes in Salima. They had old, close relationships with them. In the manuscripts that I have there are indications of their relationships: Prince Fares Abu Al-Lam'i, the prince of Beskinta who was taking care of some of the fiefs in the north (cited in El Douaihy in 1650) and Prince Abd Allah Qeidbei, the Prince of Salima (famous in history especially for the battle of Ain Dara) both of them had political ties with Sheik Abu Rezk and his son Younes. This was at the time when they were appointed the position of the counselor of Tripoli. They also shared a strong feeling for the unity and independence of Lebanon and for the Qaysi Party which made their friendship strong.

The testimony of Prince Abd Allah and Sheik Younes appeared together on a deed from the collection of deeds of El-Douaihy. After the Bachaalany moved to the Strip (Qate') of Kisrawan, which at that time was under the authority of the al-Khazen people, it started little by little to enter into the rule of the Ma'n Princes. Then, after the battle of Ain Dara, it was totally separated and became one of the fiefs of these Princes. The borders of their rule extended to the Kalb River. Thus, both Zouq al-Kharab village and Baret al-Balana village, where the Bachaalany people lived, came within these borders.

At that time, the vows of friendship were renewed between the Princes and the Bachaalany whom the Princes found to be extremely noble, outspoken and courageous.

Thus, the Ma'n Princes socialized with them and made their stay with them in Salima welcomed. They promised to give them lands there. They cooperated with them and witnessed their bravery in situations that showed they were dependable and reliable.

About fifty or sixty years ago, I asked the opinion of the knowledgeable Sheiks of my Bachaalany family about the migration of our grandfathers from the Strip (Qate') and their movement to Salima. Here I am publishing the summary of the answer of each one of these Sheiks. From generation to generation they inherited the story of their migration from Baret al-Balana and Zouq al-Kharab. This made the story so clear in their minds and so frequently on their tongues. It is the remnant of the history of these grandfathers who came to Salima for the last time about 250 years ago, after the killing of the head of their family Sheik Younes Bachaalany.

In order to be accurate in recording history, I mention the name of the narrator with the story:

After their disaster in Tripoli, the Bachaalany people lived for a while in Zouq al-Kharab and Haret al-Balana. They were used to living a life of luxury surrounded by fertile lands. In this new area the land was barren and infertile. They were not used to such a hard life. The Princes extended an invitation to the Bachaalany to join them and they accepted. The Bachaalany were credited with putting down the rebellion of Kafr Salway who mutinied against their feudal lords. After that the Bachaalany family took refuge in the rulers of Salima. Gradually the Bachaalany sold off their possessions in the Strip (Qate') of Kisrawan. (My late father quoting Nejm Andrea)

The reason why the Bachaalany came to Salima was because the Princes there knew of their fine qualities. They knew that this family had strong and brave men. They knew that they were allied with the right people and members of the same Qaysi Party. Accordingly they sent for them to come to Salima. The Bachaalany were their biggest helpers in subduing the people of Kafr Salwan who had mutinied against their rulers. The Bachaalany courageously chased down the mutineers, pursuing them until they conceded and surrendered to the government. The Princes welcomed the Bachaalany people and extended an invitation for them to join them. The Bachaalany agreed and brought their children. In the beginning they stayed in tents like the Arabs. Then they started to build houses and sold off their old houses and properties in the Strip. The Lam'is loved the Bachaalany and they, in turn, helped the Lam'is in their wars and battles. (Habib Shaiban quoting Fares Youssef Shahin).

I have gathered various bits and pieces of information from various people that can be summarized as follows:

My grandfathers came to Salima with courage as their weapon and chivalry, honor and pride as their assets. The Princes housed them in a wide place in the fief of Salima. They considered them as the first among their people who could be relied on to give wise opinions, to protect the fortresses, and to drive away any raids. The owners of the fief would be in need of men so they used to divide the houses among themselves. A Prince would take this man while another Prince would take his brother. This process is called "Charge" or "Care". Thus the man selected becomes the "Charge" of this Prince and that man becomes the "Charge" of that Prince.

Whoever wants to learn of the battles in which the Bachaalany fought to defend the nation and its independence should refer to the history of the Lam'is and their battles. The Bachaalany were with them in battles, such as Ain Dara (1711), al-Zahrani (1750), Jeba' al-Halawa (1770) and they were with Ibn Ma'n in 1650.

63

SALIMA AND ITS HISTORY

Section 3

ITS DESCRIPTION, HISTORY AND VESTIGES

Chapter 1

Salima is an extremely beautiful city.

It has a good location, fertile soil, clean air, fresh water and good weather. From a distance it looks like a fortress with pine trees surrounding it, as if it were a glove surrounding a hand. Its houses are spread on the sides of the mountains from east to west with the large palace standing in the middle like a huge giant.

Salima looks like a queen sitting on her throne with the pine forest like a crown of glory covering her head. The steady rocks under her feet are like the legs of her throne. She is leaning on a support that is evergreen on both sides while sitting relaxed in a place of peace and comfort.

If one looks at the wilderness of Salima, one will see its natural beauty. They are scenes which the eye never grows tired of seeing.

There is also the scene of the quiet valley that the Lebanese poet As'ad Rostom al- Choueiry has described in a poem written when he was absent from it:

> *"Yes, I write it in the East but it echoes in the valley of Salima."*

I swear that if De La Martine, the famous French poet, had visited the valley of Salima, then surely this valley would have made him forget all about the valley of Hamana.

I wanted to speak in detail about these beauties and wonderful magical scenes but I will leave this task to our great poets. Because of their ingenuity and inspired imagination, they are more deserving of this than me.

From their poems describing Salima, I have selected the best:

First is a poem written by the late Lebanese poet Sheik Amin Taqey al-Din, one of our Druze brothers. He wrote this in 1930 when he visited Salima and was the guest of the late Qassem Ali Said and his two sons, Sheik Amin and Sheik Naguib.

This is Salima in the shadow of the woods, city of the bride, looking from behind the veil
She came down to the valley to cool and the rays of the sun welcomed her at her hillsides
In a parade that caught the attention of the villages, the enchanting pine trees, with their loftiness, looked with admiration

The pine trees stood near the queen, surrounding her, as if they were the protectors of her throne
Souls were made to feel humble because she is so solemn, a genie guarding a garden in the forest
Green Genies (Jinns) offspring from a giant standing with bare limbs under the domes
Her people carried to the bride a unified gift
Bowing as we are allowed to sit on a green land of grass
We walked silently in her presence, to us silence is the best speech
What words cannot say, the tunes of a valley or the breeze of the mountain peaks can speak
The spring burst into bloom for us and in his laughing we sense a welcome
The scent of the flowers are stimulated by my coming and the scent strolls into the village
Greetings to you, O Daughter of Lebanon, from one who admires your beauty
When Metn brought the night to you, sleep stayed awake, the loftiest offspring to the highest descent
The books of nature about beauty are numerous and there is an introduction for each book
I looked at dear Metn with my eyes and asked my heart and used my mind
And I knew the morals of the villages of Lebanon
If you ask me about real beauty, my answer would be Metn
Salima was built with honor by those who long to live with high morals forever
You are the one who tossed aside superiority and she came back to you, your soul and offspring are noble
Your valley is deeper than the inner self, deeper than the soul of a lover
Your mountain peaks are higher than any eagle can reach
And your children, they are strong, and if they ride the sea, they spread their pearls in your presence upon their return
The most beautiful pearls are decorated with education and art
I befriended them and I took from their knowledge and I tested them, finding them ever present in disasters
We shared the spoils of love, they gained in poetry and I gained in friendship
I swear to the Almighty that my day in Salima is like a day of poetry that brushes the mind
The day sang my poem and it provoked the morning while the night slep and it did not pass by the doors
When I described the gardens with my poetry her beautiful scent spread in her time
I wish to God Who created the spring of eternal love
Do not deny the beauty of the spring and its blooming. I have given the spring my youth

The wonderful poem by the companion of my youth, the writer, Mr. Assaf al-Khuri, is a parallel poem to the poem of Sheik Amin al-Taqey. In this parallel of the poem of Sheik Amin, Mr. Al-Khuri has praised him. And in doing so he excelled in both the paralleling and the praise. Here are his magnificent verses:

This "Bride" is the destination of students and never feared one day of disasters coming from the woods
It has the crystal spring waters of heaven
Flowing in the valleys pushing itself from longing to the most beautiful mountain peaks and hill sides
Till it arrives at the valley of the bride where it touches her feet acting like a child
The pine trees are from its guards protecting her under green domes
The hands of autumn did not leave it alone like a bride that was unchaste
They characterized it with bareness out of ignorance and its shields are enough
The spring is jealous for the breasts protecting them with their chastity so it surrounded it with spears
These rocks that are embedding her valleys are filled with grass and weeds
I looked with the eye of ignorance to her destiny and I searched for the plots of the enemies
It is high so it became as the ride for the bride and it settled down so it became like a footing of those who are riding
This is Salima the home of the princes that are still in the place of education and noble descendants

In her water there is wine and in the flowers there is a scent that stimulates the minds
Her breezes are refreshing and inside her there are the tunes of abundance
A city that can give back to the old their youth through good manners
I swear to God that these leaders of the Ma'rouf folks are swaggering in the suits of the famous
And from the nobles, the children of the Cross, the men gifted with intellect and the owners of the best family names
She is a young woman in a national union whose members walk like the lions to get what they desire
They compete to sacrifice themselves for the bride with the strides of a person longing for glory
And when they are called to drive away harm, they fly like eagles.
Daughter of Lebanon, you are a queen with souls around her like protectors
You are the garden of heaven whose features are never withered over the ages
Beauty stood humble on your mountain sides in the attitude of the glorifying and the amazed
I enjoyed myself with the Madam and protected her from anything that would harm her chastity and I preserved my chastity through my youth
And arrived at the doors of love because of my love and stood hesitating not knowing
To find the Madam not enjoyable for a chaste drinker who trembled
Al-Amin has passed by and gave her a pearl so iridescent
She inspired him with poetry and he is the prince of poetry, so he wrote a wonderful poem especially for her
God bless her and anyone who cares for her so tenderly
Shawqy and Hafez and al-Khalil are the eyes of the Nile who is the builder of the greatest country
And Amin in Lebanon, the cradle of revelations and inspirations and the God of Poetry and Letters.

My relative, Sheik Youssef al-Khuri Hanna has published in his newspaper, "al-Warqa'a", that has been published in Salima for many years, the long verses that I mentioned. The newspaper, "al-Khawater", which is owned by the late Youssefal-Helw who is originally from Ba'abda, published the poem of Taqye al-Din which was taken from this newspaper by the New Yorker Newspaper, "al-Hoda", which was established by the late Na'oum al-Mekarzel who was succeeded by his brother, the writer Mr. Salloum.

Here I am publishing, in addition to the previous two poem, the verses of the late Fares, the famous writer, poet and journalist. It is taken from his long poem describing Lebanon. Part of it was published by the late Shoukri al-Kun.owner of"Abu al-Hawl" which used to come out in St. Paul.

Antone Fares said, speaking of his beloved country:

Lebanon, the most beautiful country in the East, whoever looks at it, thinks that the setting sun is stayed
I long to sing about its beauties, and describe what's in its districts
The most beantiful scenes that are in it, make you have no need to speak any compliments about its facts
And in Salima I was born and I see her beauty that touches my heart
God protected her from harm with the pine trees that are like the walls around it
"Ain al-Sawaqi" and "Zahr al-Shir" are the best picnics, in them are the dew
and the flowers and the summer. My longing for her never leaves me and in every thing in me, I have a memory of her.

There is a French poem entitled "The Violet Of Salima" written by the late Monsieur Jean Mommas who was originally from Holland. He spent many years in Salima as the Dean of the Our Lady of Lourdes boarding school that was established by the Capuchin Fathers in the palace of the Lam'i princes. He was the Dean from 1882 until 1892. I mention only the verses that are about Salima. Later I will publish it in its entirety in the chapter about the history of the school.

Mr. Momas, may God have mercy on his soul, wrote:

Look down there at this beautiful village, With a blue sky, with a good climate.
The city that dates back to the Middle Age. It is Salima,

The city with pine trees at the high mountain peak. Surrounding her humble houses Sending their pleasant odor up to the valleys.
You, Oh mountain, be arrogant.because of proud Lebanon, the adorable flower
In our eyes, like Spain, her rival sister.

Salima is an old historic city whose name is Aramaic Syriac that means "the idol and the picture or the pictured."

Perhaps it was called that because of the presence of an idol in it for worship by the idolaters. Or perhaps because Salima is like a huge idol in shape.

Salima is situated on the hillside of a rectangular hill coming out from within al- Kanissa Mountain (The Church Mountain). It ends at the tip of its western part, known as al-Rouaissa.

Salima is 900 meters above sea level.

The river al-Ja'mani runs through its valley. This river was the divider between Qate' Kisrawan and higher Metn before 1711, the date of the Ain Dara Battle. That is when the Qate was joined forever to the Metn district that belonged to the Ma'ns. Then the al-Kalb River (the Dog River) became its border.

The soil of Salima is good. A large portion of it is a black-soil where the pine trees grow. This is the reason why these areas were called the black-soil of Metn and their people used to sing when riding along: "We are the youth and the black-soil is where we were brought up".

Salima's valley was mentioned in the chronicle of Archbishop Gabriel al-Qela'ey al-Marooni.

Al-Khuri Boulos Qarali has published Archbishop Gabriel's poetic chronicle and it was included in his abridged prose under the name of "Horub al-Muqaddamin (The Wars of the Muqaddams)" (1075-1450). On page 12, he said:

> *Zar'aoun and Tarshish and the valley are inhabited by the masters.*
> *Knights and heroes and soldiers are taking care of these cities.*

Salima must have been inhabited since ancient times. This would seem to be the case because of its Syriac name that signifies its antiquity.

The same applies to the names of nearby villages like al-Arbaneiya which means pastures of sheep, and Zar'aoun, Arsaoun, and Qornayle which are all Aramaic Phoenician names.

At the beginning of this century, they found gold coins in the valley of Salima. The place was called al-Nahr on the property of Naguib Sa'ada al-Khuri al-Asmar from al-Arbaneiya. The coins are from the period of the Khalif Omar. They were found while digging at a construction site where they were to build the foundation for a building to be used as a silk laboratory.

Most probably, Salima was inhabited by Christians in the Middle Ages and in the times of the Crusades. After the destruction of Metn due to the Crusades, the Druze began to inhabited it, populating the villages and plantations.

In the period of Fakhr al-Din I (1515), the Druze came down from Metn and Gard. They inhabited Bermana and the plantations of Kisrawan that were under the control of the al-Khazen people. They did this because there was peace in those days due to the rule of the Ma'n princes and their in-laws, the Lam'i princes, who were the rulers of Metn and their alies, the al-Khazen Sheiks, who were the rulers of Kisrawan.

If it wasn't for the turmoil and revolts by the people of the Yamani Party, the lands would have been at total peace.

In the old days, the houses of the people of Salima, especially the Christians, were built on the west side of the Church of Saint John (Yuhanna), near Ain al-Hayarat which was the only public fountain.

The Sheiks said that the people abandoned their houses in the lower part of the city because of insect invasions, ants spread through the area. They have since built their houses where they are today around the palaces of the princes. In this way they were closer to the palaces which were in the higher parts of town.

The Christians called the first part where they built these houses "Haret al-Kharja" which is the neighborhood that is situated to the east of the town square and the palace of the princes.

Judging from what is left, the land of Salima, especially around the palace, from east to west, used to be forests of oak trees. A person used to build his house in the place of the cut off trees, leaving one tree standing to be a bower, planting grape vines around it.

Herds of goats used to graze freely in these dense woods where houses were built in their places.

From what I heard from the people, a shepherd used to say to his compantion:

> *"Today I was able to reach Sakyet Shaghlan with my goats."*

Sakyet Shaghlan is the winter stream that passes to the east of the old Saint John Church and the new one.

It is no wonder that the Lam'i princes too desired this city as their dwelling place and made it the center of their rule.

In the early days of their rule in Kafr Salwan, the Ma'n princes used to live in the higher parts of Metn. They were known at that time as the Muqaddams or the Muqqaddams of Kafr Salwan. Their reign included all of the fief of Metn spreading to some of the villages of the Qate until they reached the Dog (al-Kalb) River after the battle of Ain Dara (1711).

They used to visit Salima which was considered one of the important villages. Then, when Abu al-Lam'i died, his two sons, Qaidbeth and Mourad, divided their father's territory into two parts. This was in the early days of the 17th century, around 1615. Salima was part of the share of Qaidbeth who took it as his residence because of the beauty that he saw in it.

Qaidbeth built a citadel in Salima. After him, his son, Abd Allah, added a second wing as did Hussein bin Abd Allah. Then Ismael bin Hassan bin Hussein and Haidar bin Ismael built a wing or a whole palace but I will speak of this in a later chapter about the history of the Lam'i. I will describe the remains of these fortresses and palaces and tell the years in which each of these great princes built them.

Salima became important in the era of the princes and its people became proud of it, as they used to sing: *"Salima, mother of cities, in you there is a palace; and, under the palace is a valley."*

After the princes established their strong rule, they extended it. They became famous and people started coming to Salima from every direction. They sought refuge in its princes, fleeing injustice or simply wanting to a make a living in safety. Their unified strength increased until the princes were surrounded by a mixture of ethnic backgrounds and families varied in religious background and descent.

Some of them were men of swords and letters, others were men of wisdom and good management. Still others were men of the various crafts and industries including trading and farming. So it was that each one participated in the work of civilization. They worked in construction, medicine, forging, wood working, livestock management, raising silkworms, as well as defending their homeland and protecting their ports.

All this turned Salima into a civilized center and a famous place. Accordingly, its civilization grew more and more. The princes gained strength from the people of their "charge" or "care". They were able to maintain control in struggles with those who rose up against them such as the Druze in Salima and in other places.

Thus, the Christians became powerful in the days of the Lam'is and the Ma'ns as well. In the days of the Ma'n prince Fakhr al-Din, the Christians were able to hold their heads high. They populated the Churches. They rode on saddled horses. They wore white head bands and cloaks. They wore decorative belts with swords in them. They carried jewel decorated rifles. The missionaries came and inhabited the mountains and most of these prince soldiers were Christians. Most of the advisors and aids, Maronites. Thus, justice and equality prevailed there, in contrast to what was going on in the neighboring territories to Lebanon in those days.

Salima renewed its old glory and gained back its lost prestige. I will go into detail on the contributions of the "Our Lady of Lourdes" boarding school later in the history section. It made many contributions to education and refinement.

For about three centuries, Salima remained the center of rule in Metn. In the time of the princes, the beginning of the "Mutassarifiah" era, its school became the destination of students. Men of science, letters and arts came to the city where science and industry were advanced and Salima became known as the "City of Science". It became full of writers, poets, men of letters, and journalists. Some of its contractors, blacksmiths, carpenters and others excelled, as I will mention later in detail, God willing.

Many noble families lived in this city such as the house of al-Tayan, the house of Sabet, the house of Eda, the house of Saqr and others. They were in Salima during the days of the princes, then, they left.

Among those living in Salima was a group of Europeans who spent several years there in the era of the Capuchins. They came to love it like their homeland, especially Monsieur Mommas. He was considered a small king because of his luxurious lifestyle. The European teachers and those from Lebanon and Bilad al-Sham spent many pleasant days in this kind city.

The historical relics and the oral traditions of the Sheiks show that when the princes began to inhabit Salima, it contained only some notable Druze houses. These are:

1. The house of Khedr
2. The house of Yazzbakk
3. The house of Said
4. The house of Qadama

When the princes came to Salima, people began coming from all directions: the Druze from Chouf and the south, the Christians from Kisrawan and the north and many other places.

69

From the Druze:

--The house of al-Masry. They came from Ain Harsha of Wadi al-Teem and others   who joined them.
--The house of Beshr from Ras al-Metn. They joined the Qodama folks.
--Some persons who joined the house of Said.
--The house of Wahba Bu Bakr and Aisha. They converted to Christianity from Islam.

From the Christians:

--The house of Kassab, were advisors to the princes.
--The house of Bachaalany that I already mentioned. I discussed the history of their coming to Salima. Some people joined them and merged with them.
--The house of al-Nakouzi, came from Hathoun as did those who joined or merged with them.
--The house of Anton. They came from Beirut and their garndfather is originally from al-Zouq and he married into the house of al-Nakouzi.
--The house of Zein al-Shediaq from Bakfia.
--The house of al-Khawaja or the house of al-Haddad, from the same origin, came from al-Farzal.
--The house of Bshour, originally from the areas around Aleppo.
--The house of Bu Mikhayel from the areas of al-Sham.
--The house of al-Tafakjy.

There are also new Christian and Druze families who came to Salima in different times. They presently live there and among them are:

--The house of al-Asmar. They were transferred through the Church because they bought the palace of the princes from the Capuchin Fathers. They reopened the school as Our Lady of Our Lord School. They also purchased the Monastery of Mar Boutros (Saint Peter) then sold it to the missionary nuns.
–The house of Dr. Tucatjian, of Armenian origin, who lived in Salima and owned property there.

These circumstances that I mentioned were the most special reasons of the formation of each of the aforementioned families. Each family became a distinct family and officially known to the princes and others. They were competing with each other to gain power and fame. Thus each family was trying to outnumber the others with more males, more money, and more real estate. These affairs were, however, never in the hands of humans but in the hands of God. He can make one rich or poor. He make one high in rank and another low. So it was that some families increased in the number of men through birth or through those who joined them. Others decreased due to a decline in offspring, sterility and immigration. Such is life, and God has His way with His creation.

Now I start with the history of the churches and schools in Salima.

The Churches are eight:

--The old Church of St. John the Baptist
--The new Church of St. John the Baptist
--The Church of Our Lady of Deliverance
--The Church of Mar Boutros (Saint Peter) and His Monastery
--The Church of Our Lady of Lourdes
--The Church of St. Antonios (St. Anthony)
--The Church of St. Elias

--The Temple of the Druze

As for the schools, they are four:

--Our Lady of Lourdes School
--The Monastery of Mar Boutros (Saint Peter) which is now the school of the missionary nuns
--Lebnan al-Kabir School
--Al-Ma'areff School, owned by the government

THE CHURCH OF SAINT JOHN THE BAPTIST

Chapter 2

-The Churches In Metn. -The Church Of Arbaneia. -The History Of Mar Yuhanna (Saint John) In Salima. -The Churches Which Were Blessed By El Douaihy. -The Renovation Of The Church Of Saint John. -The Grave. -The Wonders In It. -Its Vestiges. -The New Church.

When the Christians started to migrate from northern Lebanon to different areas of Metn and other places, they sought comfort and security. It prevailed in this area because of the justice of the rulers, especially during the era of the government of the Ma'n princes. In the time of their rule, Christianity had become strong and people were equal in their rights even possessing freedom religion. In this condition they started to build churches and monasteries for worship. Though their numbers were small and they lacked money in those early years, still they achieved their noble purpose.

Their early places of worship were humble but because of the generosity of their rulers who assisted their Christian subjects, the goals were accomplished. This happened even though the rulers were of different religions and denominations!

It appears to me that the first church that was built in the areas of Metn was the Church of Our Lady in Arbaneia. It was mentioned by El Douaihy in his <u>Annals</u>, where he said:

"In 1636, the construction of the Church of Our Lady in Arbaneia which is one of the villages of Metn, is finished. It was headed on the 6th of July by Archbishop Youssefbin Halib al-Akouri, the Archbishop of Sidon.
The ones who took care of its construction are:
Sheik Oun al-Makari, Abu Ata Allah bin al-Qobrosi and Hajj Michael Abu Ne'ma."

It was common knowledge to the people of the old days that there was no other Church in the area in which to bury a deceased Christian. A dead person from Bekaa had to be transported to Arbaneia to be buried beside its Church. They preferred that their dead lay under the oak tree of the Church.

In the east, they used to plant an oak tree or a group of oak trees beside their worshipping places so that they would have shade under it in their life and after their death.

Still today, beside the Church of Arbaneia, the remaining huge trees are still standing. Unfortunately the largest one has been cut down. It was a most beautiful religious relic.

When the Christians started to come to the city of Salima in the beginning of the 17th century, around the year 1600 AD, perhaps earlier, they built a small church to the west of the present church. The present church is in the south of Ain al-Hayarat where their homes were located. Later they moved the church to is current location.

I did not know when this church was built but during my research, I found a written document that was sent by the late Monsieur Ne'mat Allah Awwad. He took it from one of the writings of El Douaihy that are preserved among the archives of the Vatican. He sent it with other items to be included in the archives of Bkerke.

This document says that Patriarch El Douaihy "consecrated the Church of St. John the Baptist in Salima at the end of December 1684".

Here I am publishing a list of the Churches that were consecrated by El Douaihy throughout his patriarchal period:

The Church of Our Lady in the Monastery of Mar Abda Harharia, on 11 August	1670
The Church of Mar Yuhanna in the Monastery of Harraash on 16 August	1670
The Church of Mar Shalita in the Monastery of Makbas	1672
The Church of Mar Girgis and Mar Elias al-Matin on 1 April	1671
The Church of Mar Zakhia in Ageltoun	1671
The Church of Our Lady in the Monastery of Haqla Armoun	1675
The Church of Mar Sasine Beit Shabab	1675
The Church of Mar Elias Ras Zouq Mesbah	1675
The Church of Mar Elias Haretal-Balana	1675
The Church of Our Lady in the Monastery of Ain Waraka on 21 May	1680
The Church of Mar Charbel Qaitula	1680
The Church of Mar Elias in the Monastery of Shoya	1680
The Church of Mar Elias Ghazir	1680
The Church of Our Lady Ghazir on 23 March	1683
The Church of Mar Qeriaqos Rechmay	1683
The Church of Mar Girgis Magdal Mo'awwash	1684
The Church of Mar Yuhanna the Baptist in Salima in the end December	1684
The School of the Missionaries in the Monastery of Harissa on 18 April	1689
The Church of Mar Girgis in Silfaya on 5 February	1690
The Church of Mar Abda in Beit Shabab on the first of March	1690
The Church of Our Lady in Zgharta on 17 March	1693
The Church of Mar Girgis in Ageltoun on 19 February	1696
The Church of Mar Boutros and Boulos in Zouq Masbag on 2 March	1696
The Church of Mar Elias in Sahel Alama on 8 April	1696
The Church of Mar Girgis in the Monastery of al-Rumeia on 13 May	1696
The Church of Mar Ephram Kafr Debian on 20 May	1696
The Church of Mar Antonios in the Monastery of Qazzhia on 23 April	1697
The Church of Mar Mikhail Sharya on 24 April	1697
The Church of Mar Elias Gosta on 8 September	1698
The Church of Mar Antanios Ain Waraka	1698
The Church of Our Lady in the Monastery of Mert Mora Ehden on 27 May	1701
The Church of Mar Sarkis and Bakhus in Bcharre on 29 May	1701

At that time, those who lived in this Church in Salima were the Carmelite Monks, Padre (Father) Honoratos Karam al-Rayyes and his friend, Padre (Father) Elias Basantos.

I don't know what the consecration ceremony of the Church of St. John in Salima was like because I haven't found any writings that were recorded by El Douaihy. The custom at that time was for the Patriarch and the Archbishops to present a prayer book with his personal inscription in it to commemorate the event. To illustrate the custom for you,

I am going to publish what was written by the great Patriarch on the occasion of his consecration of the Church of Mar Girgis (Saint George) in Metn.

I found this precious historic remnant on the "Shoheim of the Church" (The Book Of Prayers, in Syriac) written by his blessed hand. It is still preserved today in the house of my friend al-Khuri Louis al-Naggar who took the responsibility of preserving it in a glass frame together with other historic writings that were in the books of the Church. Here is the text of the writing:

In Syriac *"The humble Estephan Boutros, the Antioch Patriarch"*, "the seal" and then in Karchouni:

"On this date in the year 1672 AD, we came to this Metn village, protected by God, and on the first day of the blessed month of April ... we consecrated this Church in the names of the chosen Saints Mar Girgis and Mar Elias.

The reason behind its construction and the one taking care of it is the Reverend Mr. Mourad bin al-Lam'i. We ask God to protect his honored children and to support their country forever.

This was in the presence of our honored brother Archbishop Hanna al-Tulani and our honored cousin Archbishop Boulos al-Hednani and a gathering of monks and many people."

Taking what happened in Metn as an example, we can assume that something similar or even greater must have taken place in Salima on the occasion of the consecration of the Church of Saint John. It's logical and reasonable to also assume that Prince Abd Allah, the Prince of Salima at that time, was the one who sponsored and managed the construction of the Church. This is no surprise for he performed many similar glorious deeds as I will mention when I speak about the history of this prince.

I am sure that the hospitality shown to the Patriarch was huge. And it is so sad to lose the vestiges of such moments due to those who cause civil uprisings and revolts. May God forgive them.

In the Book Of Prayers (al-Fannqit) which is in Syriac, there is writing of historical importance. The book still exists today. In it is writing that tells the Church's population, the fact that it had a Monk to serve the Christians in Salima. The writing says:

This book was given to al-Khuri Moussa Abu Diwan, the server of Salima village, on July 24 in the year 1713 AD.. Youssef Boutros, the Antioch Patriarch.

He is the Patriarch Youssef Mubarak who was elected by a group of Archbishops after Patriarch Youssef Awwad stepped down. Patriarch Youssef Mubarak was returned to the Patriarchate.

There is another surviving handwritten notation in a Syriac Bible that was printed in Rome. It says:

"the humble Ya'qub al-Hasrouni, Patriarch of Antioch (and the seal is in Karchouni and there is a paragraph in Arabic) *an eternal consecration to the Church of Saint John (Mar Yuhanna) in Salima, not to be sold or bought.*

The number of Christians in the village increased until there was a dire need to reconstruct their Church due to the overcrowding.

Originally they intended to transfer it to the center of the village. The reason was that the old Church was built at the bottom of the village but now the inhabitants were building their houses near the palace of the princes.

They decided to leave it where it was out of respect to the sanctity of St. John whom, they believed, preferred to live in the woods. Actually, there was a popular story that was handed down from the grandfathers to the fathers that told a strange tale. When they wanted to move the Church of St. John from the woods to the center of the village, they would bring the stones for the building at night. Then, in the morning, they would find the stones back beside the old Church. So out of their strong piety, they left the Church where it was.

They asked the help of God and the intercession of St. John. There was never anyone born who was greater than him. They started to cut rocks from a place nearby. They made a kiln for lime which they filled two and three times to suffice their needed mud.

It must have been the Prince Ismael al-Lam'i, known by al-Mesholah, who gave them a helping hand with the construction of this deluxe building. It was said that he converted to Christianity at that time. He probably supplied them with money and skilled construction workers. The princes would bring in skilled workers from such places as Aleppo and al-Sham. One of the master craftsmen was Me'allem Elias Bshour. He was the grandfather of the house of Bshour in Salima. So it was that they carried out the construction work of this Church. It is a very beautiful style, and, rare to be found in a church of those days.

Whoever looks at this building, which still exists today, will admit that it is one of the most beautiful religious buildings in its accuracy, architecture, and capacity.

What I like in this Church is its detail and accuracy. It is similar to the houses of the princes with its wide doors and windows, unlike the narrow doors of old churches. And above its two doors, is carved, a picture of a Cross and a beautiful cup with a host above it. All of these show the accuracy in the construction. On the window sill of the southern window, there is a picture of the Heart of Jesus. Worshipping the Sacred Heart of Jesus was popular in those days. This picture was painted by the Christian builders. They took the idea and image from other paintings in the Churches of Aleppo and others places.

The Church has a large altar in its eastern forefront as was the custom of the people of the East. There are also two small altars: one on the right and the other on the left.

The Church has an inside staircase on its western wall that leads to the roof. Thus the Church becomes like a fortress. And frequently the town's Christians were caught inside it in the days of wars… like the Church of Saint George in B'abdat and the Church of Saint Elias in al-Sofaily. Both of these have a wall on their roofs where men can fire shots, just the old fortresses and citadels.

The Dome of the Church is simple with only one archway with a stone cross at its top and it is built with clean rocks like all the walls of the Church.

It was the custom of the people of the East to place a wooden lattice to separate the place of the women from the place of the men. This Church had a detailed lattice that was renewed after its wood was worn. Then, lately, the lattice was removed.

Originally, I couldn't find out when they started building the Church of Saint John. Then, after extensive research, I was able to determine that they constructed it around 1770. I say this because Mikhail Abd al-Ahad told Nejm Youssef Nasr Allah al-Bachaalany that he used to carry mud above his head during the construction. In exchange for this, his daily wage was five masary (Barat/Barsl units of money). Based on the above, and a little correction by me, I determined that this happened around 1760. Nejm also related that his grandfather, Nasr Allah, was killed in the incident of al-Zahrani. Also killed in that incident were Abu Nader Gad'oun Fasida, Sheik Bashir Sa'b Kassab and others. Sheik Bashir was like a brother to the Prince As'ad al-Lam'i. Al-Zahrani is a word that is still famous and on the tongues of my people.

What is known is that the construction of the Church of Saint John was finished in that year as assured to me by the late Fares Antone Abu Anton. It is regrettable that a date was never put in place for this Church although there was an empty place at the top of its door for that purpose.

Someone else told me that:

"The day of the burying of the knot of this Church was a famous day. The people of Salima gathered, Druze and Christian. Pots of food were put on the fire and plates of rice were extended to all. This by the command of the Princes. On the same day a call of war went out. Prince Ismael al-Mesholah, however, ordered that no one left the village until the completion of the ceremony of burying the knot. After they finished that, all the people were invited to feast. They ate, then they prepared to go off to war."

Someone also told me that they used to have a flag which they called "al-Abrash". The Prince and his men were victorious with this flag in several battles. More than once other princes asked for this flag but were denied.

The Prince and his men were victorious in this battle and did very well in it.

During this time some of the pious women were so fervent that they were competing among themselves. In their charity they gave gifts, votive offerings of jewelry and other things. They carried rocks and served water to the workers to drink. They mixed and carried mud for the construction. They were cooking in the ovens and giving what they baked for the consecration.

It was said that the time of building the Church of Saint John was about the time of the incident of Jeba' al-Halawa in 1750.

Beside the Church, there is a graveyard belonging to the Maronites and the Catholics where the bones of our ancestors lie. On the sides of the graves, there are trees. The oldest of which is an oak tree whose age is no less than 300 years in my estimation. It may be even more. This oak tree is on the eastern side standing above the graves like a mighty hero guarding the remains of the dead. It is tending to them with its branches that constantly renew throughout the years. Whenever a human branch wilts or the bones of a man wear out, this giant oak cares for them. The youth used to race from the village down to the graveyard on snowy nights. When one of them reached the tree, he stuck his knife in, pulled it out and raced back, fearless, then he was the winner.

There was rarely an easy winner because of the sanctity of the Church and the solemnity of the graveyard and the attacks of wild animals. The houses in the old days used to be in our dense woods. The mention of death would bring dread. Together, all these would send shivers down our spines and shoot fear through our hearts.

My grandfathers had piety and Christian simplicity. God did some amazing things at the hands of His Saints in order to strengthen their faith and to prove the rightness of their Christian religion among the nations.

There are many wonders, and the most important of which are these:

1. This involves one of the Sheiks of the house of Yazzbakk, from the Druze of Salima. This family has been in Salima since olden days and they rank as one of the notables. One day, while the Sheik was away, his only son fell ill. His mother did her best to treat the boy with the simple, known methods of those days. But nothing worked. When she felt that there was no way out she sought refuge in the Sponsor of the Christians (Wale ii al-Nasara), that's to say, Saint John the Baptist, whose Church was near the houses of the Druze. Saint John was highly respected by them so she sent her daughters to the Church. They entered, carrying oil. They put the oil in the lantern, then they dowsed a rag in the oil of the lantern and went home. The mother took the rag and rubbed it over the head of her sick child.

Soon he opened his eyes and asked for food. This after he had been unconscious. In gratitude, Sheik Youssef Yazzbakk held a festival for Saint John every year. (These are from the words of my late father and Mikhail Abu Dun).

2. Some of the girls from the Said folks dared to enter the Church and steal the handkerchiefs that were placed by the believers on the pictures. When any of them turned to leave the Church, she would lose her eyesight and not be able to find her way out. If she turned to look at the altar, her eyes would open again. Then they wept and kept weeping and praying to the Saint. They left the handkerchiefs. Then they went out unharmed. They say that the sound of the Church bell was heard and a Monk was seen on the roof tolling the bell.

3. During a time of wars some crude men invaded and violated the sanctity of the Church. While inside they ripped apart the old painting of Saint John and trampled the fragments under their feet. They did not get away with this act without serious punishment. I was assured by a group of Druze that all those who transgressed over the sanctity of this holy place received ill fortune. That is why the Druze of Salima and especially the Said folks respect this worshipping place as if it were one of their own worshipping places. Frequently they would make votive offerings for it.

4. In our own times, someone cut down some of the trees beside the Church. It wasn't very long before his two children caught a very strange disease and died, one after the other. This happened just recently.

5. Keng Osman Said has told this story about himself: *"Abbas Sayed Ahmad and I took some land that was consecrated to Saint John. We cultivated it and when we were about to do the threshing, we agreed with each other that we would not give any of it up for the consecration. We were going to carry the wheat on a pack animal of mine but as soon as I put the load on its back, it fell dead. Now I consider Saint John to be a neighbor of mine who protects me. Each year I offer him some of the harvest of my lands."*

6. It once happened that a woman stole some of the votive offerings of the Church. The Church's doors were open day and night. The woman could not walk away with the offerings. The priest came and saw her in this situation. He took from her what she stole and let her go away.

The people of Salima, no matter what their denomination, believe in the intercession of Saint John. They have seen his power and the results of his intercession. Whenever a plague strikes the village, the people run to his shrine and line its walls with handkerchiefs as is the custom. Soon the plague goes away. Frequently, votive offerings would come to Saint John from neighboring villages. People would make offerings from even other places besides those properties that were consecrated by the pious people for this Church.

From the vestiges of the Church that still remain today are a number that include:

1. Al-Fannqit. It consists of two parts. It contains the prayers of our religious ceremonies. There are a great many in Syriac. The book was printed in Rome and copies of it can be found in other Maronite Churches. This book was given by the Patriarch Youssef Mubarak on 24 July 1713.

2. A copy of the New Testament that was printed in Rome. It is in Syriac and Arabic and carries the seal of the aforementioned Patriarch Ya'qub. This seal consists of a picture of Saint John.

3. A copy of the book of Sheheim, which are the prayers of the week. It is in Syriac and was likewise printed in Rome. It has on it a sentence in the handwriting of Archbishop Abd Allah Beleibal, the head of the Archbishops of Cyprus with his seal. It is from his visit to the people of the Bishopric of Salima when he performed the "Sacrament of Confirmation" in 1803. There is another sentence in the handwriting of this Archbishop when he visited for a second time on 12 November 1820.

4. A copy of a book with the stories of the Saints. It is known as the Sancsar, written by the hand of a writer from the village of Salima. He was al-Shediaq Elias Sarkis. On the cover he painted a picture of Saint John the Baptist. The handwriting in the book is beautiful with very few mistakes. It dates from 1767, the time when the Church was built.

5. A copy of a book entitled "Al-Rayyesh'al-Reesh Qorian". It consists of select portions of the Prophecies and the Old Testament. It has a hole in it and I couldn't tell who wrote it. The handwriting is much like that of the Sancsar mentioned above. This has the name of Father Francis al-Nakouzi written on it in a beautiful Thuluth font.

6. Also, there is a very old handwritten book in a font that resembles the Old Style Font. This book consists of the praises of the Saints that are recited in the prayers of the Choir and which are known as "al-Hasayat" or "the Church's Speeches". The book's pages are stuck together as if they were burned. This is because of the age of the book.

7. There are also two pictures. One is of the Virgin breast-feeding her Baby and the second shows the Virgin carrying Jesus. Both of the pictures are one arm in length and two thirds of an arm in breadth. Both of them are almost worn out. I think that they date back to the middle of 18th century or before. There is no doubt that they were painted in Rome. They might have been part of the group of pictures of the Virgin sent to Prince Ismael al-Mesholah on the day he converted to Christianity. This story was told by his grandsons. They said that he sent proof of his conversion to the Pope, the Supreme Pontiff, who responded by sending a beautiful letter, the pictures of the Virgin Mary, and a picture of the Magi bowing in worship to the Baby Jesus. Some of these are still in the home of Prince Youssef in Bakfia and in the Monastery of the Jesuit Fathers.

8. There is also a small picture of Saint George killing the dragon.

9. This Church also had a beautiful picture of Saint John the Baptist that was desctroyed during the war between the Druze and the Christians in 1845. The painting that is there today was painted by the famous Roman painter Gosta. He lived in Beirut for a period of time. He died toward the end of the 19th century. It was transferred to the new Church which was built beside the square. Originally named the Church of Saint Joseph it was renamed the Church of Saint John. When this happened the painting of Gosta was transferred to it. After several years, the bell, which had also been transferred, was returned to the old Church. Mikhail painted a picture for the Church but he never finished it.

One of the Sheiks of Salima told me that Monsieur Mork, the French man, one of the owners of the Mork Store had paid to have this picture of Saint John painted. The story is that this man had been working in his laboratory in Ain Om Hamada on the day of the festival of Saint John. The laboratory caught fire and was burned down. This happened twice! Saint John was then called the "Burner". Monsieur Mork then offered Saint John the painting in atonement for working on his feast day.

In the days of the shop of the late Girgis Anton, the house of the Nakouzi refinished the altar of the Church to the appearance that it has today. This was done by the hands of the skilled carpenter Youssef Gabour who had worked in the school of Our Lady of Lourdes. In 1883 they also made improvements to the tiles of the Choir and the stairs of the altar. The Church was previously tiled with stone. Its walls were painted on the inside with bright colors, traces of which still remain today.

The Church contains a silver chalice, censers and crosses with the letter *N* carved on them. This stands for Napoleon III. All of these are among the gifts from France, the Queen of Favors. They were sent to our country after the battle between the Druze and the Christians.

In 1872, a dispute occurred between the Bachaalany folks and the Nakouzi folks which led to the division of the Church. The congregation was split between the two families so the Church of Saint John with all its belongings became of the property of the house of the Nakouzi. The house of the Bachaalany took control of the small Church of Our Lady Of Deliverance that was built in the beginning of the 19th century to be near their houses.

As for the graveyard, it remained shared among the two groups together with the Roman Catholics.

The house of the Nakouzi found it difficult to travel down to the Church of St. John because it was so far. They started to consider building a new Church close to their homes. With the permission of the Archbishop of the Bishopric, they built a church near the town square with the name Church of Saint Joseph (Mar Youssef). This was around the year 1900. Afterwards they changed the name to Saint John, so, in Salima, there came to be two churches with the name of this Saint: the old Church of Saint John and the new Church of Saint John.

Over the years, they neglected the old Church till it almost crumbled. Then they repaired it also fixing the roof. The services and rituals are often carried out in the new Church which they equipped with all the needed furniture and utensils. They transferred the old painting of Saint John to the new Church.

CHURCH OF OUR LADY OF DELIVERANCE

Chapter 3

The Old Church of Our Lady - Its Picture – Believers' Godliness And Their Strong Faith – The Dispute Between The Two Families - The Division Of The Congregation – The Establishment Of A New Church – Our Lady Of Delivrance – Blessed Revolution – Cooperation And Independence – The History Of The Church – Its Priests – Its Receptacles – Its Religious Endowment And Its Representatives – The Cupola And The Sacristy.

We previously mentioned that when the Maronites started to build their houses at the top of the village to be near the princes, then the Church came to be too far from them, especially for the old people and the invalids. So, in the middle of the Bachaalany's houses, they built a small Church called the Church Of Our Lady. It had a roof made of timbers and trunks. I remember that I saw in that Church the historical picture of the "Lady". This picture was donated to the Church Of Our Lady in Salima by the Patriarch Youssef Hebish (1823 – 1845) through Youssef Bin Daher Safi, Tanous Freha, Hanna Bin Youssef (one of the Bachaalany's), and, Shahin Ghaleb from the Nakouzy's. The picture was of the Virgin Mary holding the Boy Jesus, giving Him a grape. Then, Father Hanna El Nakouzy who was the servant of the congregation became old and weak. He was arranging for the Holy Sacrifice at the Church of Our Lady and his collegue Father Youssef El Bachaalany was sanctifying and praying at the Old Saint John Church. Both priests forbade anyone but the old and sick from attanding Holy Mass at the nearby Church of Our Lady. The rest were obliged to attend all the religious ceremonies at the Chruch of Saint John.

I remember the scene of those Maronites, with great energy and enthusiasm, coming to fulfill their religious duties. They ignored how hard it was to the travel up and down, at night or in the day, in hot or cold weather. They weren't bothered by floods or heavy snow. Whoever saw those virtuous ancestors, were astonished at their devoutness and strong belief.

Then, discord developed between the two families, something that often happens between brothers. Then it happened again and again so it seemed necessary to divide and separate the congregation. After a dispute, it was divided in 1872 during the era of Youssef Ja'ja' the Archbishop of the Cyprus bishops. It was done with the help of his assistant, Father Boutros El Zoghby (who later became a bishop). The Nakouzys have had possession of the Old Church of Saint John including its eccelestiastical receptacles. The small Church of Our Lady became the share of the Bachaalany's. There were some other properties of the Churches that were divided between the two families, the most valuable of which was an olive garden in Al Chiyah. It was made unalienable church property by Abdou Nahra El Bachaalany.

Once the division was completed, the Bachaalany's revolted. Their revolution showed the height of their zeal, their pride and strong belief. They voted to start the construction of another Church to replace the small one. They decided to call it the Church of Our Lady of Deliverance. The Bachaalany's were numerous before the immigration period. On May 28th, 1872, with the gusto of one man, they started to pluck up stones from a nearby stone quarry which was under Sa'adallah Attallah's house. They insisted on performing this religious project independently. They refused to ask for help or charity from anyone. They relied solely on God, the Virgin Mary, and themselves. Everyone participated in that project, young and old, rich and poor, even women and children. They all suffered from transporting the stones, the trunks, the sand and all sorts of jobs.

80

They faced many problems. For example, the location of the foundation did not have stones, even at the corners. This was necessary to have a solid and firm foundation. Thus, they had to dig deeper and deeper into the ground. They dug until the depth became longer than the walls' height above ground level. As an impressive sign of their collective devotion to this project, they didn't use the money which was specially set aside for the construction and building until the building was two and three cubits high. Also, they did not accept money from others except as donations from kind and charitable people. They finished the construction of the church in 1882, after ten continuous years of work. And their efforts resulted in a magnificent building, as elegant, as great and as well constructed as any of the great churches in El Metn.

The Bachaalany's had every right to be proud of their work for which they received God's blessing. As the prophet David said "Blessed are those who love the beauty of Your House." They spent their money and exerted their efforts for God's House. Everyone of them participated with whatever possessions they had and whatever labor they could expend. Their priest was that zealous and good influential man, the late Yuhanna Bachaalany. He was one of the great people who worked on bringing this dream into reality. He was the person in charge of this huge project. He gained the gratitude of the people. He received great praise from the people as well as a great remuneration and recompense from God. May God have mercy upon him for all his good deeds and kindness.

Among his papers there were verses that he composed about the Church. They have been engraved on the top of the church gate:

" A Church for the Virgin Mary
Designated by Jesus himself.
It was constructed with God's help, may God save it
For the Bachaalany's son who sacrificed his money.
And the undignified John watching
Until his very end, worn out by his lowliness.
In this Church is God's peace, relax while standing here,
Then enter with fear, and glorify God. (1882)."

The Priests Who Served The Congregation.

Here is a list summarizing the names of the priests who served the Maronite congregation in Salima before and after the division:

1. **Father Moussa Abou Diwan**: His name was mentioned in the Syriac Prayer Book (Al Fanqit), which still remains in the church. It was inscribed: *"This book was given in 1713 to Father Moussa Abou Diwan, the Servant of Salima Village. −Youssef Boutros (Mobarak), the Antiochean Archbishop."*

2. **Father Yuhanna El Nakouzy I (Father John Nakouzy):** He is the grandfather of the Khoury's, one of the Nakouzy family branches in Salima. His descendants hold his name and are known as El Khoury.

3. **Father Francis El Nakouzy,** the son of Father Yuhanna El Nakouzy I. He lived long and resided for many years with Father Yohanna II, his nephew Boutros. He died in 1810. I will refer to him in detail later.

4. **Father Yuhanna El Nakouzy II,** the grandson of Father Yohanna I. He served the congregation with his paternal uncle Father Francis. After the death of Father Francis, he became the exclusive pastor of the congregation. After the ordination of Father Youssef El Bachaalany in 1832 they helped each other in their

service. Father Yuhanna died on January 7th, 1864, at the age of 96. Later I will discuss his life and contributions in detail.

5. **Father Youssef El Bachaalany,** his full name being Youssef Bin Hanna Daham Abi 'Okl El Bachaalany. He was born in 1790 and was ordained to the holy priesthood by the Bishop Abdalah Balibel in March 1832. He died on November 22nd, 1859. We will refer to him later in the chapter about the Bachaalany family.

6. **Father Boutros Farahat El Asmar.** He was born in Al Kanaysa and was ordinated a priest of the village of Delibah where he lived with his family. From 1860 to 1862, he served the congregation of Saint John in Salima after the death of Father Youssef El Bachaalany and the disability of father Yuhanna El Nakouzy.

7. **Father Yuhanna El Bachaalany.** His name is Hanna, the son of Father Youssef El Bachaalany. He was born in Salima in 1839 and he grew up there. He graduated from the famous Mar Abda Harharia School and was ordained as priest by Bishop Youssef Ja'ja' in Novemeber, 1862. After the congregation divided in 1872, he served until his death on December 30th, 1889.

8. **Father Boutros El Bachaalany.** His full name is Nasrallah bin Youssef El Mazmouk El Bachaalany. He was born on January 3, 1839, in Salima. He was ordinated a priest by Bishop Youssef Ja'ja' in 1872. He served the Church of Our Lady's congregation after the death of its pastor in 1890. He died in October 1910.

9. **Father Estephan El Bachaalany.** His name is Youssef bin Abdou Tanous Freha Al Bachaalany. He was born in Salima on March 11th, 1876, and grew up there. On April 2nd, 1898, Bishop Ne'matallah Salwan promoted him to the Holy Priesthood. He served the congregation until 1931. He is the historian and the author of this book.

Many other priests have served the congregation after Father Estephan moved away. Pastor Sama'an Al Kharat, the Antonian monk, is but one example. There were many others. In 1936, Father Yuhanna Wahba from Qortoba, took charge of the congregation. He stayed until 1946. He was very zealous about the congregation. Our dear friend Father Yuhanna Abou Gouda, from the village of Al Maska, succeeded him. He is a great guide for the nuns and their school in Salima.

As for the Church of Saint John, many priests served the congregation following the division of the congregation. The most important of these was the late Father Joseph Nakouzy. His full name was Sabra bin As'ad Sabra El Khoury Al Nakouzy. He was born on December 4th, 1864. He studied for the priesthood through the late Father John Bachaalany, and on February 24th, 1885, was ordained a priest by Archbishop Joseph Zoghby. He was a dynamic priest and took care of the congregation right up to his death, on June 28th, 1904. I will again refer to his biography in the chapter dealing with his family. After his death , many monks and priests served the congregation. The last of these was Father Beshara Hashem. He served two congregations. The one in his village, Hassbiya, and, the Church of Saint John in Salima. He did so for a long time.

I would like to tell here, briefly, what I know of the people who have made donations and presentations to the Church.

We found a declaration written in French and dated August 22th, 1901. It was written by the late Father Andraous Laounsa, the headmaster of the Capuchin monastery of Saint Peter in Salima. He was also a priest of the Latin Congregation in Beirut. It was he who brought about many great improvements and contributions to the Church of Our Lady of Deliverance. He said that he personaly made arragements in Italy for the huge picture in the Church of Our Lady of Delivrance in Salima. It cost eighteen thousand piastres. It was paid for by the generous donations of special collections from the French made at mass. Contributions were also made by some of his priests friends as well as friends of the late Father Yuhanna Bachaalany. The same is true for the large inlayed glass, the wonderful big beam, the robes and religious garments, and other eccelestiastical receptacles. All those were bought the same way, with his endeavour and the endeavour of Father Yuhanna, the congregation's priest. The late Faragallah Tanous Freha undertook the making of a wooden frame (from an olive tree) for the picture of Our Lady. Its cost was paid by his mother, grandma Hawn. There are the two pictures, one of Saint George and the other of Saint John The Baptist. They were painted by the famous Lebanese Maronite artist, the late Habib Sourour. Their cost was paid by the sons of the late Fares Shiban Al Bachaalany. And, two other big pictures, one of the Virgin rising into Heaven, and the other of the Holy Family were for paid by Maroun Fares Ghotas. The late Andrea Girgis Al Bachaalany paid for the picture of Saint Maron. The picture of the Nativity was a gift from the late Yuhanna Girgis Anton. The late Youssef Metri Al Zaghloul donated the wonderful statue of Saint Joseph. Metri Zaghloul's sons donated two copper candlesticks for the chancel. Mary, the daughter of the sub-deacon Youssef Al Ghaziri, donated the wooden crucifix. The Statue of Saint Teresa was a donation from Handouma who is the widow of As'ad Moussa. And the foreigner As'ad Wakim (Kassab) donated about 100 dollars to make the confessional chair and a donation box. The family of the deceased Youssef Molhem Nohra contributed beautiful vases. Mrs. Jean Momasse and Barbara, the wife of Moussa Metri Al Bachaalany, donated a precious cover for the chancel. Rougina Al Bachaalany, the wife of the late Sheikh Tanious Negm Abi Gouda, offered a very nice robe. The statue of the Virgin Mary was paid for by her nieces. The late Ne'matallah De'ibass Al Bachaalany and his late mother Sa'oud, contributed a highly valued cover and a wooden crucifix to the chancel of the Church of Our Lady. Okl Habib Fares gave all the necessary electrical accessories for the Church. May God reward them all.

In the congregations of both Saint John and Our Lady, there were trustees. The ones we know are: Youssef Bin Daher Safi; our grandfather, Tanous Freha, who has been a representative for a long time; Wakin bin Boutros who was succeeded by Youssef Shahin Boutros; Girgis Tanous Freha; Abou Okl El Khoury; Youssef Wakim; Faragallah Freha; Andrea Girgis; Elias Wakim; Youssef Metri Al Zaghloul; Gamil Tanous Shiban; George Youssef Al Zaghloul; and, Hanna Youssef Sa'adallah. All them were from the Bachaalany's. And the trustees from the Nakouzy Family were: Shahin Ghaleb Girgis Anton Abou Anton and his brother Fares Anton; Boutros Salem Abou Tarbeyah; Salem Boutros Salem; Daoud Boutros Salem; and, Youssef Hanna Mansour who was known for his enthusiasm.

Around the year 1900, members of the Bachaalany's Saint George Association asked Bishop Ne'matallah Salwan for permission to construct a sacristy beside the church, at the east side. Above it, they built a large hall for religious and family meetings. The contractors were Daoud and Shahin Boutros Bachaalany and their sons, who were famous in the field of construction. Professor Ibrahim Zein and his brother Zein built the threshold. And because the late Al Mo'alem Ibrahim was the most famous builder, the threshold was accurate, detailed, perfectly engineered and elegant.

The Nakouzy family built a nice, new cupola above the portal of the Church of Saint John. Professor Ibrahim Zein designed and constructed it. He also hung a bell on it as well as a large chiming clock which can be heard from afar. It's cost was paid by the late Abdou Youssef Khattar Tarbeyah El Nakouzy. They also built another building as a sacristy and a rectory for the Church's pastor. It hasn't been completed yet, however. Among the gifts donated by the parishioners are the marbled statue of the Virgin Mary which was donated by Youssef and Hanna Metri Al Zaghloul. The late Hanna Girgis Anton and his family residing in Marseille donated the picture of Al Azer, a picture of The Sultana of the Saints, two other pictures, and the eccelestiastical receptacles. The late Louisa, widow of Hanna Gurgis El Khoury El Nakouzy, gave the choir's banister. Many other donations have been made as a sign of the parishioners' faith.

THE CHURCH AND MONASTERY
OF SAINT PETER

Chapter 4

The Capuchin Missionaries - Christianity In The East - Lebanon Mountains And The Maronites - Franciscan Missionaries - The Capuchins In The East - Mission Founders In Lebanon And Syria - The Capuchin, Father Josef   - Missionaries' Acts And Their Zealousness About Religion And Humanity - Christianization Of Prince Fakhr El Dine - His Death As A Martyr And The Oppression Of The Missionaries - Capuchins In Salima - Traces Of Their Seniors .

The light of the Bible radiated all over our country long before the Capuchin Missionaries came in 1625. Jesus descended on our land, and his two messengers followed its Roman road during their missionary trip. Antioch, Damascus and Beirut were stopping points for Christianity. It spread widely throughout the region until its light entered the innermost portion of the desert. Then that light started to be extinguished in our country because of heresies. Then it seemed that it would vanish completely when Islam appeared in the seventh century. But, then, the Crusades revived what still remained from that original glow. For a while it grew until the crusaders' shadow diminished in our land. Still a tiny ray of the light of Catholicism remained.

The Catholic missions and endeavors were almost completely lacking in Turkey. It could not reach the whole populace. But one small group, the Maronite nation, a people besieged, kept that faith in the blessed Lebanon mountains. The great Saint Francis of Assisi came to the holy lands in the early years of the 13th century. His Franciscan Missionaries followed him and stayed there to guard the Holy Places. So it was that they were the Catholic minarets. Plus, there were missioanries in Constontinople, very generously sponsored by the French Ambassador. There were also some Catholic groups without clergy who gathered.

In 1625, the French Capuchins priests came from Paris, Torino and England. They established the Capuchin mission in the East. This important job was accomplished thanks to the Capuchin priest, Father Joseph from Tremolat, the counselor of the famous Cardinal Richelieu, the minister of King Louis XIII. And Father Joseph made a great impression on that cunning man known for his intrepidity and dangerous acts, the Sublime Porte. Father Joseph was following the religious movements in Ottoman lands with an apostolic interest. He perceived that it was time to start a peaceful crusade. With his influence and slyness, he received the permission of the Sublime Porte to establish Catholic missions in Turkey. Before that, in 1622, he had established the Holy Faith Propagation Complex. It was his first achievment. Then, he decided to send the Capuchin missionaries to eastern countries in 1623. That was the first step of Father Joseph's plan. The first group of missionaries left for Saida (Sidon) in late 1625. This was when the coastal roads of Syria and Lebanon were the most important ones for trade and administration. The Saida monastery was the first mission for the Capuchins in that country. Then it rapidly spread to Beirut, Halab and Cairo in the following year.

Father Joseph, this religious genius who brought the idea of establishing missions in the East, this soul of apostolic revolution, this cleverest of men, died in 1638. After his death, the Capuchins spread far and wide... over Algeria,

84

the Roman archipelago to Istanbul and on to Asbahan; then, from Toris to Halab, and, Beirut to Cairo. Within fifteen years the number of missionaries in these places reached no less than a hundred, and the number of monasteries was thirty-one.

The Eastern countries witnessed these peaceful missionary battalions marching toward the Islamic countries, a strange and unbelievable sight. The missionaries strained to learn the languages of these countries, then they won over the hearts of their people. As they gained their positions and grew in holiness, they began establishing their monasteries and charitable organizations. They always had letters of recommendation abounding with compliments and gratitude. Pope Urban VIII wrote such a letter for the righteous missionaries in 1630 to the Patriarch of the Maronites. In the letter, the Pope expressed his jubilation in sending the Capuchin priests to the people in Maronite country. He urged that they be eagerly welcomed. The same was done by King Louis XIII, King of France, when he wrote a letter in 1628 addressed to his ambassadors in the Eastern countries. He requested that the missionaries be provided with safety. He urged the people to give them assistance and to consider them as the servants of their souls. These missionaries were coming from Italy and England. They, however, were not the only missionaries to the East. They were preceeded by French priests who settled in Palestine decades earlier to secure the Holy land. Then the Jesuits priests and others gained privileges from the Sublime Porte.

According to the written documents preserved at the mission's headquarters, the Capuchins did great things. They tell how Father Adrean from Labrosse, who established a monastery in Beirut in 1626, was special and how he gained a position of privilege with the Prince Fakhr El Dine Al Azim. The Prince was converted to Christianity by Father Adrean who baptized him and called him Louis François. That is all recorded in the documents and the mission register which are in the Saida monastery. This is a summary of what the late Father Jérome, the Capuchin's regional leader in Syria and Lebanon wrote.

We published a translation of that text in "Family Friend", a magazine which was published by our deceased friend, the Capuchi priest, Father Ya'koub Al Hadad, in Beirut. We edited it for three years, 1931 to 1933. The title of article was "Prince Fakhr El Dine Converts To Christianity And The Missionary News In Salima". It was all based on the documents and registers we obtained in the monasteries of the missionaries. Now we can summarize it here because of its importance to this research. Concerning the information about the Capuchins in Salima, Father Hilar, a Capuchin, had this to say:

"The Prince Fakhr El Dine governed Lebanon from 1584 till 1635. While the Ottomans were busy fighting the Persians and Hungarians, he seized the opportunity to, step by step, increase his political territory. He took a part of Beirut, Sayda, Ba'labak, Sour, Ajloun, and, he manacled the shoof's town, the place from which his family descended going back to 1119 . Using gifts and bribes, he managed to persuade the Istanbuln government to over-look his expansionism. In spreading out, it was his ambition and intention to create an independante state. Accordingly, he worked on making alliances with the Christians. He travelled to Italy in 1616 for precisely this purpose. He went to Florence, to the Palace of the Medici's asking for help. He received only empty promises.

The situation in the country was as we have already described when the missionaries arrived in Lebanon. The prince met them with generosity and received them as guests. Their intention was to get the Druze to join the Ca-tholic Church. In those days Druzes believed that they were the descendants of Conte Druz, a crusader prince who served Godfrey, the King of Jerusalem. The Druzes are not Muslim nor Christian. They believe only that there is a God, in Metempsychosis and in the endlessness of life. They have no churches or chapels. They have no prayers and they consider Jesus a Saint.

In 1633, Fakhr El Dine became seriously ill. He sent for Father Adrian from Labros. The missonary was afraid that the Prince would die before becoming a Christian as he intended. Accordingly, he made a vow to God, to Jesus, to

His Mother Mary, and to Saint Francis and Saint Anthony. He prayed for the recovery of the Prince as well as for his fellow missionaries. Afterwards he found the Prince had rested and was in a good state of mind. Consequently, Father Adrian seized the opportunity and talked to the Prince about his religious duties. He told him how the Lord had shown him mercy and saved him from death. Father told him that this was a warning and the Prince should carry out his religious responsibilities. Father Adrian told him that the most dangerous thing is when someone doesn't care about a bonus given by God. If one doesn't listen to God's warning, he does not deserve another chance.

Father Adrian thus spoke to the Prince and apologised for daring to be so bold. But Father added that because of the high ranking of the Prince and the special privilege that he had, he felt obligated to speak his conscience. Moreover, if the Prince should die as he is, he will lose his opportunity to share in the joy of Heaven. Father kept talking until he convinced the Prince to accept the Sacrament of Holy Baptism. Father Adrian baptized him and gave him the name Louis Francis. The prince felt so happy and blessed. After that he never allowed the visit of any other priest, only Father Adrian and his Maronite chancellor Sheik Abou Nader Al Khazen. The Prince liked that missionary, Father Adrian, so much that he told his son to remember to always show the priest his favor, and to be as generous to him as he, the Prince, was.

Then, the Prince decided that he wanted his children to also become Christians. He gave Father Adrian some jewelery and banknotes that he was saving in some Europan Christian banks. The amount was more than one million scoudy (an Italian monetary unit) in gold. The Prince also insisted that his children were to be transported on Maltese boats to Christian countries where they would be educated according to the religious teachings of Christianity. Sheik Abou Nader, however, prevented him from doing that. According to Islamic law, when a Muslim apostatizes, it is a crime and must be condemned. Thus. how would it look if such a high ranking Prince like Fakhr El Dine apostatizes. Furthermore, what will the Sultan do when he learns of it? There is nothing recorded in history that tells of someone close to the Prince denouncing him and revealing his secret. Nonetheless, this is precisely what happened. The governor of Damascus was ordered by Sultan Mourad IV to attack the Prince. He did so and twice he was vanquished by the Prince. On the third try, however, the Prince was defeated and his son, Ali, was killed. The Prince managed to escape.

This now unlucky Prince had to walk, carrying his money, passing through Asia Minor to Istanbul to beg for the Sultan's mercy. He thought he could gain the Sultan's forgiveness and mercy with gifts and persistence. The Sultan welcomed him as usual. However, the Prince's secret of becoming a Christian had been disclosed. The Prince, along with his sons, were all sentenced to death. They beheaded the Prince. His sons were hanged. Before carrying out the execution of the Prince, they asked him to reclaim his Muslim religion. He refused, honoring the promises he had made to the missionaries. Those priests were also taken prisoners because they encouraged the Prince to become a Christian. The Prince declared openly that he was a Christian. Then, at that moment, turned his face to the East, knelt down and prayed as a Christians to Jesus, his Lord.

In more detail, what had happened was that when the Prince was being pursued and sentenced to death, the Capuchin missionaries were captured in Lebanon. They were considered criminals for trying to pursuade the Prince to become a Christian. It happened that the Prince escaped to the Lebanon mountains. Meanwhile, the army plundered Beirut and captured Father Bernard de Bogea and Father Andrian of Labros. The Pasha asked Father Adrian if he was the one who baptized the Prince. Father Adrian answered: "if the Prince is a Christian so I treated him as one of the Christians". The missionary did not confirm that the Prince had become a Christian or what were his religious beliefs.

The missionaries suffered from insults and torture. They were brought to the Sultan and accused of having Christianized the Prince. The Sultan wanted to burn the five missionaries in front of five churches in Ghaltah because Ga'far Pasha the sea prince complained about them because they converted Prince Fakhr El Dine. But the missionaries were saved from that punishment by the intercession of the Ambassadors of the European countries. Instead, they were deported from the Ottoman lands. Two of them died after being tortured in prison. In Syria, the missionaries' monasteries were almost completely eliminated because the government had arrested so many of the monks. The priests were persecuted, insulted and burdened with all kinds of taxes.

Father Silvestros and Father Bonefasios took refuge in Lebanon where their escape was miraculous. The Turkish army chased them and sent spies everywhere. But they could not find them. They were hiding in the mountain caves. The priests were overwelmed by snow and they were starving. Then God sent them a Lebanese man who saved them. After suffering and being chased, they landed in Tripoli where they have been received by a tradesman who had a profound impact on the governor. Accordingly, he defended them from any harm even though the Sultan's orders were to send them to Istambul in chains. ..."refer to the book La France Catholique en Orient, by P. Hilaire Baranton: pp. 115-164".

So it was that the Capuchin missionaries came to Salima during the situation as we just described. They were received by the Lam's princes because they had been recommended by the Ma'n princes. The two families are in-laws and we will talk about that in the Chapter on Abi Al Lam's, as well as the Christianization of Prince Abdallah Qadbeh their elder. That great Prince knew about the good deeds of the missionaries and how they were devoted to the service of religion and humanity. This was clear from the way they practiced medecine, lovingly and affectionately caring for the illnesses of humanity. When these priests were allowed to reside in Lebanon, they quickly constructed monasteries and equipped them with whatever their followers could donate. All the governors, whether Muslims or Druze or Christian, helped the missionaries who have been of such great help to the town. The priests stirred an interest for the arts and science in the people. They also gave advise to resolve conflicts between them. Thus they gained the respect and love of the people of all different faiths.

There is a legend that Al Toubawy, Father Agha Teng from Vendome, the Capuchin missionary, martyred in Guinea, was the one who built the Monastery in Salima in 1634 during the era of Prince Fakhr El Din, as is mentioned in his biography. However, I have not checked that information and I know of no evidence bearing on it. What I do know is that Father Agha Teng passed by Salima and got acquianted with the Lam's princes, the in-laws of the Ma'n princes. The Ma'ns received the Capuchin priests as guests in Lebanon with warm hospitality. Furthermore, Father Ya'koub from Vendome came to help the Ma'ns and their in-laws. He then took them to Europe. He also passed by Salima but there is no evidence that Capuchins established their monastery in Salima before the year 1705 as I will show later. The missionaries did end up choosing a parcel of land in the highest part of Salima called Ain Baqha. It is an open space in a splendid place overlooking the whole town and surrounded by pine and oak trees.

Beside this land is an outflowing of water whose source comes from inside the mountain. There are some large, lofty and shady walnut trees. Underneath them can be found goat herds and shepherds. The missionaries made of this a society of soul shepherds. They were propagandists of goodness and righteousness. So, they built for themselves a monastery and called it after Saint Peter, the name of the missionaries' superior. It was known as Mar Boutros (Saint Peter) Monastery or Al Freng Monastery or El Padre Monastry. And Ain Baqha became known as Ain Al Deir.

It is obvious that this Monastery was established thanks to these zealous, religious people as well as to their devout and generous believers. Contributions were sent from Europe to the missionaries. While the support of the princes was advantageous, the work of the people participating with them aided as well. Trusted elders have told me that the missionaries were treating sick people and giving these treatments for free. They acted simply out of their religious belief, plus they performed their spiritual duties with the congregations. The princes were offering them a measure of wheat, oil and molasses, a tradition that lasted for a long time. In general, those Europeans wearing hoods and brown robes came to Salima and were a blessing. Their days were full of goodness and joy. All of the elders remember them with gratitude and praise.

The Capuchin, Father Hilar, said in his book, previously mentioned, on page 119: *"Capuchin priests practiced medicine since a long time ago, and were certified in 1735. The missionaries in Beirut established an Ecclesiastical school under the sponsorship of the King of France. The Holy See wrote to Maronite governors seeking their help for the missionaries. Then the missionaries established a print shop in Lebanon to print books in the four oriental languages.*" On page 139 he said, *"When the Capuchins arrived in the East in 1625 they found about 280 thousand Maronite Catholics.*" And he said in pages 155 and 158 *"The best thing the Capuchins did was reviving the Christian life among the Maronites and the conversion of Prince Fakhr El Din...which was the reason for the Christians' peace in the East.*"

Then, those Monks started to improve themselves with construction. They built the northen crypts where previously there was the ancient Monastery entrance. This was very well constructed, a sign of art and good taste. After that, they built a church , which was a small temple granting piety and solemnity to souls. Then, in the old building, they added an upper layer with multiple vaults and rooms at different levels. They also purchased large properties as written on the deeds which we still preserve. The monastery had grapevines, figs, olives, and pines, all signs of a high level of agricultural productivity. The missionaries were producing a good wine. Their monastery's winery was producing the best wine in Lebanon. Also, they were an example of the agricultural revolution in production.

The missionaries that we know are:

Father Michael. The first headmaster of the Monastery. He is the European Capuchin, Father Michael. He built the monastery with his friend Prince Abdallah Abi Al Lam who was converted to Christianty through him as we will discuss later. Furthermore, he had a role in establishing the Mar Avram Al Raghem Monastery for the Syriac Catholics in Al Shabania in Al Metn. The author of the book entitled The Care Of The All-Merciful For The Guidance Of Syriacs has found the mark of the Patriarch, Avram Al Rahmani. The construction of the monastery is mentioned in it. Here is a summary:

"Some Syriac Catholic deacons escaped from Halab, because of the surpression of the Ya'koubians. So, they took refuge with the Patriarch of the Maronites, Ya'koub Awad, as recommended by the Capuchins and Jesuits of that town. They asked him that they be allowed to stay in Bcharre because it wasn't good to stay where they were due to the injustice of the governors of Tripoli. Then he advised them to go to the village of Ashbania, one of Druze towns governed by Prince Abi Al Lam' . And there is a Syrian man from Rashia called Sarkis Abou Rezk who decided to build a monastery for the Syrians. Thus, they did and went to Al Shabania. From there Sarkis accompanied them to Salima where Prince Abdallah was constructing a monastery for the Capuchins. Father Mikhail, the monastery headmaster, was leading the construction. All of them, then, went to Al Shabania where they met the Maronite Archbishop, Elias Safi. All of them recommended that the people of the village treat those monks well. (the Archbishop, Elias Al Gemayel is from Bakfia and his name was Safi (1706-1713).

Thus it was that the Monastery of Mar Avram Al Raghem has been built, but it was opposed by the Patriarch of the Ya'koubians. In the beginning of 1705, they finished the construction of the monastery. Both Sheikh Abou Farahate and Sheikh Boumeghlbya - Druze chiefs - helped in the work.

The Syriac Sarkis Abi Rezk has a daughter, a zealous one for Catholicism. She bought the necessary land for a monastery from her father and sold it to the Capuchin, Father Mikhail through Sheikh Abou Shedid, Prince Abdulallah's calligrapher. Then she sent the contract to Father Mansour, the head of the Capuchins in Sayda, who encouraged the Syriacs to complete the work."

This is a summary of the Syrian's history from page 139 of the book. Now I report from the calligraphies of Karki, the text of the purchase deed between Sarkis abou Rezk and his daughter Mary (Mariam). That is followed by the deed between Mary and Father Mikhail. This appears to have taken place with the approval and consent of the Patriarch.

According to this, the establishment of the Monastery of Saint Peter in Salima occurred before 1705. Here is the exact text of deeds according to page 165, the second part of the registers of the Maronite Patriarchy:

(A copy of the Purchase Agreement of Mary, the daughter, with her father Sarkis Ibn Fahd)

"In the name of Allah, the Beneficent, the Most Merciful, He is enough for me and He is the one I turn to. This document is the means by which Mary, the daughter of Abu Rezk purchased from her father, Sarkis bin Fahd, from the inhabitants of the village of Shabbaneia in the region of Metn, belonging to Beirut, protected by God; it is the prosperous land which was known as al-Qela'i. She purchased this land for herself with her own money without any other person. It is a completed sale without any condition, corruption, reference or reversion. It was a valid sale and completed according to all proper Islamic regulations. The sale was in the amount of 25 Piasters paid by proper monetary currency, meeting all standards of weight, caliber, and produced by Islamic die. The aforementioned seller received the entire price with nothing more to claim, not even one Dirham. Two people have witnessed this willingly on the first of the Islamic month of Zu al-Hejja in the year 1120 from al-Hijra of the Prophet, Peace Be Upon Him.

The Editor

Testified to the validity of this, are: Nasr El Dine   Yehya Ibn Zein El Dine   Mohamed Ibn Armeh"

* * * * *

(A copy of the Purchase Agreement of Father Michael al-Kabushy (the Capuchin) with Mary. the daughter of Sarkis Abu Rezk)

"In the name of Allah, the Beneficent, the Most Merciful, He is enough for me and He is the one I turn to. This document is the means by which Father Michael al-Afranjy (the European) al-Kabushy (the Capuchin), the head of the Monastery of Salima purchased from Mary, the daughter of Abu Rezk Sarkis bin Fahd, from the inhabitants of the village of Shabbaneia in the region of Metn, belonging to Beirut, protected by God; it is the prosperous land which was known as al-Qela'i. He purchased this land for himself without any person. It is a completed sale without any condition, corruption, reference or reversion. It was a valid sale and completed according to all proper Islamic regulations. The sale was in the amount of 25 Piasters paid by proper monetary currency, meeting all standards of weight, caliber, and produced by Islamic die. The aforementioned seller received the entire price with nothing to claim, not even one Dirham. Two people have witnessed this willingly on the 28th of the Islamic month of Zu al-Hejja in the year 1120 from al-Hijra of the Prophet, Peace Be Upon Him.

The Editor

Testified to the validity of this, are: The mentioned seller Abu Farahat Abd Allah al-Khuri Girgis from Shabbaneia. Abu Mansour Ra'd.."

I don't know the names of the Father Superiors who came after Father Michael, the founder of the Monastery. What little I do know of the Monastery's early events is not worth mentioning. In the history of missionaries in Lebanon, it appears that weakness started to creep in after the 17th century up to the beginning of the 19th century (1800 AD). During that time the French missionary was replaced with Italian ones following the great French Revolution and the first military campaign of Napoleon into Syria.

Father Nicholas. Of the Superiors of the Monastery, I do know Father Nicholas (Niqola) Gladimir who was most probably the last of the French priests. The Holy See transferred Italian missionaries of the same Order to Lebanon. Father Nicholas was a brilliant doctor and had knowledge of the medical perspicacity, which is the ability to predict the death of a patient when he still appears to be in good health. Father Nicholas purchased many properties for the Monastery.

Father John. Father John (Hanna or Yuhanna) came to Salima after Father Nicholas, around 1830. Most probably he was one of the Italian priests. The first thing he thought about was establishing an organized school in Salima. He brought in a fellow priest from his order called Father Mansour. This was after the turmoil between the Christians and the Druze in 1845. He was a teacher of the Italian language. The Italian Capuchins spread out in our land. They established this kind of school in the Monastery of Saint Anthony (Mar Antonios) in B'abdat. This school was the seminary for the Order of Saint Anthony. Along the west side of the Monastery, Father John built a room that he turned into a school for minors. Here, Father Mansour taught Italian and al-Shediaq As'ad from Kisrawan taught Arabic and Syriac. Father John was a good hearted man, generous and kind to the poor. His moral goodness appeared most strongly after the turmoil of the year1845. Following this tragedy, he distributed money that was sent by France for those stricken by the disaster. He studied Arabic and was very knowledgeable in medicine. After he left the Monastery, Father Mansour took over.

Father Mansour. Father Mansour stayed in Salima for a long period of time. He taught Italian in the era of his predecessor, Father John. After Father John was reassigned, Father Mansour actively took over his missionary work. In Medicine, he was the most skillful priest who came to Salima. He was known for his kindness and dedication in serving the poor. He treated people of different religious backgrounds and distributed medicines to them for free. If someone became ill, the family of the patient called him from the roof. He would come immediately. In addition to his great virtue of charity, he had wisdom and piety. He was tall, good looking, and well built. He had spent his youth in the military. The people of Salima and the neighboring areas loved him and respected him. Many of them benefited from his medical treatments according to the methods of the time. They did so, just as they had benefited from the former priests of the Monastery, like, Father Joseph Bachaalany (al-Khuri Youssef al-Bshe'lani) and Sheik Haidar al-Zar'aouni of the Druze. Father Mansour gave both of these men the book <u>The Healing</u> by Ibn Sina'a. This printed copy had been in Rome for more than four hundred years. I saw it several years ago in the house of Haidar al-Zar'aouni, in the possession of his grandsons. In 1869, Father Mansour received orders transferring him to Antioch. While there, an earthquake occurred when Father was saying Mass. The congregation ran out of the Church leaving him alone carrying on with the Holy Sacrifice. The walls fell down above the altar and yet Father Mansour survived by a miracle. He died in Antioch in 1882 and is remembered with mercy and goodness.

Father Andrew. Father Andrew (Father Andraus) is the most famous of the Capuchin priests who headed the Monastery of Saint Peter in Salima. He was the most grace filled, loving, and charitable man to this town. His name will always be in our mouths and his memory will always be alive in our hearts and minds. No one can deny his great kindness which reached the rich and the poor. None can deny his blessed help to everyone. He loved Lebanon like his own country, and most of all, he loved Salima. He tried to make the best out of Salima, morally and materialistically. If only circumstances had helped him, he would have made Salima a special place of beauty in this country.

Salima regained its lost glory in his era. It regained the power which had prevailed in the era of its princes. It became the destination of men and the goal of their hopes.

Father Andrew was of Italian origin. He was born in Venice. He arrived at Salima in October of 1873. After spending some time in Beirut, he was assigned to be the Superior of the Monastery in Salima. So it was that he came to Salima with a heart burning of a missionary's zeal. The most important task which he immediately undertook was the refinement of Salima's children. He took care to upgrade the lessons in the two schools of boys and girls. For this purpose, he built a new addition on the east side of the Monastery. In this way, the teaching would be under his sight. He chose teachers known for their knowledge and virtue. He brought a teacher who received her education in the convent of al-Mahabba Nuns in Beirut. She knew Arabic and French. After he made some renovations to the monastery, he traveled to Europe as was the custom of the missionaries. Every ten years or so, they would return to their home for a while and then go back to their assignment. This was in the year 1879.

After one year, he returned. With him he brought the charity of the European believers. He returned with money and church utensils. He began to establish schools in the villages of Metn. They had long been deprived of any education. He spent much money for this project. The most important villages where he established schools for education and religion are Hassbia, Bezbedin, Kenaiessa, Kasiba, al-Arbaneia, Qornayel, Shabbaneia, Arsoun, Hamana, Aria, Matin, B'abdat, and Bakfia.

The thing which elevated Father Andrew in the eyes of the people and made him so popular and reputable throughout the country, was his creation of Our Lady of Lourdes Boarding School in Salima. With the support of his Dutch friend, Jan Momas, he performed a great service to the country. With this school he made a gift that is everlasting. Because of him, contributions came from Europe, especially France, in the name of this school. France gave a monthly donation from the government, in addition to charity given from other countries. Father Andrew was the Dean of the school and Mr. Momas was the fully accredited adminstrator. The school existed from 1882 till 1892 when it was shut down by orders of the government leaders. I will discuss this in detail later.

From the glorious deeds of that priest came provisions for the churches in Metn and the Qate' (the Strip). He provided churches with cruets and glassware, chalices and more. No church did without, each showed the signs of his favors and charity. The priests in Salima and the neighboring villages used to get a salary from the school or receive stipends for Masses or some items for the church in addition to charities. Also, he left behind the garden fence and the outside gate of the Monastery of Salima. This linked the monastery with the old schools and made it fenced. He placed on the top of the gate a marble stone which had printed on it the slogan of the priesthood. Also shown is a picture of two clasped hands with a cross in the middle of them and written on it: "a work of Father Andraus 1879".

They made the ceiling of the northern rooms of the Monastery with plaster. They established modern schools. They bought the castle of the Lam Princes from the Lebanese government for 40,000 Piasters. They turned it into a large boarding school after renovating, repairing, and adding additional buildings. This was Father Andrew's greatest achievement in Salima. He renovated the neglected real estate of the Monastery and fixed the ranch known as Ain al-Boyeet so it produced crops for the Monastery and the school. Some widows benefited from this since the Monastery raised the foundlings. There were also professors, laborers, servants, and others who have worked for the monastery and the boarding school. They all benefited from the people coming to this place. Europeans spent summers here, and all these benefits came because of this priest.

His love for Lebanon and especially Salima didn't stop at all this. He intended to build a shrine beside the Monastery for Our Lady of Lourdes. In that beautiful valley where the fountain water passed by like the water of Lourdes, surrounded by the tall pine trees, he wanted to place a statue of the Virgin in a cave just as She appeared at Lourdes. He was promised by a group of his French friends that they would visit the shrine in an official tour. Thus, Salima would become a Mecca for religion, as it was a Mecca for earthly matters. This dream, however, did not come true. The school was shut down. Father Andrew was transferred from Salima. The lucky star of this town faded when he went away.

After Father Andrew had spent about 20 years in Salima, he was transferred to B'abdat. There he served the congregation of the Latins. After being there for more than one year, he was moved to Beirut where he served the Latin congregation up to his death. Shortly before this, he visited Salima. He bid it farewell and took leave of it. He suffered from dropsy and it increased in him. He died on June 29, 1904 in the Monastery in Beirut. He had arranged his final affairs as if he was traveling. He was buried in a shrine of his own. Written on it are the dates of his birth, the date he became a priest, and the date of his death. It mentions the name of his homeland. May God have mercy on him for all of his great and good deeds.

Father Andrew was a good looking, sedate, respectable and well built man with a round face and a long beard. He was good mannered and civilized. If he became angry he never hated. He was fluent in French and Latin in addition to his native Italian language. He learned Arabic to the extent that he used to recite the bible in his Mass in Arabic. He studied Syriac until he was able to read it well. He wrote many useful articles about our country in the French Magazine "La Maison Catholique" and in the Italian Magazine "al-Tamaddun al-Katholiki". He took care of the rituals as well as religious ceremonies for the feast of Thursdays…the sacrifice that was attended by the people of the village. The students of Our Lady of Lourdes School and the students of the minor area schools, all lightened up these special parties with their music and songs that praised the Creator.

The people of different denominations respected him and loved him for he used to protect their honor out of his kindness and vigilant care. If it is possible to make statues for our good people, then we, the people of Salima and neighboring areas, should construct one for this great priest. However, since we are not able to do so, let it be known that he has a living statue in the heart of each one of us. One that never vanishes. And that great priest showed his favor on the author of this chronicle, for I was breast fed the milk of science and religion in his school. Furthermore, I taught in it for several years. Father Andrew used to take care of me whether I am near him or far away. May God have mercy on his soul.

The journey of Father Moussa Dorlian to Salima.

Father Moussa Dorlian, the Capuchin missionary, published an account of his trip to the East in the magazine "La Maison Catholique" in the issue of October 10, 1873. Father Moussa was a famous preacher in France. In his writing, he mentions his travels to Syria and Lebanon as well as visiting the Monasteries and schools. In the magazine, it also showed the painting of the Archbishop Ga'ga' and the picture of the Dean of Our Lady of Lourdes school in Salima, its teachers, and among them was Prince Khalil Saad Shihab, the administrator of the region of Upper Metn. He was staying in Salima and said:

"We arrived at Salima at 7 o'clock and the school's male pupils were lined up in the yard of the village with their teachers. As soon as we appeared to the public, they started to sing a welcoming song. They were ahead of us in the procession, singing for 15 minutes until we reached the yard of the Monastery's church. There we saw the female pupils of the school with their female teacher and they also sang to welcome us. Then, we entered the Monastery to take some rest.

As for Salima, it is a town located in the midst of the mountains and in it, there are 1500 inhabitant; 1000 are Christians and 500 are Druze. Salima is the base of government in Metn in Lebanon. It has an administrator and a division of the Lebanese military, about 50 soldiers. The Capuchin priests bought the important part of the palace of the princes in Salima and turned it into a boarding school. I will talk about it. The reader remembers that 10 days ago I fell off a mule that I was riding and suffered from a severe cut on my thigh. It was so bad that I had to stay in bed. Father Andrew, the headmaster of our schools in Lebanon, preferred to invite the teachers in the nearby schools to come with their pupils to Salima. They would take the necessary examination in the subjects they had studied. This would save me the effort of going out myself to do the examination. Thus I examined the pupils of the schools of: Hassbia, Bezbedin, Kenaiessa, Kasiba, Arbaneia and Qornayel. I could not visit the far schools due to the pain in my thigh but I learned about them from what I tested of the nearby schools.

At that time, there were two schools in Salima. The first one was for the males and the second one for the females. In the first one there were 70 pupils and in the second 50. I made the public inspection for these two schools. The party contained songs and poems. The pupils prepared clean copybooks for their French handwriting and Arabic handwriting. The girls presented some beautiful sewing and embroidery pieces. The female teacher, who was one of the students of the Lazarite Nuns in Beirut, was skillful in women's work. As for the male pupils, they answered the questions of Christian education, mathematics and French language basics. Their answers amazed us and filled our hearts with pride. Some pupils who were not more than 5 years old could read and write Arabic and Syriac. This was like nothing I had seen in France.

Unfortunately, out resources weren't enough to establish industrial schools where the youngsters receive the principles of science. In our country when a boy reaches twelve years of age, he stays with his parents where a teacher can not follow him. It is no wonder that industrial schools have great benefits for boys and girls. It protects them under the banner of the Church until they are able to form Christian associations to support the country and the Church. This is what helps to support Christian morals. The moneys that are given in the name of France as charity, this is the biggest method for spreading French authority and influence. This, also, helps to make the love and ties to the Holy Church grow.

The English tried a long time ago to spread their authority in Mount Lebanon. They sent missionaries and assigned them to open scientific and industrial schools. Students from all sects joined these schools. Thus, they established schools in Bermana, only two kilometers from Salima. They opened two boarding schools, one for boys and girls, as well as a preparatory school for both sexes. In Choueir, they had a major school and a preparatory school. In Zahle they had two schools and in Aria they opened a boarding school for girls.

During my stay in Salima, Prince Khalil Saad Shihab, the Administrator of Metn who was known for his religious, vigilant care visited me. He showed me his sorrow that the country has become a prey for the Protestant heresy. He asked me in his name and in the name of the people to build a school for the purpose of opposing the Protestants. Catholic schools would cause their efforts in Lebanon to fail. I had already undertaken to establish Catholic schools near the Protestant schools in Shabbaneia, Qornayel, Bezbedin, Bakfia, Arsoun, Aria, B'abdat, Hamana and Matin. In the last three villages, we put national teachers.

But defeating our rivals can only occur by establishing a major school, and industrial schools. This is logical. But, how can we reach this goal without the money? I came to know a man of Dutch origin who was the council of that country in Jeddah. He came to Egypt and when the revolution of Orabi happened, he escaped to Syria. He was a guest of the great Father Andrew, the head of our Monastery in Salima. When he learned of the intentions of Prince Khalil, he showed his desire to stay in this country. He pledged to help us if we wanted to build a major school. He agreed to teach in it, whatever subjects we wanted.

The circumstances were not in our favor. Establishing a school in this country requires a huge sum of money. As I was thinking about that, the Administrator told me that the palace of the Princes in Salima, which at that time was in the hands of the Lebanese government, was about to be sold through auction. In that palace, there are wide places that could be transformed into classrooms with a little fixing. Also, he said that his father (Prince Saad

93

Shihab) was the Head of the Administration and that he would make it easy for us to buy the palace. Mr. Momas promised us that he would lend us the necessary money for renovating the palace. So it happened. It was as if the heaven's protection made it easy for us to establish that institute for the welfare of the children and for the elevation of their morals and education. Thus it happened that Prince Khalil would accompany us with a letter to his father, recommending us to Rostom Pasha, the Mutassarif of the Mount."

Next, he mentioned that he traveled from Salima to Hamana on July 28, in the company of Father Andrew, the head of the Monastery. Accompanying them was Joseph (Youssef) Wakim Bachaalany, the vicar of the Monastery. They had intended to go and to stay overnight at the house of Diab Effendi, the head of the council. He is a Roman Catholic. By mistake they actually went to the house of Khalil Beshara al-Khuri, the clerk of the council. He welcomed them and they spent the night in his place. Then, the next day, they visited Diab Effendi and Prince Saad Shihab who, in turn, introduced them to Rostom Pasha. They presented the matter to him and he gathered together the members of the council since that was their responsibility. They all agreed to sell the palace for the price of 1800 Riyals. This is a very cheap price, less than one fifth of the price of the building rocks. They thanked the Mutasarrif and then left.

This is what he said about the school of Our Lady of Lourdes in Salima:

"After I left Syria, Father Andrew made the arrangements for buying the palace. Mr. Moumasse kept his promise and loaned the Missionary the necessary money. This amount paid for buying the real estate and for the necessary repairs. The renovation was started to allow for an October (of the same year) opening date for the school. The people throughout the countryside were happy with this new project, The Druze, who constitute one third of the people of Salima, said that they didn't deserve to even kiss the footsteps where Father Andrew walked. The Principal of the school, Mr. Moumasse, distributed a brochure announcing the opening of the boarding school. On the first day of October, 1882, the school was opened under the name Our Lady of Lourdes.

At the beginning of the year the number of students was 20. It reached 35 at the end of the year. The headmaster, Mr. Moumasse, made every effort to make this school a success. He truly deserves our gratitude. It was he who took care of the organization of the classes. It was he who found the three teachers who helped him teach. The students' success was magnificent. The people acknowledged it. The Association of Nashr al-Iman wanted to express its appreciation for his management and sent him 10000 Francs to continue the work. It provided the required hardware for 100 students. Unfortunately, the plague prevented this because a quarantine was applied on all imports to Mount Lebanon. He couldn't accomplish the renovations in the specified time. The number of students increased by 10 during the year reaching 45.

Here is the report of Mr. John Moumasse, the Principal of the school, he said: The second year has passed and great success crowns our works. The written examination was very satisfactory and the oral and general examination had good results. The Jesuit priests whom we invited asked the students difficult questions in French grammar. The students answered well and without delay. The same was true for the examinations in Arabic, Turkish, English, and geography. The examiners were surprised at the progress of our students in such a short period of time. With Mr. Charles, I prepared a stage for acting that cost me a large sum of money, but it was necessary and inevitable.

In the beginning of August, Father Andrew and Mr. Charles invited the French Consul Mr. Patrimonio to attend the party following the examinations. They also invited the Archbishop Joseph (Youssef al-) Zoghby and the Mutasarrif of Mount Lebanon and the Qa'em Maqam of Metn. On August 9, the night of the party, the good news came of the arrival of his Highness al-Zoghby who went to the Monastery of the Capuchins. There he was welcomed by the Superior of the Monastery. Archbishop Zoghby stayed in Salima for several weeks. Shortly thereafter, some Jesuit priests came with Father Sgak whom you knew in Lyons.

On the morning of August10. at 9 o'clock, the Consul accompanied by the Chancellor and the Qa'em Maqam of the Jurisdiction and the Administrator arrived. After they drank some soft drinks at the school, they went to the Monastery to attend the Mass. The people of Salima were shooting guns into the air. They were also singing to welcome them. After the Mass, the Consul returned to the school and, at 10 o'clock, he asked that the first part of the play be performed. The theater was in the schoolyard. Covers were spread over it to provide shade. Some 300 tickets were distributed but a huge crowd remained outside. The Consul and the Archbishop decided that the doors should be opened for them. As soon as the doors were opened, more than 2000 people entered and the performance of two plays started: the first is French and the second is Arabic. The people interrupted the plays often with their admiring applause.

After a period of rest, a French play was performed. It was entitled "The Unknowing Magician". The actors were dressed in costumes of the period of Louis XIV. They did very well. The play contained beautiful singing and it was repeated twice at the request of the Consul. Two prizes were awarded to the best performers. The first for the French, presented by the Consul, and the second for the Arabic given by his Excellency, the Archbishop. At the end of the play, one of the students gave a speech of welcome and praise, in French, to the Consul in the names of the students. Then, another student gave a speech in Arabic for the Archbishop. Then one of the people in attendance stood up and gave a speech. He welcomed and praised the Consul for accepting the invitation of the school. The person expressed the gratitude of the people of Salima. The speaker also thanked the Father Andrew, the founder of the school and Mr. Moumasse, its Principal. He then ended his speech with the following statement which he repeated 3 times in a loud voice: "Long Live France".

Then prizes were awarded. The party lasted until 5 o'clock in the afternoon. Then, the Consul congratulated us for the success of the school and for our efforts for its progress. He said: I admire your pupils. They proved their great success in a short time and, therefore, I congratulate the school for having them. I thank the teachers for their care. And, finally, I am happier than you with this success and I thank all of you. Continue forward.

He shook our hands goodbye then rode away on his horse accompanied by the Chancellor. His Excellency, the Archbishop, and the Qa'em Maqam and the District Administrator did the same. Then the pupils went on their vacation in an organized manner. Four students from Egypt remained. The reader sees that this success not only benefits the people but also enables us to spread our authority over the country. We are currently thinking of establishing an industrial school in Salima for the youth but this serious work requires great expenses. We hope that the generosity of your kind readers will extend their helping hand to us."

The author of this article makes an interesting statement about the necessity of helping this school. This was the way to oppose the Protestants who were upset at the success of the French and the spreading of their influence in the East. He asked for more help to spread this authority and to make Catholicism prosper. France and England were fighting for influence in the East through the missionaries. If the missioanries gained authority then this will increase the influence of their backers. He showed that the jurisdiction of Metn is in the middle of Mount Lebanon and has its base in Salima. He also showed that its Administrator governs the neighboring villages. He shows that at the mount of Salima, we intended to build a statue of Our Lady of Lourdes at a high elevation. Also, that for this intention, the school prayed so that its work would be successful. Then the author describes his travel from Beit al-Din to Abeia. He says: "Abeia is the first town in Lebanon to be entered by the Capuchins and that was in 1623. It was a residence for the Shihabs the same way as Salima was the center of the Lam's. The origin of the Shihabs is Islamic and the Lam's is Druze. The two groups converted to Christianity in the 18th century under the Maronite name.

Among those who helped Father Andrew in his work was Father Donato. Father Andrew (who was referred to as Father Andrew, the Junior, had a religious superior who was also known as Father Andrew, but he was known as Father Andrew, the Senior. As events occurred, Father Andrew the Senior was opposed to Father Andrew the Junior.

Father Andrew the Senior then ordered Our Lady of Lourdes school to be closed. Father Andrew the Junior was transferred to B'abdat to serve the congregation there. The last priest to head the school was Father Marshilino Dalens. He neglected the school at Salima and directed his attention to establishing a similar school in the Monastery of Abeia. He spent a large amount of money in vain on this project. He was a careless spender, a very bad planner and lacking in principles. Because of this, the religious superiors issued orders to oust him from his leadership position in the area of Syria and Lebanon. Acting according to the opinion of Father Andrew, the Junior, the authorities agreed to deliver the mission in these countries to French priests as it was the older times. This was done by the order of the Holy See in 1903.

The Antonian Priesthood. Father Marshilino bought from the late Fares Anton his house, which was a part from the palace of the princes in the past. Then all the palace belonged to the Capuchin priests. And since the school had already been closed and nobody remained in the Monastery except for Brother Fidel of the Capuchins, the superiors decided to sell the school. The priest, Father Anton, bought it and reopened it, as I'll mention later. They also decided to sell the Monastery of Saint Peter, so, it too, was sold out of the Antonean Priesthood about 1912 and was bought by Father Louis Obeid al-B'abdaty, the president of Saint John Maron in Rome and the vicar of the priesthood at the Apostolic See. It was sold for 2200 golden French Liras. Father Ash'eia al-Asmar became the president of the Monastery, followed by Father Elias Te'ma, then Father Tanious Abu Gouda, then Father Boutros Abu Gouda. They remained in that Monastery until about 1927. During that time, they were serving the congregation of Saint John in Salima.

Father Anton al-Asmar. Around 1927, the late priest, Father Anton al-Asmar, bought the Monastery. He was the one who had previously purchased the school from the Capuchin Order. He stayed at this Monastery until his death on the May 8, 1930. The Monastery and the school became the properties of Mr. Naguib, the son of his brother Amin al-Asmar. It remained his property till 1933, when it was bought from him by the Nuns of the Missionaries to become a convent for them in Lebanon.

The Nuns of the Missionaries. This religious order was established in 1876 and it had its general headquarters in Lyons. The founder was Father Blanc, the general president of the African Missionaries. He was of French origin. After the first World War, a group of The Nuns of the Missionaries came to this country by an invitation from the administration of Amsheet hospital. They took over its administration and ran it for several years. According to the request of Archbishop Anton Aql, some of the nuns took the administration of the hospital of Mar Elias in Ras Beirut. They did this job perfectly for many years. In 1933, the nuns arrived in Salima and negotiations were held between them and the Khawaja Naguib al-Asmar, the owner of the Monastery of Saint Peter. They agreed to buy it and started to build a school in the monastery that year.

In 1934, they transferred the school to the palace, which was also a property of the mentioned Mr. Naguib. They started to renovate the Monastery. The renovation ended in 1935 and they moved there. The price of the Monastery was 60,000 Francs and the expenses of the renovation and repair was 230,000 Francs. It was transformed into two suites consisting of 3 floors. It became a beautiful modern convent equipped with all that is necessary to be a center for the nuns, as well as a day and a boarding school for female students. The Convent was named Our Lady of the Missionaries, preserving within it the shrine of Saint Peter, the Missionary, with his picture. The renovation of this Monastery also brought about the renovation of the scientific, cultural, and religious movement in this town. The nuns then established some branches in Kenaiessa, Metn and Abbadeia. After several years they left these branches and returned entirely to the Convent of Our Lady of the Missionaries and the Monastery of Qabb Elias which is of no less importance.

The person in charge of this charity organization was Mother Odelle, the first mother superior of the Convent. She is a Maronite of Lebanese origin, from Aintoura Kisrawan. She lived for a time in Egypt. Her assistant at the Convent was the French woman, Mother Maximian. Mother Odelle continued in this position for 4 years (1933-1937). After her came Mother Marta, then, others came up to 1946.

In 1946, heaven sent to Salima a nun who came from French origins. Her name was Mother Marcelle. Gallantry, kindness, and wisdom shined through all her works. Even though being new to the area, she was able to capture the hearts of the people whether Christians or Druze. She took over the leadership of the Convent seriously and actively. After less than one year, she was transferred to Egypt because the order needed her there. Unfortunately, this was also at a time when the Convent of Salima also needed her wisdom and great kindness. The nuns used to take care of the patients, especially the poor. The nuns who excelled were Emilia and Georgia Wadal.

The vestiges of the Monastery. Preserved in this monastery still is an inscription carved into a stone which was put on a tomb inside the Church on the southern wall. It has the two dates for the death of Hanna bin Elias al-Tayyan, the time when his family lived in Salima. Perhaps this is when they lived in the Monastery itself when it had been abandoned. Here is the text and the two dates:

bin   Elias

-- *You who enter my shrine, sing "O mercy of God" for the one laying here.*
-- *Don't wonder that I am suddenly not among you. Do I have any power against the coming destiny?*
-- *Don't cry for me, O, you, who love me, and, don't lament me, for I am gone alone.*
-- *And my soul, after its striving, has found my rest, "it won immortal gardens of heaven".*

Hannah   1811   al-Tayyan

-- *You, Tayyan, moved from earth to heaven.*
-- *And you, Hanna (John), reached the goals of your loneliness, with the permission of God.*
-- *He called out to you in his Book "Win my mercy".*

1225

I don't know who wrote the first Christian date. It may have been the teacher, Elias Eda, the famous poet of that time who contacted Prince Bashir al-Kabir and the other princes of Salima. As for the second Hegira date, it is of the teacher Niqola al-Turk. He was the poet of Prince Bashir. He had a divan that contained poems praising the princes of Salima. I saw the text on the divan of al-Turk which I have. He wrote, lamenting his nephew, the late Hanna al-Tayyan, who died in the village of Salima:

> *"O my cousin, how much my heart has burned for you*
> *But I am sure of the goodness of this travel."*

Then he mentions the rest of the verses, which I quoted from his tomb, mentioned earlier.

A European family came to live in the Monastery. A girl of this family died and she was buried at the Church of the Monastery. A plaque was put on the northern wall with the date of her death which was written in Latin. She lived in this Monastery with others, some French and some Italian, among the people of Salima. This Austrian girl Maria was with the family of the Austrian Consul. They were spending the summer in Qornayel around 1845. She was killed and her death was mentioned by Lord Churchill in his English book "Mount Lebanon". I quoted from it about the

Sheiks of Qornayel and the priest, who was the Superior of the Monastery. He went from Salima to Qornayel with As'ad Abboud Bachaalany. He brought the daughter back to Salima and after praying over her, buried her beside the Monastery. When Father Ash'eia dug around the Church to build a fence for the Monastery about 1910, he found human remains that had been buried there beside a pomegranate that was planted there. I told him that the remains belonged to the girl, Maria, which is a fact I was assured of by some knowledgeable people. Some of the remains were of Estephan Nawfal Bachaalany who was killed in 1845, at noon, between Qornayel and Salima. Also, there were the remains of the Abu Musharraf Fahd al-Masry, who converted to Christianity with some Druze when Ibrahim Pasha al-Masry wanted to take them in to serve in the military in 1839. It was the custom of some Muslims at that time to convert to Christianity in order to escape from military service. As a consequence of this, the remains were moved to the grave beside the old church of Saint John.

Among the vestiges found in the monastery was a grapes press which my ancestor, Moussa bought from Prince Abd Allah around 1700. He gave it to the Capuchins when they built the Monastery as was shown in the old archived documents. The monastery was burnt in 1845 during the turmoil between the Christians and the Druze. News of the fire reached France. It was mentioned by the Head of the French Consul which also mentioned the Monastery of Abeia where the Capuchin Father Richar was killed in a terrible way. (refer to: the political writings of Philip and Farid al-Khazen, part 1:201 and 214). The Monastery of Salima stayed abandoned for a period of time after this. France sent large financial donations to repair the Monastery and they also donated a large bell. The bell is still there today. It has Italian writing on it saying that it was presented by John Bazouly and made in Genoa, Italy in 1845. As for the beautiful painting that remains in the Monastery still today, it has written on it that it was made in 1861. It was painted by an Italian painter and it shows Saint Peter, the Missionary, kneeling in prayer with his eyes looking to the sky, his hands folded in prayer. The look of reverence and solemnity are on his face and there is a cock crowing in front of him.

99

THE CHURCH OF SAINT ANTHONY (MAR ANTONIOS)

Chapter 5

The old Roman Catholic Church – Their new Church – Its history – Its vestiges – The names of its Priests.

I could never find any artifacts or anything in the sayings of the old men of the village that would show that the Roman Catholics had their own Church in the old days. I say this in spite of the fact that the Sheiks of the Kassab folks who were in Salima for a long time say that the house of Haddad, the house of al-Khawaja and others were members of this group. Still, I must say, there is not any proof that I can find that shows the presence of a Church or a Roman Catholic priest who would have served them.

Old men of the past used to say that the Maronite Church of Saint John had a large altar for the Maronites and two other altars, one for the Roman Catholics and the other for the Roman Orthodox. The Roman Catholics did apparently fulfill their religious obligations with the Maronite priests. It is possible that a priest of their own Roman Rite would come to them on important festivals in order to fulfill their duties according to their own Rite in the Church of Saint John or in a temporary chapel set up in one of the houses.

Around the year 1800, they built for themselves a small Church with the name Saint Anthony al-Kabir. It was at the bottom of Ain Shaqiff above the place known as the Graveyard of the Slaves (Maqbarat al-Abeed). This Church crumbled in the middle of the last century because it was poorly built. And that happened when they were attending Mass. As soon as they left the building, it fell down to the ground. After 1860, the people of this Rite started building a church under the same name in a place near their homes, beside Ain Ahmad. They finished construction in 1872 as was carved in a marble slat above its door. Archbishop Aghabious al-Riyashy gave a helping hand in building this new church by supplying money and urging the believers to finish it.

The church is well built and medium in size. At first, it was vaulted, then they made a plaster ceiling for it in 1906. They also added a very nice dome where they placed a bell. In 1911, beside the Church they built a room for the priest. Most of the real estate that is consecrated to this Church has been done so by the Kassab people. They had the power, authority, and wealth to do so. There was a woman called Salma, from the house of Boutros al-Sabbagh, the widow of a man from the house of Kassab. She consecrated her properties that she took as a dowry from her late husband. The late priest, Father Moussa, the servant of the congregation, who I will discuss later, used to mention her name in the Holy Mass until the day he died. He was acting according to her will as accepted with the consent of the Archbishop. As for the graves of the Roman Catholics, they are together in the graveyard of the Maronites, in the cemetery of the old Saint John Church. This shows that they had ties with this Church for a long time.

As for the vestiges of the church, they are the following: (1) a copy of the book of the Saints For Fasting, and at its end, there is this statement: *"Has been completed, with the help of God, all the Saints For Holy Fasting, done with the mortal hand of the sinning servant, Abd Allah bin Ata Allah al-Ma'louf, asking for the reward from God, the One, the King, the Giver. This in the year 7199 after our father Adam, the first human being, Peace Be Upon Him, equivalent to the year 1081 Hegira... Amen."* (2) The book of Atotologion, meaning the best of words, and it has on it the following paragraph: *"By the mortal hand of the ugly servant and sinning human Abd Allah bin Ata Allah al-Ma'louf in the year of 7180 after Adam."* (3) There is the book of prayers and written on it *"By the mortal hand of the poor .. Father Grigorios, the Sam'aani Priest from the city of Nassera Galeel and it was completed on Monday 16 March, 1824 AD."* (4) Also *"the consecration of the Church of Our Lady of Glad Tidings in the village of Roumeia (Metn) on March 19, 1840 AD, with the seal: Aghabios the Archbishop of Beirut."* (5) After this, there is the following statement *"The consecration of the priest, Father Mikhail al-Sayegh from Salima to the Church of Our Lady of Glad Tidings, may God have mercy on his soul"* and Father Mikhail is the brother of Father Moussa from Salima. He served the Church of Roumeia in the middle of the previous century. (6) Another book has this written on it: *"This has been completed by the help of God to serve His Holy feasts and the feasts of the Mother of God together with the feasts of the Saints. Having written this book with his mortal hand, the most humble of the creation al-Khuri Girgis Yunan from Kafr Eqab in the era of the reign of the Archbishop Beniamine and having finished this on the morning of Wednesday, June 17, 1842."*

The priests of the parish of Saint Anthony.   From these, I know of Father Elias. I have seen a will written in his own handwriting and it can be summarized as: Daher bin Safi Abu Ata Allah Bachaalany (al-Bshe'lani) has determined by a will that his 'Tal'a' (meaning the expenses of his burial) as 100 Piasters. This was in 1831. I also saw the name of that priest in the list of the "Tal'a" of Hanna Nader Gad'oun Bachaalany (al-Bshe'lani) who died at the beginning of the previous century.

Father Moussa al-Sayegh.   He is Moussa bin Boutros bin Anton al-Sabbagh or a-Sayegh and he is from the house of al-Khawaja or more truly from the house of al-Haddad as I will prove later. He studied the Eastern ritual and necessary sciences of that era. He was ordained to the holy priesthood and served the old church of Saint Anthony. When it fell down, he kept saying Holy Mass in the Church of Our Lady which was in the past in the palace of the Princes, not far from the house of the priest. That was when the Princes had migrated to Bakfia until the new church of Saint Anthony was built. He continued to say the Holy Mass up until the last day of his life. He lived about 80 years, half of it in the priesthood. His death was in the last quarter of the previous century and I will mention him again later.

Father Germanos and Father Tobia.   They are from the Hannawi priesthood meaning that they were from the priests of Saint John al-Tabshy (Choueir). I don't know anything about them anything except that they served the congregation for a short period of time.

Father Boulos Gabara.   He is originally from Damascus. He was from the priests of Saint John al-Sabegh near Choueir. He served his Rite in Salima for about 25 years. At the beginning, he used to do work from the congregation, working in the boarding school of Our Lady of Lourdes in Salima. He was good looking, with a soft voice and tender nature. He had some special quirks: he never ate food except for one meal during the day; he had a great passion for collecting birds, paintings and other pictures of birds to the extent that his room was a display room of birds and pictures. He was ascetical in his cloth, and tender in his talk and companionship. He came to Salima in 1883. He left it for the last time in 1908 and then lived in the Monastery of al-Toaq in Zahle. He died in his Monastery of Saint John al-Sabegh about 1924.

Father Mina.   He is from the village of Shabbaneia and he spent a period of time in the service of the congregation then left and migrated to Brazil. Later he came back home.

Father Metri. He is originally from Aleppo and he is from the Aleppoean priesthood. He served the congregation for several years and was of good reputation.

Father Artamios. He is from Zahle from the house of al-Qar'aan. He served the congregation for a period of time then left it and it was good riddance.

103

THE CHURCH OF SAINT ELIAS

Chapter 6

The Old Church – The new Church – Its Gate – The Grave - The Priests

We previosly mentioned that Salima's old men said that the Roman Orthodox Rite used one of the three altars of the Church of Saint John. We don't know when or where they built their own church. It may have been beside the Old Roman Catholic Church that we previously talked about and which is under Ain Al Shakeif. There are no remnants of this church except some old graves that are still there today.

In 1862, they constructed their present church near their homes above Ain Al Shakeif and called it The Church of Saint Elias. It was built by the teacher, Ghantous Bashour, and his brother, Ghaleb, who became a priest. He was known as Father Elias. Also involved with the construction was Constantin Al Hadad who became Father Constantin. They constructed a belfry there on the Church.

Concerning its gate, Father Elias employed all his wits in building that gate in such a way that nothing was missing in its sculpture. It was done to perfection comparable to the gates of the biggest Churches.

In addition to this, Ghantous Bashour and his brother, Professor Hanna Bashour, built the Church of Our Lady of Lourdes in Salima . As previously mentioned, the grave is still in its old location.

The following are the names of its priests who we knew:

Father Elias Bashour. There probably were priests who were performing the religious duties of the Roman Orthodox Rite in Salima. Among them was Father Elias Bashour who is Ghaleb Ibn As'ad Ibn Elias Bashour. He was ordinated a priest in 1863 after the construction of the Church of Saint Elias. He apparently served there until around 1880 when he died. He was kind, generous, and well mannered. Later in the book, we will make reference to his life when we will discuss his family.

Father Constantin Al Hadad. After the death of Father Elias Bashour, Father Constantin bin Nasif bin Nasr Al Hadad took over the parish. He had been ordinated as a priest around 1882 and remained in the service of his Rite for a long time until he died in the First World War, and, exactly in 1917. He was a decent priest with a good reputation and we will talk about him in detail in the chapter talking about his family.

THE CHURCH OF THE LADY OF THE CASTLE

AND

OUR LADY OF LOURDES

Chapter 7

Our Lady of the Castle.

There was among Salima's Churches, the Chapel in the Princes' castle. Prince Haidar moved it to Bikfaya when he moved there in 1846. Then, Capuchin priests came and bought Salima's castle in 1882 to establish their boarding school there and they called it Our Lady of Lourdes. They renovated the old chapel and called it by the same name as the school. In the beginning, that Chapel consisted of a large room above the existing cellar at the Southern part of the castle. Then it was demolished. Then, the Capuchins established the Lady of Lourdes Chapel in the cellar near the boarding school.

This Chapel has a long history and we should not neglect the great benefits of that history. Especialy so, since there are precious and important documents which have yet to be published. We will be content for now to present a short history of Our Lady's Chapel during the Princes' era then during the era of the school of the Capuchin Fathers.

As archived documents state, this place was built at the end of the 17th century during the era of Prince Ismail Abou Al Lam'. It was probably done quietly before the prince proclaimed his Christianity. When the Prince's children grew up, their belief and ideology was revealed. The youngest Prince Haidar, especially, was the greatest Lam's Prince who boosted Christendon. It was well known how tenacious he was of the Maronite Ara El Dine. Also, it was he who asked the religious Hierarchy in Rome and Karki to again open the Chapel of Our Lady in his castle.

At the castle there was a priest celebrating the Holy Mass everyday. The priest asked the Prince for permission to perform religious services in the chapel for the Prince, his family and everybody working in his home. He provided all eccelestical receptacles, spiritual books and religious pictures for the Chapel. All these were moved to the Prince's chapel in Bikfaya when he left his castle in Salima in 1846. These items are kept there today. They include items in Prince Haidar's own handwriting, proof of his strong sense of religion which has been a model for the people of the village. Even Europeans mentioned him in their writings and their talks with him during their journeys, as we will discuss later.

In our achives, we have a paper written by Prince Haidar consisting of prayers and supplications which the noble Prince recited at the front of his castle's chapel. Here are some of those phrases: "*Oh Mother of mercy, have mercy on me. Oh Mother of the Lord, pity me. Oh My Lady show compassion for my indigence. Oh My Mistress, do not neglect me. Without your mediation I would have been in the depths of Hell. I hope to sit in the shade of your protection and to be preserved by your attention until the end of my life. Oh, My Sweet Rain, My Refuge and the goal of my requests, accept me as your slave until my death. Do not hold me in disdain because of the unhealthiness of my sins. Do not expel me. You are aware how I am doing and Your Wisdom inspires me. Oh Empress of the Sky and the Land, have mercy upon me."*

Our Lady of Lourdes.

When the Capuchins bought the Prince's castle, they built their boarding school called Our Lady of Lourdes. In it they established a Chapel for This Lady in the same building. They put in it a picture of the Virgin just as she appeared at Lourdes. It had probably been painted by Mr. Momasse and the Frenchman, Father Charles, as both of them were very famous for their paintings and drawings.

The Holy Mass was held there during the week, but on Sundays and Feasts Days wonderful and grand religious festivities were held for the students in the Saint Peter Monastery.

When Bardiot Anton Al Asmar bought the castle, he renovated the Lady of Lourdes school and the religious festivities and ceremonies were held for the students in its previously mentioned chapel. There, the late Bardiot Anton was buried as well as his mother before him. His nephew, Naguib, is taking care of this chapel situated in the historical castle where he now lives with his family.

ASSEMBLY HOUSE OF THE DRUZE

Chapter 8

We should make a short notice about the meeting place of the Druzes in Salima. We will deal with them in more detail in a following chapter of this book. For now, we will simply say that it is known that unlike Christians and others, the Druze do not reveal themselves by saying their prayers. Rather, they hold meetings in places called the Assembly Hall of the Druzes.

It is also known that the Lam' princes of Salima were believers of Druze religion before converting to Catholicism as you will read of in more detail later.

The last person remaining of this family was a princess called Zahr or Dhahr as it is pronounced. She had inherited many large properties from her family. A house in Salima along with many other properties in Salima and elsewhere are still standing. When the lady Zahr died, she bequeathed her heritage only to Druzes. Her Castle was to be the place of their meetings, the Assembly Hall. So it is that this is the place we call the Druzes' temple, where they used to hold their religious meetings.

Around 1900, the building was split in half. The western part was taken by the Al Masrys and the eastern one was taken by Saids.

After a while, one of the Saids named Khoza'y Said bought the entire Said part and then resided there with his family. The rest of the Saids built another private assembly hall near their houses.

Meanwhile, the Al Masrys renovated their Assembly Hall and reserved a part of it to be a school for their children. Later, we will talk more about Lady Zahr, her religious endowment and her tomb.

SCHOOLS OF THE CAPUCHIN FATHERS

Chapter 9

Education in the past. It is known that modern sciences and knowledge appeared in our country in the middle of the last century introduced by the foreign missionaries, most notably by Catholic priests who had abandoned their homes and families. They brought this new view of the world along with their bibles. Yes, students of the Maronite school in Rome had learned high levels of science in the past, but in our country we lacked the schools and the means of opening schools. So it was that, in the past, knowledge and learning in the Lebanese communities was limited to the clergy and their close relatives.

Archbishop Germanous Farahat Al Halaby mastered Arabic and made it affordable for Christians . Few others did the same. It wasn't until the sciences flourished in the Ain Waraka School that the modern scientific revolution began. It covered Lebanon and Syria as well as the famous Maronite School in Rome. Up until this time, most of people in our country were illiterates. Maronites were using the Syriac language instead of Arabic because Syriac was the language of their religious rituals.

The priest of the village would teach the youth under the oak tree at the church. This was the way the famous genius, El Douahy, taught in his village, Ehden, when he returned from Rome, the Capital of Catholicism. This is why we say that in our town of Salima there was spiritual education since the beginning of the 17th century.

The teachers included Father Moussa Abu Dewan, the servant of Salima at that time, Father John I, Father Francis, and, Father John II, one of the Nakouzy people. They were teaching under the oak tree of the church, too. After them, Father Joesph Bachaalany did the same. He taught the youth of his village the basics of religion as well as the principals of the Syriac and Arabic languages.

Salima was a high ranking village, compared to the surrounding villages. It was distinguished for educated and cultured people thanks to the Lam' princes who settled there. They were keen to surround themselves with people possessing courage, science, logic and necessary manual skills. Thus, the people of Salima were of a high social class because they lived with the princes. The people were writers, poets and knowledgeable in many fields. They were especially learned in the field of calligraphy. According to the calligraphic remnants that have survived from the past, they prove that there were many Arabic and Syriac calligraphers in Salima.

Among them was Mohamed Ibn Takei (known as Abou Kamal). He was well known for his good calligraphy and writing style, as was Baz and Youssef Yazbak. The famous Christian calligraphers included Father Francis who had an average calligraphy and plain writing style but who wrote the majority of Christian's real estate deeds. Also famous were Soliman and Daher Al Sayegh and Abou Negm Andrea Ibn Negm and his son, Negm Ibn Andrea. This latter was unique with his graceful writings and elegant style. His letters addressed to the princes at that time reflect his fineness in writing. Kana'an Al Tyan, a resident of Salima, and his son Abou Naseef Elias. They were famous for their colligraphy and writing style. I saw some of the handwritten deeds and contracts of Elias Al Tyan and they show the beauty of his calligraphy and his pen's perfection. The same is true for his son Naseef and most of his family members who resided in Salima for about hundred years.

110

Father John Nakouzi was a student of Al Tyans and his calligraphy was close to theirs. He had a nice writing style. It is no wonder that John (Hanna) (Gamal) Nader Gad'un learned calligraphy in the house of Al Tyans. He was close to them and he had a nice calligraphy. There were also Abou 'Oun Bachaalany, As'ad Marun, Mansour Al Khouri, and Anton Abou Anton.

The number one calligrapher among the Christian calligraphers was Girgis As'ad Marun, a pupil of the sub-deacon Tanus Farag who is Father Girgis Farag Saghir, the first. Then his own son As'ad learnt from him. He made many developments to become with Sa'ada Mikhail Al Hadad, the best two calligraphers in the country at that time.

My late father learned much about calligraphy and was fortunate as Girgis As'ad was an inspiration for him.

There were also Fares and Girgis Anton Abou Anton. Anton Fares has been distinguished by his lovely calligraphy, fineness in writing style and perfection in composition. Habib Fares Anton's calligraphy was not bad but he was the fastest. He was so fast that people used to say that he could neatly write riding at full gallop on horse back! Fares Shiban who joined the service of Lady Malaka Abi Al Lam' was also famous for calligraphy as was the late Father John Bachaalany and his brother Abou 'Okl.

Of the Druze calligraphers, there was Ali Soliman Said, who had a very distinguished calligraphy. Mohamed Mahmoud Al Masry and his son Salman had an average calligraphy and, more recently, both Amin Salman Al Masry and his two sons Selim and Fouad were distinguished by their calligraphy.

We have concentrated in calligraphy when talking about knowledge and the sciences because it is evidence of their exsitence in the past. Usually the calligrapher was a writer also. We have to say that our ancestors did their best to keep accurate records even though their knowledge of the sciences was at a minimum. For instance, if any of these calligraphers heard or read a word, he kept it and took care of it. If he found a nice calligraphy style, he tried to model it. My late father told me that my grandfather Tanous used to pick up and gather papers that he found around the princes' Karnayl house. He would study them and the standard for the calligraphy he learned. That is how he learned calligraphy by himself. My late father used to stand by Girgis As'ad Marun in his shop to learn calligraphy. Then I, in turn, learned it from him.

As a summary, I can say simply that our ancestors took care to learn the sciences. It is not an exaggeration to say that they appreciated the knowledge that was scarce.

We have talked about the state of learning in Salima before the arrival of the Capuchin School. Then, we told of the days when Father John was appointed the Headmaster at the Saint Peter Monastery. He saw that the people of Salima were seriously lacking in educational opportunity. At that time Italy was trying to dominate Syria by spending money to have their missionaries teach the Italian language and spread their influence. This is why she established a school in Abda at the Monastery of Saint Anthony as well as in other regions. The Capuchins started to concentrate in teaching that language. One of their first teachers was from the Kisrawan, known as Subdeacon Moussa (he became a priest and served in Beirut). He sometimes used to teach lessons at the Princes' Palace during the era of Ibrahim Pacha Al Masry. At other times, he taught in a house near the old Church of Our Lady where Father Youssef (Joseph) Daham used to teach before him.

When Father John found that there was a strong demand for teaching, he brought in an assistant, Father Mansour. Both constructed those ancient buildings beside the Monastery to be an official school under their supervision.

The Subdeacon As'ad, from the region of Kisrawan, was teaching Arabic and Syriac. Meanwhile, Father Mansour was teaching Italian. Both Christian and Druze children of Salima were learning there. That was around 1840.

When Father Mansour took over the leadership of the Monastery, he appointed another person to teach Arabic and Syriac. He was a student at Ain Waraka, one of the Patriarchate Schools. His name was Subdeacon Anton Sa'd Ghiad Al Nakuzy. He started teaching a few years after the uprising of 1845.

Besides being a perfect teacher, Subdeacon Anton was using the old teaching style of being a strong disciplinarian with the boys. They were violently beaten and crudely whipped as punishment. He also used the Bastinado which was still used in our schools up to the end of the 19th century. My late father told me that the Subdeacon would beat one of his students on his fingers showing no mercy. Once he beat a student with a burning stick from the fireplace. A student, Mikhail Abdou, ran away because of this teacher cruelty. All the youth of Salima who were of Father John's era were students of this Subdeacon. The Subdeacon remained until some time after 1850 when he was replaced by his brother, Ghayad. He was less cultured. After them came the Subdeacon Sha'ia Negm Heikal Al Nakouzi. He taught there for a while and he also gave lessons in one of the Patrairchate schools for a while.

After the riots of the 1860's, and the ordination of Father John Bachaalany who had graduated from the Mar Abda Harharia School, he was appointed as a teacher by Father Mansour. He had excelled in his studies, especially in Arabic, so he taught the youth Arabic grammar and morpheme, something never done before. As a result of his teaching, a huge number of Salima's youth learned so well, and became so skilled that they went on to higher education and mastered other fields. One such example is Anton Fares Anton who learned poetry. Father John remained in his profession right up to his death. His assitant was Father Peter Joseph (Boutros Youssef) Al Mazmuk. This was during the eras of Father Mansour and Father Andrew, up to 1882. Then he has been appointed as a teacher of phraseology at the school of Our Lady of Lourdes. He died in 1890.

In the same period, a new group in Salima arose. They learned the sciences in high schools. They included people like Molhem Nohra Bachaalany, who studied French and Arabic at the famous Aintura Institute. There was also Habib Fares Anton who studied and succeeded in the sciences. His brother Anton studied at the famous Ain Al Waraka School and mastered poetry and prose. At Ain Tura School, Girgis Tanus Freha the paternal uncle of this author, studied there but did not complete his studies. Also, Shi'ya Bin Heikal Al Nakuzy studied at Mar Abda School. Amin Salman Al Masry studied at the Druzian Daoudian School. Mansour 'Okl Gueneid was at the Cleric Mar Abda Harharia School. And, finally, 'Okl Abou 'Okl Al Khoury also studied at the Ain Waraka School, then he migrated to Mexico and then to Marseilles where he became a recognized author in prose and poetry as well as a journalist.

After that, both Father Youssef Sabra Al Nakuzy and As'ad Sha'ia were teachers in the Capuchin Fathers' school. They were the ones who taught me reading in Arabic and Syriac. Before them, when I was five years old, Father John, with Father Peter, taught me the basics of reading. As'ad Sha'ia remained teaching till 1892 when he migrated to America along with all those who left Salima and migrated.

When I graduated from the Protestant School which I'll talk about later, I worked as a teacher for one year. At that time, Youssef (Joseph) Al Khoury and his brother, Boutros (Peter) had established in 1893, a private school at the Lady of Lourdes School, after it was closed. Father Peter and Naseef Youssef Wakim taught there. After I was ordained a priest and returned from Bchaaleh in 1898, I went back to teaching in that school until 1899. Father Peter Al Khoury and Elias Wakim followed me. In 1903, my brother Habib worked there as a teacher for two years. Then came my paternal cousin Naguib Youssef Negm who taught for a few years. In 1909, I started a private school. After that, I went back, for the third time to teach at the Capuchin School.

In 1850, Father Mansour established a school for girls in Salima. Before that, if a girl's parents wanted her to learn it was just the basics in reading and religion. And, they would entroll her in the boys' school, as still happens in some villages. However, Father Mansour established that school for only girls and he appointed a female teacher coming

112

from Zahle called Henna. Her comrade in teaching was a girl named Susan. Then after them other female teachers taught in that school. This included women like Katherine and Marina, the wife of Ghantous Sabra Al Nakouzy. Both of them had been educated by nuns. Some of the girls who learned, later became teachers too. This included girls like Mikhail Bo'un's daughter who was working from home, as was Meriam, the daughter of Wakim Boutros. Nesim, the daughter of Ragheb did the same.

When Father Andrew came, he brought in a young woman who graduated from a convent at Beirut, who originally came from Kfar Chima. This woman resided at the girls' school beginning in 1873. She married As'ad Sham'an Abou Rashed from Bazbadin. She taught at that school for a long time. She was then succeeded by Ms. Mary, the sister of the late Dr. Mansour El Bahout. Then came her niece Warda in 1892. Also, there was Henna Negm Ibn Youssef, Mesihia (daughter of Fares Anton) and her paternal cousin Ternga, daughter of Girgis. Then, too, came Mary, daughter of Father Peter Joseph and Mary Tanus Shiban.

After the First World War finished, the Capuchin priest, Father Ya'kub appointed Malaka, this author's sister, as a teacher for the girls. She had studied with the Nuns of El Ra'ie El Saleh School in Hamana. Moreover, teacher expenses were being paid by the French delegation.

The teaching techniques and methods used at that time are well known and are still used in the schools of some villages today. First, pupils were taught the letter "Alef" written on a paper or on a piece of cardboard strapped to a stick, or, perhaps, written on a thin parchment. The pupil was taught this way. Alef Lasheen 'alih (Alef nothing on it). Ba with a point underneath, Ta with two points above it …etc. Other teachers used another way like this… Alef wa Ba wa bubaya, Alef wa Ta wa tutaya …etc. This second way was used by Mohamed Torudy who studied at the Capuchin School and taught his community's youth for a while.

After learning the letter Alef and its use in different ways, the boy moves on to learn the remaining alphabet. Then he learns the Sanctus, then the prayer, Our Father (the Lord's Prayer), and, then. the Hail Mary, then the Psalms of David as printed at the Saint John Al Choueir Printing House. Finally, he has courses in reading Arabic and then starts writing.

In the past they would compete in having a copper inkstand made in Damascus or Hemss or Beit Nefa' of Beit Shabab. They would use black ink handmade with great care out of sweet basel, oak secretion and other ingredients, so it was an ink of the best quality. The pen was made of a local hard cane which is sharpened and put in the ink stand. The ones who boasted of possessing an inkstand were the patriarchs, the archbishops, the priests, the teachers, the writers, the calligraphers, the elders and the leaders. Most of the time they were gathering both the sword and the pen.

The teacher would write a line so that the pupil could follow the rule. Then, the student would practice it until he mastered it. People consider that he has finished his studies when he knows how to write his name.

They also cared quite a bit about learning the Syriac language. When a boy finished praying, he would stand by the priest who was preaching. The boy would join him at the chorus prayers and his parents would be so pleased and so proud of him.

Our grandparents were perfect singers in the Syriac language. They would stand beside each others when singing. Some of them mastered writing in Syriac, like Hanna Ibn Jabrael Sama'an and Boutros 'Eishy, along with his brother, Ayub, who used to correspond with each other in the Karshuni language.

They preferred teaching Syriac then Arabic, the opposite of what the teachers and parents wanted. The Subdeacon Anton was perfect in that language, that is why many of his students mastered it. He taught the language basics in grammar.

In Salima, the preaching was pefect as it was in Ba'badat and Faluga, regions of Metn.

Concerning the performance of Holy Mass, some deacons excelled in the traditional manner as they did when officiating with the Bishop. They would lead the people of their Church. This included people like Deacon Beshara Girgis Moussa Fasida, Jabrael Hanna Bo'oun, Wakim Boutros, and many others. Our own grandfather Deacon Moussa and even his father was one of those people called on to sing because of his melodious voice. The majority of his descendants were like him. So it is no surprise that both Aghnatious Hanna Eid and his brother, Ghaleb, were great celebrants of the Holy Mass. My grandfather Hanna Aghnatious was unique in his singing.

They divided themselves into two groups for major Feasts. The Church's ceremonies had a wonderful resplendence and elegance all their own. My late father with Abou 'Okl El Khoury and Boutros Hanna Ghanatious were famous for their exceptional performances. My maternel uncle, Mansour, had a beautiful voice, as did Naseef Hanna Naseef and Ghaleb Shahin Al Nakuzy.

I, myself, the author of this book, was also famous for my melodious voice. Forming a very nice choir consisting of Marun Fares Ghatas, Rashid Shahin Ghaleb, his nephew (his sister's son), Asaf Hanna El Khoury, and myself, we would celebrate the Holy Mass. After us, the late Habib Shiban, who was brilliant in the rules and principles of music, took over the celebrations together with Father Peter, the sons of Youssef Shahin Mansour and my brothers Habib, Tanous, and Khalil.

When the Capuchin priests took over the education of the youth of Salima, the students learned to perfectly sing the Latin songs. This goes back many years. They were singing the Holy mass in Latin during the days of Father John and Father Mansour. In my days, under Father Andrew, we were the singers and the celebrants.

Those priests would transliterate the songs of the Mass into Arabic and Syriac letters so that we could read them. Moreover, Father was teaching the children the Italian language. Many of them mastered the language and they would sing with the Capuchins. Students who excelled included As'ad Abud, Anton and Youssef Wakim, Ibrahim Wahba , Andrea Girgis, and Ayub Gad'un who could perfectly speak Italian.

The celebration of the rituals and ceremonies in Salima was a magnificent mixture of the beauty of olden days with the freshness of the new. All this was thanks to the Capuchins who for such a long time, carefully educated the young. They were such experts at extracting the prayers of the Latin rituals without touching our Syriac rituals. For instance, the Feast of Corpus Christi was a glamorous event, especially in the days of Father Andrew and the boarding school. Priests and believers from many of the neighboring villages would assemble at Salima on that glorious occasion. As a special reminder, we have the photo taken by Mr. Moumasse, showing the huge crowd that gathered.

There was the religious procession of Darb as-salib which was held by Father Andrew himself on fasting Sundays. Then the religious procession of the Holy Mass was held according to the Latin rituals. During the period of the old school in Salima, the Latin, Arabic, and French chanting were perfectly performed.

The first things we learned here at school was the "Angel Preaches" and "The Virgin". Those wonderful missionaries taught us those in our childhood at school.

The Monastery's bell still rings today. We hear it at dawn, mid day, in the afternoon, and after sunset. We also hear it as it tolls to announce a death.

The priests also taught the young people about religion in Arabic. These courses were taught on Saturdays, but when I was in charge of the school, I made them daily classes in the morning. Arabic classes were plain and simple due to the situation in those days.

Then, when Father John and the subdeacon Anton were there, they started to develop the program. Father John also introduced program renovations, especially after the Catholic Press began publishing some of the religion books used by the students. And again, the Arabic education declined during the years when Father Joseph Nakouzy, Father Peter Bachaalany, and As'ad Shi'ya, were the teachers. They just were not as highly educated as some others had been. At that time, I remember that I learned the Psalter and I memorized the consecration in Syriac. I learned the choir, prayers and then a little bit of Arabic calligraphy. That was all we could learn at that time because the teachers were not highly educated. We were limited in our learning, also, because the school headmasters and priests were too busy trying to develop their boarding school. The teaching gradually became too plain and weak.

Until I took charge of the school's direction in 1892, I did my best to develop it. Then I had to leave after one year. Other teachers made efforts to promote the level of teaching. My own brother, Habib, took the first step to that end and there was a measureable improvement in the students' education and studies. That was unexpected. The program taught to the students was up to date and contemporary; it consisted of the basic subjects like reading, writing (callygraphy), phraseology and the basics of grammar as well as the French language.

Until the Capuchin priest, Father Ya'kub Al Hadad, appointed me to be director of this school in 1910, that is when I started to work in developing the teaching system and including the new teaching strategies that I learned from the brothers in the Christian Schools where I taught Arabic in Ba'bada for four years. At that simple school, I taught Arabic, French, English and Syriac. Most of Salima's children, Christian and Druze. were my pupils.

The School of Our Lady of Lourdes. We previously mentioned that Father Andrew established a boarding school in Salima and called it Our Lady of Lourdes. It didn't take long for the school to be famous and well known throughout the whole country. Students from all regions attended it. This success was thanks to its headmaster Mr. Jean (John) Moumasse who was a very intellectual man. He had a virtuous soul, an elevated spirit, vigor, and has mastered six languages. He was accomplished in arts, especially in poetry, music, drawing and painting. He wrote a poem in French titled "The Violet of Salima". In it, he has perfectly described the beauty of this town, its attractive province, and showed how fascinated he was by Salima, the town he loved as much as he loved his own country. Here is the poem he wrote:

The Violet of Salima

1
Do you see that beautiful village over there
With an azure sky, with a nice climate
A medieval village
It is Salima

2
Pine-trees with elevated top
Surrounding its humble houses
Sending their perfume up the valleys

3
You, mountain, be proud
Of the proud Lebanon, lovable flower
In our eyes, and those of rival Spain sister

4

Once upon a time, it was the princes' residence
Valorous and powerful Emirs
Descended from a war race truly conquerors

5
Here they were displaying their shows
Living as happy nobles
However, too early, did an ill starred day dawn for them.

6
Still their wealth exsists
In this pleasant resort
Goods conquered by their prowess
A memory

7
It is a sumptuous building
It is their palace, a fortified castle
Built on impulse with no efforts

8
Those fragments of their wealth
Has kept itself over time
Awaiting from providence a lovely spring

9
Burnt twice by the disreputable
Originating from roaring barbarians
Those walls resisted the flames

10
After twenty years, you saw a rebirth
That spring you desired for a long time
The Lord sent a new master, unhoped for

11
The Order of Saint Francis, a priest
Noble hearted, a pure Frenchman
Saw this memorable land of the Lebanese

12
He came from France to be convinced
New Ceasar, he shook with power
he came, he saw and wanted to defeat an enemy

13
He needed some one high-minded
To finalize his great drawing
He found it in his collegue, a Capuchin !

14
Helped by the angelic zeal
And the advise of the prelate
He founded a Catholic boarding school

15
He took the ancient residence
Of the great princes and turned a rampart
To raise virtue, to make science a standard

16
Let us pray to succeed in this hard work
Of the sainted name of the virgin
Let us engrave "Our Lady Of Lourdes" on the pediment.

17
Oh, dear France, grant us
Your help and protection
And you too, Imaculate Conception !

18
Go on , have courage , we have to fight
This enemy, this English gold
It is not what will beat French hearts

19
Fight with strength and constancy
Persevere for a long time
And keep loving France, you Lebanese

20
From a zealous saint, God will vitalized you
Lyceum dutiful
Sing with a unanimous voice: Un, Te, Deum.

Salima, January 15th, 1890
-- John Momasse

This school headmaster put updated rules and policies in place. He brought in the updated teaching systems used in Europe. A student could speak French perfectly after only one year. The school cared as much about teaching Arabic as it did for French. This caused it to surpass the famous Ain Tura School. Plus, this school had an excellent culinary standard. Its tables were as elegant and diversified as those of the wealthy. Also, Salima was situated in a place where the climate was exceptionally nice, with delicious water and abundant fresh air. These were the reasons why the princes built their castle there, choosing the best place, and building four floors.

In addition, Salima's valleys were beautiful. Students used to take walks through the whole area every Sunday and Thursday. Besides, its people were so generous and hospitable. All this and more, provided comfort, joy, and encouragement to the students, pushing them to succeed.

School festivities were very well organized. Students were carefully trained in social conversation and in public speaking. And it was affordable to build a stage in the school's courtyard and it was constructed like those in the big cities. The School's music added joy to the festivities. This provided music that our town never had before. The headmaster was one of the greatest musicians and that made the school even more elegant. Compared to the music performed at the school of Our Lady of Lourdes, both the Ottoman music in Beirut and the Lebanese music directed by the famous Maestro Vencencio Avolo, both were of lower quality. The school had its own marching song composed by its headmaster. It also had its own slogan with a picture of Our Lady of Lourdes.

The students wore a special European uniform made of grey broadcloth.

The school had its own independent chapel within its walls. At the front of this chapel there was a painting of the appearance of the Virgin Mary at Lourdes. In that chapel, the students attended Holy Mass on week days. On Sundays and Feast Days they went to the Church of Saint Peter at the Monastery.

Famous plays were performed in Arabic at that theater. First was one from the novel called The Prince Beshir The Great, written by Zein Zein in 1884. It succeeded very well and played before a huge audience. The same was true for his other novel Arab's Ardor. Also performed was a play from the published novel The Tiller written by Khalil Bakhus. In addition, there were performances from French novels written by famous authors. There were also literary receptions held at the school's clubhouse. There were poems and speeches delivered on those occasions as well as those delivered on the headmaster's birthday.

The best comedians at that time were Father Charles, Ibrahim Shiban and Mahmoud Abou Ezz Eddine. They were the best pantomime actors and the audience admired them.

This splendid success that the school attained was in itself a step in the Education Revolution in the town. Salima was returning to its old days of glory and distinction.

After being a stopping point for the sword bearers in the days of Lieutenant Colonel Hussein, Prince Ismail El Mesholah, and Prince Haidar, now it became a station for pen bearers and men of knowledge. It also acquired a flourishing economic status.

The last day of the school year and beginning of the summer holiday was a memorable day every year. A huge crowd of nobles and students' parents gathered in its large town square. There would be a competition between horsemen there riding as knights of old. At the school there would be another competition between the knights of knowledge.

In general, that School had a great and wide reputation. It presented to the country a youth who served knowledge and science, who occupied high positions, and who were of great aid in its evolution and development.

The Pope awarded the School a Silver Medal. In 1888 at an Exhibition in Paris, the French Government awarded it with a Gold Medal. The students presented to the Exhibition organizers a collection of poems, articles in different languages and some oriental melodies written in musical notes. That collection had gold margins and the famous calligrapher Sa'ada Al Hadad from Salima wrote the Arabic articles. The French ones were written by Father Charles, one of the great teachers at the school. The same was done when celebrating the Jubilee of Pope Leo XIII.

In 1892, the tenth year since the school opened, a disagreement occurred. It happened between Father Andrew, the Junior, the president of the Salima Monastery and Father Andrew the Senior, the regional Superior for Syria. The first gave full authority to Mr. Moumasse, the headmaster of the school. He directed the school alone, being in sole charge. He was opinionated and he fixed the scholars' salary at 12 golden French liras. He insisted on leaving that pay as it was plus he added expenses. In addition to that, in that same year, he built a grandiose new theater in the school courtyard. He also added a stoned stairway at the west side which was very expensive. In addition, the unpaid debts of some Egyptian students added to the dispute. All of this, gave Father Andrew, the Senior, the opportunity to criticise the headmaster as being tyrannical and the Superior of the Monastery as careless.

So it happened that he obtained a formal order from the Holy See in Rome and the Superior General of the Order to close the school.

Thus is happened that this educational institute was closed. The star of that beautiful school fell. All its people have been dispersed. Anyone who knew that school, felt sorrow that this once flourishing flower had withered.

To complete this picture, we should talk about the professors who taught and educated at the school of Our Lady Of Lourdes.

The first teacher was the headmaster Mr. John Beltazar Moumasse. He taught the upper grades French, English, and Italian. He mastered the Dutch language which was his native tongue. He also knew Arabic and was a splendid maestro.

He was a very good manager for the school and nothing was done without his permission.

Also, there was Father Charles Secretain, who was well known for being widely read and competent in many different fields.

Mr. Gloa, Mr. Rambo, Mr. Bourgeois, Mr. Maksim, and Mr. Cléant, all of them were famous French teachers. In addition there was Mr. Henry Kremona from Malta, Dr. Mansour El Bahout from Deir El Qamar. He was one of the famous speakers in French and Arabic as well as being the school's doctor. There was also his nephew (sister's son) Bishop Soliman, the Capuchin priest, Father Lorensios, who died in Salima, and Farid Azba from Beirut.

The famous Arabic teachers were Father John Bachaalany, a former student of the Mar Abda Haraharia school, Professor Zein Khalil Zein one of the great poets at that time, and his brother Habib Beik. Both of them graduated from the Hekma school. There was also Khalil Bakhous from Ghazir, the owner of El Roda newspapers. There was also his paternal cousin, Dr. Khalil Ibrahim Bakhous. There was Father Joseph Jabrail El Hayek from Beit Shabab, and Sheikh Youssef Belin Al Khazen, Sheikh As'ad El Khoury from Rechmaya, Professor Said Abou Fayad El Bostani, Prince Youssef Abdel Hamid Shehab residing in New York, and the Princes Fatek, Fayez and Fayek Fares Shehab from Al Hadath, Father Ne'matallah Farag Safir from the plantation of Kafr Dhabian, Nasry Hatem from Hamana, Sheikh Habib Shiban El Bachaalany from Salima, Mahmoud Abou Ezz Eddine from Al Abadia, and, subdeacon Na'oum from Al Hadath. Those last three were graduates from the school. Also, there was Father Youssef Domt, from the plantation of Yashou', Father Ya'kub el Riyashi who took over the head position of the Hennatic monasticism, Father Boutros Salwan from Deir el Qamar, Ibrahim Zeyada from Gedida Ghazir, and, Molhem Mobarak from Aintura El Zok.

The Turkish teachers were Ibrahim El Bahout from Deir El Qamar and the Armenians Stephan and Elia. The Calligraphy teacher was the famous calligrapher of Salima, Sa'ada El Hadad. The music teachers were Soliman Al Bostani from Deir Al Qamar, Abou Ghaleb El Shedyakeya, and his son, Ghaleb, from Ba'bada.

Among the school administration staff and headmasters there were Father Peter Bachaalany, Father Joseph Nakouzy from Salima, Father Joseph El Khoury from Bazbadeen and Father Boulos (Paul) Gabara El Henawy from Damascus, Negm Daher Andrea El Bachaalany, Anton Wakim Bachaalany from Salima, and, one of the school's most valued, As'ad Ali Sheqir El Tahi from Arsoun, Saliby Zein from Salima, and others whose names I cannot remember.

Finally, we cite the names of the students of the school of Our Lady of Lourdes. We list them by their origin and we mention some information about their social life. Their names are:

From Egypt: Youssef Kahil, Ali Gebril, Amin Sadek, Michel Mata Qepti, Mahmoud Faouzy, Mahmoud Fouad, Mahmoud and Mohamed Khairy, Nasry Fanous Qepti, Habib & Naguib & Mahmoud Adly, Kaysar Borteli, Alfred Sidah and his brother Emil, Spiro Bishara and his brother George who mastered music, Pierre Caprianos, Henry Philipidis, Nichola Papayani, Constantin Cokifakes and those are Roman residents. Mostapha Hanafi the Mayor of Alexandria, the Italian Ceasar de Borteli, Elias Salibi, Mohamed Zaki, Mohamed Badr, the Greek Karno Kokoloka, the Jewish Maxlar, the Roman Sutheri, Mohamed El Sayed, Amin & Shafik Sadek, the Moroccan Khresto Waskandar and his brother Michael, Ali Sedki, Naguib El Serfi, Mohamed Tawfik, Youssef Amin, Alfred Bonard a Frenchman, Henry Fisher an Austrian, Nichola Giras a Roman, George Papgaksi a Russian, Youssef Sedik, Amin & Naguib & Tawfik & Eskandar &Youssef Howes of Lebanese origin, Philip Miscat a Frenchman, Michael Matta, Kamel Fahmi, Edgar & Hugo Fredi Italian residents, Elias Nahas and his brother Naguib Nahas who studied Law in Lyons and became a very good lawyer. All above mentioned were Egyptian nobles and among its men of letters.

From Halab: George Marach, Aziz Samian, Selim Khayat and his brother George, George and Louis Shouketly, Estephan Al Aga a Persian from Arzrum, Germanos and Bassil Hadad, Bassil Sabagh who was the school's singing nightingale because of his melodious voice, Mikhail…

From Zengebar: Leon Gulbar, Jewish.

From Marsen: Antoine & Piatro & Charles Molinari they were Italian residents, Dimitri Draki and Charle Dodah a Frenchman.

From Istanbul: the Armenian George Papazian.

From Beirut: Antone Ebeid, Habib Dimitri, the Italian Josef Lizitano one of the great clerks at the port, Jean Belatovic from Poland, François Baskoti son of the Italian musician Baskoti, Anton & Pierre & François Scou they were French, the Italian Rofael Fabri, George Nahas, Rezkallah Bash-khangi, Shokry Tarabishi, the Italian Alexandre Coriliano, Theodor Lav a Dutchman, Philip Bianci, Louis and Vincent Camiliari, Yanko-zimari.

From Zahle: Wadi' Soliman Farah Al Ma'louf the Mayor of Zahle, Khatib and Kateb Magid, Khalil Farah El Ma'louf the famous rich man in Canada .and his brother Fouad Farah who died after being one of the powerful men; George Ma'louf one of the big industrial men who migrated to Brazil, his brother Ceasar Beik El Ma'louf who was a poet, a writer, a Speaker and a journalist and he issued a newspaper in Brazil and had written a divan (a collection of poems), Gamil El Ma'louf one of the best writers and poets, he wrote several books but most of them haven't been published, he mastered the Arabic, Turkish and French languages. Rashid Balsh, Shokri an Archbishop in Shaba and Michel Beik Al Baridi.

From Batater: The Italian Louis Gowani.

From Amatur: Hussein Mahmoud Abdel Samad.

From Deir E Qamar: Youssef Azir, the lawyer and poet Shaker Azar, Naguib Shokri and Eid Adib.

From Abeyah: The immigrant writer Elias El Hadad, Farid Man Eddine, Said Nasr Eddine and Eid Nasr Eddine.

From Ba'kaleen: Selim Hamada, Selim Khedr and Said Abou Ismail.

From Mash-ghara: Ibrahim Dawood El Tarabolsi.

From 'Etnite: Ibrahim El Qayim one of the local nobles.

From Qab Elias: Ibrahim Hanush, Fares Nasr Rohana, Nemr Rohana.

From Al Mo'alaka: the Frenchman Alexandre Chivalet.

From Bakfia: Shukry (Father Louis) Belibel, one of the noble Lebanese monks and a patriotic historian, Selim Gabour, Youssef Habib Resk, Mansour Zein the brother of the two professors Zein and Habib Zein from Salima – Bakfia, Naguib and George Hashimi a writer who migrated to Colombia.

From Al Khanshara: Salem El Riyashi.

From Zabougha: Beshara Ibrahim Al Ma'louf.

From Al Metn: As'ad Youssef Okl Shedid, Shoukry Makhoul Okl Shedid, Dr. Khalil Moussa Ne'ma a well known doctor, his brother Ne'ma and both migrated to Argentina, Mikhail Daher Abou Soliman has a good reputation among our immigrants in New York.

From Ba'badat: Youssef Eskandar Lahoud, Mansour Hanna Negm.

From Beit El Kakou: Selim Elias and I think he is the famous tradesman in New York.

From Al 'Abadia: Mahmoud Abou Ezz El Dine and his brother Abulallah, the first mastered sciences and music and has been awarded the first prize in Christian Education. Abdulallah El Medwer and his brothers Nem'atallah and Shoukrallah and Rezkallah, they are good writers and among them great tradesmen in Britain.

From Falouga: The two princes Tawfik and Youssef Shedid Abi Al Lam' and this one is one of the great writers and poets and rich people in the United States. Molhem El Zaghzaghi who was a clerk at the Ministry of Finance in Lebanon.

From Hamana: Dr. Elias Beik 'Ad, he practised medecine in Paris and Lebanon where the Lebanese Government appointed him as an accredited doctor for the government. Ya'kub El Khoury who was a clerk in Al Metn Court. Lieutenant Colonel Nessib Ali Mazhar Al Tabib, he worked as a teacher then he migrated to USA where he became rich. Youssef Tanous Al Hakim from Beit Bedour of a noble family there.

From Arsoun: Colonel Fouad Beik Shaqir progressed in Military, his brother Doctor Halim Shaqir mastered medecine and died in Sudan, Daoud Shaqir, Naguib Shaqir mastered the French and Arabic Languages and wrote "The Secret of Azza Pacha Al Abed during Abdel Hamid era".

From Salima: Habib Shiban mastered two languages, worked in silk trading and progressed in the military, his brother Ibrahim was known for mastering the French language and being courageous, he migrated to Mexico where he died. Naguib Molhem Nahra became a teacher in several schools and his brother Youssef who became inspector

121

of education, Youssef Michael Abdou and his brother Abdou both mastered two languages and continued their studies at the Qornet Chahouane School then migrated to Brazil. Girgis Anton's sons Youssef and Shoukry and Hanna who migrated, Shoukry issued a newspaper called Al 'Adl (Justice) and worked as a translator at the French Council in Brazil. Hanna built a Hotel in Marseille. Youssef and Boutros El Khoury who was a writer and died very young, while Youssef worked as a teacher in many schools and lately issued a newspaper called Al Warkaa. Youssef Shahin Ghaleb studied medecine but couldn't finish because he developed a problem with his eyes and he was a philosopher. Asaf Hanna El Khoury migrated to Venezuela with his two brothers and came back with a fortune, he was a great writer and poet. Boutros Sam'an El Khoury migrated to Brazil, Abdou Girgis Kassab a calligrapher and poet, migrated to Mexico. Anton Abdelhay, Daoud Al Hadary a writer and migrated to New York, Elias Wahba mastered poetry then he departed from that for trading and he became rich. Shahin Girgis Shahin a writer. Philip Fares an orator and a writer who migrated then engaged himself in police work and became a teacher at a police school, his brother Felix Fares a famous orator and poet and journalist. The town of Salima and its school are both very proud of him.

From Karnayel: As'ad Elias Tanous Sharbel, Hassan Mahmoud El A'ouar.

From Bazbadeen: Nakhla Girgis Ghasteen Al Ba'kalini resident in Paris, he was a teacher then became a tradesman. Youssef El Khoury Girgis El Khoury a tradesman in Mexico.

From Al Arbania: Youssef El Khoury Elias 'Oun (El Daliba), Rashid Al Asmar.

From Al Kanaysa: Tanious (Father Bardiot Anton) Al Asmar he rebuilt the Lady of Lourdes School, he bought it and managed it for a while, now it belongs to his brother's son Professor Naguib Amin. Naguib (Monsignor) Ne'matallah Al Asmar who was considered one of the best poets and writers.

From Al Shabania: Gibran Youssef Abdou Yamin a writer, he migrated and gained a fortune then died in Buenos Aires. The prince Majeed (Father Mobarak) Abi Al Lam' Al Antoni.

From Nabia: Girgis and Moussa El Khoury.

From Al Harf Monastery: Shaker El Khoury Abou Gouda, he built a hotel in Marseilles.

From Al Hadath: Selim Boutros Daher.

From Al Shuwayfat: Rashid Sa'd El Dine mastered medicine.

Those are the students of that institute, students who mastered and progressed in their different fields in the Arts, Sciences and Industry. They still long for Salima and its school up to this very day.

After this school had been closed, Father Joseph John Bachaalany and his brother, Peter, both former students at the school, insisted on re-opening it. First, it was operated as a regular school then as a boarding school. It lasted for a few years. Students were successful since the school followed the same educational system as it previously had. However it was not long before it was again closed.

In 1906, Father Anton Al Asmar bought the school. He had been one of its previous students. He re-opened it as a boarding and regular school until the first World War, 1914-1918. After the War, he reactivated the school and lasted for a few years. Many students graduated from there and some of them applied for post-graduate work in other schools of higher learning. Others were content with what they learned.

123

PUBLIC AND PRIVATE SCHOOLS

Chapter 10

Now it is time to mention the schools in Salima other than the Capuchin Schools.

Protestant Schools.

Around 1875, the English and American missionaries established boarding and day schools for both sexes in Bermana, Choueir, Arya, and Zahle. Then, around 1880 they established a school in Salima. Amin al-Halaby, originally from Choueir, taught in that school. After him Abd al-Nour Abd Allah, from Bhamdoun, who was one of the very first students of the American University, became the teacher.

Abd al-Nour Abd Allah stayed in Salima for many years and he was known for his good manners and his generosity. After I had completed my primary school education in Arabic and Syriac at the school of the Capuchins, he taught me the basics of the Arabic and the English languages (1886-1891). As a sign of his good manners and unbiased nature, he never interfered with my religious beliefs. I learned many good things from him. I will always remember him. He died in Bhamdoun.

After him, came the teacher Antoine Saleh from Beirut. He was a teacher of Arabic and English and I gained some of his knowledge. I know that he later studied medicine in the American University and became a good doctor.

After him, came Girgis Qortas from Baskinta to whom I am indebted. Then came Girgis al-Tabsherani from Choueir, and then Nicola Saad from Ras al-Metn.

Next came my friend, Daoud (David) Yamin from Qabb Elias who was originally from the Yamin family of Ain Dara. He died in Aalye.

The Protestants used to teach both sexes in their schools but lately they established a girl school where Farha, daughter of Nassif Younes al-Haddad from Salima, taught.

Government Schools.

In the period of Daoud (David) Pasha, the government operated some schools in Mount Lebanon. It did so with its own money. One of these was a school in Salima beside the square in the house of Abu Daher Said.

Father John Bachaalany taught in it along with another teacher. But the school only lasted a short while and then it closed.

In 1917, the Ottoman government established two schools for boys and girls in Salima after closing all foreign schools because of World War I.

These schools used to teach the Arabic and Turkish languages but they were not popular for many reasons. The most important reason was because of the diseases that were spread, and also, because of the hunger and poverty of those days.

The teachers at these schools were Mr. Youssef al-Khuri Yuhanna of Salima, Mr. Milad Hatem Rezk Allah from al-Arbaneia and the two female teachers: Farha Nassif Younes and Zobaida As'ad Ghantous Bshour. They were both from Salima.

Before World War I, the French government used to pay for the expenses of the schools in Lebanon. Then the Lebanese government took over the task of education in the country and the French delegate still kept providing some aid to some of the private schools.

Lately, when Independence was decided, the schools came under the control of the Lebanese ministry of Education.

During the French period, the schools of Salima used to teach some of their specified educational syllabi. When the French mandate ended, the Lebanese government established a school for Salima in 1946. It appointed one teacher, Mr. Rashid Daoud Salman al-Masry.

Private Schools.

Mr. Amin Selim al-Masry, a young hardworking writer, established a private school. Most of the students there were of the al-Masry folks. Accordingly, he took good care of educating them according to the modern methods of education. He did as much as he could but he was forced to migrate like so many others who needed to earn a living.

After he spent several years in America, he came home safe and sound and victorious. He has learned much during his absence from his homeland.

Mr. Hamza Said established a school for the boys of his family, the Said folks. Soon, however, he left it to take care of his private businesses.

The Lebnan al-Kabir School.

Mr George Bachaalany received his studies in the schools of the Capuchin Fathers and in the National School of Na'eem Souaya where he taught for several years.

After World War I, he established a boarding school called "Lebnan al-Kabir School" which lasted for about 14 years. Many young people graduated from it, and many of them continued their studies with higher education. The school was noted for its programs of modern sports and school gatherings to promote public speaking activities in prose and poetry. The school also produced many plays, most of which were written by the owner of the school. These performances included his best production: "Fakhr al-Din of the Maans". This play was published at the printing shop of the Lebanese missionaries in Jounieh.

One of the things that must be mentioned at this point is the chivalry of my genius friend, Mr. Charles Qarm, a pride of Lebanon. He gave a great amount of financial and emotional support to the owner of this school. He was well known for his eagerness in sponsoring education projects. I wish that all the rich and able people of our country would follow in his footsteps. The foundations of science and education would be firmly established in our home land if we had more people like him. May God bless him.

The Lebnan al-Kabir School was shut down after the death of its owner who died young. His son, Emile, could not continue what his father started because of a lack of money.

The deterioration.

Before I conclude this chapter, I would like to mention that Salima today has sunk to a very low cultural level after its educational institutions were closed. For a long time they were so full of science and cultural life.

Reaching this low point seems to be the results of the loss of its educational facilities as well as a decline in its industrial and commercial businesses. Salima also suffered a severe decline in its tourism due to the deterioration of the roads. They became so bad that traffic between the mountain and the city almost stopped completely

This deterioration and the laziness that took over and controlled our dear beloved Salima were part of the reason why I published this Chronicle. Perhaps I would be able to treat this deterioration, waking up Salima from its sleep. Perhaps the stories of our grandfathers and fathers and their social lives would wake up Salima. Perhaps these tales would get the people to stop the deterioration and begin to progress once again.

I have high hopes of assistance from our successful expatriates. They were introduced to spiritual values and high culture here in our homeland. They tasted a great civilization and perhaps, now, they can help financially and emotionally.

BROTHERHOODS & ASSOCIATIONS
Chapter 11

Al-Habl bela Danass Association.

In 1893, Father Paul (Boulos) al-Akouri, the Lebanese missionary, together with another missionary, came to perform a spiritual exercise. They were so successful in this great undertaking that people still remember it and its benefits.

After this spiritual exercise ended, Father Boulos renewed the al-Habl bela Danass Association that was dedicated to the Virgin Mary. Its many members were both men and women. Its leadership included Abu Aql al-Khuri, Girgis Zein, Fares Murad Zein, Abdo Freha, the father of this historian, and others.

About 1912, I began serving the parish of the Church of Our Lady. This Association was renewed in a celebration. There was a strong surge of people wanting to join it, especially women after so many of the men migrated, searching for a way to earn a living.

The Association did well. It fulfilled what any religious organization should do, namely, it helped people fulfill their religious obligations and it helped the poor and the needy, spiritually and financially. Their celebrations were full of praising God and praying to the Virgin.

The girls of the Association collected a sum of money with which they bought two big copper candelabra and a beautiful statue of the Virgin. The meeting place of the Association and its altar became decorated with all sorts of contributions like covers and candelabra and vases with the result that these things gladdened the heart.

The president of the Association was Sophia Metri Moussa, the wife of Daoud Boutros Abu Asali Bachaalany. She remained a president all her life. She died years ago and is remembered with mercy because she was a wise president. She was an example of virtue and piety. After her came Mary al-Khuri Boutros, the wife of Salibi Zein. Then came Hana Assaf Girgis, the wife of Boutros Abu Asali Bachaalany. They were all virtuous women. The Association is still going steady despite the changes of the times and with so many people going their separate ways.

The Brotherhood of Saint Francis.

The virtuous Capuchin priest, Father Ya'qub al-Haddad, a man of favors and charities, established this brotherhood in the Monastery of Saint Peter. This man was so famous and charitable. I will write of his great deeds in the seciton on religion and humanity.

As for this Brotherhood of Saint Francis, it spread because of the sincerity of Father Ya'qub for our country. It also spread around the world and, still, this sincere Missionary is taking care of it without getting tired or bored. He is still running its affairs and taking every opportunity to preach and guide with his tender touching style, as did his teacher Saint Francis who followed in the footsteps of the great teacher, the Christ. So he continues to work and teach and this has brought spiritual benefits to Salima.

Al-Abb al-Ilahy Association.

This group was established in the Convent of Saint Peter by Mother Odelle Sfeir, the Mother Superior of the Convent. She exerted every effort to make it successful and it achieved what she wanted. This association has continued all these years, doing well. Its members have benefited from its good fruits. It is enough to know that it made them do their religious duties regularly, energetically, and with care. Although they had their other obligations of life still they were able to balance their spiritual interests and their worldly interests. All this, due to this blessed Monasticism.

Al-Salibeyah.

This association is popular and it has numerous branches in many countries. The group is one of the most important means to accustom boys and girls to being responsible and healthy, in an enthusiastic yet serious manner.

It has a special uniform with a cross on it. This is their declaration that its members have the mission in life of carrying their cross, being patient to the hardships as the Christ was. As He said: "Whoever does not carry his cross and follow me, doesn't deserve me."

The Association of Saint George.

This is an association for the youth of the Beshelani families in Salima. A knowledgeable person once told me that the idea for this group originated in the days of Father Mansour who was the head of the Monastery of the Capuchin Fathers in Salima in the middle of the last century.

The idea for creating this association came to the virtuous priest after he saw the disasters and calamities that had occurred in Lebanon which obliged the youth to defend themselves when necessary. Thus it was that this association was created. Its first president was the Sheik Melhem Nohra. He remained president for a long time then was succeeded by his cousin, Tanious Shahin Boutros.

Many of the youth of the Bachaalany families became presidents of this association, such as Sheik Habib Shaiban, Sheik Elias Wakim, Shahin Boutros and Solaiman Daoud.

An Invitation To Beit al-Din.

In the spring of 1876, 25 young people of the Bachaalany families who were members of the Association of Saint George went to Beit al-Din. They had been invited by Bishara Abboud Ne'ma, the cousin of the Melhem Nohra Sweid to attend his wedding.

All of them were dressed in the same uniform, wearing the Moroccan Fez (Tarboosh) that was well known at that time, and strapping a brown handkerchief around the fez.

They were heartily welcomed and they met many of the people and notables in Beit al-Din and Deir al-Qamar (The Monastery of al-Qamar).

Among these fine young men, were those who excelled in fighting with swords, those who excelled in writing and those who excelled in giving speeches. They showed great ability and control in all the situations they faced. They were exceptional in horse riding, eloquence, daring situations, and poetry.

They were accompanied by Nassif Mikhail al-Haddad, who was known for his ability to improvise poems.

Everyone who saw them admired them and said: "I swear that these are the pearls of a city, which contains youth who excel in everything".

They got the opportunity of visiting with the Blessed Archbishop Youssef al-Bostani, who received them with a gracious welcome.

One thing that must be mentioned about the intelligence of this great prelate is that when the young people approached him one by one to touch his hand – and they had among them two Druze young men: Mohammad Hamad al-Masry and Hamad Shahin Said – the Archbishop pointed them out from among the crowd though they were all wearing the same clothes. Then he made a speech praising their unity despite their religious difference. Those who were present were astonished by this amazing insight. Sheik Melhem Nohra said: "Our master, we have no foreigners among us", and the Archbishop said: "Would you hide it from Archbishop Boutros?".

They also visited the palace of Prince Bashir al-Kabir and most of the large buildings there.

Whenever the talkative Nassif al-Haddad met a notable or a prominent figure, he would sing him an improvised piece of Zagal (an Arabic form of poetry) about him that would exactly fit that person's condition. And this, without previously knowing him.

They stayed 8 days as guests of the bridegroom, during which time they were treated very kindly and generously. (Quoting Youssef Hanna Saad Allah, one of the youth of the Association).

Whenever a group of these fine young men migrated to America, the association would get weaker. Then soon it would become strong again with new members. Always another group would appear when people left. This association was very active and it prospered until it became very famous.

The most important dates when the association was renewed were 1873, 1883, 1880, 1911…etc..

In 1883, the youth of the association created a special tune that they would chant along with the famous national tunes of the day. The songs were all well known to the ear without any musical notes being written down. Also, this music playing would accompany sword games and word games. The teacher Solaiman al-Halaby al-Choueiry was at that time the music and games teacher. They would all participate in these activities whenever they got the chance. At the end of their work day they would sing the songs.

The reason that the Bachaalany folks created this special tune was that they saw that the youth of Bermana Marine in Salima had their own theme song. So, this was the motivation for the youth of the Nakouzy folks to create their own tune too. Thus, in Salima, there became two themes competing with one another.

People of those days had no fears or worries since the thought of migrating wasn't on their minds yet. Their days were full of celebrations and festivals. So blessed are those days. I remember that while I was young, I accompanied the youth to the districts of Bekaa because of an invitation of our relative Ibrahim Hanna Nasr Allah to attend his wedding. I stayed there for a whole week of happiness among the relatives. People of nearby villages would gather and watch since they were not used to seeing music being played.

This association has an old flag of its own, with a picture of the hero Saint George, painted by Elias Michael Bu Oun.

An interesting historical fact is that this flag has three colors just like the French flag.

Written on the flag is the following which the Lebanese people used to sing while they walked along together: "Go on as destined by God and what God has decided is what will be. Oh, God, on You, we depend." and, this: "Oh, Christian Saint George, save your Bachaalany Manhar", whose meaning I mentioned earlier in the book. .

Every brother who was a member in the Association had the painting of its aforementioned mediator hung in his house. They used to celebrate the festival of this Saint and attend religious ceremonies on His Feast Day.

The last renewal of the association 20 years ago was satisfactory, and the association appeared in a way that shows development and success.

The meetings were held regularly and they were united in their goals for progress and development in the future.

They also renewed the special tune of the Association in a modern style and with musical notes. This was done under the direction of Habib Shaiban who was known for his talent in music. They achieved great success because of the talents of the people of Salima and their readiness for such fine arts.

The Beit al-Masry Association.

Lately, the Masry families have established an association composed of their youth. It fulfilled what they wanted for progress and unity among themselves. Also, they created a tune of their own.

Their teacher was Mr. Boutros Abu Samra from Beit Meri and the music always accompanied them in their happy and sad times.

The House of Said Association.

The notable Naguib Qassem Ali Said has established a charitable Association. He started it the day he returned from Mexico in 1930. It was begun with a celebration to which all the notables of country were invited. In this celebration, Mr. Amin Taqei al-Din sung his poem about Salima. He paralleled the poem by Mr. Assaf al-Khuri previously mentioned in this book.

This Association didn't last too long because its founder returned to Mexico.

It is appropriate on this occasion to publish a letter that was received by the members of the Saint George Association from Habib al-Bshe'lani, the author's brother, who was an expatriate in Brazil. It is interesting reading because of what he has to say about the social benefits, memories, and historical lessons of his days in Salima.

Here it is:

My dear brothers, the respected members of the Bachaalany Saint George Association:

The feelings of love that link together nations and individuals still have their power over me. One of the prime things on my mind is the love of my country and my family.

Here I am in this long migration with seas and mountains and lowlands separating me from my beloved homeland. Still the flame of the spirit of brotherhood glows inside of me. Yes, certainly, it is the delicious memory that consoles my heart in this migration. No matter how far away I go to live, still, I long to return to my home.

I become very happy with any trinket from home. My hope is of returning to the land where by father, mother, brothers, and friends all live. That is where by dreams live. I wish to return to all those that I love to be near, all that my eyes love to see and my ears love to hear.

All these days are gone like the sweetest dreams in life. But I pray to God, Who holds everything in His Hands to join me with you and to remove the reason that prevents me from being with you.

I received your letter that showed me that you are still the hope of your expatriate brothers. I see that you are engaged with all your efforts in sincere work with good intentions and with unity.

Thus my heart was so happy because of this unity. And it was jealous for the interest of the family and preserving its pride. It is true that no matter how far I am from home, still there are emotional bonds that attached me with my homeland. This is a duty that was never forgotten and never will be.

This is the issue that we must all take care of because the lives of the nations exist on this bond which is unity and love.

And we, although we are not a nation in the sense of a huge country, our interests are not that big, but we are one family whose life requires unity and hard work to preserve its interests no matter how small these interest are. Our interests, brothers, with respect to the current social situation in the country, is that we preserve our pride. We must not tolerate any transgression against our personal rights. We live in lands that hardly respect individuals rights and, so, this social situation should make us come together and unite. We must form family unions.

These incidents of our current days teach us that misunderstandings among ourselves are the reason we have foreign interference.

This weakness that has plagued our family unity can be cured only by understanding. We must apply all our thoughts, desires and emotions to this cause of unity. Surely, this Association which was established a long time ago is our means of unity.

That's why I was so happy when I heard of the renewal of the association. It is the strong bond that holds the members of our family together. It even extends overseas binding the expatriates together so that we all become one force that works to preserve our general interest.

Allow me to express these remarks about the Association. I would love to see it last for a very long time. I would love for the sons to inherit it from the fathers after we are gone. In this way we can leave a good memory for the future.

This union was established to be, like all other associations, a power that turns a group into one and produces a huge strength coming from the unity of its members. This unity will protect their interests and their existence. But when this goal goes away, then all is lost. The bonds will break and its members will be harmed.

Although our Association was established a long time ago it has gone through cycles of being forgotten, then returning, being forgotten again, and so on. I don't know if it will continue.

Everything shows us that we need it. All these incidents were due to the weakness of our determination and the loss of our resolution. We failed to appreciate its benefits and each one saw a different goal for the Association. This diversity prevented it from benefiting all those who belonged to it. We must maintain unity in the Association so that it injects its soul into all the members of the family. So that we are all as one soul and one way of thinking. Only this can govern the general interest and strengthen it and protect it.

I say this knowing that I am in the presence of thinking minds and men who realize this power of unity. I know that we can all make this unity prevail in our lives. I know that we can not live without it. I know that we can strengthen this principle among everyone including the young so that they grow up learning this noble principle.

But, unfortunately, this principle was not supported in the past by our wise men. Because of their differences of opinion, varying goals, and the many external influences, we were led to disunity and disagreement.

I don't deny the good things brought by the Association to our city. The effects can not be denied. The good was due to the understanding between our elders and our wise men who, for a period of time, produced such goodness. But this understanding did not last a long time. And so, my brothers, this is the biggest proof of the benefits of the Association. It provides unity, it protects our interests, and it preserves our patriotism.

So, don't let us forget the past. Let us always remember and rely on the Association. Let us make it a cure for our hearts.

Any day in which this principle prevails, and in which unity and love are achieved, is a day of happiness for us. The expatriates brag about our Association and it fills our hearts with joy. Our grandfathers lived in unity and with patriotic power. They were respected and feared by their neighbors. Surely the thought of their unity will show them the great respect they deserve and bring them great joy and happiness.

It would be wonderful if you would identify and then avoid the reasons that led to the discontinuance of the Association. Please, study the weaknesses that caused its interruption. Indeed, the lessons of the past should never be forgotten. We should take good care not to commit the mistakes of the past again.

With all my strength I support this principle, believing that we can all become one soul. I will never hesitate in helping financially as soon as I see that my efforts will not be in vain.

I hope that your correspondence includes all the expatriates. Thus we can all participate with words and actions. We can all become one in the Association.

I pray to God, Who supports good ideas and noble principles, to help you and unite you under the banner of the Association. May He unite your decisions and guide your efforts to bring welfare to us all and to those who follow us. There is nothing more that I hope for than being with you again in our beloved homeland. So, please, pray for me so that God will make my affairs easy and thus make my absence brief. As for sending money needed for your charitable projects, I took care of this matter. I notified our brothers in different places. I am sending now what I have been able to gather. I will send what I can gather in the future, God willing.

Finally, I wish you steadfastness and long life in the Association. I hope that it will bring you goodness. My letter represents all the family members here who send their greetings and wish you happiness and success

From Oliveira, Brazil, September 1, 1911

Your brother,

Habib Freha Bachaalany

MANNERS, TRADITIONS

AND

SOCIAL CONDITIONS

Chapter 12

I had written something about this subject in my manuscript <u>Achieving Desires In The History Of the Bachaalany People</u>. I have also written much about this in my handwritten historical encyclopedia <u>The History of the Maronite Families</u>. I knew it would be difficult to publish this information in a specialized book like this chronicle. My love for my homeland and the place of birth forces me to exert all my effort to produce here the best of what I gathered and the best of what I have written.

This information is not excerpted or stolen from others. They are my own private observations. It is the result of long studies from which I take what is suitable in a given situation. I express honestly the social conditions of the people of Salima. Furthermore, I show them as they coincide in whole or part with the social conditions of all the people of Lebanon. This information then is beneficial, interesting, and shows good examples and lessons.

Means of making a living.

The life of the Lebanese families in the past was much like Bedouin life.

They were content with no worries. A youth may reach 20 years old without being occupied by anything.

The basis of life was raising animals, like cattle. They did agricultural and farming work. They grew silkworms. They practiced some industries. Occasionally, they went out and fought some civil wars due to the opposing political parties.

They were an energetic and active people. They cut rocks and smoothed their rough surfaces. They worked fallow lands and turned them into fertile fields. The results of their work can still be seen today.

Raising cattle is an ancient activity that has been adopted by man at all the phases of his development. Owning cattle and pack animals is essential to the Bedouin way of life, to life in the countryside and in agricultural work.

There was land given to them as fiefs by the Princes and Sheiks in the Bekaa plain and in other places. They invested in these lands turning them into the source of their bread. They used to collect their winter supplies during the summer. They would live in their home in safety. But then they were forced to leave these plains during the Ottoman period. Because of the military service, the tithes and the taxes, they turned to the mountainous land. There, they were confined to the narrow mountain.

There was also the wilderness. The pine woods that our good ancestors left is a most precious treasure resulting from their efforts and work. They raised them like someone rearing their own children. They took good care of these trees many of which still remain till the present day, hundreds of years old. They are very beneficial with their fruits, wood and the firewood that are taken from them. They used to call the pine trees "Rezk al-Arrmala" (the sustenance of the widow) since they don't need much care. People made use of them in World War I and in World War II. People even protected them, keeping them safe from the evils of need and hunger.

It is said that Man, during times of war, is forced to resort to nature. It is the occupation of his grandfathers, farming and cultivating the fields. This work keeps Man safe from the evil of need, thus, war was a good lesson for him.

They used to take into account the nature of the land and the weather conditions. Thus, they never planted a grapevine in the place of a pine tree. They never planted an olive tree in the place of a mulberry.

They didn't take courses in farming in agriculture schools but they gained their knowledge from experience, from trial and error, and from experts.

They took much care in planting grapes as can be seen from the abandoned vineyards. And there are molasses presses whose names and effects still remain in front of our eyes today. I certainly regret the current state of neglect in agriculture. It shows in the declining number of cattle and field workers. It has happened for many reasons, the most important of which are the migrations and changing lifestyles. Abandoning the lifestyle of the countryside and going to live in the cities was done by so many people. Farming the land became a disgrace when, in the past, it was an honor.

In the past, those who served the feudal lords, whether horsemen or infantry, collected a specified daily wage. This wage allowed them to take care of themselves, their family, and their horses. Each one of them would go home and take his daily wage from the Prince's official storage room. This is evident from sayings like the following: "The house of so-and-so is like the storage room of Prince Haidar". This is also the reason why those who worked in the service of a prince had their minds free from worries about their daily living or their future. They used to say of these people that their bread is already baked and their tankard is already filled with water. Serving a prince and being faithful to him was seen as an essential matter. They used to say "who eats from the bread of a Sultan will strike with his (the Sultan's) sword". Our grandfathers participated in all the famous battles with their princes. They answered the call of the ruler of Great Lebanon (Lebnan al-Kabir) in such battles as: the battle of Ain Dara 1711, and, al-Jarrmaq or al-Zahrani in 1770, where a large number of them were killed; and, in the battle of al-Mazza and Sharr al-Mokhtara in 1825, and Sanoor in Nablus in 1829, and the battles of Ibrahim Pasha in Shtoura and others. When they finished these duties, they would go back to their own personal responsibilities. .

As for their industries, they worked in construction, woodworking, forging, shoemaking, tailoring, weaving and jewel making. They were famous for making shirts and handkerchiefs of silk. They were weaving the nation's textiles, dyeing them, then sewing them into clothes known as the Dima.

As for construction work, it was, at first, limited to the house of Bshour; and, forging to the house of al-Haddad; and, jewel making to the house of al-Sayegh; and, dyeing to the house of al-Sabbagh.

Although they all used to brag about their horse riding and chivalry and manliness, they didn't like to be called "Khawajat", i.e. sellers and traders. So much so, that in their quarrels with each other, they used to say: "we are not khawajat or perfume sellers". But they used to trade in the different goods that they would bring on donkeys and mules. These would be things brought back from Sham, Beirut, Tripoli and other places. It was a rare thing that a trader would travel far. If he did travel to Sham, then he would be considered courageous. They would sing about him in their songs: "O beautiful lady, your brother traveled to Sham alone like Bu Zeid al-Hilali". (Bu Zeid al-Hilali is a courageous hero from folktales).

Jamal (Hanna) Nader Gad'oun al-Qadim was famous for his trading and the goods he brought back from Sham. So, too, was Asaad Maroun al-Henawy. From the people of national trading were Girgis bin Freha Knieser, who was rich, and his brother Tanous Freha and his son Abdo, the father of the author of this book.

Nader Gad'oun al-Qadim was the owner of a big store in the square.

Becoming famous, lately, is Youssef and Anton Wakim who both had a shop that contained all types of goods and groceries.

Abdo Freha and Abu Aql al-Khuri were famous for being tailors. They were famous for attaching the silk liners which were popular among men and women, and, also, for attaching silver decoration for women and for velvet fezzes for women.

Among those who were famous in weaving national silk were: Nejm Boulos and his son Hanna; Nejm Youssef Nasr Allah; Mikhail and Gabriel, the two sons of Hanna Bu Oun; Elias Mikhail Budalha; and, Ya'qub Ghantus and others.

Girgis Mikhail Bu Asali was famous for woodworking, especially carving doors and bridges; and Melhem Gabriel Freha and Asaad Abboud for woodworking boxes and craving and painting them.

In the same way that our grandfathers excelled with swords and wisdom and sometimes writing, so some of their grandsons were famous for their crafts. This includes people such as Faraj Allah Freha, famous in woodworking, exceeding the children of Mebawesh, the most famous woodworkers in these lands. Faraj Allah Freha's works were accurate showing his ingenuity and ability. He also knew engineering matters that he learned by accompanying European craftsmen. His nephew, my brother Khalil Freha, learned this craft from him, becoming no less skilled than his uncle in ability and engineering knowledge. And so, also, were Mikhail and Louis, the two sons of Mo'allem (Master in his profession) Faraj Allah. They have become famous in this art in the present day. And also skilled in this profession were Nejm Assaf, Nejm Andrea, Shaiban Tanous, Elias Saad Allah, Shoukri Freha and Youssef Eskandar al-Ma'luf (his mother is one of the Bachaalany folks).

Famous for forging were the Mo'allems (Masters in their profession) sons of Girgis Bu Asali; the eldest, Habib, has shown skill and ability, and, if God had extended his life, he would have made wonders. His two brothers, Boutros and Daoud, were skillful too and especially Daoud who was a unique master in all forging works.

Learning from Mo'allem Boutros in this forging industry, was his brother-in-law Boutros Daoud so he became a winner in this industry, also.

Famous in construction work were Daoud and Shahin Boutros Shahin and especially the later, who was exceptional.

Solaiman bin Daoud Boutros excelled in his profession and so did his brother Girgis.

Now it remains for me to mention working people from families other than the Bachaalany family.

The Zein family was skilled in the construction field. Among them was Mo'allem Ibrahim bin Girgis Zein, famed for his technique, attention to detail, and his reliability. His handiwork is visible in many projects such as: The new bridge over the Kalb (The Dog) River, the dome of the Church of Our Lady, and the dome of the new Church of Saint John.

His children learned the profession from him and they, too, excelled. Most notably, the elder son, Mo'allem Salibi, won praise for his detailed woodworking.

From the house of Bshour, Mo'allems Ghantous and Ghaleb (al-Khuri Elias) and Hanna Bshour, were famous in construction work and carving. They learned their trade from their father and grandfathers and then passed it on to their children. Metri al-Sayegh and his son Fares practised this profession, too, as did Qostantine al-Haddad (who became a priest) and his two sons Abu Selim Melhem and Eskandar.

Famous for forging was Nasr al-Haddad. His son Fares who excelled in tailoring, and, with his cousin, Mishal As'ad Bshour, established major shops in Beirut.

Youssef Mhanna al-Haddad, known as Abu Jaouhar, excelled in veterinary medicine, which his nephews, Girgis Tanous al-Haddad and Shebli Abu Zayyan al-Haddad, learned from him.

Also famous for forging were Younes al-Haddad and his son As'ad, the father of Niqola and Nakhla. They are virtuous expatriates. They are traders in the Transvaal, where their relative and colleague in trading, Tanous Girgis al-Haddad, is, also.

As for the Druze, they did not practice any of these professions and industries in the past with the exception of manufacturing some useful farm tools. Lately, however, they have progressed and copied some of these industries. They have also become interested in education and trading.

Haidar al-Zar'aouni excelled in woodworking and he used to make wooden bridges for homes. Into his bridges he carved his name and the date of the project, marking them "Made by Haidar al-Zar'aouni in the year … .".

Also of the Druze who were employed in woodworking are: Sloum bin Asaad and his brother and his son; also, Fares Bu Hussein and Marr'ey al-Halabi and his son Amin. They used to work in cutting wood. Today the house of Zar'aoun in Rouaissa, among many other projects, is the result of their labor.

The Prestige And Stability Of The Family.

In the family, there used to be men who are fit into all sorts of roles. In this way a family would constitute a whole group of people, each one of them providing an essential task. Thus one of them would be a swordsman, another in education and, still another in politics. The sword was very important in the past. Education was important, too, though rare. Politics was very important because wisdom comes before courage. They had a saying: "This man is for swords, this one for receiving guests, this to meet rulers, or this one for life's misfortunes." Accordingly, if all these types of personalities were available in a family then the family would be stable. They would be in an elevated social position, respected by the young and the old, alike, by the ruled and the ruler.

What would also lead to the stability of a family is learning from the fathers and grandfathers. They would teach everyone that they should obey the leaders, respecting them and being faithful to them. They should be generous to all sorts and levels of their fellow citizens. All of these values still remain today in some of the people, if only on a smaller scale.

These were the factors which built the strength of these families in the past. These were the days when everyone was conscious of himself and his position. He would never cross the lines of his role. Thus a leader, a prince or sheik would take care of the matters of his people or family. Each person in the nation was minding his own business, attending to his own affairs.

When I was young, I used to attend these family meetings in Salima. I witnessed first hand what happened in them when an incident or an ordeal happened. I saw how everyone would show his abilities. The people of wisdom and experience and the old men would state their opinions. They would share the knowledge and experience they had. They would support these opinions with lessons and examples from historical events. All the members of the family respected the words and opinions of the Sheiks. They would obey the leaders out of love and respect for national or family interest. They used to highly respect the words of the leaders. They would say: "Our leader so-and-so or our uncle so-and-so said this." Thus, the interest of a family, village or the country would stand strong in that manner. If it wasn't for that solidarity, those noble families would never have reached their prominent positions. When everyone considers himself a leader, the country and villages get divided. Then, the general interest was lost and the Biblical saying came true: "A house divided against itself, cannot stand."

Co-operation And Solidarity.

The people of Salima like all other Lebanese people are famous for their qualities of co-operation and solidarity. On happy occasions like weddings, they would exchange money gifts, like "al-Noqoot" (money gifts given to newly weds). For funerals, they would exchange invitations to food and financial aid. Also, they had something called "al-Aounat (Aids)". This would happen between members of the same family or between people of the same village, in sorrow or celebration. They would all, men, women, and children alike, all work together to accomplish a project. They would build a church, construct a home, share lumber, etc.. Through this "Aounat" they would show their virtues, their chivalry in misfortune. Working together to overcome a calamitiy, disaster, or hardship, an observer would think that they were all brothers coming together for better or worse.

Friendliness And Brotherhood

People today claim to have brotherhood and patriotism. The way I see it, the ancestors had more brotherhood, stronger patriotism and friendliness. Despite an occasional dispute, they lived in accordance with the Christian principle of brotherly love. Proof that shows their sense of brotherhood towards their co-citizens no matter what their denomination occurred in the time of civil wars. These uprisings and disputes are numerous. They used to compete in being friendly and making good relations with their neighbors. They would protect fellow citizens' honor and money as if they were all brothers.

When Nejm Andrea was in his last days, he gathered all the Bachaalany family together and told them this story. A Prince in the past gathered together the noble families in Metn for a meeting. They were asked their opinion about annihilating seven families in Metn. The reaon was that these families were arrogant and proud. It was said that they must be eliminated just like they had annihilated the house of Abu Tareyya in Bezbedin and others in Morouj and Zar'aoun. One of the princes stood up and said: "and what do you think, Sheiks, about the Bachaalany family? They are arrogant and fear no one". After debating, some of them agreed while others stayed silent. Some of those present were a group of wise men from the Me'dad family from Bezbedin and from the Helal family from Qornayel. They did not agree to this and they all opposed the Prince.

One of them stood up and explained the favors and importance of the Bachaalany family in the country. He said that it would not be right to annihilate them. A large group of the families of Me'dad and Helal and others agreed with him. When the princes saw that the Bachaalany family was strongly supported in the country, they changed their minds and asked those present to keep the whole matter a secret. Thus no one from the Bachaalany family knew about it.

Andrea ended his testimony by saying: "This is the origin of the friendship between our family and the families of Me'dad and Helal. I entrust you to keep this friendship forever.

(From Andrea Girgis, quoting his uncle Daher bin Nejm Andrea and Hussein Abu Ali Me'dad)

What the Christians did in 1845 is the biggest proof of their brotherhood. They assured the Druze that their honor and property were safe. The Christians protected the Druze women and defended them. The Druze Hatoom family from

Kafr Salwan sent their women and children and weapons to the homes of their friend Nejm Andrea and Nader Gad'oun Bachaalany. Even when the soldiers of the Turkish governments tried to plant hatred between the two groups and stir up discord, still their bond of brotherhood held.

The Christians and Druze of Salima had promised each other on the day of the turmoil of 1860 not to burn each other's houses. They promised that whoever won the struggle that they would not destroy the other's property. They shook hands before going to fight the war. This was when Assaf al-Khuri al-Nakouzi died.

Of the homes in Salima, only one house, the home of Youssef Waked was burned, and this by a stranger. So, as compensation, the Druze burned the home of Anton Hanna from the Christians. So strong was this bond that the people of the Qate' (the Strip) and the Kisrawan accused the Christians of siding with the Druze.

Hospitality And Generosity.

The Maronite families, like other Lebanese families, are accustomed to showing hospitality and generosity. It is known that the Bedouin life and the mountainous countryside life tend to make people more generous and hospitable.

The Maronite families, especially those in the mountains, were hospitable and generous and they used to consider stinginess a shameful vice. This is in contrast to the city people who always had some excuse for avoiding hospitality. Whether relatives or not, it made no difference. City dwellers became so stingy that is seemed to be regarded as their natural characteristic while generosity became that of the mountain people.

What we see today as a turnabout in the attitude of the city people seems to be due to their mixing with the people of the mountains. The cities today have become a mixture of the city dwellers and the mountain dwellers, all accustomed to hospitality and generosity. It seems today that some families and regions in Lebanon are known for their generosity while others known for their stinginess.

One of the surviving characteristics of the princes and the notables in the feudal era is the "Guesthouse" (al-Manzool). This was a room they used to build beside their houses and palaces so that strangers could lodge there. The people of the village would go there to drink coffee in an evening. These gatherings were almost totally limited to the house of the Prince. The owners of the house would rarely use these guesthouses.

People would gather in this guesthouse for discussions with the Prince. They would talk about national issues. The building which was a guest house of the princes was located to the west of the palace and square. And it is still there today. The staircase beside it is known as "the staircase of the guesthouse". This guesthouse was a shelter for strangers and there, relatives were served food and coffee.

Invitations To Funerals.

They used to invite the people of the neighboring villages to funerals. They would also invite the clergy of these villages and the nearby Monasteries. The number of invitations would be in accordance to the importance and wealth of the deceased person. Some one receiving an invitation would never ignore it, no matter how far away he lived, in Bekaa or on the coast.

This habit continues today but it has changed a little and is more limited.

The funerals of the princes used to be large. In the funeral of Prince Ismael al-Mesholah, a massive crowd gathered. He was a great man. He was the father of Prince Hassan, Prince Assaf, and Prince Haidar. The funeral of Prince Assaf was huge as evidenced by the large number of clergy in attendance besides all of the other people. The crowd was so large that the first person was in the yard of the palace (at the staircase of the guesthouse) while the last one of them was at the dome where the prince was buried, a distance of about 200 meters. Archbishop Abd Allah Bleibel was the celebrant of the funeral ceremony.

The funeral of Jamal (Hanna) bin Nader Gad'oun was attended by all the priests of neighboring villages and the Monasteries of Mikhail Benabil and the Monastery of Mar Moussa al-Dawwar and Mar Elias Shouya and Mar Girgis Bahardaq and Mar Boutros Karim al-Tin.

The stipend given to the priest for a funeral was no more than 2 Piasters and sometimes one Piaster and a half. This was a Mass and a funeral. Money was rare and the burial expenses were usually no more than 50 Piasters. This included the expense of the coffin and the stipend to the priests. They used to bury the deceased person without the coffin in the soil. Then, later, they started to bury the deceased person in a wooden coffin that cost a Zalata (30 Bars/Barat/money units). If it was expensive it could cost up to 5 Piasters.

I saw among the papers of the house of Father Edah in Beit Mri that the coffin of an al-Khuri woman, Anton, in the middle of the 18th century cost 30 Bars/Barat/money units. She was the first one to be buried in a coffin.

Civilian Dealings.

There was a custom that most of the property was shared or held in common, between relatives or fellow citizens. I remember that, in Salima, there was an old olive tree with a water fountain (Ain al-Zaitona) beside it. That fountain was shared by the members of a branch of the Bachaalany family for over 200 years.

The same was true about the oil and molasses presses, thus each house had a share of the 24.

There was also the land that was common property in each village. It was for the people of the village to benefit from its wood and crops. That property was the result of a grant to the people from the princes and the sheiks.

Lending And Renting.

When our grandfathers were in a state of poverty, if one of them owned a carpet or a fur or a cauldron or other such thing, then his brother or neighbor could easily borrow it. Often the borrower return what he borrowed with some of the crops of the soil as a sign of gratitude.

They used to borrow from each other with a deed or a promissory note that was known to them as "al-Tamassok" (the Tenacity). They would pay back the money in its due time together with its interest. They would never deny it even if the deed was lost because they were true, honest and faithful.

Medicine In Salima.

As I mentioned before, when the Capuchin Missionaries came to Salima, the Lam' Princes gave them a piece of land as a grant. That was where they built their Monastery.

What is told from our folk lore is that the monks made a vow to the princes that they would have a monk or a priest who was good in medicine. He would be present in the Monastery to treat the princes and other people. The princes, in turn, would provide a living for the missionaries. The missionaries carried out their vow and continued in it even after the princes were gone from Salima.

And it is no surprise that the head of the Monastery, Father Michael Kabushy, was an MD, a Medical Doctor. So was Father Nicholas Gladimir, Father John and Father Mansour. One of the Brothers (al-Shamas) was responsible for the medical practice if a priest was not a doctor. This was the case for Brother Chrispino, Brother Ezidore and Brother Fidale. The Monastery was sold in his days. All those mentioned were practising medicine.

Father Joseph Dahham learned this profession from the Capuchins and from Abu Nassif al-Tayyan who was a resident of Salima. Father Joseph used to treat the people of the area using the standard methods known in those days. People trusted him.

Also, Girgis (George) Aisha and his son Boutros (Peter) were very expereienced in this field. They had a deep knowledge and skill of medicine. The were often able to diagnose a patient's illness by viewing him or her and they would effectively treat the problem.

Haidar al-Zar'aouni also learned the profession. It was to him that the priest gave the copy of the book of healing by Ibn Sina'a. The book was printed in Rome and bought by his grandsons during the World War from Amin Salman Bu Ali Me'dad Bezbedin.

Haidar had a natural gift for medical practice in addition to the knowledge he had gained from his contact with Father Joseph Bachaalany, his good friend. The two of them often worked together to treat people and to compare their diagnosis.

Medicine, in Salima, continued to be in the hands of the Capuchins and al-Tayyan folks, Father Joseph and Haidar Zar'aoun and Father John Bachaalany (al-Khuri Hanna al-Bshe'lani). Frequently, on important occasions, Ya'qub Youssef Tabet would come to Salima, invited by the princes and especially Prince Haidar. The days of modern medicine arrived when a Lebanese military unit came to Salima. A member of the unit was Gorgy Effendi (a Turkish title meaning Mr.) al-Khuri. He quickly became the doctor of the people of the area besides being the unit's practitioner. Sometimes they invited Doctor Nasser Hatem from Hamana to work with them. He was one of the students of the American University. Then came Doctor Mansour al-Bahut from Deir al-Qamar to teach in the boarding school of Our Lady Of Lourdes. He became the Official Doctor. After him came Doctor Naqqash from Beirut. The late Joseph (Youssef) Shahin used to treat patients when the doctor was absent, despite the fact that he never finished his studies. Abd Allah Hanna Bachaalany who learned his medical knowledge through the experience he gained from his contact with Doctor Hash and others in Beirut, used to also treat patients. He continues to do so today, performing a great service to his patients, especially the poor, in Salima and the surrounding area.

About 1907, Doctor Jacob Tocatjian, originally of Greek origin, a student of the American School, came to Salima. He spent many years here. He married a Greek girl from Athens and had four children: Zara (Jean), Liban who died as a child, Oshine, and Jupiter. The circumstances after World War I forced him to go and live in Egypt for several years. Finally he went to Baghdad, and died there around 1943. He was a very capable doctor as well as creative. His healing methods showed his knowledge, wisdom, and creative insight. I will mention him again later when I talk about the residents of Salima since he owned a house and properties there.

After him Doctor Kiomjian came to Salima. He is one of the famous doctors. At first, he was a pharmacist, then he studied Medicine in the Institute of the Jesuit Priests in Beirut. He spent a period of time in Damascus, then he came to Salima. Finally, he moved to Beirut and stayed there with his family. He is still there today.

Of the doctors who spent time in Salima, are: Doctor Lahud Girgis Lahud, sometimes he was called on to come to Salima; Doctor Tubajian and Doctor Tanious Rezk Allah (of the Church) were sometimes also called to heal patients. The same is true for Doctor Tawfiq Salhabb. Then for a while there was no doctor in Salima, only my fellow countryman Asaad bin Abd Allah Hussein al-Masry. He studied in the Institute of Medicine in Damascus but didn't finish his studies. He spent some time in Houran in the era of the French treating patients there. He has since come back home to practise medicine. The late Mikhail (Michael) Abdo also used to care for patients when the Doctor was absent. He had a Pharmacy as did the late Youssef Mourad Zein.

Raising silkworms

The most important means of making a living in the past was raising silkworms. This job was abandoned by the Druze but practised by the Christians. It was one of the reasons for the closeness that developed between the Mann Prince, Fakhr al-Din and the Christians. Raising silkworms added to the strength of the agricultural economy.

In looking back at history, we can see that the silk crop exported by Fakhr Al-Din to Italy, as well as the crop owned by the Princes and Sheiks and other notables, was considered to be the biggest and the best harvest. So much so that they had an expression saying: "The bills are only paid in the silk season."

In the past, the Lebanese used to unravel the cocoons, turning them to silk threads, then sending them to Aleppo and Shamand then on to Europe.

The silk industry was extremely popular in the days of Fakhr al-Din. The method used to unravel the cocoons involved a special wheel that was built near a water fountain. The wheel was called "the unraveler".

The rulers and fief owners used to monopolize the selling and buying of silk. No one could hang a balance to weigh and sell silk except with the permission of the ruler and the Sheik because of the many benefits involved.

In the days of Bashir al-Kabir and in the era of Prince Haidar, the Prince of Salima, and the ruler of the Christians of Mount Lebanon, the most important centers for weighing silk were in Zouq.

At the request of Mohammad Ali Pasha, the Khidewi of Egypt, Prince Bashir sent a group from the Zend family and others in Zouq, of the Kisrawan district, to plant mulberries and raise silkworms in Egypt. That explains their presence in Egypt. The late Shoukri al-Khuri, the owner of "Abu al-Hawl" in Brazil, did the same thing there as he described in his newspaper years ago. It just goes to prove that a Lebanese is very useful to the society wherever he is.

Silk Plants, Factories, Laboratories, Workshops

Silk Plants

The first one to introduce the silk unraveling industry to our lands was Fertoni Portalis, a Frenchman. He was from a noble family and his father, Etienne, was close to Napoleon I.

After Etienne, the father, died in 1827, his five children left for Egypt. The eldest, named Etienne like his father, then lived in Aleppo. Nicholas and Fertoni and their brothers came here in 1838. Nicholas saw that silk here was cheap. The people did not know how to unravel it. Consequently, he decided to build a plant or factory (Karrkhana) for the unraveling process. However, he was prevented from doing so by Prince Bashir for what reason, I do not know. Finally, Nicholas contacted Sheik Abd al-Malek, a rival of Prince Bashir, and Nicholas bought from him a piece of land in Betaterr for 12,000 Piasters. That was to be the place for his plant. He built it and then sold it to his brother Fertoni. The plant still stands today.

Fertoni established his plant in 1847, in Betaterr, when he was 32 years old. He lived there and died unexpectedly on February 10, 1881. He was buried in the cemetery of the Latins in Beirut. His children included one son, Prospar, and some daughters. The son was, like his father, honest in his dealings and enjoyed a business. Because his harvests were of silk of high quality, he was able to enjoy success over the other plants that were built after his. He then bought the palace of Abd Allah Pasha in Ras Beirut.

His brother Robert died from the plague which he caught from his servant whom he had buried himself. His brother Joseph was a partner with Nicholas. He died unmarried. He was the one who introduced the Saint Mansour Association in the country.

In summary, this noble family provided a great service to our country by introducing the silk unraveling industry. They also made many contributions that helped the poor and the weak.

Ain Om Hamada

It is known today as Ain Hamada. It is a farm that was owned by a Druze woman from Arsoun whose name was Om Hamada.

Most probably, in the beginning of the 19th century, Abu Nassif Elias al-Tayyan, a resident of Salima at that time, acquired it with other properties that he bought.

It is on the banks of the Arsoun river opposite the Monastery of Saint Elias al-Kenaiessa. It was bought by the Khawajat (the plural of Khawaja which means a seller or a trader), Michael Faraj Allah from Beirut, along with Shlizan Chrozier and the Khawaja Mork of the French community. They formed a partnership with one of its conditions being that if one of them died, then the others would inherit his share. So it was that when the first two died, the inheritance fell to the Khawaja Mork.

At that place, after the political turmoil of 1845, the previously mentioned partners built a silk factory. There they established the spinning wheels. Then they kept adding to them until they reached 120 of them. Since 1930 they have been abandoned. They brought in a group from Ghazir to teach the employees how to unravel the cocoons.

In the beginning, the employees were of both sexes. Lately, however, the workers have been females, even the supervisors. Only one job area employed men.

The plant of Ain Hamada was one of the best plants in the area. It dealt with the works honestly and fairly. They paid the workers their wages efficiently and on time just like the Europeans.

The Khawaja Mork expanded his plant by buying neighboring properties, the plant of Arbaneia and Arsoun and al-Kenaiessa. On these properties he spread the signs of civilization by planting grapevines, mulberries and pinewoods.

From 1890 on, he purchased coal mines from the people of Qornayel. It was known as the place of Ibrahim Pasha al-Masry. Then years later, he bought Ain al-Boyeet from the manager Louis al-Hajj Boutros al-Antouny. He had purchased it from the Capuchins for 45,000 Piasters.

The business of the Khawajat Mork-Delk expanded reaching as far as Beirut and the Syrian coast. They have a branch in Marseilles and they trade also in leather, especially two types known as Shakhteian and Kazz.

Most of the employees were from the village of Salima. In construction were the sons of Mo'allem As'ad (Asaad) bin Elias Bshour, Metri al-Sayegh, and Girgis Zein. In carpentry, there were Haidar al-Zar'aouni, As'ad Abboud, Hanna Sa'b al-Henawy, Assaf Girgis Nejm, his son Nejm, and Faraj Allah Freha. The blacksmiths were the sons of al-Turk from Beit Shabab and, with them, Habib bin Elias al-Honoud who married a girl from Salima. He lived in Salima as did his descendants.

Also in the plant, was Sheik Melhem Nohra from Salima, a clerk and manager. The company hired him after the turmoil of 1860. He stayed with them for about 20 years. Abu Aql al-Khuri was a supervisor over the employees for many years, as was Girgis Metri al-Sayegh. Sheik Abd Allah al-Khuri al-Asmar was the Sheik of the brokers of the cocoons. He later established his own factory in al-Kenaiessa which was then taken care of by his son, Sheik Selim, after him.

Among those who were employed in that shop, were Abu Amin Qassem Shoqeir and Solaiman Shoqeir. Also, al-Khuri Elias Oun, his son Youssef, and the house of Kwayyes of Arbaneia.

A large number of the girls of Salima worked on the wheels in the aforementioned shop. That was when the plant first started to operate. After they mastered the craft of unraveling, they worked in the plant of Hamana, the plant of al-Motran in Shaweia, the plant of the Khawajat Qashma'ey in Bakfia, and the plant of Tabet at al-Moat River (river of death). The last one mentioned, contained many from Salima in the days when Fares Shaiban was the manager. After him came his brother Tanous. Then there were the dealers in Beirut: Selim al-Najjar and Ibrahim Gabara al-Demashqy.

The Khawaja Fabrico, the Frenchman, was a dealer of the plant of Ain Hamada in the past. Monsieur Arde and Monsieur Dilo were also.

Among their friends was Monsieur Charley Bazier. He was a bookman, librarian, and bookseller who was famous in Beirut. Frequently, he would visit Ain Hamada and Father Andrew in Salima. He had knowledge of photography, so, he photographed the plant and the Monastery of Saint Peter and the Palace of the Lam'is before it was reconstructed. That was in 1865 and 1872. In 1881, he photographed the students, boys and girls, of the elementary Capuchin school. I was among them at that time. I was about 5 years old and I was photographed with my head bare sitting among others who were seated.

The Karrkhana (plant or shop) of Louis Kempasidis

Louis Kempasidis is of French origin. His father was a stoker in the plant of Mork, the Catholic man who is buried with his wife in the cemetery of Kenaiessa.

As for Louis, he became a Lutheran. He worked with his father and mastered the language of the country and became friends with the employees. He used to visit Salima and mingle with its people and share their customs and happy occasions. He mastered a type of Zagal known as al-Ma'neii (Zagal is a type of popular Arabic poetry). He attended the wedding of Mansour Kan'aan Abu Nassar in Salima in 1852. He sang with Haidar al-Zar'aouni and Shahin Ghaleb, taking the tambourine and singing as a genuine Arab. He did, however, have a slight French "r" sound that remained in his tongue.

His friend Shahin Ghaleb once wrote to him the following line when Louis had not fulfilled a promise he made to him:

"O Khawaja Louis, isn't it a sin to compete in the trade (i.e. lying) of the Arabs?!"

By this, he implied an accusation made by the Europeans to the Eastern people, namely, that they are liars.

The Khawaja Louis kept working hard till he owned properties between B'abdat and Mezka in the place known as Ain al-Kelab. At the time, it was known as Ain Louis, and he constructed a silk unraveling plant there around 1870. Many of the men and women of Salima worked there.

He had one son called Louis, who was one of the most outstanding youth. He frequently visited the Maronite Patriarchal Shrine. He died at dawn on his wedding day. His untimely death affected his parents deeply. They died heartbroken.

The Maronite Archbishops, especially the Archbishop Youssef Ga'ga', the Archbishop of the Bishopric of Qobross, and, the Archbishop Tobia Oun, the Archbishop of the Bishopric of Beirut, issued guidelines to the owners of the plants. This was done out of their concern to preserve the religious obligations and morals of the workers. They sent these several times. This is one:

Dear Honored Sir:

May God grant you long life. With all respect to you, we offer the following:

You know that we have issued guidelines in past years forbidding the members of the Maronite community from mixing male and female workers in the silk plants existing within our jurisdiction. We know that you are aware of our obligation to do so in order to preserve the morals of our young men and women. The orders that we issued in the past years have brought about partial compliance with our wishes. This year we wish to draw your attention and that of other plant owners within our jurisdiction to our zealous desire to preserve the good moral health of our people. We wish to emphasize that you should avoid mixing men and women workers at the wheel in your plants. This mixing would inevitably lead to great harm to many of the workers. This is especially true for the dormitory arrangements at the plants if there is no barrier between them. So it is that we wish to seek your cooperation in this noble effort to save souls and prevent the corruption of their morals. We do so for the glory of God. We know, too, that this separation would not only help to avoid evil and temptation for the workers but would lead to better profits for you, the owner. The workers would face fewer distractions and thus work more efficiently. This year you could accomplish our objective by hiring only one sex, either male or female, to work in your plant. If this cannot be done, then, surely you could place cloth or wood partitions between the wheels in your plant. And for dormitories you could do the same, seeing to it that each side would have its own door. Also, if you could arrange a walking space for the supervisors to be able to view the workers, this, too, would help achieve our goal. These procedures have been followed in other plants with no ill effects. To the contrary, major harm could be avoided. Accordingly, I have alerted my sons, the priests of my Bishopric, to renew their efforts to enforce our ban on mixing employees. My sincerest hopes are: First, that you consent to this call that I make from my conscience and congregational duty to preserve the morals and welfare of all concerned; Second, that you would reply to this request telling me what it is that you intend to do so that I may, hopefully, tell my Priests that they need not enforce any ban against any of their congregation. I hope from the bottom of my heart that this process will bring happiness and prosperity to you. I ask God to grant you success in your efforts. I ask him to grant you every reward for whatever efforts you perform for His sake to prevent sin. For your efforts may He grant you long life, success, and prosperity.

The name of the sender.

Various negotiations were held between the owners of silk plants and the Maronite clergy in Lebanon. They discussed the holidays that the workers should be given as off days. They talked about not mixing young men and young women workers in the plants. And, they negotiated about the extent of the obligation of the owners for preserving the good conduct of the employees. All of this shows the role of the leadership of the Maronite clergy in caring for their subjects. They were very concerned for the religious and emotional dangers that might confront them. This ultimately led to the full compliance of the owners of the plants, whether nationals or Europeans, to the conditions put forth by the clergy. Note the following letter:

From Beirut

September 12, 1858

My dear honorable Sir:

The Khawaja Portalis, one of the French traders, has been found to own a silk karrkhana under the jurisdiction of the Bishopric of Archbishop Tobia, the Archbishop of Beirut.

Because of the announcement made by the aforementioned concerning the prohibition of women from working in these karrkhanat (plural of karrkhana) due to the many dangers, the aforementioned khawaja found himself in a state of paralysis. Accordingly, he turned to the Archbishop to seek the required permission. He came to me begging me to mediate in this matter. He told me that he should be exempt because while the women in the karrkhanat of Hamana and other karrkhanat are residents in the karrkhana itself, the women in his karrkhana, the khawaja Portalis, come with their parents or husbands or children. In the evening, they go back to their homes. Since I could find no harm due to my intercession, and whereas it could be a great help to the poor, so, I beg your excellency to enable the khawaja Portalis to continue his work without any harm done to him. And while I am waiting your positive answer, I am presenting to you all my thanks and gratitude, with all due respect,

-- Boulos Bronony the head of the Archbishops of Taron

and Missionary Vicar of Syria.

And, the following:

From Diman

Sptember 21, 1858

My Dear Respected and Exalted Sir:

Concerning the correspondence from the Khawaja Fortonato Portalis about the girls working for him, I accepted what your excellency wrote to me in the letter dated 12th of this month. Since the goal of preventing the aforementioned girls from working in the karrkhanat is to protect them from dangers, it is necessary that whenever there is no danger, then there should be no obstacle. There is, then, no ban against their employment there. I, accordingly, consider your mediation to be sufficient and that I give my permission for the girls to continue their work for him. This permission is given under the condition that every effort is made to protect them from even the slightest harm, that nothing will prevent them from practising their religious obligations, that they are of the proper age. I further declare that if any violation should occur, then, I revoke my permission. This is what I declare in response to your previous letter. Presenting my deepest regards,

Boulos Boutros

The Antiochean Patriarch

--Taken from the archives of the Bkerke Treasuries, from Bkerke. February 12, 1866.

Father Ne'ma Allah al-Dahdah
The Patriarchal Secretary

Antoine Freia, the owner of the plant in Hamana, wrote to Father Boutros (Peter) al-Zaghzaghy to present to him the issue of having girls work in his plant and to request that they be allowed to work on all days except for the six major ones sanctioned by the Patriarch. He wrote that he desired to teach the poor girls how to unravel silk so they could earn a living.

To His Holiness, Wishing For His Continued Favors:

After kissing your ringed finger with all reverence and respect, and, seeking your prayers for me forever, I pray to God Almighty that you are in good health and enjoying happiness from Our Creator:

As your excellency knows, I have been living in Metn since 1854. Since the beginning of my stay here, my thoughts have always been directed to elevate the girls and teach them how to unravel silk in my Karrkhana. I have been able to do this all these past years. I have hoped that in this way, I would be able to help the girls make a living, and, at the same time, I acquired the employees I needed to work in my Karrkhana. With this accomplished and as the Exalted and Great Creator made my work easy, I went to Europe and learned how to produce finest quality silk. I then returned and continued developing my Karrkhana which contained 76 wheel. I built a place for the girls to sleep, and in this way my Karrkhana became very special. The employees were only girls and they were all under the management and supervision of my wife.

After many difficulties, I was able to increase the number of employees to 130 girls. They were all knowledgeable in the silk process. And since it was my intention that my silk would become famous, this should make it clear to your excellency that I was always concerned to protect my girls in a way that is satisfactory to them and to all concerned. Thus my Karrkhana has been specially built so that its employees are only girls. This will be even more clear to your excellency from my comments to your excellency and my previous comments to his highness Daoud Pasha, the Mutasarrif of Lebanon. He became convinced of the truth of what I said when honoring my karrkhana with a visit. The comments of Prince Khalil to his Highness Nasry Frenqo Pasha concerning the same issue further testifies to the truth of what I write. About two years ago, a group of Karrkhana owners, out of their extreme envy for the fine quality of our silk, lured some of my girls away, even though they were obligated to work for us for a contracted period of time. Enclosed with this letter is a list of the names of these girls and the Karrkhanat where they work. Your Highness would do me a great favor if you made them return to my Karrkhana. And when they do return, then my Karrkhana will again be all girls. At that time, I promise not to let any male work in it. After that, if only one male is found in it, then I accept any religious or earthly punishment that you issue to me and them. I am hoping that you will answer my request and grant me the return of the girls that left my Karrkhana. I wish to always have the benefit of your attention. I seek your blessings and prayers.

> *August 19, 1869.*
> *Seeking prayers from your excellency,*
> *Niqola Faltaki*

Niqola Faltaki is of Greek origin. His father left Sira and lived in Athens. He was an officer in the army and was killed for his country in one of the wars. His son Niqola was an only son, so the government sent him to France where he received an education in military sciences and arts. He served in the French Navy for 15 years. He married a Greek girl of noble origin and wealth. He moved with her to the East. He so loved Mount Lebanon that he bought a piece of land in Ain Mowaffaq, between Abadeia and Ras Jarff. There he built a house for himself and his famous garden which he brought from Europe. It consisted of all sorts of fruit and flower seedlings and, also, it was built near it a silk plant.

The people of Metn loved him for his favors and generosity. The Druze never harmed him or those who took shelter in his house in 1860.

The two Sheiks Melhem and Selim al-Khuri from Rechmaya and Prince Khalil Mustafa Abu al-Lam'e from Shabbaneia were dealers at his works.

He begot: Anthony, Khristo, Constantine, Catiana, who got married to the Russian Atnas Srikaki, and, Mary, who is the wife of Qostantine Fotopolo.

His family was educated in the modern arts and sciences. His sons graduated from the famous Aintoura Institute. Of the sons, only Anthony married. He was a man of letters who wrote sentimental poems praising the beauties of Lebanon.

Catiana was able to speak six languages. She gave birth to Niqola, Chiristine, who is the wife of Rashid Ghaleb of Salima, Clota, who is the wife of Youssef al-Shaikhany of Bakfia, as well as Arazmia, Abatia and Tamz.

Mary gave birth to: Eskandar and Hilana who got married to a Frenchman and gave birth to Simona. The mother of Eskandar (i.e. Mary) is known for her favors and charity. She is the one who provided this information about her family.

At the request of the Archbishops of Qobros and Beirut, the Excellencies Youssef Ga'ga' and Tobia Oun, Franco Pasha issued an order to the Qa'em Maqam of Metn demanding the parents of the girls in the silk plants in Beirut withdraw them. He emphasized that this was necessary to prevent the mixing of the young men and women in those plants and to preserve the public morals.

In pursuit of this same cause, Archbishop Youssef Ga'ga' established a plant for unraveling silk. It belonged to the Bishopric and was located in Shaweia near Beit Shabab. In this factory, the girls of those areas and others worked. They did so because "they don't go far from home which would lead to bad experiences". Also, many girls from Salima worked there as was told to me by one of them. The girls used to attend Mass and say prayers in the Church of Saint George Bahardaq nearby where Archbishop Ga'ga' lived. For the same reason, Archbishop Ne'mat Allah Salwan established a plant in the village of Qa'qoor in 1900.

To my knowledge, the first factory established in Salima was the Karrkhana of the house of Anton. Fares and Girgis (George) Anton were the first. They established their plant in Salima in 1860. The house of Anton is one of the prestigious houses in Salima.

Next, a plant owned by the house of Maron was established. It was started by Khatar, Girgis and Mikhail As'ad Maron Bachaalany. Unfortunately, they suffered heavy losses due to the drop in the prices of silk caused by the war between France and Germany in 1870. They were forced to sell their properties to pay their debts and the plant was taken over by a trader from the Kafouri family from Choueir. It became known as "the Karrkhana of al-Kafouri". It was connected after this with the house of Wakim Bachaalany and then finally bought by Youssef Zaghloul.

Youssef and Anton Wakim established their plant in Ain Bu Atma and they practised silk trading for a long time. They were from one of the most prestigious and richest houses in Salima. They, too, finally suffered losses like the other silk traders in the country. After suffering his losses. the late Elias bin Youssef Wakim traveled to Brazil.

From the prestigious houses of Salima that practised the silk trade was the House of Shaiban Bachaalany. One of them, Fares Shaiban, had spent a period of time as a manager of the silk plant of the house of Tabet in al-Moat River (the River of Death). Most of the employees of this plant were from Salima. After the death of Fares Shaiban, he was succeeded by his brother, Tanous, who built a small plant in Salima with the partnership of the house of Wakim. It did not last long. Toward the end of the last century (1900), the sons of Fares: Habib, Ibrahim and Youssef Shaiban built a plant in Salima in Ain al-Rayhan. It's luck was better than other silk plants.

The well known Mahmoud and Amin Salman al-Masry built a silk plant. They were partners at the beginning then they divided it. Then their children practised silk trading and, still, one of their grandchildren, Mr. Shahin bin Mohammad Mahmoud, continues this trade today.

Abd Allah Hussein Saloum al-Masry established a plant in Rouaissa many years ago and still operates it today with his two sons, the two writers, Mohammad and Asaad. The first one migrated and became rich. He was the biggest help to his father.

There was also a silk trader, Selim al-Mar'ey, who, together with al-Zaghloul, Habib Fares Anton Hanna, established a plant in Kroum al-Hawa. After his death, his son 'Oql Habib kept the business going and it still continues today.

Among the silk plants that remained in business for a long time, was the plant of the late Tanious Bshour. He established it in Haql Farah as a partnership with his relative Wadee' Bshour. From what we know of his ability, courtesy, and wisdom, he managed the plant well and, like the other successful plants of Salima it was a great source of benefit to its people in those days.

Frequently there would be a change in the income of the people of Salima. It may have stemmed from the wages paid by the plant, or the price of wood fuel, or commissions paid to middlemen, or the wages of the muleteers. Whatever the change, still the value to these plants remained. And no matter what, the silk plants in Salima were of great importance. The people of Salima benefited from these plants. And it should be noted that ten plants in one town was no small matter.

Among those who came to Salima and leased some plants and managed them for a while was Boutros al-Asfar from Beirut and his son Ibrahim. They were an example to the people of great piety. And they were well known for granting their workers many rights. Also well known for his generosity and enthusiasm was Costantine bin Na'oum al-Khuri. His days in Salima were days of joy and happiness. He left in 1875. His father, Na'oum, had a silk plant in al-Bashoura.

Among those from Salima who had contact with owners of plants outside it were Mansour al-Khuri Nakouzy and Hanna Girgis. The first one was a dealer of the Khawaja Fertoni Portalis and his plants in Betaterr. Hanna Girgis al-Khuri handled some works in spite of his young age. He was able to learn some French from being in the house of these French people for so long. This helped him to become a successful guide for visiting tourists, as I will mention later.

Molhem Nohra was a clerk in the village. Later he spent about 20 years as a clerk in the plant of Mork in Ain Hamada.

Shahin Ghaleb, his cousin, Haikal, Youssef Elias, Boutros Shahin, Nasrallah al-Mazzmook (Father Peter), Ayub Gad'oon, Elias Mikhail Bu Oun and others worked in the Cocoons Choking Shop (Makhaneq of the Cocoons) in al-Swaideia that belongs to Portalis.

Boutros Shahin Boutros and his brother Ibrahim used to work in those Choking Shops (Makhaneq) for a long time. The first one died while working in Safita.

Now I mention what I can of the owners of the important national factories. By this I mean the plants, not of the Europeans, but of the Lebanese. This includes the plants established by the house of 'Oql Shadid (Matiyan), the house of Lahud (B'abadat), the house of Ghastin Bachaalany, the house of al-Khuri Girgis Laoun, the house of Ali Bu Ali (Bezbedin), the house of Mohammad Sabra al-A'warr Qarnayel, the house of Elias Tanous (Marj Qarnayel), the house of Molhem al-Khuri Rechmaya and his nephews (Falouga), Ghantous al-Qashma'ey (Bekefia), the house of Abdallah al-Khuri (Kenaiessa), the Bishopric of Qobross (Shaweia and Qa'qoor), the house of Jabr al-Ashqar, the house of al-Harbooq, the house of Tobia, the house of Hadifa (Beit Shabab), the house of Hashem (Frika), the house of Ransees Te'ma (Qarn al Hamra), and, the house of al Ashqar (House of al Kakoo and Ain 'Aar). The plants of these last mentioned people became modern plants for unraveling and weaving silk in both Lebanon and Brazil. Also, included in the list of Lebanese owned plants are those of the house of Alfons al Naqash and his sons (House of Mary and Ain Boudbess), Ya'kub Tabet and his sons (Nahr al Mout), the house of Khadra (Geonyah), the house of al Saad (ain Teraz), the house of Saleh Ne'ama (Maghouaya and Betadine), the house of Na'oum al Khoury, the house of al Gebeli, the house of al Tiyan (in Beirut), the house of Heikel (in al Damouz), the house of Shehadah (Gebil), that of Asaad Beik Karam (Ardah Zegharta), and many other houses than those in Lebanon .

After reaching its zenith, the silk trade declined considerably. So, too, did the raising of silkworms and the silk season. The decline was caused by many things, but the most important one was the migration of people and the resulting lack of a labor force. Then, too, came the international economic war, the invention of industrial silk which then developed rapidly and competed with natural silk. There is currently an attempt at a revival of those seasons and plants. We know not what the future will hold for them.

COURAGEOUS, FAMOUS, AND DOWN-TO-EARTH

Chapter 13

Many men of virtue, notability, courage, and strong conviction have grown up in Salima. They were its judges in reproaches and accidents, its assistance in times of trial and catastrophe. And. always, they were an object of pride and nobility.

It is known that countries can be happy or miserable. They can evolve higher or sink. If good people comprise its population, it will develop and flourish. They will be a source of pride for the country. The contrary will cause the country's decline.

The same can be said for big and small families, villages, and, cities as well as kingdoms and countries. This is what happens in all eras. I say this based on what we have read in history books, what we have learned from talking to people about the past, and what we have personally observed in our own time.

There is an expression that I really like. The late Tanious Beshour said it with sadness about what has happened to Salima… "Every time a wise or a rich man grows up in Salima, he leaves." When he comes back home as a returning immigrant, he spends his money in our country, Tanious Beshour would say "This small village is lucky. God sent her so-and-so, and her people took advantage and benefited from him." He was also right when he said that countries don't increase and prosper. It is the people who make it do so. A country cannot even exist without the working people. They are the ones who have strong convictions, courage, and fame. They are its spiritual strength and its economical wealth. And hereafter, we will mention as much as we know of such people who lived in Salima.

Of the Bachaalany family, in the past, there was Andrea bin Negm I. Also, there was his son, Abou Andrea Negm. He was a family elder as well as a prelude of the village's other important men. They were all men of decency, good opinion, knowledge and eloquence. Abou Andrea Negm was also the chancellor of the Lam's princes, especially of the famous Prince Haidar. So, also, was his son, Daher who was no less wise or well acquainted than his father. Both Negm Ibn Daher and his paternal cousin Andrea Girgis believed in high standard and moral principles. Father Joseph Bachaalany (al Khury Youssef al Bachaalany) was a man of note and great knowledge. His son, Father John (al Khury Hanna) was also known for his virtue. He was dedicated to helping his relatives. He was a doctor, like his father. His brother, Abou 'Okl al Khury, was one of the great men of reason.

The same can be said about Elias Abou 'Asli, Mikhail Abdou, Youssef Saadallah, Assaf Girgis Negm and many others, all men of purpose and logic. Fares bin Youssef, was the first Sheikh of Reconciliation during the mutasarrifi-yah era (the era of the Christian Governor General administration).

152

Our grandfather, Tanous Freha Bachaalany was known as a peace loving man, serving his country with patriotism and integrity. This was especially true when he was the trustee and the Sheikh of Reconciliation for the village, before and after the period of the mutasarrifiyah. His family relied on him in financial matters because he was rich at that time. During the day of the Lam's Princes and the Christian governing era, the governors used to come to his small house which still remains today. He and his brother, Girgis Freha, bought it from the Tiyan family, residents of Salima.

The same has to be said about Bishop Youssef Geagea, the archbishop and others. His sons Abdou, Girgis, and Faragallah followed in his footsteps.

In the notable Bachaalany houses, Abdou Agha Nohra al 'Eriyan grew up and I will speak of him in more detail later. So, too, did his nephew (sister's son), Nohra Sweed and his son Molhem. They too became Reconciliation Sheikhs after Tanous Freha and Fares bin Youssef. Then came Fares Shaiban and his brothers, Tanous and Youssef. Fares was given the title "Noble" the same day he became director of the Tabets' factory in Nahr al Mout (River of Death). He left a huge inheritance to his sons, Habib, Ibrahim, and Youssef. That bestowed fame on them along with their many acquaintants. This especially applied to Ibrahim who was famous for his courage and generosity. Other noble families in Salima include that of Youssef and Antone Wakim. They were well known at that time for their wealth and many connections. They owned a silk factory which was of great benefit to the people of the town as were their plants in other places. After them, we must mention Elias bin Youssef Wakim whose title was "Beik" being an administrative officer of Lebanon. Also, we must include the house of Maroune, his son, Asaad, as well as Asaad's sons. All were outstanding men of Salima.

Of the house of Nakouzy, was Mansour al Khoury, famous for being high minded and possessing great knowledge. He was well known as a man of his word, devoted to public service, and, never afraid to speak the truth. Then came his son Ibrahim Mansour, who was eloquent. He was a good speaker and his audience never grew tired of listening to his long talks. His family always consulted his opinion. Hanna Girgis al Khoury was known for his honesty, good manners, and free thinking.

Shahin Ghaleb was known by his boldness in defending his country and his family's rights. He was also highly regarded for his popular Arabic poems which were handed down, mouth to mouth, during evening talks.

Then, there was Girgis Saad, Nassef al Khoury and his son, Youssef, Asaad Sabra, the father of Father Joseph and 'Okl Genid. There was also Mansour Kanaan and his son, Daher with his son, the lawyer, Mansour Daher, and Nassef al Hadari.

The house of Anton was important in Salima and in other villages. During Ibrahim Pasha's era (1829-1840) Anton abou Anton was in the service of the princes. His son Fares grew up in Prince Haidar's house. He learned writing from the famous Sheikh Eid Abi Hatem. He was in charge of several responsibilties in Qaymiya, where Prince Mourad and Prince Youssef Ali resided in al Metn. He also estalished a silk plant with his brother Girgis which served the people of Salima well. His brother, Girgis was a noteworthy person, a smooth talker and the manager of a silk plant for a long time. We will talk about his children later in another chapter. Also well known was Habib and Anton Fares with their children.

Mourad Zein was famous in his day. The princes of Salima used to rely on him to manage their business, especialy after they left and went to Bekafeya. I have in my files correspondance between them. The letters show his sound judgment and his good organization. The house of Zein was known in Salima for their good manners and peace loving ways. Moderation was their guiding principle. They played the role of mediator and peacemaker. Their children and grand children did likewise.

We will talk in detail in another chapter about the Kassabs and their influence on the princes. We will discuss Girgis Abdou Gafal who was very noteworthy. There was also Daoud bin As'ad and his son Fares one of the generous immigrants in United States. In another chapter, we will talk about Kassab family members who migrated to other places.

We will deal with the notables of al Khawaja or al Hadad family. We will discuss Anton al Sabagh, his descendants. We will talk of the Khoury Moussa house. Also, we will talk about Youssef Mehana al Hadad (Abou Gohar) and Saada Mikhail al Hadad, and Asaad & Naseef Younes al Hadad. We will discuss al Khoury Constantine, the Hadad house.

Tanious Hanna Beshour was one of the notables of great merit. He educated his family with sound principles. He left his elder son Tawfik in charge, raising his brothers on those same principles. There was also Ibrahim al Khoury Beshour, one of Salima's great men. His descendants were very generous immigrants. Youssef Metri al Zaghloul, with great effort and dedication, built one of Salima's greatest houses.

Another great man of strong conviction from the Masrys, was Abdel Hadi Abou Ali and his brother, Salman bin Mohamed. He was succeeded by his sons, Mahmoud and Amin, who gained even more notoriety and wealth. Then, they became the respected elders of the family for a long time. Their grand children still preserve that legacy. Among the most respected and well known were Shahin bin Shahin, Selim Amin, Hussein Saloum, Haidar al Zar'ouni, Daher Matar, and others that we will mention later.

The Said's house had its celebrities. They include Abou Hassan Agha Said, Ali Beshir and his son, Qassem. Qassem gained prestige thanks to his own efforts and those of his generous sons. The same is said about Naguib, the son of his brother Beshir. Also among them were Selim bin Qassem Daher Hussein, known as Selim al Gari, and Khattar Ali Soliman. Both of them are members of Nayel Said's house. Also noteworthy was Abdulallah bin Hassan from the Bou Ali Said house. We can say the same for Qassem Said who was succeeded by his son, Selim Hussein. We can also cite Hemdan Emad and his grandson, Rashid Nasr Eddine.

Their Courage And Strength.

Many people in Salima were famous for their courage and strength. This was true for Shahin Faseida Bachaalany. He witnessed a fight between the Hatoums from Kafr Salwan and the Masrys from Salima. Accompanied by his wife, Mary (Mariam) who was known as al Hamra, they attacked and fought with the Masrys. They brought luck and, together, they won. At that time people were divided into parties. The Bachaalany were with the Masrys' party. Shahin Bachaalany was even Shahin Masry.

Al Hamra was known for her strength and bravery. So much so that people were saying: "Whoever is not an al Hamra descendant, is not a man." Her descendants were: Abdou bin Youssef Shahin, Da'ebess bin Tanious Shahin, Asaad Maroun al Henawi, and Hanna with Negm Youssef Nasrallah, Shahin Boutros, and others.

Abdou bin Youssef was a couragous knight who had no fear of death. He joined the cavalery during the Prince Haidar era, that of the Christian governor (1843 –1854). He also was one of the companions of Abou Hassan Said from Salima in serving at the Mass. Abdou was bloody and violent. He has been accused of murder. The government almost caught him in 1859 but he hid. On a Sunday, he entered Mar 'Abda Church in Baabada to attend Mass. The soldiers saw him and stayed outside the Church waiting for him to come out. When he was finished and was about to go out, he saw the soldiers. He put his hands on his carbine, which he always had, holding his pistols, and shouted "Let me pass!". The soldiers ran from him. Abdou mounted his horse and rode away.

Asaad Fares was corpulent. He had a throaty voice and was known for his strength and horsemanship. It has been said that he carried the Gebeil gate on his shoulders when he was on a mission for Prince Haidar. The prince sent him to a youth house to collect the government taxes. People were attending the Sunday Mass. He stopped them all from leaving the Church until they promised to pay him at once.

Ibrahim Shiban, the maternal grand-son of Abdou, was famous for his courage and equestrian riding ability.

De'ebas bin Tanious was an experienced and courageous knight. He was famous in both Baalbek and Batroun as being an outstanding horse back rider. He was also good with the javelin and the lance. He surpassed all of his contemporaries in his ability. He kept company with the Harafesha Princes in Baalbek and they respected him. He had a strange power with the javelin thanks to his strong arms. Stones would be broken or a piece of wood would be penetrated if he hit them with his javelin, even at a long distance. In Bchaaleh and Salima , they still talk about his shots. Other interesting tales about him include the following: Whenever people under arrest would be passing by Salima, in order to preserve his rural sense of pride at showing hospitality to people, he would loosen their bonds. He believed it was such a shame that any person should pass by the mountain with his hands tied. One day when he was walking by the stirrup of the Governor of Beirut, he arrived at the old bridge across the Ibrahim River (the bridge is still standing and it is an arch with a steep incline up and a steep decline down). De'ebas unfastened the horse's saddle. He then ran with the horse until he safely crossed the bridge. The Governor was astonished at this.

There are other heroic and courageous deeds as reported from the original documents and legal information. There are the tales of Abdou Agha–Nahra al Erian Bachaalany. He foretold certain things to Prince Beshir's father and, so, gained privilege and a strong reputation is his day. His father was courageous. He attended the wickedness of a "Maksah". He was assisted by the Moureg Katars. He killed a slave who had killed his paternal cousin. He did so out of revenge. As part of the revenge he ate of the slave. The revenge was a savage tradition at the time but it is not devoid of courage. The information about Abdou is considerable. Here is just a summary of what we know.

Abdou Nahra was an orphan. He joined the service of Prince Beshir in 1803 through his governess Marhaba Bachaalany. Thus, he grew up in the Prince's palace "Mir Yakhour" with Elias Abou Ragheb Bachaalany. Abdou brought luck and victory when he attended Lahafd battle in 1850. He had accompanied the Prince to Egypt in 1821. While there he was given the title "Agha" by Mohamed Ali Pasha for his courage. He was the first one to be granted this title in Mount Lebanon. He had also been present at al Mokhtara in 1825 and at Sanour in 1829.

After the exile of the Prince in 1840, he live at Chiyah with his wife Korgoba. Since they had no children to inherit their estate, everything they had, properties and large land holdings worth thousands of Liras, went to the Church of Saint Michael in Salima and its school. Some also went to the poor of the Diocese of Beirut.

Abdou Nahra died in 1865 and his tomb is located at the Church of Saint Michael. He was a venerable and courageous man. He was tall with a large build. We will give more details about him later.

In the house of Said, there were also courageous men such as the descendants the house of Bou Ali. Bou Hassan Said was distinguished for his courage. He was appointed governor of Nablous. He used to beat the drum with his legs, a trandition in those days. He also was appointed the District Commisioner of the government in Bakefya and Bermana at Kabashia. There was one person under his supervision from Salima. After him, we should mention Ali Beshir who grew up and was distinguished for his horsemanship, skill with the lance, and fencing. Elias Mikhail Bou'un painted a picture for him portraying these warrior characteristics. The painting still exists. It is kept in the home of his grandchildren.

Selim al Gari was audacious and gutsy. He became famous after one of the conflicts between the Druze and the Army of the Ottoman Empire at Horan.

From the Masry's house there is a group of courageous and strong people who were well known, such as Molhem Negm from Rouissa. He was tall. There are stories of his bravery. Next, there was Hussein Ali Hassoun who had a strong forearm and was the most charming young man in Salima. Also, there were the sons of Mahmoud Salman. They were delightful young men, especially Rashid who was distinguished for his courage shown in Mexico during the revolution.

The Kassab sons were divided in two groups. The first was a group of men who were working in politics and the governmental administration of the Princes of Salima. The second group consisted of men of the lance. They were known for the strength. One of them was called Zamel Kassab. He was so well known that the following story was told about him. Once, in the town square in Salima, he was trying to catch a big bull that ran away from its owner. At the same time, the Prince was watching him from a balcony of the castle. Zamel was holding the bull by its ear. The the bull bolted away. The Prince yelled to him: What a pity, Zamel!" Zamel answered him: "It's not my fault, Sir. It's the fault of the bull's ear. Then he raised his hand with the ear in it!

Some members of the Nakouzy family joined the service of the Prince. This included people like Okl Guenid and Okl bin Elias and others. They, too, were courageous. Ibrahim Mansour al Khoury was well known for riding horses. Anton Fares was known for his courage and strong forearm. He used to pick up hard almonds and crush them with his fingers. He used to tie and squeeze coin until it bent so much that the letters were erased. He would lift up many making it look as if he was raising a piece of bread. He could lift the heavy Ibrahim Rifle with the fingers of his right hand. He performed many other signs of strength.

Also showing how much courage there was in these men is illustrated in the following incident involving a chase by the men of the Wassa Pasha government. Asaad Maroun was famous for his skills as a knight, especially fencing and horse back riding. He was in the service of Prince Haidar of Salima. Asaad had a strong influence on the Prince for the favours he did for him and the country. Accordingly, the Prince promoted him to the rank of Colonel (Bikbashi, sometimes pronounced Mekbashi). Once, during the government of the Nasary District commissioner, the Prince sent Asaad to Koura. It was a difficult mission because Asaad had to defend the honor of the Prince and the honor of his own sword. Dozens of men attacked him, there in the town. They tried to take away his sword. They were beating his hand with knives, again and again, but they could not break his grip. When he went back to the Prince, he was warmly greeted. And not in the usual manner. The Prince turned his eyes to the audience and said: "Do not be surprised at my generosity to this man. He has saved my honor and preserved my dignity. He sacrificed himself for me."

Among the descendants of Asaad Maroun, there is Samih and his grand-son Asaad Girgis Maroun. Asaad Girgis was not of a large build but was nonetheless strong as well as very courageous. That was seen on the day of the funeral of Tanious Shahin in the Salima square. He was jumping on men's shoulders to reach his adversaries. There is also information saying that he mastered the Lebanese popular poem style. Furthermore, he is known for his beautiful calligraphy. His son Girgis was also strong. So too were Selim Khattar and Daher Mikhail who were likewise descendants of this family. Estephan Moussa Nofal and his nephew Estephan Metri were both also known for being strong and brave.

The sister of Asaad, name Terazia, had a son, Shahin Boutros. He was strong and has survived many mishaps which is a proof of his strength and courage. Among his sons was Tanious Shahin who was previously mentioned for being the head of the local youth and the President of the Saint George organization. He was tall, with the dignity and character of a lion. Other members of this family were also courageous and strong.

Hanna and Negm Youssef Nasrallah, maternal descendants of al Hamra, were brave knights. They became famous after joining Prince Heidar's cavalry. Later we will talk about the various incidents of his life which are proof of his sacrifice and boldness. The governmental service of that Prince is outstanding.

ABOUT THE IMMIGRANTS
AND THE EXPATRIATES
Chapter 14

Everybody knows that emigration is an old habit of the Easterners. The Phoenicians taught people how to emigrate for trade and business. Their caravans traveled by land and their boats sailed by sea. The town of Carthage, which they built on the north African coast, is one of their traveling footprints and evidence of their emigration. The Lebanese used to migrate because of oppression and wars. They migrated with Crusaders to Jerusalem and Malta. Then some of them came back home when they again found injustice and oppression. Some of them migrated to Europe for education, trade or other reasons.

It has been told that the first one from the Bachaalany family to migrated to Europe, was Abou Youssef Rezk bin Abi Rezk Bachaalany. He did so after his brother Sheikh Younes was killed. He had to leave his family and his country. He suffered through the difficulties of traveling by sea, which was hard in those days. He visited Paris where the King treated him generously. He met the traveler De La Roque. He received permission to go to Istanbul with a letter of recommendation from the King of France to the Turkish Sultan.

Among other members of the Bachaalany family to travel was the monk Anthony. He became a monk in 1752 and died in 1792. He was known as the Director Hanania bin abi Matar Saab Bachaalany. He went to Rome to gain support for his monasticism and was honoured with a personal audience with Pope Pius VI in 1772. He travelled for a second and a third time. In 1782 he received a recommendation from the Apostolic See. He also received the approval of many monastic orders and from the monarchs of Europe. He collected charity for his monastic order. He also went through Malta where he received many donations and support. He mastered Italian and other European languages. He spent most of his life in Europe. He died in Spain in 1792. He was zealous and honest. Also, we know that he was a relative of the Mazmouk family in Salima and used the visit them.

The First Immigrant From Salima

Colombus discovered America and Europeans migrated to it. The first of the Easterners to migrated there was the priest Kelmedani from Mousal. His trip was published in the magazine "Mashreq". He traveled throughout the American Continent in the late seventeenth century. Others may have also migrated there. Emigration from Syria and Lebanon started in large numbers in the last quarter of the nineteenth century . The very first one who migrated to America from our country was Anthony bin Youssef Daher Safi Abu Attallah Bachaalany. Our fathers told us about him. Then, Dr. Philip al Hitti, a professor from New York, found a book talking about Anthony Bachaalany, our fellow patriot and in-law. Dr. Hitti translated and published it. Not long ago, we read the English version of the book when Dr. Hitti paid us a visit in Salima. Here is a summary.

Anthony was born in the village of Salima on August 22nd, 1827. He was baptized eight days later in the Church of Saint John. His mother was Taqla, the daughter of Hassan Kassab. He had six brothers who died young and unmarried. The same happened to him and there are no direct descendants. Once when Anthony was 12 years old he went to Beirut where he worked with his brother in the Tayouna silk plant, near al Chiyah. He made contact with some

Europeans and was their guide during their tourist trips. When his brother Daoud grew up, he worked with him in this tourism service as a cook. Then he became a translator. He became a tour operator after mastering English and Italian.

Later, he came back to Salima as an adult and became rich. He asked to marry the daughter of one of his in-laws called Shemouna bint Youssef Nasrallah Abi Attallah. She accepted his proposal of marriage because of his tender youth and politeness. Plus, he was also rich! Her relatives, however, took note of his apparent lukewarm religious feelings. Also, they did not care for his associations with Protestants. They did not accept him and they compelled the girl to reject his proposal. Consequently, Anthony left Salima, and shortly afterwards, he left Beirut while in the company of a group of tourists.

He arrived in England. In 1854, he went to the United States by boat and arrived in Boston, Massachusetts.

A few days later he moved to New York city with a friend. He enrolled in Columbia University and learned the English language and higher studies in science. His professors and fellow students admired him. He was clever, courageous and gentle. His professors nicknamed him "School Champion" because he could deliver speeches in English at school festivities. The audience could not believe that he was Lebanese and not American. What was remembered, however, during his stay in his new country, was how he wore his Lebanese clothes and the Morrocan Tarboosh on his head.

Sadly, our hero died two years after enrolling at the university. Strangely, he died on his birthday, August 22nd, 1856. The university headmaster wrote a book in English talking about his life. The book has 250 pages. Dr. Philip Hitti, a Doctor in Philosophy and a professor of the Eastern Studies, came across it at Columbia University. It talked about this young translator's origins, his age, the reason for his immigration, his noble anscestors and his village, Salima. He also mentioned some of Anthony's relatives, especially Hanna Saadallah Bachaalany, his brothers and sisters, as well as his mother.

In the book there is a picture of Anthony Bachaalany, written in English in his own handwriting, inscribed to a friend. He is wearing the clothes so well known in Lebanon in the middle of the nineteeth century. On his head is the Morrocan Tarboosh, which has a large tassle. On his outergarment you can see the button holes. A shirt appears in the middle of his chest, around his neck a pressed collar with a European tie. Around his waist is a wide belt. Because this is just an upper photograph of him, there is nothing showing of his large trousers, his leg swaddles of silky lace, which he wore, as did his brothers, when he was in Salima.

From the details in this book, his grave was located. It is a tomb especially made for him in the Mount Olive Cemetary in Brooklyn, New York. On his tomb is engraved a picture of the Morrocan Tarboosh, the slogan of our country and the picture of a lion, a viper and a lamb. The picture of the lion is to show he was courageous. The snake shows he was clever and the lamb represents his gentleness. Then the engraving shows his name in English: Anthony Bachaalany along with the dates for his birth and death. In 1919, the immigrants Shiban Tanious, Elias Youssef Shiban, and Khalil Girgis Khalil visited his grave. All of them are from the same Bachaalany family.

According to my files and documents, Anthony wrote about the wealth and opulence in America when he arrived there. He was studing Arabic as well as English. Also, he wrote to his relatives informing them that he was sick and that the doctor had predicted that he would die within three days, which is precisely what happened. The newspapers for that day which reached Beirut told of his death. They talked about his intelligence and ability. Anthony's father was one of the wise men and notables of Salima. He had a nice callygraphy and writing style. He was one of the trustees of the Church of Saint John and he visited Patriarch Youssef Hebeish as we previously mentioned.

Youssef Daher died in August of 1839 and left seven young sons. Anthony was one of them. His mother, Taqla bint Hassan from Bani Kassab al Mashayekh, raised the boys. When she lost her husband and the boys, she was filled with mourning and sadness. It is said that she locked her house and threw the key off the roof saying: " Here is the key, God!" She was out of patience because of her losses and was almost going to deny God. Her remaining boys met the following fates: Daoud was accompanying tourists to Egypt and other places. He came back to Beirut and no one knows where he was buried. Ibrahim was the supervisor of Anton's factory in Salima. He died in Sharkh al Shabab on September 26th, 1860. Daher died on December 10th, 1848.

We have the list of presents given to Naseef Bo'oun on his wedding in 1843. The names of his brothers, Anthony, Daoud and Ibrahim are mentioned. His mother, Taqla, died at the beginning of August, 1882. It is so strange that Anthony was born on August 22nd , and his father died in August, 1839. His house in Salima is still there. It is just as it was when his father was still alive. The owner of it now is the family of Girgis Khalil Daham Bachaalany.

Our old ancestors migrated but they did not go outside Lebanon and Syria. A number of them went and lived in the places of the princes, in Beit ed Dine, Ghazir, Bekafya, Shamlan and other places. Others were traders, and travelled to Damascus, Beirut, Tarablous, and other towns where the caravans went. When the silk factories were established they went to them to make a living. They worked in groups and they lived happy. They were content with the little that they had. They came back to Salima for feast days and other celebrations. Then, along came the idea of migrating to the regions of Egypt. They started to prosper. So, a group from Befefya migrated there and they succeeded. Then, from Salima, in 1869, Molhem Azar Khashan travelled to Egypt. Later he came back home. Also, Khalil, Guenid and Said Guenid went in 1870. All of these men are members of the Nakouzy family.

After a few years, members of the Bachaalany family left Salima. Estephan bin Metri Moussa went to upper Egypt and its countryside in 1876. There is a story that he came back to Lebanon in disguise during the Orabi movement. Reportedly, he then went back to Egypt. Some years later, his brothers, Moussa and Hanna, went there trying to bring him from the countryside to Cairo. However, it didn't take long before he went back to the interior where he lived with Bedouins. He practiced simple medecine. There was never any news about him after that. He was one of our strong young men.

In 1877, Khalil Boutros Wakim travelled to Egypt. Others who did the same include Fares and Maroun Khattar Asaad, Ne'ma Daham, Nader Gad'oun, Asaad Youssef Ghaleb, Mikhail Abou 'Asala, and Saab Fares Saab. All are from the Bachaalany family. But they did not stay there for long. They came back, probably around 1882, because of the Orabi Pasha revolution. From the Nakouzy family many have migrated, like Youssef Hanna Guenid and his brother Abdou, Ragi and Hanna Ghandour, Shahin Saab and his brother Tarbeya, Francis and Eskander Rahal, Selim 'Azar, Asaad 'Okl Elias, Ghastin and Mandar Elias Mansour, Abdou Habib, and Mansour 'Okl. Mansour 'Okl first traveled in 1888, then came back. He went on to travel back in 1893 and returned the final time in 1920. He died a few years later in Salima. At that time, the main activity drawing them in Egypt was the tobacco trade and the production of cigarettes.

Immigration to America

In the year 1888, a number of Lebaneses immigrants came back from American countries as winners. However, due to the lack of job opportunities and of security, it was difficult to make a living. There was injustice from the government. People's debts increased. Hunger became intense. So it was that immigration increased. Modern civil plagues reached us. The Lebanese found an outlet for their ambitions. A group from Salima includes Mikhail Elias Abou Assaly, Naguib Molhem Nohra, Ibrahim Shiban, and Shaker Hanna Youssef, all from the Bachaalany's. From other families there was Ghaleb Shahin Nakouzy, Hussein Ali Hassoun Masry, Maguid bou Daher and Fares Amin from the Saids.

In that year, Abdallah Habib Saloum Bachaalany travelled to Brazil by the Taraboulos route. Meanwhile, Naguib Molhem and Ibrahim Shiban went to Marseilles. Naguib came back home after many years. Ibrahim went to Algeria and his brother Habib joined him. They later returned together to Salima. Mikhail bou 'Assly and Ghaleb Shahin went to Buenos Aires. Shaker Hanna Youssef went there too. Later he moved to Brazil and then travelled around the American states, untimately ending up in Africa. Because of all his travels, our maternal uncle, Mansour Ghanatious, called him "Naval Sinbad". Maguid Abou Daher and Hussein Hassoun went to Buenos Aires. Fares Amin came back from Marseilles to Salima with Ibrahim Shiban.

This is all the available information we can provide about the early years of our immigrants abroad. Later, immigration took fifty percent of the Lebanon population to foreign places. It became the material and spiritual force of our people. We will continue talking about Salima's immigrants in later chapters. We will try to provide the latest information after checking on them in their new locations.

SPIRITUAL AND SCIENTIFIC LEADERS

Chapter 15

In previous chapters we wrote at length about our leaders and the guardians of our heritage. They were the ones who created our civilization, our culture, and our reputation. They were a blessing from God for Salima. It remains for us now to cite some of our other spiritual and literary leaders. We will write, in brief, about those from Salima who contributed to Lebanon's spiritual and cultural areas. While in previous chapters we wrote in detail about the religious movements and spiritual accomplishments of our village, here we will focus on Salima's participation in monasticism. Salima's past is evidence of its renaissance and great concern about spiritual values.

Monasticism

1. **The first Monk** from the Bachaalany family that we know of was the leader, Hanania, of the Antonian Monasticism. We mentioned him briefly in the previous chapter, "The Immigrants And The Expatriates" but we will talk about him in more detail in the Section Four which deals with the kinship of the Bachaalany families.

2. **Pastor Zakaria Ne'ma al Salamaoui (Bachaalany).** He received his monk's hood, on November 20, 1742, from the hands of Father Bernardus, the headmaster of the Tamish Monastry. This was recorded in the register of the Louisa Monastery. Also, in the book, The History Of Monasticism, written by Father Louis Belibel, (Part II, page 145), his name was mentioned: "Among the names of the monks who lived in the monastic community … in the seperation time, 1753, is Pastor Zakareya al Salamaoui." Also, the name of Pastor Zakareya was mentioned in the kinship tree which was dictated by Negm Andrea Bachaalany, the in-law of Pastor Zakareya, which we preserve in our files. We do not know when he died, but we know that he is the son of Elias Ne'ma from Andrea's house.

3. **Pastor Mobarak al Salamaoui.** His name is Girgis bin Fares al Henawy Bin Moussa Youssef Rezk Nasr Bachaalany. He joined the Halab Monasticism on June 29, 1828. He wore the monk's hood at the Monastery of Saint Peter in Karim al Teen. This was under Father Boutros Karaita al Ashqar. Pastor Mobarak became the headmaster of the Louisa Monastery for a duration of three years, then of the Sayedat al Tala in Deir al Qamar for 14 years. After that, he entered the seclusion of the previously mentioned Monastery of Saint Peter. He remained there until he died. He was buried there on January 22, 1889. He was deeply devoted to the rules of monasticism law, forsaking worldly pleasure, and safeguarding the monastic properties. However, some of the monks in the Louisa Monastery were jealous and envied him. They added to his burden. But he was a strong and courageous man. He made renovations to the monastery. He also purchased large additional properties for the monastery after paying off all its debts, about 70,000 piastres.

4. **Pastor Abdel Mesih Bachaalany.** His name is Shebli bin Saab Fares Youssef Al Henawy Bin Moussa, the nephew of Pastor Mobarak who we just mentioned. He joined the Halab Monasticism, taking his vows under his paternal uncle. But his mother opposed his choice and called on Pastor Mobarak for help, hoping he would persuade him to withdraw. Pastor Mobarak answered her: "This is none of my business. I neither forbid him nor encourage him." Thus, she returned to her home empty handed. Her son obeyed the calling of this celestial order. He was of a gentle nature with a clean reputation. He was lovable. He served at the Sabnaya Church, near Baabada. While there, he baptized some Shihab Princes, according to what I read in the records of the Church's Bible. He died after an accident, falling from the roof of the Saint Elias Shoiya Monastery. He was burried there in February, 1889.

5. Pastor Igidios al Salamaoui. His name is Geadios bin Saadallah Abi Attallah. He was born in Salima. Like those mentioned above, he joined the same monasticism on May 14, 1836, at the Karim el Teen Monastery. He received the monk's hood from the hands of Father Francis Poiret, the Monastery's director. According to the monastery register, he died and was buried there. But from what I personally know, is that he died in Salima in the house of Father Boutros Youssef al Mazmouk, his nephew (sister's son). It may be that he was ill and frequented his sister's house, and then, died at the monastery.

6. Pastor Arsanios al Salamaoui. His name is Arsanios bin Elias Abi Attallah Bachaalany. He was a pure man, tall, with a nice voice. He joined the Halabian Monasticism and spent the majority of his life serving the congregations in Beshara. This was during the era of Bishop Boutros al Boustani. The bishop used him as his confessor because of his piety. He died in Monastery of Saint Peter in Karim el Teen on April 14, 1912.

7. Pastor Francis al Salamaoui. He is Francis, son of Father Yohanna (John) al Khoury Nakouzy. He was born in Salima and joined the Halabian monasticism . On the morning of Thursday, June 30, 1860, he was killed in Deir al Qamar with many of his fellows as they were being slaughtered. This information is according to the register of the Louisa Monastery and the register of the municipal presidency.

8. Pastor Mobarak Bachaalany. His name is Naseef bin Wakim Boutros Bachaalany. He was born in Salima and joined the Lebanese monasticism. He was the President of the Kahlouneya Monastery and provided the religious services at its schools in Shabania village, Ras al Metn, al 'Abadia, Mariam and al Hawash. He died suffering from hemophilia at the Saint Moussa al Dowar Monastery in 1880. He was a genuine ascetic. He is the brother of Anton and Youssef Wakim.

9. Brother Beshara Bachaalany. His name was mentioned in the register of the Antonian Monasticism at Mar Sha'ia Monastery, as follows: "Brother Beshara from Salima village, Ibn Yohanna Bachaalany. The identified came to our Monastery of Saint Anthony in Baabada, wore the novice's clothes, and once his training period ended, we legally cast his lots, and we had the recommendations of acceptance from the priests and brothers. Then he received his monk's hood from the hand of Father Gregorious al Kanaysi, the President of the mentioned Monastery during the era of Father Superior Egnadious Shoufi, the eloquent, most respected, on April 2, 1823." Then, there was also this text "Brother Beshara Salima Bachaalany flew up to the merciful God, may he be exalted, after having served as a monastic for 63 years. He was armed with secrets and his spiritual necessities according to the orders of the Church of Peter. His death occurred at the Saint Domt Romia Monastery (Al Metn). He was burried there, the funeral being presided over by the Father Superior of the Samaan Blouni Monastery, on June 10, 1886."

10. Brother Lebaos Salima Bachaalany. He passed away after 25 years of service at the monastery. He died at our monastery called Saint Roukz Dahr el Hussein. He was armed with God's secrets. This was during the Presidency of Youssef al Baabadati (The General Superior of the Antonian Monasticism) in 1863.

11. The Capuchin, Father Francis Zein. He is Daher the son of the subdeacon Girgis Daher Zein. He was born at the end of January, 1861. He was baptized by Father Boutros Farahat al Asmar from al Daliba. He was the parish priest in Salima at that time. Father Francis Zein's baptism name was Yohanna (John). His godfather was Elias Abou 'Assly Bachaalany and his godmother was Hannah, the wife of his uncle Mourad Zein. He was educated at the Capuchin Fathers' School in Salima. From his early childhood days, he showed a strong desire to join the monastic life. He was sent to Europe where he completed his basic studies, then he continued his education by studying Latin, Italian, and French, along with Philosophy and Theology. After his ordination, he came back to the Middle East where he spent many years in the Beirut Monastery. A few years ago, he died in Italy where he had been living during his final years. To the end, he kept performing the duties and deeds of a virtuous monk and a true priest. In the chapter on the Zein family in Section III we will refer to his life in more detail.

There is a beautiful family heirloom which is a picture of Father Francis' family. It shows his father, mother, brothers and two sisters. I saw a copy of it in an Italian book called "The History of Capuchin Monasticism". The photograph was presented in a section where they wrote about this holy family which has produced such a virtuous monk.

In reading the biographies of these monks, it is very clear that what produced so many vocations was the good example of earlier monks. It seems that each monk who joined the monastic order was following the strong effects of a monk who preceded him. And, he, in turn, was the example for one who came after him. What a strong impact they had on the spirituality of society and the eras that developed. We are sorry to say that Salima today is a far cry from that religious society of the past. The village that contributed so much in the ecclesiastic past, today, has no monks and only a single nun, Sister Madelaine. She is the daughter of Shahin Ghaleb Nakouzy. At present, there is not even a single seminarian responding to the call of the priesthood. So it is that Salima has lost the great force of its spiritual powers.

New Fields Of Learning

Since the middle of last century, the Lebanese emphasized the learning of languages and the value of higher education. Some of the boys of Salima studied at various schools, such as, Ain Waraka and Mar Abda Harharya which were the most famous Ecclesiastical Maronite schools. Some attended the famous Ain Toura School. There was, also, the great boarding school of Our Lady of Lourdes of the Capuchin priests, especially during the eras of Father Joseph Peter and that of Father Anton al Asmar. There was also the Lebanese school of Saint Joseph in Qornet Chahouane, the Debs school of the Hekma Institute, the Jesuit school in Beirut, the National School in Baabadat, the Great Lebanon School in Salima, and many others.

Then, there were those who became a savant, professor, writer, poet, journalist, doctor, lawyer and engineer. Others became traders and other job careers and industries either locally or where they migrated.

The Lawyers from Salima. The following are attorneys who were born and raised in Salima. They are: Youssef Shiban Bachaalany, Habib Fares Anton, his brother Anton Fares, Tanous Freha Bachaalany, his son Youssef Freha, Youssef Hanna al Khoury, Mansour Daher Mansour, and Pedro Khoury.

Youssef Shiban was intelligent and hard working. He studied on his own and learned much by adaptation and actually practising law before the Lebanese courts. This was in the days when no certification was needed to practise law. The most famous lawyer at that time and in these regions was Tanious Abou Nadar from Beskinta.

We previously mentioned how both Habib and Anton Fares acquired higher education. Lately they have been performing as defense attorneys. Habib took a leave from his practise and went on to study law in French and Arabic here in Lebanon as well as in Egypt. He also mastered municipal law and appelate law. He had some memorable cases that he handled because of his courage and intelligence. He was a lawyer, a journalist, a writer, a poet, and a farmer, all at the same time! His two sons followed in their father's footsteps in the legal field. His son Felix Fares practised law for a while, and his son Emil Fares is still practising today.

Concerning Tanous Freha Bachaalany, he is the brother of the author of this book. He studied law under the tutelage of Selim Beik al Ma'oushi and Mikhail Afendi Eid al Bostani. Both of them were very famous at the beginning of this century. He was also trained by other lawyers. He was the first one to ever be appointed to a Lebanese court right after the Bar Exam. The famous Bishop Youssef Negm said "Tanous Freha is a rising star." In fact, he passed his exam before a special committee held in Beitedeen. It included Selim Baz, a unique lawyer at that time. Mohamed Abou Ezz El Dine was one of the famous Lebanese geniuses. He surpassed his fellow lawyers and was appointed Attorney General at the Metn court. He continued in this post until World War I. At that time he left for family reasons and started his private practise again. He continues to practise today with his usual intelligence and perfection.

His son Youssef Freha Bachaalany studied at the Hekma Institute where he graduated with a degree in Philosophy in 1944. After that, he studied law at the French Institute in Beirut. It is a most elegant and modern school. He passed his bar exam in front of the examination committee headed by the greatest and most famous law professors in France. This was in October, 1947. His degree was bestowed on him and his fellow graduates in a grand ceremony attended by dignitaries of the government, including many judges. Todays, he is completing a probationary practise at his father's law office in Beirut. The French Director of the Institute said about him: "This is the first time a 20 year old has received his certificate. May God help him to succeed".

Youssef al Khoury, is the son of Hanna Girgis al Khoury Nakouzy. He studied Law under Mikahil Afendi Eid al Bostani and other judges working in Lebanon. He acquired through hands on practise what could not be gained through classes alone. A few years ago, he was elected the President of the Law Association in Beirut. He is still practising law before the courts today.

Pedro Khoury is the son of Assaf Hanna al Khoury and the nephew of Professor Youssef al Khoury. He studied at the Jesuit Institute where he learned law and received his diploma. Beside his regular law practise, he translates legal documents. He has mastered Arabic, French, Spanish and English. Before that, he was a translator at the Spanish Embassy in Beirut.

Mansour Daher is the son of Daher Mansour Nakouzy. He began practising law after an apprenticeship with the courts. He was courageous and talented in his courtroom performance, even though he never attended law school. Naguib al Asmar and Shahin Mohamed al Masry studied law under the previously mentioned Mikhail Afendi Eid. However, they didn't continue in that profession.

There is a group of our expatriates' sons abroad who have studied law, medecine and other fields of higher education. We will refer to them in Section 3.

Houses of Knowledge

In 1861, Molhem Nohra was a student in Aintoura. Then he worked for the owners of the silk plants in Salima and in Ain Hamada. He was also the Reconciliation Sheikh in Salima. His son Naguib was a student at the school of Our Lady of Lourdes. He spent his entire life in education, teaching at the school of the Jesuits in Zahle and the Hekma School and The Fréres in Beirut. His brother Youssef Molhem studied at Our Lady of Lourdes School and the GhAintoura School. He has been a teacher for many years at the Eastern School in Zahle. He joined the Education Ministry during the French era. He was appointed as an inspector. His son Henry studied at The Fréres and then learned engineering at the Jesuit Institute. He was then appointed an engineer for the Lebanese government. The second child of Youssef Molhem is Beshara, a clerk at the Lebanese Education Ministry, appointed after finishing his studies at The Fréres in Beirut. Tawfik bin Naguib Molhem studied at the National School owned by Na'im Sawaya in Baabadat. He joined the Lebanese Army and has been promoted to Lieutnant colonel. His sons are now pursuing their college studies.

Habib Fares Anton acquired his higher education in the Aintoura Institute (1865-1870). In 1871, he started to teach the French Language at the Lebanese Monastic School in Metin. Then, he taught at the Zahle School for the Roman Catholics in 1873. In 1875, during the Rostom Pasha era, he was appointed to the Foreign Department. This appointment shows how perfectly he mastered the French language since he became the private translator of the administrative officer.

In 1878, he quit the government service and joined Gabour al Tabib in the money exchange. Then in 1879, during the era of the Medhat Pasha of Damascus, he entered into political life. He practised law in 1882. In 1888 he left for Egypt and remained there until 1892 pursuing his intellectual activities.

He became the editor of Arab and French newspapers, such as Al Mahrousa, El Nile and Al Bosfor. Then he established and created a newspaper called Sada Al Sharq (The Echo of the East) which was highly respected in Egypt.

Through that newspaper, he charged Wassa Pasha and his government with wrong doing. He fought against the injustice and bribery that was occurring in Lebanon. Because of this, the administrative officer asked the Egyptian government to deliver Habib Fares to him. However Lord Kromer, the British ambassador in Egypt, refused to allow this. Then, the administrative officer sent a military force to Salima in 1891 to arrest his brother Anton Fares. It was well known that he was writing and helping his brother in publicizing the government scandals in the "Sada Al Sharq" newspaper. Anton learned of the military raid from some friends so he went into hiding. The government sent spies to find him. When they failed, they placed guards at his father's (Fares Anton) house. Because of this the old man has suffered physically. The oppression continued until Anton secretly fled to Marseilles as Bishop Youssef el Debs had advised him. He was assisted in his flight by the French Consul.

In 1893, after the death of Wassa Pasha, Habib Afendi come back to Lebanon. He refused to join the government service. He practised law as well as some agriculture. He also had a construction business which dug charcoal mines and produced baked bricks and pottery. In 1910, he returned to journalism through the newspapers of his son Felix. The newspaper was called "Lisan Al Etehad" (The Union Tongue). . He has written several publications in Arabic and French, some of them have been published and many remain in manuscript form.

Among the published materials are: books entitled The Innocent's Scream, In Liberty's Horn, and Secrets of Lebanon. There is also a book about French grammar and a novel called Yesterday. He also wrote some books in Arabic and French which have not been published. Before his death, he gave his writings and papers to the National Archives to be kept there. He died in Beirut and his remains were transported to Merigate where he previously had a home. The house was surrounded by large statues and gardens and he was buried there in a new family cemetery in 1932.

Anton Fares was born in Salima in 1857 and grew up there. It was there that he first attended school. Then he studied at Ain Waraka. He learned French from his brother Habib who was a master in that language. Anton was a master in the Arabic langauge. He was a glorious writer and an illustrious poet. His talents appeared in his written articles in the "Al Mersad" newspaper which he started in Marseilles at the beginning of 1897. In 1905 the newspaper ceased publication. Anton played his own role in immigration because he was a great help to the expatriates who passed through Marseilles. He wrote wonderful poems which showed his great talent as a poet. The most important one was the poem ending with the "Noun", which he sent to his brother-in-law Khalil 'Okl Shedid after his arrival in Marseilles. He expressed in this poem what he had suffered with his family and how much the Lebanese government had opressed them. It was a wonderful dramatic desciption of the events.

He wrote many other poems. The last one was a long poem describing the beauty of Lebanon. A part of this poem was published by Shoukry al Khoury, the owner of "Abou El Hol" in Sanboul. During World War II, around 1942, he died in France.

He had two sons who died young, Naguib and Rashid. They were among the best of the young men of Salima by their culture and good manners. His son Farid is one of the national revolutionary leaders. He did much for the development of this village.

Felix bin Habib Fares was the most famous writer, the most innovative poet, a great orator and a rising journalist. His ingenuity and moral fiber were evident in his writings. He was born in Salima in 1882. He studied on his own in his parents' house. When he was 14, he was able to write poems. He undertook translating, writing, and publishing in Egyptian and American newspapers. He often published what was forbidden in the press in his country. Until the modern Ottoman constitution was announced, he had taken dangerous stands on issues which illustrated his outstanding usage of language. He established a nice position for himself in the history of modern revolutionary literature.

He wrote memorable material calling for the overthrow of the corrupt political system and the adoption of the new constitution. He became famous throughout the country. In 1909 he started a weekly newspaper "Lisan Al Etehad" (Union Tongue), which soon became a daily. He delivered fiery speeches which showed his courage and boldness. Even when those opposing the constitution threatened him with death, he showed no fear.

When the leaders of the Union and Advancement Organization changed and the members became radical, he stopped publishing the newspaper. He went to Halab to teach classes in the arts, literature and French oration at the School of the Sultan for 9 years. When World War II ended, Felix returned to Lebanon. He continued his literary and patriotic activities. He became more experienced and was doing more creative writing and he was delivering speeches in Arabic, French and Turkish. He was widely recognized, of strong argument and clear logic. He had the ability to improvise in his writing as well as on stage. He had the ability to hold an article written in French and translate it while reading it. It was as if he was reading an article written in Arabic. On top of all this, he was a sweet and generous man of good manners. He spent his last years in Alexandria where he was working in an important position in its government. He died in 1939. His body was transported to Lebanon and buried in Al Merigat. He had compilations of translated books and valuable literary manuscripts which we will refer to in a later chapter. What he left behind is evidence of his brilliance, his distinction as an author, and his fertile mental creations. All this made him a glorious writer, poet, orator and exceptional journalist. He lived his life philosophizing and he died a philosopher.

Hereafter I have included a few paragraphs of the letter sent by the Maronite Patriarch Elias Farah el Wakil in Alexandria, addressed to Bishop Mobarak, the Archbishop of Beirut. The letter is dated June 6, 1939: "…The death of Felix was like a Saint's death. He called us in his last hour. Father Mohasseb from the Patriarchate went and assisted him in the difficult situation. He confessed with total repentance and embraced the holy oil. We held an elaborate funeral for him in our Church. A huge number of writers and poets came from all over Egypt. Also, there were representatives present from the government where he was the director of the translation department. We wept for him and his children. About his religious feelings, we noted: 'We remember with great emotion the hours we spent at his bedside. He was restless. Laying on his death bed. We remember with humility and admiration his great, living faith that was supporting him throughout this sickness right up to his final breath. Professor Felix Fares brought out people's enthusiasm with his great eloquence and irrefutable arguments. Professor Felix Fares' writings are still inspiring intellectual minds. Professor Felix Fares was a spirited orator, a delicate poet, and an experienced politician. Professor Felix Fares was the intellectual philosopher ready to face death with the simplicity of a pure infant. He called us twice when he was ill to perform his religious duties. He confessed with full repentance for every human weakness. He consecrated himself and his senses to embrace the holy oil. Then he raised his eyes to the sky crying and sighing as if he was looking at the spirit world of God. He shouted "My God I am leaving my soul in your hands." (Documents of the Maronite Bishopric in Beirut).

His brother Philip Fares was born in Salima and studied in its boarding school. He wrote articles in American newspapers where he migrated. His articles and speeches were thoughtful and revolutionary. He joined the army when he came back home. Due to his competency he was promoted to Commissioner. He was put in charge of the education of the soldiers in Baabada. Then he retired from the military. He is now a free man, loves his country and serves it with devotion. His children, Edmon, Fernan and Emlie, the writer, are educated and cultured.

His brother Emil Fares was mentioned in the chapter on the lawyers from Salima. He studied in his parents' house, learning from his father and mother. His maternal grandmother played a great role in educating the children of this family. She was very knowledgeable.

Youssef, Hanna and Shoukry Girgis Anton Abou Anton studied at the Salima School. The most succesful was Shoukry who became a teacher at the Lebanese School in Qornet Chahouane. He went to Marseilles where his paternal cousin Anton Fares lived. He helped him in a business he had there. After that, he traveled to Brazil, living in the capital where he started a newspaper called "Al Adl" (Justice) in 1901. Of all the newspapers published in the capital, it was the only one that lasted long enough to celebrate its Silver Jubilee. It ceased publication when its owner died in 1934. With his newspaper, Shoukry was defending his religion and his country. He was a translator in the French Consulate and was its devoted friend. He felt he could serve his compatriots with his connections there.

One of the houses in Salima that was noted for being educated and intellectual was the house of Father Hanna Bachaalany. He wasn't just one of the genius' of Salima but he was one of its greatest with his knowledge of theology, literature, poetry and so many other fields. In those days learning was a rare commodity. He studied at the Ecclesiastical Institute of Mar Abda Harharia where most of the genius' of the Maronite Rite were educated. They were the shining examples of Maronite culture and the church's educational system. Father Hanna (John), in his time, was the only educated person in the Metn region. In addition, he was a man of great piety and deep-rooted virtue. He was a living reference in matters of theology and Arabic literature. Many students at Our Lady of Lourdes School in Salima learned Arabic grammar from him. He was the most outstanding teacher at that school. He was very strong in his conviction that his sons, Joseph and Peter, would study at that school. If he lived longer he would have been so much more useful to his family and his country. His knowledge was so great. He made so many contributions to his principals and in his job.

Joseph and Peter (Youssef and Boutros al Khoury) studied at Our Lady of Lourdes School. After it closed they reopened it and it lasted for a few years. Then, Joseph went to 'Abiah and was a teacher there in the Capuchin school. After that he travelled to Marseilles and helped Anton Fares, his brother-in-law, in editing the newspaper and in some other business ventures. After that, he came back to Salima. He worked as a teacher in Qornet Chahouane, and, then, in the Khoury Anton school in Salima for many years.

He created a newspaper called "Al Warka" about 25 years ago. He is a writer, a poet and an orator. He wrote several poems with different themes. He also wrote plays. His brother Peter (Boutros) wrote poems and novels. Some of these items have been published and some remain in manuscript.

'Okl Bachaalany is the son of Abou 'Okl al Khoury. He studied at the Eccelesiastical School in Ain Waraka. He taught in the Qornet Chahouane School. Then he helped Anton Fares in publishing the "Al Mersad" (The Ambuscade) newspaper in Marseilles. At the beginning of this century he created a newspaper called "Matameer Lebnan" (Lebanon's Cemetaries) for a few months. After that, he left for Mexico and worked in journalism there until his death. While there, he began a newspaper called "Al Sharq" (The East) in 1906, and "Al Matameer" (The Cemetaries) in 1909. In this latter paper, the martyr Said Fadel 'Okl al Damouri helped him. Said Fadel went back home to start a newspaper called "Al Bayrak" (The Flag), which was the cause of his execution in World War I.

Amin Salman al Masry studied at the Daoudian School in Abia. He did not finish his studies. However, he was a good writer and has a nice calligraphy style. His children followed in his footsteps. His son Fouad studied basic science and joined the Army. After some years he retired and he was appointed Mayor of his village. During his term in office he served his people with dedication. His brother Aref Amin al Masry was educated at the Great Lebanon School. He joined the police. After a while he resigned from that and took a government job in charge of road development. His brother Raouf is a rich expatriate. The three brothers are among the senior landowners in our village.

Some of the educated students and their families from Salima include:

Shahin bin Mohamed Mahmoud who is a silk trader. His children are studying the sciences at the Hekma School and at other schools.

Kamel Shahin studied at Our Lady of Lourdes School and then at other schools. He has been a teacher for a while. He migrated and then came back home.

Amin Selim studied at the Salima schools and established the school that we previously mentioned. Also, there was Negm Bin Youssef Haidar who studied at the National School in Baabadat, then he migrated to the United States. He wrote articles for some newspapers.

Mostafa bin Ahmed Soliman studied at Salima's schools. He became its mayor for a number of years. During that time he served his country well. He has a tender style of writing and very nice calligraphy. He is migrant to Argentina with his brothers Aly, 'Okl and Soliman.

Rashid Daoud Salman studied at Salima's Schools and he was appointed as a teacher there at the School of Modern Knowledge.

Youssef Daher Matar was one of our fellow students at the Salima Primary School. He took care to teach and educate his children, then migrated and then returned after acquiring wealth.

Then, there was Abdallah Hussein Seloum who loved learning. He made sure to educate his son Mohamed who migrated and came back with his riches. His other son Asad who studied in Salima spent some years in a medical school in Damascus and he is now practicing medicine in our country.

From the Said House there was Gamil bin Selim Hussein who studied at the Great Lebanon School and then migrated to Australia.

Naguib Beshir who has nice calligraphy and a good writing style. Amin and Naguib Qassem Said did not have the opportunity to study. Amin, however, took his son Salah to the Aintoura School where he is enrolled in higher education. Naguib took care to educate his two sons Afif and Anwar at the Mexico schools, where they are now tradesmen with their father.

Hamza Said did not go to school but he migrated to Brazil where he learned the skills he needed, like calligraphy, writing and other material. He learned this as did many other immigrants. His older son Raslan is a good reciter of the popular Arabic poems. He is employed as a clerk at the Mail and Telegraph Service offices.

One of our most generous emigrants in United States was the late Fares Daoud Kassab. He was a wise man and valued education and literature. When we sent him our book entitled <u>Lebanon and Youssef Beik Karam</u>, he replied that the amount he sent us was not worth the value of one page of our book.

Hanna Girgis al Khoury was one of our intellectuals of great spirit. He accompanied the tourists in their journeys throughout the East and the West until he arrived in Moscow, Russia. When the school of Our Lady of Lourdes was opened in Salima, he took his older son Assaf there to learn. He studied at the school for five years until it was closed in 1892. He was a teacher at the 'Abia School, then the Mar Youssef School in Qornet Chahouane.

In 1896, he traveled with his brother Girgis to Venezuela where they worked in commerce for 15 years. By working in this field, he mastered the country's language. He was as fluent in Spanish as the people born in the country. He worked as an Education Inspector there, proving how intelligent and capable the Lebanese are. In 1911, he came back to his country with his family and his brother. Being far from home for so long, he had forgotten some of his Arabic and his ancestral traditions. After returning he stayed silent for a while but soon again found his ancient ways, writing and composing good poetry like he used to. You can notice his perfection in the poem he wrote opposing Amin Taki Eddine on page 79 of his book. There are other marvelous verses he wrote in that book. He was concerned about his children's education so they took their higher learning in the schools of Beirut.

His brother Girgis died in Brazil, the second country he migrated to. Their good mother took care to educate them. One of them named Caesar studied the Portugese language at the university. He took his father's place in the business.

The third brother Selim, was concerned that his children receive their higher education in Beirut. The fourth brother, Mr. Youssef Hanna al Khoury, is the one we discussed in the chapter about lawyers. He is educating his children at the Jesuits' school. And we want to be sure to mention that he received the award of Lebanese Merit when he was the president of the lawyers association. The fifth brother Nassib is a rich emigrant in Brazil. He has a son studying medecine.

Ghaled Nakouzy was a wise and literate man. He educated his sons Ghaleb, Youssef and Rashid. Youssef studied at school of Our Lady of Lourdes in Salima and was successful there. After he graduated, he worked as a teacher in Qornet Chahouane School, then joined the Medical Institute in Beirut. He was forced to stop his studies in his last year because of a disease which attacked his eyes. He was mentally exhausted and was reading countinuously. The disease progressed to the extent that he became blind. Still, because of his patience and devotion, he managed to serve our suffering humanity and his relatives with his medical and scientific knowledge. He devoted himself with piety, worshiping God like an ascetic monk, dying as a genius philosopher. The educated members of this family also includes the sons of Ghaleb: Emil, a clerk for the Railroad, Shahin who works at the Observatory of Kasara and at the radio station in Beirut where he occupied a high position; and George who worked at the Syria-Halab Bus Transport Company, and, finally, Philip working for the Kasara Radio station. The sons of Rashid: Jean, Antoine and Josef are all educated and work in business.

The house of Daher Daabis Nakouzy are also highly educated and successful. They include: 1. Their elder and dean Abdou, who worked for the railway and reached their highest position, manager of the Reyak El Kebir depot. He retired after forty years of service. His three children are educated. 2. Khalil has worked with his brother at the railway for a long time and his children are educated. 3. Anton migrated. 4. Hanna has joined his children at the Hekma School for higher education. 5. Tawfik has children in school and all of them are today in Al Dakwana.

Shiban Daham was working at the house of Lady Malak, the wife of Prince Assaf Abou al Lam'. He was managing the house and the family's properties. His son Fares learned calligraphy and composition, so he was appointed a clerk, then manager of the Thabets' plant in Nahr Al Maout (The River Of Death). There he acquired money and prestige. He died in middle age. Eida, his wife, took care of her children and she was powerful and intelligent. She enrolled them in the school of Our Lady Of Lourdes in Salima where they received their advanced studies. The older Habib Shiban became a writer and a poet. The second, Ibrahim Shiban, mastered the French language as well as his brother Habib mastered the Arabic language. Then, Habib came to be in charge of the Sheikhdom of Salima for a long time. The youngest child, Youssef Shiban, studied in Salima and, then, at the Hekma School.

The three of them established a silk plant in Salima and managed it for many years. They were trained in this business and its techniques, but, then, it turned into a disaster, as it did for all the silk traders in Lebanon at that time.

Sheikh Habib has wrote poems for different occassions and compiled written works discussing many different subjects. Those manuscripts are kept by his only son Boutros who studied at the Fréres school in the Hekma Institute. Ibrahim migrated to Mexico where he died a few years ago, but his brother Youssef is still in Mexico. Their sister Assine was educated at the Aintoura School and was married to Youssef Ghastine Al Baaqalini.

Tanous Shiban took charge of the previously mentioned Tabet factory after the death of his brother Fares. We can say that he was intelligent, honest and free. He educated his children at the Qornet Chahouane School and others. Three of his children migrated to Mexico, working in trading. Then they established a big plant there. Amin died first and a year ago Louis the older one also died, leaving a large inheritance. Amin was mastering many languages and loved reading. He bought a library full of books in different languages.

Youssef Shiban I had a son called Elias who is an emigrant in the United States. He is married and has a son.

Among the educated families in Salima is the Mikhail Abdou family. He was wise and cultured. He married an educated woman, so both parents took care of teaching and educating their children. They were Youssef, Abdou, Moussa, and Milia who married Hanna Metri al Zaghloul.

They studied at the school of Our Lady Of Lourdes in Salima, and at the Qornet Chahouane School, and at other ones, too. When the railroad company was established in our country, both Youssef and Abdou were employed there. Then, they migrated to Brazil and their brother Moussa followed them. There, the three brothers gained a high rank and a solid reputation in the trading business, especially the older brother Youssef, who was wise, very logical and always vigilant. Abdou had guts and was fast. Youssef died before World War I, on his way to Lebanon, accompanied by his family. Abdou died a few years ago. Moussa lives in Rio De Janiero with his family and the family his brother, Youssef.

Asaad Maroun Bachaalany was a man of the sword and the pen. His son Girgis became a calligrapher and writer. Then, his son, Asaad bin Girgis, surpassed him in calligraphy. He was the most famous calligrapher of his time. In addition, he was well known for his talent of composing and reciting popular Arabic poems. He wrote a story about Youssef beik Karam, in which he opposed the popular famous story written by the Halabian Monk, Pastor Girgis al Sahelani (from Alma Coast). First, it was published by Na'oum al Karzal, then several times in Beirut. He employed all his poetic and patriotic wits in his Asaad Girgis' story, which is still in manuscript form.

When Asaad migrated to Brazil, he wrote a popular Arabic poem composed of about a thousand verses, describing his journey, and, how he suffered some accidents and terrors during that journey. It is handwritten and has never been published.

His published works consist mainly of his arguments and debates between himself and the Lebanese, popular, Arab poets living in Brazil. They were published at the Al Asma'ey newspaper and at the Abou Al Houl newspaper directed to their owner Shoukry al Khoury. How nice it would be if all his works were published.

His son George Bachaalany grew up under the guidance of his grandmonther and paternal aunt because his parents were expatriates. He had the opportunity to learn at the Capuchin School when Habib Bachaalany was teaching there. Then, at Our Lady Of Lourdes School when Father Anton al Asmar was its headmaster. Then, he went on to the National School under its owner, Na'eem Sawaya, where he was a student, then a teacher.

In 1920, he established the Great Lebanon School in Salima and it remained until his death in 1935. Many students graduated from that school.

George Bachaalany was an elaborate poet by nature. He was also a perfect, influential orator with a remarkable voice and speaking style. His poems, however, are not widespread. We hope that his children will succeed in gathering and publishing them. In general, he was one of Salima's intellectual giants of whom she was very proud. He wrote poetic plays, the most important one was the story of "Salah El Dine Al Ayoubi" which he had published. This story contained the most noble patriotic themes and principles.

His children grew up in Beit Alam, and the elders Emil and Alfred inherited much of their father's talents for poetry and oratory. Emil joined the Ministry of Finance while Alfred joined the police.

There was another educated and cultured family in Salima and Bakfeya, the Zein family. This noble family was known for its gentleness, piety, and gracious manners. A group of its members were distinguished for their knowledge and literary accomplishments. There were people like the sons of Khalil Zein: Youssef, Zein, Habib and Mansour. They were living in Bakfeya and continued their higher education. Zein and his brother Habib graduated from the Hekma School in Beirut after 5 years and where their names were mentioned in its handwritten student register (1874-1925):

"The Subdeacon Zein Khalil Zein from Bakfeya and his brother Habib from 1879 until 1884. " The scribe of this book took care to gather and organize the information recorded in 3 volumes.

After their graduation, the headmaster of Our Lady Of Lourdes school in Salima requested they become teachers at his school. They came to be among the best the school ever had. Their talents and cultural capabilities rose, especially the genius of Zein with his exceptional knowledge of Arabic and French literature. This was shown in the wondeful verses he wrote, along with those of Halab, which echoed throughout Syria and Lebanon. He was highly skilled at writing plays with historic and patriotic themes, such as "Prince Beshir" which was admired by numerous people when it was performed at the school. They wrote poems which brought acclaim to these rising modern writers. Such is the poem written by Zein congratulating Bishop al Debs when he came back from Rome.

Then there were two great poems written by his brother Habib. These were fully published in the book titled <u>Rayhanat Al Ouns</u> (The Sweet Basil Of Good Fellowship), on pages 63, 64, and 156.

Both of them had written wonderful poems about Pope Leo XIII which were published in the congatulatory book printed on the occasion of his Jubelee, pages 40, 34, and 159. When the previously mentioned school was closed, they left for Egypt where Zein wrote the poetic play "Mohamed Ali Pasha", which was highly regarded in the literary world.

This great writer died before World War I in the spring of life. The historian Issa Eskandar al Maalouf said in the Al Ne'ma magazine (1:394): "The Lebanese Zein Khalil Zein had made a place in history for Syrian literature of the 19th century. When he was in Halab in 1891, those assembled wrote his biography and he was applauded by writers and poets alike."

In the generous house of Fares Mourad Zein, were his sons Habib, Mourad, Gamil and Louis. Their father saw to their education at Our Lady Of Lourdes school in Salima and the National School in Baabadat. The oldest child, Habib Zein was skilled in literature, well known for his wonderful poems about the nation and the immigration. He wrote for several occasions. They show the natural poetic impression of that literary man on his work and its simplicity.

The "Al Hoda" newspaper in New York has published some of his glorious verses. And I read in the "Al Mashrak Al Yasou'eya" magazine (The Eastern Jesuits) in Beirut some of his poems copied from that newpaper which were written to mark the day when our constitution was announced. Our literary man was writing and composing poems at the same time that he was busy with his trading business. He published some of his poems while others still remain manuscripts. His poems are as wonderful as the poems of his paternal cousin Zein.

His brothers did not follow him in the field of literature and poetry. However, they participate with him at the national projects and the charitable deeds performed in our country and the country to which they migrated. This gave them a good standing and high rank among the residents and the expatriates. Gamil, who was one of them, was known for his generosity and the favors which he performed. Most notable of his favors was that done especially for the sake of this history which would not have come to be without his assistance.

We must mention the unforgetable project of Louis Zein who brought running water to the houses of Salima. He brought into our lives drinking water, irrigation water, and washing water. This was something the inhabitants never dreamed of. This is also something that the whole country could use.

While Mourad Zein was taking care of educating his sons Fares, George and Josef, the oldest one received his college degree.

Also, Emil Zein grew up within this family. He is the son of Salibi Girgis Zein. His father enrolled him at the available schools at that time in Salima, and then, in the Fréres (Brothers') School in Beirut where he finished his higher education. His area of expertise was in the Arab and French languages. He was fond of literature, poetry, composition and oratory. He wrote poems with nice modern syllables. He also made speeches which made lasting impressions and had a great influence. The youth of this family seems to have made a strong impact in the literary field, especially poetry. This is truly a gift of God given to those he likes.

There was also Khalil Ibrahim Mansour al Khoury, an expatriate who died in the United States in the spring of life. He studied at Salima's school and at the school of the Jesuits in Taanayel. He studied the Arabic and French languages. He mastered the English Language during his migration. He had a great sense of diplomacy, politness, and strong ethics.

Among the emigrants going to Africa was his brother Mansour al Khoury who was known for his bravery and courage. He had a high literary standing among trademen and expatriates. There was also Aziz al Khoury and his two brothers, Rashed and Tawfik, all expatriates in Africa. They have greatly succeeded in trading and become wealthy. All this, thanks to Aziz. Aziz and Rashed died, and Tawfik remained there working in the business with his sons George, Aziz and Khalil.

Among the expatriates originating from Salima was Daoud Nassef el Hadary who obtained a great deal of learning from Our Lady Of Lourdes school as we already mentioned in that earlier chapter about the school. He has been in New York for a long time. He and his family have gained a great deal of prestige in their new country. Also among the men of Salima who migrated to the United States is Asaad Wakim, known as Ernest Kassab. He is a man of revolution and very active in patriotic projects.

Among the Nakouzys there are the sons of 'Okl Guenid. They migrated to Egypt a while ago and became wealthy. They gained great prestige and had a wide spread business. Guenid was a wise and intelligent man. He educated his sons Farid, Philip, Fahim and 'Okl. They were the picture of happiness in their youth growing in knowledge and ethics. They achieved a high, respected status in the United States. Meanwhile, their paternal uncle Mansour was educated at the Ecclesiastical Mar Abda Harharia School. However, he did not go on to become a priest. He went with his brother to Egypt, then, he came back to Lebanon where he died.

Also among these expatriates was Salem Boutros Salem. He was the trustee of the Church of Saint John for a long time. His brother Daoud followed him in this task. Both were zealous and generous. Salem educated his sons Elias and Moussa and then they migrated to Charleston in the United States. With hard work and honesty, they gained wealth and a solid reputation. They inherited these good characteristics from their father. Elias performed some remarkable deeds for the writer of this history. Both of them have children occupying high positions in business. They have served in the American army in the war.

Also, I must include the children of Shedid Saad, one of our generous traders who migrated to Charleston. In that city there is Tanious and Boutros, and that is where Youssef Khattar is, one of our intellectual young men. Tanious died. His brother died last year in Senegal. He was a remarkable man in the business. He mastered many languages. He had chivalry and strong feelings of love and patriotism. He donated a big clock to the Church of Saint John in Salima. It is a large antique with religious and patriot sentiments. Also mong the intellectuals was Girgi Nassef Youssef Naseef al Khoury who studied modern science. He occupied important positions in the financial department in Al Ladheqihay. His children learned much about science at the Fréres School. This family holds a special high intellectual rank there.

The House of Freha Bachaalany

I think I can modestly talk about our own house here, too. Like the other families mentioned, I will briefly discuss our levels of culture and learning. Our grandfather Tanous Freha grew up a self-made man. He adopted the characteristics of our ancestors which are piety, virtue and the performance of good deeds. He held the responsible position of being the sheikh of reconciliation. He was also a trustee for many years. He was still young when he gained fame and fortune. He then focused on the education of his children Abdou, Girgis and Faragallah. The oldest acquired the most knowledge and his father did not want to lose him because, as he used to say, this son was the cane of his old age. He joined Girgis at the famous Aintoura school where he spent three years. His son Elias learned much about science. For 18 years he has been tax collector in the Upper Metn.

Faragallah learned capentry and was one of the most distinguished. His two sons Mikhail and Louis mastered that same craft after completing their basic education. Abdou became a tradesman and a tailor and worked in various jobs.

He spent a considerable sum of money to educate his sons: Youssef, Boutros, Habib, Tanous, Khalil, Milia, Malaka and Anissa. They acquired a good deal of modern scientific learning.

Abdou had a nice calligraphy style with good composition. He was an experienced bookkeeper. He was wise and a good manager. He thought about becoming a priest but he could not afford the education. However, before he died, his son Youssef was ordained to the priesthood, thus fulfilling that ancient desire.

Father Stephen Bachaalany (Al Khoury Estephan Al Bachaalany)

This person is Youssef bin Abdou Tanous Freha. He became a priest and took the name Father Stephen. He was born and grew up in the village of Salima. He was born on March 11, 1876. He studied at the Capuchin schools and others during his elementary school days. Then he was self-taught, learning a good deal of knowledge as well as the languages of Arabic, Syriac, French, and English.

He worked as a teacher in many schools: the Capuchin Fathers' School, Our Lady Of Lourdes School, the Great Lebanon School in Salima, the Lebanese Mar Youssef School in Qornet Chahouane, and the Fréres School in Baabada. Before being ordained, he opened a school in Bchaaleh and stayed there for five years.

He spent 13 years at the Bishopric of Beirut. He stayed at the bishopric itself, its schools and the Al Matrania office. Also, he was the Chief Librarian in charge of documents, as well as a registrar and a member of the Archbishopric.

He was in charge of managing "Jean D'arc", the printing house of the Capuchin Fathers. He was the Editor of the "Sadik Al 'Ela" (Family Friend) magazine, which was founded by the Capuchin priest, Father Jacob (Yaakoub) three years before. From his early childhood days he loved History, especially the history of his country. He gathered many historical documents and manuscripts pertaining to this. The greatest thing he presented to the public was his book Lebanon and Youssef Beik Karam which he published in 1925. He also wrote The History Of The Maronite Families, and Memories. Also, he wrote the Al Hekma School Student Register and The History Of the Bishopric Of Beirut.

On the whole most of these are still unpublished manuscripts. He authored this family history which you are now reading. It was finally published with God's help.

Habib Bachaalany

Habib Bachaalany is the son of Abdou Tanous Freha Bachaalany. He is the third child and grew up in a house of piety and knowledge. He studied at the primary schools of Salima. He continued his studies on his own and sometimes had private tutors. He mastered Arabic and French. After he migrated to Brazil in 1910 he came to understand Portuguese. He was a teacher at the Capuchin School in Salima, and at the Lebanese Mar Youssef School in Qornet Chahouane. From his childhood days, we was fond of journalism. He even started a handwritten newspaper which he sent to the expatriates. He was the Editor of the "Al Roda" newspaper for its owner Khalil Bakhos. He was Editor of the "Lesan Al Etehad" newspaper for its owner Felix Fares in Beirut. In 1910, he migrated to Brazil and worked as a sales representative for some stores and he did other jobs. At the same time, he was working in the field of literature, writing social and reformation articles in Arabic newspapers and magazines issued in Brazil and other places.

Around 1935, he started the "Al Ahrar" newspapers in Sao Paulo, Brazil. It was continually issued until World War II, in 1941, when a court order shut down newspapers in foreign languages. It was a literary, political and critical newspaper. It had a good reputation and was one of the most important Arabic newspapers in its language, communications and quality.

In general, Habib Bachaalany was a literary man, a creator, first class journalist and a reform minded critic and orator. He took a strong interest in the education of his only daughter Anreat. She was schooled at institutions run by nuns. When she graduated from her higher education she understood Arabic, Portuguese, French and English. She married a young Brazilian writer and had children.

Tanous Freha

We previously mentioned "Bachaalany" on an earlier page 2XXX17 as one of the lawyers. He studied at the primary school, but he studied only Arabic. That is why he mastered it. Then, he went on to specialize in legal studies working with the greatest information researchers and the most famous judges in Lebanon. After his bar exam in front of the examining committee delegated by the government, he was appointed by the Administrative Officer as a Clerk and Attorney General at the Al Metn Court. This was during the Yohanes Pasha Qioumigian era. He was very successful. After four years, he quit his job for family reasons and engaged in private practice which he continues to do today. People who know him, certified that he is exceptionally capable in this field because of his intelligence, and the knowledge he had acquired. He can get to the core of the matter with diligent examination. In addition to being well known for his sincerity and devotion to this job, he has proven his righteousness and his patriotic convictions. People of intelligence have vouched for his loyalty, zeal, sincerity, and patriotism. His stand on the issues involving his country will be evaluated on the basis of events yet to unfold. History will be the judge.

He did his utmost to educate his children Youssef, Salma and Salwa. Youssef studied the sciences at the Hekma Institute, graduating with a degree in Philosophy. He studied Law at The French Institute in Beirut and graduated from it. He is performing a probationary period at his father's law office, which is traditional. His sisters are studying at the School of the Virgin, run by nuns of Al Ashrafeya, Beirut.

Khalil Freha Bachaalany

Khalil Freha Bachaalany learned the principles of knowledge in Salima. Then he migrated to Brazil after the War where he had to learn Portuguese. Like the other expatriates, he was engaged in commerce. He had the opportunity to improve his understanding of the spoken and written language which he did, just like many other Lebanese expatriates. He came back to Lebanon in 1928 and worked at many different jobs in commerce and other fields. His children Mariam, Terase, Abdou, Rezk, Younes and Maha are studying in Salima with Abdou at the Hekma Institute in Beirut.

Andrea Girgis

He is Andrea bin Girgis Negm Andrea Bachaalany. He was born in Salima in 1863 and learned his knowledge and religious principles at the Capuchin School. He joined those respected Fathers in their monastery in Salima and in Beirut. He spent thirty years there as a cook. He spent ten years with the Christian Brothers' School in Beirut until he died around 1929. He was a wise man, zealous and generous. He cared greatly about his family's interests and how to improve their lot. He narrates many stories and passes on the tales about our ancestors. He related honestly to us the many serious events and news that he learned from his paternal uncle Daher. Daher learned them from his father, the famous Negm Andrea Bachaalany. The two of them are the most trusted transmitters of the past, confirming many memorizes.

The late Andrea was providing a special service care to the expatriates' affairs in Salima. He got them organized when they were leaving. Doing the same during their migration and when they returned. He made travel arrangements from Beirut through the ships because, at that time, the traveler was not safe from those corrupt sailors. There was violence in the port of Beirut against the many Lebanese travelers as well as those returning. He arranged for correspondence of the expatriates with their families. There was no Post Office in Salima at that time, so Andrea handled it. Andrea would accept the mail from the muleteers. The mail would consist of the letters and money arriving from America. He would handle it honestly and with no charge from the people. He would then distribute the letters and money to the respective recipients in Salima. Because of this and his other charitable deeds for the church and the poor, people remember him fondly. Simply put, he was a good and charitable man. May God have mercy on him.

Molhem and Selim Azar Nakouzy were the first expatriates to Egypt. They possessed intelligence, knowledge and good ethics. They worked in commerce. Death came early to Molhem. He has a large family which has been well educated in Egyptian schools. The girls married young men from notable families. Naguib 'Azar still holds a high position in the Eyptian Government. His paternal uncle Selim favored the family of his brother. He never married and died.

At present, the family of the lawyer Mansour Daher, who died 24 years ago, reside in Alexandria. His wife took her children and went to Alexandria. There she worked and became a famous dressmaker. She raised her children and educated them all the way to college.

Among our noble expatriates in United States are: Maroun, Ghatas, Youssef and Habib, all sons of Fares Ghatas who emigrated a long time ago. They took care of raising their children and educating them in the ways of modern sciences. The special one was Ghatas. God blessed him with a big family along with wealth and fame. The children grew up learning his good principles and ethics. His intellectual sons participated in commercial, charitable and patriotic projects, here and where they migrated, in war and in peace.

Other educated people of Salima include Hanna Gebrail Abou 'Oun who mastered calligraphy and book keeping. He worked at the silk plants and in stores. His sons Elias, Guergi and Mikhail learned the basics then migrated with their father to the United States. They were successful in their business endeavors. The sons Elias and Guergi learned many different fields in the sciences. Some became doctors and soldiers in the American army and became famous after the last world war.

Also among the generous expatriates in the United States are Daoud, Hanna and Mikhail, the sons of Boutros Sowan. They were known in this country and in the country to which they migrated. The were of a soft nature and straight and true. Daoud took great care in raising and educating his children.

Abdallah Saloum Bachaalany has worked at some stores in Beirut and Tripoli. He migrated to Brazil in 1888. He was a very vigorous man with a high sense of honor and noble manners. He had a pleasant personality, plus God blessed him with a cute face. He was perfect in nature and manners.

He descended on the Brazilian capital when the trading market was popular. The country was fresh. The money was abundant. The American people did not know what trading was. He established a trading company in the capital with another Lebanese man. He was lucky and acquired great wealth thanks to his honesty and activity. His business spread when he employed peddlers to travel the countryside. He helped the needy and the new expatriates. He gained the friendship of notables and high ranking people. He was intelligent, sedate, wise, of genuine opinion and of good organization. He was distinguished by his generosity and zealousness.

Unfortunately the age of easy money turned its back to him. He was afflicted with a great financial loss and illness. One of the jealous traders in the capital provoked him and there was a big dispute between them. It ended with a financial action being brought against him. It cost him a share of his wealth and considerable time. Even his fellow Lebanese were not faithful in their transactions with him. And this, despite the fact that he showered them with care and donations. So it was that his money was spent and business came to an end. All this affected his health and he became ill. With sorrow for his lost youth, he died in San Joan De Lara, a stranger and alone in 1904.

He was a literary man. He liked authors and he helped them. For example, he aided Na'oum al Labki who issued "Al Manadher" (The Sights) in Brazil and then later in Lebanon. He was one of the famous journalists, noted for his literature and politics. His children inherited the same characteristics from him. The most distinguished ones were Salah and Kasrowan, the first excelling in the Arabic language and the second in French.

From the Bachaalany's who migrated were Youssef Wakim's sons. The first one was Selim, who migrated to Brazil in 1895. This was after he finished his schooling at Our Lady of Lourdes School in Salima, and the Hekma Institute in Beirut. When he migrated he was less than 16 years old. He worked at stores in the capital, then he started to travel around the country, working in commerce. After some years, his brother Elias went to him and they helped each other. Their commerce succeeded thanks to Elias' commercial capabilities and because of Selim's honesty in dealing with others. In addition, Selim had learned how to read and write Portuguese perfectly.

The times then fluctuated between profit and loss. Elias came back home. Then his family did, too. However, it wasn't long before he became ill and died in 1934. He left three sons: Josef, Anton, and Milad. They went back to Brazil, joining their paternal uncles.

Salima Natives In Oliveira

Oliveira is a town in the Minas Gerais state of Brazil. So many of Salima's expatriates went there to live that it was called Salima 2. Among the expatriates was Hanna Metri al Zaghloul who accumulated wealth with his high position in commerce. The same was true for his brothers Youssef, Elias and Mikhail. They were not people of great knowledge or education. It just goes to prove that knowledge is not a guarantee of success. Good manners, the ability to seize opportunities, and using wisdom to accurately and cautiously manage your affairs will help success considerably.

Hanna, Youssef and Elias have educated their children in Brazil and they are managing their fathers' businesses.

Also in Brazil are the sons of Naseef al Zaghloul: Rashid, Metri and Guergi. They are working in commerce. They are married and have educated their children.

One of our old expatriates in Oliveira is the generous patriot, Rashid Said. He is the son of Nasr El Dine Hamdan Emad Seif. Rashid, accompanied by his nephew, Adeeb, (his brother's son), and his family, came back to Lebanon. They had joined him in Brazil a few years ago. Despite their love for Lebanon, Rashid and Adeeb are emigrating again because of the bad economic situation here.

Also among the expatriates in Brazil are the sons of Mansour Deeb Bachaalany. They gained prestige in commerce and the industrial markets due to their efforts and good ethics. Abdou bin Mansour is successfully working in trade. Fouad, the son of his brother Naguib, is a partner in a modern glass manufacturing plant. And Hanna is a tradesman. All of them are living with their families in Belo Horizonte, the capital of Minas Gerais.

Glorious Deeds Of Our Poets

We finalize this chapter by sharing with you a couple of the glorious examples of our genius poets' works. There are so many outstanding ones that we wish we could publish them all.

Here are some verses from Sheikh Youssef al Khoury Bachaalany's poem where he praised Mr. Soir, the French Consul in Beirut:

> *Sheathe the eyes which are like swords*
> *Untie the chains which are like bracelets*
> *Do not let the statue pierce a heart which is in submission*
> *To that which the fascinated eyelids forbid*
> *You put the granite bridge over the eyes*
> *You protect the legs which are like sharp edged swords*
> *I built for this source a honeycomb fence with pearls*
> *All covered with precious purple*
> *The jealous and beautiful women lay down prostrate*
> *As did nobles before the bracelets of the gallant .*
> *People of glorious deeds and prohibition*
> *He possesses a great reward for knowledge certified*
> *In this region for a night spent a gallant one*
> *Of a country of honor whose God is its representing supporter*
> *France has an eternal debt that we owe*
> *Which our ancestors and their grand-children recognize*

George Bachaalany also wrote a wonderful poem about poetry. Here aresome of its lines:

> *Poetry was created when light was came to be after fire*
> *There was injustice in the kingdom of Caesar*
> *The prince of word was in the Palace*

Art in Egypt was flourishing
Two pyramids became beautiful by their shadows
It was the key of every thing unknown
A journey to the treasures of knowledge in Greece
It was the voice of religion in the people of Moses
It was the messenger of peace our land
It was the sword of justice in the hand of Rome
The judgment of the sword in the Roman hands.
It is the last word of an oration of any occasion
And the soul's discussion inside of bodies
It is an inspiration, wisdom and a light
It is the voice of God in our minds
It is the recital of life and the meaning of mortal existence
And with immortal meanings
There is a poem which cherished a throne
And a poem which demolished a throne
There is a poem which brought about peace
And a poem which overwhelmed the earth with bloody retreat
In poetry is a magic for our sentiments
Which is the magic we find in phrasing.

FACTS, EVENTS AND TALES

Chapter 16

In this chapter we will talk about many different events that happened in Salima. These are based on the many documents we have in our possession and the many tales we have heard. During the era of the Ma'ns, there was much fighting, especially between the Qays and Yamani parties. Struggles between the two existed and worsened for about hundred years, from 1600-1711.

The Lam'i Princes who were in Salima were the brothers and sons-in-law of the Ma'n Princes who were ruling Lebanon. The Ma'ns were the main group of the Qays party who were struggling against the Yamani party whose leaders were the Alam El Dine Princes. The people of Salima participated in the fights which occurred between those two big parties. The last one was the Ain Dara battle in 1711. It was in this fight that the Qays defeated the Yamani who then became extinct. After that, there was no more talk of the Yamani in Lebanon.

Among the events told is one that occurred at the Ain Dara battle. A man looked at Lieutnant Colonel Hussein while he was attacking one of his enemies. The man said to him: "May God keep your right hand safe, Lieutenant Hussein." Hussein became furious. He struck the man with his sword and said: "I killed three Princes and you call me lieutenant!". Hussein, himself, liked to be called Prince. This tale has been recorded and is kept in Salima, the native land of Lieutenant Colonel Hussein. Later, when we talk about the history of The Lam'i Princes, we will tell how they were Princes before Shar'endara (the victory of Ain Dara). They were called muqaddam (some times spelled muqata'jis), meaning Lieutenant Colonel. Muqaddam was a word used to refer to the Maronite governors and others in Lebanon. The Princes demanded their rights to their lands and titles. It was something that they inherited from their fathers and grandfathers. It was after the Ain Dara battle that the higher ruler, Prince Haidar, gained their right.

Salima, The Persecuted Refugee

Father Nicolas al Sayegh, the monk who was from Halab (Aleppo), of Shuwayr (Choueir), as well as being the famous poet, was establishing his monasticism. In 1723, the Roman Catholics tried to take over some monasteries. Father Nicolas went knocking on the doors of the Lam'i Princes in Salima. He demanded his monasteries be returned. The Princes saw that they were returned. The Prince and his children, together with the monks, retained the Monastery of Our Lady of Tamish Maarouf. And when the foreigner, Patriarch Silvestros, opposed the monks of Shuwayr and expeled them in 1724, even from the Mar Elias Al Mahidetha monastery and the Mar Yohanna Al Sayegh monastery, Father Nicolas requested the help of the Lam'i and got it.

Furthermore, when this Patriarch Silvesteros launched a violent war against the Patriarch Kirles Tanas and his followers, who were loyal to the Roman Catholic Church, Father Nicolas sought a decree from the Sublime Porte to exile Silvesteros from Halab and Syria. Then, Kirles escaped to that blessed mountain, Mount Lebanon, in 1725. There, Yaakoub Mourad, the Patriarch of the Maronites, together with his priests, won for him a decree confirming his rights. It was presented to the Ambassador of France in Istanbul. Because of that, Silvestros denounced them to the governor of Syria who oppressed them. He stole their homes and the village of Geba Beshray.

So it was that the Patriarch Kirles came to Salima and met Prince Hussein Abou Al Lam'i. This was arranged through the mediation of one of his followers who was living there, Sheikh Beshir Saab Kassab. Sheikh Abou Nader Nofal al

Khazen attended the meeting. The Prince calmed him. The Patriarch stayed under his protection for three years. (from The History Of Pastor Rofael Karama).

Covenants and Pacts

On this occasion we will now tell how the Kassabs gained the respect and consideration of the princes governing the fiefs of Metn. The Kassabs were men of the sword as well as men of the pen. They were the custodial parents and consultants of the Salima princes. I have in my filing drawers and bookcases some of their written covenants and pacts with the princes of Salima and other governors in the Metn fiefs.

These documents are statements of the mutual interests of the governor and his citizens. They are the most important proof showing the good policy the princes implemented, in being kind fair and fair to the citizens. They also prove the obedience of the citizens to their governing princes. They show the people's loyalty and their dedication to the public benefit.

These covenants were between the princes and a group of citizens, or, sometimes, just one. Each contract consisted of promises by both parties so as to avoid any type of suspicion or accusation. The parties to the agreement rarely broke their oath or misused the contract.

In those days, citizens were divided according to their covenants. For example, this family is the covenanter of prince so-and-so and that family is the covenanter of prince so-and-so. Also, the same family can be the covenanter of two or three princes. However, if a family is related to a prince then they become his sole property. They can serve only that prince. They can receive orders from no one else. There are other aspects of this bond that we will mention in a later chapter talking about the princes. Here, I now present some of those pacts between princes and citizens with their original texts:

Covenant between Prince Fares Abou Al Lam' owner of Al Shabania and the two Sheikhs Beshir and Fares Kassab of Salima:

"Being present for the purpose of writing this agreement, on this date, we affirm and transmit our solidarity to Sheikh Bou Ali (Beshir) and Sheikh Bou Hussein Fares, in words and decision. We so solemnly swear by God, the prophets and the saints, the Bible and on the Holy Koran that we are with them. We are dedicated to their interest and will not oppose them, neither in secret nor in public, neither intentionally nor morally. Every notice, whether old or new, will not be followed. We will pursue only that which will please them, just as they please us. We will support them just as we support our family. We will give them full compliance in any matter. We will allow no one to corrupt this agreement. We will allow no one to oppose this agreement. We will deal only with those who recognize and respect the terms we have sworn to in this document. They have sworn to us upon the Bible. They have accepted from us a sacred obligation. Anyone who makes changes in what has been stated, either from our side or from theirs, he is considered a traitor. He is a traitor to God, his prophets and messengers, and to himself and his money. And whoever serves this agreement with a steady faith, God will be with him along his road and with his children. Written by their hand, in the month of Ramadan 1140 Hegira (One thousand, one hundred and forty), 1728 AD.

The Humble Fares M"

The Pact of Prince Mourad Abou Al Lam'i, the governor of Metn, to Sheikh Bou Ali Beshir Kassab Salima:

"These written words attest to that which we have sworn and confirmed to our dear Sheikh Bou Ali Beshir. They are to be cherished and honoured between us. They are to be obeyed. We will intercede in every matter that demands our attention, holding him as dear to us as we hold ourselves. If anyone should oppose him, we will be his enemy. We swear this on God's Holy Word, on the prophets, His saints and His Holy Book. We so swear to this document

with no changes or exchanges. If we should change anything to which we have sworn, we have then betrayed God and His Faith will become our enemy. Written in the year 1731, AD, one thousand seven hundred thirty one. (The stamp is on the back side, in front of the signature).

    Merciful God, have mercy on your servant Mourad.   *The humble Mourad "*

The Murder Of Prince Asaad

History is full of crimes committed by Princes and Kings, killing their rivals. They killed their competitors for power, even if they were their closest friends and relatives.

In Egypt, Mohamed Ali Pasha killed the Mamluks. Prince Beshir the Great killed Girgis Baz and his brother Abd El Ahad. He gouged out the eyes of the sons of Prince Youssef al Shehabi, and the eyes of Prince Fares Sayed Ahmed Shehab. Napoleon ordered prisoners in Aka killed. These incidents happened in the East and the West. In such matters, some historians describe how horrible such deeds were and how cruel and tyranical were those who committed them. At the same time, other historians excuse those same rulers for what they did and consider them as political crimes that were necessary to control the people, to strengthen their authority, to establish their security and comfort, or to end sedition. The use of the sword was common at that time.

We think that the tale we are about to tell to you, faithfully reported from its narrators, is one of these types of incidents. We leave it for the reader to judge it.

Prince Assaf, the son of Prince Hussein Abou Al Lam'i, was one of Salima's Princes. Prince Assaf died. He had been locked in a constant dispute with his brothers for the right to rule. The struggle was particularly intense with his brother Hassan. The people of the village of Salima were divided into two groups, a party supporting Prince Hassan and the other, which was the majority, sympathised with the other group. After Prince Assaf's death, his heir, his son Asaad bin Assaf, was still a child. Sheikh Shebli Kassab was appointed to be the custodial parent of the young heir. Shebli had a brother called Youssef Kassab, and together, they had their supporters, among them was the Senior Governor Prince Molhem Shehab. He was the uncle of Prince Asaad, being his mother's brother. The Kassabian sheikhs took charge of the government. It was their intention to run the government until the young Prince was old enough to rule. Because the Prince was in their possession, their standing in the community increased and more and more people supported them. Then, the bitter opposition of the boy's uncles, Prince Hassan and Prince Soliman, increased. They put together a plot to get the Prince under their control. Hassan had gone to a village called Zar'oun. He invited the young Prince Assad to leave Salima and come to Zar'oun. Prince Assad was now twenty years old. Prince Hassan invited Assad to Zar'oun under the pretense that he wanted him to marry his daughter.

The right to govern went to the maturest and oldest person in the family. The children would share the fiefs. It seems that the Kassabs, who were the custodial parents designated by Prince Assaf, took steps to ensure that they kept his fiefs in the high Metn until his son Asaad came of age. It is said that this Prince was naïve and never matured, so the Kassabs monopolized the government. The other princes saw that their right to rule had been taken and they plotted to kill Prince Asaad. His death would eliminate the whole situation. Prince Hassan was corresponding with Asaad and his mother. They were hesitant about the invitation. Then in November, 1725, he decided to go. His guardian, Shebli Kassab advised him not to do so. He said that he was afraid of the evil that might be disguised in this visit. But the Prince refused to listen. There are tales saying that his mother accompanied him to Zar'oun.

Thus it was, that as he was about to reach his majority year, they killed him just as his guardian feared. There was a story that Ismail, the son of Hassan, killed him with the help of his uncle Soliman. He was reportedly killed at night while he slept. Other stories say that Prince Soliman hired someone to kill him, a Druze from Kafr Salwan by the name of Ghid. And, it was said that he killed the Prince and his mother. Afterward, Soliman himself killed Ghid saying that he feared that he would kill him as he had killed his nephew.

Then, the sound of gun fire was heard at night coming from Salima. Shebli Kassab yelled at his family. They were living at the castle of Prince Asaad. They started to gather and move their furniture to their homes. Before they could finish, Prince Ismail and his men surprised them. His uncle Soliman soon joined him. They entered the castle wanting to attack and kill Shebli with his brother Youssef. Shebli and Youssef had called for the help of the people of Salima. The town's citizens quickly gathered at the castle and found the gates closed. They screamed aloud and fights began. After the insistance of the people, Ismail and Soliman opened the gates and released Shebli and his brother Youssef. They were saved from certain death.

After this, the Kassabs could no longer stay in Salima being the object of such anger. So they escaped to Qarnayel, asking Prince Youssef Ibn Mourad Al Lam'i, the governor of Qarnayel at that time, for his protection. He granted their request and protected them from his paternal cousins' anger for two months. Then they finally had to flee to Kisrawan, where the Khazens, their allies, protected them and they resided in Zok Mesbah.

Prince Molhem heard about the murder of his nephew (his sister's son). Then Prince Mansour went to the Metn in 1753, destroying the buildings of the Lam'is, their harvest and their crops. They seized the remaining properties of Prince Hassan and his son Ismail. Later, he forgave them and made them pay twenty thousand piastres.

Thus it came about that the Princes Soliman and Haidar shared the properties of Prince Asaad. Together they ruled his governnment in Al Metn. After three years they made peace with the Kassabs. They came back to Salima in 1756. (This is reported from my late father, the late Guigis Zein, Asaad Beshir Kassab and the late Fares Khatar Bachaalany. This was also printed in the history book of Pastor Rofael Karama.)

Next I will present some of the agreements made by the people of Salima to their governors, the Lam'i Princes, to resolve disputes or other issues that might arise.

The Contract between The Bachaalany's And The Nakouzy's With Their Princes:

"WHEREAS we, the below mentioned two families, on the below mentioned date, agree to henceforth be one state, one hand, and one opinion. We have removed any wrong and any bitterness with our complete consent. We agree to be at the disposal of the highly respected, beloved Prince Hassan, Prince Assaf, and Prince Haidar. Being committed in writing, we hereby agree: First, that in any case arising between the two families, if it cannot be resolved, we will present it to Their Excellencies. Both families will cast off the two adversaries, and no one from our families will be friendly with whoever the accused is. Rather, we will exercise our full abilities to find the appropriate solution between the two adversaries. Whosoever shall commit a cruel act against another, we shall, all of us, be as one hand against him. We shall have nothing to do with him. No one will be his friend or be kind to him or join in fellowship with him. If we cannot stop him from so acting, we will present him to Their Excellencies and ask for his punishment. No one shall receive any special treatment because he appears to be good or because there is a case between him and another one from the two families.

No case should be kept from being presented to the governor. All cases and action showing just cause, will be resolved with no partiality, hatred, or discrimination. Their excellencies will solve any referred case justly as they have done in the past. No matter who shall commit a wrong, we will be the first to claim and ask for punishment. Whoever shall trespass, we will all be one arm against him. Whoever shall take sides with the accused, he will be expeled from his family and we will ask for his punishment, as God is our witness. If we should change our commitment, may God be our adversary in life and after death. We bind ourselves with our full consent. If any of us cause

183

any misunderstanding, he will be bound by this legal record. If we change our will and show any violation, then the offending party shall pay a legal fine of one thousand and five hundred piasters to the Treasury of Their Excellencies. And if only a part of the whole group are in violation of this agreement, then they will pay five hundred piasters as a fine with no right to seek any mediation. And if there is just one individual who makes changes he will be ousted from the group and the governor shall have the final judgment concerning his punishment. We will ignore him and no one will keep his company. This is made with our full consent, with no force or reservation, but with our full and voluntary consent.

Our relations in dealing with each other, acting according to our agreement, are very old and eternal. Accordingly we commit this to writing, in the month of Hegira Shaaban, the Hegira year twelve hundred and thirty four, 1818 A,D..   Committed to writing by Elias Al Tyan

Accepting for themselves: The Bachaalany house in general and the Nakouzy house in general.

Witnesses: Mohamed Mahmoud al Masry, Hussein Ibn Daher Said. "

And, also, the following:

The Contract Of The Bou Ali Said Family In Salima:

"WHEREAS on the mentioned date, we, the previously mentioned individuals, promise to be at the disposal and service of our Afandeyate in Salima. We promise to obey them by following their orders, whether many or few. We will do so to our fullest extent, with our blood, our lives and all that we possess. We will not be concerned or sorry for whatever would be a benefit for them. Whatever they ask for we shall strive to accomplish. We cannot be dedicated to any other but them. We cannot deviate from their service or their desire. Should anyone oppose Their Excellencies and be opposed to their good, we will not agree with them. We will not participate with them. We will not request anything of them. We will not shelter them. We will give them no assistance. To the contrary, we will always work hard in our endevours, listening to and obeying the orders of Their Excellencies. And should any one of us fail to perform this union, we will all be as one arm to force compliance. If he does not perform, then, he will be presented to His Excellency, and whatever he judges will be considered fair. There will be no mediation or intercession for him. Our hope is in what they have planned and reassured us. The expectation and recognition is that they own and guard us jealously, giving us their consideration and obligations. Such has been for both of us our traditions and manners inherited from our ancestors. So we will continue to be in accordance with each other, in accordance with justice and righteousness.

With full knowledge of this, we have made this written agreement with our complete and voluntary consent, with God, the Judge of our circumstances, our money and our children, as our witness.

Written and signed in the Hegira year twelve thirty six, and accepted by: Bou Ali Ezz El Dine, Kiwan, his brother Hassan, Hamoud his nephew (brother's son), Ahmed Hamdan, the sons of Seif, Qassem Gouha and his brothers, the sons of Bou Ali, Mahmoud Ibn Ezz Eddine, Soliman and his sons and Saab ibn Hussein and his sons."

Al Zahrani Battle

The Matawels (Matawilahs, as the Shi'ite Muslims were called in Syria) were plundering in the South, revolting against the government of Prince Youssef al Shihabi. So, in 1770, the Prince prepared to punish them with a force of thirty thousand soldiers. But despite the great courage shown by the Lebanese fighters, they failed. The battle occurred in the area between the rivers of Al Zahrani and Al Qasimeya. In this battle, Beshir Saab Kassab, the guardian of Prince Assaf was killed. Along with him, Nasrallah Attallah and Gad'oun Fasida Bachaalany also died. There is a saying that two hundred pairs of brothers from Lebanon were killed in that battle.

Shar Al Mokhtara

This was a battle that happened between Prince Beshir and Sheikh Beshir (1824 – 1825). The Sheikh and those standing with him were against the Prince who lost and he and his forces were dispersed. They escaped to Houran where they were captured. They were then sent to Akka and sentenced. A group of Prince Haidar's men from Salima supported Prince Beshir. There were other men, followers of Prince Assaf who supported the Sheikh.

The Sanour Day

This is one of the famous Lebanese days of celebration. Prince Haidar, the Prince of Salima, along with his men originating from Al Metn attended that battle and other ones. Briefly, the history of this Battle of Sanour Fortress is as follows: At the end of 1829, the chiefs of Nablous originating from Bani Touqan, Al Gerar and other places, disobeyed Abdallah Pasha. He was the regional leader of the Ottoman government in Akka. He wanted to use force to bring these people into compliance with his rule. They, however, revolted and made a stand at the fortress at Sanour. This was a fortified stronghold built on a rounded rock. The soldiers of the government attacked them but lost and retreated. Then, the leader from Akka called for military assistance from Prince Beshir who immediately moved in to help on January 3, 1830. He joined in with his Lebanese men, among them the Maronite hero Abou Samra Ghanem from Bekassin, and Hanna al Shantiri from Bekefya. The famous Youssef was not among the fighters because some of the people thought he was too young.

Prince Haidar and his strong powerful men of the Metn strengthened the siege. Those under siege, at the risk of their lives, defended the Fortress for four months but were finally forced to surrender. The Sanour Fortress was demolished.

Prince Beshir went back to Lebanon with his victorious fighters, celebrating and waving victory flags above their heads.

Prince Haidar Al Shihabi, the Lebanese historian, was the one who reported that battle. Then Al Shedyak, Al Debs and Al Maalouf took that story and embellished it. In the Al Manara magazine (2:501,588) we published four letters of Prince Haidar Abou Al Lam', who witnessed the battle. The letters were sent to his wife. They contain interesting news of the battle that was previously unpublished. In the letters he tells the names of some of the Prince's men who participated in that battle.

The Governors Tyranny

Among the events that took place in Salima, there is an interesting one which happened in July, 1865. These are the details: Ward was the wife of Hanna Khokaz. He was an Armenian from Beirut and the personal secretary of Daoud Pasha, the administration officer of Lebanon (1861 – 1868). He went to Salima to spend the summer there. Ward's maid commited a violation against the property. The keeper, a man by the name of Asaad Fares, reprimanded her. This led to a full confrontation as the two of them hurled insults at each other. The lady, Ward, complained of this incident through government channels. The government officials gave her full consideration because of her husband's position. He was, at the time, accompanying Daoud Pasha in Istanbul.

As a result of the complaints, the government commissioners wanted to catch the keeper who was a member of the Bachaalany family. He escaped arrest and his relatives were accused of helping him to escape. This led to a major dispute between them and the commissioners. Then, the district commissioner sent a large military force to Salima to capture the keeper and his relatives. They had insulted and fought with the lower officials there. The strongest of the

Bachaalany's left the houses and went out into the rocks. The soldiers were afraid to approach them. The Bachaalany's refused to surrender because they feared the government would betray and oppress them.

Finally, they decided to ask for help from Youssef Beik Karam, the protector of oppressed people and friend of all Lebanese. He was particularly close to the Bachaalany's since most of them were his supporters.

Three of them, Daher Negm Andrea, known for his fast talking, his brother Girgis who used to be one of the government's cavalry, and D'ebis Tanious, known for his enthusiasm, walked down the Al Gerd road towards Ehden. On the way, they met the Beik. Once he learned of the events taking place, he said: "May those tyrants of the government perish." Then he wrote to the Patriarch that the local government was mistreating his sons, the Bachaalany's. He said that if the government's men did not treat this family with justice, then he would be obliged to come to their aid.

After they rested at his house, they excused themselves to go. Then he told them as they were leaving: "I swear on my father's grave, if the government doesn't treat you right, I will personally come to save you, the ones who went with me to Al Thaghra (near Al Choueir), who can take me to Bahnas and Beit El Dine (the Government Headquarters). Then, the Patriarch wrote to Bishop Geagea who negotiated with the District Commissioner. When the governors saw that, they feared that Karam could be behind the whole affair, so they became very tolerant of the Bachaalany's. The Bachaalany family heavily armed themselves and left their hideout. They went to the government headquarters where they reconciled with the officials.

The following is the biography of "The Hero Of Lebanon", summarized from our book <u>Lebanon And Youssef Beik Karam</u> which was published in 1925, and has since become very scarce.

Youssef Beik Karam

Youssef Karam was born in the middle of May, 1823. His birthplace was the village of Ehden, the Bride of the North and the origin of geniuses and heroes. The great Patriarch Estephan Al Douehi and the famous Youssef Beik Karam are but two examples.

Karam's father was Sheikh Boutros, one of the notables of Ehden. He followed in the footsteps of the piety, patriotism, pride, and generosity of his ancestors. His mother was Mary, the daughter of Sheikh Antonios Abi Khatar Al 'Entorini. She was raised in a home filled with knowledge and virtue. Youssef learned all these good traits and integrity from his parents. His father hired private tutors of the highest learning and the best character to teach Youssef the principles of religion and literature. The best of these was the Spanish priest, Father Amaya, who taught him many subjects, especially the French language. It is no wonder that he developed such a high degree of culture. It is no surprise that his learning stimulated his mind and made his personality grow even more. He mastered the Syriac language so well that he was able to write poems in it. He also learned to read, write, and speak French and Italian. He was considered one of the best Arabic writers, exceling at Kathir, Yaalou, and Yanhat verse.

Youssef was also exceptional at horse back riding, being taught by the unique Sheikh Emad Al Hashem Al 'Akouri. The student surpassed his teacher because of his great intelligence and physical strength.

His father's high political position brought to him people of virtue, high ethics, and great knowledge. Kings, princes and notable travelers were his acquaintances, so it is no surprise that he came to characterize the best of the ethics of his era. Before reaching his full status of manhood he had already become accomplished in his knowledge of religion, literature, history, administration, and fighting.

Some of the stories of his younger days show his uncommon intelligence and great courage. Sheikh Hussein Talhouk, a well known Druze, once heard Youssef speak at a meeting of country ministers in Beirut. He was astonished at the courageous comments and the solid logic of his arguments. So much so, that he commented: "This boy will be great. If he was one of ours, we would have worshipped him!"

After the death of his father, Youssef became the governor of the region and performed great deeds showing his sense of justice and honesty. He was an example for the youth to learn his courage, patriotism, and religion, all at the same time.

When the insurgency of the 1860's happened and anarchy spread throughout the whole country, Youssef was the leader that people obeyed. He was their soul and financial security. He sacrificed his mind, his pen, and his wealth to help those afflicted by the disasters of those days. His sword remained sheathed for just reasons. When the French military expedition arrived, its men so admired him that they called him the "Prince of Lebanon" and "Youssef The First". They could feel his deep devotion to freedom and independence for his country.

After gaining considerable power and sovereignty, Fouad Pasha, the Ambassador of the Ruler, appointed him the Governor of North Lebanon. He maintained justice and stability as well as the special privilege that Lebanon enjoyed. He proved the capability of a citizen to govern with impartiality and perfection. This was the judgment of leaders throughout the country. He was the first person elected to govern Lebanon.

There were detractors who were jealous of his position. There were even some who plotted against him. Some, who did not like his policies. Some, who wanted their own personal gain. So often, the pretext given was that Karam was too religious.

Then, an international committee appointed a foreign governor for Lebanon. Thus it was deprived of its own patriotic governor. Youssef Beik Karam resigned from his post, but his influence remained powerful. Daoud Pasha, who was appointed to rule Lebanon, could not get the approval of the people for his reign. The people still supported Karam and they viewed his resignation as an act of honor and courage. They continued to support his efforts to defend their rights of self rule.

Daoud Pasha saw that he needed help so he called on Foad Pasha who paid a personal visit to Karam. This alone is proof of the high standing of Karam. He refused the recommendations of Foad that he should take a position in Daoud Pasha's government. Karam went into exile. This increased the bitterness of the Lebanese against Daoud Pasha. He tried to gain the support of the people by giving their chiefs jobs and pretending that he cared for them. None of this was successful.

Karam traveled from Egypt and Turkey all the way to France trying to negotiate Lebanon's self rule. He even presented his case to the Emperor, Napoleon III. Karam then ended his exile and returned home to Lebanon. This caused considerable tension in the country even though he promised to remain neutral.

Daoud Pasha saw Karam's popularity increasing day after day. Convinced that Karam was receiving outside help from some unknown power, Daoud Pasha insisted that Karam work in his administration. Karam refused and retired from active opposition. Still, his mere presence was enough to keep the people's faith in democracy alive.

Youssef Beik Karam held no extremist positions. The people did not love him because he resisted unjust Turkish rule. They loved him because he supported the oppressed. He was straight-forward. He was brave. He defended his country with his soul and his wealth. The clergy supported him because of his patriotism, his sense of revolution, and because he wanted to preserve the Maronite religion and stand up for the rights of men.

Daoud liked to rule by force, so he sent the Turkish Army back into the mountains. He increased the taxes on the people and this provoked intense indignation. The Patriarch opposed these actions and the people revolted by refusing to pay the taxes. Karam decided to lead the people in revolution. The Patriarch tried to mediate the crisis but Daoud refused his efforts. Daoud then used military force and arrested some of Karam's friends. The revolution had started!

Karam protested this injustice. He spoke to a peaceful crowd that included a group of chiefs from Bcharre, the house of Abi Saab, Al Dahers, and Al 'Azars. He thought that they did not share his opinions. The country was suffering and there was no one more powerful and better than him. The people all forgot about their internal and petty disputes. They agreed that Karam should take charge and nothing less than seeing him in the Governor's seat would be acceptible.

While mediators were trying to resolve the dispute, Daoud Pasha sent a force to capture Karam. They attempted an ambush near Jounieh and they attacked his followers. The fighting was intense and Karam's backers forced Daoud's troops to retreat to Zaghrata.

Daoud Pasha then tried to entrap Karam by secretly attacking him at Bnasha. Anyone who knows about the Battle of Bnasha sees it as a brilliant victory. Karam and his troops certainly erased any hint of dishonor or weakness of which some had accused them.

The government was only printing news that it felt was suitable and enhanced their image. They were afraid that they would be embarassed by their losses and that the people's bitterness toward them would increase. Contradictions in their different stories, however, made people suspicious. Their efforts were in vain.

It wasn't long before the news of Karam's victory spread by word of mouth. He had completely vanquished the Ottoman Army and shown great bravery and ability. This victory by Karam's small military force was the catalyst for his future victories. Karam wisely took shelter in the mountains.

Daoud's army, however, was chasing after him everywhere he went. The army cruelly treated people whose only crime was that they loved Karam. Furthermore, Daoud ordered Karam's beautiful castle in Ehden to be plundered. Seeking revenge, he ordered it to be burned, destroying great historical treasures, many presented by royalty and the famous who had been guests in Karam's home. But the people shouted: "You did not burn Karam's house. You destroyed the house of our Country, the house of the poor!"

Karam was suffering through this sorrowful situation. He was homeless, living in icy weather in the rugged mountains. But he treated his personal suffering as minor. He was absorbed by the calamities affecting his people. He saw the destruction of his castle as an attempt to destroy the freedom of his country.

The injustices that were occurring pushed him out of his den into battles to oppose the savagery that was spreading. In his concern, he wrote to the Patriarch and Bishops pleading his case and explaining the truth of what was happening. He explained the fairness of his case and his attempts to defend the rights of the people. He called them to solidarity with his cause. The French newspapers and the newspaper, "Al Gawaeb" of Al Shediyak in Istanbul were supporting and defending Karam. His friends in Beirut offered to help him escape to Europe. His friend Mohamed Arselan offered him his home in which to hide. Karam thanked them all, and, refused all offers.

More military expeditions were seeking him out and the number of soldiers committed to his capture increased after every attempt. Then at the Ain Qarna and Meziara (Wadi Miziari) Battle, there were nine thousand soldiers led by the greatest Turkish commanders. The Turkish soldiers faced the great Lebanese mountains in fear and awe. The commanders desparately wanted to kill this revolutionary who fought them at Badishah and escaped only by some divine miracle.

Inevitably, violence erupted. Men from North Lebanon and Kisrawan joined with Karam. They were followed by the men from the Metn. As he moved on from one battle to another, his followers increased. Meanwhile, Daoud's forces were constantly retreating all the way back to Bekefya.

Daoud Pasha abandoned his headquarters at Beit El Dine, fleeing to Beirut. There, he rallied support from the European Ambassadors who negotiated with Karam to stop the fighting.

At the same time, news arrived from the French Ambassador that the Emperor offered Karam safe passage and haven in Algeria. Karam saw that it was inevitable that he accept the Emperor's offer. He stopped his advance on Beit El Dine and, with his followers, went to Bkerke where he met with the Patriarch, his Bishops, and other notables. A crowd numbering in the thousands gather outside the Patriarch's residence. Karam and the Patriarch convinced the crowd that this exile was necessary for the benefit of the country and the welfare her people.

Karam left Lebanon with his head held high, drawing his sword like a conqueror as he entered Beirut. His cortege was magnificent. The country never saw anything like it before. He walked between two rows of people from the Dog River to the town. Those who were waiting to see him shouted "God, let him triumph!" as he passed by. He was the guest of the French Consul who put Al Dare'a at his disposal. When it was time for him to leave, people said their farewells with voices cracking from emotion. Even as he tried to be brave and calm with these people, he was impressed. He said goodbye to his country. He looked at his beloved mountains and gave them his final salute.

When he arrived at Alexandria he was welcomed by a crowd. The same happened when he arrived in Marseilles. The French people watched the great Lebanese prince wearing his unique uniform. In front of him, walked his eight comrades in their bright uniforms. The people were shouting "Long live Youssef Karam, the Hero of Lebanon!" He shouted back: "Long live the Emperor Napoleon!" and "Long live France, the protector of Lebanon!" Then he sailed to Algeria where his friend Marshal Mekmahoun met him with respect and affection. The French newspapers were full of long stories about him. His name was the subject of admiration by the whole world.

He went on to Paris where he was honored by standing before the Emperor Napoleon III and the Empress Eugenie. The Emperor placed a high ranking decoration on his chest. At the same time, the famous Sheikh Youssef Al Assir said: "France has welcomed Youssef Beik Karam as a king. The Archbishop has visited him. Emperor Napoleon III has overwhelmed him with his concern and generosity. The people and dignitaries have glorified him. The government, the clergy and the people of France have given him great sums of money and promised to help him achieve his goals and name him the Prince of Lebanon."

Karam began to travel throughout Europe visiting its capitals. He wanted to learn more about them and he wanted to survey their politicians about his country. He negotiated with Kings and their ministers about the Lebanese reformation. Everywhere he went, he was the subject of admiration and discussion. He even traveled to the capital of Turkey, gaining privilege with high ranking officials in the government who promised him good things. Karam was not satisfied with the progress of his efforts and he started laying plans for a military expedition under his leadership. He would enter Lebanon as a conqueror through Egypt and Latakia.

He negotiated with some countries who considered him a great leader of Lebanon. He made treaties to provide the necessary funds for such an invasion. He agreed with his Algerian friend, Emi Abdel Kader, to free Syria and Lebanon. At the same time, he was making proposals to the French government through his friends, to get financial backing for internal improvements in Lebanon. These included the construction of a railroad, opening coal mines, and constructing water works, all of which would benefit the Lebanese people.

His ideas, however, did not become realities because of opposition he encountered. In addition to all this, he was managing his own affairs in Lebanon. He was relying on the income of his properties to pay for his many expenses including contributions to his friends and the many people who sought his financial aid to overcome their crises. He also gave special attention to spiritual affairs. He wanted to raise the standing of the Maronite Rite of the Catholic Church and, to this end, he performed many great deeds.

On April 7, 1889, at 11:50 A.M., the tragic news arrived from Razinia, near Naples. It spread throughout Italy, then to France and Syria. "No more Hero of Lebanon. The noble Prince Youssef Karam has died."

After an elaborate funeral, he was buried. A few months later his body was moved to Ehden. This was a glorious ceremony and his body was entombed in the Church of Saint George. Renowned people made pilgrimages to this place, and still do.

On September 11, 1932, a statue of Karam was dedicated in Ehden. It was made by the sculptor Youssef Saadallah Al Howeik and paid for by some generous expatriates from Ehden. The ceremony was led by Patriarch Anton Areda and Mr. Charles Al Debas, the President of the Republic of Lebanon.

Such is the distinguished life of the Hero of Lebanon. He was so noteworthy because of his many talents and great characteristics. He was so exceptional for his great deeds and the heritage he left for us. It is rare to find a great man who was so free from faults in his behavior and deeds.

He was a shining example of good ethics, piety, chastity, courage, patriotism and self sacrifice. All that he did, said, or wrote was so perfect and beautiful, showing his brilliance, abundant knowledge, strong faith, energy, and noble opinions. He gained victory honestly through dedication. There are many similarities between him and Napoleon. If France is proud of its Napoleon, so Lebanon is proud of its Karam. He is great. A leader. A fighter. A hero. He is a hero of life and faith. He has been named the Hero of Lebanon, a special honor. He was a firm believer and his religion was the secret of his greatness. It was the factor which pushed him to sacrifice his life and wealth for his country.

He was unique in his love of purity and chastity. He was never dishonored by meanness. He never submitted to base affections despite the temptations that came with his fame and wealth. He was one of our great exponents for establishing our independence and rewriting our historical glory. Even if he did not succeed in his objectives, at least he built a strong base for the next generation to build their glory and independence. He spread in their heart an immortal soul. The last thing I have to say: Every Lebanese must visit the tomb of the Hero of Lebanon in the Church he loved, with his statue in front, compensation for the many favors he did for his beloved country.

THE HISTORY OF
THE FAMILIES OF SALIMA

Section 4

We have talked about the social and religious life in Salima based on the materials and documents we have on hand. Lest we forget, we must now discuss the families of Salima and their history and geneology.

The first family that we will portray is that of the Al Lam's. Although their story has been recorded in two large volumes, it still remains in manuscript form. It is too long to present here so we will summarize it. Following that, we will write about the history of the rest of the families of Salima, those who still reside there as well as those that have become expatriates. After that, we will talk about the old and new families of Bchaaleh including families who migrated. Thus, the history of Bchaaleh will be the first and the last topics of this book, the A and the Z, the alpha and the omega. How wonderful it would be if our financial condition improved and we could expand our treatment to two or, perhaps, three volumes. This would allow us to publish the documents, the updated news and the miscellaneous remnants relating to the families of Salima during the era of the Princes, especially the days of Prince Haidar which were full of important and interesting historical events.

THE HOUSE OF ABI AL LAM'

Chapter 1

Origins and Residences

The Lam' (Lam'i) Princes are descended from Prince Abi Al Lam'. His lineage comes down from Fawares al Tanukh. The Tanukh is one of the most noble of the Arab tribes that came from Al Hira, an ancient city in Mesopotamia located south of what is now Kufa in south-central Iraq, to the high mountain near Halab, the ancient name of Aleppo in northern Syria.. From there they moved to Lebanon where they settled and can still be found today.

The Tanukh origins go back to Al Nu'man Bin Mundhir. He was known as Ibn Ma Esama Al Lakhmi. He was one of the Arab conquerors and one of the Kings of Al Hira. He assisted the Persian Kings in their battles. His reign passed to his sons after him and ended with Al Nu'man IV (594 AD). Ali Khosrow, the King of the Persians, had disputes with Al Nu'man IV and fought with him for many years. Finally, Khosrow tricked him and killed him. Then, Nu'man IV's son Al Maary emigrated with his tribes. They ended up in the area between Halab and Al Me'ara. This was when Islam was appearing.

In 779 AD, the Abbasid Caliph Al Mahdi came to Halab, the ancient name of Aleppo in northern Syria. The Tanukhs who were living around the city of Halab went out to welcome him. In those days the Tanukh were tent dwellers and rode horses attired with beautiful saddles.

Some one told the Caliph that the Tanukhs were all Christians. At that news, the Caliph was furious. He demanded that they become Muslims which they did, approximately five thousand men. The women had fled and escaped from the Caliph. One man called Laith was martyred. After that, they moved from the desert to the high mount. There they built villages and established farms.

A serious incident then occurred. A representative of the Halab governor sent to the people attacked some of their women. One of the men called Naba pounced on the man and killed him. He then fled to Lebanon. When the governor learned of this the people became fearful for their safety. They followed Naba's lead and likewise went to Lebanon (820 AD). There were ten tribes governed by Prince Tanukh. First they settled in the Southwest of Lebanon. Then they spread throughout the country.

The references for this information consist of the following: a handwritten manuscript of the history of Prince Haidar Al Shehabi, in his own handwriting; The History of the Notable Sheikh Tanous Al Shediyak; the manuscript history of Sheikh Antonious El Aintorini; Mount Lebanon by Lord Churchill Beik (in English); The History of Celdo Wathor Told To Mr. Odoshir; The Syriac History Of Ibn El Ebry; documents taken by Sheikh Philip Al Khazen from the Tuscany Treasury, then published by Father Boulos Qarali in his book The History Of Fakhr Eddine Al Maani; "Lebanon During The Era Of The Mamlukes" by Professor Ibrahim Awad in The East, 1940; and, from the documents in our own possession.

As these tribes spread, their might strengthened. Their standing in Lebanon rose consistently until its people became governors and elders. The tribe of Bani Fawares, also known as the Tanukhs of Fares governed the fief of Al Metn.

194

Then, for the first time, they settled in the upper area in the village of Kafr Slowan. It was there that Abou Al Lam', the founder of this famous family, emerged.

At that time his familly was known as "the Lieutenant Colonels" of Kafr Salwan. When he became well known and famous, it started to be known as his surname. It continues to be tied to him right down to the present time.

The family embraced the Druze religion. The religion had appeared in Egypt at the end of the fourth Hijra century. It spread to Syria and Lebanon. The ancestors of the Lam' followed the religion prevailing in the country they were governing.

The Genius and Government of the Lam'.

The importance of the Lam' increased and their reputation spread. They were men of genius. They were distinguished by their courage, generosity and sound policy. Their boldness and patriotism showed itself from the very beginning of their rule. They were Lieutenant Colonels and they governed Al Metn, the Gorge, and the surrounding area. They made an agreement with the Maronites of the Kisrawan. They fought against the soldiers of Syria who crept into Lebanon in 1294. They defeated the Syrian Army in the Battle of Ain Sannine near Bakinta.

The Lam' were partisans of the Qays Party and major supporters of the Ma'n House. The Ma'ns were the governors of Lebanon and the leaders of the Qays. This party originated in pre-Islamic days from two leaders, Qays and Yomn. It existed among the Arab tribes for a long time. The tribes who descended in Lebanon absorbed the ideas of that party and held them. In the seventeenth century those beliefs intensified.

Their Relation With The Ma'n House.

Prince Fakhr al-Din al Ma'n II was related by marriage to the Lam's. The marriages were arranged to form an alliance between the two families as well as to seal their bond of friendship. After the disaster of the Ma'n's in 1635, they and their allies were pursued by their enemies. Sheikh Abou Nader Al Khazen, the Commander of the Army of Fakhr al_Din II and his counselor went to Rome to seek the help of the Pope. They sought his assistance to save Prince Mulhim, the son of the brother of Fakir al-Din II, and his brothers-in-law, the Lieutenant Colonels Lam's. After their 1635 disaster they were hiding from the Turks in the Lebanon mountains. The only ones to escape from the Turks were a young son of Fakhr al-Din, Hussein bin Oloa bint Sifa, his nephew (brother's son), Prince Mulhim, and his daughters who were married to the Lam' Lieutenant Colonels.

In 1636, the Pope wrote to the King of Tuscany, Ferdinand II, through Sheikh Abou Nader, asking him to send the ship "Gholion" to Lebanon to rescue them and bring them to Europe.

Abou Nader held a special position in Rome and was highly respected in the court of Tuscany. Accordingly, the Grand Duke fulfilled the Pope's wishes and prepared the rescue boat stating that it was ready to receive them as guests. Abou Nader sailed on the "Gholion" and stopped by Malta with his children. He sent his son Nader with Father Ya'koub from Vendome to Lebanon. They arrived there and met with one of the Lam's houses but could not locate Prince Mulhim who was in hiding. They could not extend their stay to wait for him because plague was spreading throughout the country. They returned to Malta. Abou Nader returned to Rome with two letters, one, for the Pope and the other for the King of Tuscany. They were letters expressing gratitude, apologies and prayers from Alam al-Din, Qayed Beih, and Mourad Abou Al Lam'.

Father Ya'koub presented a report to Cardinal Berberini, Minister to the Pope. In summary, it said:

Prince Ali, son of Prince Fakhr al-Din is alive, and he and his paternal cousin Mulhim are hiding in the Damascus regions. The Lam's, bothers-in-law of Fakhr al-Din, mobilized two thousand men in the woods, under the command of their father Lieutenant Colonel Alam al-Din. They are in fortified places north of Beirut. They are creating fear throughout all the regions of Syria. They all agreed on what should be done. This is what they wrote about in their letters to the Cardinal and the Grand-Duke. The Lieutenant Colonels like many of the Christians are ready to do their utmost. They are prepared to assemble about twenty-five thousand men, among them a large group of Christians. They are eagerly awaiting word from the Princes of the Christians verifying their commitment. They will be assembling a military excursion of 25 fighting ships, 15 transport ships, and mobilize 25,000 fighters to take possession of the Holy Lands and occupy the island of Cyprus. This will not be a difficult task for the virtuous Apostolic Chair, the Knights of Malta, the State of Tuscany, the Kingdom of Spain, and the various other Christian countries."

Their Three Houses

In the past, the Lam's were living in Kafr Salwan, in upper Metn. Probably around 1616 they left there. The exact time when the grandfather Abou Al Lam' existed is unknown. It probably is not as some historians have written. They said that he moved with his children from Kafr Salwan then died in Al Metn and that he was buried in the Prince's cupola. However, this is based on an incorrect reading of the date engraved on the tomb. I personally went to al Metn and have read the inscription. It states:

"In the name of God, the All Merciful, this blessed tomb was constructed by His Excellency The Lieutnant Colonel Alam Eddine, the son of the late Excellency The Lieutenant Colonel Abou Al Lam'. He was buried here on the morning of the unique Sunday, in the Hegira month Safar, in the Hegira year 1058."

People understood this inscription to mean that Alam Eddine constructed that tomb for his father who was buried there. However, the written words do not necessarily mean that. It is not proof that Abou al Lam' is the father of Alam Eddine or his grandfather. Anyone who has studied the terminology of those people knows that the meaning of the words used varies. Often the sons of Abou Al Lam' and his grand children wrote "The Son of Abou al Lam'a" or "Known as Ibn Abou Al Lam'".

Nevethless, we do know that the Lam's were divided in three houses or three family branches: 1) Qayed Bayeh in Salima, 2) Mourad in Al Metn, and, 3) Fares in Beskinta.

Qayed Bayeh had a son called Abdulallah who had four sons. Of them, Hussein, lived in his father's house in Salima; Negm, resided in the Ras El Metn house; and Mohamed, was the owner of the Al Shabania house.

The families which are descended from the house of Mourad in Al Metn include the house of Prince Youssef in Qarnayl, the house of Prince Shedid in Falougha, a house in Abadia and a house in Broumeya.

The offspring of Prince Fares stayed in Beskinta.

The offspring of Prince Youssef moved from Qarnayel to Beit Mary. The offspring of the Princes of Salima moved to Beit Eshabab after the events of Ibrahim Pasha, and then resided in Bekefya. When Prince Haidar took charge of the Hakemeyaet El Nasara in 1846, he built his castle there.

The majority of the princes and sheikhs in Lebanon were nobles of great generosity. Talk about their tyranny and oppression do not flaw these wise and noble men. They were human beings who made mistakes. They had power and possessions and they made mistakes like all people do. Their advantages outweighed their inconveniences. The noble and virtuous men far outnumbered the uneducated ones. These leaders were the strength of Lebanon who took charge and fulfilled her needs. They are the pride of Lebanon which would not have existed without them.

The Lam's preserved the country's rights and independence. They faced oppression and misfortune when they became partners with the Ma'ns and the Shehabs and all the others who ruled over Lebanon. They revived the region's agriculture and promoted industry and the arts. Many of them were masters of the sword and the horse as well as of writing and poetry. Their houses were meeting places of the talented and the wise.

They were the safeguards of Christianity and the builders of Churches and monasteries. They did this before and after they became Christians. We are deeply indebted to them for their great and memorable deeds. We saw how they drew Christians close to them being their governors' and trustees. We also saw how that pursuaded the Christians to settle in the fief of Metn, especially in Salima. This village possessed prestige and fame during their era. Many oppressed people asked for their assistance because the princes were known for their generosity, chivalry and ardor. This further added to their power and sovereignty. It added even more life and civilization to the country. The fortresses that the princes constructed, which remain to this day, are proof of their power and capability. These buildings also show the high level of the art of construction, sculpturing and engraving that existed in their days.

Prince Abdullah.

In the beginning of the 17th century, Qayed Bayeh Abi Al Lam' left the village of Kafr Salwan to reside in the historical village of Salima. It was there that his son Abdullah grew up. He then enlarged the castle that his father built. He also constructed a fortress in Ras Al Metn.

We previously mentioned that Prince Abdullah's son Hussein fought in the battle of Ayn Darah. This was according to report of the historian Prince Haidar Ahmed Al Shehabi. However, we found a book printed in Rowan in 1717 written by the French traveler Paul Lucas. He travelled to the East in 1714 on orders of King Louis XIV. Like Prince Haidar, he reports as being an eyewitness to the Ayn Darah (Ain Dara) Battle. However he does differ with the Prince concerning some dates, some events, and the role of Prince Hussein. The following is an honest and accurate translation of the French version:

"Among the dangerous events that occurred which were very harmful for the Christians in Lebanon was the deposing of Prince Abdullah. It was well known that he favored the Christians and supported the Maronites. He treated them kindly. He asked for their help against the Turkish governors.

The local governor was a Druze Prince and he had exclusivity in governing his territory. However he was under the supervision of a Turkish governor and was obligated to provide him with soldiers when needed. Being obedient to their rule was not a problem for the Prince. However their despotism and constant constraint were. This forced Prince Abdullah to pay large amounts of money to try to please them. Prince Abdullah tried to take all possible precautions but because of their greed he was unable to meet their demands. He could not please the governors of Syria and Sayda. The greediest was the governor of Syria. He was known for his brutality and boldness. Everyone feared him. Prince Abdullah was surpassing Al Sadr Al Aazam in his influence and power. He was even more proud of himself when he conquered the Arab rebels in Palestine and Gaza. This made the Syrian governor Al Sadr Al Aazam decide to remove him. To accomplish this he committed one injustice after another against the Druze. He imposed harsh penalties on them. He made an alliance with the governor of Sayda to the effect that if Prince Abdullah could not pay the excessive taxes then they would strip him and his family of their rule, a rule that they inherited from their ancestors. Then the Turkish governor would give their territory over to a family well known for their hostility against the Prince.

The two governors mobilized their soldiers. They gathered accomplices to help them fight the Prince and his partisans. The Prince, the grand-son of Fakhr al-Din, had to leave his castle and hide in caves in the mountains along with other princes.

Prince Abdallah was caught by his enemis who had plotted many traps to bring it about. The Christians and especially the Capuchins were so sad about that. He had loved them so much, brought them together, and built a monastery for them in his fief. In those days he even thought about becoming a Christian. Now that the venerable old prince was in prison he was destitute. He lacked life's necessities. The missionaries smuggled the basics to him.

So it was that the Prince became afraid that he would die. He asked to be baptized. One of his Maronite men performed the Sacrament with the guidance of the missionaries. He received the sacraments with joy and piety as fitting the Christian forefathers. He joined his hands to his chest with his eyes looking up at the sky and weeping. Then, with courage and firmness, he declared to his faithful servant that he wasno longer afraid of death. He asked that the Capuchin priests be informed of that.

When the missionaries learned of this they were relieved. They prayed for him to find fullness and long life. They made attempts to have the governors forgive and release him. They made an agreement with a tradesman to ransom the Prince. But the Pasha refused it and wanted ransom to be paid for him and all the followers of the Prince together. That was impossible. So the Prince remained in prison.

That cruel treatment influenced the Prince's children. Everything they had was worthless, their houses and all their possessions. None of it could buy the freedom of their father. Accordingly they worked on plans to save him. Among the Druze Princes was his elder son Prince Hussein, the bravest prince. He gathered together his brother, their men, as well as the men of their allies. When the army was completely mobilized, they attacked their enemies resolved to either vanquish them or die.

They reinforced themselves in Ayn Darah. After two hours of intense fighting, they totally conquered them. They killed anyone who resisted them. They plunder the vanquished.

They did not attack the government workers or its army so as not to provoke it. So it was they got back their stolen freedom and their extorted fiefs.

Prince Abdullah was the only one who remained captive as he could not pay the ransom for all the prisoners. He was taken to Al Basra, near Persia, which is the same place to which the governor of Sayda was transferred.

The oppressed Prince considered his baptism to be the only consolation in his life. He wanted nothing more than to meet God. The first thing his children did when they regained their fiefs was to call for the missionaries who had performed such great charitable deeds for the country, especially since 1710 when the uprising began.

Under the strict orders of Al Sadr Al Aazam, neither the governor of Syria nor any other governor, was to make troubles for the Christians or the Druze from that date forward. Prince Abdulah died in 1717 A.D.."

Lieutenant Colonel Prince

Now is a good place to mention how we replied to Prince Nessib Shehab in the *Al Belad* newspaper in an issue of the year 1937. It concerned the fief of the Lam's and was as follows: The important writer Prince Nessib Shehab wrote some historical articles in the *Al Belad* newspaper. We need such articles. However, sometimes he contradicts the statements of a great number of researchers, follows weak opinions, and gives himself too much authority. Such are not the characteristics of the honest historian who follows his mind and aims for noble purposes and goals. A good historical writer does not resolve a historical matter unless he is sure of its correctness. He must distinguish between the current facts which all trusted historians voted for and the narrated traditions still under investigation. When historians are in disagreement about the facts, they need to be reviewed. All this is necessary so as not to accuse the Prince by spreading rumors. This we will not accept.

The Prince has written in the "*Al Ahwal*" newspaper an article about the Lam's princes. In it he wrote that Prince Haidar al Shehabi, the great governor, became related by marriage to them after the Ayn Darah battle, and, also, that their rank rose to "Prince" after having been "Lieutenant Colonel".

Then he wrote in the "Al Belad" newspaper a lengthly article where he decided, as he usually does with historical events "that the majority of the present Lebanese people are of Noble Arabs, and that the Lebanese families whether Muslim, Druze or Christian are of Arab origin, not the transient tribunes of the past who lived in this country, which is the opinion of some Europeans and Lebanese people because of some political reason they are afraid of or because they are ignoring their country's history".

And in that article he again opposed the ranking of the Lam's princes, so he listed them in the third position in the listing of the Tanukhs ranks, i.e after feudal sheikhs.

We wanted the Prince to take into consideration the historical and logical rules, especially since he is one of the men of history and logic. We do not want to attribute to him that which he has attributed in his article to some Europeans and Lebanese. Namely, that there are some people, who due to some internal motive or just a complete ignorance of history, are of the opinion that the Lebanese people are not Arabs. But we must draw attention to this because what he has done is an insult to the great historians and pillars of knowledge of the past. It is an affront to those who have spent their lives in searching and investigating, traveling the world over seeking out manuscripts and collecting historical vestiges.

Thus, based on their long experiences, they wrote. Their works are the only justified references for researchers. Their writings are proofs for investigators in the East and West. Among these great names are El Douaihy, Al Samaani, Mosaad, Al Debs, Daryan, Lamens, Al Maalouf, Mr. Hitti, and many others.

We wanted to engage in debate with him, but because of the critical national political situation today, it is better not to disturb those responsible. They will discover the realization of the Lebanese union and be part of the gathering of the different dispersed ethnic groups in the country. The Prince had to avoid those critcal matters which evoke rage and disputes, and cause divisions among the people of one country. Whatever his reasons for his statements, he still should have respected the writings of the great trusted historians with regard to the ancestry and origins of the people.

Now we would like to focus on a purely historical issue which he brought up, namely, "The Princedom of the Lam's".

Prince Nassib erroneously wrote: "Prince Haidar, the great governor of Lebanon raised the rank of the Lam's. After being Lieutenant Colonels, they obtained their status as Prince on the day of the Ayn Darah battle." However, we have logical and written proofs that they were originally princes.

The logical proofs: The Arabic word "Muqaddams" (sometimes spelled Mokkadems) (meaning "Lieutenant Colonel") was the name given to those showing courage and power. At that time, it was the name applied to the governors of the fiefs. Then, successively, it became a position rather than a rank or status. Thus, it does not delay the princeliness.

The Lebanese people used to surname their governors like that since the 14th century. Then as their standing rose, especially the Maronite Lieutenant Colonels in the north of Lebanon, so the Lieutenant Colonel grew to be as superior as the prince.

When the Lam's, who are the princes of the Tanoukhs, took charge of the feudal government and were princes, then people surnamed them, as per the country traditions, with the name of "Mokkadem" (Lieutenant Colonel).

In history, it is mentioned that when Sultan Selim conquered the Sham territories, he was addressed as Fakhr al-Din Lieutenant Colonel, the first so mentioned. The governor of Ghazir, surnamed Gamal al-Din Sifa Assaf Bin Sifa, had the same title, and, both of them were Princes.

Princeliness was the highest rank in Lebanon. Consequently it is not reasonable that the great governing prince would bestow a rank on someone else that is equal to his own. It is well known that the princes and the people were covetous with ranks and titles in their conversations, correspondence, and in all their interactions and transactions. Even if such a thing was possible, we have never heard of a single Lebanese governing prince or of one Ottoman governor who ever raised the rank of someone to the status of prince. Even the Sultans themselves, never bestowed any such title on a person in Lebanon. Furthermore, princes remained princes. The only thing the great governor could do was to draw attention to it by addressing them as "Dear brother" and thus making him a Sheikh. If the governors were recommending someone to the sultan he would address him by the title "Pasha" or "Agha".

We must say here that when the Lam's noticed that the title of Lieutnant Colonel was taking higher precedence than their title of prince, and that it was being considered as a rank between Prince and Sheikh, they began to reclaim their princeliness, their inherited title. That is why we noticed that some of the people were calling them princes and others calling them Lieutenant Colonel, as will be discussed later.

The situation remained that way until the battle of Ayn Darah where the courage of the Lam's manifested itself. This was especially true for their leader Hussein bin Abdullah, who showed vigor, courage, intrepidity. He brought them the victory. Thus, when the governing Prince Haidar saw that the Lam's were demanding their inherited right, through their bold leader, and that they preferred their role as prince over the title of Lieutenant Colonel, he gave them the recognition they desires. After he saw their deeds, he acknowledged them. Thus, he officially declared them princes and then became related to them by marriage. He also enlarged the area of their rule.

Hereafter I cite historical evidence and original texts which prove our statements. We have revived them from their obscurity before they disappear. We published some of them in our book Lebanon and Youssef beik Karam and also in the magazines "Al Mashrek" and "Al Manara". Unlike some historians we know who improperly pass on information, we want to do so properly, so we are citing our sources. Here they are from their handwritten passages.

1. A letter from Prince Ahmed bin Ma'n to Prince Fares Abi Al Lam', the governor of Baskinta. It was kept by one of the Prince's grandsons, Fouad Amer Abi Al Lam'. It says:

"To the attention of the dear brother, Prince Fares, May God preserve him:

First, we wish you good health; and, next, we wish to inform you that Sheikh Abou Ander and his Sheikh brothers, have presented to us their payment in a letter marked by Sheikh Sharaf Eddine (the judge) with his stamp and written by his clerk. The total of their taxes, revenue and tobacco is 86 piastres minus two yellowish Shahits. Last year they brought you the mentioned amount , and they now intend to pay the mentioned amount , and it is enclosed. ... best regards.

(The stamp on the paper back) Moheb Mokhles Ahmed Ma'n.

The letter has no date but Prince Ahmed Ma'n died 15 years before the battle of Ayn Darah.

2. The construction date of the Mar Girgis (Saint George) Monastery in Deir El Haref in Al Metn, still there today, has an inscription above the church gate as follows:

"In the name of God, Eternal and Forever Alive, who I call on for help, His excellency, the respectful Prince Abdullah, son of the late Prince Qayed Bayeh, known as a son of Abi Al Lam', may god forgive him, has constructed, with

God's Will, and obedient to God and his care, that blessed monastery in the month Dhi Al Hejjah, of the year 1102 Hegira (1691 AD)". "Made by the teacher, Girgis, teacher Samaan, and teacher Girgis Al Shamy."

3. In the margin of a book of Syriac prayers, kept in the Mar Toqla Monastery of the Lebanese monks in Wadi Charoun, is written, in Syriac and Karshouni:

"This was completed, Glory to God, on October 20, 1695, when our Holy Patriarch was Mar Estephanos, and the teachers were of Bishop Boutros (Makhlou) Al Ghastawy (Bishop of Cyprus), by the most humble one by the name of Deacon Yaakoub from the blessed village of Hasroun" (He may be the one who later became Patriarch). *The title of the book is:* <u>*The Memories of Saint John in the Bikfaya Fief, A Continuation of Beit Al Shabab*</u>. *The person who wrote that was, the pastor Father Moussa from the village of Beit Shabab. He was a descendent from the Al Hawat family. He was the headmaster of the mentioned monastery. The fief's governor was His Excellency Prince Abdullah Abi Al Lam'. "His Excellency Prince Ahmed Ibn Ma'n was expelled from his throne, then, with good reason he got his throne back. Glory to God always."*

This vestige is a proof that the Lam's were called "Prince" before the battle of Ayn Darah and another proof that they were governing the fief.

4. In a book of Syriac prayers kept in the Mar Toqla Church in the fields of Al Metn, there is a handwritten note by a monk. It concerns the construction of the Mar Ash'eya Bermana Monastery for the Antonian monks. It says:

"In 1698, I, Pastor Boutros, a lowly sinner from the Tamish Monastery, was sent by Bishop Gabriel Al Belouzani, my Superior for many years, to the Mar Ash'eya Monastery which was in ruins. I was alone and the first monk entering the place. In 1699 Pastor Moussa joined me. Together we made ovens and cut bricks for the construction of the church. In 1700 we completed the church, thanks to God's care and the owner of the land, and, to the supervision of Prince Abdullah Abi Al Lam'. He gave me 200 lion piastres. May God keep him and safeguard his children. Also my teachers paid much from his money for the Monastery. With his supervision, vigor, effort and insistence, the Monastery has been built. I pray that God, may He be exalted, will compensate him for his effort in this life with longevity, and, in the next life, with eternal rest in Heaven. Amen!"

5. In a book of Syriac religious duties, there is a handwritten notation. The book is, still, today, preserved in the Saint Elias Church in the village of Al Sefily, near Ba'abadat in al Metn. It states:

"Yaakoub, the Metropolitan of Tripoli (He is Yaakoub Aawad who later became a Patriarch), *in the holy year 1702. I am the lowliest and most humble of the leaders. I have consecrated this Church to the honor and name of Saint Elias, the living prophet. This Church is that of the village of Al Sefeli. I have also consecrated the chancel and the baptismal fount basin. Our friends are gathered here for this consecration, consisting of a group of priests, monks, deacons, and, the people of the neighbourhood. This happened during the tenure of his Holiness the Blessed Estephan (El Douaihy), the magnificent Patriarch, and, the era of the Princedom of the Lam's. May god bless it for the people of the mentioned village on the blessed September 23."*

6. There was a granite stone placed above Ayn Ahmed in Salima, the center of the Lam's reign. When the drinking fountain was demolished, the stone was moved to the castle of Prince Haidar Abi Al Lam' in Bikfaya where it still remains. It was engraved with these words:

"This holy drinking fountain was constructed by his Excellency the honoured Prince Abdullah Ibn Abi al Lam', on the day of Tuesday, of Ragab the Hegira month, of the year 1117, (1705 AD). Thanks be to God."

I am sure that Prince Haidar Shehab and Sheikh Tanous Al Shediaq having read such clear and straightforward passages would not have erroneously reported the time for the "Prince" status of the Abi Al Lam' family.

Thus it would seem that Prince Nessib has made light of these two historians and, as a result, has wrongly commented on the Princely status issue.

In addition, the Lam's were the in-laws of the Ma'ns. They were the most noble governing families in Lebanon. That was enough for them to be proud and to be opposed by the Shehabis. There was no need for such competition as some princes from the Shehabis are insisting. We are all Adam's offspring. If we must compete, let it be with good deeds of which we can be proud in the face of the people and of God.

The Lady Zahr (Al Set Zahr)

The only things the Druze of Salima know about this princess are that she was the owner of the famous endowment, and, she was the only one who did not convert to Christianity as did all the other princes. They light her tomb, as if glorifiying and dignifying her as a saint. They surname her Al Set Oum Soliman (the lady, mother of Soliman), which is wrong. She was, in fact, known by the surname of Oum Ali as we will discuss later. According to the narration of Hussein Saloum El Masry, she never married and her father left his entire estate to her. She, then, left her estate to the Druze Assembly.

The mother of Maguid Abi Daher Said told me that Al Set Zahr was the wife of Prince Qassem, and I have verified that from the register of the department survey of the year 1705, written by Sheikh Youssef Yazbak. This survey is in one of my files. Also, we have ascertained that she was the daughter of Prince Mansour Mourad Abi Al Lam'. She had no children and willed her estate, which she received from her husband, to the Druzes.

Hanna Youssef Nasrallah and Andrea Girgis Andrea say that she is the paternal aunt of Prince Haidar Ismail and that he wanted to bring legal action against the Druzes feeling that the inheritance should be his. However, he was persuaded not to do so thanks to the mediation of Nejm Andrea al Bachaalany from Salima, Salman Bahmed from Kafr Salwan, and Eid Abou Hatem from Hamana.

Lord Churchill states in his book, Part I, p99: "The family of Abi al Lam' were Druzes then they became Christians, except for one old princess who died embracing the Hamza religion". Surely this was Al Set Zahr who died in 1230 Hejeri.

In Salima, the princes have two remaining tombs in the Druze cemetery, one at the east side of the castle and the other at the north of the Saint Elias Church. The first tomb is known to be that of Al Set Zahr, which was changed when the Druzes renovated the cemetry. They made a special grave for her. The second tomb is known as "The Cupola", where Prince Fares "The Christian" has been buried along with Prince Assaf Ismail with his son and other christian princes. And the Druzes preserve both the cupola and the tomb of Al Set Zahr.

We have five documents about The Lady Zahr. One of them is a very valuable document which we found among the papers of the 'Aishi family. They are the descendants of the Muslim Ali bin Ahmed Yassin. He converted to Christianity with his mother Aisha and lived in Salima. The original text of that document is as follows:

"Purchase deed from her excellency Al Set Oum Ali (the motherly lady of the Lam') in Al Madouara. In the name of God the All Merciful, my only need and source of help. This is what the man called Mohamed Abou Ghezlan has bought, with his money, for himself not for anyone else. He purchased it from her excellency Al Set Oum Ali during one meeting, with one contract, and with one transaction. This agreement includes the mulberries, pears, cinnamon bark, vines and figs; her whole share, without any share of the residents of the place known as Al Medouara. The agreed price is sixty piastres. In addition, a half interest in the mineral water rights is ten piastres. This makes the

total amound to be seventy pieastres, paid in cash, with no amount remaining to be paid by the buyer. There is no commission to be paid to anyone for the transaction and the amount due has been paid to her Excellency Al Set, the seller of this property, by legal contract with nothing left to be paid. The property has become the buyer's own without any interest of the mentioned seller. The deal was completed after legally viewing and inspecting the property. The sale is irrefutable, clear, and signed, with no conditions, no corruption, no retreat, and no repetition. The transaction has occurred as per the Islamic rules and legal laws for selling. We reviewed and registered this contract and voluntarily witnessed it. What has been mentioned is within the jurisdiction of our Sultan, may the meciful God always grant him success. This agreement became valid in the month of Shaaban, in the year 1122. It has been implemented as of that date with God as our witness. The assesor is Noaman Said.

She accepted	*Witneses*	*Written by the mean*
Zahr bint Mansour Bel Lam'a	*Dhaher ibn Mohamed from Zar'oun*	*Ahmed Ibn Hussein Khalil*
	Ezz Eddine Bou Ali	*from Bezbedine*
	Bergas ibn Soliman from Zaaroun"	

(The stamp is on on the back)

- - - - - - - - - -

And, another document:

"It is true and correct that this writ has been transfered from us to her excellency Al Set Oum Ali Zahr. The cash amount has been received and there is no additional amount due to her .... This has been written in the month Dhou Al Hejjah of the Hegira year 1230, exactly.

Witnessed that	*Witnessed that*	*Written by*
Salman Khatar	*Bergass Al Masry*	*Mohamed Ibn Mahmoud Al Masry"*

- - - - - - - - - -

And, still, one more document:

"This writ has been transferred from the Assembly representatives to Ali Yassin, and has became his property, to dispose of as he wishes. The price of the property is one hundred and sixty piastres according to the evaluation of Noaman Said, The money was paid in cash with not one Derham remaining to be paid. This agreement excludes the water rights. Those rights remain to the assembly. Written exactly in the month Dhou Al Qei'da, in the year 1231.

Witnessed by	*Written by*
The Humble Youssef Porcelain	*Khalil Karim Eddine"*

- - - - - - - - - -

The Princes' Castles.

There are four Princes' castles They are:

1. The grand castle consisting of four floors: two partitions; at the south was the house of Prince Hassan, at the north was the house of Prince Haidar.

2. Prince Assaf died before his house was finished, so Amin Slaman built his house at that place.

3. The House of Prince Soliman was demolished and the new Church of Saint John at the east side of the square now occupies its place.

4. The house of Al Set Zahr is today the Assembly Hall of the Druzes.

Anyone who looks at this Castle which has been standing for three centuries will be astonished at its large size, its solid construction, the thickness of its walls, and the height of its four floors. In their old popular songs they used to sing: "From the window above four floors…Like the Lady in the Salima Castle."

Its west gate was built by prince Ismail. It is beautiful with its ornate carvings. On both sides of the gate are the images of two lions, a traditional theme at that time. In the center is an engraved poem. The verses almost totally illegible due to fires during the civil unrest of 1845. The only part that is totally legible is the date of the construction "1171 Hegira year". We can still decipher half of the first verse which says: "This place surpasses similar structures…" and "Abi al Lam'".

Everyone knows that our castles look like those built by the feudals lords in Europe. They are magnificent, solid with high balconies. All of it was strengthened to be a fortress to provide defense whenever necessary.

In the Salima Castle there still remain some written vestiges. For example, there is carving on the pillar of the window in the west hall, known as Al Qamandoul. It says: "Hussein Ibn Abdullah, who hopes for the forgiveness of God, has built this place with God's help. It was finished at the beginning of the month Dhou Al Qei'da in the year 1134."

Above the doors an inscription says: "Built with God's help for the generous Hussein Al Lam' with the full hope for the joy of the Lord's resurrection. 1134." Around the door it says: "May God forgive its writer and composer." And, also: "Oh, house, built with joy and giving happiness to its viewers, upon your gates geniality is written, so enter, all, in peace and safety." And, also, "May the glory of your four sides remain and your inhabitants feel stability in the building of cheerfulness. The best of things have been raised up with you so that the Haj Hussein may live in a retreat."

There is a proverb about the characteristics of the Princes' castles. One says: "The height of the Salima house, the gates of the Falouga house, and the hall of pillars of the Betedine house."

The history of Bermana House was engraved on its gate: "Prince Abou Shehab Abi Al Lam' built a house constructed of corners and pillars. There was Ahmed Fakh during his reign …etc. to remind us of what is left forever. 1127 "

This was constructed by Prince Ahmed, surnamed Abou Shehab, the grandfather of the Bermana princes. He is the son of Prince Abdulallah of Salima. His grandchildren's characteristics were an example to all. For example, "The generosity of Prince Nejm, the throne of Prince Ahmed and the sword of Prince Mansour." These were the children of Beshir Ahmed.

Prince Haider Ismail built a beautiful castle in Bikfaya when he took charge of the government of the Christians in Jibel Lebnan (Lebanon Mount). It still exists. Above its gate he had two verses of a poem engraved. The poem is about the building's construction and remarks made about it:
        "I built it from God's prosperity
        It has remained with thanks and an abundance of praise

I need only an empty life because
I will fulfill it with my God in the life to come.   --1849"

Prince Haidar Salima   (his name is also spelled Haidar, Haydar, Haider)

Prince Haidar of Salima is the son of Ismail Bin Hassan Bin Hussein Bin Abdulallah Bin Qayed Baih Bin Abi Al Lam'. He was born in 1787 in the castle of his father and grandfathers. It still stands in Salima, the capital of Al Metn during the Princes' era. His father, Prince Ismail, was the most famous Prince of his time. Only "The Great Governor of Lebanon", Prince Youssef Al Shehabi, surpassed him in politics and governing methods. His mother was a pious Christian woman and urged that her son Haidar be baptised. His baptismal name was Elias.

Some people say that his father converted to Christianity and presented a certificate of this to Rome. He probably did not do this even though it was common knowledge that he cared deeply for the Christians and provided for them.

Prince Haider inherited justice from his father and piety from his mother. In addition to his inherited nobility, he grew up with Christian values, becoming a strong Catholic.

He governed his anscestors' fief, Al Metn and the partition, for a long time, until the events of Ibrahim Pasha. Due to him and Prince Beshir Al Kabir, Prince Haidar and fifty-three Princes, Sheikhs and Lebanese notables fled to Senar in Al Khortoum in 1840. Ibrahim Pasha and Prince Beshir thought that Prince Haidar was a leader of a revolutionary movement. In fact, many people were taking note of Prince Haidar and he was growing in popularity. When the Lebanese held a meeting at the Public Hall of Antlias seeking to elect a patriotic governor, Prince Haidar was chosen upon the advice of the Patriarch of the Maronites. He knew of the patriotism, intelligence and vitality of the Prince.

Before the end of 1842, after Lebanon was divided into two governorates, he was appointed the Governor of the Christians. He chose qualified men for his government. He ruled with wisdom, authority, and maturity. All things ran their course and the administration grew larger, various special interests grew, and parties and doctrines became more diverse. The employees of his administration were the most capable men in their fields. They knew how to get things accomplished, great and small. There is nothing strange about this since Chistianity provided their ethics which were learned early in life.

Prince Haider would personally listen to the complaints of his people. He would initiate legal actions even opposing the precedents of his own office. Often, he would accept pleas brought to him from lower individuals and would write eloquent guidelines so his clerks could implement policies accordingly.

He was solving problems not only with justice and fairness, but also with patience and compassion. All the people loved and respected him. He took charge of the peoples affairs ruling as the kind hearted father he was. He preserved peoples' rights and kept injustice and wrongdoing far away.

He was democratic when dealing with people. Even that idea was a new policy at that time. Feudalism and tyranny started to disappear after he introduced his ideas and policies. It became well known that if a feudal lord oppressed an individual, that person had recourse in the justice and equity of Prince Haider.

If the government of Prince Beshir was most noted as a government of justice and influence, then the government of Prince Haidar was one of patience and compassion.

The Prince mixed feudal martial law with constitutional law. He was like a spiritual judge who interceded to stop decisions based on personalities. Instead he brought cases to the state council. This body consisted of judges who were members and representatives of all doctrines. Judgement was made by men of honesty and justice.

He dealt with his men as a homemaster who treats his family with compassion, not as a tyrant prince. With all that, he cared about people's feelings. He respected their rank and aptitude.

In general, he was accomplishing what God would want. He brought peace and justice to his people. This made the Sheikhs say: "Lebanon has never seen a better governor. We have never lived in a happier time than in his."

Concerning his preservation of the country's rights, judge for yourself. In his era, Gebeyel and the north were taken back from Turkish rule. They wanted to separate them from Lebanon. He was eager in defending the frontiers in Baalbek, its environs and in other places. He used arguments, irrefutable proofs, all based on his experience, using the best of the knowledgeable people he knew.

Attempts to divide Lebanon into two governorates was a Turkish attempt to disrupt the peace of those days and cause insurrections. Prince Haider, in his wisdom, prevented that. Instead, he brought about just the opposite. He reconciled the differences in people's doctrines and beliefs so that every one was satisfied with his government. They lived an era of tranquility and peace.

Prince Haidar was well know for his kind heart and good manners, his honesty and generosity. He displayed the best characteristics of his nobility and the way he was treated by his people was proof of his honor and virtue. He was a firm believer in Catholicism, famous for his piety and his devotion to the Virgin Mary. Rumors spread that the Virgin was the one guarding him, something of which he was very proud! In 1846, he built a private chapel for the Virgin Mary in his beautiful castle in Bikfaya. It is still there today.

The chapel is a marvelous work of creativity and beauty. There are wonderful historical pictures which were moved from his castle in Salima, and which are precious antiques. Some of them were gifts to him from the Pontiffs and Kings of Europe. The Prince used to go to his chapel after he finished his work. There, he would prostrate himself before God and, in a low voice, utter his ardent prayers.

He died on May 11, 1854, at his winter residence in Serba, near Junieh. His body was transported to Bikfaya for his funeral. He was buried, as per his instructions, in the Church of Our Lady of Deliverance of the Jesuit Fathers. The Jesuits did this to acknowledge the many favors he performed for their mission and to recognize what he did for his religion. On his grave the date of his death was engraved along with the following:

This is the tomb of the prince of glory, Haidar,
Who governed this country and who did so much.
One of the Lam's, the sons of glories, he built
*   on earth a fixed reputation.*
Like the full moon, with its light shining on creatures,
That is why he deserves to be lifted so high.
If that full moon should disappear, still he is in the sky ...etc
His light shines in the best land." --1854.

Then, written in Latin: *"The Jesuit Monastery has built this grave for his Excellency, Prince Haider Abi Al Lam'."*

The Lam's In Our Present Time

The above is just a short summary of the Lam's' history, marking a glorious page in the annals of Lebanon's past. It is a summary of the manuscript <u>History of The Lam's Princes</u> which we have put together over many years.

It contains precious vestiges, documents, and current news of the Al Lam's. It reveals the truth of their origins and the glorious deeds of their ancestors. It is an object of pride for them in all centuries. How nice it would be if they could help us to bring it to publication as a service for the history of Lebanon. The history of our country still lacks some details and even some corrections of wrongs written by those who don't know this fine art.

The present accomplishments of the Lam's show many things for which we should be grateful. They have worked actively for progress, not resting on the laurels of their past nobility. They have participated in revolutionary works transforming our culture and our professions.

Before ending this section, we will mention the names of those still living, in brief, per their three houses (families):

Princes of Salima and Bikfaya:

Prince Youssef bin Qaysser (Caesar) bin Youssef Ismail bin Hassan Ismail, Prince Beshir bin Mansour Bin Hassan bin Ismail, the sons of Prince Amin Mansour: August, and Moris, and Antoin bin (the son of) Moris. Wahib and Soheil are the sons of August.

From Bermana:

Prince Beshir bin Neguib ibn Prince Beshir Ahmed, the Governor of the Christians in Jibel Lebnan (Lebanon Mount) (1854 – 1859). The children of Prince Beshir: Khalil, Shafik, Malek, and Youssef.

Prince Khalil had a son called Samir. Prince Shafik had Naguib and Rafik. Prince Yousef had a son called Raef.

Also among those from Bermana was Prince Selim, the son of Prince Mansour. His sons are: Edward and George. Ferdinand, the son of Prince Fouad Amin Mansour. His two children Amin Amin Mansour: Edkar and Youssef. Youssef and Emil are the sons of Prince Maguid Amin Mansour.

Ras Al Metn, in Qartada:

Among the Princes of this place are:

Prince Amin Abbas and his brothers: the Princes Nessib, Fares, Youssef, and Gehgah. Prince Fares has children living in the United States of America.

Shabania:

Prince Maguid Qaysar (Ceasar) Khalil Mostapha is living in Brazil and has children.

Prince Tawfik Rashid and his children, the children of Prince Youssef Gehgah: Fouad, Shafik, and Gamil with their children, too.

All those are the offspring of Prince Abdullah Qayed Baih Salima.

Al Matyan.

Among the Al Matyan Princes are the sons of Prince Mahmoud Salman Mourad. They are Assad, Magued, Youssef, and Malek. Prince Assad has a son called Adel. Prince Magued has two sons, Fayez and Fayek.

Prince Qablan bin Mourad Qablan, and Prince Victor bin Asaad Qablan, and the two Princes Youssef and Shafiq who are the sons of Moussa Youssef Nasr. There is also Prince Fouad Selim Mourad, and the two Princes Shafiq and Halim, the sons of Prince Farid Mourad.

Qarnayel:

Prince Youssef Selim Said Mourad and his sons, Fouad and Selim. The Prince Qayssar (Ceasar) Mahmoud Ali, and Prince Youssef Mourad Ali and his son Mourad.

Falouga:

From the Falouga Princes are Prince Tawfiq Shedid Abdulallah and his son Adnan; Prince Doctor Raeef Shedid Abdulallah and his two sons, Farouk and Gehad. There is also Tawfiq, the son of Prince Mourad Ibrahim. These are the offspring of Prince Mourad, the Prince of Al Matyan.

Beskinta:

From the Beskinta Princes are Prince Amin bin Abdulallah, Prince Bel Lam' bin Beshir. Also, Princes William, Afandi, and Qaiss who are the sons of Prince Youssef Afendi; all of them are in the United States.

Prince Abdel Hamid bin Hassan and his sons in Qaa' El Rim.

Among them, also, are the sons of Prince Amer Taroudy: Fouad, Shakib, and Youssef who was on a ship that sank and died. Prince Fouad died in an accidental fall down the stairs at the Bishopric in Damascus. Losing him meant losing a national and cultural gem. He was our dear friend. Prince Shokeib is in the United States, and his son Fradi is living with his grandmother in Junieh.

In the book The History Of Beskinta, written by our fellow priest, Bishop Boutros Hebeqah, there is much information about the Prince Fares family. He is the grandfather of the Princes in Beskinta.

Conclusion

We have listed the family of the Al Lam' in the first position among the other families of Salima. Some parts of that family have lived in Salima for three centuries! It is fitting now to follow their history with that of our good fathers and grandfathers. They were the ones who remembered the favors shown by their princes and kept their promises to preserve the rank and dignity of the nobles.

THE HOUSE OF THE BACHAALANY

Chapter 2

Their Origins

In previous pages we made it clear that the Bachaalanys are related to the historical village of Bchaaleh which is in the Al Betroun district. We also showed that some views of the family's origins and background were wrong. We used reasonable proofs to verify all of our positions. We said that the Bachaalany family is one of the noble Lebanese families, being the descendants of Phoenician and Maronite families. Its ancestry goes back to Sheikh Abi Rezk Al Bachaalany and his in-laws. They were all famous Maronites. Trusted historians reported all this. It is probable that they are the remnants of the Mardaites who moved from Bchaaleh to Tripoli in the North of Lebanon.

We talked in detail about Abu Rezk, his brother Abu Saab and the children of Rezk: Younes, Abdullah and Rezk. We talked of the disasters and ordeals of the people and the village. We told of the murder of Abu Rezk and his son Younes, who died as a martyr. We also talked how that famous father and son died for their religion and their country.

We gave the historical details of how the Bachaalanys escaped to the Kafr Kisrawan fief after their disaster in 1697, fleeing and hiding from the tyrant governors. They lived for a while in Al Belana quarter and the Al Kharab Alley. We made reference to the departure of the majority to Salima in the Upper Al Metn region. Also, how two of them emigrated to Bikfayah and and Al Mehidetha, being the ancestors of the Al Qash'ami family and the Abi Nakad family.

Two others went to the Chouf area: the ancestors of the Harfoush family and the Abi Rashed family. Then, their offspring settled in Niha, Bekaseen and Wadi Shahroor.

* * * * * *

Their Offshoots

The Bachaalany family in Salima consists of many original offshoots from Abu Rezk, his brother Abu Saab and some of their in-laws. The family also consists of offshoots from families that merged with this family through marriage. Despite the varied and many people who came together, still, they were forming one family bound with firm commitment, under one name which is the "Bachaalany House." Here are the names of the branches.

1. Youssef (Joseph)	2. Neama	3. Abou 'Okl
4. 'Abssy	5. Karam	6. Attallah
7. 'Erian	8. Mazmouk	9. Saweed
10. Karargey	11. Ghatass and Aboud (Gutas)	12. Heriz (Harris)
13. Salem Al Guelkh	14. Soliman Beshara	15. Falouty (Flute)
16. Gabour.		

The Sheikhs agreed that five of our ancestors were the first to come to Salima, and, they were: Youssef, Neama, 'Okl, 'Abssy, and Karam. However, in the documents we possess, it is mentioned that the offshoot of Attallah came with the first five. Then, the other above mentioned branches came. Some people have said that the Attallah Bachaalany house originated from Ghabala in Kisrawan from the Attallah house there. They are wrong. Those from Ghabala originate from Yanouh which is near Afoura and they have no connections with the family of Attallah Bachaalany. The similarity in the name is just a coincidence.

Their Residences

The six ancestors came to Salima at the end of the seventeenth century and settled there. Then the others came in different waves and time periods. The house of 'Erian came from Kafr Salwan in the middle of the eighteenth century and there were four of them: One of them lived in Saadanayel, the second in Geditah, the third in Shabania at El Metn, and the fourth in Salima. At the beginning of the nineteenth century, Gabour Bashelany left Salima and went to the west of Lebanon and he is the grandfather of the Bachaalany house in Abia and the West Market. At the same time, Hanna Nasrallah Mazmouk joined the service of Prince Haider Shehab in Shamlan, then he left Salima. He was the grandfather of the Bachaalany house in Shamlan.

Salima people, especially the Bachaalanys, were frequently going into the rural areas to farm. When their work day was finished, they returned back to Salima. But some of them were obliged to reside where they worked. Consequently, at the end of the last century, one by one, they started to sell their properties in Salima. They lived in Makse, Thaalabaya, Shatoura, Merigate, Qab Elias, and Zahle. Merigate was a municipality of the Salima Sheikhdom which owned the majority of its properties. It remained that way until 1920 when it was separated. A private reconciliation Sheikh was appointed for it, then, it became a municipality of the governorate of Zahle. The first Sheikh who was appointed at the Merigate was our in-law Sheikh Qablan Asaad Ghaleb Bachaalany. He remained a Sheikh for twelve years.

Their Homes

The Sheikhs say that in the past the homes of the Christians were near the old Church of Saint John (Mar Yohanna), on the west side, beside the Ain Al Hiyarat. Ain Al Hiyarat was known as "Al Ain": which was also known as Ain El Shaqif, Ain El Qamar, Ain Ahmed, Ain El Deir, Ain El Zeitouna, Ain Al Magd, and many others names. It was said that because of "ants", the Christians moved their homes from the bottom of Salima to its upper part where they are now. However, it is much more probable that they moved so as to be nearer to the princes who built their castles in the upper part of the village. Their first neighbourhood was called "Harat Al Kharga". It is near the Saray square, as we previously mentioned.

The construction of homes in the past was like this: the man gathered stones, either from a stone quarry or from the land where he wanted to build his home. Then he cut those stones into pieces as much as he could. He moght leave the site as it was or he may try to find a high wall. Salima is situated on a sloping hill side. Thus a home builder would use the hill side as one of his foundation walls. The other three walls were built of the stones he gathered. From the stone base he might raise up four poles, firmly blocking them with bricks and small stones mixed with mud. Then he made a ceiling with wood braces, covered with thistle, then thin stones, and finally light dirt. The roof is then compressed with a roller. The small pressed stones help to prevent leaks during the winter.

Homes in Salima were not precisely built, except for those of the princes and the upper class. People started to build good homes whenever their financial situation allowed, which was usually after the period of emigration when friends and relatives would send money back from the new lands.

Now we will begin with the lineage of each offshoot of the Bachaalany family, providing their stories and circumstances in brief.

211

The House Of Abou Youssef   (The House of Joseph)

Abou Youssef Rezk Bin Abou Rezk Nasr Al Bachaalany (Joseph Rezk Nasr Bachaalany).

Joseph (Abou Youssef) is the brother of Prince Jonas (Younes) who was martyred in 1697.

Their other brother was Abd Allah. They were the sons of Sheikh Abu Rezk, also martyred by Muslims, in 1654.

Abou Youssef had three sons: **(A.) Youssef (Joseph), (B.) Moussa (Moses), and (C.) Abdullah (Abdullah)**.

We don't know anything about **(A.)Youssef**.

(B.) Moussa had three sons: **1. Nejm, 2. Girgis (George), and 3. Youssef.**

(C.) Abdullah had two sons: 1. **Mansour and 2. Eid.**

(A.) Youssef, the son of Youssef, the brother of Prince Younes. We know nothing of his life or possible children.

(B.) Moussa (Moses), the second son of Youssef (Joseph), the brother of Prince Younes (Jonas), had three sons: 1. Nejm,   2. Girgis (George), and Youssef (Joseph).

(C.) Abdullah, the third son of Youssef, the brother of Prince Younes. This Abdullah had two sons, Mansour and Eid.

(*Editor's Note: It should be emphasized here that all of these men undoubtedly had some, probably even many, daughters. Their names were rarely recorded. When the women were noted, it was usually in connection with the men that they married. In other rare instances, it was because they performed some deed of remarkable significance and/or bravery. Dna studies of the future will most likely shine the light on many family connections which, for now, are unknown.)

Moussa's Three Sons:

1. Nejm Bin Moussa. Known as Abou Knieser Nejm Bin Moussa (Knieser, Crooked Little Finger on the Hand, Nejm the son of Moses).   He is the grandfather of the Knieser family (Khnesar, Konaycer, Khnaisser, Khenaisser, Khonaysser, Khneiser, Khuneisser, Kenicer... all these are just some of the spelling variations of the same name). This Nejm was nicknamed "Knieser", "Crooked Little Fingers On Your Hands" (explained later). He had six sons.

Nejm's six sons:

a) Knieser (Crooked Little Finger), who died without offspring,
b) Youssef (Joseph) surnamed Freha (Happy),
c) Boutros (Peter),

d) Boulos (Paul),
e) Gibrail (Gabriel), and
f) Tanious.

The last two sons, Gabriel and Tanious, died unmarried.

a) Knieser Bin Knieser Nejm Bin Moussa had no children.

b) Concerning **Freha (Happy)**, the grandfather of the Freha Bachaalany family, he had Girgis, Tanous, and Gibrail. Girgis never married. Tanous had Abdou, Girgis, and Faragallah. Abdou had five sons: Youssef who became an ordained priest named Father Estephan (Stephen) Bachaalany (the author of this book), Boutros who died young and single, Habib, Tanous, and Khalil. Habib had only one daughter, Henriette. Tanous had Youssef, and Khalil had Abdou, Rezk and Younes.

Girgis Bin Tanous Freha had Elias who had George, Beshara and Abdullah.

Faragallah Bin Tanous Freha had Mikhail and Louis. Mikhail had Fouad, Faragallah, and Philip. And Louis had one boy.

As for Gibrail Freha, he had Molhem and Hanna. Molhem had Shoukry and Tanious. Shoukry had only one daughter named Victoria, and Tanious had Molhem, Youssef and Abdou. Molhem and Youssef died as children and Hanna Bin Gibrail had Mansour and Girgis. Mansour had sons and daughters in Brazil as did his brother Girgis.

c) Boutros (Peter) Bin Abou Knieser Nejm had Shahin. Shahin had Boutros, Knieser, Ibrahim, Youssef, and Tanious.

Boutros the son of Boutros Knieser had Daoud and Shahin. Daoud had Soliman, Tanious, Girgis, Boutros, Lotfallah, and Youssef. Soliman Bin Daoud had Philip. And Tanious had Gamil, Anis, and Tawfiq. And Girgis had Alam, and Soliman who died when he was a child. Boutros had Shafiq and Hanna. And Lotfallah had Badi', Edmond, and Elias. Youssef Bin Daoud had Edward, Naguib, Fouad and Michel. And Shahin Bin Boutros Shahin had Farid who had Emil.

Concerning Knieser Shahin, he had two sons, Nejm (March 21, 1875-July 12, 1922) and Abdou (July 15, 1878- 1918), and a daughter, Nejmi (d. 1918).

[The following details of Nejm Knieser, on this page and the next, are supplied by the Editor, Paul Knieser, his grandson]

[Nejm came to the United States in 1895 by way of Le Havre, France. He sailed from Le Havre on November 25, 1895, on board the ship La Bourgagne.

Nejm was twenty years old and traveling with four companions, Betros Rezk, Gabriel Diab, Boutros Daoud, and Joseph Kalil, all most likely, like him, from Salima.

Nejm's name on the ship's manifest was spelled "Najim Konaycer". Three years later, the ship he had sailed on was in a collision and sank off Newfoundland on July 4, 1898, with the loss of 549 lives. This sad fact points to how dangerous travel was in those days.

After staying a short time in New York City, Nejm soon moved to Olean, New York, as a representative for a wholesale company who supplied pack peddlers (the original door-to-door salesman). Nejm himself would sometimes travel the backroads selling, even occasionally taking one of his children with him.

Nejm, like so many fellow immigrants, wanted to adopt a name that was more American and typical. The sound of Nejm was similar to Jim, and so Jim Knieser came to be! It wouldn't be until the 1920 US Census that this name was officially established. Even when he became a US Citizen, his official document spelled his name as Gem Kaneser, also declaring him as previously a citizen of Turkey. Syria and Lebanon had not yet become seperate, independent countries.

In 1897, Jim Knieser, as Nejm was now known, took over the business using a room in his home as his office and supply room. This was at 202 Whitney Avenue in Olean, New York. There, too, is where he also manufactured suspenders for a number of years.

At the turn of the century when the great migration was in full swing, Jim Knieser had as many as 40 agents covering his entire territory, which was mostly Northern Pennsylvania.

On December 23, 1902, he married Anna George Saab (1882-1940) at St. Mary's Roman Catholic Church in Olean, NY. She was also from Salima, Lebanon. Anna and Jim were actually distant cousins, sharing Moses Joseph Rezk Nasr Bachaalany as their common ancestor. Their witnesses were Kattar Beshara and Mary Faris.

Jim and Anna had ten children in all, three sons: Joseph, John, and Michael. They also had seven daughters: Helen, Julia, Rose, Josephine, Teckla, Olga, and Mary.

Jim (Nejm) Knieser died on July 12, 1922. The cause of his death was a reaction to an anesthetic after undergoing an operation for cancer. Anna died in 1940, only 58 years old, from heart disease.

Nejm and Anna's children had many children of their own.

Joseph married Louise Thomas and they had Thomas, Richard, and Mary.

John Knieser married Josephine Dwaileebe and had Betty Ann, James, Robert, and Christine.

Michael Knieser married Lena Ehrhart and they had four children: Kenneth, Martial, Anna May, and Paul (the chief editor of this English translation).

Of their daughters, Helen married James Teppas and they had no children.

Rose married George Sader and they had William, Raymond, Margaret, and Robert.

Julia Knieser married Phillip Farris and they had Patricia, Theresa, Phillip, and Alice.

Josephine Knieser had Adele.

Mary Knieser married Emil Ash and they had Emil, David, Peter and Paul.

A daughter, Tekla (Hammam) died in child birth. Her child also died.

And a daughter Olga died as a child in 1916 from an infection.

Nejm's brother, Abdo, had Khalil and Knieser. Both of them died during the First World War.

Nejm's sister, Nejmi married and had two children, George and Adele. She was in an unhappy marriage and she died in the 1918 flu epidemic as did Abdo, Nejm's brother. Nejmi's two children were taken in by Anna Knieser, Nejm's widow. George Knieser lived in Buffalo, NY, and Adele Elias Zabougie married and lived in California.

Abdo's death, like his sister's, occurred quickly during the 1918 influenza epidemic. After his death, he was quickly buried without any funeral home ceremonies and even without a Church funeral. During the epidemic period it was urgent that the deceased be disposed of quickly in an attempt to halt the spread of the disease.

We might mention here that time has taken its toll on the material vestiges of heritage of Jim and Anna Knieser. Their home on Whitney Avenue was torn down many years ago and is now just part of the athletic field of the Olean School District. Jim, with other Olean, NY, Lebanese immigrants, spearheaded a movement to establish a church of their own in Olean. Nejm was a driving force for this Church, reportedly having even been involved in a fist fight with a fellow Lebanese, to get some feature of the Church adopted. I believe that Jim was also instrumental in naming the Church, honoring that early "grandfather" of the Bachaalany's, Joseph Rezk Nasr Bachaalany. Not only was St. Joseph the name of this new Church but Jim also named his first born son Joseph.

Sadly, not only is the old homestead on Whitney Avenue now gone, but so is the Church that Jim helped to establish, having burned down a few years ago. An interesting side note is that Jim Knieser's early death at the age of 47 saw his funeral as the first funeral of St. Joseph's Church! He was so widely admired and respected in Olean that his funeral was one of if not the largest Olean had ever seen. From the front of the funeral procession to the end, it measured two miles. When the casket arrived at St. Bonaventure Cemetery in Allegany, NY, the end of the procession was still at the main intersection of State and Union Streets in Olean!

Just as Father Stephen Bachaalany took a little liberty to detail his personal family in some detail, I will likewise do the same. Michael and Lena Knieser had four children. Kenneth, the oldest and an established accountant, in turn raised two children, John and Ken with his wife Mary. Martial, who became a doctor, with his wife Susan had two children Michael and Christine. Anna May, their only daughter, suffered from Down's Syndrome. She never married because of her condition. Interestingly it was her condition which alerted her younger brother, Paul, the Editor of this translation, to the medical facts which related to the "Knieser" meaning. Paul Jerome Xavier Knieser had one son with his first wife, Darlene Suich, Paul Jerome Knieser Junior. Paul married Sarah Elizabeth Tommasino, the love of his life, on December 8, 1990. Together they had five children, Nigel Orest Joseph Knieser, Abraham Paul Knieser, Sarah Colette 'Missy' Knieser, Ruby Anna Knieser, and John 'Jack' Roland Wilson Knieser.

Paul and Sarah stayed in Olean, NY, caring for their aging parents and relatives. After the last of them died, they headed to the Orlando, Florida, area. The many joys and adventures of Paul and Sarah can be found in a privately issued book to be published soon in 2017 or 2018.]

Ibrahim Shahin had only one girl Teckla, the wife of Shahin Boutros, her paternal cousin. Youssef and Tanious Shahin died without offspring.

d) Boulos (Paul) Abou Knieser had 'Okl and Nejm. 'Okl died as a youngester and Nejm Bin Boulos had 'Okl and Hanna. 'Okl had Elias who had Edmond and George in Egypt. Hanna had Nejm who is an expatriate in Olean, New York.

2. Girgis Bin Moussa Bin Abou Youssef. He had three sons. He had Khaled who is surnamed Boutros, Taleb who is surnamed Mikhail, and the deacon Beshara. Boutros had a son called Wakim and Wakim had Nasef, Boutros, Anton, and Youssef.

Nasef became a monk and he is known as the Pastor, Father Mobarak. Boutros had Khalil and Hanna. Khalil had no children and the sons of Hanna were born in America. Youssef Wakim had Wakim, Nasef, Selim, Elias, Tawfiq, and Naguib. The sons of Wakim were born in Brazil: Josef (deceased), Antonio, and Alfons. Nasef died in Mexico unmarried. Selim did not have sons, and Elias had Josef, Milad and Antonio. Naguib had Geofer and Edwardin. Taleb bin Girgis died unmarried.

3. Youssef (Al Henawy, meaning "The Red") Bin Moussa Bin Abou Youssef. This son of Moussa, Youssef, had three sons. They are **Fares, Maroun** and **Abdulallah**.

Abdulallah had Youssef who died youngester.

And **Fares** Al Henawy had

(a) Saab,
(b) Guad'oun,
(c) Girgis,
(d) Maroun,
(e) De'ebess,
(f) Khalil, and
(g) Saloum.

> (a) Saab had Shebli, Hanna, Fares, and Girgis. Shebli became a pastor surnamed Abdel Messih. Hanna died with no offspring. Fares had Saab and Hanna, neither of whom married. And Girgis Saab had Ne'matallah who died during World War I, and a daughter, Anna, who went to Olean, NY, and married Nejm Knieser on December 23, 1902.

> (b) Guad'oun Bin Fares Al Henawy had Beshir who had Daher, Guad'oun, Mikhail, and Hanna. Daher Beshir had Habib and Hanna. Habib had George, Josef, Jean, Daher, and Guad'oun. Hanna died as a child. Guad'oun Bin Beshir joined the Jesuit monasticism and Mikhail Beshir had Naguib, Girgis, Boutros, and Beshir. Naguib had Anis, Antoin, and Josef. Girgis Bin Mikhail was ordained a priest and was known as Father Beshara. Beshir had Michel, Moris, and Nabih. Hanna Bin Beshir was ordained a priest and known as Father Hanna.

> (c) Girgis Bin Fares Al Henawy bacame a priest in the Halabian Monasticism. His brother Maroun had Daher who had Abdou and Maroun. Abdou had Habib, Mansour and Daoud. Habib had Naguib, Abdou, and Boutros. Naguib had Fouad and Malkoun, while Abdou had one son, Emil. Mansour Bin Abdou died leaving daughters. Daoud Bin Abdou had George, Milad and Michel. Maroun Bin Daher had Wadi', Youssef, and Gamil. Wadi' didn't get married and Youssef had Maroun in the United States.

> (d) Maroun Bin Fares Al Henawy, he had Asaad who had Khatar, Girgis, Moussa, and Mikhail. Moussa died as a youngester and single. Khatar had Fares, Selim, and Maroun. Fares Khatar had Rashid who had

216

sons and daughters and they are in Brazil. Selim had Abdou and Girgis. Abdou died too young and Girgis Bin Selim had Assaf, Youssef, Selim, and Elias. Assaf had Abdou, Jean, and Milad.

Maroun Bin Khatar had Wadi' and Louis. Wadi' died unmarried, and Louis Rezk was young and died in the War. Girgis Bin Asaad Maroun had Asaad and Abdou who died single. Asaad had George. George Bin Asaad had Emil, Asaad, Alfred, Edmond, Antoin, Albert, Edward and Elly. Mikhail Bin Asaad Maroun had Said (who died when he was a kid), Mo'awad (died a youngster), Said, Daher, and Shaker. Both Said and Daher died and had no offspring. Shaker had sons in Brazil.

(e) As for De'ebess Bin Youssef Al Henawy, he died young.

(f) Khalil Bin Fares Al Henawy had: Asaad, Daoud, Elias, Amin and Daoud. Both Daouds died when they were kids. Asaad had Qablan and Saada who emigrated and there is no news about him. And Elias died confused. Amin had Shaker, Eid, and Khalil. Eid and Khalil both died in Mexico when they were teenagers. Shaker Amin had Camile, Gamil, and Emil. Camil had George, Josef, Mounir, Khalil, Eid, and Elias.

(g) Saloum Bin Fares Al Henawy had Khatar and Habib. Khatar had Abdou, Fares, and Hanna. Then, Abdou Khatar had Tawfiq, Gamil, Boutros, and Wadi'. Tawfiq had Michel, Jean, and George. Boutros had Milad and Abdou. Wadi' had Philip and Samir. Fares Khattar had: Habib, Ghatas, Michel, George, Elly, and Antoin. Michel had Afif, Nazih, and Nabih. Hanna Khatar had Naguib and Josef who had Romeo and Rolan. Habib Saloum had Selim and Abdulallah. Selim died without children and Abdulallah never married.

(C.) Abdulallah Bin Abou Youssef Rezk had **Mansour** and **Eid**. **Mansour** had Gad'oun and Shahin. Guad'oun had Nader and Mansour. Nader Bin Guad'oun had Guad'oun and Hanna who was surnamed Gamal. He never married and has died. Guad'oun Bin Nader had Hanna, Ayoub, and Nader. Hanna Guad'oun had Mansour and Guad'oun. Mansour had sons in Mexico and Guad'oun did not marry and died where he emigrated. Ayoub Guad'oun did not marry. Nader had Gamal and Abdulallah who died young and unmarried. Gamal Bin Nader had Michel, Abdulallah, and Josef. Michel had a son. As for the second Mansour Ibn the first Guad'oun, he had Asaad who had Hana, Mena, and Jana.

Shahin Bin Mansour had Youssef and Tanious. Youssef Bin Shahin had Fares and Abdou. Abdou had Eida and Fares had Asaad, Habib and Hanna. Habib did not marry and died. Asaad Fares had Abdou and Habib. Abdou had girls who died in the war. Habib had no children. Hanna Bin Fares had Youssef who had three boys, but the one named Fares died.

Eid Bin Abdulallah Bin Abou Youssef, he had Hanna who had Khatar, Ghanatious and Ghaleb. Khatar never married and died. Ghanatious had Hanna, Boutros, Girgis, Youssef, and Abdou. Hanna had Boutros and Mansour. The two Boutros' died young and never married. Mansour died unmarried. Abdou didn't get married. Youssef had Ghantious and Fares. Ghantious had Youssef and Abdou and both of them died in the First World War, with no one remaining from Ghantious' children except Fadoa. Fares died in that same war with his two young boys. Girgis Ghanatious had Assaf and Elias. Assaf died in Brazil and left one boy and two girls there. Elias is also in Brazil and his boys and girls.

Ghaleb Bin Hanna Eid Bin Abdulallah Bin Abou Youssef had Youssef, Mar'ei, and Elias. Youssef Bin Ghaleb had Asaad, Khatar, Mansour, Mikhail and Elias. Asaad had Qablan, Girgis, Francis, and Youssef. Qablan Bin Asaad had Edmond, Albert, Asaad, Antoin, and Elly. Girgis Bin Asaad had only girls. Francis had Raymond, Pierre, and Jack. Khatar Youssef Ghaleb had Fares and Boutros. Fares didn't get married and died a youngster. Boutros had Josef,

217

Antoin, and George. Mansour Youssef Ghaleb had Habib, Naguib, Boutros, and Boulos. Boulos had George. Naguib had one boy. Mikhail Youssef Ghaleb had Youssef, Ibrahim, and Louis. Youssef did not marry and died. Ibrahim had one daughter. Louis had three boys, the oldest one is named Josef.

Elias Bin Youssef Ghaleb had Ceasar, Hanna, Nayef, Josef, Halim, and Michel. Halim didn't get married and died young. Ceasar had Henry, Jean, and George. Hanna Bin Elias had Philip, Moris, Samir, and Elly. Michel had Elly.

Mar'ei Bin Ghaleb had Ghaleb and Eid. Ghaleb had Elias, Mar'ei, and Girgis. Elias had Nasef who had two boys. Mar'ei didn't have children. Girgis had two daughters. Eid Bin Mar'ei Ghaleb had Rashid and Youssef.

Tanious Bin Shahin (Faseida) had De'ebess and Elias. De'ebess had Neamatallah who had George in the United States. Elias Bin Tanious had only one daughter called Eida.

Their Offshoots And Surnames

According to documentation and traditions, Abou Youssef Rezk is the great-grandfather of this offshoot. And per the narration of Father Yohanna Al Bachaalany as passed down from Nejm Andrea Al Bachaalany, he is the famous Abou Youssef Rezk Bin Abou Rezk Nasr Al Bachaalany. This offshoot of Abou Youssef is surnamed "The House of the Deacon" and sometimes called the "Faseida House" which may be Syriac meaning water brook. It has been said, too, that it is the name of a bird which frequents the water brook.

The offspring of Abdulallah Bin Abou Youssef were surnamed "Faseid". Meanwhile, the offspring of Nejm Bin Moussa Bin Abou Youssef were surnamed the "Abou Knieser House". The word "Knieser" being a nickname for a "crooked (or curved) little finger of the hands". The offspring of his brother Youssef Bin Moussa was surnamed the "Al Henawy" meaning "The Red" because of a prominent red garment worn by Youssef Bin Moussa, and the offspring of Youssef Bin Nejm Abou Knieser was surnamed "Freha" meaning "Happy" because he was always in a happy state of mind. The surname of the offspring of Wakim Bin Boutros Bin Girgis Bin Moussa became the "Wakim House". And, Maroun Al Henawy was known as the "Maroun House".

The offspring of Ghanatious Bin Hanna Eid were surnamed the "Ghanatious House". The surname of the offspring of his brother Ghaleb was the "Ghaleb House". And the surname of the offspring of Guad'oun Bin Nader was the "Guad'oun House", etc. for the many other surnames.

Besides being the surname of the Abou Youssef House, "The Deacon" was also the surname of the offspring of Andrea and Metri Moussa from the Ne'ama House. This indicates that they were brothers or paternal cousins, and Andrea, who is the son of the old Nejm, used to call them "Cousins".

The Neama House and Abou Youssef House were mixed and lived in the same neighbourhood ever since they settled in Salima. That offshoot was rich because, as we previously mentioned, Abou Youssef Rezk went to France and returned with a large amount of money. As a result of this financial grant, his son Moussa started to buy real estate from Prince Abdulallah and others. Moussa built a house on some of this land. The deeds that survive are many. The offspring of this offshoot have increased that heritage and enlarged their holdings and means of living. Still today, and for more than two and a half centuries, the oldest child inherits the father's real estates. That, in itself, proves how our family preserves the ancestors' inheritance.

It is with gratitude to this family residing in Salima for such a long time that our heritage has been preserved. They lived in comfort. They lived content. They preserved the inheritance of the ancestors by ignoring many of life's interests. They continually worked hard until they possessed the majority of the East side real estate in the rural area of Salima. They planted that area with pine trees, starting from the "Place of the Press" to the high upper area. The area still belongs to the Abou Youssef House. It encompasses the place known as the cave of the Abou 'Okl House, the Matar ditch of the Matar Karam house, the Al Henawy ditch of the Henawy's, and the majority of the wall belonging to the Al Abssy House. Our ancestors bought all these properties from the Princes and the Said Family who were the oldest habitants there.

Among the remembered glorious deeds of this offshoot is all that they did to help with the endowment of the Saint Peter Monastery to the Capuchin Fathers. Basically, what we know about this is that they donated the land and the building. Accordingly, the Capuchin Fathers were beholden to them and promised to appoint one of them as supervisor or curator of the properties of the Monastery. This established the tradition of our ancestors being in charge. This has been proven by their actions and deeds over the years. The history of the Monastery shows this. It can been seen during the era of Taleb Bin Girgis Faseida, who was the Monastery Curator who was killed as we will talk about later, up to the days of both the late Anton and Youssef Wakim Boutros who were in charge of the monastery during their entire lives.

Our ancestors had two olive trees in front of Ain Al Zeitouna. One was big and the other of medium size. They were divided between the three offshoots, the Moussa, Mansour, and Eid. Then, Eid duped them and took the medium size Olive tree for himself and did not pay the others. Accordingly, the Princes surnamed him, as tradition says, "Hilik" (Crook).

Then Moussa and Mansour took the big olive tree. Those two olive trees remained as an important proof of their kinship. They are the real kinship tree and not one of our ancestors requested their division. Their age is about two hundred and fifty years. In the past our grandmothers used to take their laundry there. They would sit on the well rock, under the shade of the two olive trees. They would hit the clothes with a bat, washing them in the traditional way.

Recently, their owners donated them to the Church of Our Lady. They were valued at about two hundred piastres. They were then cut and sold.

In the middle of the last century, some of those from the Abou Youssef Al Bachaalany House moved from Salima to the countryside. Among them was the offspring of Ghaled Bin Hanna Eid known as the House of Ghaleb Al Bachaalany, the offspring of Nader Guard'oun who were known as the House of Nader Al Bachaalany, the offspring of Guad'oun Bin Fares Al Henawy known as the House of Beshir Al Bachaalany, and the offspring of Saloum Fares Al Henawy who are from the Khatar Saloum Al Bachaalany House. All those are living in Makse, Shatoura, and the Merigate.

Their Homes.

The homes of the Abou Youssef Al Bachaalany families were in the same neighborhood, next to each other, showing the division of the offshoots and their gathering of small families. The area situated on the eastern side of the Princes' Castle in Salima. They are:

1. Wakim Home. Our grandfather Moussa Bin Abou Youssef bought his place from Prince Abdulallah. In 1847, Wakim Bin Boutros renovated it. Then his two sons, Anton and Youssef, renovated it for the third time.

2. Maroun Al Henawy Home. It is situated on the eastern side of the Wakim home.

3. Boutros Bin Wakim Home. Situated on the eastern side of the Maroun home.

4. De'ebess Bin Tanious Home. It is situated on the eastern side of the Boutros Wakim home. And the last three homes were adjacent with Andrea's home, with their roofs at the same level.

5. Abou Knieser Home. (Abou Khnesar Home) This consists of two parts: the eastern part of his son Boulos and the western part of his son Freha. The two homes today belong to Girgis Bin Selim Khatar Maroun.

6. The home of Boutros, the third son of Abou Knieser, is occupied by the sons of the previously mentioned Shahin Bin Boutros. Those homes are situated in the northeastern side of Andrea's home.

7. The home of Ghaleb Bin Hanna Eid. It is situated to the north of the above mentioned homes. It is divided into two parts and was occupied by the Ghalebs before they moved to the countryside.

8. The homes of the Fares Al Henawy sons: Saab's home , Saloum's home and Guad'oun's home. In their place, Khalil Abdou Freha has built his present home.

9. The home of the sons of Khalil Al Henawy: Asaad and Amin.

10. The home of Guad'oun Bin Nader is situated on the southern side of Abou Knieser homes.

11. The home of Ghanatious under the Mar Boutros monastery: a part of it is for Youssef and the other is for Girgis.

12. The home of Hanna Ghanatious is situated on the north.

13. The home of the Freha sons is situated at the eastern side of the castle. They bought it from the Al Tiyans and gave their old home to their nephew (sister's son) Selim Khatar.

14. The home of Fares and Abdou Youssef Shahin in the Al Kharga district is on the eastern side of the square.

15. The home of Asaad Mansour is beside it.

Their Vestiges And News

We are now presenting here some of the documents which we found in the home of the Abou Youssef offspring. They include items such as contracts, deeds, agreements, judgments, testaments and many others. They present us with a good picture of what their social life was like in those days. The documents have been very helpful in establishing and confirming relationships, especially when coordinated with other items, including the Church registries.

Our grandfathers used to roll these documents into small cylinders and keep them in their turbans when they were moving from one place to another. Here are some of the events and information they reveal.

"The reason for writing these letters is that we have sold to our friend Moussa a property in Bou Assy fields. The price is five piasters and has been paid in full to us in cash. Nothing further is due from him. The mentioned property is completely his and he can dispose of it as he wants. We have written this contract as a declaration and to prove its existence.

Written by	*Stamp on the back*
Abdulallah M	*Abdulallah Abi Al Lam'*

   --Written in the beginning of the year 1114." (1702)

The one called Moussa in this document is the son of Abou Youssef, the greatgrandfather. He was the companion of Prince Abdulallah and the one who baptized him in prison with the guidance of the Capuchin Fathers.

The following certificate was probably written during his exile:

" The reason for writing this letter is to verify the following: we were in Salima at the residence of his excellency, Prince Abdulallah. in the hall. Moussa and his brothers came to his excellency and he declared in front of us all that he, the Prince, sold to them the field for sixteen piasters, deducting from the said amount four piasters. We acknowledged it and that is what happened in our presence.

Sheikh Abou Nejm Assaf and Sheikh Abou Farahat had also come to his excellency, Prince Abdulallah's place. So Moussa asked the Prince for a girder bridge going from the boundary of the Al Sawaf House. He gave him one and asked Sheikh Abou Nejm to show it to him. Accordingly, Sheikh Abou Nejm cut a girder bridge for him. He mentioned that it cost two and a half piasters. Abou Nejm mentioned that his excellency had cut and given him a girder bridge but refused to take any money at all for both of them.

Written by Baha Eddine Ibn Ezz Eddine. "

- - - - -

"The reason of writing this is that Abou Hussain Sharaf Eddine Ibn Abou Fayad and ourselves have sold to Abou Nejm Moussa the press situated under Ain Baqha. We have received its full value in cash with not a derhem due. Also his paternal cousin, the son of Abou Nasef, has sold his share with full consent of all concerned.

Written by   The stamp on the back in front of the Signature

Abdulallah M   Abdulallah Aba Lam' "

- - - - -

"This is what Moussa Ibn Faseida, from the village of Salima, has purchased. He bought it with his own money, for himself, with no one else. He purchased it from Abou Ali Fares Ibn Yazbek ... under Ain Baqha. Its price is eighteen and a half piasters. It was paid completely in cash and no remaining amount due. It has been so testified in the month Geomadi Al Aoual, 1115, Hegira Year, of the year of the prophet's journey, giving our full salutation to him.

Written by   Witness

Ahmed Ibn Abou Mora from Arson   Abou Faysal from Zar'oun, Saab, Mazhar, from Bezbedin .

- - - - -

"This is what Sheikh Moussa, son of the Deacon, and his brothers purchased with their money, for themselves and not for anyone else, from the man called Sheikh Abou Ali Ibn Youness, and his paternal cousin Mohamed Ibn Naser Eddine. All parties involved are from Salima and what the sellers have sold is their own. They dispose of it freely, evidenced by this contract. It consists of all the uncultivated lands in their places known as Ain Baqha Sham Al Hawa for the price of two piasters and five shawahi. It has been taken from the mentioned buyers and given to the mentioned sellers, and there is a remaining amount due. The assessor was Abou Moussa Barakate. Whatever has to do with any intercession or prevention of this sale falls necessarily upon conscience of the seller. Also, whatever refers to the money of this transaction falls upon the conscience of the buyers. By our own choice we hereby certify this agreement in the month of Moharam, in the beginning of the Year 1121. (1709)

Witnesses: Mohamed Abou Ridan, Soliman Ibn Abou Bakr, Ahmed Ibn Abou Ali, Rezk Ibn Abou 'Assy.

Written by: Al Haqir Mohamed Bin Taqiy"

- - - - -

The reason for writing this is to verify that Abou Ali Breqaa Ibn Said has sold to the Deacon Abou Nejm Moussa Ibn Abou Youssef, a parcel of land in Ain Al Sayfeya. Bordered from the East the big Shahar stone, from the North Al Shir, from the West the known fountain, and from the South the road. The price of that land is one piaster. The assessor Abou Qansowa Mohamed has taken the amount from the buyer's hand and given it to the seller's hand. The land became the property of the mentioned buyer. He may dispose of it as he sees fit. There are no obligations upon the buyer. This is what they ordered us to write and certify. Written on the year 1145. Written by Witnessed that this is valid

Mansour Ibn Nasr Eddine   *Abou Ali Ismail."*

- - - - -

"The man called Abou Nejm Moussa from Salima village has bought from the man called Abou Farahat Hanna Al Beiruty, residing on this day in the mentioned village, the trellis which are in the Ain Al Sawaky land. It is bordered from the South with the property of the buyer's brother, from the East the great Shahar Stone, from the North a property of the seller and from the West the property of Abou Badr Eddine Al Fafoush, for the price of one piaster. Year 1131.

    Witness: Shahin Tarboush from Bezbedine. Written by: Ismail Bou Ali from Rawas Al Balout."

- - - - -

" The reason for writing ... is that Nejm Ibn Moussa Faseida from Salima Village has bought from Sha'ia Ibn Bou Karam Boutros from Al Arbania village, the vines which are in Al Wariz forming two water sources and air. Its price is twenty five piasters according to Estephan Ibn Mikhail's evaluation. This transaction is irrefutable and valid ...written in 1177.

    Witnesses   *Written by*

    Yaghi Bin 'Oun, Mikhail Al Gamal, Sarkis Bin Mikhail   *Fares Matar*

- - - - -

Knieser Nejm

He is Nejm Bin Moussa Bin Abou Nasr. My father related this story to me, passing it down from his father and grandfather.

The story is that Nejm known as Abou Knieser was in love with his kinswoman, a distant cousin, the daughter of Abou Andrea Nejm. One day, knowing that she went to the place of the presses, on the east side of Salima, he followed her there. She was climbing up a pine tree, collecting its fruits. He told her "I want you to come away with me and elope to Bezbedine. If you refuse, I will cut down this tree with you in it!" The girl was afraid, so she climbed down the tree and accompanied him to Bezbedine which was not far. They told a priest about their situation and he agreed to mediate with Abou Andrea, the father of the girl. They all reconciled. Shortly thereafter they were married. They went back to Salima with the priest and Abou Andrea was content. Still, today, the place where the incident occurred

222

is known as the Abou Khnesar threshing floor. The properties of the Abou Andrea house and the Abou Khnesar house are neighboring!

Freha Abou Knieser

Abou Knieser Nejm had six sons: Knieser, Youssef known as Freha, Boutros, Boulos, Gibrail, and Tanious. The last two died young and unmarried. Concerning Freha, the Princes gave him his new name of "Freha" because he was always cheerful. He lived a long life and died in March, 1830. His wife was Khashfa, the daughter of Estaphan Abou Nofal his negihbour and his maternal kinsman. Freha was a tradesman and Nader Guad'oun was his partner according to his records. He died and left three sons: Girgis, Tanous, and Gibrail. He also had a daughter called Rahja who married Khattar Asaad Maroun.

His sons had to work after his death. Girgis joined the service of the Princes of Qarnayel for a while. Then he worked in commerce. His brother Gibrail took his place in the service of those Princes and remained in the house of Prince Beshir Bin Hussein Youssef Mourad and his son Prince Said. They lived in Qarnayel and Beit Meri. He worked for them until he died. Tanous joined the Princes' service in Salima.

I am now showing the last will and testament of Knieser Bin Abou Knieser Nejm who died and had no children. His wife was Matra, the sister of Ghanatious Hanna Eid.

"In the name of the Father, the Son, and the Holy Spirit, the One God, Amen.

I, Knieser, in sound mind and body, wish to write my last will and testament, giving my full consent. First, I certify and declare my faith is the faith of the Roman Catholic Church of Peter. I believe in whatever it believes and I oppose whatever it opposes. I wish to die in its obedience and faith. Second, when I am called to my Creator, my share of the presses, my holdings of Ain Bouatma and the Wariz Cinnamon Bark must be sold immediately. The income of the mulberries and vines, as well as the house and its furniture are to provide for our paternal cousin until her death. Then it shall fall permanently to our brothers and our nephew (brother's son) to share. The three mulberry trees which are in front of the house shall not be assigned to anyone. Instead, each year their harvest is to be sold and its money used to pay for requiem Masses on my behalf. Concerning my wife, if she should die at the house, also, then the income shall be used for requiem Masses on her behalf. People of good conscience will provide this on our behalf. When our properties and means of living are distributed, whatever remains shall go to our brothers and our nephew in equal shares, as already mentioned.

It is totaly forbidden to change a single letter of this testament. No one has the right to object about anything in our testament. One of our stipulations is that our paternal cousin not sell our properties, nor mortgage them. Instead, she is to make her living from the crops that they produce. We have delegated our paternal cousin Saab Ibn Fares (Al Henawy) to execute this testement. Whenever the time of our passing shall come, it falls on him to immediately carry out the terms we cited and to properly distribute our fortune. If he should neglect any aspect of this testament, we pray that God punish him accordingly. We expect and pray that his conscience will be clear having carried out our testament. If he does not do so, may he have to answer before God. We have written what God has inspired us to seek. We have explained it to Father Hanna (Al Nakouzy) who has written it down as requested. If one of our brothers or paternal cousins should change any condition of this, may God be his adversary in life and after death. We will ask for our rights on the Great Judgment Day. This has been written on April 28, 1819, in the presence of Pastor Rofael Al Shababi.

Written by Father Hanna according to the dictation of the mentioned Knieser

Also, concerning the house, after the death of my wife, it will become the property of Shahin, the son of our brother Boutros. He should sell his share of the Al Atiq building to his paternal cousins and take the fair value of his share. The reason that we are giving the ownership of the house to Shahin is that our deceased brother Boutros did much of the work in building it.

(The Capuchin Father Nicolas wrote this notation in Italian).

After this testament was written, it is our understanding that a furnished home be provided for his wife and the other properties sold and the money sanctified. Nothing contrary to this is to be allowed."

Written by Father Hanna

- - - - -

"The reason for writing this on this date: Boulos, Freha, and Shahin shared the house. Freha took the upstairs rooms of Shahin. Freha paid sixty five piasters to Shahin for his share in his uncle Knieser's house. Freha paid to Boulos, 117 piasters for his share in the house and the upstairs. He also paid for the extention under the upstairs. He paid the remaining amounts, 80 piasters and 27 piasters, in Derhams cash, to Boulos and the family of his brother Knieser, and we gave it to our nephew Shahin. And anyone who had a part of the house, it was his property and he had the right to dispose of it any way he wishes. Anyone who might make a claim on the house, his claim is worthless. We have written this contract with the consent of all parties involved. They have entered into it voluntarily with no force or sense of obligation. -- Written in November, 1235. (1819).

Witnessed by	*Written by*
Boutros Ibn Anton	*Wakin Ibn Boutros*
Saab Al Henawy	
Fares Al Henawy	

A Valuable Document

I am now publishing a document which was among the items in the archives of our friend Sheikh Edmon Blebel. My generous friend Mr. Ibrahim Awad presented it to me. The names of Knieser Bin Nejm Moussa Al Bachaalany and his maternal uncle Andrea Nejm Al Bachaalany are mentioned in the document. From its content, it is evident to me that the mentioned consignments were from the Lady Oum Habib, the wife of Sheikh Ghandour Al Saad, and were deposited in Salima, Al Arbania, and the Mar Elias Shoya Monastery. It took place just before the day when the butcher Sheikh Ghandour was killed in 1790. I think that Oum Habib was from the Blibel family, the sister or daughter of Sheikh Youssef Blibel, but I am not positive. Here is the original text of the document:

> *"The reason for writing this is that the Sheikh Youssef Blibel asked us to certify the consignment. What he has received has been deposited with His excellency Afandina Prince Fares when they were in Manin. This consignment consists of two green boxes which have been engraved on sides. One box is bigger than the other and is a money-box. One box was received at the Mar Elias Shoya Monastery of the Roman Catholics. The second from Knieser was received in Salima. The money-box was at the residence of lady Zahr, deposited there by Youssef El Khoury. With all the consignments there is a basket (a big basket made of sticks) which is medium black. It was kept in Al Arbania at the Abou Haidar house. When the family of the late Sheikh Ghandour (Al Saad) moved to Ghazir, the mother of Sheikh Habib asked for the basket. We*

sent it with her messenger and it is still there. This is what we know and how it happened. I swear that this is the truth. Written by Andrea from Salima with his own hand."

The Ain Al Sayfia Press

"Fares Saad, Freha Bou Knieser, Girgis Saad, Nejm Andrea, Saab Al Henawy, Asaad Al Henawy, Wakin Ibn Boutros, Shahin Ibn Boutros, Nejm Ibn Boulos, the sons of Hanna Eid; the share of Ghanatious and his brother Ghaleb, Elias Ibn Shahin, Tanious Ibn Shahin, Father Nichola Gladimir, Sabra Al Khoury, Elias Al Tian.

"The reason for writing this: On this date, we, the above named individuals, sixteen in number, renovated a vine press in the trench called the Bou Knieser trench. We paid the price of the land to the mentioned Freha and the sons of his brother. Also, the price for the water rights was paid to Fares Saad and his brother Girgis. We, the above mentioned persons, have equally paid the salary of the master Bshour and the wages of the men who did the work. We paid all of the expenses involved.

The shares are equal. The agreement covers a four year cycle. Every year, four of the named individuals sit and collect the tithe... everyone paid his share of all the mentioned expenses. And if something on the press needs to be repaired, it will be paid and used equally. Concerning the shares, each one has one carat and a half. And the sons of Nemr, they have only one share, a carat and a half. Of the rest, each name has one share. This is how all have been satisfied and agreed. They have delegated us to write this contract with their wish and satisfaction, and all done voluntarily with no force or obligation.

It has been written for clarification and to avoid having any of its terms forgotten.
Written in the holy month of June, 1241. (1825)
Contract written by   *Witnesses*
Assad Al Henawy, delegated   *Qassem Ibn Hamada Hatoum*
by the above mentioned.   *Fares Daham and Girgis Bou Waked*

Ghanatious Hanna Eid

He married Raheel the daughter of Elias Khatar Bou Tarbeyah. He had So'oud the wife of Abou 'Okl Zidan Al Asmar from Al Arbania, Hanna, Girgis, Youssef, Abdou, and Boutros.

Hanna Ghanatious married Moheba, the daughter of Nejm Andrea. Girgis married Terazia, the daughter of Samaan Tanious Raad from Beit Mery. Youssef married Shomouna, the daughter of Youssef Nasrallah, and they had: Shams, the wife of Hanna Guad'oun; Saada, the wife of Youssef Shahin Mansour; Ghanatious, Fares, and Mariam, the wife of Youssef Eskandar Abou Shakra who had a son Abdou in Mexico. Abdou Ghanatious died in middle age and unmarried. He was an expert at horseback riding. His horses were famous because they were pure breds. He had a horse called Saada which was once stolen. To prove that it belonged to him, the horse was allowed to hear his voice. It neighed, and he was allowed to take it back.

A document citing this name reads:

"...we have sold to the children of our sister, Knieser and his brothers, the vines which are in Lezaq Al Hariq, below the vines of the children of our uncles Guad'oun and Shahin, for the price of thirty five pias- ters. ...It bordered on the north, the properties of Saliba Bou Bakr and those of the assessor Bou Nejm Heidar, in front of his.

--Written by the seller of this property himself, the mentioned Andrea. "

Tanous Freha

He is Tanous Bin Youssef (Freha) Bin Abou Knieser Nejm Bin Moussa Bin Abou Youssef (The Deacon) Rezk, the direct descendant, the great grandson, of the famous Abou Resk Al Bachaalany.

Tanous was born in the beginning of the 18th century, around 1810. In 1843 he married, and he died in 1883 at the age of 73. When he was young he used to go to the Saint Peter (Mar Boutros) Monastery of the Capuchin Fathers in Salima. There he learned the basics of his Maronite Catholic religion. He learned other elements of knowledge from his teachers in their small village school. Because he had to work to help support himself and his family he could not continue his studies.

He told my father, and my father told me, that he used to collect the papers that were thrown out in the trash from the Princes' houses. From these, he learned calligraphy and essay writing. This ambitious endeavor, alone, shows his intelligence and ability. He relied on himself to learn and earn a living throughout his whole life. He bought large real estates and by working hard, he earned no less than a hundred thousand piasters, which was very wealthy in those days.

The Lam's Princes trusted him greatly. They delegated him to manage their properties and to keep the accounts of their many partnerships in Salima, in Al Deliba, in the Al Houz neighbourhood, in Al QaaQour, in Al Douar, and in coastal Beirut.

He had various businesses including loaning money, with moderate interest rates. Together with his two brothers, he bought the house of the Tiyans which they had built in Salima. There his children and grandchildren were born. The house still stands today. He also bought other properties which the Tiyans used to own in Salima, including pine trees, vines, etc. He didn't like risking his money in commerce like his brother Girgis did. Girgis and his brother Tanous Freha were among the men exiled with Prince Haidar to Senar in Khortoum in 1840 by the order of the Egyptian Government and the Great Prince Beshir. Tanous took advantage of that occasion and gained a huge amount of wealth from taking charge of the affairs of the exiled people.

Our grandfather Tanous was kindhearted, of a good reputation and self-sufficient. He was pleasant company and loved by everyone. He was generous in taking care of his house. He liked cleanliness and order. He was a strict disciplinarian in his own house. He managed his house with authority. He disliked having an opinionated child, even when my father was fully grown and with a family of his own. He liked keeping his religious duties done. And, he was emphatic that his children attend to the rituals and prayers at Church. It was his daily habit to pay visits to his inferior relatives every night after work. He would ask about them with tenderness and affection. He was charac- terized by his loving sincerity and truthfulness. He enjoyed dealing with people who helped others because he, too, liked to help people.

He was in charge of the Sheikhdom of Salima before the era of the admistrators. At that time, the Sheikh had the same authority as the governor, especially if he was famous, decent and elderly. He would reprimand his adversaries and imprison the youth to keep them from doing bad things. In those days, life was simple. Familiarity and a sense of brotherhood prevailed.

For many years he was a trustee because the leaders and the common people knew they could rely on his honesty. When Bishop Youssef Geagea was visiting Salima, he stayed at Tanous Freha's house, in the small room which still exists. The Governor also stayed there. Although the house was small, it was the best home in which to receive the Bishop and the Governor.

Our grandfather used to wear a red cloak with blue cotton poplar pants. He wore shoes called "Al Beheiriya Al Meqitna" which were the common shoes of the day.

Once, he went to the Aintora School to pay the tuition for his son Girgis. It was the first time the headmaster ever saw him. He was so astonished to see Tanous wearing those clothes. He asked the headmaster in which exchange he would like him to pay, golden liras or Magediyan riyals or any other type of money. He did the same with the mayor of Al Metn when he came asking the people of Salima to pay their taxes. When Tanous found him insisting on it, he offered to pay the requested amount on behalf of the citizens, in whatever monetary currency desired!

He was of short stature, light brown in complexion, with a look of action and intelligence appearing on him. Elias Mikhail Abou 'Oun drew his profile many years after his death. He was standing up, lighting his small pipe, with a bottle, under the sun's light. He also drew him with his friend Abdel Hady Al Masry, and both pictures accurately portrayed him.

He had many droll stories. For example, he related that one time, he met his friend, Haidar Al Zar'ouny, a Druze from Salima. Each of them started to recount their bad times. Haidar said: "Oh, Sheikh Abou Abdo, I was living in my little house, content and satisfied. Whenever someone came to visit me, they would say: "How stupid this man is! He weaves the stick and canes pieces, he hews bridges, windows, and boxes. Meanwhile, he lives in this miserable house." They continually said this, so I built my new house. Now they say: "How stupid is this man?! He is living in this beautiful house and he is too old and advanced in years to enjoy it!"

Thus, our grandfather Tanous told him: "Don't be sad, Sheikh Abou Nejm. I am paying the taxes for the people of the village every time the government insists on it. I do this to spare us the oppression of the army, and especially on the poor and miserable. But when the survey and assessors' committee of the government came, I was a victim of my chivalry. I tried to economize for the benefit of the people. But by doing so, the government treats me with injustice by increasing the taxes on my properties.

I carry out the people's interests. I defend the oppressed and the poor. My house is open and everybody is welcome. With all this, they don't see any of the merits or favors. And you were right when you said that a man cannot satisfy people. We must be satisfied with God being content with our actions, and our treatment by those who are fair."

His last disease was edema and paralysis. It came on suddenly and it gave him no time to deal with it. He died within ten days. He received the final sacraments from the holy parish priest, Father Yohanna Al Bachaalany. He died a pious death in the company of his family. His wife Helen, the daughter of Abou 'Oun, and his children: Abdou, Girgis, Faragallah, Moheba, the wife of Daher Nejm Andrea, Ragoun, the wife of Youssef Nejm Nasrallah, and, Mary, his daughter-in-law (the wife of Abdou) and her children: Youssef (the author of this book), Boutros, Milia, and Habib…all were present. Many other relatives were also present. That was on February 28. His funeral was held at the new Church of Our Lady. He was then buried on March 1, 1883, beside the Church of Saint John. After a while, his body was moved to our family's tomb.

The following is a letter written to him:

"To our noble son Sheikh Tanous Freha: May God bless you and we wish you good health. Having received this order, we ask that you pay to our son, FatherYoussef, your generous servant, his annual wages as usual. We ask that you be patient with him concerning the amount he owes you which is guarranteed by the document you have in your hands. We ask you to wait until next season for payment because things were not good for him this year. He has been unable to pay because of the bad seasons. Because you are a person of great perception, understanding and insight, I need not explain further.

September 26th, 1859   *The Humblest, Youssef Geagea, the Bishop of Cyrus*

Another letter from him sent to Tanous says:

"Pay to our son, the Subdeacon Hanna Al Khoury, three hundred piasters on our behalf now and we will settle the account with you. Please, keep this message until we settle it. "

November, 12th, 1861.

Hanna Eid Faseida

His sons are: Ghanatious and Ghaleb who were famous for their melodious voices. As the offspring of Abou Youssef Rezk, known as The Deacon, this is not surprising. The offspring of Rezk all had wonderful voices and were famous for it in Bchaaleh and Salima for a long time, continuing right up to today. It is no wonder that their great-grandfather was surnamed the Deacon because of his nice voice. The children, the grandchildren and even the other offspring have inherited this talent.

Ghaleb Hanna Eid with his brother Ghanatious, and Ghaleb Bin Shahin Bin Sha'ia Safi Al Nakouzy were known as the masters of voice because they were singing at the funerals and weddings. If by chance they should ever be absent from a function, people asked about them. Their offspring continue to inherit that talent still today. The grandfather has passed his voice on to: the family of Hanna Eid, the family of Guad'oun and Shahin, the sons of Mansour, the brother of Eid.

The wife of Ghanatious Hanna Eid was called Raheel, the daughter of Elias Khatar Tarbeih Al Nakouzy. Raheel is the sister of Rahal and this how the Rahal house is related to the Ghanatious house.

Ghanatious had a sister called Matra who married Knieser Bin Abou Knieser Nejm and he died with no children. Thus, Matra came back to her brother's home. She served for a while at the house of the Princes of Qarnayel after her husband died. Later she went blind. Because of that, she again returned to her brother's home even though the Princes were generous with her because of her honesty and devoutness.

My maternal grandfather Hanna was the paternal uncle of Ghanatious who loved her and cherished her when she became old.

During the sedition, people were fleeing Salima, so he carried her on his back. She insisted that he leave her behind because she was afraid that he would get hurt. He refused and took her to a safe place. It is my belief that because of his actions, God blessed him. God gave him a good family and home. He blessed him with a son to take care of him in his advanced years. That son was my maternal Uncle Mansour.

Hanna Ghanatious

He is Ghanatious Bin Hanna Eid, from the offspring of Abou Youssef Rezk Bin Abou Rezk Al Bachaalany. He had a brother called Boutros who died in September, 1833. He was a teenager not having reached his twentieth birthday.

Boutros was distinguished for his pleasant voice. With his friends he performed the play "Al Badaweya" (The Bedouine) in the Salima town square. In the drama he played the role of a bedouine who lost his child. He started to seek out the child speaking impressive words. Boutros stood upon a fountain and two of his comrades were holding him. He was playing his role and he sang verses blaming himself. He imagined that he was dying so he said farewell to life. Prince Haidar heard him from the balcony of the castle and wept. He called to the boys playing and said: "get him down, get him down". That play was the last thing Boutros did in his life.

A strange coincidence involving this was that my mother was the niece of that Boutros (the daughter of his brother), thus it was her paternal uncle who died as a youngster. Plus, she had a brother named Boutros who also died as a youngster. And, then, her own son (my brother) who was named Boutros died as a youngster.

The ethics of our grandfather Hanna Ghanatious focused on tenderness mixed with a sense of humour. He told the story of how, one day when he was in Beirut, he heard a street seller shouting: "Thyme! Biscuits with Thyme open the mind." He immediately replied: "If Thyme could open the mind, my donkey would be reading books!"

He had a nice voice as did the other members of his family. He used to sing at the Mass, when he was at Prince Haidar's house in Bikfaya. He would sing along with Nakhla Khadra, famous for his melodious voice.

Our grandfather Hanna was a good looking man, with beautiful eyes. He was a good lecturer and a gentle companion. Prince Haidar liked him and made him one of his drinking companions. Prince Haidar would never drink coffee made by anyone else other than him because he trusted him so deeply.

He gave him a gift of a "Shabia", a prayers book written with colorful letters. It had gilt page edges and had thick paper. I keep this manuscript as a precious treasure, especially for its wonderful calligraphy. I have been told that it is in the handwriting of Subdeacon Tanous Farag Safir who was ordained a priest and named Father Girgis. Others told me that it was handwritten by Sheikh Amin al Dahah. I haven't investigated to see which might be true. Hanna was the best of his brothers in capability and knowledge. People liked him the most.

He died at the age of 70, on October 28th, 1872. He had always remembered the death of his son Boutros who died in Makse at Al Beqaa. He was singing at the Mass in the Gedita Church, when he felt pain in his head. They took him to Makse and he died very shortly thereafter.

Lawsuit, Dispute and Judgements

Tanious Bin Shahin Faseda married Fasouh, the sister of Mourad Al 'Aqoury, a resident in Salima. She was married before to Mansour Bin Guad'oun and had a child called Asaad. Then, from her marriage with Tanious Bin Shahin, she had: De'ebes and Elias. Her brother Mourad Al 'Aqoury died unmarried. After his death, there was a dispute about his estate between Hanna Mikhail Habaq Al 'Aqoury, a resident of Salima, and the three children of his sister: Asaad bin Mansour, De'ebes, and Elias Tanious.

Hanna Habaq presumed that he was the one who deserved the inheritance of Mourad Al 'Aqoury because he claimed to be his paternal cousin. Because of that, a dispute and struggle erupted. The Bachaalany's were divided. One party sympathized with the children of Fasouh, the sister of Mourad Al 'Aqoury, and the other side supported Hanna Habaq.

When I was young, I used to hear about the disputes. Some blamed Father Youssef Al Khoury who sided with his son-in-law, Asaad Mansour, the husband of his daughter Ester. They accused him of favoritism. The whole matter remained secret and hidden until I found the papers preserved in the house of Nasef Metri Al Zaghloul, the husband of Mena, the daughter of the mentioned Asaad Mansour. Among those papers was the judgement of the right of inheritance. It eliminates any doubt about the issue and reveals the truth of the lawsuit. Furthermore, it confirms the right of Fasouh's children and the lack of any validity in the claim of Hanna Habaq who left Salima after his claim was denied.

He escaped to Beirut under the protection of Prince Fares Sayed Ahmed Shehab being one of his peasants' partners. He died around 1890. He did marry a woman from Al Zok and had only one daughter. He called himself Hanna Al Bachaalany.

Hereafter is the text of the original judgment, which I have preserved. It has eloquent meaning, clear expressions, and nice calligraphy. It expresses justice, righteousness, and honesty which the famous Bishop Hanna Habib has blended into the beginning and end.

It also contains a memorable lesson for anyone who fraudulently claims a kinship which is not legitimately his, whether for material or moral reasons. Such improper behavior will always end in failure and deprivation, particularly if the judge is fair, wise, and intelligent, as was Bishop Yohanna Habib. The text reads:

> *"Thanks be to God. May he always be exalted. The reason for writing this is as follows: Fares Bin Nasr Karam Al Bachaalany the legal lawyer of Hanna Bin Mikhail Habaq came to my court as his confirmed legal representative in the matter that will be explained.*
>
> *Previously, the above mentioned Hanna went to the Council of the Christian Governorate. There he gave the above mentioned Fares the power of attorney in the following case. With this power of attorney, Fares presented his claim against the attendant in the Court, Abdou Bin Youssef Shahin Al Bachaalany, the legetimate lawyer of Asaad Bin Mansour Faseida Al Bachaalany, De'ebes, and Elias, the half brothers of Asaad, from their mother. They are the sons of Tanious Shahin Al Bachaalany. Both parties are from the village of Salima. The testimony of Sheikh Yazbak Bin Lahoud Yazbak from the Kafr Debian farm, and, that of Nasef Bin Elias Al Khoury 'Oweda from Ghizir village, will be heard along with the presentations of the two parties involved.*
>
> *The first attorney in his petition and pointing at him in his speech said: 'My client Hanna is the son of Mikhail Bin Habaq Bin Mourad Al 'Aqoury. It is well known that Mourad Bin Hanna Bin Mourad Al 'Aqoury had many properties as we have established. Some are in Salima. Whereas Mourad had no heir other than my client, Hanna, his paternal cousin, the properties should pass to him. Furthermore, it should be established that Asaad, De'ebess, and Elias have tried to establish their heritage by transgression. Therefore, it is requested now to deny their claim and grant my client's claim.*
>
> *However, concerning the properties cited, the lawyer Abdou denied his opponent's claim saying that Hanna was not the heir of the deceased...*

...because there was no legal evidence supporting his claim, the above mentioned Hanna's claim is denied. This verdict is legal and correct and pronounced in the presence of the attorneys. This verdict is rendered by request and on demand, taking effect this day, August 28ᵗʰ, 1851.

The Humble	*The witnesses*
Father Yohanna Habib	*Shiban Al Khoury Samaan Al Shabani*
	Subdeacon Mourad Bin Daher Zein
	Al Khawaga Abdulallah Saliby Qazah
	Father Elias Sorour

- - - - -

The Home of Wakim

Wakim Bin Boutros has renovated the home of our great-grandfather Moussa Bin Abou Youssef in 1848. Then his two sons, Anton and Youssef, renovated it again in 1870. When they did this, they had two verses composed by Father Yohanna Bachaalany engraved on the sides in the front door. It reads: "Oh God on High, remove the cover of ignorance from us and show us all things clearly. Grant us peace. Your Glory is forever." Then is says: "This blessed place has been constructed by Anton and Youssef Wakim, with God's help and generosity."

Boutros Knieser (Peter Knieser)

He married Terazia the daughter of Maroun Al Henawy. Her mother was Mary Bint (the daughter of) Ragheb Teama Bou 'Okl surnamed Al Hamra. This latter was famous for her beauty, intelligence, and strength.

After becoming a widow, Al Hamra married Maroun and had Asaad, Terazia (the wife of Boutros Bou Knieser, and they had Shahin), Mary (the wife of Youssef Nasrallah Abou Atallah), Bahga (the wife of Ghaleb Hanna Eid), and Frooseen (the wife of Youssef Al 'Erian).

Shahin was short, handsome, and with a strong voice like his father. He married Negma the daughter of Soweed and had Boutros, Knieser, Ibrahim, Youssef, Tanious, Terazia (the wife of Girgis Abou Assla), Marina (the wife of Assaf Girgis Negm Al 'Erian).

The mother of Boutros inherited part of the estate of her maternal uncle, Abdou Agha Nohra Al 'Erian.

Boutros Shahin

He was of medium stature and olive complexion. He lived with the Frenchman, Bartalis who was residing in Lebanon. He mastered the stifling of the pupae and the management of the silk plants that the Bartalis family built in Beirut, the Tripoli port, and Al Sowediya. His brothers, Youssef and Boutros, were also qualified in that field. It was through this firm that many of the people of Salima found work in the silk industry.

Boutros Shahin died in Safita where he was managing the silk plant of the Bshour family who were notables of that town. They were generous with him in this life and after his death.

The wife of Boutros was called Hana, the daughter of Mikhail Bin Hanna Bou'oun. She was intellectual and virtuous. She gave birth to Daoud, Shahin, Mariam (the wife of Elias Mikhail Rabiah from Bar Elias), and Ragoun (the wife of Sheikh Tanious Negm Abou Gouda).

Daoud Boutros married Boustine, the daughter of Fares Metri Al Sayegh. They had Soliman, Tanious, Girgis, Boutros, Lotfallah, and Youssef. All of them are workers and artisans. Daoud is a historian.

Shahin married Toqkla, the daughter of his paternal uncle Ibrahim. They had Farid and Mounira (the wife of Fouad Youssef Abou 'Assla). The father of Farid Shahin was known by his logic and his activities. He performed many praiseworthy deeds that the Druzes and Christians alike will always remember. In addition, he was famous for his skill in construction.

He lived for a while in Istambul with his two sisters, Mary and Ragoun. He donated a valuable chandelier to the Church of Our Lady in Salima which I failed to mention earlier.

Ragoun took a job teaching and educating Mounira, the daughter of Rashid Pasha, the Governor of Beirut, and the land Registrar in the capital of Turkey. She gained honor, presitige, decorations, and gifts from the Sultan Abdel Hamid and his wives. Ragoun was their translator when they went to the various Ambassadors' wives. She was skilled in Arabic, French, Turkish.

It was she who saved the house of Rashid Pasha, his money, and his dignity in the overthrow of 1908. At the same time, she maintained her religion and ethics, They were all taking note of her holiness and weighing her opinions.

Father Hanna Beshir

He is the son of Beshir Bin Gad'oun Bin Fares Bin Youssef known as Al Henawy Bin Moussa Bin Abou Youssef Rezk Bin Abou Rezk Al Bachaalany. Bashir lived in Al Merigate and had four sons: Daher, Gad'oun (who joined the Jesuit Monastery. He became a brother and died there in 1944), Mikhail, and Hanna. Hanna first joined the Jesuit Monastery then left it and became an ordained priest in 1921. Thanks to him, his nephew Girgis, the son of his brother Mikhail, was able to join the university of the Jesuits in Beirut. When he finished his studies he was ordained a priest, called Father Beshara.

Father Beshara Bachaalany

He was born on June 22, 1895, in the village of Merigate. He took his primary studies in Moalaket Zahle. His paternal uncle, Father Hanna, encouraged him to join the Eastern Clergy of the Jesuit Fathers in 1911. After he completed his higher studies, he obtained a Diploma in Philosophy and Theology in 1921. He was ordained a priest on May 16, 1925. .

He was delegated to serve the congregation of Moalaket Zahle. Then, Bishop Augustin Al Bostany called him and charged him with the spiritual service in his hometown village of Al Merigate. There, he was a good pastor, an experienced teacher, and a valuable educator. During his service there, he created the brotherhood for men and women and made interesting modifications in the church.

Through his actions, he was an example of honesty, abstinence, zealousness, and he dedicated himself to the salvation of souls. His praiseworthy efforts educated the children of his parishioners. He taught them the Christian religion and good manners. He struggled like a courageous soldier until he fell sick with pleurisy. He bore that with patience and acceptance. He died shortly after that, completing his Christian duties and being a fine example of a true priest. He passed away on May 21, 1931, in the prime of his youth. He was buried in the Church of St.Girgis in Al Merigate.

The House Of Neama

The House Of Andrea Neama

Neama Bachaalany had a son called Elias. Elias had: Negm, Estephan, and the pastor Zakaria. Negm had Girgis, Andrea, and Elias who died single. Girgis died with no children and Andrea the first had Negm who had Andrea II, Girgis, and Daher. Andrea II died young. Girgis had Andrea III who had Youssef, George, and Anton. George Andrea had Andrea, Samir, and Sami. Anton had four sons: Nadim, Emil, Nessim, and Nasry. Daher Bin Negm had Negm who had Daher, Emil (deceased), Elly, Francois, and Emil II. They are living with their mother in Brazil since the death of their father in 1944.

The House Of Nofal Estephan

Estephan Bin Elias Bin Neama had Nofal and Moussa. Nofal died having no children, while Moussa had Estephan II and Metri. Estephan was killed in the Sedition of 1845. Metri Bin Moussa had Estephan III, Nofal, Moussa, and Hanna. Nofal II died when he was a teenager. Estephan Bin Metri never married. Moussa had Sofia who got married in Brazil. Hanna Bin Metri had Metri and another son who died young in Brazil.

Their Surnames And Homes

It seems that the house of Neama (or Abou Neama) was, in the past, given the name "the house of Al Shamas". This surname was also that of the house of Abou Youssef, which proves that these two offshoots are related, namely, paternal cousins. In addition to this, their homes were neighboring.

This offshoot of Neama divided into two houses (families): the house of Andrea and the house of Abou Nofal Estaphan. The house of Abou Nofal Estaphan became known as the house of Metri Bin Moussa. Their homes were not far from each other.

The offspring of the house of Abou Neama did not increased in the past and today there remains only one, from the offspring of Metri Bin Moussa Estephan. He is Metri Bin Hanna Metri living in Olivaira, Brazil. This is in great contrast with the house of Andrea, whose descendants, today, are many.

The members of the Andrea house were famous by their common sense, intelligence, and good judgment. The house of Abou Nofal Estephan were known by their bravery and courage as well as their good voices. Estephan Bin Moussa and Estephan Bin Metri were among the bravest of men. Metri Bin Moussa was also a good speaker with a pleasant voice. His children have inherited these talents from him. Their names are Estephan, Moussa, Hanna, Alia (the wife of Youssef Mourad Zein), Gamila (the wife of Tanious Naseef), and Sofia (the wife of Daoud Abou Assla). Alia and Gamila were famous for their melodious voices in singing spiritual hymns, performing at many wedding celebrations and funerals.

Their Vestiges and News

The following are taken from documents we possess:

"Estephan Abou Neama ... bought in Ain Al Mahata land from Abdulallah Abou 'Okl in 1198 Hegira (1783). Written by Youssef Al Khoury."

- - - - -

" ...Moussa Bin Estephan bought ....from Teama Bou 'Okl ...in the year 1208 (1793). Witnesses: Moussa Al 'Erian. Father Francis (Al Nakouzy) Hanna Bin Nasr.
(Karam). Soweed Bin Nofal. "

- - - - -

" .. Moussa Bin Estephan bought from Hanna Ibn Mousa Bou Issa ...a piece of land (with pines) which is above the Priests' Monastery, for the price of thirty four and a half piasters. Written on March 1214 Hegira (1799). The assessor Hanna Bin Nasr Karam and his witnesses, written by Youssef Al Khoury (Francis) and witnesses."

- - - - -

" ...Andrea has bought one Carat of the press of Gibrail Bin Samaan (The Ghousha Press) in 1809. "

- - - - -

" ... That records that we sold the rotating fountain which was the property of Elias Al 'Erian. Its borders are known to our dear Sheikh Andrea Al Bachaalany. We received from him the price according to the evaluation of Noaman Said, ...was written on Shaaban, 1222 Hegira (1807), Hassan."

- - - - -

The Son Of Prince Ismail Abou Al Lam'

Negm Bin Andrea Al Bachaalany bought from Bedah Qadama the vines in Lezak Al Hariq (Al Wariz) at the price of fifty piasters, in 1240 Hegira (1824). It was written by Bou Ali Said. The Witnesses were Ismail Bin Bergas, Ezz Eddine Bou Ali, Bou Hassan Al Zar'ouny. In another document he purchased from Ismail Bin Bergas Al Masry the property bordering the pond, for the price of 140 piasters. He bought from the Lam's Princes a piece of property in Makse, Al Beqaa. He also bought many other things that would take a long time to list.

Andrea Bachaalany

The elder Andrea Bin Negm was a famous man in his time. He was known for his logic and sound judgment. We previously mentioned him in a couple of places in this book including the story of the kidnap of his sister and her marriage to Abou Knieser Negm, the contract between his nephew (sister's son) Knieser and himself, and the situation with his nephews (his sister's children).

My late father passed down this story from the sheikhs. He told me that there was hostility growing between the Qayed Beih family in Salima and the family of Mourad in Al Matiyan of the Lam's Princes.

At the end of the 18th century, their guardian and councelor, Abou Andrea I or his son Andrea was thinking about a way to mend the rift between the two parties. His efforts were in vain.

So, he sent someone to the Al Belana quarter and held a meeting with the grandfather of the Al Mazmouk family who were the remaining part of the Bachaalany House in that village. He sent him secretly to Hasbeya which is situated between Salima and Al Matyan and among the plantations belonging to Al Matyan princes.

The man did what Andrea ordered him to do. He set fire to a house belonging to one of the partners of the Murads Princes in Hasbeya. He then returned to Al Belana at night.

Those Princes saw the fire and thought that the people of Saayate were executing a plot. Thus, they came to a balcony overlooking Hasbeya and started to threaten the perpetrator. News reached their paternal cousins, the Princes of Salima. They overlooked the plantation. They started to make threats. Then, the fire burned itself out.

The next day the Princes of Salima knew that the princes of Al Matyan were coming. Accordingly, they went out of the village to welcome them. They hugged each other and reconciled.

Then, the princes of Salima, in turn, paid a visit to their paternal cousins in Al Matyan. Abou Andrea worked on bringing Al Mazmouk from the Al Belana Quarter to Salima where he settled and lived with his offsprings. They are still there today.

After that Abou Andrea revealed the secret to the Princes who praised his chivalry and wisdom.

A dispute occurred between Prince Beshir the Great and the Princes and the people of Al Metn. They held a meeting in the place of "Gel Bin Hiyato" situated between Salima and Bzebdine. Meetings were also held either in that place or in Ain Basenbil in Qarnayel. They kept discussing the matter, and, in the end, Abou Andrea Bachaalany was called upon.

He stood up and a summary of what he said is: "In my opinion, we have to go to Prince Beshir and talk to him personally about what is good for the country and the people. That will be better than worthless letters." Everybody shouted and said: "That's right!" and at once they went to Deir Al Qamar and met the Prince. They achieved what they wanted.

Negm Bin Andrea

He was born around 1780 and grew up in a big house. He followed the ways of his father who was known for his virtue, wisdom, and management skills. He was distinguished for his speaking ability and eloquence in expressing his thoughts.

After his father died, Negm took his place. He was the property of the Salima Princes and their number one manager. He married Mary the daughter of Nader Gad'oun and had Girgis and Moheba. Moheba married Hanna Ghanatious. After the death of his wife, Mary, he married Afifa Al Qardahy, the widow of Hadj Khelo Halwa, one of the notables of Zahle. She had seven sons, three of them died and four remained. The older was Abou Shahin Halwa. She was a good woman, and from her marriage with Negm had: Daher and Youssefeya, the wife of Negm Bin Youssef Nasrallah.

According to oral traditions handed down, when the great Patriarch Youssef Hebesh was a child, he was accompanying his father to the house of the Lam's Princes in Salima. Negm was accompanying his father Andrea there. The house was a well known stopover for the notables of the country.

Thus, the two boys, Negm and Sheikh Hebesh, met and they were playing in the beautiful meadow of Salima. Years later when Al Hebesh became Patriarch, Andrea went to congratulate him. The Patriarch didn't recognized him at first. So Negm started to remind him about the days they spent at the Salima house. Then the Patriarch started to remember and hugged his childhood friend with a brotherly hug.

On many occasions Abou Andrea took charge of negotiations concerning the country's affairs with this Patriarch, representing Prince Haidar Ismail, his intimate friend. Negm was well known for his patience and knowledge.

In 1845, the uprising happened between the Christians and the Druzes. Mohamed Shakib Afandi, the ambassador of the Sultan, was delegated to Lebanon. He held a meeting which the princes, the sheikhs, and the notables of the country attended.

It was a memorable day. People from everywhere attended. Shekib Afandi put together a reading of the rules for Lebanon. They were known as "Shekib Afandi Arrangements" and they consisted of 38 clauses.

He asked the fiefs' governors to give their opinions and to note their remarks. The feudal lords appointed representatives for that, and the most capable and important ones were Sheikh Negm Andrea Bachaalany and Sheikh Hussein Talhouk, known by the Druzes. Each one of them was offering the other prioirity. When Sheikh Hussein insisted, Sheikh Negm came forward and started his speech by invoking the Sultan and his Ambassador. After that he listed the thirty-eight clauses, clause by clause, and commented on it. Shokeib Afandi asked him: "Where are the borders of Lebanon?" So, he answered: "One day, the borders of Lebanon are Al Merigate, and, another day, they are Bawabat Allah in the Sham. This is so because when the governors surpass the Lebanon frontiers they link their end to Al Merigate in Al Beqaa. And if they were vanquished by the Lebanese governors, the borders would become Bawabat Allah in Damascus." After Abou Andrea finished his speech, Shokeib Afandi asked in Turkish "Ke Min Bo?" and that means "The property of whom?". Then Prince Haidar Ismail the governor of the Christians answered "He is mine, my Lord."

Prince Haidar had a right to be proud of Andrea Al Bachaalany, his counselor and representative. He performed well in front of that crowd of presidents and notables. (passed down from honest Sheikhs of Salima who witnessed the event).

In 1847, Negm Andrea received a letter from the Princes of Qayed Baih, the Lam's, saying:

"To be brought to the attention of our loving, most respectful excellency, dear Sheikh Negm Andrea the respectful, may God save him.

Longing to see you in good health and asking about your desired safety. We wish to inform you of a meeting intended to take place between notables of the Jibel (Mountain) and the two councils' owners. The purpose is to resolve issues concerning our country. We require your attendance asking you to be our representative along with the other Al Metn representatives. We will work until God's will is done, without compensation.

Accordingly, full care should be given to this meeting. Being certain of your maturity and knowning our reliance on you, it was inevitable that we select you for this assignment. Delay is unwanted and apology is unacceptable. The mentioned meeting will be held on next Monday, Rabie Al Awal 14, in the morning. Thus, we want you to be present at the assigned place before the appointed morning. God willing, we will see you there in good health. --Rabie 1263 Hegira (1846). --Written by our loving Sheikh Soliman (Abou Ahmed). Stamped wiith a seal and sent it to him immediately by recorder delivery. The house of Qayed Baih: Hassan, Beshir, Gehgea, Beshir, Fares, Ali, A-min. "

His son-in-law, Nader Gad'oun, personally told me about him. He said uncle Negm used to sit under a large mulberry tree in front of his home, behind the Aboud home. He was surrounded by men of the neighbourhood and others who were listening to his talks and his interesting news. He said that when he was a boy, he used to sit between his arms. He would give him the tobacco bag to fill his pipe and roll a cigarette for each one of the attendants. Then they would drink coffee and smoke their cigarettes. When the people were gone he said he asked him: "Are we going to serve cigarettes and coffee to those people every day?" He answered: "My son, the subsistence of men is an obligation on men. It is an act of charity to those less well off." That is why his words were always a piece of wisdom. They were passed from mouth to mouth. And usually they attributed sayings to him adding: "...As our uncle Negm Andrea says."

During the era of Prince Beshir and the Egyptian Government, Abou Andrea was a clerk with Sheikh Salibi Al Ramy from Falougha in Al Beqaa (the countryside). They were giving orders and issuing prohibitions like governors do.

Abou Andrea owned 500 head of goat and cow cattle. However, he lost his cattle in 1840 during the events of Ibrahim Pasha.

Only forty cows were saved: 30 able to plow and ten were unable to plow. Their herder, Shahin Saad Allah Attallah, was the one who saved those. He used a ruse, telling the soldiers: "May God grant long life to Afandina Ibrahim Pasha because he approved that we should take the cows." Thus, the soldiers could not object. He rode Abou Andrea's horse and drove the cattle back to Salima.

When the insurgence of 1845 occurred, he possessed forty thousand piasters. A great part of it was saved by the lady Lam', the wife of the Prince Haidar Ismail. Negm Andrea did not buy things to earn a living with his money. Instead, he spent it on his house without considering the future.

He was appointed the ambassador of Prince Haidar in the town of Jbail for three years during the era of the Christian governorate.

Negm Andrea died on Monday, May 8, 1865, at midnight, armed with the necessary sacraments. In attendance was the congregation's priest, Father Yohanna Bachaalany and the Roman Catholic priest Moussa Al Sayegh. At the time of his death he was conscious. Death came while prayers were being read and he was making the sign of the Cross.

Abou Andrea was tall, erect, and corpulent. The exsisting picture of him was drawn by Elias Mikhail Bou'oun and we published it in our book Lebanon and Youssef Beik Karam. Among our preserved documents, there are many written items either from him or to his attention. They show that he was dealing with important affairs relating to the country, the Princes, especially Prince Haidar for whom Abou Andrea was a counselor. About Andrea was one of the pillars of his government and Prince Haidar's ambassador, responsible for his dealings with religious and governmental leaders.

His composition was eloquent even though he was not formally educated. Also, he knew the Syriac language.

Daher Negm Andrea

He was born in Salima where he received the Sacrament of the Holy Baptism in March, 1839, from Father Hanna Nakouzy. He grew up in a house of advantages and notability.

From his father he acquired his intelligence and broad base of knowledge. He was educated on the Christian principles and a high standard of ethics. He followed in his father's footsteps in serving the public interest and the affairs of the Salima Princes. This was at a time when their governmental power was slipping away.

He solved their problems. With complete honesty, he divided and sold their properties for them. That is how he managed the properties of the house of Tabet in the Beqaa (the countryside) regions. It caused him many problems.

He worked in the sheep business with his neighbour and in-law, De'ebes Bin Tanious. This, however, turned out to be a fiasco and, as a result, he had to sell many of his properties. He was a patient man, always thanking God and saying that what he did was not for money and not for men. He said that even though he may have lost everything, his honor, his peace, and his clean conscience were preserved.

Abou Daher Negm had an unusual memory. He could narrate events, stories from his father as well as long and numerous histories of families. My father and I recorded the majority of the ancient tales he handed down. Moreover, the Capuchin missionaries took from him the history of the Salima Princes which they published in a magazine called "The Catholic Mission."

He married my paternal aunt Moheba, the daughter of Tanious Freha. She was sedate and wise. They had: Negm, Afifa (the wife of Abdulallah Hanna Youssef), and Julia (the wife of Khalil Hanna Moussa).

He was tall, with a small head. He was good looking and his skin was half white and half brown. The time and the events of his life left lines and creases on his face, so much so, that in his last days, he always appeared to have a frown on his face.

He was a very devout man always giving his compliance to God's judgments. Even if he went to a morning or evening religious service, he would still hold his weekly "Kyrie Eleison" litany of the saints. He would recite his familiar prayers, particularly the Syriac Mar Avram prayer which he would recite by heart.

I used to see him at the Church, listening to the Holy Mass and following the priest's movements. Or, he would help the priest, reciting the Syriac Chorus prayers which he mastered as do all Maronites.

And how wonderful it was when the priest would ask him to read the "Al Senkisar" (the stories of the Saints). He would open his mouth and utter words of pearls, speaking as if he were an eloquent orator. He was understood by the educated and uneducated, the young and the old.

His final illness was a terminal disease. Dr. Mansour Al Bahout treated him but the medicines were useless. He knew that his death was close at hand. Thus, he told his sister Moheba (my maternal grandmother): "Save your efforts. It is time." He died after confessing and receiving Holy Communion and the Last Rites. He never lost consciousness. He continued reciting the prayer of Mar Avram and repeating: "Jesus, Mary, and Joseph" until he drew his last breath. On January 30, 1892, his soul went up to His Creator to receive the reward awaiting good Christians.

The House Of Abou 'Okl

Their In-Laws

Abou 'Okl had three sons: Teama, Neama, and Abdulallah. Teama had Ragheb and Daham. Ragheb had Elias and Abdullah. Elias Bin Ragheb had Ragheb and Daher. And Ragheb had Negma (the wife of Yakoub Ghantous), and Nassim (the wife of Maroun Khatar). Daher had Shaker (deceased), and, Abdullad Bin Ragheb died with no children.

Neama Bin Abou 'Okl died without having any children. Abdullah Bin Abou 'Okl had Bou 'Okl, Teama, Youssef, and Aboud. Then, Abou 'Okl Bin Abdulallah had 'Okl who also died without having any children. Teama Bin Abdulallah had four children: Anton, Abdullah, and Negm. Three of them never married. The fourth, Tanous, died without children.

So it was that the offspring of Teama Bin Abdulallah Abou 'Okl ended after they died. Youssef and Aboud, the sons of Abdulallah Bin Abou 'Okl, died without marrying. So the line of Abdulallah Abou 'Okl ended.

Daham Bin Teama Abou 'Okl had Hanna, Fares, and Neama. Neama had Daham who had Neama who died single. Fares bin Daham had Shiban, Ghantous, and Hanna (who died). Shiban Bin Fares had Fares, Youssef, and Tanous. Fares Shiban had Habib, Ibrahim, and Youssef. Habib Bin Fares had Boutros. Ibrahim had no children. Youssef Bin Shiban Daham had Soliman, Elias, and Rashid. And Elias had Youssef who is residing in the United States. Rashid had children while Soliman did not, and he died young. Meanwhile, Tanous Bin Shiban had Louis, Amin, Shiban, and Gemiel. Louis had no children, and, Amin did not get married. Shiban had Fares. Gemiel had George, Tanous, and 'Okl.

Hanna Bin Daham Bin Teama Abou 'Okl had Mansour, Youssef, and Khalil. Mansour had Hanna who had Mansour who died in Brazil without having had children. Youssef became an ordained priest with his same name and he had Hanna and Abou 'Okl. Hanna, too, became an ordained priest using his own name and had Youssef and Boutros (who died very young and single).

Abou 'Okl Al Khoury had 'Okl and Soliman. 'Okl died single and Soliman married a Mexican woman and has two daughters still living in Mexico.

Khalil Bin Hanna Daham had Ibrahim, Girgis, and Abdulallah. Ibrahim died single. Girgis had Khalil who had children living in the United States. And, Abdulallah Khalil had Ibrahim who had Khalil, Soliman, and Abdullah.

Meanwhile, Ghantous Bin Fares Daham had Yaakoub and Teama. Yaakoub had a son who died when he was a child. Teama had Negm and Eid who died when they were teenagers.

Father Youssef

He is Youssef Bin Hanna Bin Daham Bin Teama Abou 'Okl Bachaalany. Youssef was born in approximately 1790. He was received a Chritian education. He learned Arabic and Syriac, and, he helped his father doing farm work at Shatoura, in the Beqaa Plain.

He was one of those who accompanied Prince Haidar Abou Al Lam' at the battle of Sanour in 1830. He was married, around 1825, to the daughter of Abdulallah Abou Ragheb who died six months later.

He then married 'Akela, the daughter of Hanna Nasr Karam. They had many sons, but the only remaining children are: Ester (the wife of Asaad Mansour), Yahoodette (the wife of Hanna Dib), Hanna (who became the ordained priest), and, Abou'Okl.

In March of 1832, he was promoted to the Holy Priesthood. He was ordained by Bishop Abdulallah Blibel, Bishop of the Cyprus Diocese. This was after he had completed his studies at Zakarit Monastery.

We have already mentioned him as one of the priests who served the congregation in Salima.

Father Youssef was a generous and active priest. He served the congregation with an apostolic zeal. He helped the people with their diseases and poverty. He encouraged them to bear the difficulties and troubles that confronted them. We already mentioned that he learned and practiced Medicine. He treated the people with the standard medicines and methods of the time. He was known for his sound judgment and for being.amicable. Much of what he learned was from practice and experience.

He was short, brown, with piercing eyes aflame with intelligence and boldness. According to the drawing by Elias Mikhail Bou'oun, he used to wear a turban, sometimes a fur turban. The handdrawn picture of him still exists. It is in the house of his grandson Youssef. He died on November 22, 1859. One of his literary vestiges, is the Church registery which he gathered and organized in 1826.

Father Yohanna

He is the son of Father Youssef Bachaalany. We already told a little about his life and apostolic deeds. This pious priest was born in Salima and was baptised by Father Hanna Al Nakouzy in February 1839. He received a good Christian education from his virtuous father. He first studied at the Capuchin School where his teacher was the Sub-deacon Anton Nakouzy from Al Shabania, a former student of Ain Waraka. Then, he joined the Ecclesiastic School in Mar Abda Harharia at Kasrowan. Then, in his higher education, he majored in the Arabic Language. Thus he studied morphology, syntax, grammar, and various aspects of Arabic Literature such as vocabulary, phrasing, poetry, and rhetoric. After that he studied logic, philosophy, and theology. He also learned Syriac. Thus, in three years he acquired what would take most people many more years. This was due to his dedication, hard work, and great intelligence.

When he graduated from school, he married on December 8, 1861. His wife was Negma, the daughter of Guad'oun Bin Nader, a very virtuous woman. His father died in 1859.

Bishop Youssef Geagea ordained him to the priesthood in 1862. He worked hard in the service of his congregation. He showed great involvement with many activities, outstanding zeal and true devotion. He would preach without fear or apprehension. The congregation was admired and revered him for his generosity and virtue. He was a pastor as well as working as a teacher. He also treated patients with the traditional methods of medicine that he learned from his father. He also acquired much medical knowledge from various books on modern medecine.

He worked on the construction of the Church of Our Lady as we previously mentioned in another chapter. For all his efforts and virture, he undoubtedly gained a great reward from God, not to mention the undying pride of the entire Bachaalany family.

He worked as a teacher in the Capuchin Fathers' regular day school, then in their boarding school of Our Lady of Lourdes. There he was the teacher of vocabulary and phrasing up until his death. He worked continually at his interests, his courses, and he faced many troubles. He became ill with asthma and lost much of his weight. However, four days before his death, he appeared to be in good health and said Mass in his Church on Christmas Day, 1889. It was the last Holy Mass he celebrated. May God have mercy on him.

He has literary vestiges. The most important one is a poem he wrote to celebrate the Golden Jubilee of the priesthood of Pope Leo XIII. You can read it in the book of Gomaa Khalil Beik 'Okl Shedid and his son-in-law Watanina Anton Fares.

I remember that Father Yohanna composed this poem and came to our house to read it to my father. My father was no poet but he was intelligent and he liked Father Yohanna. At that time, I was young and listened to him very carefully and with delight. My father encouraged him and told him: "Bravo !"

Here is a small part of this poem:

"Temper has come to an end to those whose government has likewise ended.
Friends and enemies have talked of his favorable characteristics
He is in the upper rank
Notables were proud of him and his name became strong.
It is as if God kept him alive till our days so filled with problems.
He is the desired leader for the humiliated armies of tyrany in their awful day.
With sharp-edged truth, not the warrior's sword, justice and the earth support him.
If he spoke a word of wisdom, our deaf youth uproot the meaning.
Men with ornate chests had recourse to him to solve their problems.
He is Pope Leo dedicated to end the poison of this catastrophe.
The baptizer of the people, the chosen one of felicity, and the Shepherd of justice, the gallant Lion.
And when he rose to the Throne of Leadership, he ruled. He humiliated the army of injustice and the arrow was broken.
His letters traveled from north to the south, from east to the west with growing notice.
They had their roads in the East and West to carry justice, but they ended it.
They were for guidance but went astray…
Oh, our dear Pope! May your highness's footing remain steadfast, untouched by dishonour.
With you, minutes bring us pride; hours, clearness. Your days are triumphant and around are your rewards.
Making you content is the best for anyone, whether they are full of hope or a beggar.
History will be praising you.
     --Signed with a stamp, 1887 ".

- - - - -

The House Of 'Oun Al 'Abssy

Their Kinships

Abou Dagher known as Al Abssy had Abdel Messih. Abdel Messih had Abou 'Oun who had Gibrail who had Abou 'oun and Hanna.

Abou 'Oun had Naseef who had Hanna. Hanna had Youssef, 'Oun, and Naseef. Youssef had children living with him in Mexico. 'Oun died there and never married. Naseef had Fouad who had sons and he is with his offspring in Brazil.

Meanwhile, Hanna Bin Gibrail Bou 'Oun Abdel Massih had Gibrail and Mikhail. Gibrail had Hanna who had Elias, Girgi, and Mikhail. The three of them are living in the United States with their children. Mikhail Bin Hanna was given the name Abou Dahla and had Elias who was the end of the Mikhail Bin Hanna offspring.

241

Their Vestiges and News

" ... Abdel Messih Bin Abou Dagher from Salima, a coal miner of Al Metn near Beirut, has bought from his maternal uncle Girgis Ibn Abou Farahat, all being from the same mentioned village of the same mentioned job, all the mulberries planted in front and around the house .... This includes all except the roots of three mulberries planted in front of the house and a fig-tree ...at the price of thirteen piasters according to the evaluation of Abou 'Oun Ghadoub from Al Arbania ... written on Gomadi II 10, 1146 (1733), written by Baz Ibn Yazbak. Witness: Mohamed Bin Yazbek, Fakhr Eddine Ibn Yazbak. "

- - - - -

" ... Abou 'Oun Abdel Messih from Salima Village has Bought from the wife of his paternal uncle Oum (the mother) Farahat and the wife of Abou Farahat Ibn Al Shamas from Al Arbania Village, the unemployed above the pond of Al Abssa at the price of three piastres according to the evaluation of Hussein Abou Mora. And the contract is for his wife, the daughter of Oum Farahat. Written on Ragab 10, 1163 (1749), Written by Baz Ibn Yazbak. "

- - - - -

"Abdel Messih Al Abssy has bought from Hassan Bin Rafea, of the boundaries of the waterwheel of Al Dahr, at the price of eleven piasters, save a quarter, according to the evaluation of Haidar Radi ... the borders in the South being the ancient road. At the East the boundary if Qoblan up to the border of the black stone. In the north, the waterwheel, and at the west, the crossroads. ... Written in the year 1173 (1759) by Soliman Al Sayegh. The Witnesses: Sharaf Eddine Masry, Ali Bin Youssef, Daher Yazbak, Qoblan Masry. "

- - - - -

" We sold to Father Francis and to Bou'oun Abdel Messih, two thirds of the field owned by Qassem Ibn Shahin and which is above the quarter of that mentioned. Exempt are two fig trees beside the house of Nofal. They still owe us 127 piasters...save one third ... Written in Ragab 1179 (1765). Oum (the mother of) Ali accepted for the sale.

(stamp) Malaka Shehab. Written by Qassem Ibn Mansour (stamp). Witnessed by Said Ibn Farahat. "

- - - - -

"The reason for writing this is that Abdel Messih Al Abssy has come here before us with his wife and the children of Moussa Faseida. They have pleaded to us about the purchase of an uncultivated land which is a property of the father of the Wife of Abdel Messih. The above mentioned bought it from Shahin Habib the nephew (sister's son) of the mentioned woman. She is claiming intercession and presented her mother's testimony as well as the purchase agreement. After their pleading before us, we ruled in favor of her right of intercession for the mentioned uncultivated land. We so ruled because it is the closest and its intercession is still valid and it was the first contract made according to the division between her and her sister. Thus her subsequent one became invalid. Thus, the wife of Abou 'Oun should pay the price of the mentioned uncultivated land to its buyer as she has the right by intercession and this case. God knows. Written on November 27, 1762. Written by Father Elias Al Gemail on behalf of Bishop Philipos. "

- - - - -

"Gibrail Bou'oun and his children have bought from Abdel Kahlek Al Masry and his brother's sons Salman and Saab Al Masry ... the property bordering on the waterwheel of Al Dahr at the price of forty-three Piaters ... the bor-

ders: at the south, Marah Khatar road, from the east, the properties of Mahmoud Ibn Hassan ... Written in February, 1206 (1791). Written by Daher Al Sayegh. Witnessed by: Abdel Wahed Said, Refaa Beriqaa Said, Nabhan Al Hadj Ali. "

- - - - -

One of the Sheikhs of the Abou Oun House told me that one of their ancestors was a priest and was known as Father Sader. His remaining vestiges are a portion of the Torah (the Old Testament) written in Arabic and Latin. Gibrail Hanna Abou 'Oun was one of the three deacons elevated to the priesthood: the above mentioned Gibrail, Wakim Bin Boutros, and Youssef Daham, ordained a priest of Salima by Bishop Abdulallah Blibel.

On the first page of the ancient register of the Salima congregation, I read this paragraph written in 1826:

"This is a contract which is a testimony of the heritage of Bou'oun Ibn Mehana of the year 1779, legalised by the late Bishop Elias Al Gemail to sanctify from this money that which is over and above the cost of the testator and his deed. Written by Father Youssef Daham Bachaalany. "

Their Three Houses

This offshoot has not procreated and the family of Abdel Messih Al Abssy divided into three houses: 1- the House of Naseef Bou'oun Bin Gibrail Bou'oun. 2- the House of Gibrail Bin Hanna Gibrail Bou'oun. 3- The House of Mikhail Bin Hanna Gibrail Bou'oun. The last perished after the death of Elias Bin Mikhail.

The offspring of the first house are expatriates. They consists of Youssef Hanna Bou'oun and his children in Mexico; and, his brother Nasef with his family in Brazil. The second House offspring consists of the children of Hanna Gibrail Bou'oun who are Elias, Girgi, and Mikhail with their children living in the United States. We have already mentioned them in this book.

Mikhail Bin Hanna Bou'oun was surnamed "Abou Dalha" because he continued to wear the "Dalh Tarboush" which had been out of fashion for some time.

He lived to be over one hundred years old! He used to weave silk shirts and handkechiefs on the loom. He would also weave baskets canes. I used to see him, when I was a child, leaning on a mulbery tree in front of his home, praying the weekly Kyrie Eleison Litany of Saints.

His son Elias drew his picture wearing his familiar clothes. He accompanied his sister to that place, before her marriage with Shahin. She used to be the governess of the children of Mr. Charles Bazier, the French librarian in Beirut.

Since his childhood, Elias was fond of drawing. If he had studied it, he would have been one of the great painters. Among my documents, I preserve his old papers which include an accumulation of pictures drawn over a period of thirty years.

They include:

The pictures of Andrea Bachaalany, Hanna Youssef Bachaalany, and Ali Beshir Said. I published these three pictures in my book titled: <u>Lebanon and Youssef Beik Karam</u>. In addition, there are the pictures of the Capuchin Father Mansour, and Father Youssef Bachaalany which is preserved at the house of the grand-daughter of Youssef.

There are the pictures of Father Moussa Al Sayegh, Haidar Al Zar'ouny, and Tanous Freha Al Bachaalany. He has also drawn Abdel Hady Al Masry, Abou Hussein Amed Al Masry, Hanna Khatar Al Nakouzy, Ayoub Eishy, Tanous Shiban, and Elias Tanous Al Makary from the prairie of Qarnayel with himself.

He drew the picture of Youssef Beik Karam riding his horse. He also drew the picture of Saint Yohanna Al Me'me-dan. This art style disappeared after his death because, it seems, this often happens when its master dies. He was very ascetic in his life, and, intensely pious.

Moreover, I found the papers of Naseef Bou'oun among the papers of my grandfather Tanous Freha who had the custody of his child Hanna after his death. My grandmother Helon was the sister of the mentioned Naseef.

According to those papers, that house was a wealthy home. Its expenses were about 800 piasters per year, a high sum for that time. It included charity and money for sanctifying various feasts, as well as moneys for the monasteries. The donation for having a Mass said was no less than two piasters. Also, there were the costs of weaving and knitting …etc. which shows how managing the matters about the home was based on saving and accuracy.

Hanna Bin Naseef Bou'oun grew up very active and self-reliant. He educated a large family. He was also keenly zealous about matters of Bachaalany interest.

Abi Attallah House

Their origin

Some researchers thought that this house belonged to the Attallah family in Al Fotooh. However, after accurate research, we found out that this, like other supposed kinships of families, was due to similarity in names. Additionally, Attallah folks in Ghobala and Wehshoush and other places agreed that their origin is from Yanouh and Magdal Aaqoura, not from Bshe`le. Bchaaleh is the original source of the folks of Abi Attallah Bachaalany in Salima. We deduced the same from old documents where their ancestral line is mentioned in documents involving the buying and selling of properties. These confirm that their great-grandfather was from one of the grandfathers of the Bachaalany's who came to Salima in their early emigration. The following passages are some of their valuable vestiges: documents and stated papers that we publish here in brief, keeping the terms as mentioned in the originals in our possession. The passages are:

Their Vestige

"In the name of God, the All Merciful, sufficient for me, Whose help I seek. This is what Samaan Ibn Nasr, his brother Moussa, and his paternal cousin Nasr Ibn Wahba from Salima of the Shehar of Al Metn, following the safeguarded Beirut, have purchased from Abu Nasef Khalil of the same mentioned job and follower: the land known as the island at the foundry. Its borders from the Honoured Kiblah, the land of the Mohalhel family, from the east, the white waterwheel, ,from the north, the Great River, and from the west the rivulet at the Oven. This includes everything known to belong to Abou Nasef and others in the island land, in the valley land, and, he has nothing more left. He fully gave his somplete right..Also the price of the island land is four piasters ... in the year 1148 (1735), Hegira.

Written by the humble	*Witnessed by: Safy Ibn Rezqallah*
Ahmed, son of Harfoush.	*Sharaf Alden Ibn Khalil*
	Basher Ibn Alam Eddine

- - - - -

"The reason for editing this is that Andrea Ibn Nejm admitted and acknowledged that he owes his wife Hendia, the daughter of Samaan, an amount of sixty piasters for her dowry. This document was edited to the satisfaction of both parties and they asked us to write it as a declaration and to avoid forgetfulness.

Written in the month of December, in the Christian year 1776. This document was edited by Father Francis and witnessed by Ibrahim Ibn Shahin, Mikhail Ibn Elias."

- - - - -

"...That is Ibrahim Ibn Shahin admitted and acknowledged that he owes the daughter of his paternal uncle, Samaan Ibn Nasr, an amount of fifty-five piasters for her dowry and post-dowry... in1181 Hegira (1767). Edited by Father Francis. Witnessed by his paternal uncle, Khatar, and his paternal cousin, Samaan."

- - - - -

"Gibrail Ibn Samaan has purchased from Daham Ibn Teama (Abou 'Oql) the portions at the White Sheir at the price of thirty piasters ...bordering from the East is the seller, from the North, the properties of Ragheb, from the West, up to the border of the Sheir, and from the South, the Cinnamon Bark .... Edited by Father Francis; witnessed by Sheikh Abou Fares Rahal (Kassab), the assessor Nejm Ibn Fayad."

- - - - -

"... Gibrail Ibn Samaan has purchased...from Mustafa Mansour Al Helow, all are from Salima... the Circled Mulberry... at Ain Al Mahata at the price of twenty-four piasters ... it borders from the South, the vines of Hatem Ibn Abdel Karim, from the East the waterwheel, from the North, the mulberry trees belonging to the seller`s brother, and from the West, the vines of Nofal Ibn Hanna.... In the month of Safar the Hegira year 1190 (1776). Edited by the humble Youssef Yazbak. Witnessed by: Mohamed Ibn Mahmoud, and Nayel Ibn Nejm."

- - - - -

"Gibrail Ibn Samaan purchased from the sons of Deeb Ibn Hanna, the vines they own under the press, the borders of all of them are known from the waterwheel up to the borders of Nofal`s properties .. in 1193, Hegira (1779). Edited by Father Francis. Witnessed by Bo Dammra Ibn Girgis."

- - - - -

"We received from Gibrail Ibn Samaan, six piasters for the price of the quarter of the mulberry trees belonging to Ali Al Helow at Ain Al Mahata. The price of the crop is two piasters; and, five piasters as the price of two and a half crops of leaves at the house. The whole is paid to Boutros from the previous year, and from this year on Shawal, 1197 (1782). Written by Abu Ghosn."

- - - - -

"...We sold to our paternal cousin, Gibrail, the uncultivated lands which we own at the Matar field ... bordering from both the South and the West the sons of Bou Kheir, from the East and the North terraced land of Fares .... The assessor, Hanna Ibn Nasr witness. Edited by Father Francis. Accepted for himself, Youssef Ibn Nasrallah."

- - - - -

"We sold to our brother Daher Ibn Mikhail Alhaj Boutros, the mulberry trees and a cinnamon bark which are in the lands of our late paternal cousin Elias, a waterwheel, and a brocaded piece at the price of thirty piasters ... their borders from the East of the brocaded to the East by three mulberry trees as they appear to the Cliff, from the West to the Za`roor well on the river bank as they appear to the border of the land of Fares Ibn Nasr, from the South the property of Fares Ibn Nasr, and from the North the river ..in May, 1210 Hegira (1795). Edited by Y-oussef Al Khoury. Accepted on himself, Gibrail Ibn Samaan. Witnessed by Andrea, Hanna Ibn Nasrallah Bou At-tallah, She`ea Al Shediak. With the knowledge of Hanna Ibn Karam."

- - - - -

"This title deed was transferred from us to our brother, Gibrail Ibn Samaan.

Gibrail Ibn Samaan has purchased from Girgis Saady the vines.... located at Ain Al Mahata owned by his paternal cousin Moussa, for the price of eighteen piasters, and the land of aconite located at the edge of the property of Sardy Kassab towards the press. In March, 1211 Hegira (1796)."

- - - - -

"We sold to our brother Gibrail Ibn Samaan our share of the caldron which is between us and his Excellency, at the price of eighty three piasters... On the first of September, 1211 Hegira (1796). Edited by Daher Al Haj Boutros in his own handwriting."

- - - - -

"...We sold to our dearly loved Gibrail Ibn Samaan Al Bachaalany, three quarters of the properties he runs, whe-ther buildings, mulberry trees, vines, cinnamon bark, water and air, except the edge (pine... We received the price of the three quarters from him, three hundred, seventy five piasters. We received the amount through the assessor, Hamad Fakhr Eddine and Andrea Al Bachaalany ... in Shawal, 1222 Hegira (1807).

Hassan (the seal). This took place to our satisfaction and should be carried out. Assaf (stamp)."

- - - - -

"...Gibrail Ibn Samaan has purchased from his paternal cousins Marhaba and her daughter, (Zabla), the wife of Youssef Ibn Shahin, their share of Al Ghoushy press, four carats, and the vines located at Ain Al Fawara, for the price of twenty eight piasters according to Hamad Fakhr Al Eddine's evalulation. They received the fixed price from the buyer ... the boundaries of the mentioned vines, from the East, the property of Fares Ibn Nasr Wahbi, from the South, the sons of Abdel Salam,, from the West the rivulet, and from the North, the buyer. Edited in the month of May of the year 1223. Edited by Bou 'Oun Ibn Gibrail. Witnessed by She`ya Ibn Safi, Girgis Al Aqouri; Segaa Said; Youssef Nasr Karam, Fares Daham, and Fares Ibn Nasr Wahbi."

"Hanna Ibn Gibrail Ibn Samaan has bought from his paternal cousin, Elias Ibn Neama, the grand mulberry tree beside the house and the aconites in front of the furnace for the price of seventeen piasters save one third... their western border is as it seems, the furnace pillar, and on the other borders, the buyer's properties. In July,1815. Witnessed by Shahin Ibn She`ya Safi; Fares Ibn Nasr Wahba; the assessor, Bou Ali Brekaa."

- - - - -

The furnace among the sold items, for the price of two piasters and one third, paid to the seller. Edited by Father Hanna. Witnessed by Abdo Ibn Nohra; Ghaleb Ibn Hanna Eid; Latouf."

- - - - -

"...We gave permission to our dearly loved: Sheikh Elias Ibn Ragheb, Sheikh Hanna Ibn Moussa, and Sheikh Y-oussef Hatem, to rent at Al Belana at Ras Hakoura Al Hammra with my profit in the one third we owe. We will take for each house, three piasters per year. The year 1241, Hassan (1825)."

- - - - -

"...She`ya Ibn Safi has purchased from Abdel Hay, the cinnamon barks at Ain Al Rehan for the price of twelve pias-ters and a quarter. 1711."

- - - - -

"She`ya Ibn Safi has purchased from Hanna Deeb and his brothers, the mulberry trees located in Ain Al Majd and the wasteland which are all at the mentioned place, and the weathercock located beside Moussa Attallah's house, Khensareen and all what they own at the mentioned place for fifty two piasters. The Year, 1777."

- - - - -

"She`ya Ibn Safi has purchased from Abdel Hay the mountain terrace located at Ain Al Mahata, Its borders: from the East, Estefan Ibn Moussa, from the West, the open road, from the South, the properties of Moussa Attallah, and, from the North, the properties of the sons of Samaan Bou Mikhail. Edited by Soliman Al Sayegh."

- - - - -

"...we exchanged with She`ya Ibn Safi for what we gave him in the Mantara trench and took in its place a compen-sation for Ain Al Mahata in 1190 (1776) (Prince) Ismail."

- - - - -

"She`ya Ibn Safi has purchased from Hatem Ibn Abdel Karim, his mulberry trees, located at Ain Al Majd at the price of nine piasters....in March, 1190."

- - - - -

"Daniel Ibn Neama sold to his paternal cousin, She`ya Ibn Safy, the mulberry trees located at Shahin Al Erian's house and their price is forty-four piasters... they are bordered from the East by the properties of his Excellency Prince Haidar, from the North by Shahin Saadallah, from the West by the road, and, from the South by the pro-perties of Bou Saqr. In 1809."

- - - - -

"She`ya Ibn Safi has purchased from Wahba Bardaouil in 1225 (1810)."

- - - - -

"We sold our raspberry field which belonged to Elias Ibn Ne`ma to the mentioned below, for the price of 723 pias-ters. Malaka (Prince Assaf's wife), Lam's (Prince Haidar's wife). The sold property was transferred from Elias Ibn Neama to the children of his paternal Uncle She`ya Ibn Safi in July, 1230."

- - - - -

"Nasrallah Ibn Sawan has purchased from Girgis Al Sayegh..."

- - - - -

"...the sons of Bou Attallah: Saadallah, Neama, and Abdelahad have purchased from Mourad Ibn Abdel Samad, the mulberry trees at Alhawa vines for fourty eight piasters...

Its borders: from the South, the cavern, from the North, Bou Ali Beshir`s fig trees, from the West and the East, the waterwheel ... in August, 1171. Witnessed by Said Ibn Farahat; Moussa Ibn Dhaher."

- - - - -

"...Abdel Ahad has purchased from Nasser Eddine Ibn Beshir at Alhawa vines, a circle of fig trees, evaluated by Haidar Ibn Fakhr Eddine. The borders are the waterwheel at the East, at the West, the seller, at the North, the buyer, and, at the North, the real estate of Mehana Al Hadad. The year 1177 (1763), Edited by Soliman Al Sayegh and witnessed by Teleb Ibn Zein Eddine."

- - - - -

"...we sold to our sister's son, Nasrallah, and brothers, the mulberry trees we possess in Ain Al Mahata at the price of ninety one piasters, acknowledged by Badah Ibn Haidar Qadamy; And to mention the borders, instead of determining them, will be enough ... on January 9, 1243. It has been edited by their maternal uncle Youssef Ibn Daher in his own handwriting. Witnessed by our paternal cousin, Girgis Ibn Shahin Saadallah."

- - - - -

"...Sheikh Abu Nasef Elias Al Tiyan and Soliman Kadama... exchanged the vines that are at Ain Al Sawaka under the press belonging to the Kadama house... in 1235, Hegira."

- - - - -

"This document was transferred from Elias Al Tiyan to Soliman Dolican Kadama in 1250. Witnessed by: Bou Mehanna Ibn Qassouf from Alarbania, and Hanna Ibn Salem Al Khoury. Then, it was transferred from Soliman Kadame to Sheikh Nasrallah Ibn Sawan in its date with Nasef Al Tiyan's handwriting."

- - - - -

"Sheikh Kanaan Al Tiyan, a resident of Salima at the time, has purchased from Mohamed Ibn Nasser Dine Kadama, the vines, crops... at the presses for the price of 67 piasters ...in 1233. Edited by the humble Mohamed Ibn Mahmoud Al Masry. This document was transferred to Soliman Deliqan. In 1250, Elias Al Tiyan. It was transferred to our brother, Sheikh Nasrallah Ibn Sawan. Written by Nasef Al Tiyan. Witnessed by: Nasrallah; Attallah, and their brother, Moussa in 1245, in title, the document of Nasef Bou 'Oun."

- - - - -

"Abdo Ibn Mikhail has purchased from his father, the vines of Al Hawa through the assessor, Mikhail Bou Assly, for the price of fourty piasters in March, 1835. Witnesses: Nasef Al Tiyan, 'Oun Ibn Daniel. Edited by Father Youssef, the Pastor of Salima."

- - - - -

"Abdo Ibn Nahra purchased from Mikhail Abdel Lajd, two mulberry trees... through Nasef Ibn Hanna for 24 piasters." "This act was transferred to Abdo Ibn Mikhail in April 1839."

- - - - -

"Nasrallah Ibn Hanna and his brothers purchased from Mikhail Bou Assly the property at Al Shaweya, the exit of Arsoun for 150 piasters. The borders from the South, the property of the sons of Bou Habeeb Al Tiyan, from the East, the property owned by Elias Beshir, from the West, the waterwheel, and from the North, Shahin Ibn She`ya... In December, 1242. Edited by Youssef Ibn Hanna Daham. Witnesses: Nader Ibn Gad'oun; Elias Ibn Shahin Ibn She`ya; and, Saab Bou Qayed Baih."

- - - - -

"Elias Ibn Shahin Saadallah Al Bachaalany and Nasrallah Ibn Sawan bought from Neama Ibn Nayel Said, the cinnamon barks at Ain Al Rehan, for the price of 58 piasters... the borders are: at the South, Bou Fares Ibn De'ebess, the East, Kanaan Bou Nassar. 1247 (1831). Edited by the humble Aly Said. Witnesses: Bou Nejm Ibn De'ebess Said; and Youssef Ibn Hatem Al Bachaalany."

- - - - -

"We sold the vines located at Ain El Sawaki on the back side of the cliff which we took from Sardi Kassab for Hanna Ibn Nasrallah at the price of 110 piasters. This document was transferred to Youssef Shahin Al Masry Al Bachaalany in 1245. Edited by Domat Moa'wad. Witnesses: Zeidan Raad from Ghazeer. Father Youssef Al Rozee, a student in Ain Warka school. This document was transferred from us to Abdo Ibn Mikhail in 1252 (1836). Accepted and admitted by Youssef Ibn Shahin. Edited by his son, Fares."

- - - - -

"The reason for recording this document is that Daher Ibn Safi said before us that his crop would be sold for one hundred piasters. This is what his children would be paid, crops sold for one hundred piasters from the vines of Ain Al Mahata. This is what he said before us. It is forbidden for anyone to disobey his will. Edited on March 16, 1821. For each one of his daughters, he permitted one olive tree only. Edited by Pastor Elias, servant of Salima."

- - - - -

"Nasrallah Ibn Sawan purchased Girgis Al Sayegh, a crop of grapevine and figs at Ain Al Sawaki, neighbouring the mentioned, for the price of 27 piasters, through Fares, son of Soliman Said ... in 1246 (1830). Edited by the humble Ali Said. Witnessed by Girgis Ibn Nasr Al Hadad, Hanna Elrian."

- - - - -

"A reconciliation and satisfaction took place between Nasrallah Sawan and his brother upon the partnership of the Acre, the money, the store activities and transactions according to the partnership agreement... Attalla gave his brother Nasrallah the acre and the she-mule, whereas Nasrallah left to his brother Attalla what he owes him from the income of the partnership contract and debts. Neither of them has any right upon his brother and should either of them accuse his brother, his claim will be invalid and inactive of all legitimate right... This is what they accepted and for which they gave permission, to be protected from any actions, accusations, or excuses. Agreed in the presence of witnesses mentioned below. Edited on September 9, 1256 (1841). Accepting and admitting by themselves, Nasrallah and Attallah. Edited by Moussa Erian from Al Showier. Witnessed by Moussa Al Germany from Bezbedeen."

- - - - -

*"Hanna Ibn Saadallah has purchased from Moussa Sowan the share he inherited from his paternal uncle Fares...
for the price of 120 piasters.... at the beginning of 1252 (1836). Admitted what was mentioned by Moussa Sowan.
Witnessed by his brother Abdo (may be Abdulallah) Sowan, Girgis Ibn Shahin She`ya. Edited by Nasef Bou 'Oun.
This deed has been transferred from Hanna Saadallah to the hand of Nasrallah Sowan in 1858. Edited by
Ibrahim Youssef Daher. Witnessed by Abdo Mikhail and his son Girgis."*

- - - - -

*"...Sabra Ibn Shahin Saadallah sold to Abdo Ibn Mikhail three pounds and a half of leaves near the buyer's
house at the price of 52 piasters and a half. Written in February, 1849. Sabra Shahin accepted it. Edited by
Mansour Al Khoury. Witnesses: Khalil Daham, Hanna Saadallah."*

- - - - -

*"Nasrallah Bachaalany and his paternal cousin Hanna Ibn Saadallah, from Salima, purchased from Molhem Ibn
Qassem Seif Eddine from Saad Nayel the vines located at Al Hendiyat land...in 1268 (1851)."*

- - - - -

*"...the sons of Attallah Sowan sold all their properties in Salima to their paternal uncle Nasrallah Sowan at the
price of 450 piasters ... in August, 1864. Edited by the assessor Elias Bou Assly. Witnesses: Hanna Saadallah;
Hanna Youssef Nasrallah; Nejm Youssef Nasrallah; and She`ya Ibn Hanna."*

- - - - -

*"Girgis Al Showery sold to Abdo Bin Mikhail Bachaalany, both from Salima, a circle where there are olive trees
located at the Hawa vines for the price of fifty piasters. This has been acknowledged by Elias Bou Assly, the assessor at that time, on April 13, 1852. Edited by Father Hanna Bachaalany. ...Admitted and accepted by Girgis
Al Showery. Witnessed by Youssef Al Kelargy. Mikhail Bouhriez dropped his right of intercession to Abdo."*

- - - - -

Though necessarily brief, these extracts from the many documents we possess, show some of the various familial ties
and dealings related to the Abi Attallah house.

Their Kinships

Abi Attallah Al Bachaalany begot: Safi, Wahba, Nasr, Nasrallah, Saadallah, Sowan, and Abi Neama. Safi begot:
Abdel Ahad, Daher, and She`ya. Abdel Ahad begot: Mikhail who had Abdo and Hanna known as Al Maka`ee.

Abdo begot Mikhail and Girgis. Mikhail Abdo begot Youssef, Abdo, and Moussa. Youssef begot: Fou`d and Pedro.
Abdo died unmarried and Moussa had two sons. Mikhail Abdo's family lives in Rio De Janeiro. Girgis Abdo begot:
Anton and Hanna, who are in Brazil and have children.

Concerning Hanna Maka`ee, he begot Nakhla and another son who was living in Beirut and we have no news of
him. Nakhla died in Serbia and had no children.

Concerning Daher Bin Safi, he had: Youssef and Saadallah. Youssief bin Daher had Anton, Ibrahim, Daoud, Daher,
and two other sons who died young. Ibrahim, Daoud, and Daher died in Salima, young and unmarried. Anton is,
Anthony Bachaalany, the first Syrian-Lebanese immigrant to the New World. He died unmarried. Saadallah Bin
Daher Safi had: Hanna, Pastor Egnaduous, the monk from Halab. Hanna Saadallah had: Saadallah, Youssef, and

Abdo. Sa`adallah Bin Hanna had Youssef and Boutros. They are at Lawrence, Massachusetts, in the United States and have children. Youssief Hanna Saadallah had: Elias, Hanna, and Anton. Elias is in Brazil and has children. Anton lives in Brazil but has no children yet, that we know of. Hanna had: Nasri and Abdo. Abdo Bin Hanna Saadallah had Khalil, Ibrahim, and Najib. They are all in Mexico and have children.

As for Sha`eya Bin Safi, he had: Hanna and Shahin. Hanna had Abdo, Sha`ey, and Tanious who had no children. Sha`ey Bin Hanna did not marry. Abdo Bin Hanna had Hanna who had Abdo and Sha`ey. Abdo died young in Brazil whereas Sha`eya died there and has a daughter here named Bade`aa. As for Shahin Bin Sha`eya, son of Bin Safy had Girgis who had Shahin. The latter died in Lawrence, Massachusetts and had children there.

Concerning Wahba Abi Attallah, he begot Nasr who had Wahba. The latter had Fares who died with no children. His inheritance was distributed within the Abi Attallah house. Nasr Abi Attallah had Samaan and Moussa. We know of no offspring for Moussa.

Samaan Bin Nasr had Gibrail who begot Hanna who had Elias, Wahba, and Gibrail. Gibrail died unmarried. Wahba died and left no children.

Elias Bin Hanna Gibrail had Daher, Youssef (known as Al Zeer), and Hanna. For Daher, none of his children remain except for Rasheda, the wife of Youssef Al Qasouf. Youssef Al Zeer had Rashid, Beshara, and Selim. Rashid emigrated to Brazil and we have not had any further news of him. Beshara died young and unmarried in Etna in the First World War. Selim lived in Zahle and had children. As for Hanna Bin Elias Bin Hanna Gibrail, he had Gibrail, Mansour, and Elias, who lived in Al Merigate. Gibrail had George, Michel, and Selim. Mansour had Elias and perhaps others. We think Elias had at least one child.

Nasrallah Bin Abi Attallah had Youssef who begot Nejm and Hanna. Nejm Bin Youssef had Youssef who had Najib and Selim. Najib had Youssef (who died), Emil, and Youssef II. As for Selim Bin Youssef Nejm, he had children who are with their parents in Brazil.

Concerning Hanna Bin Youssef Nasrallah Abi Attallah, he had Mansour, Shaker, Daoud, Abdou, Abdulallah, and Fedaa. Mansour had only Alice who married Selim Bin Youssef Nejm. Shaker had Elias who had sons in Lawrence, Massachusetts in the United States. Daoud had Soliman, Ibrahim, Selim, and Hanna. Soliman and Ibrahim disappeared in the First World War. Hanna had Youssef, Daoud, Soliman, and Moussa.

Abdo Hanna Bin Youssef died in Brazil unmarried. Abdulallah had Youssef and Michel. Youssef had Farid. Fedaa had only one daughter in the United States.

Saadallah Abi Attallah had Shahin who had Girgis and Elias. Girgis had no children whereas Elias had Saadallah, and Pastor Arsanuos, the Halabian monk.

Saadallah Elias had Elias and Girgis who died young. Elias Bin Saadallah had only Laila. Also, there is Daniel Neama Abi Attallah who had 'Oun who died young in 1835, unmarried. We did not know who from the Abi Attallah's is Daniel's father.

Sowan Abi Attallah had Nasrallah, Attallah, Abdulallah, Moussa, and Mikhail. Nasrallah had Hanna who had Ibrahim, Youssef, and Nasrallah.

Ibrahim begot Molhem and Hanna. Molhem is an emigrant in Cleveland, Ohio, in the United States. His brother Hanna moved from Qab Elias to Tha`labaya.

Youssef Bin Hanna Nasrallah had Abdo, Elias, and Girgis. Abdo and Girgis died young. Nasrallah Bin Hanna Nasrallah migrated in 1895 to Oliveira in Brazil, married a Brazilian woman and had Jane and Joseph.

As for Attalla Bin Hanna Sowan Abi Attallah, he had Mansour and Nasr.

Mansour moved from Tha`labaya to Damascus and died there on 1921 without children. His brother Nasr settled in Beirut and we have never heard of any news of him. Concerning Abdulallah Bin Hanna Sowan, in Tha`labaya he had Youssief, and Zeon (the wife of Saadallah Hanna Saadallah. Youssef had only Mary (the wife of Nader Gad'oun), and Henna (the wife of Mikhail Moussa Sowan).

As for Moussa, the fourth son of Hanna Sowan, he also lived in Tha`alabaya as did his offspring. He had Elias, Mikhail, Anton, and Daoud. Elias had Youssef, Girgis, Tanious, Boutros, and Shokry. Youssef had Louis. Girgis had Elias and George. Tanious had Moussa and Elias. They are both married and live with their father in Buenos Aires.

Boutros Bin Elias Moussa Sowan is in Buenos Aires and has a son. Shokry died shortly after getting married and had no children. Mikhail Bin Moussa Sowan had Youssef, Abdo, and Qazahya. Youssef had Elias. Abdo died young, and we don't know about Qazahya.

Anton Bin Moussa Sowan begot Hanna and George. Hanna had Tawfik, Anton, and Elias. Anton Bin Hanna had Jean and Elias. George Bin Anton Moussa had one daughter, then his wife died.

As for Daoud Bin Moussa Hanna Sowan, he had Soliman, Abdulallah, Mousa, and Soliman. The first Soliman died young. Abdulallah is single. Moussa had Aziz, Jean, Dawoud, Sowan, and George. The second Soliman had Anis, Emil, and Youssef. As for the fifth son of Hanna Sowan, Mikhail, he stayed in Salima and had Boutros, Sowan, and Nasef. Boutros had Daoud, Hanna, and Mikhail. Daoud Bin Boutros had sons in the United States. Hanna had no children.

Mikhail married recently. Whereas Sowan Bin Mikhail had only Marhaba (the wife of Shaker Al Erian), Mary (the wife of Abdo Girgis Sabra), and Marta (the wife of 'Oun Neama Bou Neama). Nasef Sowan died unmarried.

Abou Neama Abi Attalla had Neama, Girgis, and Sabra. Neama had Elias, 'Oun, Fares, and Youssef. Elias had Nasef. 'Oun had Neama, Mikhail, Attallah, and Eid. Neama Bin 'Oun had Mikhail, 'Oun, and Wadee`. Mikhail had Neama and Joseph. 'Oun had Fouad and George. Wadee` had Anton.

Fares Bin Neama had Girgis, Daoud, and Elias. Youssef Bin Neama had Elias who had Youssef, and the latter had children. Girgis Abou Neama had Assaf who died leaving no children. Sabra Abou Neama had Daher and Girgis Daher had Youssef who died young. Girgis Sabra had Abdo, Sabra, and Youssef. Abdo had Elias and Tanious. Sabra and Youssef are married in the United States and have children.

The House of Gibrail Bin Samaan

This is one of the most important offshoots of the Abi Attallah family. Also, it is one of the oldest houses in Salima, well known for the virtue as indicated in previously mentioned documents. The oldest item is the title deed for the purchase of a piece of land at the island place of the Agmani River at the Bozbla River, not far from Hasbiya. That land still belongs to them today.

The previously mentioned Samaan Bin Nasr had two daughters, one of them married to the old Andrea Bachaalany and she was named Hendia. She was one of the most perfect and honourable women. The second daughter was married to Ibrahim Bin Shahin Abi Tarbia, one of the noteworthy people of the Nakouzy house. Hanna Bin Gibrail Bin Samaan was an educated man of note. He had the second lead in the chorus after Andrea as we already mentioned in the section on the Maronite traditions in churches. Hanna was surnamed "The Half World" due to his power and popularity.

Safi House

This house is divided into two parts: one known for bravery, which are the houses of She`ya and Saadallah. The other part was known for knowledge and brilliance. This includes the houses of Youssef Daher and Mikhail Abdo. Youssef Bin Daher Bin Safi was a man of insight. He was the Trustee of the Maronites in Salima for a long time. He married Taqla Bint (the daughter of) Hassan from noble family of Kassab. He had many sons. Those we knew of are Anton, Ibrahim, Daoud, and Daher. They were the best of the youth. And they all died unmarried.

Here we mention the eldest son, Anton (Anthony) who is the most important and most popular. Especially since he was the first immigrant from Lebanon and Syria to the New World. We published his biography in a book called <u>Lebanon and Youssef Beik Karam</u>. We will give a brief presentation of his life here based on what we have been told by the old men and the biography in English which our friend Dr. Philip Hitti discovered, summarized, and published in a special notebook.

Anthony Bachaalany.

He is Anton Bin Youssef Daher Safi Abi Attallah, born in Salima on August 22, 1827. He was raised like all his kin in that beautiful village between rocks, under the shadow of the trees, and resting on the banks of the streams. Thus, he took his firmness and intellectual independence from the mountains of Lebanon. From the breezes of Salima came his intuition and his congeniality. From the perfumed air of Salima's violets and roses came the fragrance of his good qualities and his ethics. He was raised in a house of virtue, piety, and knowledge. His father was raising his family and earning his living from growing silkworms and tending to mulberry trees, olive trees, grapevines and pine trees. He was taught the principles of his religion and science by the Capuchin Fathers at their monastery in Salima. He also learned the Italian language from them. On August 5, 1839 his father died. The family suffered the loss of their house and crops which were burned during the sedition that occurred after the fall of Ibrahim Pasha Al Masry and Prince Beshir The Great of Lebanon. Thus, with these disasters befalling the family, Anthony, only twelve years old, had to assume the duties of his late father and support his family.

As a result of all this, his family moved to a village near Beirut. It was there that he made contacts with the Italian Consul who appointed him to be one of his translators since he knew Italian. After being away for many years, the family returned to Salima.

Anthony had met an English Protestant Missionary in Beirut and gave him a copy of the Old Testament. This caused a dispute between Anthony and some of his friends which resulted in his arrest. After he was released, he went back to Salima where he learned that the news about his "heresy" reached his family. He was received rudely and this caused a hard feelings on both sides.

He let it be known that he wanted to marry Shamouana, the daughter of Youssef Nasrallah Abi Attallah, one of his kin. Her family, however, refused to marry off their daughter to him. They did not forgive him for the deviation from the beliefs of his ancestors. So, Shamouana married Youssef Ghanatious Bachaalany. And Anthony angrily left Salima and his relatives, who were divided, some for him and some against.

He went back to Beirut to continue working with the Consul until 1850. Then he changed his career and worked as an interpreter accompanying European and American tourists traveling to Syria, Lebanon, the Holy Lands, and the Nile Valley. This made him want to visit the Western countries and to learn more about them and the growing science field. He had made friends with many Westerners. One, in particular, was a wealthy merchant from New York. He met him in Beirut ni 1852. The merchant greatly admired Anthony for his strong characteristics and his good manners. More specifically, he admired his wit, nobility, gentility and eagerness to work.

In August, 1854, Anthony sailed from Beirut with 300 Ryals, going to London and, then, on to the United States. He arrived at Boston in October of that year. He entered the office of his friend, wearing the Moroccan tarboosh and Lebanese clothes. He also wore a brilliant, smiling face. The merchant was surprised to see him. He stared at him for a moment, recognized him and warmly welcomed him.

It did not take long for Anthony to renew his friendships. People welcomed him warmly and generously invited him to their homes.

He was moving from one family's mansion to another with no confusion or embarassment. He felt at home at each place, his friends having opened their hearts before their doors.

The young man from Lebanon devoted himself to study. He applied himself to the English language once on his own and another time with an American teacher. He taught Arabic upon request and this paid for his living and educational expenses.

At the same time he was employed to help establish a union for Italian expatriate workers. He was hired for this because he spoke Italian. With his friends' help, he was able to enroll in school, and soon became the school hero. He was loved by both students and teachers alike. They admired him for his gifted brilliance and determination.

All this exertion, however, affected his health. Due to the difference in weather, he developed a cough and contracted the flu. His physical strength was drained, and even more so when he added Latin and Greek to his course load.

His friends tried hard to show him their love compassion. They took him to summer resorts where his health improved slightly. Then he returned to class and became ill again.

Some people advised him to return home, however, it was too late for that. The disease had already conquered him. He went to the hospital, leaving behind his studies and education.

Then, his friends, even more, showed their compassion and love for him. This evoked memories of his homeland and his family. In particular, it made him think of his mother, whom he longed to see. She had not approved of his decision to emigrate. She was afraid for him, having to travel by boat. She feared that he would forget his principles, beliefs, and Maronite traditions, because he was living among Protestants. We wonder if, at that time, he regretted having traveled without his mother's approval.

Finally, he knew that there was no hope left that he would recover. He prepared for his impending death. He wrote his last will and testament. In it he mentioned that he had no money for an inheritance because he spent all that he earned on doctors. He bequeathed his books in English to his American friends. Concerning his Eastern clothes, he requested that they be sent to his family in Salima, where they could be of use.

Then he wrote a letter to his brother Ibrahim and his paternal cousin, Hanna, the son of Saadallah. In it he said *"to be delivered by M. Hearter in Beirut, with advanced thanks. Sincerely, from Anthony."* Then, he wrote on it: *"It is forbidden to send this before my death."*

Here is Anthony's letter in brief:

"Time gathered us but we separated
And the heart is deeply inside burning
The eye cries to be separated from beloved
Time is long when we will meet?

Respectfully to my brethren: Hanna, son of uncle Sa`adallah, and, my brother, Ibrahim.

I miss you very much. I hope this finds you in good health and prosperity. If you should ask about my health, I am, at this time, in serious condition waiting for God's mercy. It started in April, 1855, when I developed a very severe cold. The doctors refuse to perform bloodletting for me, because they do not practice that here in this country. The cold attacked me again with with a cough.

I took the medicines which the doctors prescribed for me. That cost me 800 piasters. I continued with my lessons and education. In June, 1856, the illness came back again. I am certain that death is near. Thus, I am writing this letter to you so that, should I pass away, it will be forwarded to you by a friend of mine. Death is the end of every one, so, I am lying here, hoping for the Resurrection. I look forward to meeting you again in that state of purification and charity, before God, sitting in glory in the world immortal. Do not think of what happened to me as a result of negligence or carelessness. I have been treated very kindly. I am not sorry to be leaving this mortal world. I have enjoyed it. I spent many good days with my Christian brothers and loyal friends. Even King Soloman, with all his glory, did not have a better life than I. As for you, my soul mate, brother Ibrahim, kiss my mother's hands for me. Take care of her and brother Daoud. I pray to God to help you in what you do, hoping that you will present to all my relatives and friends, my last farewell. I end this letter by saying "Peace be with you. Do not weep for me, but be happy for me and feel calm. May God always protect you and grant you long lives."

Your brother

Anton Youssef Daher Bachaalany.

P.S. I wrote this letter without a date because I do not know when I will die."

The news of our hero Bachaalany was transmited through the majority of the Arabic newspapers and magazines both here and abroad. Afterwords, our learned friend Dr. Hitti published an article about him.

Here is some of what was published in the "Mera`t Al Gharb" (The Mirror of the West) newspaper by its editor, the great writer, Nessib Aredah, about Anthony Bachaalany. He said "…he walked the same path as his ancient Phoenician ancestors. That young man pursued his conquest with no weapon but his deep hope. From his tools, came a wonderful dream. From the transient things of this world, 300 Riyals collected by hard work, he was able to seek out the America he had heard about but never knew. Neither he nor those he left behind, at home, ever knew that he was at the forefront of a huge army. An army of emigrants who would soon follow in his footsteps to the land of Columbus. There is a way to new conquests and it is not by weapons or battalions. It is by the power of a firm will and hard work…that young man with his ambition motivating him went to the land of the unknown America to join the warriors' army of those who established the American nation. …He is the inspiration of the adventurous generations who conquered world. He was educated in the past, then he came to ask for that which his ancestors had spread throughout the world, the treasures of knowledge and accomplishment. This young man was forgotten, his tomb unknown. Then, Professor Philip K. Hitti discovered it. He found the biography that his friends had published to preserve his memory and to acknowledgement of his virtues. What a beautiful tribute it was. The most wonderful recognition we can make is to trace the footprints of the people who knew his favors, and, renew his memory by renovating his forgotten tomb. We should sow a rice plant of Lebanese rice at the tomb of this forgotten stranger, Anthony Bachaalany, the first Lebanese immigrant."

Saadallah Abou Attalla

He was afflicted by the plague. His wife feared that the princes who ruled the country. would banish him to the wilderness where he would die out of fear and neglect. Thus, she pretended to be insane. She would to throw rocks at any one who passed near her door. So, people thought she was crazy and stopped going near her home. This situation lasted until her husband was cured. No one knew of his disease and suddenly she was cured from her disease. Then people learned the truth of what had happened.

When the rulers heard of her trick, they praised her and granted her the robe of honor. When Nada, the daughter of Tanous Teama Abi 'Okl, was infected with the plague in 1840, catching the disease from the policemen of Ibrahim Pasha Al Masry, who were camping in Hamana, Tanous nursed his daughter, and he, too, was contaminated. He died with plague, whereas his only daughter was cured.

Sowan House

The majority of this house has emigrated from Salima to Makse and to other regions in the countryside. They settled in Taalabaya where they have reached positions of power. They have acquired large holdings of property and have had a huge number of offspring. They have become honored in this country.

Abdulallah Sowan was a hero known for his bravery. He was a living example of strength and all the people of the countryside feared him. For his strength and good fortune he relied on God and on his kin, "Marhaba", the great Prince Besheer`s governess as we will see shortly. Once, twenty knights went to him. Their intent was to kill him. He was armed with only his sword. So, he mounted his horse, and fought them viciously. After wounding six of them, the rest scattered, fleeing in fear. Then, there was the time he was attacked by a tiger trying to kill and eat him. With his bare hands, he broke its jaws.

On another occasion, a finger on his hand was infected with a severe boil. He took an axe and cut off the finger, then, cauterized it with boiling oil.

Among his good deeds, he donated a huge sum of money to build the Church in Taalabaya, as the inscription over the front door indicates.

His brother, Attallah Sowan, was known for being corpulent. He used to carry the big bridge pieces and large stones easily. Once, he hit a wrestler in the Dar Betadeen square. He threw him down and was about to kill him. In recognition, Prince Beshir granted him the robe of admiration for his strength. His son, Mansour Attallah, attained fame in Damascus in Al Sham. He was the most renown tailor there, used by rulers and senior officers.

My brother, Habib, and I paid him a visit in 1902 and saw his prestige. He married the sister of Habib Khaled Al Helow from Baabada. They had no children. He died in 1921 in Damascus.

Nowadays, there are Sowan folks in Taalabaya and expatriates in many places, all known for their activities and hard work. Some of them are intellectuals and of outstanding manners.

Youssef Nasrallah House

Their grand father, Nasrallah Abou Attalla, was one of those killed in the battle of Al Zahrany in 1770. He had two children: Youssef and Marhaba. She was the governess of The Great Prince Beshir. Let me tell her story.

Youssef Nasrallah married Mary, the daughter of Boutros Abou Khnesar. She was very wise and virtuous. She was an expert at nursing sick people. Her husband was a knight of a powerful arm.

Youssief died in 1839 and his two sons, Nejm and Hanna, served in the Princes' houses in Salima, Betadeen, Ghazeer, Bikfaya, Bermana, and Gouniah. That was during the era of the feudal governors: the Great Prince Beshir, Prince Haidar Ismail, Prince Beshir Ahmed and Youssef Beik Karam. Nejm and Hanna were cavaliers known for their ability of riding horses as well as for their bravery.

Some memorable events occurred in Hanna Bin Youssef's life. We will mention some of them as proof of his chivalry and bravery.

In 1858, Hanna was in the service of Prince Beshir Ahmed. He was out one day, in the company of some of the Prince's knights. They were in the high, barren Kisrawan mountains. On that particular day, the Prince's horses were in their pastures in Besabina in the town of Jbail. The men heard screaming. The Prince's enemies were trying to steal the horses. The cavaliers of Abou Saab and the Bachaalany's hurried to help the guards. When they reached Besabina, a group of men from Kisrawan and Jbail were standing in their way.

Hanna started acting like the hero he was. So much so that people were in awe at his bravery. He was in the company of some other cavaliers: Abdo, Ghanatious, and Girgis Nejm Andrea from the Bachaalany folks. Hanna and his company stood at the Jbail gate. So did their enemies, who numbered about 300. They stood on the sand near the Church of Our Lady, it the middle of the city. The three Bachaalany men attacked, riding their horses into the three hundred! They were screaming threats that they would open fire if onyone dared to touch the Prince's horses.

It so happened that Father Youssef Frefar (who later became Bishop) was there. He stood up between the two groups and each of them withdrew, back to their original places.

In the morning, a huge crowd of the residence of Jbail gathered. Together with the other people from Kisrawan the number of people grew to about two thousand. They confronted the Prince's men at the grave yard to frighten them away. Showing no fear, the Bachaalany horse soldiers attacked!

Girgis Andrea shouted: "Hear me, people! Don't think for a second that you will win a single thing from us. We are the Bachaalanys. Everybody knows us. We are the fish bones that will stick in your throats. Don't get near us, or you will fall in failure and disgrace. I swear by God Almighty that we are the ones who twist the Dog River! We cut roads of the high and barren mountains… etc.."

When the people heard that, they ran in fear. The power of the Prince and the fame of the men from Metn overwhelmed their hearts with fear!

The Prince's men, then advanced and took the horses out of Jbail. They counted twenty- five horses.

When they were some distance away, they remembered that they forgot the horse of Prince Khalil, the son of Prince Beshir. It was called "Farha".

Hanna Bin Youssef went back alone, riding his horse named "Sabr Ayoub". He reached the place where the horses were. He did not dismount. Instead, he came up next to the horse. He cut its rope. When his horse started to whinny, he hit it to shut him up. Then, he dragged the horse behind him. He walked with it into Jbail Souk (the market). People stepped aside, looking at him with admiration for his bravery and courage.

The brave knights rode until they reached Shemestar. There they left the horses with the guards. They returned to the house of Prince Beshir which at that time, was in Beirut. The news of their actions had preceeded them. The sheikhs of the Abi Saab house had been talking about their bravery, and, how, without them, the Prince's horses would have been stolen.

Prince Beshir welcomed his brave men, showing them all great respect and honor. He greatly appreciated their bravery and their sacrifice for duty. Then, the Prince ordered that the forage for each of their horses should be three quarters of the barley portion. The usual feed for his men's horses did not exceed a half a portion.

Samaan Al Labki Al Baabedati, the Prince's counsellor, protested saying: "Sir, we served you for all this time and our horses' forage never exceeded a half a portion." The Prince answered him, "Listen, Samaan. While you were in the mountains throwing pieces of rice to the chickens, those heroes saved my horses. They bought my honor with their blood. I would prefer to die rather than see my horses stolen from my pasture." (Quoted from Hanna Youssef, himself, and Andrea Girgis Nejm).

Marhaba Bachaalany And Prince Beshir

There was a woman raised up from the Abi Attalla Bachaalany house. Her name should be mentioned whenever the name of the Great Prince Beshir Shehab is mentioned.

She was Marhaba Bachaalany. She had a singular grace, exceeding that of the Prince's mother who left him when he was young. Marhaba replaced her, raising and caring for him. She nurtured him when he was young, then, serving and accompanying him when he became an adult. It was obvious that this great man respected her and was very generous to her. He used to call her "My Mother" and with just cause. She was the best mother and governess as well as the most loyal servant.

Among the documents of the Abi Attallah house was one that we previously mentioned in this book. It was the one whereby Gibrail Bin Samaan bought from his paternal cousins, Marhaba and her daughter (the wife of Youssef Shahin), their share of the Ghoushi Press (between Ain Al Sawaqee and Ain Al Mahata). It consisted of four carats. In addition were the vines in Ain Al Foura (between Al Qabou and Ain Al Sawaqee).

Originally, the name of Marhaba was unknown and information about her was lacking.

Historians who wrote about the Prince's life often had inconsistent stories about her. Some of them said that she was his slave. Others said she was just one of his slaves. Another one assumed that she was a Negro and was treated like the other negro slaves who were living in the castles of the princes in Lebanon.

We will set the record straight. The governess of Prince Beshir was of Lebanese origin, belonging to Maronite Catholic Church and from the Bachaalany house of Salima. We discovered her name when we searched records and documents about fifty years ago. We were, at the time, intending to write our biography which we are doing now with this book. We recorded every detail about her that we found. We even wrote down information we gathered from witnesses and even from people who personally knew and lived with her.

No one wrote about her other than the late Dr. Shaker Al Khoury in his book Mogamaa At Lassarate (The Collection of Pleasures), printed in Beirut in 1908. The following is a summary of what he wrote on page 290:

> *"Sheikh Farahat Al 'Azoury was the teacher of the grand-children of Prince Beshir. He accompanied him in his exsile until he died. The Prince told his grandchildren, in the presence of Azoury, about his attendants. Specifically he talked about his governess. He said she was from the house of the Bachaalany of Salima. She took care of him after the death of his father and after his mother left him. He was just a few months old. His mother married Prince Sayed-Ahmed Shehab in Hadath, Beirut. He told them how he packed his luggage, put them on a camel and made his governess also ride on it going to Deir Al Qamar. He ended his talks about his childhood but didn't mention the name of this governess at the time."*

However, we proved in our research that the governess of the Prince was Marhaba, the daughter of Abi Attallah Al Bachaalany who was born in Salima. Her father, Nasrallah, was killed in the Al Zahrany battle in 1770. She married Elias Eid Abi Samra, one of her relations. She had only one girl, Dhabla, the wife of Youssef Bin Shahin, the offspring of Abou Youssef Bachaalany.

When Marhaba became a widow, she contacted Prince Qassem Shehab through the Salima Princes. He authorized her to be a governess for his house in the village of Ghazeer. Then, Prince Qassem died on April 18, 1767. He had two boys, Hassan who was 4 years old, and Beshir, who was three and a half months. Beshir had been born on January 6, 1767. He had been baptized with his father and his mother when they were converted to Christianity by Bishop (Patriarch) Youssef Estaphane Al Marouni. After a while, the widow of Prince Qassem married, after his death, Prince Sayed-Ahmed Shehab in Hadath, Beirut. Thus, Marhaba Bachaalany undertook the job of being a governess of Prince Qassem's house and educating his children, especially the little Beshir.

Once Prince Hassan grew up, he left Ghazeer, and lived with his in-law, Prince Youssef, the Governor of Lebanon, in Deir Al Qamar.

After that, Marhaba and Prince Beshir moved to the village of Borg Al Baragna, near Beirut. It was next to his mother on property with a mulberry garden that his father had previously owned. Sometimes Beshir would visit his mother and sometimes he would live in Bashamone where he would go hunting.

When Prince Beshir reached manhood, his excellence and intelligence appeared in full bloom. One day, he packed his luggage, rented a camel from the Borg, made his governess, Marhaba, ride on it. And he walked with her to Deir Al Qamar. Then, he went to Betedine. He was still only sixteen years old.

He did as his brother, Hassan, had done. He joined the service of Prince Youssef. Then he married the Lady Shams, the daughter of Prince Mansour and the widow of Prince Shehabi from the Teem Valley. In 1788, he governed Lebanon. Now, he was still only twenty-one years old.

As things settled, he undertook many tasks. He constructed the famous commissary house, the greatest remaining vestige of his reign.

Then, it happened one night. One of the enemies of the Prince sent a man called, as they said, Fares Al Hakim, to kill him. He climbed a tree which was beside the castle. He worked his way through the building until he could enter the Harem next to the Prince's bedroom .

He approached along the wall. He took the Tabanjah (a type of carbine) belonging to the prince. It was silver plated and decorated with prescious stones. Then, Marhaba woke up. She grabbed the intruder by his clothes. He bit her hand and pushed her away. She fainted and fell down due the shock of it all.

The Prince was awakened by the commotion. Being aware of the fighting, he shouted with his gruff voice: "Marhaba! Mother!" But she did not answered because she had lost consiousness.

As for the intruder, he heard the voice of the Prince and he panicked. He didn't know what to do or, even, how to escape. He ended up taking the Tabanjah and fled the castle through the water canal. He ran away as fast as he could.

The Prince got up and awoke Marhaba. She told him what had happened to her. The Prince sent his men to search everywhere for the would be assassin but they could not find him.

Time passed. And it happened that one of the Prince's men was with his son picking up figs in the Prince's orchard. A stranger passed by them and was holding the Tabanjah. The man knew at once that it was the gun belonging to the Prince. Thus, he asked the stranger: "From whom did you buy that Tabanjah?" The stranger answered: "From so-and-so.:" Then the Prince's man said: "May God bless them for you." And he told his son to give the fig basket to the man, which he did. Then he said to his son: "Take the tabanjah from our friend and try it out. Let us see if you have become a man." The stranger gave the tabanjah to the boy and continued eating figs. The boy took the gun while his father was getting down from the fig tree. When he down, he grabbed the weapon and shouted at the stranger: "Turn around right now. Give me your hands to tie you or I'll kill you." The stranger was very afraid and obeyed the man's orders. The Prince's man then walked the man, in front of him, to the commissary building. There, the man confessed to the Prince how he entered the castle and how he was convinced to try to kill him. He said that he had regarded the Prince as such an important man that he had decided to take the gun to show as proof that he was the one who had broken in and killed the Prince.

He told the Prince how Marhaba stood as brave as any man to stop him. She held on to his clothes so he bit her with his teeth, pushing her away and fleeing through the canal.

We don't know what the Prince did to the intruder after he confressed. As for Marhaba, this incident only increased her respect in the court of Prince Beshir.

Her daughter, Dhabela, married Youssef Bin Shahin, who was also one of the Prinnce's men. And when the Prince's daughter, Saa'de, married Prince Selim Bin Abdullah Hassan Shihab, Dhabela accompanied her to the house in Ghaz-eer where she stayed for a long time. Both Qamara and Sabat (Bachaalany) were in service with her. They were the daughters of Shedid Sharbel from the Qarnayel pasture, known by the surname of Bachaalany.

Qamara married Fares, the son of the previously mentioned Dhabela. And Sabat, was married to a man from the house of Al Gorr and was in the service of the House in Ghazeer. She is the maternal grand-mother of George Beik Zouin and his brother Monsignor Louis Zouin.

The popular poet chanted the beauty of Sabat Bachaalany when he said:

> *"In the whole world,*
> *From East to West,*
> *From North to South,*

I've never seen a beauty, like you, Sabat!"

The presence of Marhaba Bachaalany in the castle of Beit ed Dine was reason enough for her many relatives to visit and come into contact with the great Prince of Lebanon. This included her brother Youssef Nasrallah and his two sons Hanna and Nejm. Nejm even named his daughter Marhaba after his aunt. Also, her son-in-law, Youssef Bin Shahin Faseda, the husband of her daughter Dhabla, would come to call. The same was true for his maternal half-brother Asaad Maroun Al Henawy whose mother was Al Hamra. Other frequent visitors included Andrea and his son Nejm Andrea Bachaalany, Abdou Nohra Al 'Erian, Abi Ragheb Abou 'Okl, and many others. There were so many visiting that people started saying that the palace of Beit ed Dine was a Bachaalany house!

It is worth mentioning on this occasion that once we published, for the first time, the story of Marhaba, the governess of Prince Beshir, in our book <u>Lebanon and Youssief Beik Karam</u> in 1925, some new historians began to mention her name and her story. They did so without the least notation of reference to us. Most of those historians are our friends like our fellow cleric Isaac Armala, Sheikh Edmon Blibel, Mr. Youssef Emadand, and Mr. Lahd Khater. All of them are aware that doing so is illegal and unusual.

Even Sheikh Edmon changed his mind about Marhaba as is indicated in his book <u>The Extended History of Lebanon</u>.

The strangest thing is that Mr. Lahd Khater in his article in "Al Bashir (The Forerunner)" newspaper, published on the day when the mortal remains of Prince Beshir were transferred to Lebanon, he mentioned the story of Marhaba Bachaalany as if it were his own.

And our friend, Father Girgis Abi Samra, the Lebanese missionary, said in his book <u>The History of the Al 'Oun Family</u>: "The will of Prince Beshir was published by Mr. Eissa Eskandar Al Ma'loof in the magazine "Al Manara" in Gonia." The truth is that we were the first to publish it in our book <u>Lebanon and Youssef Beik Karam</u> in 1925. Then we also printed its text in letters in "Al Manara (The Minaret)" magazine and Mr. Al Ma'loof had nothing to do with that.

When the mortal remains of Prince Beshir were transferred, both Prince Abdul Kader and Prince Abdul Aziz, the grandsons of Prince Beshir, published an engraved photocopy of the Will. It was taken from our original text and done so without mentioning that fact.

Also, the "Al Aa'mal (The Work)" newspaper printed the text also without giving proper credit.

The strangest of all is that we have another friend, Mr. Samaan Khazen who took about one hundred pages from our book <u>The History of Karam</u> and published them word for word in his book <u>The History of Ehden</u>, Volume One, without mentioning at all that they were taken from us. He ignored the term "Rights Reserved" written on the front page of the book. All these are some of the wonders of these days in Lebanon. We don't see similar actions in the developed nations.

Among our records are many original documents and written vestiges about Prince Beshir and his Shehabi family. It is a rare gathering, no less in size or importance than our collection of historical material on the Al Lam's Princes. We are preserving these collections and others of precious rarity until God deems it time to publish them. Then, with the help of those who also value such literacy treasures, and with God's assistance, they will be published.

The House of Al Qassouf

The first member of this family who came to Salima was Youssef Bin Elias Al Qassouf. Magdelania, the daughter of Hanna Salem, one of the Bachaalany's in Salima, married the man called Elias from the Qassouf family. That family had lived for many, many years in the village of 'Arbania near Salima. Elias and his wife died leaving two sons, Youssef and Louis. Louis lived in Boushria on the Beirut Coast. The other son, Youssef Al Qassouf, took up residence with his maternal grand-mother in Salima, after the death of his parents. Thus, she raised him until he grew up and he, in turn, took care of her until she died. Then, he married Rashida, the daughter of Daher Elias Abi Attallah Bachaalany, thus he belongs to this family through his mother's side. He then lived in Salima with his children. Because of all this we though it was better to discuss them after the House of Abi Attalah, talking about their origin and kinships.

Their Origin

Their ancestors lived for a long time in the village of Douma which is near Bchaaleh in the town of Bratoon. Around 1620, three brothers (we think three) emigrated to Kisrawan. They were fleeing injustice, taxes, and seeking relief and safety.

One of them lived in Dar'oun in Kisrawan. His offspring was called the House of Al Moqawem (the appraiser), because their grandfather was famous for his work in determining the value of various things including their crops.

Then, the house of Natin descended from the Moqawem House and from them, came the Al Dar'ouny folks and the Kanaan folks in Zahle and Beirut. All of them are Maronites.

The second brother lived in Al Khenshara and his offspring was known as the house of Al Qassouf. They are Roman Catholic and Orthodox and live in Al Khenshara, Al Shower, Zahle, Zabougha, and in Egypt.

The third brother resided in Al Shower and from him came the house of Qeyama, who are Roman Orthodox. (References: The Province of Kisrawan by Al Hadathounee, 73; Al Dowany by Al Ma'loof, 692, and, Douma's History by Father Constantin Al Pasha, 109). There was, however, a part of the Qassouf house who lived in the village of Arbania near Salima. They lived there for a long time and are Maronite. One of them, called Abu Mehana Qassouf was mentioned in two purchase (previously shown) agreements as a witness in 1250 Hegira. He is one of the forefathers of the Maronite Qassouf house in Al Arbania, who went to the Coast of Beirut at the end of the last century. Thus, they have lived in Al Boushria and Al Sad. Among them was Youssef Bin Elias Al Qassouf whose mother was from the Bachaalany house. She had married one of them, so Youssef belonged to the Bachaalany family through her. Since that time he lived in Salima with his sons and the family still lives there today.

Their Kinship

Those that we know of as living in Al Boushria, Al Sad, and Salima are: Asaad, Elias, Salibi, and Rokz. Asaad died unmarried. Elias had Youssef and Louis. Youssef who lived in Salima, had Elias, Boutros, Girgis, and Louis. Louis Bin Elias had Alfred, Na'eem, and Youssef. Salibi had Halim, Mikhail, Elias, and Selim.

Halim had Shehada and George. Shehada had Antoin and Halim. George had Jean. Mikhail Bin Salibi had Fouad, Abdo, and Deeb. Elias Salibi had Michel, Salibi, Tanious, Jean, Moris, and Youssef. Selim Bin Salibi had Antoin, George, And Michel.

As for Rokz, he had Namer, Michel, and Said who died as a youngster. Michel had Youssef, Hanna, Elias, and Shehada. Namer had Said and Rokz who died as a child and unmarried. All of them lived in Al Jadida, Al Boushria, and Al Sad.

The Ghaziry House

The Ghaziry house follows the Abi Attallah house because, in the middle of the previous century, Youssef Bin Hanna Nakhoul Al Shediak from Jadida Ghazir in Kasrowan was one of the workers in a silk plant (Karakhana) of the Thabet House in Al Moot River off the Beirut Coast. At that plant there were many workers from Salima and Ghazir as well as from other places. Youssef Al Ghaziry became acquainted with a girl from Salima called Raheel, the daughter of Hanna Bin Safy Bin Abi Attallah Bachaalany. They married. Raheel lived in Salima to the end of her life. She had Youssef (who died too young), Lucia (who married Abdulallah Khalil Daham Bachaalany), Mary (who never married who now lives in Mexico where she traveled to many years ago).

The Falouti House in Taalabaya

The Falouti folks are those families that belong to the Bachaalany house. They lived with the Bachaalany's in Salima and they all migrated together to the Beqaa district, namely Makse, Shetoura, and Taalabaya.

Once, one of our knowledgeable old men told me that the origin of the Falouti house is from Deir Al Qamar and from the Bahary folks. I knew one of their men in Bekefiya, who died there leaving no children. In the Church register of the Maronite Congregation in Salima, there are the names of some of them in Salima. The oldest entry is for Fares Al Falouti in 1826, as a godfather of Tanious Bin Melkoun Al Henawy, and, a best man for Melkoun.

Fares Al Falouti had Mikhail who had Hanna and Elias. Hanna had Youssef, Fares, Elias (known as Al 'Abassy), and Mikhail. Hanna Al Faloti came to Taalabaya and contacted Nakhla Beik Al Toweini, the rich man with numerous properties in Taalabaya. Hanna became his partner and his holdings broadened and his living conditions improved. His son Youssef is now one of the noble men in the country. He has a family and many properties in Taalabaya.

Karam House

This is one of the old offshoots of the Bachaalany folks. Boutros Nasef, one of their Sheikhs, told me fifty years ago that "Nejm Andrea Bachaalany, when he was dictating to Father Yohanna the kinships of the forefathers of the Bachaalany, he was unable to determine the great-grandfather of the Karam house offshoots. He said it was too long ago in the ancestry.

Today we notice that there are so few members of this house, especially when considering how old the house is. Sadly, the plagues that afflicted our country caused many deaths. This is especially true for the period between 1775 and 1800. Coupled with this is the recent immigration trend. Few of their numbers remain in the country today. Most of properties now are in Salima in Ein Al Sawaqee, and, in the place known as Matar's trench which is at Al Qabou. Matar is one of their ancient forefathers.

One of the evidences of their ancient existence in Salima is that the greatest feasts at the Maronite Church was theirs. Easter, our greatest feast, was prepared by the family of Hanna Bin Nasr Karam. Christmas was prepared by the family of Deeb, who migrated from Salima to Hassbia but still remained in charge of preparing for that feast day. They would come to Salima to attend Mass at Saint John's Church on Christmas day. Then, they built a church in Hassbia, so they stopped preparing the Christmas Day festivities around the year 1870. Father Abou 'Okl then took it over.

The feast of the Ascension was also prepared by Fares Nasr Karam and was handed over to them by Assaf Girgis Nejm Al 'Erian. As for the Assumption feast, it was prepared by someone called Hatem Abdel Karim.

The Karam house made many donations to Saint John's Church. These consisted of many donations of property. It is also worth noting that the Church which was build since the end of the 17th century was near the houses Karam families .

Deeb House

According to what the old men told me, the reason for which Deeb Matar Karam Bachaalany moved to Hassbia near Salima was that the house of the mentioned Deeb was located to the north of the Lam's Princes' palace in Salima. The princes asked to buy his property from him, but he refused to sell them his house. As a result, they oppressed him. So, he left Salima asking for refuge at the Lam's Princes of the Mourad folks in Al Matyan. They let him live in a ranch of theirs in Hassbia.

Some of the documents that we previous published in this book illustrate that the sons of Deeb Bachaalany from Hassbia sold all of their property in Salima around the year 1777. That was when they left Salima and went to Hassbia. They continued to live there as did their offspring who can still be found there.

In the past, before the last survey in the year 1861, their homes were located in the tax district of Bezbedeen, including Hasseba. They were, however, still burying their dead near Saint John's Church in the old cemetery of their forefathers.

Their Vestiges

"The reason for writing this document is that, Nasr Ibn Al Hadad has purchased from Abou Hatem Ibn Bachaalany, the arbours located at Ein Al Sawaqee for the price of seven piasters. He paid the whole amount. The mentioned individual sold him an irrefutable, valid, and signed agreement with no right of redemption, change or corruption. The other mentioned party bought this with his own personal money for himself and not for any one else. As for the money, it is the buyer's responsibility. Recorded in the month of Zee Al Heja, in the year 1107, by Nasser Eddine Ibn Abdel Hady. Witnesses: Sheikh Abou Hussein Sharaf Eddine, and, Sheikh Abou Ali Fares".

- - - - -

We found the above mentioned document among the papers of the Hadad house in Salima. It is one of the oldest Christian vestiges proving that the Bachaalany and the Hadad houses were in Salima at the end of the 17th century. We will also publish among the vestiges of the Hadad house other important documents which are older than this. It is interesting to point out that "Abou Hatem Al Besh'elany" at that time with this obvious term "Bachaalany" is proof that this is the actual name that these people were called. We wish to draw attention to this just to show, as we did in the beginning of this book, that the name "Machaalany" is not correct. And, that there is no truth to the story that the Bachaalany family originated from Houran.

Their Kinships

Karam Bachaalany had Hanna, Nasr, and Attallah. Hanna had Matar and Abou Hatem known as Abdul Karim who had Hatem. Hatem had Youssef and Tanous who died without having children. Meanwhile, Youssef Hatem had Girgis, who had Assaf, Youssef, Hatem, and Boutros. Hatem died young and unmarried. The remaining three emigrated to Brazil. Assaf died unmarried. Youssef married a Brazilian woman, had children and died. As for Boutros, he married the daughter of Father Azaar Beshour, one of Salima's immigrants and had four sons and seven daughters. The eldest son died young.

As for Matar Bin Hanna, he had Deeb who emigrated to Hassbia with his three sons: Youssef, Elias, and Hanna. Youssef had Andrea and Girgis, who died unmarried. While Andrea had Nejm and Youssef. Youssef died young. Nejm had Girgi, Gamil, and Youssef. Girgi had Abdo and Andrea. Gamil died young. Youssef is still unmarried.

As for Elias Bin Deeb, he had Nassef who had Shebl, Boutros, Matar, and Elias. Elias died young. Shebl had Deeb, Philip, Nassef, Habib, and Nassib. Boutros emigrated to Colombia, married an American woman and begot children whose names we do not know. And Matar had Me'awad.

As for Hanna Bin Deeb, he begot Mansour who had Abdo, Najib, Hanna, Daoud, and Karam. The two latter sons died young. Abdo and Hanna emigrated to Brazil. Abdo married the daughter of one of Hassbia's immigrants there and had children. Hanna married, like his brother, one of his nationalities and had sons there. One of them is Emil, the doctor. Najib had Fou'ad who emigrated to Brazil to his uncles' place. He married an immigrant of Lebanese origin and had children.

Concerning Attallah Bin Karam, he had Moussa and Hanna. Hanna died without having children. Moussa Bin Attallah Karam had Elias surnamed Abi Assla, the grandfather of Abi Assla Bachaalany house. He had Mikhail who had Elias and Girgis. Elias had Mikhail, Youssef, and Moussa who died unmarried. Youssef had Fouad who had Youssef possibly others. As for Mikhail II, he had Elias (who died unmarried), Hanna (the expatriate in Mexico), and Philip who has only had two daughters up to now. Girgis Bin Mikhail Abi Assla had Habib, Boutros, and Daoud. Habib had only Rashida, the wife of Khalil Girgis Khalil from the Abi 'Oql family. Boutros had Girgis who had Emil and Boutros. While Daoud had only Mary (the wife of Tawfik Makhloof), Malaka (the wife of Habib Tanious), and Marina (the wife of George Andrea Girgis Al Besh'elany).

As for Nasr Karam Bachaalany, he had Hanna who begot Nasr and Nassef. Nasr had Abou Karam Fares who had Karam and Ziedan. Ziedan emigrated to Egypt and, then, returned back from there around 1914. He then died during the First World War. Karam had only a daughter who married Boutros Saadallah Hanna in the United States, where Karam has been with his family. Concerning Nassef Bin Hanna Nasr Karam, he begot Boutros, Hanna, and Tanious. Boutros had Daoud who died and had no children. Hanna had Nassef and Youssef and both of them emigrated to Brazil. Then, Nassef died there childless. Youssef married a Brazilian woman and had sons and daughters. He probably died there. As for Tanious Nassef, he had Moussa, Girgi, and Habib. Moussa and Girgi left for Brazil and their children are there also. Lastly, Habeeb had Selim and Hanna.

Nasr Besh'elany

We have to pay attention to this man. This is a very critical point concerning the history of the Bachaalany people. Namely, knowing the name of Abou Rezk, the great-grandfather of us all. His surname was always the one mentioned. His actual name was never declared.

However, during our research in the documents belonging to the Maronite Apostolic See, we found a purchase agreement which took place in Tripoli. There, as the name of the witness, was "Rezk Bin Nasr Al Besh'elany". Undoubtedly, he is our grandfather. Abou Youssef Rezk was in Tripoli at that time. This is the reason why we mentioned in the kinships series Abou Youssef Rezk, his father's name, Abou Rezk Nasr Bachaalany. Also, the name 'Nasr' is repeated three times in the kinship tree of the house of Karam Bachaalany, which emphasizes the authenticity that is derived from that grandfather. Also. the names of Nasr, Abi Youssef, and Rezk are mentioned in the ancestry of Rezk, and that of the Shediak houses in Bchaaleh, and the relations of Abi Rezk's offspring in Salima.

The Karam house was distinguished with the profession appraiser of real estate, basic subsistence items, and crops. They excelled in this field. Some of those who were distinguished in it include: the old Nasr Karam and his son Hanna; Mikhail Abou Assla and his son Elias. Elias seems to have surpassed all of them in his profession. He was prudent, wise, and truly patriot. He estimated the properties and assessed the crops by himself. Also, he divided real estates to brothers and sisters; resolving the problems and disputes about properties borders. On his own, he would write agreements and deeds of sale, division, agreements, and devotions, and other things that needed logic, honesty, and truthfulness.

Also known for this profession are: Andrea, with his son, Nejm, and, Daher Bin Nejm of the Bachaalany folks; Fares Bou Ali Nayel, from the Said folks; Fakhr Eddine from the Masry house; and, many others whose names were mentioned in the selling and buying agreements of Salima.

Tanious Karam

We failed to mention in the family tree of the Karam house, Tanious Bin Nasr Karam. He had Boutros and three daughters: Naasa, Saada, Fawza (the wife of Nader Gad'oun). Boutros died and had no children, and the inheriters disagreed about the inheritance. The case was brought before the archbishop, Gibrail Al Nasery, the judge of the Christians, at the time. We publish here the related documents which are full of details into the lives and people of that time:

"The reason for recording this document is that Hanna Ibn Nasr and the daughters of his paternal uncle Tanous Karam came before us. They acknowledged that they sold to Nader Bin Gad'oun, two loads of grapevines in Ain Al Sawaqee... the borders of the mentioned location are: to the south, Khaled Faseda; to the North, Hanna Al Aqoury; to the East, Mikhail Habak; and, on the West, the waterwheel ... the price is thirty piasters... the appraisor is Hanna Ibn Nasr. This was edited in September, 1207. Written by Kanaan Al Tyan. Admitted and accepted by Hanna and his paternal uncle's daughters. The witnesses: Gibrail Ibn Saman, Hanna Eid, Hatem Abdul Karim. Nassef certified the contents were legal. The humble Gibrail Al Nasery."

- - - - -

"... Daher Al Sayegh bought from Boutros Ibn Tanious Karam...the sugar cane press

known by 'Girete Al Shari (the buyer's neighborhood)", at the price of three piasters ...estimated by Haidar Qadama, in Ramadan, 1207, edited by Kaaan Al Tiyan. The witnesses: Tanious Ibn Khataar, Rameh Ibn Qadama, and Yaakoub Al Siqly. It has been transferred from our hand to Nadir Gad'oun's hand. Edited by Daher Al Sayegh."

- - - - -

"To Nadir Ibn Gad'oun Fasedat from Hanna Ibn Nasr Karam and the daughters of Tanious Karam, the vines located above the press at the price of eighteen piasters ... in the year 1208, The Witnesses: Hanna Al 'Aqouree, Mikhail Al Sayegh, Fares Al Henawy and Ossman Seif ... Edited by Daher Al Sayegh."

- - - - -

"Nader Gad'oun bought from Nassef Ibn Nasr...in the year 1234 (1818). Edited by Shahin Said."

On all these documents there are footnotes written in the handwriting of Archbishop Gibrail Al Nasery, and with his seal, stating: *"Nassef Bin Hanna has certified the content of these agreements."*

A will

"Be it known that Naasa has paid, after the death of her father, as she said: paid 7 piasters to Hanna's wife for requiems; 7 piasters paid to Adwan; 10 piasters paid to Father Antoin Al Jomayel; 15 piasters paid to Haidar Al Zar'ouni.

In the name of the Father, the Son, and the Holy Spirit. God is One. Amen. This is me, Naasa, daughter of Tanious Karam; sound in both mind and body; I admit and acknowledge that I am a follower of the Catholic Church of Saint Peter. I believe in all that it believes and I reject all that it rejects. Since death is a fact, with my sound mind, I wish to write my will to my full satisfaction.

First, concerning the wastelands we had at the mill, we sold them to our kin, Nader, according to a deed and we received the full price. I gave him, as written above, on behalf of our father, with nothing left owing to Nader. Concerning the rest of our crops: Al Qalaa, fig trees at Ain Al Sawaqee, mulberry trees by the house, exempting our donations and the house, our share in these places is to be sold immediately. The money is to be distributed for requiems for my soul and our fellow deceased, without losing one piaster. As for the vine leaves, the load is valued at twelve piasters. Our share in the press is subject to a debt owed but any amount over that will be for requiems. I strictly forbid any one to reject this will. Anyone who does so, I will litigate him in the afterlife.

Recorded and edited by Father Hanna by his own hand. We do not owe nor have loaned anything but the price of a piece of cloth and the revenue taxes to our kin, Nader.

This document was edited in January, 1818. Witness: Nassef Bin Hanna Nasr"

- - - - -

"Nassef Ibn Hanna and Nader Ibn Gad'oun settled their mutual account according to the legal opinion... Each took his legal right from the other... in 1243. Witnesses: Abdo Ibn Nohra, Badah Qadama, Youssef Bin Shahin, Asaad Bin Maron, Mikhail Bou Assly, Hanna Moussa Al Erian, Tanious Bou Saber, and Hanna Bin Gibrail.

Editor of this document, Elias Al Tiyan."

- - - - -

Below is the legal opinion and the judgement resulting from this suit:

After the legal pleading of both Saab Elias. Nader Gad'oun, Nader's wife, Nassef Hanna, and Nasr Karam all from Salima, upon the distribution of the inheritance of Helena, daughter of Nader, who died without leaving an in-

hertance to her parents and her husband, Saab, and, according to their testimony before us: we judged the following: Her inheritance will be divided into three parts. One part for her funeral arrangements and requiems; one portion which is to be half of the remaining amount, to her husband; and, the remaining portion to her parents. As for the earrings and the golden chain: Saab has claimed that Nader's wife gave them to her daughter, Helena, his wife. Then, when she was alive but approaching death, she took them back.

However, Saab proved that the testimony of Nader was false because Helena never owned the items in question because they were only loaned to her, this judgment made after the appropriate testimony was made by Nader's wife; thus, the claim is denied. Nassef, Saab, and Nasr Karam claimed a share in the inheritance of their paternal cousin, Naasa.

It was established that she had received father's inheritance and managed it making it increase in value during her life. What is left belongs to her two sisters; Foza and Saadi. Therefore, the claim of the others was denied concerning Naasa's share. As for Nassef, he claimed that his father should have a share in the inheritance of Boutros Ibn Tanious Karam, which Foza had received. It was proved that he had a claim and from her share he is entitled to forty five piasters. He has taken half of the house ruins worth thirty piasters, and is still owed the remaining fifteen piasters.

It was agreed between him and Nader that he will take from Nader the mentioned sum for Foza's share in the mulberry trees which are in front of his house. Then an exchange and accounting would take place between Nader and Nassef. According to it, Nader would give the rest of the mulberry trees and take, instead, money from Nassef's share in some other appropriate place; all legal suits exchanged between them were denied. This is our judgement and edited for statement in March 3rd in 1828. (the official seal)

The humble Archbishop   Witnesses:
  Gibrail Al Nassry   Father Hanna Salamboly, and,
                               Nicola Al Khoury from Ghazir

The Archbishop Gibrail Al Nasery

He is the honorable Maronite judge who was appointed by Prince Beshir Shehab the Great as the judge of the Christians of Lebanon Mount (Jibel Lebnan). He took over the position and held it for a long time. When he was a priest, he was known as Father Yohanna Al Nasery (Father John Nasry). When he became the Archbishop of Al Nassera he was honored with the name of Gibrail.

Among our documents, we have many of his judgements in various legal suits and disputes between claimants, Christians and others as well. All of them show how that virtuous prelate was characterized by justice and honesty. In addition, he possessed eloquence and an ability to express his thoughts well while still being brief. The rulers of Lebanon Mount relied on him because they trusted his knowledge, his pure intentions, and his sense of fairness. Also, Maronite spiritual leaders trusted him as much as civilian leaders.

Here is a brief summary of what we know about his life. He is of Israeli, Jewish origins. More precisely, a Nazarene. He left Nazareth, his home land, due to the poverty of his parents. He took refuge in the hills of Mount Lebanon. He was named Hanna Al Khayat Al Nasery. Pastor Nimutallah Natin, the master of the Harf Monastery in Der'oun Kisrawan hired him to be the shepherd of the monastery.

One day, he met Father Kheirallah Estefan (the Archbishop Youssef). The priest was so impressed with him that he hired him to do service work at the Ain Waraka School.

After he converted to Christianity, the famous Patriarch Youssef Al Tiyan ordered him to be enrolled in that same school in 1797. There, he studied Syriac and Arabic under the Sub-deacon Sam, the son of Father Antonios Shahwan. Once he finished his studies, he was appointed to be a teacher in the same school in 1808.

He then went to Ghazir with his school mate, Moussa Abou 'Akr Beskintawy (Archbishop Karam Boutros, the Archbishop of Beirut), to learn theology from the previously mentioned priest Kheirallah. He was a judge at that time, by order of Prince Beshir.

About the year 1811, he was ordained a priest with his friend Moussa Al Beskintawy. The Prince appointed them as judges in Ghazir and fixed their salary at 500 piasters per year. Then, the Prince issued an order for them to travel around the Mount Lebanon fiefs to judge in various cases, making it easier for the citizens. Their deacon was Yohanna Al Islamboly who later became a priest.

In 1820, Al Nasery was ordained as an Archbishop by Patriarch Yohanna Al Helow and he was given the name Gibrail. He stayed in charge of his jurisdiction until 1824, when he took over the administration of the Ain Waraka School.

When Patriarch Youssef Hebesh entrusted the management of the school to Father Yohanna Abi Rezk Al Gezini (Archbishop Youssef Rezk), Archbishop Gibrail returned to his position as a circuit court judge. Then he was appointed Abbot of the Mar Sheleta Makbas Monastery in Kisrawan until 1828. After that, he devoted himself to his judgeship.

His residence was often in Ghazir where he bought a building and a house. Toward the end of his life, he was afflicted with dropsy. Then he began to prepare for his death. He bequeathed all of his estate to the organization of the Missionaries, to support their works of charity. His death cane on April 22nd, 1838. He was buried at the Church of Our Lady in Ghazir.

The date of his death was noted by his pupil, Father Abdulallah Al Maqeer, who said that Al Nasery tried hard to convert his mother to Christianity, but he failed. Also, his pupil, Father Arsanuos Al Fakhoury, the famous judge and poet, dated his death in verses which have been engraved on his tomb. (see the article of our kinsman the notable Father Ibrahim Harfoush in the magazine "Al Manara" 9:572. Also, see the book The History Of the Al Shorafa Library, pg. 128, written by our friend, Monsignor Isaac Armala).

Teama House And Bachaalany House

Our sheikhs never told us that there was an ancestral relationship between these two families. However, the documents that we found at the Teama house convince us that there is a kinship between the Teama house in Qarana Al Hamra and the Bachaalany in Salima. It was never mentioned either because the connection occurred so long ago, or, for some other reason that we still do not know. Our basis for the connection are as follows:

1. There is a comparable succession of names in the past in the two families, such as Abi Rezk, Rezk, Abdulallah, Younes, Karam, Nasr, Fares, Teama, and Youssef.

2. The Teama folks say that their grandfather called Karam emigrated with his children from North Lebanon to the Kisrawan fief at the end of the 17th century, Also, they say that their grandfather, Teama, is the son of Rezk Bin Karam, which agrees in some aspects, with the history of the immigration of the sons of Abi Rezk Bachaalany to the Kisrawan fief and their dwelling first in Al Bellana district and in Zouq Al Kharab, not far from Karanat Al Hamra. This was before their immigration to Salima and other places.

3. Some offshoots of the Bachaalany house still live in the Bellana district, such as the family of the prelate Hanania Bin Abi Matar Saab Bachaalany and his relatives. They belong to the house of Nasrallah Al Mazmouk who went to Salima, as we will mention.

4. A family exists in Qarana Al Hamra known as the house of the priest. The members of the family say that they came from Zouk Al Kharab.

5. Some names of the Bachaalany's from Salima are mentioned in the documents of Teama house in Qarana Al Hamra in the Hegira year 1172. These names are of our grandfather Abou Knieser Nejm Bin Moussa Bin Abou Youssef and the name of Tanious Bin (Nasr) Karam whom we previousely mentioned. This and other similarities has drawn the attention of writers to keep investigating the kinship of these two families.

Al Gibely House

Members of this house are related to the house of Karam Bachaalany by marriage.

They originate from the town of Gibel. They came to Salima at the beginning of the previous century, when they were known as the house of Al Tabsoul. One of them is Fayad Al Gibely, who died in 1830. There are three brothers raised from this house, the sons of Yohanna Al Tobsoul. Two of them joined the Antonian monasticism and died there. They are Brother Beshara and Brother Lebawes Bachaalany. We have previously mentioned them. As for the third, he joined the Al Baladya monasticism. We could not trace any details of his life. By those monks, the offshoot of Al Gibely house in Salima was interrupted.

The House Of Samaan And Al Salmany

Long ago, there was a family known as the house of Hanna Bin Samaan in Salima. He was mentioned in the register of the Survey Department which we keep among our documents. Its date goes back to the year 1770. It mentions " the properties of Hanna Bin Samaan Al Faran". His home was located at the place called the Al Kharga district in front of the house of Fares Bin Youssef and the house of Hatem. His wife was the daughter of Wakim Bin Shamouna and the sister of Asaad Wakim from the house of Bou Mikhail, the Roman Catholic.

Hanna Bin Samaan had a boy called Youssef who married the daughter of Nasr Karam Al Bachaalany. They had a daughter named Tranja who married Dr. Basila Al Roomy in Beirut.

I found the purchase contract of Youssef Bin Hanna (Samaan) Bachaalany in which he sold his properties in Salima and his house in the Kharga district to his daughter, Taranja, on July 26, 1864. The house was bought by Girgis Abdo Mikhail.

After Girgis' family emigrated to Brazil, the house collapsed and nothing remains but its ruins and the pomegranate tree which stood in front of it. As for Taranja and her mother, I used to see them frequently in Beirut. Then, Taranja had a neural disease and her mother died. Then her husband, Dr Basila died. Thus, she inherited money from his estate. A young man from Gonia coveted that money. He lured her and then married her. After the marriage he took her money, he left her, and she died from the shock of it all.

In Moalaket Zahle, there is a family known as the Al Salmany house. They claim that they originate from Salima and that they are kin of the Bachaalany house there. They are notable people and own considerable properties in Zahle, in Al Moalaka, and, Beirut, too. Also, they are related to our famous friend, Dr. Tawfik Rezk. Their relationship is from the mother's side since the relations were his maternal uncles.

Abu Rashid Fares Khatar Maron, who is one of our knowledgable Sheikhs, told us that the Salamany house in Zahle had their origin from Salima. He said that they are the relatives of Hanna Bin Samaan, who we already mentioned. Their grandfather is originally from Bahr Saff. He came to Salima and belonged to the Bachaalany house…and he may be from the family of Al Hajj Boutros in Bahr Saff.

The House Of Nasrallah Al Mazmouk

Their Kinships

Nasrallah Al Mazmouk had Samaan, Youssef, and Hanna. Samaan had Girgis, Asaad, and Boutros. Girgis married a girl from the house of Abi Gouda in Al Zalaqa on the coast of Beirut. There he and his offspring lived. He had Selim, Amin, Rashid, Najib, and Samaan. Selim had, from his first wife, Elias and George. From his second wife he had other children whose names we do not know. Meanwhile Elias Bin Selim had Beshara and Eid.

Amin Bin Girgis died young and unmarried. Rashid had Youssef, Girgis, and Masoud. Najib had George and Michel. Samaan had Youssef and Aazar. As for Asaad Samaan, he had Youssef, Ibrahim, Khalil, Francis, and Hanna. Youssief had no children. Khalil died young and unmarried. Ibraheem had George, Michel, and Asaad. George had Roger and William. As for Francis Bin Asaad, he had Elia and Abdo. Hanna had Mansour and Henry. Boutros Bin Samaan had Mikhail, Abdulallah, and Elias, who died young. Mikhail had Elias and Boutros. Elias died young. As for Abdulallah Bin Boutros, he had no children.

Youssef Bin Nasrallah had Nasrallah, who became an ordained priest and was called Father Boutros. He had Raheal (the wife of Selim Habib), Mary (the wife of Salebe Zein), Olina (the wife of Ibrahim Zein), and Henna.

Concerning Hanna Bin Nasrallah, he lived in Shamalan and had Mansour and Rashid. Mansour had Khalil, Ibrahim, Najib, and Nassib. Khalel had Dr. Mounir, who lives in Palestine. Ibrahim married an English woman and had children living with their mother in England after their father died with the sinking of the Titanic. Najeeb died in Egypt and had children there. Nassib lived in Egypt and had Edward and Alfred. As for Rashid Bin Hanna, he had Selim, Naji, and Karam. Selim and Naji have had no children so far. While Karam had Richard, Gilbert, and James.

Their Origin

Their ancestry goes back to Sheikh Abi Saab Bachaalany who was appointed as a governing Sheikh of Beshray Well. At the time, his brother, Sheikh Abou Rezk Bachaalany was the highest ranking Sheikh in the government of Tripoli, as we already mentioned in detail. This is from the most famous authoritative source of all historians, Archbishop Estefan Douwehy.

After their terrible events, the Bachaalany folks lived in Tripoli, in the Balana district and in Zouk Al Kharab. Then, they migrated to Salima at the end of the 17th century and the beginning of the 18th century (again, this already described in earlier pages). The reason for which the forefather of the Mazmouk folks came to Salima was, according to Abou Andrea Bachaalany, that he was brought from the Balana district to Salima. His offspring still live there today.

One of Sheikh Abi Saab's sons was still in the Balana district. That is where the Bachaalany family resorted to when they escaped from Tripoli. His name is Abu Matar Saab, father of the prelate Hanania Bachaalany, the Antonian monk, about whom we previously talked. He is also a relative of Nasrallah and surnamed Mazmouk, due to his European garment known in our country as "Mazmak. That happened after he came back from a trip to Europe where he was accompanied by his brother-in-law, the already mentioned prelate, Hanania. It seems that there are no relatives of the prelate left other than Nasrallah, the grandfather of this family in Salima, Shamlan, and the coast of Beirut.

Their Vestiges

"Brother Hanania Ibn Matar Saab: This man was from the Balana District. He was an orphan, so he traveled wherever he liked. He went to Mar Girgis 'Oukar and he worked for them for seven months. And, because he stayed with monks, he decided that he wanted to be one of them. He asked the prelate, Father Benjamin, to allow him to join with the beginners in the Mar Ash'iay Monastery. Father Benjamin agreed to his request and put him with the novices in their uniform. After he finished his training period and was approved, he won the holy certificate from the brothers. Then, he wore the angelic hood of the Brothers, bestowed by the hand of Father Youssef Al Shabq, the vicar of Mar Ash'ia.

That day was the feast of Ash'ia, on October, 15, the Father Superior was Father Ibrahim Assaf, in the Christian year, 1752."

"Father Hanania passed away after spending forty years in Monasticism. He was very zealous in his Monasticism performing many good deeds. He went to the Christian countries three times, for the sake of his monasticism. His origin is from the Harat Al Balana village. He died in Spain, after making a pure confession and receiving the last rites of Extreme Unction. This information is based on the testimony given by his Christian Brother Eugene in 1792, at the time when Father Tobia Oun, was the Father Superior of the Monasticism." (This is according to the monastery register.)

- - - - -

"... At the appointed date, agreement and acceptance took place between our sons Youssef and Samaan, sons of Nasrallah, about the dwelling: the eastern attic room and the room under it are given to Youssef. what follows it from east, the mulberry and other trees belong to him. The western attic and its field and the mulberry and other trees are given to Samaan. Each have the full right to manage what he owns; they will not be allowed to claim from the other anything, not jewellery, nor furniture, with the exception of the cooking pan, frying pan, pick axe, ladder, and the craft tool (tools of shoemaking). ......we edited this contract ...on November 26, 1843... and the plants, mulberry at the garden at the end of the field, the border of the twisted mulberry tree, they are part of the western attic. Edited by Father Youssef. Witnesses: Daher Bou Ragheb, Youssef Hatem, Hanna Bin Moussa, Khalil Daham, Nassef Bou 'Oun, Sabra Abou Neama, and Daham Ibn Neama."

- - - - -

This is the statement of the shares of Karam of the Jowana trench to Youssef and his brother, Samaan, in 1845.

"Samaan's share is: the Shaboq garden and its divisions. The fig garden at the end of the field of the fig tree at the west and a vine tree with a fig tree at the east, in the recently ploughed land four strips of lands with trees and a

shelter at the bottom, two pieces under the Al Bayad Cliff, ...belong to the above share. The oak garden and whatever the oak garden looks over at the east side and a fifth above the Maghara garden of mulberry and vines, at the border of his share towards the east, five mulberry trees in the Maghara garden at a waterwheel, saplings and bearing tree at the east side under Fares house; in Al Hayarate, three fig trees at the west side, a garden above the waterwheel of Youssef.

Belonging to Youssef: two fig trees at the bottom in half of the garden and... which is above it and a garden above Osman, in the path of the Bayad cliff, four strips of lands with trees and...the border of Al Bayad cliff to the west side at the head of the recently ploughed land. Three pieces above the olive tree at the border of the Hadad house. From the strips of fig trees up to the Bayad cliff. A strip of land at the top and the waterwheel beside the mulberry tree under the Hussein house and its surroundings in the Maghara garden, four vine transplants up to the cliff; at the south, three transplants and its grapevines. A waterwheel, mulberry tree,...and a mulberry under the house of Fares, under the Refaa house a garden and three mulberry trees at the west side, and charcoal, six fig trees at the east side in the Hiyarate, a waterwheel at the bottom and four strips of lands with trees, belonging to it a transplant of fig at the west side, and, that which the twisted fig tree is overlooking. Written by Nasef Bou 'Oun according to the dictation of the two parties. Witnesses: Nasr Karam, Youssef Al Erian, Youssef Salem, and, Mikhail Bou 'Oun."

- - - - -

Prince Haidar Ahmed Shehab was the friend of Shamlan and he often went to the house of the Princes Al Lam' in Salima. Hanna Nasrallah Al Mazmouk was employed by those Princes as a Cook. So, Prince Haidar asked the Princes if Hanna could be the cook of his house in Shamlan and they agreed. The same Hanna agreed to join this glorious Prince, so he accompanied him to Shamlan and lived there in his house until the Prince died in 1834.

Through Prince Haidar Shamlan, Samaan Nasrallah, the brother of Hanna, was allowed to join the service of one of the sheikhs of the 'Aqily house. They are the Druzes' dwelling in the Shouf county. He became his housekeeper for ten years then returned to Salima. His brother Hanna, meanwhile, stayed in Shamlan and dwelt there with his family. Hanna had become engaged to one of his relatives' daughters in Salima. But he had to leave Salima without marrying her because he had to accompany Prince Haidar when he joined his service.

The girl's parents insisted that he marry her but he didn't. As a result, there was a rupture between them. The girl married another man. In Shamlan, Hanna married Frouseen, the daughter of Jabour from the Qobel Monastery. Jabour had a melodious voice. The Prince had brought him to Shamlan and made him live there.

The origin of his family is Ehden, from the Ebeid House who moved to Aarmoun Kisrawan, then to 'Einab. They were known as the Shahin House. After that, they went to Ein Kesour. Because something happened there between them and the Druzes, they went to the Qobel Monastery and were known as the Jabour Semia House.

Hanna preserved the religious principals he inherited from his ancestors. I saw the name of his son, Rashid, mentioned among the names of those who were been baptized in the year 1847 at the Maronite Church in Shamlan. He was baptised by Bishop Tobia 'Oun, the attendant of the Bishopric of Beirut, as follows: "Rashid, the son of Yohanna, the Cook."

He also preserved "preaching prayers" as you can see mentioned in his letter below. He sent it to his relatives of the Bachaalany House, in answer to a letter they sent to him. This was after the rupture between the two families because of his engagement. He apparently gave them land (in Salima), part of an inheritance from his father.

Here is the text of the letter with its original terms. It was written in nice handwriting by his son Mansour. It is preserved in our archives:

"January 28th, 1864.

To the attention of our respected, glorious father, and to our paternal cousin,

May God keep them

We kiss your respectable hands and ask about you. We have been honored by your letter in which you expressed your good health and praying God for us. May god have mercy on you and be generous with you. We are hoping that you are always well, mentally and physically. From our side, we thank God that you are well and wish you every success. According to what you wrote to us, namely, that we have forgotten you but that you have not forgotten us. Even more, that you are continuingly longing to see us. So, we are saying to you that we, too, are thinking of you all the time. If some important matter has preoccupied us, still, we wake up and think about you. We long to come to see you and fulfill your request. However, we must confess we have been negligent in this. And, we thank you so much that you forgive us our negligence and that you are not angry with us. We understand from your letter that you have decided to come to visit us. This makes us so happy. We, also, have decided that we will come and visit you. We are sending this letter with the thought that it can, perhaps, temporarily compensate for not seeing each other at this moment, but knowing that the moment is coming. God willing, we will come soon and fulfill our duties. We are looking forward to that next occasion to arrive when we can kiss your hands and see with our own eyes how you are doing. Then, our spoken words will express what we are thinking. We are asking the Creator, may he be exalted, that when we are next honored to be in your presence, that you will be in good health and happy.

So it is that we have understood from your letter and so we hope that this is what has been explained. With our best regards, from all of us, to all the family and, specifically, to you. Our children and everyone here is kissing your hands and asking about you, sending greeting after greeting. May God keep you safe and preserve you with a long life.

Praying for you.

Yohanna the Cook

The Address: Salima Al Metn. Upon its arrival, received with honor by the respected, glorious Father Yohanna, and our paternal cousin. May God give you long life!"

The document we mentioned proves that there was a division of the properties of the Nasrallah Al Mazmouk House, between Youssef and Samaan, without their brother Hanna, who left his share of the inheritance in Salima to his two brothers. What we are unable to ascertain is whether he donated it to them, or sold it to them.

The Bachaalany family who were raised in Shamlan and lived in Beirut, Egypt, and Palestine, are all houses of knowlege and culture.

Hanna's son, Mansour had Khalil, Ibrahim, Najib, and Nassib. They have studied the sciences and languages at the high schools of Lebanon. They have excelled in writing, journalism, and management. Khalil took over his father's job at the Water Works of Beirut.

I paid him a visit in his home in Beirut on April 25th, 1921. We talked about the past eras of our ancestors. We rebuilt the relationship that was almost broken. Khalil at that time was about fifty years old, decent, and handsome.

When ending our visit, he told me: "I consider this visit, the best day of my life." As for his son, Dr. Mounir, he was one of the most brilliant doctors. He occupied important positions in Al Nasra, Hayfa, and Jaffa.

Ibrahim Mansour excelled in the English language and its literature. He worked as the treasurer of the famous ship, the Titanic. What should be mentioned is that he issued a newspaper in English. He was preparing, printing, and distributing it on board that giant ship which sank in 1911. He was one of the fatalities. His English widow took their children with her back to England.

As for Najib, he is the famous writer and journalist. He was in charge of editing a newspaper called "The Voice Of The Present" as well as other newspapers. With his magic pen, he also translated into Arabic many important novels such as <u>The Brave Of Venizia</u>, <u>The Flower Of Love</u>, and many others. He died in Egypt around 1921.

Nassib was famous for his novels published in the magazine "Al Diya". Its owner, Sheikh Ibrahim Al Yazejy, was the Imam (leader) of the Arabic Language. Then, one of the Sheikh's relatives re-published them in San Paolo, Brazil. Nassib has been residing in Egypt with his family for many years.

In general, this house is one of our greatest intellectual families. We are so proud of them. We are hoping that they have maintained the religion and the beliefs on which they were raised, and for which, their ancestors spilled their blood and gave their lives.

And, historically speaking, we have a wish. It is our deepest desire to see those using the name "Machaalany" return to the proper, original, historically correct name, "Bachaalany". The difference in names has hurt the union of our house and caused doubts about the validity of some of our kinship.

As for Rashid Bin Hanna, he grew up in Shamlan and died there in 1912. He spent his life teaching the Arabic Language and Arithmetic in the village school. His two sons, Selim and Nagui, emigrated after 1910 to the United States where they married with foreign women but had no children.

Karam studied at Souk Al Gharb then continued at the American University in Beirut. In 1927, he married Alice, the daughter of Dr. Wahba Al Salebe. Karam is an employee of the Secony Vacuum Company. He resides with his family in Beirut.

Prince Haidar Shehab

He is the son of Prince Ahmed. He is the Prince Haidar Shehab who governed Lebanon after the reign of Prince Beshir Shehab the First.

Prince Haidar was raised on the values of piety, goodness, and love for his religion, and especially its pious monks. He was known for his honourable companionship and high ethics. He loved peace and hated hostility and disputes. He donated many of his properties to the monasteries and the churches of the region. His last will and testament showed how much he was a firm believer of the Catholic Church.

He died embracing the Maronite doctrine, the religion on which he was raised. He also loved and donated much to the Roman Catholic Church. He bequethed 1500 Golden Liras to the Church. Among our archives, we possess a list of his expenses during his life and after his death.

I visited Shamlan during the First World War, on February 13, 1916, and went about visiting the historical monuments there. The first ones I went to were those of Prince Haidar Ahmed. I saw his home which is still standing but on the verge of collapsing. Still, I could see the hall roof, full of carvings and painted in the old beautiful style. There were verses and wise poetic sayings still legible. The bathroom's flagstones are still the same.

The Lady Oum Abass, the daughter of the Prince, sold the home and its surroundings to the Khawaja (the European) Scott, a British man. Then, the Bishop Tobia 'Oun, the Archbishop of Beirut, bought it from him to make it into a big school. However, he died before that took place. Thus, Bishop Youssef Al Debs sold it to Moussa Frij and with its money he built churches and large schools in Beirut.

The location of that house is beautiful, overlooking the sea. The glorious Prince spent his days of power there. In the house, the remnants of a chapel exist. There the holy sacrifice of the Mass was celebrated by the priest of the pious Maronite Prince. He donated much to the Shamlan Monastery of the Antonian Monasticism.

That Prince made many donations to the churches of neighboring villages, in addition to many churches and monasteries throughout Lebanon.

In the Monastery Church, there is a picture of the Virgin, drawn by Rafael and dating from Prince Haidar's days. It expresses a deep solemnity.

Signs Of Esteem

"We have distinguished and allowed this honest Prince, His Excellency Prince Haidar Shehab to install a chapel in a room or special place as he sees fit. He may do so when he so desires. In this chapel, only Holy Mass is to be held. We permit him to hold more than one Holy Mass per day. It is permited that anyone shall be allowed to fulfill the requirments and practice all religious duties, even the Easter duties in his prosperous house or in any other one, between him and whoever lives with him, or whoever is present with him then. On November 26, 1827.

The Humble Youssef Hebeish, Patriarch. "

- - - - -

"We acknowledge the requiems requested from us every year for His Excellency Prince Haidar Ahmed, as it is described below. This is in return for the income and the properties donated to our Monastery from His Excellency, ,from the leaders of our Monastery. and from the headmasters who preceded us: Father Martinous in the year 1799, until the era of Father Tobia, Father Matia, and Father Nicholas up to today; all, with their full and complete satisfaction. Among those councillors who were at that time and according to their documents, previously sent to His Excellency, as it will be correctly explained later:

'From the grinding mill of Bou Hassan, two hundred requiems during his life and after his death, so be it. A requiem every Saturday morning for a whole year as well as on every Friday evening, the total of that, forty-eight requiems each for every year, so be it. Following that, the requiems of the day of Saint Elias Antelias' feast, from the priests present on that day, at the Saint Elias Antelias Monastery. And half of the grinding mill lease will be left during the life of His Excellency, which is 30 piasters; and, after his death, the whole lease amount of the grinding mill, to be used for the requested requiems and the charity of Saturday. So be it.'

Also, every year, all the priests present in the Saint Elias Monastery in Ghazeer, shall present requiems on the day of Saint Elias' Feast, for the intention of His Excellency every year during his life and after his death, as long as the Monastery shall exist. This is to be done in return for paying fifteen piasters and a half from the lease paid to His Excellency every year for the mentioned Monastery, and for our income in another Valley. So be it. Also, we present two hundred requiems every year for the intention of His Excellency during his life, and, after his death, on behalf of him, as long as our Monasticism exists, and for that, as repayment for the properties endowed for us by His Excellency at the borders of the Ibrahim River and Beqaq Eddine, that according to deeds we received from His Excellency and that we have in our possession. The total is 455 requiems.

The purpose of writing this is that we, the below mentioned names, the headmaster and the Antonian councillor monks of Saint Sha'ia, are sworn in what we should do for His Excellency, Our Beloved Prince Haidar Ahmed, the respected. And. that every year, they will present requiems for him during his life and on behalf of him after his death, four hundred and forty-eight requiems every year, as it is registered above. Moreover, all the priests present on the day of Saint Elias Antelias' feast and at Saint Elias' Ghazeer Monastery, will present their requiems for His

Excellency's intention every year in his life and after his death. All those written requiems are requested from us and from our children after us, as long as our Monastery exists.

We have written this document from us to His Excellency to our full satisfaction, and affirm that we have done so without obligation or force of any kind.

Written on December 1, 1811.
Abdulallah, Fourth Councillor;   Morqos, Third Councillor;
Guanadious, Antonian Councillor;   Samanous, First Councillor; and,
*   Youssef (Al Shababi), General Superior, Antonian Priest*

These historical documents which we have transferred in their original texts are from the registers of the Patriarchal See and the Mar Sha'ia Monastery of the Antonian Order, which the Prince enriched with endowments and donations. In exchange, he put the condition of presenting the requiems for his intention during his life and for the peace of his soul after his death.

All this shows the great charitable acts of that very pious Prince, his strong faith showing through his benevolent deeds and prayers; especially the sanctifying of the holy Mass, which he attended daily with sincere worship.

The endowments of Prince Haidar were to be found in most of the Maronite Churches and Monasteries, in addition to the Roman Catholic Monasteries in Al Shouf, at the west, in Al Metn, Kisrawan, Jbail, and in the North. In all parts of Lebanon, we find one of the Prince's kind vestiges, which makes him a shining example of benevolence and charitable deeds. This example for the princes of the Christians and their rich people is to gain the benediction for themselves in this life. They should be doing as the saying of the Prophet David expressed it:

"God, bless those working on the beauty of Your House. "   The diadem of glory is in the happiness of the afterlife.

The Historian Prince

It is one of our duties to mention the patriotic and scientific contributions of this great man, not just generous and religious ones. He created, without intention, his famous history, just by writing down the details about the governement of Lebanon during the era of the Shehabians from 1698 until his death in 1834. This history has many lines and verses, different in their length and abbreviation. At the end of last century, the Lebanese Professor Naoum Meghabgheb published it in Egypt. Then, the Lebanese Ministry of Education published the last chapters talking about the government of the Shehabian Princes by two Professors, Asad Rostom and Fouad Al Boustani, in 1933.

Although there was enormous benefits from publishing that book, neither publisher had the original handwritten copy.

This writer has succeeded in finding the original copy, the only remaining one, the precious manuscripts of this great book. It is a precious manuscript written with the generous Prince's own hand, but was unknown for many years. When it was reviewed, and the hand writing compared, we became certain that it is his.

This precious antique manuscript was almost taken out of Lebanon, because when it was quoted to some friends, they refused to buy it, saying that it wasn't of any significant value and that the book had already been published.

Our friend, the gifted Dr. Philip K. Hitti knew about it. So, he asked to buy it on behalf of the American Princeton University, where he is the Director of the Oriental History Department. The price was 1650 Lebanese liras.

However, those at the Ministry of Education, who knew its true value, became involved in the dealings. They informed those responsible individuals about it and about the necessity of keeping this precious vestige in Lebanon. They pointed out that it is one of the great proofs of Lebanese history, virtue, and nobility. Therefore, the ministry bought the manuscript at the mentioned price and put it in the National Library.

The last thing remaining to be mentioned is that from the offspring of Prince Haidar, only five daughters remain. They are: 1. The Lady Fanous, surnamed, Oum (the mother of) Effendi, and the wife of Prince Beshir the Great. 2. The Lady Badie'a surnamed, Oum (the mother of) Fa'our, and the wife of Prince Hassan Ali in Charoun Valley, and the mother of Mansour and Khalil. 3. The Lady Jamila, the wife of Mostafa Abi Al Lam' from Al Shabania. 4. The Lady Habous surnamed, Oum (the mother of) Abbass. 5. The Lady Asma. Their mother died in 1842.

Al Erian House

Their origin

The forefather of the Al Erian house was living in Kafr Salwan since the begining of the Lam's princes era. Erian died around the year 1750 and he begot four sons: Fares, Saad, Girgis, and Youssef. The four sons emigrated after a dispute between them and the citizens. So, Fares and Saad went to the countryside regions. Fares lived in Saadnayel and Saad in Jediteh. Some say that the Nahra House in Jediteh are the offspring of Saad; and, a remaining number of them lived in Zahle and are still known there today as Ashy Al Bachaalany.

Girgis emigrated to Al Shabania in Al Metn. As for Youssef Al Erian he lived in Salima under the protection of the princes of Abi Al Lam'.

Fares Al Erian who lived in Saadnayel, he begot Youssef who begot Elias, the famous faithful man.

Once, an English tourist was passing by Saadnayel and forgot a big suitcase. Elias found it, so he took it home and hid it in a secret place so that even his family did not know about it. Then, he went to Zahle and appointed a crier to call out in the Souk (popular market), and, he requested the priests to announce at the churches that: so-and–so in Saadnayel has found something that was lost. Whoever has lost something declare its marks we will return it to them. Three days passed and nobody clamed it.

Thus, Elias went to Beirut and there he did the same thing he had done in Zahle. On the third day, a messenger from the British Consulate came to the crier asking for the lost suitcase. He asked him to go to the Consulate with the person who found the suitcase. The British tourist, the owner of the suitcase was there and described its marks, shape and the content. The description matched the suitcase, so Al Erian went with someone from the Consulate, to Saadnayel. They came back with the suitcase to Beirut where it was opened because it was closed with an iron lock. It was opened in the presence of the Consulate's clerks and the owner of the suitcase, who was one of the Noble British Princes, with his spouse. When the big suitcase was opened, the following items were found in it: **1.** Four golden bags containing two thousand English pounds. **2.** A collar of diamonds costing no less than one thousand pounds. **3.** A pair of gold ornate items with precious stones priced at 500 pounds. **4.** Four pairs of earings costing 300 pounds. **5.** Rings with diamonds costing 100 pounds. **6.** Three items mostly table ustensils: Gold spoons, forks, and knives. **7.** A box containing gold ornate drinking glasses. **8.** A box containing an inkwell and pencils to write made of gold. **9.** Wedding pictures of the Lord and his spouse in golden frames. **10.** Precious antiques and different marriage staffs belonging to him and to his spouse.

The audience noticed that the man who found the suitcase wasn't astonished at seeing the precious antiques which dazzled their eyes. And, he showed no signs of regreting that he had returned the lost suitcase with honesty to its owner. On the contrary, he was calm and cool, happy that he accomplished his duty with honor and honesty.

The Lord asked him with the typical British coolness and said: "What do you wish and want?" Al Erian answered: "I won't ask for more than 6 Beshalek, the amount I paid to the crier." That made the audience laugh when they heard it. The Lord said: "Whatever I give you, will be no where near as rare or as valuable as your honesty and honor deserve. However, I would like you to accept this small amount as a souvenir." Then he gave him 25 English pounds. Also, he gave him a promissory note that every month, he will receive from the Consulate in Beirut a monthly salary of 5 golden pounds for as long as he lives. So, Elias Al Erian left and went to his home. And, for a long time, he was cashing a monthly payment until he died.

The British Prince published the story of that honest Lebanese man, in his country's newspapers. Then, Elias Al Erian died, and he had no children. Thus, the offshoot of Al Erian ended at Saadnayel.

Al Erian House In Al Shabania

As for Girgis Al Erian, he held a position in the countryside. One of his offspring was Girgis Bin Shahin, who was famous. He was the one who contacted the Harafish in Baalbek. He was surnamed "the flagholder" because he would hold the flag, use his sword and carbine, all while riding horseback! He frequented the house of the Lam's Princes in Al Shabania. He married Almaz, the daughter of Al Namar from the Roman Catholic congregation in that village. He lived there and his descendants still do today. His children and grand-children have followed the doctrine of the Roman Catholic Church. Girgis died around 1880. He begot two sons, Assaf and Youssef. Youssef had only girls. Assaf begot Girgis, Najib, Hanna, and Anton. The first three died during the First World War and were unmarried and young.

As for Anton, he is the last one remaining from this family whose offspring has not increased in Al Shabania. He is one of the old employees of the Singer Company that makes sewing machines. He is in Beirut in the good job because of his honesty, action, and capability. He has a good standing in his country and is one of its notables. He has had four sons and three daughters: John, George, Najib, and Josef. As for the girls, they were lucky. Two of them, Helene (Marie Madelaine) and Georgette (Antoinette) joined the Hanaweya Convent of the Roman Catholics.

Their Lineage

Youssef Al Erian, who lived in Salima, begot Moussa, Elias, Shahin, and Nahra. Nahra begot Abdou Al Agha who died in Al Chiyah and had no children.

Shahin begot Youssef and Fares. Fares begot Mikhail. This latter had Daher who had no children.

Moussa begot Nejm and Hanna. Nejm had Girgis and Youssef. Girgis begot Assaf and Hanna. Assaf begot Nejm and Abdou who died young and unmarried in Mexico. As for Nejm Bin Assaf, he begot Youssef and Jamil who died when he was a child. Youssef is an expatriate in Africa and has daughters. Hanna Bin Girgis Nejm begot Mansour and Girgis, who are expatriates in Brazil and have children.

Youssef Bin Nejm Bin Moussa begot Ibrahim and Boutros. Ibrahim begot Melhem and Elias. Melhem begot Halim who begot Samir and Melhem. As for Elias, he had only Malaka who married a young man from Ras Al Harf.

Boutros Bin Youssef Bin Nejm begot Daoud and Youssef. Daoud has emigrated to Brazil and has a son. Youssef begot Abdou.

Hanna Bin Moussa Bin Youssef Al Erian begot Mansour, Moussa, and Elias. As for Mansour, he begot Shahin, Boutros, and Khalil. Shahin begot Youssef who begot Habib, Naguib, Ibrahim, and Rashid. The three died unmarried. Rashid is an emigrant with the Texaco Company in the United States and has children.

Boutros Mansour begot Mansour and Daoud who both died young, and only Saady, Shams, and Mary remain. Khalil Mansour begot Selim and Ibrahim. Selim had Aziz the emigrant in the United States who has children. Ibrahim had only Liza, the wife of Fedaa Hanna Youssef. Moussa Bin Hanna begot Hanna, Noaman, and Asaad. Hanna had Moussa, Khalil, and Moussa. The two Moussa's died young. Khalil had only Rose and Helene.

As for Noaman Bin Moussa, he died young and unmarried. Asaad begot Tawfik and Noaman. Tawfik had children and died in Brazil while Noaman is still unmarried.

Elias Bin Hanna Moussa begot Tanious and Nasef. Tanious had Moussa and Karim who died young. Only Mary, the wife of Youssef, the son of her paternal uncle Nasef, remained.

Meanwhile, Nasef Bin Elias begot Youssef, Qablan, and Elias. Youssef begot Michel and Nasef. Qablan begot Raymond, and others whose names we don't know. Elias had children whose names we don't know. Both of these latter are expatriates.

Elias Bin Youssef Al Erian begot Youssef who had Abdou, Hanna, and Girgis. Hanna died young and Abdou begot Youssef, Elias, Shahin, and Mikhail. Youssef Bin Abdou begot Abdou, Amin, and Khalil. Abdou had Habib and George.

Amin and Khalil are in the United States and had children. Elias Bin Abdou lived in Qabelias and begot Halim, Selim, and Najib. The two first are in Argentina and Najib is in Africa.

Shahin Bin Abdou begot Fares who begot Shahin and Mikhail. Mikhail Bin Abdou is an expatriate and has children.

Girgis Bin Youssef Al Erian begot Hanna, Shaker, and Assaf. Hanna begot Mansour, Melhem, Daoud, and Michel. As for Mansour, he begot Girgis and Boutros. Melhem begot Philip, Heikel, 'Oql, and Louis. Daoud begot Antoin, John, and Josef.

Michel Bin Hanna begot Morris and Elias. Shaker Bin Girgis Bin Youssef begot Shokry, Youssef, and Elias. The two first died and Elias begot Nasef and Shaker.

As for Assaf Bin Girgis Bin Youssef, he begot Girgis, Najib, Qazahia, and Mikhail. Girgis Bin Assaf begot Khalil, Assaf, Elias, Michel, Antoin, Boutros, Josef, and Edward. Khalil and Elias died young. Assaf begot Fawzi and others whose names we don't know. The same is true for Michel who also had children.

Abdou Agha Al Erian

We previously said that Youssef, the forth son of Al Erian, was the one who moved from Kafr Salwan and lived in Salima during the era of Prince Ismail Abi Al Lam' around the year 1750. He begot four sons: Moussa, Elias, Shahin, and Nahra who begot Abdou.

We also previously talked about Nahra, saying that he was known for his strength, as well as the biography of his son Abdou. Now we should briefly talk about Abdou Agha and his vestiges which are many. We should start by saying that he is Abdou Bin Nahra Bin Youssef Al Erian Bachaalany. He was orphan and frequented Hasbeya which was near Salima. When he was a child, he played with his friends, and his arrow almost always won the game, beating his fellows in the popular games in Lebanon such as Tangook (Knukle-bones) and Dokook (using wooden sticks).

It happened one day that Prince Beshir the Great was passing by Hasbeya, coming from the Princes' castle in Salima. He was going in the direction of the Princes' castle in Al Matyan. It was around the year 1795. He saw a boy carrying under his arms a number of wooden sticks. On his shoulder he had a bag of knukle-bones which he won from the children of Hasbeya. So, the Prince asked his servants about the boy. They informed him that he was from Salima from the Bachaalany clan. Then, the Prince asked him: "What's your name, and what are you doing here?" The boy replied boldly: "My name is Abdou and I played with the boys of Hasbeya and won all of their knukle-bones and wooden sticks. If any of those boys wants to attack me, I'll hit him and defeat him." The Prince, with his usual perspicacity, knew that the boy had a promising future. The marks of genius and courage could be seen in his face. After that he turned to Elias Abi Ragheb Bachaalany, who was accompanying him. "Mir Yakhour" was in his castle, so, he ordered him to take Abdou and keep him in Beit ed Dine.

The boy learned horse riding and all types of skills of knighthood. He mastered tham all and became one of the greatest swordsmen and army commanders in the Prince's government. He rose to a position of high privilege with the Prince and accompanied him in many of the well known battles, as previously mentioned. He was given the title Agha in 1821 by Mohamed Aly Pasha, while accompaniying the Prince on his visit to Egypt. It was a reward for Abdo, recognizing his bravery and spirit of knighthood.

In 1829, Abdou was one of the commanders of the Army of Prince Khalil, the son of Prince Beshir, at the Sanour Battle, as well as in the Shabaa battles of 1835.

While Prince Amin, the son of Prince Beshir, appointed him treasurer and his counselor, and this was even after his father, Beshir The Great, had gone into exile. Prince Beshir was exiled in 1840 to Malta and Istanbul. Prince Amin died in 1850 and had no children.

It seems that Abdou Agha did not accompany Prince Beshir into exile. Instead, he remained in Lebanon managing the properties of the Prince and his children.

I noticed the name of Abdou Bachaalany in the Register of Compensations after the national riot in 1845. The register was kept by Shekib Effendi, the Ambassador of the Sultan. Abdou's name was among the names of the afflicted people in Rechmaya. He was probably there, at that time, supervising the properties of the Shehabian princes, the properties of the previously mentioned Prince Amin, and those of his wife, the Lady Fanous in Al Set (the Lady) Valley, which was named after her.

Abdou Agha chose a wife for himself from the beautiful bondmaids who were in the service of Prince Beshir the Great. She was Hosn Gihan (Beauty of Life) and they wed. They begot Saady and So'oud. That was after the death of first wife Shams Shehab, the mother of his children Qassem, Khalil, and Amin. He spent the last years of his life in Al Shieyah and died there after buying up a large number of properties. We ascertained this from the vestiges we print below:

"Attention, our dear and respected Abdou Agha Bachaalany, God save him.

Longing to see you in good spirits and healthy.

We received your letter and we knew that you are well, and, when you mentioned that you are missing us, we prayed God to bless you. From our side, we thank God that, at the present, we are living in complete luxury. And to please you, we so inform you, our beloved, and keep in contact.

On November 26, 1843. (Stamp) Amin Shehab.

Note: Concerning the clothes, deliver them all to our son, Sadek Agha, sending them to this address. Also, show him the box of papers so he can make copies of some them and send them to us. The original agreements he will return to the box and send them all back to remain with you in its proper place. (Stamp) Trusting in God. Amen. (Under this expression there are the Masonic symbols: the scale, the compass, and the yardstick)."

- - - - -

"We received from the Excellency, uncle Abdou Agha, five electrical aperture, complete with their accessories, as usual, among them an aperture with a ring made of Zaghir Diamond. They are to be handed to His Excellency, Our Beloved Prince Amin Al Shehabi, in Istanbul. We wrote this reference for clarification. It was written by the mentioned uncle according to the known procedures for doing so. Written on January 10, 1843, by Sadek Mamlouk."

- - - - -

"A list of the items that we have received from Abdou Agha and which belong to His Excellency, the Beloved Prince Amin Al Shehabi: One red tablecloth made of Silk; 7 engraved pipes; 1 Mirror box; 1 Musket with silver bracelets; 1 Musket with copper bracelets; and, 1 Silver plated Islambouly Sword. – The reason for writing this is that the above items are per the order of Prince Amin Al Shehabi. I received them personally from his servant Abdou Agha in order to sell them and deposit the monies received of the above to the hand of his representative. And in order to confirm this, I gave him this receipt on Shaaban 3, 1261.

(Stamp) Written by Mikhail Abdulallah Antaki."

- - - - -

"The reason for writing this, upon the order of the respected Affendem Prince Amin Al Shehabi, I have received the horse which was with Abdou Agha and made him swear concerning all the items belonging to His Excellency, namely, that there are no other remaining items. I gave him this receipt as requested. Written on March 9, 1261 Hegira. Mikhail Abdullah Antaki. (Stamp)"

- - - - -

"The reason for writing this is to confirm that I, undermentioned name, Fanous, the daughter of Prince Haidar Ahmed Al Shehab, with my full satisfaction, stating that I am completely alert and healthy, have received from our dear servant, Abdou Bachaalany, sixty-nine thousand, five hundred piasters, and, sixty piasters in Derham coins, with one piaster equaling forty coins, and that I gave to him from my own property which I dispose of, with my consent and full satisfaction, in the attendance of the assessors Metri Wahbi and Girgis Wahbi from E. Choueifat, and Faragallah Barbour from Kfar Chima, four hundred and fifty banknotes.... The whole or any part are limited to the mentioned money and have no right to require or sue in anyway, and there is no suspicion of missing money during his entire terms of service. And, in order to clarify everything before everybody, and to stop any suspicion and any objection, we wrote this act, clearing him from any suit. We permitted this to be witnessed by the undersigned names, with our signature and stamp. This was done with our representative. We have so authorized Elias Madi and his son, Beshara. Written on Shawal 7, comparable to October 9, 1845.

Its writer – The mother of Effendi Shehab M

Witnesses: Beshara Madi, Elias Madi Mikhail,
Abdulallah Antaki, Fanous Shehab.
(The stamp)

- - - - -

" .... *His Excellency Prince Najib, his sisters their Excellencies, the Ladies: Khadouj, Hola, Zahr, Miss, Leila, and the children of the late Prince Gehgeah Al Shehabi, have sold what is their own, and that which they legally purchased from Her Excellency, the Lady Asma, the daughter of the late Prince Haidar Ahmed Al Shehabi .... The sold items are two carats from the twenty four carats of the Al Akss garden situated in the Al Shieyah lands, and containing Mulberries ...etc. They are bordered from the South with the properties of Her Excellency, the Lady Jamila; from the North and the East, the property of the buyer; and, from the West, the properties of the children of Habib Al Melhama ..... This mentioned sale includes the right of using the water of the famous Al Chiyah canal, as per our shares of incomes and that of the keeper of this act ...our dear Abdou Agha Bachaalany ...and the price is eight hundred piasters ....and by finalizing this, validating and concluding it, the mentioned sellers have sold to the mentioned buyer twenty two carats in Al Akss garden at the price of one thousand and four hundred piasters and twelve and a half piasters ... written on April 24, 1847. We acknowledge what has been set forth here by: Prince Najib, the son of Prince Gehgeah Al Shehabi, the Lady Khadouj, the daughter of Prince Gehgeah, the Lady Khola, the Lady Zahr, the Lady Miss ..the lady Leila ..the witnesses of the act: Ali Shehab, Asaad Shehab, Haidar Shehab, Ali Shehab, Melhem Shehab, Ibrahim El Shene'e, and. Salouma Bou Moussa."*

- - - - -

" ...*we sold what belongs to us ...what belongs to us through legal heritage from our deceased father, may God shelter him with his mercy and satisfaction ....twenty carats from twenty four carats of mulberry grove Al Shieyah. It contains buildings and a wall of 150 mulberry trees ...the mulberry grove is bordered from the South by a road, from the North by the properties of our sister, Her Excellency, the mother of Prince Abass, from the East the properties of our son, His Excellency, the referred to Prince, and, from the West by the properties of our sister, Her Excellency, the mother of Prince Fa'our which is well known by the quarters separating all those other properties from each other. Included are the vines and the wall in Al Chiyah field bordered from the South by the road, from the North, the properties of the Endowment and of Mansour Al Berbary, from the East, the properties of our sister, Her Excellency, the mother of Prince Fa'our, from the West, our properties and those of our mentioned sister ... to our dear Abdou Agha Bachaalany, for the price of ten thousand piasters for twenty carats ...at the end of Ramadan in the year 1260, acknowledge and admitted by the mother of Effendi Shehab. (Stamp) Fanous Shehab, Witnesses: Domt Me'awad; Hatem Al Ashqar; Beshara Madi; Elias Madi."*

There is another deed, with the same date, place, and content for four carats of the mentioned property at the price of twelve thousand piasters from the Lady Fanous to Abdou Agha.

" ... *His Excellency, the respectable Prince Najib Gehgeah Al Shehabi, came and sold what is his property, and which belonged to him through a legal inheritance ....to Abdou Agha Bachaalany from the village of Shieyah ...a piece of land situated along the irrigation ditch of Al Shieyah known as Al Akss garden, containing plants of mulberry, pomegranate, and .... Along with this sale are the water rights, the right of irrigating from the public water, bordered from the East, the properties of the mentioned buyer; from the West, the water canal, from the South, the property of Her Excellency, the Lady Oum (the mother of) Abbass, the Shehabi; and, from the North, the properties of the buyer. For the price of one thousand and two hundred piasters ....written on October 6, 1851, Christian year. The acknowledging and admitting, is Najib Shehab. (Stamp). Witnesses: Ibrahim Al Shamayel from Kfar Chima, the authorised Tanous from Al Shieyah, and, Asaad Zakaria from Kfar Chima."*

- - - - -

"I, the undersigned name, testify before God and his servants, that Mansour Madi from Rechmaya is owed by the Lady Oum Effendi, the wife of Prince Beshir Shehab, one hundred piasters, as part of his salary that he deserves for his work as her servant. The mentioned Mansour has asked her for the mentioned money through me. However, she has not paid him. Instead, she kept the money, holding it, trying to oblige said Mansour to return to her service. This is what we know and testified to. as God is our witness. Written upon request on August 6, 1852. Abdou Bachaalany. Beshara Madi. Written as it was given in the presence of its writer, Father Youssef Nejm."

- - - - -

From Aintoura to Al Shieh on July 12, 1861

Dear Uncle,
This year has been short and long at the same time. It seemed to me that it was endless when I was thinking about the pleasure of seeing you again and kissing you. But when I thought about how much I have to know for tests, I become afraid of how short it is.
How can we ever complain about how long time is if we only stop to think how quickly it disappears. It is long only for those who don't know how to spend it.
Things are so busy around this house: my studies, practices of piety, games and entertainments. All that makes the day so short.
August 14 is the day of they distribute the awards. Thus, this will be the last letter you will receive from me for this school year. Also, I will be busy with preparations for the feast of St. Vincent de Paul which is coming in just eight days.
We have all submitted our essays for the awards' presentation. I am hoping mine will receive one. So, uncle, only the final exam remains and we have been studying for that since Easter.
Dear uncle, I never fail to mention you and my grandmother in my prayers, asking him to give mercy and all his blessings.
Goodbye, dear uncle, I kiss your hands as well as the hands of my grandmother.
I am your everlasting,
respectful and affectionate nephew.
Melhem Nahra

- - - - -

"In the name of God, Father, Son, and Holy Spirit, One God, Amen. – I, Abdou Bin Nahra Bachaalany, dwelling in Al Shieyah, admit that my belief is in all that the Roman Apostolic Holy Church believes. With this belief I have lived and I will die embracing it. Since death is a divine duty, we should fulfill it properly. I am fulfilling this divine duty and I accept the obligation by issuing my will, and paying for my many sins. God, may He be exalted, has told us to prepare for death because it is certain, and, so, I already wrote my last will and testament which I am now renewing.

Since God, during this life, has granted me wealth as a reward for my efforts, I acknowledge that they consist of properties which are known and situated in the village of Shieyah, including houses, outstanding loans, movable items, and everything else known to be mine. Thus, accepting my generous God's desire, and coveting the great reward of heaven, I order that a percentage of my estate be spent on my funeral, then, distributions are to be made, such as the value of three carats of my whole estate for the priests of my Maronite Congregation with a kind request for requiems and kindness to be shown on my behalf at my funeral. And I wish to give two carats of the original 24 carats of my entire estate as a donation for poor of the new Maronite Bishopric School of Beirut in Bait Mari. From the whole written inheritance, I wish to give 1/3 carat as a charity to the poor of the two Maronite parishes at the mentioned Bishopric of Beirut. Also, to give one carat, a third of a carat and half of a third carat to be under the disposition of Saint Michael's Church in Al Shieyah. For the poor of Elm Al Awlad in al Shieyah, I give them one and a quarter of a third carat. All of this mentioned above is to be given and distributed to the parties as described above, with the exception of my funeral expenses which shall consist of a third of my entire estate, i.e eight carats from the original twenty four carats.

I appoint as executor of my estate, Bishop Tobia 'Oun the Bishop of Beirut, most respected, who I am asking to accept this assignment and carry out the terms of this last will and testament. I plead that he will be responsible for making the donations and distributions as I have stated above. For this I have assigned up to a third of my entire estate. All this, to gain God's pleasure and hoping for his great reward. I rely on His Eminence to fulfill and execute this testament. Whatever remains of my estate after my funeral and the mentioned thirds, is to be divided among my heirs according to law. I bequeath this to them with the instruction that each shall be content with his share and not covet what I have given to others. There shall be no disputes or conflicts as that will only bring spiritual and physical losses. My dictates in this testament are within my legal rights and the results of a good conscience with no violations of anyone else's rights. Finally, I ask God to fogive me, and I ask the forgiveness of anyone who I may have ever offended in anyway. And, I forgive anyone who has offended me in anyway. I leave my soul to My Creator, wishing this to be my last testament. I ask it to be witnessed as that by those whose names appear below. Written on May 23, 1865. Admitting to all that is written and it is attributed to Abdou Nahra Bachaalany from Al Shieyah. (stamp). Raji Lotfallah Abdou 1,250 Hegira. Written by Father Youssef Nejm. The witnesses: Estephan Kanaan Neama; Hanna Kanaan Neama; Khalil, the son of Anton Effendi from Baabada; and Nejm, the son of Antonious from Majdel Meouch."

- - - - -

"The accounting of the estate of the late Abdou Agha Bachaalany, August 6, 1865.

Bearing mulberry groves, 180 of them, at the price of 225 each = 40,500; olive and vines, 5 thounsand; house furniture, 4,470; outstanding debts to be claimed, 12,737; cash money and other liquid holdings, 9,792. Total, 72,498. To pay from this amount, the fees of the funeral: 2,600 for Father Youssef Nejm; 700 for debts; 247, the quarters of the mulberry groves' partners, 2,190. The total, 4,737, leaving a balance of 67,761.

The above mentioned amount is to be divided as indicated in the last will and testament: a third for requiems, 8,470; the Bishopric See, 5,647; its poor, 1,176; the Church of Al Shieyah 4,235; the School of Al Shieyah, 3,058 piasters. The total, 22,586. The obligation for the wife, a quarter of the remaining portion, 11,294. For the paternal cousin, a sum of 33,881. The total, 67,761."

- - - - -

This paternal cousin is Nejm Bin Youssef Al Erian, the only heir of Abdou Agha. The amount was cashed in by Nahra Sowayd, the son of the sister of Abdou, but his name was not mentioned in the accounting of the heirs nor in the legal parties, because Abdou Agha gave Nahra, the son of his sister Zahri, all the properties and homes in Salima. Accordingly, he left Beirut where he had lived for a long time and went to live in Salima.

"... a detailed declaration for the fundamental heirs of the inheritance of the lateAbdou Bachaalany: Mansour Hanna Moussa Al Erian, and, his two brothers, Elias and Moussa, 3000 piasters for each. Girgis Youssef Shahin and his brother, 2000 piasters, 1000 for each. Mikhail, the son of Fares Shahin and his brother, 2000, 1000 for each; Girgis Bou Saber, 500; the wife of Daher Al Eishy, 500; the wife of Shahin Boutros. 500; Nour, the wife of Metri Al Sayegh, 500; Youssef Bin Nejm, 1000 piasters.

An amount of 1,200 piasters interest with the debt balance, was paid before its due date, making a total of 8,800 piasters received. Fares Anton Abou Anton, from Salima, who was at that time the treasurer of the Metn district, has received this amount from Bishop Tobia on May 22, 1866, with directions to distribute it to the mentioned heirs."

- - - - -

"In the name of the Father, the Son, and the Holy Spirit, the One God. Amen. – I, Mary, the wife of Abdou, the son of Nahra Bachaalany, living in the village of Shieyah, declare and admit that I belong to the Roman Apostolic Holy Church ....etc.. I want to write down my last will and testament. As I am a stranger in this life, and since I have no surviving relative with a right to my inheritance, except for my husband, Abdou Al Agha, the son of the mentioned Nahra Bachaalany. Whereas my estate consists of properties in the village of Shieyah including the lemon garden, are managed by Girgis Mofawad who takes a third of its crop as his salary, but who has no legal right of inheritance in it. Also in the estate are the grove of mulberry and different type of fruit trees, with two houses ...and a third house situated in the district near the Endowment Building, as well as jewelries, etc.. From this estate, I wish for it to be spent as such: for my funeral, seven carats; charity to be donated to the Saint John Endowment in Salima, one carat, to complete the third. From the seven mentioned carats, it is spent for requiems and the funeral. Another part is to be distributed as charity for the two Maronite congregations in the Bishopric of Beirut. The rest, which is the remaining two thirds: one third, which is half of the remaining amount, is for my mentioned husband and it his share as per the law. The remaining third will be an eternal endowment, seizing forever a blessing of the generous God and seeking an eternal reward. This last third is for the poor of the School of the Maronite Bishropric of Beirut, which recently has been moved to Beit Meri. If some of this is not permissible, should my husband's death come before mine, so he will not be able to take his legal share of my estate, then, I wish for his portion to be added in and donated to the poor of the school already mentioned. As the executor for my last will and testament, I appoint His excellency Father Youssef Nejm, the attendant of the mentioned location under the supervision of the Supreme Bishop Tobia 'Oun, Bishop of the mentined Bishopric, who deseves all respect ... written on June 28, 1865. Admitting what have been dictated, Mary, wife of Andou Nahra Bachaalany. Witnesses: Hanna Al Khoury Bou Diwan from Al Sefily, and, Anton Neama from Al Shieyah. Confirmed by Abdou, husband of the mentioned woman. (Stamp) Written by Khalil Lahoud Al Labkeh from Baabadate."

- - - - -

The beautiful Mary, wife of Abdou Agha, died in Al Shieyah on May 11, 1867. She was buried on the 12th, in the cemetry of her husband. Her will was executed with the inheritance that she received from her husband's estate.

The Jewelry Of The Widow Of Abdou Agha

"These items included: one pair of golden bracelets; one pair of golden cub-braclets with two quarter chains hung on it; a coniferous golden chain with 30 big hearts hung on it, then with 30 half smooth jehadi, then also hung on it, three gold pieces, and, between each heart, a golden ring; a big golden necklace with a golden crucifix on which are hanging three full golden soft-mint ottoman coins and, on the necklace, hang six gold pieces. Also, a golden necklace with 32 hearts hanging on it, 32 quarter chains, then a golden heart, with three personalized gold pieces; a golden Buckle with a curled knit on the circle with five chains, each chain being personalized gold. There was also a golden amulet with 5 halves of ancient Ghazi hung on with a golden chain; three pairs of silver bracelets; ...and a silver pan for cloth; earings made of gold with silver plated hooks; a silver buckle having three small jewels; one small silver relic. And, one large silver garb with a silver chain; 3 pearl-studded silverware items; 3 silver plates and 2 silver pins; a silver pocketwatch; one silver watch with coral; a golden box; 8 silver rings; a small silver

amulet; ...one silver bracellet. All items comprise 32 pieces only, and no more. Written by Father Youssef Nejm. (stamp)."

Her Clothes

"Broadcloth with new silver threads; a new broadcloth overcoat; a new embroidered broadcloth with new silver thread; 8 pieces of weaving; a muslin curtain; a cotton tunic; ... an embroidered broadcloth with heavy threads; yellowish tunic; a black tunic made of linty; am ancient silk piece; 2 tunics made of cashmere; 5 silk shirts; an untailored veil; 10 coloured pieces and 10 others; 3 large bourgeois towels; half a cotton shawl or scarf; embroidered pleated ruffles; embroidered cloth; 2 combs made of bone; and, a mirror. All items make 47 pieces and no more, except for silk and miscellaneous pieces.

Written by Father Youssef Nejm. (Stamp)."

In Shieyah, there remains an eternal remnant of the life of Abdou Agha Bachaalany, the Lieutnant Colonel of Prince Beshir, the Great. It is found in the Church of Saint Michael. This is the same church and school to which he donated holdings of real estate which cost thousands of Liras, not to mention the donations he made for the poor of the Beirut Bishopric, as you read in his last will and testament and that of his wife.

This relic consists of historical verses carved in a marble piece. Abdou Bachaalany supervised the construction of it when he was alive. He built it beside the Church of Saint Michael in Shieyah. It bears these verses:

God cultivated this Bachaalany grave. He called to him and he responded and God bestowed on him his reward.
On his grave is his history: 'God came to his house calling him, the Lord has chosen his servant'.
1865
When the Bachaalany people came, asking where he was going, God's Angel replied that he knew: 'Our wish is for this servant of the Lord to glorify Him in Heaven.'
1865

Sadly, when they renovated the church, they demolished the tomb and transported the remains of Abdou Bachaalany to another place in the Eastern Church Wall. On the outside portion they placed a piece of marble with the date on it. Then, when they built the annex to the school next to the church, the marble was moved inside one of the rooms, now hidden and unseen. It was put in an unsuitable place for such a man. He performed so many good deeds and made so many donations to the Church and school .

We have brought this matter to the attention of the individuals responsible for endowments. We tried to make our case that it end the years of neglect and give Abdou Agha his proper honor. Especially, the Church should perform the annual requiems which were imposed as part of the endowment when the will was executed. They should fulfill the requiems just as the Bishop does.

In Shieyah, there was a priest named Father Youssef Nejm from the Moubarak family of Bqatoute. He left his village and became a servant in Shieyah during the era of Bishop Tobia 'Oun who appointed him as Bishopric Representative in Al Sahel.

The funerals of both of Abdou Agha and his wife were performed by this hounorable priest. He also was the executor disbursed their donations.

Nahra Soward House

Their Origin

The late Melhem Bin Nahra Sowayd has a manuscript in which there is a handwritten historical biography of the Bachaalany family. The origin of the family is mentioned in the manuscript without any references to documents or papers that the author relied on. That is probably why he wrote rather loosely in some of his narrations and information. This is especially true of him when he was talking about the ancient origins of the family and the family name. This approach is contrary to the established method for historical research and reporting. It easily results in stories that are incompatible with reality, and with facts relayed by genius historians like El Douaihy, De Le Roque, Al Debs, and many others.

Besides the above historians, we have cited the original documents preserved in our archives. They are our proof for what we have described in this book about our family origins and its name.

It was appropriate for Sheikh Melhem to mention, at the very least, his origins and his relationship with the Bachaalanys, but he didn't. He simply mentioned the following phrase below:

> *"After Abdou Agha Nahra Al Erian, the son of his sister, Nahra Sowayd Bachaalany, received the title of 'Notable...'"*

He then continued with his narration but without mention of how there would be an in-law connection or, specifically, what the maternal relationships was with that family. He doesn't give us any real information about his origins.

Accordingly, we have seriously considered denying his claim of origins. It is an honor to belong to the family of his maternal uncle and to hold that name. And we recorded that he even called himself "Machaalany" not "Bachaalany". He actually gave up the wrong name! He abandoned the Bachaalany name for himself, as well as his children and grandchildren. This has caused a mess and a great deal of confusion for so many good people. Many believed his rediculou tale which was just trying to pick a name that sounded a little nicer than the real name.

From the Sowayd Family, we know only the name of "Sowayd Bin Nofal" which we saw in an ancient document in our archives; and, the name of "Girgis Sowayd who died in Ras Beirut in the year 1842". Further, we know that Sowayd married "Zahri", the daughter of Nahra Al Erian and the sister of Abdou. We know that Sowayd and Zahri begot Nahra, Nejma (who married Shahin Boutros Abi Khnesar Bachaalany), and Nour (the wife of Metri Al Sayegh). Moreover, we know that Nahra was the servant of Prince Amin, the son of Prince Beshir The Great while he was in Beit ed Dine at the same time that Abdou Agha, his maternal uncle, was there.

When the Prince travelled with his family, in 1840, to Malta then to Istambul, Nahra became the servant of his son, Prince Amin. And among his female servants, was Helen, the daughter of Aboud Neama from Beit ed Dine. He married her and lived in Beirut for a while. Later they moved to Salima in the house and properties endowed to him by his maternal uncle, who lived in Shieyah. Then he continued to live there as did his offspring.

After that, he joined Prince Beshir Ahmed Abi Al Lam' in Ramana who occupied the position of Christian Governor in Lebanon after the death of Prince Haidar Abi Al Lam'. Prince Beshir appointed him to be the teacher of his son Prince Najib and he accompanied him to the Aintoura school. There, Melhem Bin Nahra got an opportunity to study in that famous institute.

Then, Nahra came back to Salima. He was appointed as the Sheikh of Reconciliation of the village after Tanous Freha and Fares Bin Youssef. After the death of Nahra in 1883, his son, Melhem, succeeded him in the sheikhdom of Salima as we previously mentioned. We talked about him and about his children Najib, Youssef, and Selim who studied in Salima at the Aintoura School. Then, they worked as teachers in the Eastern School at Zahle. We talked also about the appointment of Youssef as the Minister of Education, and his son Henry, the engineer, and his son Beshar, a clerk at the Ministery of Education. And we mentioned that Tawfik, the son of Najib Melhem, joined the army, staying there until he reached the rank of Lieutenent.

Their Lineage

Sowayd Bin Nofal begot Nahra who begot Melhem. Melhem begot Najib, Youssef, and Selim. Najib begot Tawfik and John, who died young. Tawfik begot Fouad and Nabih. Meanwhile, Youssef Bin Molhem begot Henry and Beshara. Henry begot Anton. Beshara begot Youssef. As for Selim, he had no children and died in the United States. All of them were the geniuses of the Bachaalany family of Salima. And, we refer to them as Bachaalany even if they deny it calling themselves Machaalany.

To preserve the historical vestiges, we are publishing the text of a letter written in French from Melhem Nahra Sowayd to Abdou Bin Nahra El Erian, the maternal uncle of his father. He sent it from Aintoura at Kisrawan where he was studying in its school. He sent it to Shieyah at the coast, where Abdou Agha was living with his wife Mary. That letter is in our archives and contains beautiful memories. Besides, it is interesting and entertaining. Youssef Melhem Nahra learned the French language and many other things at the same desk that he father sat at and learned. All at the Aintoura French Institute. Before his death, he was awarded a medal from the Academy of France as well as the Lebanese Medal of Merit.

As a final addendum to this matter of family name, we will publish, below, some paragraphs from the memorendum of Sheikh Melhem Nahra which have been preserved in our archives. They are in his own handwriting. This should be proof of what we have said about the name "Machaalany" even though he personally didn't use it. We hope this will put the matter to an end. Here is the material from the original text:

" ...in this year, 1863, a dispute took place in Salima between the two Christian congregations, the Bachaalanys and the Nakouzys. The dispute occurred because a group of the Nakouizys organized against a young Bachaalany man, seeking revenge.... A complaint was sent to Prince Mourad Abi Lam', the governor of the Metn .... The chief of the region, Prince Khalil Mostafa Abi Al Lam', came and took the testimony of both the Bachaalanys and the Nakouzys. People from both sides were sent to jail.... Some relatives of the Bachaalany family, like Nahra Sowayd Bachaalany, Fares Bin Youssef Bachaalany, and Elias Abou Assleh Bachaalany came and presented a petition to the district commissioner .....and finaly the arrested people were released."

In July, 1865, there was news about the Yellow Fever ... the people of the city went up to the mountain ... and some accidents and losses happened there. This was because some people caused troubles to the local citizens. ... and briefly, what happened in Salima was because of the maid of Ward, the wife of Hanna Khoukaz. She committed a violation against the properties, and the concierge issued her a warning. However, she became angry and insulted the concierge. In turn, he got angry and insulted her back ... She lodged a complaint against him with one of the officers who came quickly because of her husband's importance. He was the councillor (Kenkhdar) of the provencial governor in Istanbul .... When the officer learned that the concierge was a member of the Bachaalany House he asked the soldiers there to bring him in. But they informed him that they couldn't ... The officer got angry and talked very rudely to them. He pushed people and, then, raised his sword. The people wouldn't tolerate that so they attacked *him with his fellow soldiers and insulted them .... The officer went to the Prince Youssef Ali, the Governor, and informed him about what happened with the Bachaalanys .... He was afraid that this was all a plot by Youssef Beik Karam against the governmentt ....*

... In the end, the Governor sent about 600 people to Salima. Those who were upset told the government that the Bachaalany House came out of their houses holding their weapons high, intending to resist. .... Thus, the Governor was fearful when he saw that there would be rebellion which would do the country no good. The Bachaalany family was the protection of the village.... ...the people coming to see the happenings were frightened and stopped at the Je'many River ...and it happened that some of the Bachaalany family were coming back from the funeral of Abdou Agha Bachaalany, one of their own who died in the village of Shieyah. The people knew that they were the Bachaalany's and that they would not have heard yet of the events that happened in Salima during their absence..."

He ended the story of what happened between the Bachaalany folks and the government just as we mentioned earlier in this book. Also, he mentioned the name Bachaalany and the Bachaalanys more than twenty times. So how could he possibily believe in the Machaalany name!

Beshara Nofal House

Their Origin

We have ascertained that Nofal, the forefather of the Sowayd house, had another son called Beshara. The sheikhs of Salima knew that this Nofal moved from Al Showeir seeking refuge with the Lam's Princes in Salima. They knew that he had three sons: Sowayd, the forefather of Sowayd house; Beshara, the forefather of Beshara house and who died in 1829; and, Abou 'Ekr. They were mentioned in the documents of the Salem house which we will talk about later. In the accounting books of Nahra Sowayd, Beshara Bou Soliman, the grandson of Beshara Bin Nofal, was mentioned as: "Our paternal cousin Beshara." The children of this house emigrated to Mekseh with those who emigrated from Salima to the countryside.

Their Lineage

Nofal begot Sowayd, Beshara, and Abou 'Ekr. Sowayd begot Girgis who died in Ras Beirut in 1842 according to the register of the Salima Congregation. Nahra, the forefather of the Nahra and Abou 'Ekr families perished. As for Bershara Bin Nofal, he begot Rezk and Bou Soliman who both were killed in Shershetoura, in the countryside, at the battle of Ibrahim Pasha Al Masry in 1840. Bou Soliman begot Soliman who was mentioned among the records for 1843.

Beshara, who we knew as a Sheikh, wore a long beard and looked just like the typical pictures of the sheikhs of that time. He begot two sons: Rezk and Soliman, and, both are expatriates.

Rezk went to Buenos Aires in Argentina and begot three sons: Beshara, and two others whose names we don't know. As for Soliman, he married a girl from the expatriate Abi Soliman from Al Matiyan family and he begot a son who died when he was a child. He has five daughters who remain. He now lives with his family in Utica, New York, in the United States.

Salem House

Their Origin And Lineage

The Salem folks belong to the Bachaalany house. Their forefather, Salem, the son of Father Gibrail Al Gelkh moved from Bahr Saf, near Bikfaya, at the beginning of last century. The Gelkh family originates from the Jaj village in the upper Jbail county. They came to Bahr Saf a very long time ago. A group of them moved to Al Arbaniea in the Metn. After a long time there, they moved to the village of Louisa near Baabada, with Rezkallah family. From that group, there were those who went to Forn Al Shebak. A group lived in Deir Al Qamar in Beirut.

Salem Gelkh was in Salima and known as Salem Al Khoury or Salem, the Muleteer, because he used to rent the mules of the Lam's princes in Salima and Bikfaya.

In the book entitled The Evaluation of Bikfaya, on pages 254 – 255, written by our friend, Sheikh Edmond Blibel, he said "Ibrahim Gelkh and his children went, in 1815, from Bahr Saf to Al Arbaniea, and, among them were the Salem folks in Salima and the Gelkh folks, whose forefather Boutros Gibrail emigrated to Al Louisa (Baabada). That Father Gibrail succeeded Father Beshara Al Gelkh as the priest of the Congregation of Bahr Saf. His name was mentioned in a document in the year 1766."

Father Gibrail Gelkh is the father of Salem, the grandfather of the Salem House in Salima. He used to visit the house of his son frequently. From his vestiges there is a copy of the Holy Book in Arabic and Latin printed in Rome. It was in their home in Salima and it was stolen during the riot of 1860.

Salem begot Ibrahm, Youssef, and Hanna. Ibrahim had no children and died. Youssef begot Salem and Hanna; Salem died young and Hanna Bin Youssef begot Youssef who begot Salem, Ibrahim, and Mansour. Meanwhile, Hanna Bin Salem begot Ibrahim who had only two daughters. They emigrated with their father to Brazil where they got married and he died.

Their Vestiges

We found among their papers, documents that informed us of the following: The Lady Lam's, the daughter of Prince Fares and the wife of Prince Haidar Abi Al Lam', sold to her sister, Malaka, the wife of Prince Assaf, in the year 1223 Hegira, the house she had with "Sowayd" in Salima. She sold it for 150 piasters as per the appraisal of Girgis Kharat (from Bikfayah). Then, the Lady Malaka transfered the property to "Oum 'Ekr, the wife of Bou 'Ekr Ibn Nofal". Her husband, Prince Assaf, certified the sale. Then, Oum 'Ekr transferred the property of this home "to our son, Salem Khoury", then "the mentioned Lady Malaka sold to Oum 'Ekr a garden and a buffet under the house of the old Church of Our Lady. The borders were: from the East, Mikhail Abdel Ahad; from the North, Abdou Ibn Nahra; and, from the South and the West, Bou'Oun. The sale price was 115 piasters according to the appraisal of Bou Ali Said and Soma Al Bejjeni (Beit Shabab). Also belonging to that was a part of the cinammon bark in the field of Bou Kheir Eddine. In the year 1230". This was written by the Lebanese Pastor Germanos Al Ashqar and certified by Prince Assaf. An expression was written by Sharaf Eddine Al Qadi with his seal… "the order is valid upon this act as well as its transfer; and any opposition or encroachment is legally forbidden, in Shaaban 1223."

- - - - -

"And the Lady Malaka sold to Salem Al Khoury from the Gelkh House of Bahr Saf, a mulberry garden in front of the Salem house. It borders: from the East, Teama; the West, the Church endowment; … a mulberry tree on the wall belonging to Beshara. Also, mulberry trees, grapevines, figs, a third of an olive tree in the field of Ein Al Mahata, with their border: from the East, Gibrail Bin Samaan; from the West, Youssef Khoury; from the North and South, Abdou Ibn Nahra. For the price of 85 piasters … in February, 1230."

- - - - -

"Ibrahim Ibn Salem Al Khoury and his brothers have purchased from Salman Naaman Said, Abdul Malek, and Bahga (the wife of Wahba), the cinnamon barks which are in Merigate. Also a trellis, a sampling, a fig tree, and three pear trees for the price of 68 piaters. This is done with the acknowledgment of Ismail, the son of Berjas Masry, in the year 1245 Hegira."

- - - - -

There is also the last will and testament of Oum 'Ekr:

"I bequeath the mulberry trees in front of the house of Abdou Nahra to our children Haloun and Warda. The lot for a house, behind the house of Youssef Nasrallah, uncultivated and with trellises, at the bottom of the press district, I bequeath to our son, Mikhail. If he should wish to bring legal action against his sisters, they have no objection... in the year 1833."

In these documents we find the names of Nofal's children mentioned. Sowayd (the grandfather of the Sowayd house), Beshara (the grandfather of the Beshara Bou Soliman House), and Abou 'Ekr (the husband of Oum 'Ekr who was mentioned above) and their offspring have perished. The homes of the three were on both sides of the Church of Our Lady.

Ghatas And Aboud House

Their Origin

This family belongs to the Bachaalany house of Salima. They originate from Qornet Chahouane, one of the villages of the countryside where there is still a group of them. They are known as the Abi Karm House and they belong to the Zoghby House. The Zoghby house is one of very noble birth, Maronite, and known everywhere by the name Al Zoghby. Among their old surnames was the Shouwaysha House. Three brothers from that house came to Salima in the beginning of the last century. They were Ghatas, Aboud, and Father Maroun, the children of Tanious Bin Romanos. Thus, in Qornet Chahouane they belong to the Zoghby House and in Salima to the Bachaalany House.

The Zoghby House is one of the old Maronite houses who lived in Aaqoura in the upper Jbail county. They moved from there around the year 1600 because of a dispute between them and the Sheikhs of the Hashem folks. They separated in Kisrawan, the North of Lebanon, Al Metn, Al Shouf, and in the South. In Kisrawan they first went to 'Ejeltoun and approached the Khazen House who were the Governors of the fief. Then a dispute occurred between them and a sheikh from the Khazen folks. This was the cause of their departure and going over to Kafr Tiyeh, the Alma Coast, and Qarna Shehwan. Then, afterwards, moving to Al Kehala and Alma Al Shaab. In addition, there are those who, in the past, went to the northern villages: Al Koura, Al Zawya, and Halab, which is where the Abdini House developed. They, then, moved from one northern village to another. All this has been described in detail in our book, The History Of The Maronite Families.

Ghatas House

Father Maroun was a virgin priest who spent his life in Salima. He was a priest and worked another job to earn a living. His brother Ghatas married Helena, the daughter of Girgis Eishy. They begot Fares and Habib. Habib died in Egypt, young and unmarried. Fares Ghatas married Katerin, the daughter of Youssef Al Khoury from the Ghibril house in Bayt Shabab. Also, she is the sister of Augustin Ghibril, the Halabian monk originating from Bayt al Shabab and one of the students of the Maronite School in Rome. He was a man of virtue and knowledge. He was especially learned in the Syriac language. He bought a library full of books written in that language.

Fares Ghatas was an intelligent man and very eloquent. He was often telling us what he knew about the monasticisms and the present governors. He begot Maroun, Youssef, Ghatas, and Habib. Abou Maroun and Oum Maroun took great care to see that they all received a good Christian education.

Maroun emigrated to the United States around the year 1890. He lived in Baltimore, then moved to Atlantic City. Then he settled in Washington, D.C.. He married an American girl and begot Metil and George. Metil married a young Irishman. George helps his father in his trade, operating a French pastry shop for which they have became famous. He learned that profession from a Jewish man. Maroun developed many relationships with men of religion, especially Cardinal Gebnez. Maroun gave me, for my library, some books written by this well known American. After Maroun's success, Youssef, Ghatas, and Habib successively migrated to the United States. Youssef married his maternal cousin, the expatriate, and they lived with his brother Habib in Charleston, South Carolina. Then he died, leaving children. Habib married a girl from the Hensh House and had children.

As for Ghatas, he left Lebanon in 1892 for the United States. He was obliged to go to Rio de Janeiro and spend a few months there because of Yellow Fever. Then, he left and went to New York and to Baltimore in April, 1893. In 1906 he came back home and married Jamila, the daughter of Salem Boutros Nakouzy. After that, he went back to the United States and had ten children, five boys and five girls. Their names are: Alice, Felix, Josef, Isabelle, Emil, Helen, James, Frederic, Avlin, and Florence. Ghatas was held in high standing in the American community. He participated in patriotic deeds, especially during World War II. He showed us what the expatriate Lebanese is known for: sharing with his neighboors in their sorrows, doing construction work, and doing charitable acts. During his stay abroad he acquired a great amount of money, knowledge, and prestige. He did his utmost to educate his children and teach them the best of culture.

Ghatas, with his wife, visited Salima after the First World War. He renovated his house here and, then, went back to America.

Aboud House

Aboud married Sa'oud, the daughter of Moussa Estephan, in 1829. He built a house not far from the house of Nejm Andrea Bachaalany, the maternal uncle of his wife. As I remember, this house was shaky and collapsed before it was completed. The workers were in the house at the time and one of the was lost in the rubble. They had to search the wreckage for him. Girgis Bin Asaad Maroun, the noted poet, wrote a popular poem about it. Some of its verses are:

> *He is appearing, dear, he is appearing*
> *Aboud from Qornet Chahouane.*
> *Aboud constructed for me,*
> *For the youth and the others.*
> *A wind from the east came,*
> *And made all its walls fall.*

Aboud begot Asaad, Youssef, Girgis, and Satout. Asaad married Mary, the daughter of Mansour Bin Hanna Moussa Al Erian, and they begot Youssef, Aboud, Rashed, Edma (the wife of Boutros Sowan), and Asma (the wife of Hanna

Abdou). Youssef Bin Aboud and Youssef Bin Asaad Aboud died young and unmarried. As for Girgis Aboud, he married Sawsan, the daughter of Wakim Boutros. They had no children and he died. Aboud emigrated to Colombia with Mary, the daughter of his paternal aunt, Satout (the wife of Selim Hashima). We have had no news about them lately.

Rashed, known as Rashid Bachaalany, lives in New York. He migrated there before the First World War. He worked for many years as a clerk in one of the well known Sarsaq Houses in Beirut. Then, he married Cecilia Nomeir from Moalaket Zahle in New York. She is one of the most virtuous women. They had Asaad and Youssef. He has lived there for many years operating a restaurant frequented by the Lebanese. His children have now taken over the business from their father.

Their Vestiges

" ... Aboud Showaysha bought from the wife of Elias Bou Heriz, the grapevines ...in Kroum Al Hawa for the price of ....twenty five piasters .... Their names are enough and there is no need to determine their borders...in April, 1830. Written and witnessed by: Youssef, the son of Daher Bachaalany. Witnesses: Saab Al Henawy. and Abdou Ibn Nahra Bachaalany."

- - - - -

" ...we sold the terraced land we have, above the well, to our paternal cousin, Gad'oun Nader, at the price of fifteen piasters ...its location is from the oak sampling of our paternal cousin, Asaad, at the west, up to the rivulet; at the East ...in February, 1253. Written by Khalil Al Henawy who acknowledged this for himself. The sale is valid for Aboud and was paid for by him. Witnesses: Tanous Ibn Shahin; Ali Bou Ali Said; Asaad Al Henawy; Girgis Freha, the son of our brother, Shebly."

- - - - -

"... the sons of Saab gave to his Excellency, Father Maroun, and his brother, Aboud, the uncultivated land that they own at the vines of the cliff. The priest will cultivate it. Once its vines grow and became mature and beautiful, they will divide the land in half, between themselves. The priest and his brother will receive half, and half will go to the sons of Saab. ...on October 2, 1245, Written by Asaad Al Henawy. Witnesses: Shahin Ibn Boutros. our paternal uncle, Abdulallah ..."

- - - - -

"Aboud Ibn Tanious and his brother, Father Maroun, bought from Tanous Ibn Shahin .. the mulberry tree which is beside the two terraced lands at the corner of the house to the east... and three pounds of leaves, for the price of 39 piasters ... in September, 1256. Written by Gad'oun Nader. Witnesses: Shahin Ibn Boutros and Ghaleb Ibn Hanna Eid."

- - - - -

"Aboud Ibn Tanious purchased from the children of Freha and their paternal cousin, Nejm Ibn Boulos, a carat and a half at the press which is at the back side of the cliff. They bought this from the Capuchin, Father Hanna ...the price is 12 piasters and a half .... on September 26, 1257. The persons acknowledging what has been described here are the children of Freha and Nejm Boulos. Written by Tanous. Witnesses: Shahin Ibn Boutros, and Youssef Rahal."

- - - - -

"...Aboud Showaysha and Helena, the widow of his brother Ghatas, came before us .. they acknowledged before the undersigned witnesses that they have reconciled over the dispute involving the inheritance of the late Ghatas. Aboud was claiming that the woman was keeping the purchase deeds of these properties in her name and were bought during her husband's life for the price of the value of her jewelry; and, that was illegal.... ...Whereas Helena claims that everything bought with her money is her property. She is asking for her share of the inheritance left by her husband, a carat and a half, written for her by a deed which she has in hand, except for the two above mentioned deeds in Karm Al Sanasel and Karm Al Mantara from Gad'oun Al Henawy and Nasr Karam in Ain Al Sawaqy ... and they have reconciled, and Abdou paid one hundred piasters to Helena to her complete satifaction; and she has given to her children all that she inherited from her late husband's estate. The income, jeweleries, and cloths remain hers. She abdicates her right to anything else for her sons, Fares and Habib. And she has discharged them from their paternal uncle Aboud who is their legal gardian.... Aboud withdrew all suits against his nephews. They reconciled and shook hands and discharged each other On October 18, 1852. Written by Ibrahim Al Gelkh. Admitted by: Abdou Showaysha, and Helena, the widow of his brother Ghatas. Witnesses: Ibrahim Bin Hanna; Nejm Bin Youssef Nasallah; and 'Oql Ibn Genid."

- - - - -

"...on this date we have deputized our son, Aboud Al Showeishy, to sell from the properties of our sons, his deceased brothers, Maroun and Ghatas, to cover the amount of their debts with the approval of our son, the Antonian Pastor, Father Youssef from Bait Shabab. He is not allow to sell any more than that from the mentioned properties, not one piaster more.... ...on March 12, 1855. The Humble Youssef Geagea, Bishop of Cyprus. (stamp)."

- - - - -

"This is to acknowledge a barter between Youssef Nasef and the widow of Mikhail (Mekhoul) Daher and her daughters.... Both parties were satisfied as agreed upon ...on February 26, 1868, admitting what have been described: Youssef Daher Al Nakouzy; Asaad Aboud; and Youssef Nasef Al Khoury. Written by Khalil 'Oql Guened. Witnesses: Youssef Azam Fares Al Nakouzy; Mikhail Saad Fares; Boutros Salem: Girgis Aboud; with the acknowledgement of Elias Abou Assleh. This is valid: As long as the acceptance was of both parties, as written. We witnessed this on February 27, 1868. Written by: Tanous Freha, (stamp), the Sheikh of Salima Village."

Zaghloul House

The Zaghloul House is one of the Bachaalany families. They came from the Matyan to Salima where they are known as the Zaghloul house. They are an offshoot of the Hadad house.

According to the stories of the Hadad House, they originate from the Christian families who escaped from the oppression of Houran and took refuge in Lebanon. This happened a long time ago. They escaped to the safety of the Al Lam' Princes. We talked in detail about that when we described the Hadad House. The first one who came to Salima from the Zaghloul house is Nasef. He came with his mother who was widowed in the Metn. She joined her two daughters in Salima where they been married.

When Nasef Zaghloul grew up, he worked in a black smith shop with Nasef Al Hadad, the husband of his sister Banout. He married Badou', the daughter of Hanna Anton Hanna from the Hadad family. We will talk about this family a little later. Nasef Zaghloul was assassinated in the national sedition between the Christians and the Druzes in 1845.

About The Zaghloul And Their Lineage

Nasef Al Zaghloul begot Youssef and Metri. Youssef died young and unmarried. Metri married Henna, the daughter of Wakim Boutros from the Bachaalany house after she had been engaged to his late brother. They begot Nasef, Hanna, Elias, Youssef, Mikhail, and some daughters. Metri joined the Capuchin Fathers after being Roman Othodox. The Zaghloul folks became Catholics. All of them are Maronite except for one of their houses, the Youssef family who are officially with the Roman Catholic congregation.

As for Nasef Metri Al Zaghloul, he begot Rashid, Metri, and Girgi. Rashid begot Alberto and Marberto. Metri had one son in Brazil. Girgi begot children in Brazil.

Hanna Bin Metri begot four sons: Tawfik and Shafik drowned in a river in Brazil, such a terrible loss of young lives. Elias begot Badie' and others whose names we don't know, except for Youssef. Youssef begot George, Edmond, and John.

Mikhail Bin Metri is still unmarried today. The children of the Zaghloul are all expatriates in Brazil except for the Youssef House. Edmond is the only expatriate from that house.

The first from this house who emigrated were Hanna and Elias. They went to Brazil in 1893. They lived in Oliveira which, today, has become a colony of Salima people. Then Nasef and Youssef travelled there in 1895. Hanna came back in 1900 and got married. After that he went back returning to Salima in 1914 with his two sons, Tawfik and Shafik. Before the World War I started, he went back to Brazil and left his two sons in Salima. They stayed there during the war. After the War was over, they went back to Brazil where they died.

Elias came back from Brazil to Salima around the year 1906. He got married and went back to Brazil where he died.

Their Vestiges

" ...Nasef Ibn Zaghloul bought from Ahmed Ibn Kheir Eddine Zein Eddine from Salima ...the mulberry trees at Ein Al Sawaqi in the Motamani trench, The price was 22 piasters based on the acknowlegment of our brother Fares ... they are well known so there is no need to determine their borders ...in Dhou Al Qe'da, 1246. Written by the humble Ali Said. Ahmed sold this on behalf of his brother. Witnessed by Soliman Ibn Daliqan."

- - - - -

"We sold that which belongs to us. It is what we were in charge of by the direction of our dear Sheikhs, Soliman, and his brother, Bou Ali, children of Ali Said from Salima. We sold the lands situated in Al Wariz at the bottom of the Masry house including figs, vines, and olives. We sold it to our dear Sheikh Nasef Zaghloul, from this same place. It is bordered from the South, by Sayed Ahmed Ibn Ezz Eddine; from the East, Girgis Ibn Boutros; from the North, Bou Hassan Ezz Eddine and Yaqdan Ibn Daher; and, from the West, Shahin Ibn Soliman and Khalil Ibn Yazbak. The price was four hundred piasters with the appraisal by Shiekh Elias Bou Assly ... Written on May 14, 1865. Accepted for herself .... Badoura the daughter of Assaf Qayed Baih. (stamp) Witnesses: Youssef Daher Al Nakouzy. Ghantous Daham Bachaalany."

- - - - -

Wahbe(a) House

Their Origin

Among the families who have been affiliated with the Bachaalany house in Salima, is the Wahbe Abi Bakr family. They are originally Muslims. In the past, they joined the Lam's Princes of Salima. Some of them say that they came to Lebanon from Bakr lands with the Shehabian Princes and then settled in Salima.

Since the general rule was that the people embraced the religion of their rulers, so it was that the Abi Bakr family followed their Princes in Salima. They converted to Christianity toward the end of the 18th Century.

We found a handwritten piece, written by Bishop Abdulallah Blibel, the archbishop of Cyprus, in the register of ordinations, annexed to his ordination:

"On April 11, 1816, we baptized Zamel Bou Bakr from Salima. He was surnamed Girgis and on June 3, we baptized his wife, his son, and his daughter."

And in the Regiter of the Congregation of Salima, this expression was written: *"In 1826, Youssef Bin Saloum Bou Bakr and his wife Nassim converted to Christianity and were baptized in the Arbaniea Church. His godmother was Al Khouria."*

The occasion of the conversion of Abou Bakr and his wife, Nassim, the daughter of Salebe Abou Bakr, has been handed down by the sheikhs as follows:

One night, Nassim dreamed of the Virgin Mary saying to her: 'Wake up and go to the priest to be baptized'. She woke up, called for her husband, and told him what she saw in her dream. He told her that he had dreamed the same thing! Therefore, they went to the priest of the congregation and told him what they saw in their dreams. He welcomed them into the group of believers, teaching them the rules of the religion. In the village of Arbaniea, they were baptized.

Wahba Ibn Saloum Abou Bakr was married to Nassim, the daughter of Salebe Abou Bakr. She was his kin and had a sister called Habous. The only thing we know about Zamel Bou Bakr is that he had two sons, Abdulallah and Nabhan. They sold a piece of land in Salima to Hanna Al Khoury Moussa at the back of the cliff, in 1857. There is no news about them after that.

Their Lineage

Wahba Bin Saloum Bou Bakr begot Khalil, Asaad, Saloum, and Ibrahim. Khalil begot Youssef who had a son who died when he was a child. Asaad Wahba begot seven sons who all died. Saloum Wahba begot a son called Amin who had no children. As for Ibrahim Wahba, he was the Business Agent of the Capuchin Fathers in Beirut, so he lived there and begot Elias and Hanna.

Elias studied at the School of Our Lady of Lourdes in Salima. He worked in commerce in Beirut. He begot Kamil who begot Elie and Nadim. Hanna, his brother, studied at the Hekma School in Beirut, then in the Eintoura School. He begot Emil.

The Wahba house was related by marriage to the Bachaalany House. It was through Hawa, the daughter of Wahba, who married Hanna Youssef Nasrallah; Labiba, the daughter of Saloum Wahba who married Mansour, the son of the previously mentioned Hanna; Mary, the daughter of Ibrahim Wahba who married Andrea Girgis. All of these are Bachaalany folks.

Bou Heriz House

Their Origin

They are one of the families who came to Salima and became related to the Bachaalany family. The name of Mikhail Bin Elias was mentioned in a deed which we previously published in this book. We think that it is most probable that he is the father of Elias Bou Heriz. We also mentioned earlier the name of Daher Ibn Mikhail Al Haj Boutros. So, the house of Abi Heriz originates from those of Al Haj Boutros house, the famous family in Bahr Saf, in Saqiyet Al Mesk, with some in the Joar Al Houz, and others places.

The family of the Boutros are a Maronite family of noble birth. I remember that the Abi Heriz house used to follow the Roman Catholic Congregation. Then they moved to the Maronite Congregation. From a very long time ago, the Heriz house were living among the Bachaalany houses. They belonged to the Bachaalany houses by marriage. So much so that they fully became members of that family.

Their Vestiges

"...Mansour Al Showayri purchased from Mourad, the son of Abdel Samad, the grapevines that are in Koroum Al Hawa above Ein Al Sawaqy. He bought the grapevines and the disabled trees. At the bottom of the grape vines are two oak saplings, as per the appraisal of Beshir Bin Nasr Eddine, at a price of eighteen and a half piasters , ..the borders from the South, the grapevines of Hussein Ibn Fakhr Eddine; from the East, a pond divided in half, a half for the buyer and the other half for the seller, and the half of the pond belonging to the buyer, no one has any right over it. From the West, Ali Al Helow; and, from the North, that of Serhal Seif. Written in February, 1171. Written by Soliman Sayegh. Witnesses: Hussein Yazbek, and Said Farahat. '

- - - - -

"Elias Abu Heriz, from the village of Salima, purchased from the children of Ali Al Helow of the Said House, the grapevines and half of...   ...in Koroum Al Hawa at the price of twenty piasters .. the borders from the South, Mansour Al Helow; from the North and the East the buyer. The assessor is Hamad Ibn Fakhr Eddine Al Masry .... In Shaaban, 1219, Written by the humble Ibn Mahmoud Al Masry. Witnessed by Mansour Al Helow, and Hamdan Qadama."

- - - - -

"Elias Bou Heriz and Tanous Al Siqily, each acknowledging the other about the mulberries of Elias .. in the neighbouhood of the Press on the terraces of Gibrail house; He acquired them from His Excellency, Prince Assa. The mentioned Elias paid for them with the working waterwheel in Ras Al Khandaq .... The borders, from the West Gibrail; from the East, His Excellency, Prince Haidar; from the North, the cliff; and, from the South, His Excellency ... in the year 1229. Written by the humble Mohamed Al Masry. Witnesses: Hamdan Bergas Al Mar."

- - - - -

"...Mikhail Ibn Abdelhad from the Bachaalany's and Elias Ibn Heriz from Salima came to our house and asked us to write this deed for them. They have exchanged the grapevines; Mikahil gave him a grapevine in Al Wariz at the bottom of the stream and Elias gave him a grapevine in Koroum Al Hawa. Those are the grapevines he bought from Abou Bakr's house, belonging to them, two terraced lands in the grapevines of Al Showayri House ...in Ramadan, 1219. Written by the humble Mohamed Ibn Mahmoud Al Masry."

Their Lineage

Elias Bou Heriz begot Boutros who begot Mikhail. Mikhail then begot Boutros who begot Dawoud, Youssef, and Mikhail. They emigrated to the United States at the beginning of this century. There, they married and lived in Olean, New York.

Daoud had children whose names we do not know. Youssef had no sons, but he did have daughters: Saady, the wife of Asaad Wakim (Kassab); Edal, the wife of Youssef Shahin Samaan Al Khoury who was from Bezbadine; Rogina, the wife of Tanious Avram Saad from Beskinta, and an unmarried girl. As for Mikhail Bin Boutros Bou Heriz, he had no boys. All those we mentioned are expatriates in the United States.

I have special memories of Daoud Abou Heriz who was our school mate in childhood. We used to sit beside each other at the village school in Salima.

Ateia House

Among those who belonged to the Bachaalany by marriage was Edward Ateia. His father, Youssef Bin Khalil Fares Al Haj Ateia, moved from Souk Al Gharb to Beirut in 1910, and he lived there. He begot Wadie', Alfred (who died), and Edward, who married Eugenie, the daughter of Mikhail Abou Assly and lived in Salima. They built a nice house there.

Edward Ateia had a unique child, a son, called Alfred. He has five paternal uncles: Selim, Tawfik, Ibrahim, and Amin (we are missing one name). Amin stayed in Souk Al Gharb. The first four uncles emigrated to Brazil where their cousin, the son of Rashid Shahin Al Haj Ateia, was already living. Among their paternal cousins was the professor, Shahin, and his son, also a professor, George.

Bou Saber House

They belong to the Erian Bachaalany house. However, Sheikh Melhem Nahra did not mentioned them in his biographical manuscript. Nor were they mentioned as one of the offshoots of the Erian House. The house of Abi Saber was adjacent to the house of Abdou Nahra which he gave to his sister's son, Nahra Sowayd. There is nothing mentioned in our archives other than a statement that they belonged to the Erian House.

The following is all we know and can provide about their lineage: Abou Saber begot two sons: Tanious and Abdulallah. Abdullah was killed by his brother Tanious. Tanious begot Girgis and then he was killed in 1840, in Shar Makseh. Girgis had Tanious who died young and unmarried. There was a girl who died in the First World War, and, thus their line has ended.

Al Kerarji House

From their surname, it seems that their forefather who came first to Salima was "Klergy" of the Princes of Salima. The word "Klergy" means "the keeper of the stores of provisons". The Klergy belonged to the Bachaalany family by marriage so he became one of the in-laws. We tried to determine what village they originally came from but our search was in vain. We know that their forefathers include Elias Al Karargy who begot Daher who died in 1849 leaving two sons, Youssef and Fares. Fares died in 1851. Abou Daher Youssef who I became acquainted with when he was an old sheikh, begot Daher who emigrated to Africa. Daher then came back and he begot Elias and four daughters. Elias emigrated to Africa, then came back and got married. After that he went back to Africa and begot Sami and Youssef.

Shamrawy House

They originate from Deir Shamra in the countryside. They are from the Abi Anton house who moved, in the past, from the village of Tertej to Metn. They took refuge with the Lam's Princes. A group of them lived in Deir Shamra and another group in Al Qaaqour. The latter group are known as the Abi Anton House and the Madhloum House. There was a group of them, in the past, found in Bezbedine and they were known as the Khoury House. They are the Al Khoury House who are in Thaalabayia.

As for the forefather of the Shamrawy House in Salima, he is Abou Mourad who died in 1869. He had Beshara who begot Abdou, Khalil, and the wife of Asaad Fares Bin Youssef Bachaalany. Abdou begot Raheel, the wife of Tanious Daoud. Khalil had only one daughter.

Metri Al Sayegh House

Their Origin

The Sayegh folks in Salima are the descendants of their forefather Wahba Al Sayegh. His offspring was the only one in Salima with that name.

Because a group from the Hadad House (who we will talk about later) have been called Sayegh for a long time, their children decided to choose another name which we will also mention in more detail later.

We have tried to determine the relationship between that Sayegh family and the Sayegh Al Hadad family through the documents we have in our archives. We had no success. Thus, we have left the matter under study. All that we will say about the Sayegh House is that they might be the offspring of the Sayegh Al Hadad in Salima, or, possibly, of the Sayegh family known in Al Showier, in Beteghrin, and in Beirut. The title of "Sayegh" (Jeweller) like the names of other professions, have been given to families with very different origins and kinship. The Sayegh clan that we are interested in are the offspring of the previously mentioned Metri who became Maronites and who belonged to the Bachaalany family.

Their Lineage

Wahba Al Sayegh begot Girgis, Mikhail, and Naqoul (who had no children and died). Girgis begot Metri and Habib (who died young and unmarried). Metri Bin (the sons of) Girgis Wahba Al Sayegh begot Fares and Girgis who emigrated with his family to the United States and died there. He left two daughters Nour and Matil. As for Fares Bin Metri, he begot Habib, Khalil, Abdou, Youssef, and Selim. Habib died young and unmarried. Khalil begot Fares who had Habib and Anton.

Abdou, known as Abi Shahin, begot Shahin. Youssef Bin Fares Metri begot Najib and Milad. Najib died when he was a boy and Selim died in the United States unmarried and young.

The offspring of Metri Sayegh became Maronites because Metri married Nour, the daughter of Sowayd Bin Nofal, as we previously mentioned. Thus, they belonged to the Bachaalany's.

Mikhail Bin Wahba begot Youssef who begot Mikhail. Mikhail begot Youssef who begot Michel and Tawfik. Both of them died in Africa, young and unmarried.

ZEIN HOUSE

Chapter 3

Their History

The Zein people come from their forefather, Zein, the son of Shediak. Shediak was of noble Maronite birth of the family of Jemeyel. The children of the Jemeyel family left the village of Jaj in the upper part of Jbail county in 1545 and went to Kisrawan. Leaving at the same time were the Khazen people and the Kamid. This was during the era of Prince Mansour Al Assafy, the Governor of Ghazeer. This was where they found safety and justice.

The Jemeyel folks moved to the Bikfaya fief where they settled and grew. They also spread to the neighboring fiefs. They lived and mixed with other refugee families from Jaj and various villages of northern Lebanon. They were all running away from oppression and injustice. (see The History of Al Doueihy for the years 1545 – 1587).

One of the offshoots of the Jemeyel House was the Shediak House. A boy growing up in the Shediak clan grew to manhood and was named Zein. He is the grandfather of the Zein House that is found in Bikfaya and Salima.

The Jemeyel Folks are divided in three parts:

The first part is composed of the original Jemeyels. They are the offspring of the children of the Jemeyel who fled Jaj as Doueihy described. There is a group of descendants who claim to be the only ones who are the related to the original settlers.

The second part are the Hashemite Jemeyls. They moved from the village of Wadi Shahin. They are descended from Haj Hashem Al Jemeyel. Rumors say that they stole the name Jemeyel and claimed it as their own. The original Jemeyel folks then abandoned their name and chose to be known as Abi Jamil in order to be distinguished from the new group. The late Anton Pasha Jemeyel kept and preserved a document written by Father Youssef Jemeyel. He lived during the middle of the last century and was a man of virtue and goodness. In the document he explains this story which is our main proof for passing it on.

The third part is made up of the Shediak Jemeyels. They descended from a man from the Jemeyel House. He was a subdeacon, one of the ecclesiastical ranks. His offspring are divided into two groups:

One group has maintained both surnames: Shediak and Jemeyel. They are the ones who lived in Shawaya. From this group have come a famous Patriarch, Bishops, and Priests. Their signatures literally showed both names: " … Ibn (the son of) Al Shediak Ibn Al Jemeyel"; or, "from the Shediak House of the Jemeyel family."

Then, the second group was content with just the Shediak name only. They lived in Bikfaya and Showaya.

Zein, the forefather of the Zein House descended from that Shediak House. Zein is the ancestor of those who lived in Bikfaya and Salima.

Some researchers, however, don't think that they descended from the Jemeyel House. They think that their relationship with the Jemeyels is a maternal one, resulting from being in-laws of the Jemeyel House. These researchers believe that the Zeins were originally from the Shediak House, then married into the Jemeyels and mixed with the majority of them. They believe that there is nothing indicating the true origin of the Shediak House.

A curious thing appears in the book The History of Bait Shabab, by Father Mikhail Ghibril. It is found in Volume 2, Chapter 3, page 217. He says that the Shediak House is the offspring of Matar Al Jemeyel. On page 218 he adds that they are the offspring of the Shediak (the Subdeacon) Elias Al Hasrouni. Douaihy mentioned that Elias drew a picture of the Church of Mar Abda, built by Father Anton Al Jemeyel in Bikfaya. However, Ghibril never mentioned that reference.

Other researchers could not clearly prove any relationship between the Shediak and the Jemeyel Houses. Some of our new historians seem to be making claims on poor investigations, neglecting some documents and exaggerating oral traditions. It is precisely for these reasons that we cannot rely on them for the truth concerning the origins of any of the Lebanese Families. Rarely do we seem to encounter this type of flawed research in Western historians.

With all of the published and unpublished documents dealing with the Jemeyel Family no one has yet been able to definitively describe the early origins or lineage dealing with the Jemeyel and Abi Jemeyel, the Shediak and Al Haj Hashem. I hope to be able to sort through all of the material and clarify these topics in my book The History of the Maronite Families which will hopefully be published after publishing this book.

With the research that I have performed so far about this family, we have come to the conclusion that the Jemeyel people, Abi Jemeyel and the Shediak are most probably from the same origin. The different offshoots, the different names of the grandfathers, all the different names seem to be just the result of each trying to distinguish themselves from each other. The origins, we think, are the same, only the names are different. We are making this our position until some trusted historian emerges or some ancient, original document appears to prove otherwise.

As for those who did write about the Jemeyel House, they are: Douaihy in his famous Annals, Hadathouni in The Fief of Kisrawan, Father Mikhail Ghibril in The History of Bait Shabab, Sheik Edmond Blibel in An Evaluation of Bikfaya, and, Father Elias Al Jemeyel in his biography. Also, there is the biography of Bishop Youssef Dagher by Amin Jemeyel which was published by Professor Abdulallah Hashima. Professor Youssef Ghastin has written a critical article about the families of Bikfaya, especially the Jemeyel family but he has not published it yet.

Their Lineage

Zein Al Shediak begot Aboud and Khaled whose offspring is surnamed Al Shediak and they lived in Bikfaya. Aboud lived in Salima and begot Daher who begot Mourad, Abdulallah, Girgis, Khalil, and Abdulallah II who died when he was a child.

Abdulallah the first died unmarried in 1838. Khalil settled in Bikfaya and begot Youssef, Zein, Habib, and Mansour (who died and left children). Youssef and Zein died unmarried. Habib had no children. Mourad Zein married Henna, the daughter of Shayboun Kassab and begot Fares, Asaad, Youssef, and Toqla (the wife of Fares Metri Sayegh). Fares Mourad married Hedba, the daughter of his paternal uncle Girgis, and begot Habib, Mourad, Jemeyel, Louis, Nadhira, Mariam (the wife of Moussa Salem Nakouzy), and Leila.

Mourad Bin Fares begot Fares, George, Josef, and Louis. Louis married Emily, the daughter of his maternal uncle Salebe Girgis, and begot Anton and girls.

As for Asaad Mourad, he married Lamia, the daughter of Youssef Azam Kassab. They had Nessib, Boutros, Mansour, and girls. Nessib married Kafa, the daughter of Metri Al Zaghloul, and begot Asaad, Youssef and others. Mourad married Alia, the daughter of Metri Moussa Bachaalany, and begot Najib, Rashid, Lisa (the wife of Nejm Daher

Andrea), Rashida (the wife of Khatar Abdou Khatar), Khatoum (the wife of Youssef Fares Shiban), (the three from the Bachaalany House), and, Anissa who died in Africa with her brother Rashid.

Meanwhile, Girgis Zein married Refqa, the daughter of Father Shediak Ibrahim from Showaya and begot Daher, Salebe, Ibrahim, Zein, and Rosa (the wife of Amin Nasef Asaad Kassab).

Daher joined the Capuchin Monastery and became a priest named Father Francis. Zein died unmarried. Salebe married Mary, the daughter of Father Boutros Youssef Bachaalany, and they had Emil, George (who died when he was a child), Emily (the wife of Louis Zein), and Leone (the wife of Elias Sahyoun). Emil Salebe married Emily, the daughter of Ibrahim Hashem from Hasbeya, and begot Feras, Gerge, Francis, Alexi, Jemeyel, and girls.

Ibrahim Girgis Zein married Olina, the daughter of the previously mentioned Father Boutros, and begot Khalil, Boutros, Zein, and girls. Khalil married the daughter of Khalil Fares Metri and begot Raymon.

About Them

Abou Daher Aboud Bin Zein Al Shediak Al Jemeyl was the first of the Zein folks to come to Slaima. He joined the service of the Lam's Princes. Their rule extended to the Bikfaya fief as we already mentioned. He married the daughter of Sheikh Zamel, one of the sheikhs of the Kassab house who were the guardians and counselors of the Salima Princes. They held positions in their government. Abou Daher Aboud was the brother-in-law of Asaad Maroun Bachaalany. Both of them were married to daughters of Shiekh Zamel. Aboud begot Daher and, then, his wife died. He married a girl from Bikfaya and lived in Zahle where he died.

After his death, his son Daher went back to Salima and re-joined its Princes. He married Rosa. She was the daughter of Sheikh Jaffal Beshir Saab from the Kassab folks who were his maternal uncles. He begot Mourad, Abdulallah, Girgis, Khalil, and Abdulallah II. We will content ourselves with information already mentioned about these individuals.

Wedding of Jemeyel

As a favor, and, in recognition of the generosity of some of our friends, we wish to talk about the ceremonies surrounding the wedding of Jemeyel Zein and Miss Josephine Nejm, the daughter of the Lebanese lawyer, Mr. George Nejm, from the Shouf district. He is just one of the many generous expatriates in the United States. This young lady has excelled in school receiving advanced diplomas in the sciences and arts, and especially in music.

We will mention some of the poetry written for this occasion as well as some of the material from articles in the "Al Hoda" and the "Al Samir" newspapers. There were also stories published in other Arabic newspapers as well as local newspapers in English. They described the engagment and wedding ceremonies. These rank as some of the greatest and most glorious of Lebanese festivities held in the places of emigration.

The engagment party was held on December 14, 1947, at the house of the parents of the fiancée, in New York. (Editor's note: The Arabic wording was not precise on the location. It would appear that this took place in either Poughkeepsie, NY, or Brooklyn, NY.) The wonderful wedding ceremony was held at the Church Our Lady. The marriage was performed with splendor and glamor equal to any other festivity held at the Church.

The church was full of guests. There were expatriate Lebanese as well as great numbers of Americans. It was in February 1948. After the wedding ceremony, the guests walked to the Hotel where an elegant banquet had been prepared for 250 people. When they finished eating, an intellectual festivity was held. First, speaking in English, was the governor of the state, the mayor of the city, the Chief of Police, judges and other notables. Then came the Arabic poetry and orations. Habib Zein, the brother of the groom, delivered a speech of thanks, then recited a poem he composed as well as another poem which Emil Zein, the matenal cousin of the groom, sent:

As the year ended, came omens of the approaching wedding
Then the time and dream became true.
A dream that I always saw and today it became true.
Jemeyl looked at the stars, longing for its splendor and a beautiful smile.
So he chose from them a sparkling light "Nejma" (star),
She was shining, surrounded by her inspiring beauty.
Love shot its arrows and hit both their hearts.
So they promised each other to be faithful,
The promises of virtuous people is an obligation.
Brother, you have been entrusted with the best charge,
To care for the one who the mighty and the nobles raised.
She is a flower raised in the meadow of virtue,
Covered with the floral leaves.
For her to be honored is nothing new
Among generous she gives her generosity.
In the middle of the young girls, she is as a full moon surrounded by the stars.
With their beauty they appear as if in a picture,
A picture the painter has invented.
So, take care of her. She is a gift.
By loving her you will be blessed.
Be the protector of your charge and keep your promise.
The days will strengthen you.
You will find your happiness and joy beside her.
Your life will be surrounded by peace and felicity.
Year after year you will find love from above.
   -- New York, February 1, 1948.   Habib Zein.

You are the best of our youth, Jemeyel Zein.
Your bride is gentle and beautiful.
You, who fill my heart and governing all of me.
I sacrifice my soul for the moon, as if the eyes of a human took its light.
You were soaring and longing for a star, "Nejma"! Did you find comfort from it? You fulfilled a debt but do you have another?
You are of no less ardor and she is not half of you.
Both of you are fulfilling promises and I am the witness of that.
So enjoy, for she is fascinating. Sip with a smooth mouth her
Sweet shaped lips, cheeks and eyes.
She is a star (Nejma) in the sky...

...In her wedding, I thought her a nymph from heaven.
No one is as beautiful as she.
On the east and west, the celebration walked from the Campbell Hotel.
New York has never seen such joy.
I choose you to be the poet delivering poems from two poets.
You are the chosen, precious beloved, able to stir two champions.
Take this poem from a poet among those standing.
If the rain will permit, I would like to stand up between the two halls.
I would voluntarily write two compositions about the faithfullness among people.
You are the one who I grew up with. I just need two hours to tell.
You are lucky, you, "Negma (star)". You see, there is no other such beauty in the Jemeyel folks.
... Sweet scented star (Nejma), you attracted Gemeyel Zein."
      -- February, 1948.   Emil Zein.

After that reading, a group of our intellectual patriots spoke. They were: Farid 'Oql Genid, Nasry Mansour Ebeid, and Boutros Youssef Khatar. Then, the Corporal and groomsman Asaad Wakim (Kassab) read the congratulation letters which numbered more than 150. When he read the letter of Louis and Emil Zein, which was sent from Salima, the loving hometown, the whole gathering stood up and applauded.

They celebrated with enthusiasm and joy. In the evening, a dance party was held. There were many people who attended the wedding ceremonies having come from far away places. After the honeymoon, the groom and bride went back to Charleston, West Virginia, where they took up residence. The groom is in business there with his two brothers, Habib and Mourad. May God help them to succeed.

Their Vestiges

The following are some choice verses from the poem of Zein Khalil Zein, which his teacher, the famous Sheikh Abdulallah Boustany, included in his volume of collected poems. The theme of the poem was to congratulate the late Bishop Youssef Debs when he came back from Rome as a victor, having been proved innocent of accusations brought against him in 1886 to 1887.

Let it resound loudly throughout the land, so loud that the quivers cause pain.
It will shut the mouths of the oppressors who will plead for forgiveness.
You want to bring the truth into the light, and only the truth wil help you and support you.
Oh, you, who want to humble the party which was our strong support even in bad times!
You must stop. It appears that you adore the impossible. Demanding the impossible, as you do, is insane.
We, the people of Maron, we are happy just being Maronites.
Time cannot shake us or move us. We are sons of the mountain!
Because of all this we are not afraid of death if it overtakes us! In one disaster after another we bury the centuries.
Villains will not steal the glamour from our pride. Not as long as our pride is founded on our union.
They thought that virtue would be hidden, that justice would be buried. ...
They have no reason to be jealous that the virtues of Youssef appeared despite all the accusations; because truth will always win! ...

The truth is his strength whenever he speaks. His mouth will trap the words that others speak in evil.

It is enough for us to be proud because we have been freed from those who became liars and thieves for the famous.

Honest Youssef, Jesus is your comfort against those who would dare to humiliate you. Your Excellency, in the past the tyrants were plotting against you. But see what happened to them.

They were happy when they thought their plots against you succeeded. But now they are weeping at the feet of the Pope.

They thought that the successor of Saint Peter would be attentive to their pretentions. But, instead, he freed the accused!

Your Excellency, Youssef, you were the jailer who became a prisoner.

Beirut acclaimed and welcomed you even during those black days.

You bade them farewell and their eyes were full of tears. They longed to see you.

Every patriotic one of them was longing for your arrival.

Oh, you ignorant souls, what did you intend to do by your deeds. If only you retrace the steps of truth.

Let us go. There is no time for regrets. The Glorious Pope is still full of kindness.

We ask our ruling Pope to forgive those who misbehaved, for he is still the father of all of us.

May God preserve your rule and keep you in happiness. May you always live in joy.

Go forth and continue to be the rare composition that you are, you who originates from the holy Al Ghar.

Below we have chosen some verses from the wonderful poem that Zein Khalil Zein composed when he was the French teacher in the Lady of Lourdes' School in Salima. Khalil Beik 'Oql Shedid included it in his book of congratulations for Pope Leo XIII. It marked the Jubilee of the Pope's ordination to the priesthood which was being celebrated in 1887–1888.

Stop at Rome and pass by its congregation. You will meet its protector, the valiant lion.

You'll find there the rock of faith, with the strength of the vicar of God, giving glory to Him.

Fear not the days of black for God will transform them.

He took care of His Church through Jesus, its Saving Corner stone.

He said, "Peter, you are a pure rock, and so I will build upon you.

I will give to you the keys of heaven. Anywhere you go, it will be   there with you.

It is like Noah's boat. Jesus will carry us in the flood in this unfaithful world. He will keep us safe.

A vessel driven by a pious sailor "Leo", he will be the protector.

He has followed the path of the Popes before him and added to   their glory.

How many cataclysms happened to him! They sounded and the whole earth endured them.

With his wisdom, Life and Religion became compatible. It was as if he was the owner and the guardian of life itself.

The festivities shook the Mountain of Lebanon. His men around the world celebrated.

If you succeeded, continue to seek our support; and if you write history, tell us there will be help for those who hope.

Below are a few verses told by Habib Khalil Zein, the Arabic teacher at the School of Our Lady of Lourdes in Salima. He added his congratulations to Pope Leo XIII. The one who collected the material, made it the sweet finale:

When the poetry spoke of his characteristics he rejoiced. When the brave illuminated him, he exulted in their attention.

When he spread the fragrance of his knowledge throughout the west and eastern sky, poetry drew attention to it.

Because of you, pride has been brought to all of our people through the poems of our eastern writers.

They did not write their poetry to uplift themselves, they wrote it to be your ornamental crown.

It is good to be thankful to those who have been generous, and I mean that it was magnificent, the best.

He is "Ibn Oql", who became, like his ancestors, a lover of the Church, from the bottom of his heart.

It was he who gathered the poems of his grandfather and voluntarily published them.

Josef, the son of "Aql" (another pronunciation of the name "Oql" meaning "the mind"), you will be generously rewarded and repaid by God for your kindness.

And Leo, you remained the cornerstone of the Lord's Church which is overcome with joy.

And, so, just as this collection started by asking that the Lord's will be done, so I end with a prayer for the same request.

THE ASMAR HOUSE

Chapter 4

Their Origin

At the beginning of this century, the Priest (Bardiot) Anton Al Asmar came from the village of Knaisse to Salima. He bought the castle of the Lam's Princes from the Capuchin priests who had transformed it into a boarding school. It was named "Our Lady of Lourdes" (1883–1893). They had puchased it from the District Government of Lebanon who had taken it by force.

So it was that Father Anton bought it and re-opened the school. He operated it for years before and after the First World War. He also bought the old Monastery of Saint Peter from the Monks of Saint Anthony who had purchased it from the Capuchin Fathers. When the Bardiot Al Asmar died, the monastery and the castle came to be the property of Mr. Najib, the son of his brother, Amin Al Asmar. He sold the Monastery to the Apostolic Nuns and kept the castle as his personal residence.

The great-grandfather of the Asmar House is Al Haj Khalil Bin Ayoub Al Bashrani. He emigrated with his two brothers: Hebesh, the forefather of the Hebesh House, and, Haj Yonan, the forefather of the Edeh House. They first moved to Deir Al Ahmar in Baalbek to Yanouh, near Al Aaqoura, at the upper Jbail. The Haj Yonan Edeh lived in the cities of Jbail and his offspring spread to Beirut, Beit Meri, and Baabda. Sheikh Hebesh and his people lived in Ghazeer in Kisrawan. Meanwhile, Haj Khalil lived in Hbaline, in the heart of the Jbail cities. He is the great-grand-father of the family of Asmar the Hbalians. His children are known to be originally from Yanouh. Then they moved to Hbaline, only to leave it later and spread over the country: Kisrawan, then in the Metn, Jezzinee, at the coast of Beirut (especially in Hadath), as well as in Baabda, Damour, and, in other places.

In the Metn, they were under the protection of the Lam's Princes. They lived in Aarbaniye, then in Knaise, Qartaba, Zandouqa and Dlaibe. A group from those who were in Qartada moved to Beit Meri and Ain Saade where they are known as the Asmar House and the Qartada House. Those who lived in Jezzine extended to the neighboring villages, in the Bcharre towns and in Baabda where they were known as the Asmar or the Hbaline House. In Hadath, it was the same, and among them was the Kharma House. We have collected the information and the documents of those families in our manuscript "The History Of The Maronite Families". So, hereafter, we will just state the offsping of Father Yaakoub, the great-grandfather of the Asmar House in Salima. Father Yaakoub is Tanious BouHaidar, one of the Asmar offshoots. He was married and lived in the village of Knaisse. On November 27, 1807, Bishop Abdulallah Blibel ordained him to the priesthood in the chapel of Saint (Mar) Ash'eya, in the Church he built in Qatada. So, he moved there and lived a very long life. He lived to be 115 years old and was in full control of his mental abilities.

He was generous, zealous, and pious. These qualities are still passed on from one generation to another. He built the Saint Ash'eya Monastery in Qartada and donated large holdings of land for it. He appointed his children its supervisors, then successively, the supervision was passed down from the oldest on down. It was a building for residence as well as a church, named after Saint Ash'eia. He renovated the building in 1831 as mentioned with the date on the Church door.

Father Yaakoub was succeeded by his son, Father Ash'eia, who took charge of the endowment. After him, came Abdulallah, who was married. He resided for a long time in this monastery and was, like his father, a very generous man.

In his time the endowment property grew considerably. He died, leaving sons, who are:

1- Pastor Shawoul who became the headmaster of the Antonian Monastery. He was famous not only for his generosity but also for his management skills and his counsel.
2- Pastor Ibrahim the first.
3- Pastor Ignacious.
4- Hanna.
5- Father Ash'eia who was the headmaster of the Qartada Monastery. He begot Sheikh Abdulallah Khoury who moved to Knaise. He built a house there and a silk plant and he lived there. He was very well known in the area and he firmly established his nobility and wealth. He begot A- Najib "Monsignor Nimatallah", B- Sheikh Selim, and C- Khalil who begot two daughters: Lea and Bahga.

In addition to his own knowledge and generosity, Sheikh Selim inherited from his father the same high degree of nobility, notability, and wealth. As for Hanna, the son of Father Yaakoub, he begot: Abou Zeid, Father Boulos, Pastor Ibrahim, Khalil, Youssef, and Father Youssef. Abou Zeid begot Salebe, Pator Shawoul II, Fahd, and Neama. Father Boulos took charge of the presidency of the Saint Anthony Knaise Monastery. Father (Monsignor) Youssef Asmar was the headmaster of the Saint Ash'eia Monastery in Qartaba and the bishop. This position was undertaken by Monsignor Nimatallah Asmar, who was a man of generosity, literature and, especially, poetry. He has left behind many printed and manuscript literary pieces, such as: The poems of Kalila and Demna, previously written by the author Ibn Habaria, he completed the missing verses and corrected the edition printed in Beirut. He also translated the book The Martyr by one of the famous Spanish writers; he translated it from French to Arabic and it is a good historical and religious book. They were succeeded by Monsignor Anton Asmar. As for Youssef Bin Hanna, he begot: Louis (Father Boutros) and Hanna. Fahd, the son of Abi Zeid, begot Ghatas and Youssef. Neama Abou Zeid begot Youssef, Shoukry, and Yaakoub.

Khalil Bin Hanna Al Khoury Yaakoub begot: Amin, Mansour, and Tanious. Amin begot Najib with his first wife, Frenja the daughter of Father Elias 'Oun from Arbaniea. With his second wife, Helena, the daughter of Habib Hosher from Beirut, he begot Maroun. Mansour begot Khalil (Father Youssef), Youssef and Fouad. Tanious is the Badriot Anton Asmar who bought the castle and re-opened the school of Our Lady of Lourdes. He travelled many times to Europe and America for contributions for his building projects as we have already mentioned.

After his death, his nephew, Najib, the son of his brother Amin, inherited all of his properties. Najib married Adele, the daughter of Sheikh Mahmoud Belibel from Bikfaya. With her, he begot: Josef, Anton, Henry, and two daughters. He is a very intellectual man and his children are attending the famous Eintoura School. He lives with his family in Salima and he participates in its cultural and patriotic matters. Also, he has been appointed the Mayor of Salima. In addition, he was the generous one responsible for having the nuns in that village.

As for the rest of the information about the Asmar House, it is all written down, in detail, in our book The History of the Maronite Families which is now being printed.

THE NAKOUZY HOUSE

Chapter 5

Their History

The Nakouzy family is a noble Maronite family coming from Aramean and Phenician roots. We don't have any detailed history about them because of the wars and catastrophes of the past. There are just a few unproven vestiges of their past. This includes documents as well as oral traditions.

The Maronites faced many catastrophes after the departure of the Crusaders and the destruction of Kisrawan in the years 1303 to 1307. The Christians emigrated to the upper Jbail towns and were confined to the area behind the Ibrahim River. It was there that they found some relief during the reign of the Assaf Princes. This was particularly true during the rule of the greatest of these Princes, Prince Mansour Assaf. Safety prevailed in those days. Therefore, the Christians came back to Kisrawan, and, at the end of the 16th century and beginning of the 17th century, they gradually moved to the Metn, the Shouf, and the South during the rule of the Ma'an Princes. Comfort, justice, and safety were the order of the day.

The number of Maronites emigrating from the Northern parts increased because of the oppression of the Muslim governors. This was after the retreat of the Maronite lieutenant colonels and their feudal leaders. Many of the villages of the North became empty with all of their inhabitants taking refuge in the areas surrounding Kisrawan.

The Hebesh folks approached the Princes of the Assaf people. The Princes became stronger and more noticed after they were joined by the lieutenant colonels. Then came the Khazan folks who were influential during the government of the Ma'an.

The migration of the Maronites expanded to the province of the Lam's Princes who were, at that time, embracing the Druze religion. They brought the Christians nearer. They liked them because they were honest and dedicated in their service. Even more, the Princes liked them because the Maronites excelled in agriculture and in raising silkworms; things that the Druzes of Metn neglected. The Maronites filled other jobs too.

Among those who migrated to the Metn were the Nakouzy folks. According to knowledgeable people, the Nakouzy's originated from the village of Hadtoun in the mountains of Batroun where the old native Maronites towns are located. From there, many families emerged, such as: the Tiyan, the Hadtouni, the Maroun, and many others. Also, there are many beautiful monuments showing the area's antiquity. Furthermore, there are old buildings and antiques which show the development of Chritianity.

Again, the reason why those families migrated was because of oppression. And, there is another reason which anscestors mentioned, namely, a great fire which occurred in Hadtoun around the year 1600. Consequently, its people left and seperated into the country. Some time after its destruction, some families went there and populated it. Today, most of its inhabitants are from the Khalifa House. They came from Bejje in the Jbail area and they still remain even after some moved away.

As to the name of this family, there are many stories:

Youssef Khatar Ghanem handed down this story about the name "Nakouzy" from the families of Hadtoun. This story says that the name Nakouzy was given to this family as per an incident which happened to one of their forefathers. He killed an employer working for the governor of Tripoli because he had talked badly about his sister. After that he ran away with his family, and since then, has been called "Nakouzy" or "Nakhouzy" or "Nakhoussy". This word is a Syriac word deriving from the verb in Syriac "Nakhassa" which means "to slaughter", so "Al Nakhoussy" means "The Slaughterer".

Another story told by some is that the Nakouzy House is related to Nicosia in Cyprus and that they are of those Lebanese Maronites who migrated to that island during the period of the oppression. This is the story that was mentioned by historians like Douaihy and others. This may have been what happened after the catastrophes that occurred when the Maronite towns were destroyed after the Crusaders left. Some Maronites went and lived in Nicosia, then came back to Lebanon and lived in Hadtoun. Ever since then they were known as the Nakouzy.

Still another story was told by someone to Monsignor Dagher which he mentioned in his book <u>General Views of Lebanon,</u> on page 386 it says: *"The historian, Prince Haidar, has mentioned that the Nakouzy House came from Nicosia in Cyprus and were tied to it."* However, this story is not true. It has not been mentioned in the Prince's history nor in any other histories.

Their Offshoots

Of the Nakouzy families, some of them are original and others are derived from it. The original ones are those who went to Salima at the begining of the first migration. They are six. The subsidary families are those who belong to the Nakouzy family but joined to it by marriage, as well as by a union of concepts, opinion, and cooperation. Thus, there has been a mix of people with the original offshoots and they have became one family, even if some of them still call themselves by their private sub-surname.

Those original houses are:

1- The Tanious House which is divided in two parts: the Khoury House and the Abi Safi Hanna House.
2- The Tarbeia House and the Khatar House.
3- The Abi Eissa House.
4- The Moussa Daher House.
5- The Abi Mehia House.
6- The Abdel Hay Badran House.

The subsidary houses are:

1- The Anton Abi Anton House.
2- The Kanaan House.
3- The Hanna Bin Tanious House.
4- The Hadary House.
5- The Sahyoun House.
6- The Hanoud House.
7- The Eishy House.
8- The Bou Saqr House.

However, those who are surnamed Nakousy from this family are:

1- Those who lived in Salima in the past and who include a group who migrated to Dekouane at the Coast of Beirut.
2- Those who lived in the past in Mtain and the group who migrated to the countryside, to Baouchriye and Sadd; they are the Khalil Nakouzy House, the Moussa and Khalil Safi House.
3- Those who were at Jbail.
4- Those who, in the past, lived in Beirut, and most of them originate from Jbail.
5- Those who live in Berga near Jounie.

As for those who are related to the Nakouzy House:

1- The Abi Karam House in Broummana, some say that the Bou Soliman House is among them.
2- Bou Kanaan House in Abeia.
3- The Hatouni House in Dlebta who moved with the Nakouzy House from Jetoun.
4- The Maroun House who are on the Alma Coast.
5- The Tiyan House in Beirut and from them came the Kanaan Tiyan house who lived for a long time in Salima and then returned to Beirut. And there are also those are also originating from Hadtoun.

God willing, we will talk in detail about these families in our The History of the Maronite Families.

Those who have written about the Nakouzy House are: Father Mansour Harouni in his book entitled The Province of Kisrawan printed in Beirut, page 67; The Printed Lineage Tree, 1907; the Historical Biography about the families of Dlebta, and the Register of Saint Yaakoub for the Harouni which Father Boutros Rofael published in his book The History of Dlebta, page 12. Also, there is the program by Youssef Khattar Ghanem and his letters to the Ghanmes people.

However, we must mention that we possess a document in our archives which was with the inheritances of the Genuid Abi Safi Nakouzy family. In this paper, it is mentioned: "Abou Safi Hanna from the Salima village, from the Nakouzeh ..."

This document is dated close to the date of the murder committed by Nakouzy, and the victim was an employee of the Tripoli governor. The time of the conflagration in Hadtoun was in 1600 and it was followed by the departure of the Nakouzy folks. They left there and took refuge at Kisrawan, then Salima, and Ras Al Metn, where they were protected by the Lam's Princes. This was around the year 1616. Also, this date is close to the date of the mentioned document, 1074 Hegira (1663). In this document, which we will present with its complete text when talking about the Abi Safi House, the word Nakoussy or Nakhoussy were not mentioned, only the word "Nakouzeh" was mentioned. This clearly proves that the story of Youssef Khatar Ghanem about "The Slaughterer" is untrue.

The Khoury House.

Their Lineage.

At the beinning of the 17th century, Tanious Nakouzy left Hadathoun in Batroun. He begot Father Hanna and Abou Safi but there is a possibility that they may be paternal cousins. Father Hanna begot Father Francis and Boutros who begot Father Hanna II.

Therefore, the Khoury the Nakouzy people became two houses: the Father Francis House and the Father Hanna Ibn Boutros House.

The Father Francis House

Father Francis begot Youssef who was known as Youssef Al Khoury; he begot Nasef, Sabra, and Girgis.

Nasef begot Shebl and Youssef. Shebl died young, while Youssef begot Nasef who begot George. George then begot Josef and Antoin.

As for Sabra, he begot Mikhail, Asaad, Francis, and Refqa (the wife of Mansour Kanaan). Mikhail didn't get married. Francis had no children, and, Asaad Sabra begot Sabra and Youssef. Sabra became a priest named Father Youssef. Youssef had only Josephine.

Girgis Bin Youssef Al Khoury begot Assaf and Hanna. Assaf died unmarried and Hanna Bin Girgis Al Khoury begot Assaf, Girgis, Selim, Youssef, and Nessib. Assaf begot Pedro, Anibel, John, Edward, and August. Girgis begot Ceasar and we don't have further information on others. Selim begot Moris and Emil. As for Youssef, he begot Alexi and Elie. Nessib begot children, we believe, but we don't have the details.

The Father Hanna House

Boutros, the son of Father Hanna I, begot Father Hanna II and three daughters: 1. the wife of Shahin Saadallah Al Erian who died and had no children; 2. the wife of Nemr Bou Eissa Nakouzy; and, 3. Warda, the wife of Abdulallah Bin Sha'ia Bin Safi. Father Hanna begot Mansour, Boutros, Ragi, Tanous, Rashed, Elias, and Mary (the wife of Daher Bou Ragheb Bachaalany. Mansour Khoury begot Ibrahim who begot Khalil, Mansour, and Najib. As for Khalil, he died unmaried and young. Najib joined the local Monastery and became a pastor and priest. Mansour, so far, has had no sons.

Boutros Khoury begot Daoud who died unmarried. Tanous Khoury begot Elias who died unmarried. Girgis begot Aziz, Rashed, and Tawfik. Aziz and Rashed died unmarried. Tawfik begot George, Aziz, and Khalil. Meanwhile, Ragi, the son of Father Hanna, became a pastor in the Halabian Monastery. He was killed at the Lady of Tala Monastery in Deir el Qamar in 1860. As for Rashed and Elias Khoury Hanna, they died unmarried.

A statement issued by the Governor of Sayda to Girgis Hanna Khoury:

"No. 258. The reason for issuing this travel pass: namely, that from the five hundred pieces of weapons which have been reserved for those in the army, and those mobilized in the Chritian governorate: twenty one pieces of weapons have been sent to the province of Metn, the Coast, and to Rechmaya for the Princes, the sons of Prince Ismail in Salima. The person holding this pass no. 258 who will give his name and description at the border of the Christian governorate, is traveling armed. No civil officers and no other person should stop him. That is why this travel pass

has been issued from the office of Ayalet Sayda Hegira, Mohamed Kamel, the Mayor of Aylat Sayda and Tripoli (Stamp) …year 1262 Hegira."

"Holding this travel pass is Girgis Hanna Khoury, the servant of Prince Hassan Ismail in Salima: Medium height, Brown tint, blond moustache. This has been issued as per the honoured order of the statement dated Sh. 15th, 1262 Hegira, by the governor of the Christians of Lebanon Mountain (stamp) Haidar Ismail."

The Abi Safi House

Their Vestiges

"The reason for writing this is that the wife of Abou Dhaher Aziz gave to her son-in-law, Abou Safi Hanna from the Nakouzy House in Salima Village, the uncultivated lands which are the field which is in the Thagra, the field which is in Deir Qanat, and that which is in Kafr Hiyan, as well as half of the house. He will cultivate them and give half of their crops for the lady for as long as she lives. After her death, her daughter Maania, the wife of Abou Safi Hanna, has the right to dispose of them. And, as long as she is alive, they are not for sale or mortgage. Written in Rabie Al Awal, in the year 1074 (1663). And, there will be nothing for Dhaher or for …. Written by the humble Ali Salman. Certified by Sheikh Nasr Eddine."

According to that document, it is clear that Maania, the daughter of Abou Dhaher Aziz from Ras Al Metn, was the wife of Abou Safi Hanna Nakouzy from Salima. Her mother donated to Abou Safi half of her house and parcels of land at the exit of Ras Al Metn. The places are still known by their names today. The Thagra is a district between Benkhnieh and Deir Al Herf; and, Kafr Hiyen is between Ras Al Metn and Al Qasiba. Deir Qanat is a place not far from Al Ras where there is a monument of an old bridge. Some say that it was part of a monastery.

Moreover, from that precious document, we can know when the Christians were returning to those regions.

Hereafter, is a second document from the historical items belonging to this family. It is as valuable as the first one. The name of Abi Assy from the offspring of the mentioned Abou Safi is mentioned in it. He died without having any children:

"This document has been written because Abou Assy has purchased from Abou Hassan Yaghi, the cinnamon bark which is in Ein Al Sayfiyeh at the price of thirty-two piasters, according to the evaluation of Abou Hassan Ibn Sengueskh (This may be Segaa or Geahgeah). The cash was received by the seller with satisfaction and the agreement accepted by both parties without any hidden restrictions or obligations. The Seller accepted the full payment from the buyer and there is no amount due. Written in the year 1103 (1691), correct and proper. The buyer guarranteed all right of intercession and full succession to the seller. Written by Abou Kamal. Witnessed by Abou Mahmoud Al Masry, Hassan Ibn Shahin, and Bahmed Said."

"…the sons of Sha'ia, the Sheikhs Shahin and his brother Abdulallah, from the Nakouzy House of Salima have purchased from the Sheikhs of the Khawaja House, namely, Professor Elias, Gueris Ibn Nasr, and Anton Ibn Mehana, the mulberries behind their district. Also included were two fruit gardens looking over the mulberries from the Genina, a fruit garden which is at the bottom of the fruit garden of her excellency the Lady Zahr…. Its borders, from the South, the properties of Nasef; from the East, the road; from the West, the waterwheel and the cliff which is in front of the Azarole; and, from the North, Anton House…on Geomadi Al Awal 1231 (1815), Written by the humble Mohamed Ibn Mahmoud Al Masry. Witnesses: Bou Ali Breqaa. Elias Al Tiyan."

"Shahin Ibn Sha'ia bought from Sheikh Abou Saab Kanaan Al Tyan, the grape vines which are in Ein Al Sayfeyeh at the price of 80 piasters, in 1231. Written by the seller, Kanaan Al Tiyan. We agree upon this with our full satisfaction. Written by Elias Al Tiyan."

Their Lineage

We previously said that the offspring of Tanious Nakouzy, who left from Hadthoun, was divided in two families: the family of the Khoury and the family of Abou Safi Hanna. We already mentioned the family of the Khoury's, so, we will now talk about the family of Abou Safi.

Abou Safi Hanna begot Safi who begot Hanna and Sha'ia. Hanna begot Genid, the forefather of the Genid House and Sha'ia, the forefather of the Sha'ia House.

As for Genid Bin Hanna Bin Safi, he begot Khalil, Hanna, and 'Oql. Khalil Genid died without having children. Hanna Genid begot Youssef and Abdou. Neither of them had children. 'Oql Genid begot Khalil, Mansour, Said, Genid, Ibrahim, and Hanna. Khalil 'Oql had no children. Mansour didn't get married. Said had children living in Egypt. Ibrahim and Hanna died young and unmarried. As for Genid, he begot Farid, Philip, Fahim, and 'Oql. They are expatriates in the United States and have children. Today, there is no one of Genid House remaining in Salima. The only ones surviving of the descendants of Genid 'Oql are those living in the United States, and the Said offspring in Egypt.

Sha'ia Bin Safi begot Shahin and Abdulallah. Abdulallah had only girls: 1-Taranjeh, the wife of Anton Abou Anton. 2- Badou', the wife of Assaf Bin Nemr Abou Eissa. 3- Qanou', the wife of Mansour Bin Hanna Tanious. 4- Dalila, the wife of Nasef Youssef Al Khoury Francis. And, 5- Mahaba, the wife of Shahin Bin Sha'ia Bin Safi Al Bachaalany.

As for Shahin Bin Safi Nakouzy, he begot Ghaleb, Elias, and the wife of Bou Saqr. Ghaleb begot Shahin and Girgs. Girgis was killed in Beirut in 1883 and Shahin Ghaleb begot Ghaleb, Youssef, and Rashid. Ghaleb Bin Shahin Ghaleb begot Emil, Shahin, George, and Philip. Emil Ghaleb begot Marcel and Josef. Shahin begot Anis, Moris, and Charlo. Philip begot Edward. As for Youssef Shahin, he died without ever being married. Rashid Shahin begot John, Antoin, and Josef.

While Elias Bin Shahin Bin Sha'ia begot Youssef who begot Asaad who died young and unmarried. He was killed near Marseilles, on his way to America.

Heikal Bin Sha'ia Bin Safi begot Nejm and Mar'e. Nejm begot Dhaher, who had no children, and Sha'ia. Sha'ia later begot Asaad who had only Adele, the wife of Tanious Sahyoun. Mar'e Bin Heikal begot Heikal and Ibrahim. Heikal begot Nejm, Mar'e, and Selim. Mar'e begot Youssef who married in the United States. Nejm and Selim are expatriates in Venezuela. Ibrahim Mar'e begot Melhem who begot Edmar in Brazil.

The Abi Tarbeia House.

Their Lineage.

Boutros Abou Tarbeia begot Khatar and Shahin. Khatar begot Elias, and Tanious (the forefather of Abou Tarbeia Al Nakouzy family in Dekouane at the coast). Elias Khatar begot Khatar, Salem, Hashim, Rahal, and Rahbel, the wife of Ghanatious Bachaalany. Khatar Elias begot Fares, Girgis, Hanna, and Boutros who had no children. Fares Khatar Elias begot Khatar, Youssef, and Habib. Habib died in Brazil, unmarried. Khatar Bin Fares begot Fares who begot a son and a daughter in Brazil. As for Youssef Fares Khatar, he begot Abdo, Tanious, and Boutros. Youssef Fares Khatar was killed by slaves in Africa. Abdou died in Africa young and unmarried. Tanious died in Charleston in the United States and has left a son and a daughter. Boutros became an expatriate in Charleston and, as yet, is still unmarried. Girgis and Boutros Khatar have no offspring.

Hanna Khatar begot Shaker, Boutros, and Girgis. Shaker is an expatriate in Venezuela and has boys and girls living there. Boutros is an expatriate in Africa and begot girls. As for Girgis, he died and left a daughter.

Salem Ibn Elias Khatar begot Boutros who begot Salem and Daoud. Salem begot Elias and Moussa who are both expatriates in the United States. They are married and have sons and daughters.

Daoud Boutros Salem begot Boutros who is an expatriate in Brazil and has sons. As for Hashim, he begot Khatar who lived in Dekouane and he begot Youssef who begot Elias. Elias begot Youssef who has children.

Rahal Bin Elias Khatar begot Youssef, Elias, and Mosaad. Mosaad died unmarried. Youssef Rahal begot Francis, Raji, Sasin, Yamama (the wife of Girgis Gibrail from Bzebdine), Saida (the wife of Shahin Saab), and Boutrosia (the wife of Saad Heikal Khairallah, originating from Bhamdoun). Francis, Raji, and Sasin died without having children. Elias Rahal begot Eskandar (who died unmarried), Henna (the wife of Father Elias Al Haj Boutros from Jouar el Haouz), and Mena (the wife of Anton Rokz Al Haj Boutros from Jouar el Haouz).

As for Shahin Bin Boutros Abou Tarbeia, he begot Ibrahim who begot Shahin. Shahin begot Saab who begot Shahin and Tarbeia. Shahin begot girls, while Tarbeia known as Youssef had no children.

Abou Tarbeia In Dekouane.

As for Tanious Bin Khatar Bin Boutros Abou Tarbeia Nakouzy, he emigrated from Salima to Dekouane at the Beirut Coast. He probably begot Daher and Ayoub.

Daher begot De'ebs who begot Daher. This latter lived for a long time in Salima. Then, he went back with his family to Dekouane. He begot Abdou, Khalil, De'ebess, Hanna, Anton, Elias, Tawfik, and Soliman. Abdou begot Josef, George, Pierre, Paul, and Gabriel. Khalil begot Antoin, Louis, and Badi'e. Hanna begot Elias, Josef, Abdou, and George. Tawfik begot Philip, Labib, and Nabil.

Anton begot George in the Transval (Republic of South Africa). Soliman begot sons and died in Argentina. De'ebes had only girls. Josef, the son of Abdou Daher begot Jack. Daher De'ebes lived to be more than 90 years old.

Today, they are in Dekouane and Borj Hammoud except for those expatriates who are in Transval and Argentina.

Ayoub Bin Tanious begot Khatar who begot Tanious, Ayoub, and Hanna. Tanious is an expatriate in Venezuela and has two sons. Ayoub begot Girgi, Khatar, John, Francois, and Jemeyl. As for Hanna, he died young and unmarried.

And in Dekouane, there is Neama Nakouzy who begot Girgis, who is a paternal cousin of Ayoub who lived in Dekouane.

Their Vestiges

"...Boutros Ibn Fahd acknowledged before us, that he legally owes the keeper of this document, Khatar Ibn Elias, an amount of seventy piasters.... We agreed to write this document for clarification and to avoid forgetness. Written and valid in April, 1839. Written by Nasef Bou'oun Ali as dictated. Witnesses: Mansour Abdel Hay. Mansour Ibn Hanna Bin Tanious."

"...Fahd Al Masry and his sons, Fa'our and Hamdan, admitted before us that they owe to Khatar Ibn Elias the amount of one hundred forty piasters and a half ... and in case of death, they vow that ten days from the date of their death, the amount will be repaid to the mentioned Khatar ...on February 1, 1253 (1837). Witnesses: Youssef Ibn Tarad. Qassem Ibn Hussein Daher Said. Girgis El Efish from Mehidtha. Written by Shebli Ibn..."

"...We owe to Fares Ibn Khatar, 15 piasters and vow that they will be repaid by the next crop in February, 1255. Written by Hanna Ghanatious. Bou Soliman Beshara accepted. Witnesses: Metri Ibn Moussa. Khatar Ibn Asaad."

"...Tanious Serkis from Dlaibe acknowledges that he owes an amount of 67 piasters to Khatar Ibn Elias from Salima. January, 1259 Hegira. Written by Hanna Ghanatious. Witnesses: Youssef Ibn Mikahil Abdel Nour. Elias Ibn Asaad Me'lem Elias."

Abou Eissa House.

Their Lineage.

Abou Eissa Nakouzy begot Abou Nejm Moussa or Abou Eissa begot Eissa and Saad. Eissa begot Moussa who begot Hanna and Nemr. Nemr begot Asaaf, Shahin, Boutros, Nader, and Boutrosia who married Nasef Abou 'Oql, a resident of Moalaket Zahle and the brother of 'Oql Shedid from the Metn.

Assaf Bin Nemr begot Nasef, Daoud, and Shahin. Nasef Assaf begot Youssef, Louis, Caesar, and Nakhleh. Youssef died without having any children. Louis begot Emil who has no boys up to today. Caesar died unmarried and young. Nakhleh had Edmond who begot Nakhleh. As for Daoud Assaf, he had no children. Shahin Assaf begot Anton and George. Anton begot Michel.

Nader Bin Nemr begot Habib and Asaad who died young. Habib begot Asaad and Abdou. Asaad Habib begot Said, Rashid, and Boutros. Said and Boutros were unmarried and died young. Rashid begot, with his first wife, George, and, with his second wife, he begot Josef and Raymond. George begot children, we believe. Josef died young and Rashid died in the United States where his family lives.

Abdou Habib begot Anton who lived in Egypt, while Shahin bin Nemr begot Mary (the wife of Shahin Ghaleb Nakouzy) and Zahra (the wife of Asaad Khalil Bachaalany). As for Boutros Nemr, he begot Dharifa (the wife of Habib Al Hanoud), and Shams (the wife of Youssef Dhaher Nakouzy).

Saad Abou Eissa begot Girgis who begot Mikhail, Saad, and Hanna. Mikhail begot Shedid, Eid, Hanna, and Said. Shedid Mikhail begot Mikhail, Hanna, and Shaker. Mikhail had daughters and one son whose names we do not know. Hanna Shedid begot children, we believe, as did Shaker Shedid.

The family of Shedid Mikhail Saad is in the United States. Eid Mikahil begot Abdou who died young. Hanna Bin Mikhail died young, too, and Said emigrated to Brazil and begot Josef and possibly others whose names we do not know.

Their Vestige

"The reason for writing this document is to acknowledge that on this date we have promised and vowed to his excellency, the respectful Prince Haidar, that we will be his servants. We will obey his orders and act upon his wishes, providing an honest service, for as long as we are alive. We will keep his secrets. We will do our utmost to obey his orders without deception or fatigue. We will not participate in acts against him or against any of his interests, either secretly or publicly. God is our witness to what we are saying. If we show any objection to what we have previously accepted and promised, his excellency has every right to blame us and punish us with the appropriate punishment, after making his investigations and having reports.

We must not serve anyone else other than him, unless with his permission. We wish to be sheltered by his zeal and concern. .... We accept all this for ourselves, with our complete satifaction and desire. To certify this agreement, the undermentioned names are witnesses. Written on February 23, 1236 Hegira (1820). Accepted by Girgis Saad Nakouzy. The Witnesses: Father Hanna Salima. Written by Father Daniel (Jemeyel)."

The House of Moussa Daher.

Their Lineage.

(It should be noted here that sometimes the author writes the name as Dahar and at other times, as Dhahar.)

Moussa Daher Nakouzy begot Sabra, Elias, Tanous, Fares, and the wife of Fares Al Henawy Al Bachaalany. Sabra begot Ghandour, Ghantous, and Youssef. The two last ones had no children and Ghandour begot Hanna and Raji. Hanna Ghandour had no children and Raji begot only Matilda, the wife of Nasef Sham'oun originating from Jouar el Haouz.

As for Elias Bin Moussa, he begot 'Oql and Asaad. Assad was killed in the battle of Ibrahim Pasha. 'Oql begot Asaad who had no children.

Tanous Bin Moussa begot Khalil and Nasef. Nasef died young and unmarried. Khalil Tanous begot Francis, Girgis, Tanous, and Nasef. Francis and Girgis both died young. Nasef emigrated to Brazil. He didn't get married and died there.

Tanous Khalil emigrated to the United States, then, came back to Salima in his last days to die there. His sons, Khalil and Emil, are in America.

Fares Bin Moussa Daher begot Azam, Jabr, and Khashan. Azam begot Youssef and Hanna. Hanna was killed in the fighting with Ibrahim Pasha. Youssef never married. Jabr Bin Fares begot Daher who begot MAintoura (the wife of Girgis Bou Saqr), Haloun (the first wife of Hanna Fares Bachaalany), and Farfoura (the wife of Daoud Assaf Nemr).

Khashan Bin Fares Bin Moussa Daher Al Nakouzy begot Azar who begot Melhem and Khashan surnamed by Selim (and who died unmarried). Melhem Azar begot Najib, Mary (the wife of Boutros Al Soury), Emily (the wife of Habib Beik Gueris), and Rosa. Najib begot only girls thus far.

The Abou Mhaya House

In the newspapers talking about the parcels of properties in Salima dated 1770, I saw the name of their forefather, Elias Bou Mhaya, written that way.

Elias begot Daher who begot Youssef and Mekhwel. Youssef Daher begot Daher and Mikhail who both emigrated to Brazil. Daher begot Josef and four daughters. Mikhail begot Nessib, Najib, and a daughter.

As for Mekhwel, he married Satout, the daughter of Aboud Showaysha and begot Mary, and Khristine (who died unmarried). Mary married Selim Hashimeh from Bikfaya. Today, no one of this family remains in Salima.

The House of Saad Ghayad

The House of Saad Ghayad came from the House of Nakouzy living in Shabanieh (Charbine). It is said that they are the closest offshoot of the House of Abi Mhaya in Salima. Saad Nakouzy married the daughter of Mansour Abdel Hay Badran Nakouzy from Salima and begot Ghayad and the Subdeacon Anton, who died young. While Ghayad married Amina, the daughter of Daher Abi Mhaya Nakouzy, and begot Shedid who begot Fares, Faram, Youssef, and Anton. Ghayad and Subdeacon Anton were students of the famous Ein Waraka School, and, were studying by turns at the regular Capuchin Father's school which was near their Saint Peter's Monastery in Salima. Subdeacon Anton mastered the Arabic and Syriac languages. He taught many of Salima's youth during the mid 1800's.

The Abdel Hay House

It is said that they are the closest offshoot to the House of Moussa Daher and are known as the Badran House. Badran begot Abdel Hay who begot Mansour, Badran, and Mandar. The last ones died young. Mansour begot Elias and Abdel Hay. Elias begot Mandar, Youssef, Ghastine, and Mansour. Mandar migrated to Venezuela and married a woman from there. They begot two sons and a daughter. They are all there. Youssef died young. Ghastine migrated to Mit Ghamr in Egypt and died unmarried. Mansour had no children and died.

As for Abdel Hay Mansour, he begot Anton who migrated to Brazil. He died and left children. Elias Mansour joined the Capuchin Fathers when he was a boy. He was a cook and counselor in the Monastery and he was known for his courtesy and good taste.

The House Of Kanaan Abou Nasar

According to old sayings, they are from Beit Eirbid of the Chouf region. Their forefather, Kanaan Abou Nasar, came to Salima a long time ago. He became related to the family of Moussa Daher Nakouzy because he married Saoud, the daughter of Elias Moussa Daher. Thus, he became one of them.

He begot Mansour who married Rafqa, the daughter of Sabra Khoury, and begot Daher who begot Mansour, Hanna, and Habib. Habib migrated to the United States and died there. He had Halim, Selim, John, and daughters. Halim and Selim got married there and have children.

As for Mansour Daher, he begot Albert, John, and four daughters. He has since died. Their mother Aziza Sayegh took the children to Alexandria. She saw to their education and gave two of her daughters in marriage. All this, she accomplished through her own efforts and hard work. She was a famous tailor. Hanna died in the United States, unmarried. He was brave and strong.

The House Of Hanna Bin Tanious

People say that they came from Baabdat and married into the Nakouzy family. They also say that they have relatives in the Qanaba of Salima and were known as the House of the Head Cutters.

Others say that they originated from Bikfaya. A group of them lived in Zahriye, opposite Salima, and another group lived in Salima. Of this group, the one we know about is their forefather, Tanious, who begot Hanna who begot Mansour. Mansour married Qanou', the daughter of Abdulallah Bin Sha'ia Nakouzy, and begot Hanna and Tanious. Tanious had only Satout, the wife of Fares Sahyoun. Hanna Bin Tanious begot Mansour, Girgis, Youssef, and Rashid. Three of them migrated and are married in Venezuela. They have boys and girls, and only Youssef has remained in Salima where he lives today.

The Hedary House

The Hadary family originates from a small village not far from Deir el Qamar, called "Had Edeir". They moved from there and went to Deir el Qamar and were called "the Hedary House."

According to oral traditions, this family originates from the Kierouz House in Bcharre (Bisri). They are from the Anahelians or the Helow house who came from the North at Ain Helia, near Damascus at Sham. This is what is acknowledged by the family. We will talk in detail about this in our book The History Of The Maronite Families.

Nasef Hedary came to Salima around the year 1875. He was one of the Lebanese Military troops detached from the Metn and who made its post in the Castle of the Lam's Princes. The District Commissionary office seized it, as we had previously mentioned.

Nasef Hedary married Foutine, the daughter of Boutros Khoury Nakouzy, so he became one of the family. He begot Daoud, Youssef, and two daughters.

This family migrated to the United States with the mother after the death of the father many years ago.

The Sahyoun House

They originate from Baiqoun in the Chouf. They are from the Eid family, one of the old families who moved from Haqil in the middle of the towns of Jbeil. Fares Bin Sahyoun Nejm Eid came to Salima with the military troops. They were sent there by the District Commissioner of Lebanon in 1872. He was one of the soldiers. He married Satout, the daughter of Tanious Bin Hanna Bin Tanious related to the Nakouzy family, so he became one of the family members. He begot Abdou, Najib, Tanious, Habib, and Moussa. Habib and Najib died young and Moussa migrated to

Africa. Tanious begot Najib, Elias, Habib, and Philip. Elias begot a son whose name we don't know. Habib also begot a son whose name we don't know.

The Al Hanoud House.

The Habib Al Hanoud.

They originate from Ehden, from the famous Douaihy family. They came to Deir el Qamar during the days of the Ma'n Princes. Most of them worked as goldsmiths and in the field of medicine. As for the ones who came to Salima, they are three: Habib Al Hanoud, Said Al Hanoud, and Hanna Al Hanoud.

After the incidents of civil unrest in 1860, Habib Elias Hanoud left Deir el Qamar with his father Elias and his brother Hanna. They spent a long time in Ghazir where they practiced their profession. Then, Habib moved with his brother Hanna to Beit Chebab. After a while, he left his brother in Beit Chebab and went to Ain Hamada where he worked in a silk plant for its owner, the Frenchman Morc (as we previously mentioned). At that time, he got acquainted with Dharifa, the daughter of Boutros Nemr Bou Eissa Nakouzy from Salima, and married her. They lived in Salima with the Nakouzy family. He was an understanding man, eloquent, practicing as a tinsmith, goldsmith, and dispenser of medecine. He begot Youssef, Elias, and Girgis. All of them migrated to the United States.

Said Al Hanoud

He is Said Bin Hanna Bin Nasef Bin Gibrail Al Hanoud, originating from Deir el Qamar. He came to Salima around the year 1890. He lived there for a long time and practriced medecine as his father did, with traditional methods. He married his kinswoman. Mary, the daughter of the previously mentioned Habib Hanoud and begot Shafik, Hanna, Tawfik, Philip, Felix, and a daughter.

Doctor Said traveled from Salima to Akar as a doctor. That was until the First World War started. Then, he left Salima and lived in Kaftoun with his family. He died there a few years ago after the death of his wife and some of his sons. His loss was terrible, especialy the loss of his son Dr. Shafik who was one of the best of all the young men. He was known for his high standard of ethics, his great intelligence, and his knowledge of modern medicine. He was a famous doctor. He was loved by everybody and used to be one of my students. Today, he has been succeeded by his brother Hanna who learned Medicine by practicing it in the town of Akar where this family remains.

Hanna Al Hanoud

Hanna Hanoud belongs to the Hanoud family who came to Salima at the end of the 19th century. He married his kinswoman Dhahoura, the daughter of Habib Hanoud and begot Mansour, and Tawfik. Both of them moved with their mother to Tripoli.

Mansour has, for a long time, been one of the government commissioners living in Halba with his family.

We found some interesting historical information attached to the manuscript books of medicine belonging to the father of Doctor Said Hanoud. We present a couple of them:

"Abou Hanna Nasef Hanoud died in Deir el Qamar with the Halabian pastors (the monks) on March 30, 1856. Ghaleb Bahout, one of us (brother of the wife of Abou Said Hanna Hanoud), passed away on March 3, 1853. Shahin Bin Abdou Hanoud died on January 11, 1855."

"On May 1, 1832, Ibrahim Pasha (Al Masry) invaded Deir el Qamar, so, Bou Nakd, the Druze family, escaped to Ham and Hamat. Abou Adbdulallah Boutros Boulos Abou Karam died with Father Youssef (Mourad) Hadshity in Beirut Sabt Al Nour on March 30, 1861."

The Al Charouny House

Their Origin

Stories say that they originate from Salima from the Nakouzy family and that their forefather, Assaf Nakouzy emigrated from Salima after an accident happened to him there. He sought refuge from the Shehab Princes of the Charoun Valley in the middle of the 18th century.

Assaf begot Mansour who moved to Bsous and was known there as Charouny after the Charoun Valley and begot a son called Youssef who went to Beirut with his familly after the First World War. He died around 1939 leaving children: Najib, Selim, and others whose names we are not sure of. They acquired a large fortune through their hard work.

The Aishy House.

Their Origin.

The Aishy Family is originally Muslim from the Yassin folks in Tripoli. They left Tripoli and moved to Beirut because of the injustices they faced. At the end of the 18th century, they joined the Princes of Salima, the Lam's. Ali Bin Ahmed Yassin took refuge with those Princes and lived with his mother in Salima. She was called Aisha and after her name the family was so named, Aishy. In 1824, Ali Bin Aishy converted to Christianity. He was given the name Girgis. When the Muslims learned of his conversion to Christianity, they were watching for his return to Beirut so they could kill him. Because of that, he stayed away for a long time, afraid of what would happen.

He bought properties in Salima, such as the house of Gehgeah Jombolat Said located at the east of the Salima square. He shared the building with Abou Nasef Elias Tiyan Beiruty, residing in Salima. Thus, Girgis Aishy lived in the west side of the house and Abou Nasef took the east side. When the Tiyan family left it and went to Beirut, Tanous Freha, our forefather, and his two brothers, Girgis and Gibrail, bought the house in 1847. This is where our forefathers lived and where our fathers and we were all born. The house of the Aishy family turned to ruins after the death of its owners. They had emigrated and had no offspring.

Their Lineage

Girgis Aishy married Habous, the daughter of Abou Nasr from the village of Mchaikha. He begot Boutros and Ayoub. Boutros married Sayagha, the daughter of Elias Shahin Saadallah Atallah Bachaalany, and begot Elias, Girgis, and Hawa (the wife of Yooussef Saad) …from Qanaba of Salima.

As for Ayoub, he didn't get married. He took care of his brother's children as if they were his own and lived the life of a meek Lebanese. How excellent a neighbor he was! We were always amused at hearing his old stories and funny anecdotes.

Boutros Aishy was aware of the traditional medicinal techniques and the medical insights which he learned from the practical experiences provided by his father. He was a master. Elias and Girgis were among the best youth in Salima. At the end of the 19th century they went to the United States. Elias didn't get married and Girgis married the widow of Nasef Hedary and didn't have a son. Both of them died a few years ago and their lineage perished.

The Abou Saqr House

In Saqiet el Misk at Bikfaya, some say that their forefather came to Salima seeking refuge in her Princes. That was in the middle of the 18th century.

What we do know of them is that they are Roman Catholics. Their forefather married Nakhla, the daughter of Shahin Sha'ia, so it was that they became related to the Nakouzy family. Abou Saqr begot Mikhail who begot Boutros, Girgis, and Daher. Boutros died young. Girgis had no children and Daher begot Mourad, Warda (the wife of Asaad Youssef Ghaleb Bachaalany), and Henna (the wife of Qablan Asaad De'ebes Saada from Merigate). As for Mourad, he begot Daher, Girgis, Boutros, and Mikhail. Daher migrated to the United States and there has been no news about him. Girgis begot sons and daughters. Boutros died young and Mikhail lived in Merigate and had sons and daughters.

THE ANTON HOUSE

Chapter 6

Their Origin

The first one of the Anton House who came to Salima was their great-grandfather Anton Abou Anton. Probably, the real name of Abou Anton is Fares. The date of their arrival in Salima was around the year of 1820.

It is said that Anton came first to Ras el Metn when he was running away from either an epidemic or from an injustice he had endured. This would have happened when he was living in Beirut. The time would have been around the year 1830. He joined Ibrahim Pasha when he invaded the town, so he appointed him the supervisor of the workers at the charcoal mines in Qarnayel. Then, he went to Salima which was nearer to his work and he lived there alone, with no family.

His first real estate purchases date from 1823. His name is listed as "Anton Abou Anton Al Beiruty, residing in Salima at this time."

The late Abou Habib Fares Anton told me that his father Anton had a brother called Mikhail. He said that he was living in the village of Bhannis where he was conducting business. Then, he left for Cyprus and they had no news about him after that. He met a Lebanese man coming back from that island and the man informed him that the brother, Mikhail, had died and that he saw with his own eyes, the grave where he had been buried. He probably died unmarried.

The late Habib Fares told me that the above mentioned Mikhail was killed by the Muslims when he refused to deny his Christianity. He died in the regions of Tripoli and had no children. According to the word of the late Fares Anton, his family is related to the family of Farzan in Al Zok. Youssef Khatar Ghanem says that the Anton House are his relatives.

Thus, we can say that the Anton family came to Salima at the end of the last century from Beirut. Also, that they had previously descended from Al Zok in Kisrawan where their relations, the Ferzan family, still remain today. They are just like the rest of the Maronite families. Raised in the north of Lebanon and, because of catastrophes and injustice, they left to go to the Kisrawan. From there, they, then, spread over the entire country. We don't think that there is any relationship between the Anton and the Nakouzy houses, except for the marriage of their forefather Anton with Tranja, the daughter of Abdulallah Bin Sha'ia Safi Nakouzy. The same applies to their relationship with the Tiyan House who migrated from Beirut to Salima and lived there for approximately one hundred years. They had no kind of kinship with the Anton House or with the Nakouzy house.

In all the investigation and research I have conducted, I have found nothing to prove the pretended relationship that Youssef Khatar Ghanem talked about.

Their relationship with the house of 'Oql Shedid who are from the Salama House in Mtain was because of the marriage of Anton Fares Anton with Saadi, the daughter of 'Oql Shedid, and then, the marriage of Farid, the son of Anton, with Edna the daughter of his maternal uncle, Shedid 'Oql.

Their Vestiges

"...Anton Bou Anton from Beirut, residing in Salima at Shahar Al Metn, bought from Abdulallah Ibn Sha'ia Nakouzy of the same mentioned village ...in 1239 (1823). The accessor and writer Bou Ali Beriqaa'. Witnesses: Nader Gad'oun, Youssef Ibn Shedid Al Aawar."

"Thank God, to him alone, ... Anton Abou Anton from Beirut residing in Salima at Shahar Al Metn, bought from his uncle, Abdulallah Ibn Sha'ia Nakouzy of Salima, the mulberry trees which are at the yard and around the house; at the West in Al Sira, five mulberry trees, at the East up to the waterwheel and in front of the northern gate up to the level of the cliffs and homes to the extent the level is seen, he has bought them with his own money ... the price of that is two hundred and sixty piasters ...their names are enough to determine their locations. Written in Jomad Al Akhar, 1239 ...the accessor and writer of this deed the humble Bou Ali S'eid."

From the two above deeds, it is clear that Anton was married in 1239 Hegira (1823), which is around the year 1823. That is the reason why, in the second deed, it was mentioned that Anton from Beirut residing in Salima bought from his "uncle" which means his father-in-law, the father of his wife, Tranja. Furthermore, Anton wrote the original deed in his own handwriting. We are preseving it with us. And it is worth noting that he uses the expression: "the deed of our uncle, Abdulallah, for the house, yard, and the mulberry trees which are around it."

Here is the third deed:

"...this is what Anton Ibn Abou Anton residing in Salima ...has bought from the daughter of our uncle who is our wife, the mulberry trees whose location he knows at the yard of Salman's house, and, a terraced land starting from Al Edbeta in the East going to the road. Their quantities are evaluated at three loads and two pounds and their price is two hundred and fifty one piasters ...with the acknowledgment of Bou Ali S'eid ...written in Rajab, 1240, by the humble Mohamed Mahmoud Masry; in the presence of our children: Bou Ali, Saloum and Salman. Witnessed by Hassan Abdah."

Their Lineage

Anton Bou Anton married Tranja, the daughter of Abdulallah Bin Sha'ia Bin Safi Nakouzy and they begot Fares, Girgis, and Warda (the wife of Ghandour Sabra Nakouzy). Fares Anton married Dala, from the Abi Hatem House in Hammana, and begot Habib and Anton. Habib Fares begot Philip, Felix, and Emil. Philip begot Edmond and Fernan. Felix begot Habib and Adeeb. Emil begot Samir and Felix. While Anton Fares begot Najib, Rashid, and Farid. Najib and Rashid died in Marseilles where their father was living. They were unmarried and young. Farid begot Najib, Rashid, and Anton.

As for Girgis Anton Abou Anton, he married Handouma from the Amoury House in Zahle and begot Youssef, Hanna, Shokry, Selim, Beshara, and Nakhla, who died young. All of them migrated to Marseilles and Brazil. Youssef and Selim died unmarried. Hanna begot Nasri, Na'eem, George, Albert, and Antoin. Nasry begot Raoul. Shokry had children in Brazil as did Beshara who also moved there.

Hanna Girgis Anton built a hotel in Marseilles to welcome the expatriates who were passing through its port. Next to it, he built a home. It is in a beautiful neighborhood location of Marseilles. The family currently resides there. Hanna Girgis Anton was well known for being full of life and zeal. He really cared for the expatriates coming from his country.

Shokry was a lieutenant at the French Embassy in Brazil. He issued the newspaper titled "The Justice" in Brazil. When he died, the French Ambassador said that France had lost one of her best employees. He said that Shokry was the best advocate for the Lebanese community and the Arab press.

About Them.

We have previously talked about the Anton house. We know a lot about them. We have a considerable amount of old documents relating to them, especially to their role in the incidents that happened between them and Wasa Pasha, the District Commissioner of Lebanon in 1891.

Habib Fares has given the majority of his literary collection, both printed and manuscript times, to the National Library. The rest was generously given to us by Philip and Emil Fares, the sons of Habib Fares. We will publish some of his material in this book, some in full and some in edited form. We previously mentioned that Philip and Emil were raised in Salima and both became lawyers. (See page 158).

We also previously mentioned that Habib Fares went to Egypt to live and that he issued a newspaper there called "The Orient Echo". In it, he strongly criticized Wasa Pasha and his political administration. He repeatedly published articles showing the defects of the government, their misconduct and the injustices they were committing. His criticism caused much embarassment and pain to the district commissioner and his employees. People were eager to read his stories and the government forbade the papers to be distributed in Lebanon. None the less, they continued to circulate by various means. Habib Fares's greatest supporter and correspondent was his brother, Anton. Anton was at that time living in Salima. Other supporters included Youssef Beik Shediak from Hadath Beirut. He was probably a classmate of Habib at the Aintoura School. Also, there was Beshara Shediak, the kin of Youssef Beik, the famous journalist Selim Serkis, Youssef Khatar Ghanem, who was then residing in Alexandria, Sheikh Philip Khazen, and Prince Shekib Arslan, and many others.

From Anton Fares to his brother Habib. September 5, 1891. (Abridged)

"My Dear Brother Habib,

...when our father told you that he does not know my whereabouts, it is true. Nobody knows my location except for my one friend who is taking care of me in these circumstances. (He is Khalil 'Oql Shedid, the brother of Saadi, the wife of Anton). *There are many lookouts. Fishermen and sellers are spying on me. Officials are inspecting and controlling the mail. For this reason I write letters to no one. Khalil reassures my family. Concerning the book* The Secrets Of Lebanon, *do not put your name on it. Put down the name of a foreigner. Or, make up a name. No one knows what will happened in the future. His excellency Zehrab Pasha is in Istanbul. Tell him what is happening to us. Tell him of the oppression we endure and ask for his zealous intercession. I am thinking of publishing the poem you composed. Let it be lifted up to the highest governmental power. If the publishing house here refuses to publish it, I will send it to Egypt for publication. Then you can send it to Istanbul through Zehrab Pasha.*

I don't know anything about the people who oppress us or the ones who help us. I only know what I hear from people's chatter. (People say that they are Nasef Rayess and Ibrahim Beik Aswad). We have ascertained that Gir-gis Safa is doing his utmost to support us. The governor of the Metn has helped us as much as he can, secretly, and by still following his orders. Hassan Agha Abou Shaqra kept calling us but he certainly didn't do anything wrong. Habib Agha Meghabgheb is being judged for having left our home unattended. Our paternal cousin, Daher (Mansour Kanaan), is also in court being charged with having alerted us. Prince Khalil Saad and his servant Y-oussef Mansour (from Hammana)both went to Egypt as spies. If he couldn't get written evidence, then he relied on oral reports. That, alone, was sufficient reason to oppress those who were arrested.

And here is (Guawish) taking over the position of our cousin, Daher Mansour. What our father told you about us is true: once, the army saw us in a shop but couldn't catch us. So, they arrested the concierge and put him in jail. The rumor was spread that I had been arrested and that the order has been given to condemn me.... Meanwhile, the losses which have afflicted us from the injustices of the district commissioner are innumerable. For four months we have managed to hide in the prairies. And during this time, our Karakhinas (silk factory) is left in God's care. Our business has come to a complete halt with no hope of ever getting back what we have lost. We have lost our capital and that of our clients. No one dares to entrust their money under the control of Wasa Pasha. As for Mansour Youssef, the rumors are not true that he is in possession of the manuscripts.... I have no idea about what Selim Effendi Thabet did. I don't have any news from anybody. I don't know who is my friend and who is my enemy. Also, I don't know anything about the helpers. I only know of those from whom I am taking refuge in their house ('Oql Shedid house in Mtain). They are the only people who know where I am hiding. Khalil has stopped meeting me for fear he would be seen. Now, he just writes to me if he thinks there is something important. The lookouts are planted around all these people, especially Khalil...

Our son-in-law (Girgis Lahoud) asked to meet me a month ago, so, we fixed a place and a date to meet. During the meeting, he showed his utmost concern and interest in our well being. However, since then, we have been unable to meet with or write to anyone. ...attached you'll find some verses of a poem we composed. It tells about our situation. Publish it at the end of your book. The rest of the poem will be sent to you ....keep writing to me. And, remember to send the mail the way I instructed you. ...I am looking forward to the opportunity of coming to you, unless something should prevent it. May God keep you safe."

Here are some of the verses:

Men of power in this country have pointed their arrows at me.
So, I took refuge in the mainland and raised my case to the Lord.
He is the refuge of honest souls and He hears the call of those who ask.
He does not discriminate between the poor and the rich. they are all alike because they are oppressed.
They wanted to arrest me so they mobilized all their forces, putting spies of blue eyes to observe me.
They refused to look to the sky, to be reminded of what God says and to be fair.
I was afraid of betrayal there, before the help of my benefector could reach me.
That is why I chose the Fiyafi as a refuge....

From Fares Anton to his son Habib in Cairo. (Abridged)

"Dear Son,
      May God keep you safe. We received your letter dated the 6th of this month. It was delivered through Al Khawaja Eskandar (Kanaan originating from Abiea). We felt reassured about you. We were astonished when you said that you didn't receive our previous letters. Is there another Youssef Mansour in Egypt who steals the mail...
      The Khawaja Eskandar stayed for two days at the house of his son-in-law (Girgis Lahoud, the husband of his daughter, Leila) in Baabdat. After that, he changed his mind about coming here because he saw the government's oppression over our house.
      Recently, Melhem Beik Bou Shaqra came to us with sixty soldiers to inspect and look for your brother (Anton). They intend to arrest him, dead or alive. ...Your brother stopped in his travels to hide where ever he could. He saw that the roads were all surrounded. However, three days ago, the Creator helped him to arrive at Beirut. From there he travelled directly to France because his entry to Egypt, where you have been for the last two years, was refused.
      You asked about your cousin (your wife) and your son, and Felix our son. Your cousin intends to enroll (your son) Philip in the School (in Salima) and to take Felix to her mother (Shtoura). We have presented a petition on behalf of your cousin about the encroachments on the properties in Mraijat and Ein Al Zarda, but there has been no response. ... Briefly, the oppression is from everywhere. The absence of your brother has weakened us. Concerning your book _The Secrets Of Lebanon,_ no one dares to buy a copy ... The Khawaga 'Oql (Shedid) endured a great

deal of trouble because of what happened to their brother ... We ask God, with our continuous prayers, to help you succeed...from Salima. September 18th, 1891".

The poem below was composed by Anton Fares congratulating Bishop Youssef Debs upon his return from Rome where he had been found innocent of accusations brought against him in 1887:

Thank God you came back. Spread the good news. Winning is the most beautiful thing. Be optimistic and spread the good news.
Hear the acclaim. The heart is overjoyed to hear it. Those with the grudges, their hearts are filled with grief and afflictions.
Let it be said that the road of God is truly fair. Just to be on it is to be proud.
His judgments are for the truth. He compensates the pious, giving them glory and victory.
Like he compensated Ayoub, afflicted with sickness, and giving power to David in battle.
Goliath with his might, could not win in the field of battle.
The youth of Babel survived the fire of Atoun, then sang praise and thanksgiving ...
And the handsome Joseph who was sold because of envy, he came to be the ruler of Egypt.
And so He glorified and proved the innocence of Youssef Debs when evil doers plotted against him...
Their plots turned against them and destroyed them, turning affairs upside down ...
With their force they bound up a Pope known for his generosity, virtue, pride and glory.
Excuse my fondness for him, but I vowed to give him my eulogy, and God is asking me to fulfill my vow.
You can exagerate as you like, but be sincere in praising him. Don't be afraid of the exaggeration. Instead, say and chant it loudly ....
His writings and translations have been of great benefit. He has confronted the misleading and the unbelievers ....
He has an eloquence mixed with wisdom and piety. From it you can make a vaccine against the sorcerers' spells ...
He has the clear heart of David, the chastity of Joseph, and, with knowledge, he spoke with the Pope.
His piety is built on a foundation of purity. Whatever is hurled at him, is like a wild goat butting his head on a rock.
The Maronite people proudly celebrate with dance, as well as breathing a sigh.
You have proved to the people that God is enough if He believes you.
His vote is free of evil so the innocent do not fear betrayal from Him.
...Don't be surprised that he is innocent after being wrongly accused. This is what happened to Joseph in Egypt.
He went away making our hearts bleed but he came back so they were filled with joy.
Beirut smiled when he came. All Lebanon rejoiced.
Beirut was like Jerusalem when the Redeemer came, everything shook.
...Having returned, his companions are delighted to hear him declare that the Lord is his support, his counsel,
The Lord is the one who gets me out of the traps laid for me, and I believe only in Him.
...In my life, I have been given more than I ever wished for, so what is given by Him is better than can be imagined.
My heart was full of happiness and joy when the Lord's deputy informed me of the good news.
By mentioning His name, I mean to thank and glorify Him. The deeds of Pope Leo have been reknowned in this era.
He brought about peace between great nations as they applied his solutions to their problems.
Kings recognized his favors and politicians looked so small next to him.

Among the writings of Felix Fares were the following lines:

Oh, neighbourhood of mine, is there anyone who will stop reminding me of the pain and of Satan.
I removed it from the bottom of my heart, and its roots have pulled up my feelings from the bottom of my heart.
Students went up to the podium, and my ideas came out of the past tense with breaths of ecstasy.
And so, my soul became clear for the people around me, while it remained hidden from me.

I bring out a light with my poesy and unveil the past to remind those who forgot.
My soul became clear with its splendor, and the poetry hid the light from my view.
I searched for my soul in the hard times, I sought it under the shadows of the flowers and the myrtle.
I looked for it in the eyes of the betrayers, who greedily try to revive my pains.
The sparkles of life in it frightened me, and the darkness of my despair in my silence frignhtened them.
People imagined me walking on their lands, but I am just a mirage in the air.
If I sat amused among my brothers, I see an illusion of myself sitting with them.
I seduce the glass of drunkness to make me feel intoxicated but I find only imaginary inebriation in it.
The Year, 1929.   *- - Felix Fares.*

THE MARONITE FAMILIES AND COUNT TERAZI

Chapter 7

A book written by our great savant and friend, Count Philip De Terazi, appeared when we were almost finished with the history of the Nakouzy House. The book is entitled The Truth Of Lebanon's History And The Syriacs. He graciously gave us a copy of the book. We praise his wide culture, his abundant knowledge, his vitality, and his diversified writings that he has published. We particularly admire those published in his old age. We wish that the publishing of this book will be an important event for Lebanese History, a great educational service. The history of the Lebanese families is sorely in need of men of investigative skills, virtue, and objectivity.

Educated people know that there is mystery and confusion in trying to decipher the history of the Lebanese families. There are fables and illusions that have been attached to their origins and lineage. There are no trustworthy sources. One cannot rely on stories and oral traditions. Furthermore, there are no specific or general dates to refer to. Nor do antique manuscripts reveal the true history of each family. The exceptions are the noble families. For them, historians could collect information from different sources, or, they were mentioned in general histories. Other than that, most resources are incompatible narrations and private manuscripts which are of little help to the historian unless he has a broad range of reading material, numerous preserved documents, a deep cultural understanding, and a special critical analysis skill which enables him to distinguish between the true and the false, between the inadequate and the proper.

We did not neglect the Maronite intellectual scholars who searched and investigated the history of their country. However, they concentrated on what proved their origins and the collected general information about them. The greatest one of those people is Douaihy, the master of Maronite history, I should say of Lebanese history. His concern was to prove the origin of his religious group, the truth of their belief, to publish their objects of pride, and to defend their possessions. The Maronite scholars and historians did the same. They followed the manners of Douaihy. They could not be impartial in recording a history for all their families because of the reasons we previously mentioned: separation, emigration, being refugees because of wars, the battles, the riots, injustices and oppression. In addition, there was poverty, social and emotional distress. These all occurred to that struggling country. And, all these things have kept them from recording their history and from being able to discover their origins and developments. Their main concern was to preserve their religion and independence in that narrow mountain. A man doesn't care about his history until he is free of major problems and not constantly dealing with crises.

Some of them published the history of one province or village or family. Others tried to record a general history of all the families but they were never able to complete it. We do know that our historian friend, the patriotic Mr. Eissa Eskandar Maalouf, a long time ago, started to write an extensive encyclopedia of Eastern families in 14 volumes. As of today, it still has not been published. And, we, too, have been preoccupied with writing an encyclopedia called The History Of The Maronite Families, arranged in alphabetical order and comprising several volumes. We intend to publish it, God willing, once we have completed the publication of this book.

In general, right up to today, all that has been published about the history of the Lebanese families has not met our expectations. We need a history of our Lebanese families that rises to the same high position that our intellectuals

333

and scientists have reached. Our historical writings must be compatible with the new technology and the most accurate data available.

Accordingly, we proceeded with great anticipation to read the book of the Count. Unfortunately, it did not measure up to our expectations. It is inconsistent with our intellectual standards and doesn't follow the proper principles of historical research.

Since we don't have the space in this book to elaborate on all the errors and flaws in this book, it will have to suffice to make a general comment on it. We will answer the many specific problems in our encyclopedia.

The History Of The Maronite Families is where we treat each family which the Count discusses as being of Syriac origins. And, we wish to make it clear that our friendhsip with the Count will in no way restrict our comments. Scholarly research has nothing to do with personal relationships.

The first thing that jumps out at us when reading the title and contents of the book is that the author, Count Terazy, wants to emphasize the idea that the majority of the Maronite families originate and have the blood of the Syriacs. He makes his assertion that the Lebanese ties to the Syriacs are not only language and religious rituals but actual blood ties.

He has the intention of renewing the old tone and violent compaign incited by Father (the Bishop) Youssef Daoud. He was the Syriac scholar who was anti-Maronite. He accused them of being heretics like the rest of the Eastern Rites professing physitheism. He complains about how he was opposed by people like the courageous Maronite scholar, Bishop Youssef Debs. He stood against that campaign and freed the Maronites from that false accusation in his book The Spirit Of The Answers. After considerable conflict the issue finally died down.

When Bishop Daoud died, as did Bishop Debs, someone published the forbidden book on this debated issue. Thus, Bishop Derian replied to it in a way that the Maronites did care for and were not satisfied with.

And now, today, the Count has returned to the attacks against the Maronites. He does so in the same way a submarine attacks a ship, underwater. He uses a gentle approach with camouflage. He makes the majority of the highborn Maronite families to be of a Yaakoubian Syriac origin. He uses these historical claims to conceal his real objectives which is to once again accuse Maronites of being heretics. He makes this claim by tying their supposed origins to the Yaakoubians. Imagine the hard feelings this book creates in the hearts of the Maronites.

We had expected the Count, who has experienced the difficulties and the mess our population was suffering because of the history of the families, to be in the vanguard of the reconciliation process. We thought he would be in the forefront of those helping to eliminate the false illusions. Instead he helps to record and publish false information in a way that seduces those who don't know any better. Perhaps his approach deceived scholars because of its appealing outlook and logical approach. The illusion becomes more established and the different little stories increase. Then the illusion is so impressed on people's minds that it is difficult to undo, just as happens with heresies and folktales.

Does the Count think we don't know that the people he uses as sources are merely a convenience for him to make his improper historical claims? We don't even want to mention the people he refers to because we want to preserve their dignity. He makes claims of historical facts that the greatest scholars have been unable to prove. Does he know that the people he relied on for their stories are not to be trustworthy sources just because of their associations and rank? Historiography is not based on educational level or rank. It needs experience, intelligence, a foundation of experience in patriotism and national history, and, an ability to be objective.

Moreover, it is simply not justified to claim that the Maronites are Syriac in origins just because they use that language. We recognize that Syriac is used in the religious rituals, in the names of their saints, their churches, their lands and even the names of many of their villages. But all that , of itself, is not proof that the Maronite families are originally Syriacs, as the Count has claimed.

The Maronites are originally Armenians and Phoenicians, and so is their language. They have in common with the Syriacs, the names of saints and churches. The Saints were Eastern and the Church as one unit, indivisible, accepted these Saints and their names. That is just logical. It doesn't mean that they are all Yaakoubian Syriacs. They Syriacs are different from the Maronites in many ways: their history, their dialects, and their rituals. Even if they were related in the past, each sect has its own established history with its own language, beliefs and rituals, as well as other social characteristics. The common things among them are due to being participants in one Church.

Also, it is not surprising that some Syriacs who became refugees in Lebanon joined the Maronite religion. This happened in different time periods. The friendly relations they would have established can explain the influences in language and rituals.

But to claim that this or that Maronite family is originally Syriac, that is just something that needs to be proven. It needs sound and continual documentation as proof. The Count does not have that basis of proof.

The Count cannot take as proof of the doctrine he mentioned by citing what the scholar Douaihy said: that people came from the East, Nablous, and from other places to Lebanon in the 15th century. That the reason they came was because of Lebanon's serenity and safety during the era of the Maronite lieutnant colonels. Douaihy never mentioned what their doctrine was. Even if it were to be confirmed that they are Syriacs, they still were Maronites and we can't know or confirm their offspring from that alone.

As for the incident of the Yaakoubians who were in Lebanon under their Patriarch, Duosqors Do, known as Ibn Al Nabky, we know that the Maronites revolted against them in the year 1488. We know that the Maronites expelled them from the country because they had interfered in the Maronites' religious affairs. This is not a proof that the Maronite Do House is originally Syriacs. One must present other proof or evidence to support such a claim. Actually, to the contrary, this would make better evidence to support that the Maronites were not Yaakoubian Syriacs. The Maronites revolted against the Yaakoubians residing among them and who wanted to deceive them. Thus, they kicked them out of the country and any who remained joined the Maronites. Their offspring is unknown.

Furthermore, the Syriac Bishop Youssef Daoud, well known to be a great enemy of the Maronites, made horrible accusations against them. He made all kinds of malicious claims against them. But, even he never mentioned what the Count did. To the contrary, he separated from them. So much so that they became helpless foreign residents among the Maronites. That is the truth. And, that was when he tried to defend them from the accusation of the Maronite Patriarch Mikhail Razi who accused them of having damaged religious books of the Maronites in 1578.

In addition, the Count said that the Razi House and the other highborn Maronite families are originally Syriacs and not from Lebanon (Book titled The Collector of the Actual Proofs, page 324).

But how could that be? When the Maronites revolted against the Yaakoubians and expelled them from the Maronite country, as Douaihy said in his book, in the year 1488, there wasn't any one, such as Count Terazy, who knew the origins, the lineages, the kinships, and the relationships between the Maronites and the Yaakoubians. If there had been, wouldn't they have tried to preserve the rights of brotherhood and had mercy upon those brothers and paternal cousins in such a time of calamity caused by the Maronites?

Finally, we can say that the author of the Syriacs' history regarded everything as lawful to attain his hidden aim. The Count made changes, exchanged, distorted, fabricated, invented, added, deleted, used ruses, cunning and, very simply, was vile. Anyone who is knowledgeable and perceptive will find in his history unexplained wonders, mysteries of legends, superstitions, anecdotes, and childish jokes. He will be astonished that such a scholar and great sheikh had the audacity, so late in life, to write such a book. It is unsuitable to his rank. In addition to what was already mentioned, it is an intentional, indirect defamation of the origins of the Maronites and their beliefs. In addition, it is an attempt to ruin their history, their social and religious entity. May God forgive him.

THE KASSAB HOUSE

Chapter 8

Their Origin

According to stories from unknown sources the Kassab folks belong to the Salebe folks, attributed to the Helenians who came to Damascus in the fourth century. Then, they moved to northern Syria, to Tripoli, Aaqoura, and they spread all over Lebanon.

Among them are the Salebe folks in Souq el Gharb and Batloun, the Nafaa House in Batsheiya, the house of Shamas and Abi Haidar, the Hawy House in Choueir, the Hashim House in Aaqoura and the Kassab house.

Father Boulos Kassab from Qolei'ate who died in 1946, told me a story. It was told to him by Patriarch Boulos Mosaad, namely, that the Kassab folks originate from Kassba, in the regions of Halab. They were Maronites. A group of them left for Damascus Al Sham and followed the Roman Catholic doctrine after a dispute between them and a priest of the Maronites in Damascus. Then, a group of them joined the Roman Orthodox Church. In Damsacus and Beirut, they are Roman Othodox and Roman Catholics.

As for those who are in Lebanon, they left Kassba Halab and went to Aaqoura, then to Hardine, Kisrawan, and Jezzine. All of them are Maronites. And, it is said that those who went to Aaqoura came from Damascus.

The Maronite Kassab folks are found in Hardine in the Batroun district, at Qolei'ate, and Aajaltoun, in the Zouq, and Balloune in the regions of Kisrawan. Those in the Zouq are known as the Moolay (My master) Kassab House. Those in Balloune are named the Halaby House according to the priest Samaan Balloune, the Antonian Archmonk. They are the relatives of the Moolay Kassab House in Zouq. The surname of "Al Halaby" proves that the Kassab House is originally from the regions of Halab as told by Patriarch Boulos.

There is a story told to me by Sheikh Tanious Girgis Makhlouf Kassab from the district of the Kassab family. It was told to him by his father and from Eskandar Baroudy. It is as follows:

The forefather of this family is a Hungarian. He came to Halab and joined the service of the Lord of Ghith in Aaqoura. He married this noble's daughter and begot three sons: Selim, Kanaan, and Leonardo, who stayed with his father in Halab. Kanaan and Selim lived Aaqoura. Then, Selim moved to Damascus and lived there with his children. As for Kanaan, he left for Kisrawan and lived in Aajaltoun and Qolei'ate. So, Selim is the forefather of the Kassabs of Beirut and Damascus. Kanaan is the forefather of the Maronite Kassabs in Lebanon. However, we must state that we are not certain how reliable this story is. There are Kassabs living in Aabadiye at the Metn.

Youssef Khatar Ghanem wrote <u>Al Bernamej</u> (The Program) and talked about this and said on page 190:

"Some people claim that the Kassab family emigrated from Houran or Ghouta in Damascus and went to live in Aaqoura. The famous one was Malek Gheith and his sons: Jabour, Fadel, and Moussa .... Jabour is the forefather of the Melhema and Abi Shelha families in Beirut and Jbail, as well as the Rezkallah family in Saida. Fadel is the forefather of the Fadel family in Beirut. From them came Patriarch Fadel, the Bishop Fadel, and the priests of the Fadel House.

Moussa left for Jezzine and he is the forefather of the Moussa Kassab House there and in other regions. From them came Bishop Boulos Moussa Kassab...."

It would not be surprising if the forefathers of this family were of different origins even though they share the same name. However, we could not come up with resources to prove either situation.

The Kassab in Salima

There are so many different stories about this family that we could not determine who was the first Kassab to come to Salima. What we do know about them is that they came to this village a long time ago and they got to be very close to the Lam's Princes. Ever since their arrival there, they have been Roman Catholics, supporters and defenders of the Church's doctrines and leaders. We saw occasions when those religious leaders asked for the Kassabs' help against the governors. They protected them with their swords and eliminated those bearing resentment and oppression. They removed them from Halab and Lebanon. The Kassabs were able to do this because they were powerful and had authority and influence. For that reason, the Lebanese historian Pastor Rofael Karama told of their deeds in his book, Historical Resources, published by Bishop Qatan.

In previous pages of this book, we talked about the members of this family who achieved fame, privilege, holiness, and thoughtful regard for others. They were knights of the sword as well as men of the pen and of opinion. Because of all these qualities, the Lam's Princes, the governors of the country at that time, chose them as guardians, consultants, and their military commanders.

However, after a while, the same policy that they used to acquire their status and possessions ended up causing them to lose it all. Changes in the government and disputes between them and the Princes brought about strained relations and a decline in their prestige and wealth. Step by step, the Kassabs joined the rank of the general public after being among the status of the Sheikhs of the country during the feudal era.

Their Lineage

The Kassab house was divided in two groups: the upper offshoot and the lower offshoot. The first one was composed of men of opinion, culture, politics, and notability. They were the Beshir Saab House consisting of the Houses of Jafal, Rahal, Beshir, and Bou Hussein Fares which is the Kisrawan House. The other was composed of men of the sword and physical strength. These were the Deliqan House, Azzam House, and the Hassan House known as Abou Leila. We have already talked about them and their deeds.

The Beshir Saab House

Beshir Bin Saab Kassab begot Jafal and Rahal who was killed in 1777 at Qab Elias. Jafal begot Beshir and Abdou. Beshir begot Asaad, Khatar who died unmarried, and four daughters who were: 1- Leiya, the wife of Fares Saab Kassab, 2- Hawa, the wife of his brother, Deliqan, 3- Satout, the wife of Melhem Gibrail Freha, and, 4- Baz, the wife of Elias Ghaleb Bachaalany. As for Asaad, he begot Khatar who begot Nessib, Tawfik, and George. Tawfik begot ......

Abdou Jafal begot Girgis and De'ebess who died unmarried. Girgis begot De'ebess, Abdou, and Mansour. All of them are expatriates in Mexico. De'ebess begot Najib and Tawfik. Abdou begot ....and Mansour begot ......

The House of Bou Hussein Fares

Bou Hussein Fares Kassab begot Youssef and Shebly. Shebly had no children. Youssef begot Kisrawan who begot Youssef who begot Kisrawan, Elias, and Shebly. The last two died unmarried. Kisrawan begot Youssef and Fares. Youssef begot Qablan and Mikhail. Fares begot Habib who emigrated to the United States and Youssef who died young.

The Deliqan House

Deliqan begot Saab, Girgis, and Kassab. Saab begot Fares and Deliqan. Fares Bin Saab begot Saab and Elias who begot Deeb. This later begot Elias.

As for Saab Bin Fares, he begot Selim, Amin, Fares, Tanious, and Shokry. Those last three are expatriates in Brazil and each one has his own family. Amin Bin Saab died young and unmarried and Selim …. Deliqan Bin Saab begot Abbass, Girgis, Eid, and Kassab who died young. Eid begot Emil, Alfred, and George. Girgis begot Assaf and Fawzy. Assaf begot Girgis and Ghassan. As for Abbass Bin Deliqan, he begot Khalil, Deliqan, Fouad, Najib, Girgi, and Boutros who never married. Fouad died young. Deliqan and Girgi emigrated to San Salvadore. The first is unmarried and the second is married and has children.

Najib begot Kassab, Fouad, Philip, and Aniss. Khalil begot Ibrahim, Michel, Josef, Fayez, and Edmond.

As for Girgis Bin Deliqan, he was killed in Shtoura during the government of Ibrahim Pasha in 1840. Kassab begot Daher who lived in Beirut and begot Elias who begot Daher, Michel, and Gibran.

The Zamel House

Zamel begot Azzam and Hamam. Azzam begot Zamel, Tanous, and Youssef. Zamel had no children. Tanous begot Asaad who begot Tanous and this latter begot Asaad who begot Elie and George. As for Youssef Azzam, he begot Qablan, Nasef, and Girgis. Girgis had only one daughter. Nasef was in Egypt when he begot Youssef who married the daughter of his paternal uncle Girgis. Qablan did not get married.

As for Hamam Bin Zamel, he begot Gehgeah who had only Mahaba, the wife of Daoud Bin Asaad Girgis.

The Hassan House

Hassan Kassab, known as Abou Leila, had only Taqla, the wife of Youssef Daher, the son of Safi Bachaalany and ……the wife of Tanous Azzam Kassab.

The Shiboun

From them, there was Shiboun Kassab who had only two daughters: Henna, the wife of Mourad Zein Shediak, and Ghorra, the wife of Gehgeah Hamam Kassab. When their father Shiboun died, their mother Fahoum married Abdou Jefal Kassab and they begot Abou De'ebess and Girgis.

The Serdy

There is also someone called Serdy and we could not locate his origin. He was very rich and owned cattle. People said that he had many goats as it was said that they actually owned over a thousand. They claimed that Serdy had a bad eye, which made the shepherds forbid him looking at any goat. They were afraid that he would hurt it with his bad eye.

There is even one story that says Serdy once looked at the door of a shanty of goats and all the goats he looked at died. Fortunately, Serdy did not get married and had no children.

The House of Girgis Bou Waked

Girgis Bou Waked Kassab begot Asaad who begot Daoud, Nasef, and Ibrahim. Daoud Bin Asaad begot Fares. With his first wife, Nazha Kassab, Fares begot Habib. From his second marriage with Milia Daher Mansour Kanaan, he begot Aniss and Edmon. Habib begot George and Aniss begot ......

As for Nasef Bin Asaad, he begot Asaad and Amin. Asaad begot Nasef and Hanna. Amin begot Selim amd Louis. Selim begot Emil and Antoin. Louis emigrated to Africa and begot ......

Meanwhile, Ibrahim Bin Asaad Bin Girgis begot Marchy the wife of ... Kefoury from Joweiqat, Mary (the wife of Selim Khalil Erian Bachaalany), Loulou (the wife of Elias Fares Kassab) and that is enough.

THE KHAWAJA HOUSE

Chapter 9

In Salima, the Anglican Roman Catholics and the Orthodox are families of different origins and consist of the Kassab and the Khawaja Houses. We just finished talking about the Kassab House, so now we will discuss the Khawaja House.

This is a surname which, in the past, was given to those who came to Salima from the Angelicans, excluding the Kassabs. The majority of the Khawaja House are from the Haddad folks, originating from the Fourzol family. In the beginning, some of them were tradesmen, so they were named the Khawaja House. Others were jewelers and goldsmiths, so they were named the Sayegh (the jeweler). When they worked in tinting and dyeing, they were named the Sabagh (the dyer). A group of them have continued to pratice their old profession, so they continue to be called the Haddad house still. The families which became related to them were the Bashwar family, the Tafkajy family, and the Bou Mikhail family. As a whole, they were surnamed as the Khawaja House. Hereafter, we will talk about each family separately.

The Haddad House.

Their Origin.

According to the old stories, the Haddad people came from the village of Fourzol in Lebanon. It was said that they are the remnants of the Christian Ghasanians who were in Horan and at the extremities of the Sham. Then, they spread over the country. They took refuge in Lebanon because they had heard that they would find safety and peace there during the era of the Ma'n Princes. Thus, the story continues, in the middle of the 16th century, they left Adhra'a in Horan and went to Fourzol to the East of Zahle. After an incident that happened between them and one of the feudal lords, they moved to Zahle. However, they had to flee from there because they were afraid that the lord would track them down there. They took refuge in various places in Lebanon. First, they lived in Beskinta, then they spread to various Lebanese villages as times and events changed. The majority of them worked as a smithy, a trade they practiced from a very long time ago which is why they were named after it. One of them lived in Khinchara and his descendants were known as the Riyashi folks. They have since spread to different villages.

Some of them worked as jewelers and were known as the Sayegh House (the jeweler). A third group was known as the Mesalem House.

That is a summary of the story passed on by Mr. Eissa Eskandar Maalouf which he proved in his family biography Under The Picked Fruits and in the book by Bishop Boutros Hebiqa The History of Beskinta and Its Families. It was published by the "Saneen" newspaper in Beskinta. Its contents were approved by Patriarch Gregorious Haddad.

However, with our full respect to the author of that story, to its publisher, and to the Patriarch who gave his approval, we did not find any document or an act that historically supports it. That is why we did our utmost to investigate the history and origins of the Haddad family in our village of Salima. We succeeded in finding some original, precious documents dating from 300 years ago. We don't believe that any of the members of this family or anyone who has

341

written about the family, have ever had access to such documents. Therefore, we are publishing them in brief, because history without documents is like a body without a soul.

Their Vestiges

"...Mansour, the son of Moussa from the village of Fourzol has purchased from Raslan, the son of Bou Nowayhed from the Ras (Ras el Metn), the grapevines located at the end of the road in the village of Salima. Bordered from the South by the grapevines of the son of Bou Neama; from the West by the grapevines of Bou Sharaf Eddine; from the East, Mohamed Ibn Heriz; and, from the North by the fruit garden of Abdel Hady. For the price of four piasters, gida derham, paid in full by the buyer to the seller. The seller was delegated by his wife, with her consent and satisfaction. It was authorized to witness them in Ramadan 1064 (1653), written by ...Ibn Raslan, witnessed for its validity by the son of the seller, Qaiyed Bai. Witnessed and written: Ali Ibn Ismail, H....Ibn Marsel."

- - - - -

"...Sheikh Bou Jamal Eddine Fakhr Eddine, the son of Yazbak Yazbak, and his brother, Bou Mohamed Qorqomas, from Salima village, came and sold to Abou Mansour Moussa Ibn Al Haddad, the non-Muslem freeman, originating from Fourzol and living on this date in Salima. They sold him the antique site of ruins located at the East of the village together with all that is on it, namely, its stones, its paths, and all its gates and yards. Also, the mulberry trees which are at the district's home. For the price of thirty-five lion piasters ...in the month of Jomady, the second, year 1096 (1684). Written by Yared. Witnessed: Mohamed Ibn Masry, Selim from Kafr Selwan: Abdel Wali Ibn Qadama, Bou Mohamed Alam Eddine. Safi Ibn Mohamed bin Yazbak."

- - - - -

"...Nasr, the son of the Haddad who lives in Salima village, bought from Abou Hassan Yaghi and from Abou Kheir Eddine, the son of Jabr from the same mentioned village, the attic which is of the same size as the attic of Ghadban, the son of Saad Bin Said. It is full sized ...and the furnace is in half, and the paths and everything related to it. And that is excluding the estimation of half of the addition which Ghadban made ...at the price of twelve piasters ...in the year 1085 (1674) ...in the presence of Abou Jamal Eddine. Abou Mohamed Merdas Abou Sharaf Eddine Ali Mikhail."

- - - - -

"...Nasr, the son of the Haddad, bought from Abou Hatem, the son of the Bachaalany, the trellis located at Ain el Sawaqi at the price of seven piasters ...in the month of Dhi Al Hedja, 1107 (1695). Written by Nasr Eddine, the son of Abdel Hady. Witnessed by Sheikh Abou Hussein Sharaf Eddine, and, Sheikh Abou Ali Fares."

"...Abou Moussa Sayegh, living in Salima Village...bought from Ghanem, the son of Abou Ghanem, from the same mentioned village ...the cinnamon barks located at the bottom of the Hayarate at the border of the Ain el Tehta waterwheel...in Shawal, 1157 (1744)."

- - - - -

"...Soliman Al Sayegh ...bought from Dhaher Bel Kheir, both from Salima, ...the mulberry trees ...located at the grinder mill ruins ...year 1164 Hegira (1750)..."

- - - - -

"We sold the mulberry trees ...located at the bottom of the house of Elias, to Fares Ibn Anton. Its borders: from the East and the West, Youssef Yazbak; at the South, our uncle Youssef, in 1189 (1775), Written and sold by Rehal Kassab. Witnessed by Father Francis and Hanna Eid."

- - - - -

"Anton Sayegh bought from Qassem, the son of Shahin ...in Mairjat ...year, 1194 (1780)."

- - - - -

"...Hanna Ibn Anton ..bought from Sejaa, the son of Said, all from Salima ...the addition of which is in front of the quarter at the East side ...and half of the furnace which is in front of their attic, above the mentioned addition... for the price of seventeen piasters and a half ...in 1197 (1782). Written by the humble Youssef Yazbak. Witnesses: Kanaan Tiyan, Ali Beriqaa, Nasr Eddine, the brother of the seller..."

- - - - -

"... Boutros and his brother, Fares, have agreed upon the attic which they share. Boutros received from Fares the cost of half, fifty piasters, in 1204 Hegira (1789). Written by Kanaan Tiyan. Witnesses: Hussein Bin Daher; Bergas Soliman Masry. Fadoul Rebat, and Hanna, their brother."

- - - - -

"...Fares, the son of Anton Sayegh, bought from Marcel Ibn Hussein Beshr ...in 1205 (1790) ..."

- - - - -

"...By this document, Dhaher Youness Sayegh bought from Azzam, the son of Kassab, the Amer House ...bordered by the District, where the mentioned house is at the West side and the Rowaqa in front of it at the East side .... For the price of twenty-nine piasters...in 1209 (1794)..."

"...We sold the mulberry trees... located in front of Daher Sayegh's house to the mentioned person at the price of three piasters...in 1210 (1795). Accepted by Moussa Estephan..."

- - - - -

"...Kanaan Tiyan bought from Mikhail, the son of Elias Bou Assly, the citadel which is at the edge of Qamou'... in 1216 (1801) .... This selling act has been transferred from our hands to the hands of our brother, Sabra Hamoud, 1216, and accepted by Kanaan Tiyan. Witnesses: Fares Henawy. Hanna Ibn Anton. And we have received the amount from him after we sold it to Sabra ...written by Kanaan Tiyan."

- - - - -

"...We have sold to our cousin, Fares Ibn Anton Sayegh, our properties at the ruins of the Grinding mill, and at Ain el Sawaqi, Halboun, and at the end of Marihna ...at the quarter: the big house, its Western house in Tanoura ...and the surroundings, the Eastern house and the Sharka house beside the alleys, and the attic in the neighbourhood. For the price of six hundred piasters...in the holy month of March, 1800. Written and accepted by Daher Ibn Youness Sayegh ... in the presence of our cousin, Father Moussa Al Matiyan..."

- - - - -

343

"...Fares, the son of Anton Sayegh and all the children of his sisters, the paternal uncle of his children, Boutros Sayegh, and the children of his brother Hanna .... The small house which is jammed together with my land at the quarter of the buyers... in 1817. Written by their paternal cousin, Aghnatious Sayegh. Witnesses: Darwish Gharzouzi; Anton Ibn Mehana; Nasef IbnYounes Khawaja; Girgis Ibn Nasr Al Khawaja."

- - - - -

" .. we sold to Boutros Ibn Anton three aconites fields ...at the top of two terraced lands belonging to the Assembly of her excellency, the late Lady Zahr, a field of constructions, for the price of thirty piasters. Bordered from the South, the bottom of the enclosure; from the East and the West, the properties of the mentioned endowment which overlooks the Beik road at the cliff, which is at the Southern enclosure.... At the upper fruit garden, the large mulberry tree is his own, and, she has a part of it at the West. The lower fruit garden at the corner: the cut antique mulberry tree is for him and a part of it, at the east side of seven spans of the hand... year, 1234. Written by the humble Ali Taqiy. Witnessed: Qassem Taqiy; Bergass Masry. That happened at our request with their satisfaction (the Princes) accordingly, Hassan, Haidar... (the stamps)."

- - - - -

"...Our son, Boutros Sayegh, from Salima, came to me with his sons: Girgis, Mikhail, and Moussa. He has accomplished what he promised to do, dividing that which he has given to them, the properties, buildings, and furniture. Nothing was left for any of them to complain about... ... written on August 6, 1833. The humble Aghnatious Ajoury, the Bishop of Fourzol and the countryside. (stamp). Accepted by Boutros Sabagh. We, Girgis, Mikhail, and Moussa have accepted it."

- - - - -

"...On this date, we requested from Sheikh Fares Ibn Anton that he write down this legal document. It states that he gave to his son Youssef, the attic which is at the south of the attic of his brother Habib. The western house is to be divided among his three sons: Samaan, Habib, and Youssef. Moreover, the store under the summer residence is likewise divided among the three of them ...year, 1250 (1834). Written by the humble Ali S'eid. Witnessed by Girgis Ibn Boutros with his own hand. Sheikh Fares Anton came and spoke before us: Father Boutros from Aarbaniye; Father Girgis from Al Dlaibe."

- - - - -

"...Before us, Mikhail, the son of Boutros Sabagh, declared that he gave a fifth of a grapevine in the enclosure of Ain el Sawaqee ... to the Church of Saint John in Salima, in 1250. Written by Nasef Tiyan ....this deed has been transferred from the donor to Girgis Ibn Boutros Ibn Anton ...year, 1841. Written by Wakin Ibn Boutros, the delegate of the endowment..."

- - - - -

"...Girgis Sabagh confessed before us that he has to pay to the holder of this legal act, his wife, Morta, the daughter of the Gharzouzi, the amount of 500 piasters, the cost of jewelry and copper utensils which have been sold ... Written on December 8, 1839. Written by the Deacon Mikhail Sayegh and accepted by Girgis Sabagh. Written by Neama, the son of Professor Elias Bashwar."

- - - - -

About Them And Their Lineage

Those documents presented above are the most truthful sources regarding the name of this family, the Haddad, and the name of Fourzol as the place where they grew up and came from. The story saying that the Haddad folks originate from Adhra'a in Horan and that they are the remnants of the Ghasasnians, remains under study. We don't have any documents to prove it.

Thus, Mansour Bin Moussa Ibn Haddad (from the Haddad folks) from the village of Fourzol took refuge in Lebanon asking for the protection of the Lam's Princes at Ras el Metn and Salima. He was running away from the tyrannical rule of the governors and feudal lords in the Sham states. He had heard about the tendency of those Princes to provide protection to Christians.

In 1653 he wemt to Ras el Metn and bought grapevines in Salima. Then, we saw that the son, Abou Mansour Bin Mansour bin Mousa, the free non-Muslim from the village of Fourzol, bought the ruins of a Druze's house. He renovated it and settled in. That was in 1684.

The Sayegh House

Abou Moussa Al Sayegh appeared around the year 1744. He is the son of the previously mentioned Abi Mansour Haddad. He was surnamed "Al Sayegh" because he was a jeweler, a profession that has been handed down to his children and grandchildren, from generation to generation. The offspring of Moussa Sayegh are: Soliman, Younes, and Daher Bin Younes. The Sayegh family in Salima probably are descendants of them. The only remaining Sayegh family left in Salima are those who became Maronites.

What we should say is that this Haddad family, which has been surnamed Sayegh, then known as Sabagh, then known as the House of Al Khoury Moussa, and, after that, by the names of their children; all of them were Roman Catholics.

The Haddad House

The offspring that we already talked about, saying that they belong to the Haddad House, according to published documents, has a group who still maintain the name "Haddad" today. They continue to be smithies and are the only ones to be so named.

I consider it more probable that the great-grandfather of that Haddad House is Farah Haddad after whom the field of "Haql Farah" is still called today, after him. It is a place where there is a water source, and, beside it, a silk plant owned by Tanious Bashwar.

Furthermore, the ruins of his first house still remain today in that field. The names of Farah, Moussa, Nasr, and Mehana are frequently used among the Haddad folks. However, the offspring of Mansour Bin Moussa Haddad used different names like Sayegh, Sabagh, Khoury, and others. They have used so many different names and gotten so far removed from their old ancestor Nasr Farah Al Hadda that many of them forgot their heritage. They no longer knew that they were of one origin and the children of the two parties. They were astonished when I assured them that they were all from the same origin. The lineages of those two parties are as follows:

The Lineage of Sayegh Haddad, Moussa begot Mansour who begot Abou Mansour Moussa. This latter begot Abou Moussa Anton Sayegh (and Soliman and Younes Sayegh). Anton Sayegh begot Fares, Hanna, and Girgis who are the forefathers of the three known families in Salima:

345

1- **The House of Fares Anton Sayegh:** Fares begot Nichola, Samaan, Habib, and Youssef (who died unmarried). Nichola begot Ibrahim who died unmarried. Samaan begot only Ward who married Shebly Bou Zian Haddad of whom I will talk of later. Habib moved to Beirut and married a woman from the Roman Orthodox Sect and embraced their doctrine. His offspring are all Roman Catholics. Together with his children, he went back to using the name Haddad. Habib begot Asaad, Selim, Ibrahim, Gibran, and Wasta. Asaad emigrated to Greece and got married there. Since then, there has been no news about him. Selim emigrated to Brazil and begot Elias and Girgi. Girgi died unmarried. Ibrahim emigrated to Brazil and begot George and Michel. Gibran Bin Habib Haddad begot Tawfik, Michel, Habib, George, and Fouad. Wasta Bin Habib begot Elias and George. Both of them practice their ancestors' profession. They are goldsmiths like their father.

2- **The House of Hanna Bin Anton:** Hanna Bin Anton Sayegh Haddad begot Anton, Ibrahim, and Elias. Elias was sterile and died. Anton Bin Hanna begot Fares, Girgis, and Ghaleb (who didn't get married). Fares begot Habib and Anton. Habib Bin Fares Anton Hanna begot Selim and 'Oql. Selim begot Jemeyel, Tawfik, and Anton. They are expatriates in Colombia. As for 'Oql Habib, with his wife Heloun Faragallah Freha Bachaalany, begot Habib, after more than twenty years of marriage. Anton Fares Hanna begot Fares (who died young), leaving only Saida as the last surviving offspring of Anton. She married a Frenchman named Alfons Ferman. Ibrahim Bin Hanna Bin Anton begot Hanna who begot Ibrahim who lived in Beirut for a while. and then, emigrated with his family.

3- **The House of Boutros Bin Anton:** The name of Boutros Bin Anton Sayegh was mentioned as Sabagh because he was a dyer as well as a jeweler. He begot Girgis, Mikhail, and Moussa. Abou Boutros Girgis begot Boutros, Daoud, and Youssef who both died with no children. As for Boutros Bin Girgis, he begot Anton. But when Anton's father died, he was raised by his grandfather, Abou Boutros, and was known as Anton Boutros. He begot Girgis who emigrated to Mexico and called himself Girgis Khoury, the surname of the paternal cousins of his father Moussa, not his.

The Moussa Khoury House

Mikhail and Moussa Boutros Anton Sayegh were ordained to the priesthood. Mikhail became a celebate priest with his own name. He served the Romy el Metn village. Moussa was ordained a priest with his own name and begot Nejm, Abou Elias, Samaan, Hanna, and Naoum. This offspring is known as the Moussa Khoury House. Abou Daher Nejm begot Daher and Ibrahim who died young in Brazil. Daher begot Nakhla who begot George and Michel, both of whom lived with their father in Choueir. As for Hanna Khoury, he begot Habib who emigrated to Brazil and begot Abdou and Hanna .... Abou Elias Khoury begot Elias, Said, and Abdulallah who are expatriates.

Samaan Khoury begot Eid (deceased), Shaker, Andraous, and Moussa. Moussa had no children and died. Boutros Samaan begot Girgi, Selim, and Nasry. As for Shaker Samaan, he begot Gibran and Michel. Andraous had no children. All of them are in Brazil.

The Lineage of Farah Haddad

Farah Haddad begot Nasr and Mehana. Mehana begot Anton, who begot Youssef and Mehena who died unmarried. Youssef, known Abi Gohar Haj, had no children. As for Nasr, he begot Girgis who begot Nasr. Nasr begot Girgis and Nasef. Girgis begot Tanous, Nasr, and Mikhail. Tanous begot Girgis who begot Tanous the expatriate in the Transval. He is married and has a family. Nasr Bin Girgis begot Fares and Hanna who died unmarried and young. Fares Nasr begot Nasr known as Nasry, and he begot a son…. Mikhail bin Girgis Nasr begot Nasef, Elias, and Andraous. Nasef emigrated to Brazil with his family. His children are Mikhail, Khalil, and Anis who died young. Mikhail begot ten children: Nersizo i.e Nasef, Moris, Walson, Elias and…. Nersiso was one of the best doctors in Brazil. Khalil Bin Nasef didn't get married. Anis died young, while Elias and Andraous Mikhail Haddad had no children.

Nasef Bin Nasr Haddad begot Younes, Elias, Mikhail, and Constantin. Younes begot Asaad, Boutros, and Nasef. Asaad Younes begot Nichola, Nakhla, and Elias. They are with their children in Transval. Boutros Younes begot Daoud who emigrated to Olivayra in Brazil. He has children, however, Nasef Younes begot only daughters. Elias Bin Nasef Nasr Haddad begot Qablan, Daoud, and Khalil and we couldn't find out any information as to the possible marriages or children…. As for Mikhail Nasef Nasr Haddad, he begot Saada and Nichola. Saada begot Mikhail, Emil, and Youssef. Mikahil Saada died young. Constantin Bin Nasef became a priest, then he begot Melhem, Eskandar, and Mata who died young and unmarried. Melhem Khoury begot Selim, Girgi, Tawfik, and Milad. Selim emigrated to the United States and had a son…. As for Tawfik, he died young and unmarried in Africa. Milad begot ….

The House of Shebli Bou Zian Haddad

We previously mentioned that Ward, the daughter of Samaan Bin Nichola Bin Fares Sayegh Haddad, married Shebli Abou Zian Haddad. He had come from Mo'alakat Zahle to his uncle Youssef Anton Mehena Haddad (Abi Gohar). He and Ward lived in Salima and begot Nasef, Samaan, and Elias. Nasef Shebli begot Girgis who died unmarried and young, and, a daughter, Mary. She married Fadoul Bashwar. Samaan died unmarried, while Elias Shebli emigrated with his family to Mexico. His children are Mikhail, Gibran, and Samaan. All of them are married and have children.

The Bashwar House.

Their Origin.

The members of this family who seemed to know, said that they originally came from a village called Seqilbeiya, next to Halab. Some family still remains there. Its Sheikh was called Rostom Bashwar. Some of those who moved from there because of the tyrannical and despotic governors, lived in Safita (Sfaile?). Their numbers grew and they came to own a considerable amount of property there as well as becoming well known. Their Lieutenant Colonel there was Nassib Pasha Bashwar. He inherited the title of Pasha from his father and grandfather. Another group from this family went to Beirut and in the middle of the last century they were living in a building still known as The Tower of Yaakoub Bashwar. He was the leader of his people at that time. He gave part of that building to his children. He died at the age of 115.

What we know is that the first one from that family who moved from Beirut to Salima was the teacher, Elias Bashwar. In his time, he was one of the famous builders. He moved to Salima before or in 1750 when the famous Prince Ismail Abi Lam' renovated his castles in Salima. Most assuredly, it was he who built the old Saint John's Church around the year 1770. The fact that these religious and civil buildings still stand, today, is proof of the development of art and industries at that time in Lebanon.

We think, in all probability, that the "Ibn Abou Neama" mentioned in the document dated 1064 Hegira (1653), is the forefather of Neama Bashwar. That means that this family has been in Salima for 300 years. We don't know of any other person from that time period who had that name in Salima.

Their Lineage

The teacher Elias Bashwar begot Asaad, Bashwar, and Neama. Asaad begot Elias, Ghantous, Hanna, and Ghaleb. Elias Bin Asaad begot Selim who had no children. Ghantous begot Asaad, Girgis, and Saba. Asaad Ghantous begot Michel who begot Asaad and Roro. Girgis Ghantous begot Metri and Asper. Saba Ghantous begot Gibran, Elia, Bashwar, and Hanna. Those four emigrated with their parents to Oliveira in Brazil where they are married and have children.

As for Hanna Bin Asaad Bin Elias Bashwar, he begot Tanious and Boutros. Boutros died young and unmarried in Mexico while Tanious begot Tawfik, Victor, George, and Pedro. Ghaleb Bin Assad, the son of the teacher Elias, was ordained a priest and was named Father Elias. He begot Ibrahim and 'Azar who begot Wadie' who is in Brazil. Ibrahim Khoury Bashwar begot Melhem, Girgi, and Elias, who are all expatriates in Mexico, married with children. As for Bashwar, the son of the teacher Elias Bashwar, he begot Hanna and Fares who begot Beshara, Fadoul, and Tamer. Beshara begot Elias. Fadoul and Tamer migrated to the United States and are married.

Neama Bin Elias Bashwar begot Shedid who begot Neama and Najib. Both of them migrated to Brazil and have children. The only one from this family remaining in Salima is their sister Mary.

About Them And Their Vestiges

Many of them are mentioned in the documents we have published in this book. And probably, the "Bou Neama" mentioned in the old document of the Haddad House dated 1064 Hegira (1653), is their forefather. In another document dated 1259 Hegira (1843), we read *"Witnessed by Elias Ibn Asaad teacher Elias"*. This is Abou Selim Elias Bin Asaad, the son of the teacher Elias Bashwar, the forefather of this family in Salima. This mentioned Elias was one of Youssef beik Karam's knights and one of his close friends.

Daher Nejm Andrea, with his brother Girgis, and De'ebess Bin Tanious from the Bachaalany folks, went to Ehden asking for refuge from Karam Beik, as we previously mentioned. Elias Bashwar was, at that time, in the house of Beik Karam and served him with honesty and devotion. Thus, he was appointed a knight at the office of the governorate of el Metn. After that, he was promoted to the rank of Sergeant in the army, during the era of the district commissioner. Finally, he moved to Safita and lived with his in-laws. Then, there is no additional news about him.

The teacher Ghantous Bin Asaad was exceptional in the field of construction. The Church of Our Lady in Salima is one of his accomplishments. It shows accuracy, solidity, and perfection in construction, the characteristics he was noted for. Hanna, his brother, was his greatest assistant in building that Church. Hanna converted to the Maronite doctrine. We have already mentioned the help of Father Elias Bashwar in building Church of Saint Elias in Salima in 1862. Also, he was the one who built the tribune of the Church of the Capuchin Fathers in Beirut.

Today, in Salima, the only ones remaining from the Bashwar House are Tawfik Bin Tanious Bashwar and his brothers & sisters. The rest are all expatriates, as we previously mentioned.

The Tafkaji House.

Their Origin And Lineage.

All that we know about them is that they are Roman Catholics. Their forefather took refuge with the Princes of Salima. He used to walk with the Prince, preceeding him, and smoking his pipe, thus he was named "Al Tafkagy" which is a Turkish word. Their lines of descent are: Shahin, Mikhail, and Gibrail, all the sons of Al Tafkagy. Shahin begot

Girgis and Elias. Elias begot Eskandar, Najib, and Nakhla. Eskandar emigrated to Colombia and when he was on his way back to Lebanon, he died at Marseilles. He had Eskandar and Edgar. As for Najib Bin Elias, he begot Pedro and Najib who are all in Colombia. Girgis Bin Shahin begot Selim and Amin who both died unmarried in Beirut.

Mikhail Tafkajy begot Nichola and Tanious. Nichola begot Girgis who begot Mikhail. Mikahil migrated to Mexico where his maternal uncle Girgis Anton Boutros lived. In Beirut, Tanious Bin Mikhail Tafkajy begot Hanna and Nakhla who migrated to America. Gibrail Tafkajy died unmarried.

The Bou Mikhail House.

Their Origin and Lineage.

They were known as the Bou Mikhail House. Their forefather came from Damascus – Al Sham (Syria) asking for refuge from the Lam's Princes in Salima. Abou Mikhail begot Youssef begot Nejm, Nasef, Girgis, and Wakim. We only know the names of these first ones who are mentioned in old documents. Wakim had seven sons but only Asaad remained. Assad begot Nejm and Wakim. Nejm begot only girls: Mary, Marta, and Henna. Wakim begot Asaad who begot Theodore. Asaad and his family are in the United States where he is known as Ernest Kassab (Kassab is the name of his maternal uncles).

349

THE S'EID HOUSE

Chapter 10

Their Origin

The S'eid House is a noble Druze family. It is one of the oldest families that lived in Salima after its restoration. That is the reason why we could not determine its origins or its time of arrival. At one time, the S'eid folks were the greatest owners in and around Salima. The newcomers to Salima would have to deal with them. And, when the Lam's Princes came to Salima at the beginning of the 17th Century, the S'eids and some of the other old families were the most powerful and wealthiest. Then, their numbers increased as did their real estate holdings which reached to the Qaaqour at the northern end of Salima. However, it was not a lasting things. Sometimes they were strong and at other times they were weak. This is something that happens to every generation.

The S'eid folks say that there is a relationship between them and the Do House in Zaraoun and Qraiye. From the S'eid House come many offshoots which migrated to various places, such as to the region of the Chouf, Aaqbe, Hasbaiya, Rachaiya, and Horan. Other groups and individuals from them have migrated to the region in the countryside. They lived in Makse, Establ, and Mraijat. Others have lived in Germana in Syria and the Qobl monastery. Then, there are the S'eid folks who emigrated to the United States.

Once the taxpayers of this family numbered no less than 500, however, today, in Salima, they are less than 40.

The offshoots of the S'eid House are: 1- S'eid, 2- Nayel, 3- Bou Ali, 4- Seif, 5- Bahmad, and 6- Abdel Wahed.

The offshoots of 1- S'eid House consist of the following Houses: Salman Bou Daher, Sajaa, and Hussein Qassem.

The offshoots of the 2- Nayel House consists of: the Noaman House, Ali Soliman House, Fares House and the Shahin House.

As for the offshout of 3- Bou Ali, they consist of the House of Bou Hassan Ezz Eddine, the House of Hassan Abdulallah, the House of Hassoun Refaa, the Saab Qassem House, the Bou Saadi House, the Sayed Ahmed House, and the Ezz Eddine House.

The offshoot of 5- Bahmad, consist of the House Ossman Meshref, Wahbeh House, and the House of Abou Jemeyel Selim Hussein Qassem.

As for the offshoot of 6-Abdel Wahed, they are the House of Ali Beshir.

The Abou Hassan Sajaa

Abou Hassan Sajaa is one of the S'eid folks. He lived for a long time in Makse and Marj in the countryside where he cultivated the fields and raised cattle. He worked for the government and was a lieutnant colonel during the era of the Princes Haidar Ismail and Beshir Ahmed. He commanded 50 knights, among them, a group from Salima.

Abou Hassan was a short man, of strong will, who drank alcohol like the Christians. He was a bold man who had no fear of death. He was famous for his participation, with his men, in the battle of Nablous. Because of that, the Ottoman government bestowed on him the title Agha. When he came back from Nablous, he was a military and civil governor. He accumulated a large amount of money, most of which was retained by his daughter-in-law, Kenta, the wife of his

351

son Abi Daher. Of his famous knights were Ali Beshir Said, Asaad Mohamed, and their paternal uncle, Ali Al Jari from Kfar Nabrakh. He built himself a beautiful home in Salima with a stable for his horses. It was just like those of the princes. People used to say: "the horses of the Princes went out and they came back the horses of Abou Hassan". He died about the same time as his son, Abou Daher. That was around the year 1876.

Selim Al Jary

He is Selim Bin Qassem Daher Hussein, from the offshoot of Nayel Said. His mother was the sister of Asaad and Mohamed Al Jary from Kfar Nabrakh. Selim was surnamed after the name of his maternal uncles. Al Jary's children were mostly in Broummana and Salima. One of them married a girl from there. Selim was born in Salima and grew up with his maternal uncles. When Mohamed, his maternal uncle, was hung, he lived in the house of his maternal uncle Asaad. He surrendered after the revolt against the government. He also accompanied Shebli Al Erian to Baghdad, where he was appointed its governor. Asaad was an officer with Shebli and Selim, the son of his sister, Tatounji. At that time he learned the Turkish language. When Shebli Al Erian died, Selim came back with his maternal uncle to Damascus where he was appointed a policeman. After the death of his maternal uncle, he inherited his entire estate. He then moved to Snaya to join the service of Ali Pasha, the son of the Algerian warrior, Prince Abdel Kader.

When the Druzes of Horan revolted against the Ottoman government, Selim was there. Hassan Agha Bozo arrested him because of the hostility between them. He sent him to Damscus. After three years, he was appointed to the Secret Police. In Damascus, he lived through hard times. Because of that he went back to the Druze Mountain where he lived with "the Kasars". Then, Mamdouh Pasha arrested him and delivered him to the Government. He came back to Horan and worked, like his maternal uncle, as a high ranking officer.

The second war happened in Horan, and Selim was a commander. It has been said that he roused his men and attacked an Ottoman battalion passing by a river at the Druze Mountain. He wiped out the battalion and was wounded in the process. As a result, he acquired great influence with the government. However, some have denounced him and said that he was the cause of the murder of the battalion because it was done at his recommendation. Therefore he was arrested and exiled with the other Sheikhs of Horan to western Tripoli.

After that, an order was issued sending Selim to Istanbul, but he never reached it because of the war the Ottoman Empire and Greece had started. Instead, he seized the Ottoman ship and captured all the exiled Druzes. He then transported them to the island of Cyprus.

The Greeks treated Selim generously because he was an experienced knight and was also a veterinarian. Thus, he practiced that profession in Athens and remained there till the constitution of the Ottoman Republic was announced. Thus, Selim came back home with a sizeable estate. He lived for a long time in Salima with his parents and relatives. He built a large home. However, he became ill quickly, so much so, that he could not finish his new home. He died in 1911 and he had no children.

He was of tall stature, with a majestic look. And, he was courageous. His two half-brothers, from his mother's side, lived in Salima. They were named Fares and Rashid and were the sons of Fares S'eid. They both died without children.

Ali Beshir

He is Ali, the son of Beshir Bin Abdel Wahed Said. His father, Beshir, and Sheikh Ali Al Emad, were both killed. Ali was accompanying Sheikh Khatar Al Emad.

Ali fought in many battles with him. He was an experienced knight. While riding on horseback, he was able to carry his lance and wield his sword at the same time. After watching him for ten years, Elias Mikhail Bou'oun drew a picture of him in exactly that position.

The two authors of The Political Liberators (Chapter 3, page 180) talk about the Lebanese Druzes who were exiled during the sedition of 1860. They cite a letter from Ali Beshir to Hassan Beik Shaqeir Arsoun. Ali sent the letter from his exile in Belgrade, primarily as a bequeath to his family. In it he said that someone had poisoned him to prevent him from disclosing the secrets of the national slaughter.

He begot Beshir, Abbass, and Qassem. Qassem begot Amin and Najib who are among our greatest expatriates in Mexico. Beshir begot Najib who died and left two sons.

A'wary and Helaly

Civil unrest broke out on October 5 and 17 in 1856 between the Helaly folks and the A'war folks. They are the two famous families in Qarnayel. People from both sides died. Prince Beshir Ahmed Al Lam', the governor of the Christians, in the presence of Sheikh Hussein Talhouq, as he was known in the Druze's tongue, was ordered to reconcile. Through an agreement signed by the notables of the Druzes of the Metn they agreed not to renew the fighting.

The noticeable thing about the agreement is that the signatures of the notable Druzes of Salima preceding all others. Salima was in the avant-garde position among the Metn villages.

Here are the names of the people who signed that document, in the same order as they appear in the original register of the Governorate. We are preserving that register. It should be noted that it also contains the details of that uprising and the reconciliation. The names are: "Abou Hassan (Sajaa) S'eid Soliman (Ali) S'eid; Abdel Hady Al Masry; and Salman (Mohamed) Al Masry."

The people of the village of Salima at that time, were split into two parties: The A'wary and the Helaly. The Christian Bachaalany's and the Druze Masry's were on the side of the Helal House. The Christian Nakouzy and the Druze S'eids backed the A'war. The first belonged to the Janbalati party and the others to the Yazbaki party. That is how the parties were organized in Lebanon in the past, more political than religious.

The Lineage of the Druzes

We have tried to make a family tree, organizing the offspring in such a way that the kinships of the Druze families of Salima are shown. We want to do this just as we did for the Christian families. Unfortunately, we were unable to complete it for the following reasons:

1- The necessary references are unavailable because the Druzes don't have old recording registers as do the Christian Churches. The Christian registers show marriage, birth, and death records which allow us to determine lineage and kinship.

2- Although we conducted many searches, we did not locate any old household documents such as old deeds, contracts, etc..

3- There aren't any Druze leadership positions like the Sheikhs of the Christian families. These Sheikhs are often the repository for considerable oral traditions and information relating to their families.

In the past we collected some information about the old families, like the Yazbak House, the Khedr and Qadama Houses. Those families became extinct or nearly so.

In our archives we possess a register of the real estate lots belonging to the people of Salima. It is from a work entitled The Newspapers of the Sheikh Youssef Yasbak, written by himself around the year 1760. It includes the names of the owners of the properties. Also, we have many old documents mentioning many people of Salima, both Druze and Christian. However, all of this, still does not allow us to compile even half of the kinships. And, as researchers examine the documents published in this book, he will find the names of many Druze families. Actually, he will probably find more than he will in any other place.

The Yazbak House

In the past, in Salima, there was a noble Druze family. Its children were known as the Sheikhs of the Yazbak folks. This family probably belongs to Sheikh Yazbak, one of the forefathers of Emad House. They were famous in Barouk and its neighbouring area. He was the leader of the Yazbaki party. The opposition party, the Janbalati, is related to Sheikh Janbalat, the forefather of the Janbalat family in Moukhtara. The Yazbaki sheikhs were well known and had large real estate holdings, some of which were known by their names.

It was said that the Yazbak and S'eid folks were fighting against the Lam's Princes when they came to Salima at the end of the 16th century. It was a struggle for power and the right to rule. The most famous of these fighters was Sheikh Youssef Yazbak. I am preserving many of his handwritten compositions in my archives. His house was located where Hamad Darwish Masry's house is now.

Sheikh Youssef died at the beginning of the last century and with him the offspring of the Yazbak house ended. He had a nephew (sister's son) known as Sheikh Selim from the well-known Bou Elwan House in Barouk. He came to Salima claiming the inheritance of his maternal uncle and lived there for a while. He was eloquent, an author of popular Arabic poems, and, writing proverbs and maxims. I came across his name in connection with the S'eid house. He was in the vanguard of those who went to Bikfaya in 1854 to attend the funeral of Prince Haidar Ismail. He delivered a popular poem there, on behalf of the people of Salima. The poem was to eulogize their great Prince: *"You, daughters of the notables, embroider even the borders of your veils. Hide even from his horses, so your path will be safe."*

Shahin Ghaleb Nakouzy started his elegy by saying: *"The scythe of eternal departure has picked up the best of us and left the rest bewildered. Oh, poor soul, how low we feel after your demise, Prince Haidar...."*

THE MASRY HOUSE

Chapter 11

Their Origin

According to the narrations handed down from the Masry people themselves, they came from the village called Ein Hershi at the Tim Valley around the year 1057 Hegira (1647). They went to the Lam's Princes in Salima. The Princes welcomed them warmly as they usually did with those who were seeking refuge, whether Christian or Druze.

The first to come from this family were the brothers Ali and Ahmed Kheir Eddine. Thanks to the Princes, they quickly bought a place to live and lands from which to make a living. So it was that they lived under the shelter of the Prince of Salima in full comfort and peace.

At that time in Salima, there was a strong, radiant, and famous family known as the S'eid family. They were related to S'eid Qarb Lam'. They were proud of themselves and of their men. It happened that Ahmed Kheir Eddine went to the field known as the Hayarate at the north of the village, to water his land. A man of the S'eid family, named S'eid, met him. He also wanted to water his lands, so, he kept the water from Ahmed. This caused a fight between them. S'eid was the first to strike, hitting Ahmed with a fatal blow. He died immediately. This happened at night. In the morning, the news spread and people, including the Princes, went to see the murder victim. Ali came and found his brother's body on the ground. He was so furious that everything in front of him went dark. But there was nothing he could do. He went back home with the intention of leaving. The Princes refused to let him do so. The S'eid folks did the same.

However, Ali Kheir Eddine no longer wanted to live there. So, one day, with his family and the family of his brother, he moved to Horan, to a village called Rima. He was with his four sons: Abdel Hady, Jabr, Matar, and Soliman. With him as well, were the three sons of his brother: Younes, Shahin, and Abou El Kheir. Soliman had two sons, Henedy and Yazbak. When Henedy grew up, he became a Sheikh of Rima which was called after him "Rimat Henedy". Matar Bin Ali begot three sons: Youssef, Nejm, and Omar. Youssef was the toughest one and he was named "el Shater" (the Clever). He lived in Majdal Horan.

Jabr begot two sons: Fakhr Eddine and Soliman who shared the Sheikhdom of Majdal with his paternal cousin Youssef. Their paternal cousins Youness, Shahin, and Abou El Kheir lived with them in those two villages for a while.

Ali Kheir Eddine traveled to Egypt and worked in the horse business. He had sold everything he owned, staying in Egypt for many years, self-employed in his own business. Then, he came back home. First, he went to Salima to see what had happened during his absence. He had Egyptian products which he spread on the ground. He saw the Sheikhs of the S'eid house and their youth walking and having fun. They didn't recognise Ali Kheir Eddine after more than 25 years. In the crowd, Ali was unable to find his adversary, S'eid. The Princes had exiled him to Qarnayel. Then, the Prince saw Ali Kheir Eddine and asked him: "You are Ali, aren't you?" He answered negatively. After he had sold his merchandise, he left Salima and went to Horan. There, people warmly welcomed him with joy and happiness, congratulating him for his safe return. Then, all of them lived there in peace and happiness.

After a period of time, both the S'eid and the Masry Houses reconciled. The Masry House came back from Horan to Salima after being away for a long time.

355

Certainly, the reconciliation between those two families happened in an unusual way, a way that honours and suits the two parties. However, what has been told about it is, in fact, unbelievable. What is described is contrary to Lebanese traditions, those of the Maarouf folks and others. Furthermore, there wasn't a single document or a trusted narration that could prove the supposed story. Nevertheless, we decided to pass it on:

As the story goes, the forefather of the Masry folks was so named because he migrated to Egypt (Misr) at some unknown time. We are now going to publish a previously unknown document that we discovered in the treasury of the Maronite Patriarchy. From it, it is deduced that the Masry family was in Salima before 1057 (1647)Hegira. Also, that they had large property holdings which spread up to the Kanaysi village, near Salima. Here is the text of the document:

"In the name of God the all merciful, I ask for his help and know that by him I will succeed. On the day of Sunday, of the month Jomady Al Awal, of the year 1047 Hegira (1637), Abou Ibrahim Herika and Abou Moussa Girgis Ibn Herika from the Aarbaniye village of Choueir at the Metn county, affiliated with Beirut, have bought from Sheikh Abou Soliman Ali Ibn Marsel from el Ras village in the same mentioned county and the same mentioned deal. They bought from him a part of the plantation belonging to the Church, containing mulberry trees, cinnamon barks, woodland, trellis, disabled trees, and, half of the water source located at the mentioned part, the ruins of the monastery...for the amount of six hundred ninety seven piasters according to the evaluation of Abou Mounes Ibn Makarem. The mentioned sum has been completely received in one meeting. He made with them an irrefutable, honest and valid sale. Any sort of claims are the responsibility of the mentioned seller, including that which has come to us from his excellency, the Sultan, according to the boundaries, the borders of which are, from the South, the great Al Shemshar, which is above the source at the bottom of the Ibn Al Masry properties and the road. From the West, the waterwheel of the source and the waterwheel of what comes down from Arsoun. At the East, the waterwheel which is in front of Arsoun up to Ras al Hersh, to the bottom of the Masry land. Thanks be to God, the boundaries have been determined and witnessed to its correctness, its writer is the humble Fayad Ibn Saray Eddine from el Ras village. Witnesses: Sheikh Abou Nejm Ezz Eddine from el Ras, Sheikh Qassem Abou Zaanaf."

That document proves that, a long time ago, the Masry House owned property at the outskirts of Salima. It contains evidence that the Mounes House belonged to the Makarem House from the Druze of Ras el Metn of that time. And, it is the oldest vestige of the habitation of the Kneiese village and the renovation of the Saint Anthony Monastery there by one of the Asmar folks in Aarbaniye who built the endowment for that monastery.

The Masry and Hatoum Houses

At the end of the 18th century, a great dispute happened between these two families. It ended with a crime and victims on both sides. The cause for the situation centers on a strong man, called Selim, from the Hatoum folks in Kfar Selouane.

When this man wanted to water his lands in Jdita in the countryside, he dug with his knife at the water pool to let some water go. He apparently also placed his knife beside the water basin as a threat, so no one would dare to divert any water to their lands. It happened that one of the Masry House, called Meqled Bin Wahab Bin Matar, didn't care about the threats of the Hatoumy or his knife. So, he freed the water in the basin. Then Selim asked people who did that. The dispute started. It was between him, Selim, and the son of the Masry. It ended in a violent struggle in which the son of Hatoum died.

After that, the son of the Masry, with his companion, went back to Salima. The news of the death of Ibn Hatoum reached the Hatoum folks in Kfar Selouane. They revolted and attacked Salima. But, on their way, they met Mansour Khedr from the Druzes of Salima. They encountered him at the gate at the outskirts of Qarnayel, and, they killed him.

Then they returned. Each group started to find one of their enemies alone, and, they killed him. Finally, the Hatoums attacked with all their power and force until they reached the borders of Salima. The Masry folks started to retreat with the Hatoums close behind them. Then, the Masry arrived at the Sabaa Cliff above Hasbaiya.

At that time, the people were divided in parties. The Masry and the Bachaalany folks belonged to the same group. Thus, the Bachaalany helped them in that battle. It was in that fight that Shahin Fasida Bachaalany became famous. He attacked with his wife, Mary, surnamed Al Hamra. She was so courageous and strong that together they succeeded and vanquished the attackers. The Hatoum folks retreated to the frontiers of Al Hoz. It was at that time that Shahin Bachaalany was also given the name Shahin Masry.

Abdel Hady

Abou Ahmed Abdel Hady Masry was considered a rare man, generous, extremely honest, and highly ethical.

In 1860, he was in the village of el Merijat. One day, a fugitive named Mikhail Shamy was running away from the masacre happening in Damascus, Syria. He was the agent of the Capuchin priests in that village, so Abou Mohamed saw him and saw three others coming up behind to attack. So, Abou Ahmed used tricks and succeeded in keeping the enemies away. He hid with him in the stable with the animals until the enemis went away. He then took Abou Ahmed Mikhail Shamy and accompanied him to a safe location. Then, he went to Beirut.

Mikhail Shamy knew that this hero was Abou Ahmed Abdel Hady and he knew the location of his farm. So, he went to the Capuchin Monastery in Salima, and, with the priest, went to visit the one who saved him and to thank him. Abou Ahmed was living at that time in the assembly room at the castle of Lady Zahr.

Abou Ahmed was a close friend of our grandfather Tanous Freha Bachaalany. The friendship of these two men was firm. Nothing would separate them but an act of God. They called each other "my brother" and they raised their children and grandchildren on those values. That friendship was their inheritance. What we remember is that the artist, Elias Mikhail Bou'oun Bachaalany, 30 years after their deaths, painted a picture of our grandfather Tanous and his friend, Abdel Hady. Those who knew them said that the painting is an exact representation of how they looked.

Abdel Hady begot Ahmed and Mohamed. Mohamed lived in Bzebdine and begot Shahin, Youssef, and…. Ahmed begot Abou Hussein, Ali, Nejm, and ….

Haidar The Zaraouni

He is Haidar Bin Abi Hassan, belonging to the Zeid folks in Zaraoun. His father left and lived in Salima where he became related to the Masry folks. He was extremely generous and intelligent. He was famous for his knowledge of medicine which he learned from Father Hanna and Father Mansour, the headmasters of the Saint Peter Monastery of the Capuchin Fathers in Salima. He was also a friend of Father Youssef Bachaalany who knew medicine as much as Prince Haidar did. Thus, they would help each other to solve problems and cure the sick, especialy the poor.

Haidar had a strong influence over his people. He was very well thought of and highly respected by the people of Salima. He had that special medical perception which often allowed him to determine the illness of the patient just by seeing him. Father Hanna gave him a book entitled <u>The Cure</u> in which the author, Ibn Sinai, discussed medicine. The book was printed in Rome approximately 400 years ago.

It is said that Prince Haidar converted to Christianity during the era of Ibrahim Pasha Al Masry, when military service was an obligation for the Druzes of Lebanon. We also discussed other things about his life which appeared in a previous chapter, so, please, review them.

Haidar begot Nejm (died young and unmarried) and Youssef who begot Nejm, Haidar, and Selim who begot ….

At that time, many of the Druzes of Salima converted to Christianity, such as: Beshnaq from the S'eid House and Abou Meshref Fahd from the Masry House. They did that in order to avoid military service. Fahd Masry died in 1839 and was buried beside the Saint Peter Monastery. His remains were moved to the cemetery of Saint John in 1912.

Their Offshoots

The original offshoots of the Masry folks are four: Abdel Hady, Matar, Jabr, and Soliman or Behay Eddine.

1- From Abdel Hady came: the Abdel Hady House, the Mohamed House, the Borhan House, and, the Shahin Saab House (in el Roweisa).

2- From Matar came: the Matar House, the Masoud House, the Saleh House, the Teroudi House, the Fa'our House, and, the Wahab House.

3- From Jabr came: the Fakh Eddine House, the Soliman House, the Fares Bou Hussein House, and the Mar'ei Qassem House.

4- From Soliman or Behai Eddine in el Roweissa came: Hussein Saloum Bin Hussein Behai Eddine House, the Behai Eddine House, Molhem Nejm Daher Bin Hussein Behai Eddine, the Daher Sonjod Soliman House, and the Hamoud Behai Eddine House.

In Horan

Among the offspring of the Masry family who migrated, in the past, to Horan, are the Henedi family who are in Rima in Horan. It was said that they went back to Salima, then they migrated elsewhere at some unknown time. The two groups, Henedi and Masry, are in a good relationship and they often visit each other. I remember their notable, Hazima Henedi. He paid a visit to his relatives in Salima, then, a few years ago, his son Fadl Pasha, one of the well known Druzes in Horan, did the same.

In The Qalaa

The Amin Masry House is one of the Masry folks, and Fares Salman is one of them. He lives in Qalaa, near Hammana. They are a large, distinguished family, coming from Jabr, one of the Masry offshoots in Salima. As for the relationship between them and some other families, like the family of Melhem Qassem the Metwelians and others, they are probably all just fanciful stories with no basis in fact. People just continue to pass on the tales.

The Families Related To The Masry House In The Past

Families From Srifa

From the renowned Druze families of Salima, there are some who became related to the Masry folks:

1- The Khedr House. A group of them are in Baaqline. Selim Bin Hassan Beik Khedr and his brother attended the School of Our Lady of Lourdes. People said that they came from Kfar Selouane where they were tyrants and people revolted against them. So, they came to Salima, but their victims took revenge. They agitated the Lam's Princes against them. Later, they invited them to a banquet and killed them during the presentaion of the food, just as they had previously done with the Abou Tareiya family in Bzebdine. Ahmed from the Khedr family was the one who survived that plot and took refuge with a friend from the Qadama House in Salima. This friend talked to Prince Al Lam' who took a liking to him and protected him.

Ahmed married the daughter of Qadam and lived in Salima. His children were surnamed after their maternal uncle. From them came the Bou Shaqra House and the Talb House. Then, they joined the Masry house. Abou Shaqra is Mahmoud Bin Ahmed Khedr and he begot Hussein who begot Qassem. This latter begot Hussein and Youssef. Hussein begot Qassem and Salman who migrated to Argentina. Qassem begot Selim. Youssef begot Amin, Mejid, and Selim. Talb Bin Khedr begot Asaad who begot Qassem and Talb. Talb begot Asaad, Daher, and Shahin. Qassem begot Mansour.

2- The Qadama House, of the old inhabitants of Salima, were the in-laws of the S'eid House but because of a dispute between them, the Princes moved them to Sarfa, to the east of the village and they became related to the Masry house. They were powerful men, and rich. They had a molasses press beside Farah field (Haql Farah), bearing their name still. From them came the assessor, Abou Nejm Haidar, and his brother, Deliqan. There was also, Ataf, the grandfather of the De'ebess, the father of 'Oql, as well as Mohamed Hamad Ataf who died during the war and had no children.

3- The Beshr House originated from Ras el Metn. They became related to the Masry house and lived in Sarfa. Abdulallah Beshr begot Amin, Seif Eddine, and Marcel. Marcel became insane. Amin Beshr begot Bou Ali and Fendi who had no children and died. Bou Ali Amin begot Abdel Karim who begot girls and died. Seif Eddine begot Abdulallah and Soliman who had no children, while Abdulallah begot Hassan, Mahmoud, and Soliman. Soliman begot Farid.

4- The Hourani House is the inhabitant of Sarfa and are related to the Masry house. It was said that they are the remaining offspring of Younes, one of the children of Kheir Eddine Masry. Their forefather was called Al Horani because he emigrated to that village, then came back. Al Horani begot Abou Hussein and Abou Ali. Abou Hussein begot Ali who begot Hussein and Mohamed who begot Shahin, Jemeyel, and Radi. Hussein migrated to the United States. Abou Ali Hourani begot Hassan who begot Hassan.

The Families Who Recently Became Related To The Masry House

The Haidar House

Their forefather is Haidar Zaraouni. His father, Abou Hassan, is from the Zeid House and had come from Zaraoun to live in Salima. He begot Nejm and Youssef. The first one died young and Youssef Haidar begot Nejm, Haidar, and Selim.

The Bou Ghezlan House

It was said that they came from Hasbaiya Rachaiya a long time ago. Their forefather is Mansour Bou Ghezlan who begot Mohamed. Mohamed begot Nejm who begot Daher, Qassem, and Amin. All of them had no children. Some members of that family were famous for training and riding horses.

The Halaby House

They are one of the Druze families brought up from the Upper Mountain by Prince Beshir Shehabi the Great. That was around the year 1820. They, then, spread into villages all over Lebanon. So, in Salima, it was Hamoud Halaby. He begot Marei' and Qassem (who had no children). Marei' lived a very long life and begot Amin who begot ....

The Khatib House

They originated from Kholowat, near Hammana. Hussein Khatib came to Salima and lived in Al Roweissa. He begot Hamad and Mohamed.

The Zaraouny House

Abdulallah Adnan came from the village of Zaraoun, from the Zeid House. He settled in Roweissa in Salima, then he became related to Masry House and begot Mejid and Khalil.

The Mohamed House

Mahmoud Abdel Hady Masry begot Mohamed and Shahin. Mohamed begot four sons: Abou Ali, Salman, Hassoun.... Abou Ali begot Darwish, Beshir, Selim, Abou Daher, and Mahmoud. Mahmoud had no children. Darwish begot Nejm, Hamad, and Khatar. Hamad Darwish begot Ali, Youssef, and Nejm. As for Beshir Bou Ali, he begot Bou Ali, Marei', and Mansour. Bou Ali Beshir begot Ali who begot Hussein who died and had no children. Marei' Beshir begot Selim and Amin who begot .... Mansour Beshir begot Fares who begot Selim. Selim begot Hassan and Selim. Hassan begot Mahmoud. Selim begot Mohamed, Najib, and Rashid.

Abou Daher begot Daher who died young and unmarried. Salman Bin Mohamed begot Mahmoud and Amin. Mahmoud Salman begot Mohamed, Salman, Ahmed, Rashid, and Najib. Mohamed Mahmoud begot Shahin and Salman. Shahin begot Hassib and .... Ahmed Mahmoud begot Nessib. Salman and Rashid died young and unmarried.

Najib Mahmoud begot …. Amin Salman begot Selim, Fouad, Aref, and Raouf. Selim died young. Fouad begot …. Aref begot ….

Hassoun Bin Mohamed begot Ali and …. Ali Hassoun begot Hassan, Hussein, and Hassoun. The last two died in Argentina, while Hassan begot Daoud. As for Saloum Bin Mohamed Mahmoud, he begot Mohamed, Shebli, and Asaad. Assad begot Qassem and Saloum. Qassem begot Mohamed who begot Jemeyel and Kamil. Saloum begot Hassan. Mohamed Saloum begot Salman, Ali, and Youssef. Youssef begot Najib.

Salman Mohamed begot Halim, Na'eem, and Anis. Ali Mohamed begot Jemeyel and Kamel. Shebli begot Asaad, the father of Qassem.

There is also Saab Bin Shahin who begot Youssef, Shahin, and Qassem. Qassem had no children. As for Shahin, he begot Shahin who begot Kamel and Jemeyel. Kamel begot Karim…. Youssef Bin Shahin Saab begot Amin who begot Selim. Selim begot Qassem, S'eid, Asaad, and Amin.

The House of Fakhr Eddine Jabr

Fakhr Eddine Jabr begot Hamad and Omar. Hamad begot Fakhr Eddine who begot Hamada, Qassem, and Abbass. Hamad Fakhr Eddine begot Youssef, Selim, and Mahmoud. Youssef Hamad begot Fares and Selim. Selim Hamad begot Rashid who begot Ramez. Mahmoud Hamad begot Nessib and Adeeb. As for Qassem Fakhr Eddine, he begot Hussein who begot Qassem who begot Melhem. Abbass Fakhr Eddine begot Shahin, Ali, and Amin. Ali Abbass begot Najib and Kamel.

Amar Fakhr Eddine Jabr begot Beshir and Qassem. Beshir begot Mahmoud who begot Mohamed. Mohamed then begot Beshir, Shahin, and Selim. Qassem Bin Amar begot Soliman and Mar'ei. Soliman Bin Qassem begot Ahmed and Mohamed. Ahmed Soliman begot Ali, 'Oql, Mostapha, and Soliman. As for Mohamed Soliman, he begot Qassem, Selim, Asaad, and Youssef. Mar'ei Bin Qassem begot Hassan, Fares, and Salman. Hassan begot Mar'ei. Fares begot Selim who begot Fayed. Salman Mar'ei begot Mahmoud, Daoud, Amin and Shahin. Daoud begot Rashid.

The Siqly House

In Chapter 9, we failed to mention the Siqly family, one of the families known as "the Siqly House". They took refuge with the Princes of Salima. They were surnamed with the name of their profession which was probably making weapons and polishing them (Siql). The only thing we could find out about them was the name of their great-grand-father who was Yaakoub Al Siqly. Yaakoub Siqly begot Tanous who begot Abdou who begot Beshara and Elias. Elias had only a daughter named Olga. She married the son of her paternal aunt, Najib Shedid Neama Bashwar. As for Beshara, he begot Abdou and Shokrallah. Shokrallah disappeared during the First World War (1914 – 1919). Abdou emigrated to Brazil.

The Vestiges of Salima

Among our archives, we possess newspapers listing the real estate lots belonging to the citizens of Salima from 1750 to 1800. According to them, our grandfather Tanous Freha was the property tax collector. He had this job from the time he became the Reconciliation Sheikh and before the changes of the layout that occurred during the era of the District Commissionary in 1861. That old newspaper was written by Sheikh Youssef Yazbak from one of the famous families of Salima. From that record, we will give the names of the properties' owners. Some are illegible because they were written in red ink. We present the names as they appear in the original:

"His excellency Prince Soliman...Prince Ismail... Prince Fares... Prince Ali... Prince Hassan... Prince Qassem. The humble writer of this (Sheikh) Youssef Yazbak. Sheikh Beshir Kassab; his brother, Sheikh Saab; Sheikh Zamel; Sheikh Bou Leila; the son of his brother, Sheikh Deliqan; Sheikh Waked; Sheikh Kisrawan; his brother, Sheikh Sardy; Sheikh Jafal; the children of Bou Shaqra; the children of Talb; the children of Shams Eddine; Mohamed Beshr; his brother, Seif Eddine; his brother, Marcel; Bou Nejm Haidar (Qadama), children of Mahmoud; Hamad Bin Ali; Deliqan (Qadama) Mohsen Bin Shahin; his brother, Fares; the children of his brother, Bou Ali ...Hussein Ibn Jamal Eddine; his brother, Ismail; Nasr Eddine Bin Bahmad; his brother, Salman; the heirs of Hussein Ibn Sharaf Eddine; Khatar ? Bin Yaqdan; Mahmoud Ibn Hassan; Borhan Ibn Ali (from the Abdel Hady house) his brothers, Mohamed and Ahmed. Abdel Khalek; his brother Ismail; Salman Bin Shahin; his brother, Saab; Meqled Ibn Abdulallah ...his brother, Toroudy; has ...Ibn Shahin .... Allah Ibn Soliman ...Othman; his brother, Bergas; his brother, Waked; Hamad Ibn Fakhr Eddine; his brother Omar; Qassem Bahaa Eddine ...Fares Ibn Ibrahim... Jamal Eddine; the children of Bou Ali Ibn Yaqdan; Ibn Nejm Ibn Ezz Eddine; Mansour Bou Ghezlan; Naser Eddine Ibn S'eid; his wife; his brother, Beshneq; his brother, Sajaa; Ferhat Ibn Naser Eddine; Waked Ibn Youssef; his brother, Beshir; his brother Jeneid; Mohamed Ibn Mahmoud; Hussein Ibn Dhaher; Morat Hamada Ibn Shahin; Salman Ibn Nayel; his brother, Emad; Ahmed Ibn Abdullah; Beshir Ibn Nasef; Berges Ibn Bahmad and the children of his brother, Fasres. Beriqaa Ibn Bahmad; Riman Ibn Ismail; his brother, Salman... Sayed Ahmed Ibn Shahin; his brother, Hamada; his brother, Hamad and his mother; Ali bou Soliman Ali; his brother Sayed Ahmed; Hussein Bou Hassan; his wife and daughter; Salman Ibn Dhaher; Emad Seif; his daughter, Naasa; his brother, Serhal; his son Seif; Nejm Ibn Ismail; his wife; his brother, Jombelat; Mahmoud Ibn Qassem; Youssef Ibn ... Abdel Wahed; his brother Naser Eddine; Youssef Fares ... Fadoua, the daughter of Ismail; Nichola ? ...the children of Fares; Shahin Ibn Kanaan; Bou Darwish; Youssef Al Khoury (Francis) Boutros Al Khoury; Shahin; his brother, Heikal; his brother, Boughoush; Professor Elias (Bashwar) Genid Ibn Safi; the children of Elias Bou Mehiya ...his brother, Nemr; the children of Saad; Morshed; Hanna Andraous; Lias Ibn Khatar (Tarbeiya) Youssef... his brother, Boutros; Andrea Ibn Nejm ... Neama; the children of Nejm Bin Moussa; Youssef El Henawy; the children of Gad'oun Ibn Mansour; the children of Girgis ..Safi; his brother Shaiya; Gibrail Ibn Samaan; Lias Ibn Ragheb; Daham Ibn Teama; Bou 'Oql Ibn Abdulallah; the children of Nofal Ibn Hanna; Shahin Ibn Sadaad Allah; the children of Nasrallah ..Neama. Gibrail Bin Abdel Mesih; Hanna Al Aqoury, the daughter of 'Oun; Lias Ibn Moussa Atallah; Fares El Henawy; Hanna Ibn Samaan, the baker; Mansour and Hanna Al Showeiry; the son of his brother, Youssef; his brother, Hanna .... Lias Ibn Moussa Ibn Nasr. Hatem Ibn Abdel Kerim).

Those names starting from Andrea Bin Nejm up to Abdel Kerim are all from the Bachaalany House.

Fares Bin Anton (Al Khawaja) his brother, Hanna; his brother, Boutros; Daher Ibn (Al Sayegh) Ossman Bou Bark; his brother, Saloum; Girgis Saada; the endowment of the priests' monastery, Al Zereqi; Nasrallah, the fellow of his excellency Prince Soliman; Haidar Abdel Al Salam; the son of Mohamed Sharaf Eddine; Daher Ibn Masoud Heriz; Hamad Ibn Mahmoud from Arsoun; Anton and his brother, Shehada; Dorgham Mehawesh; Abdulallah Mehawesh; Bou Yaghi; his brother, Ibrahim; Lias Ibn Ziada Boutros; Youssef El Nieyi ...Rezkallah; his brother, Zeiyada ..." (the last names mentioned are living in the Dlaibe village near Salima).

362

THE EXPATRIATES FROM SALIMA

Chapter 12

In this chapter, we will briefly talk about the people of Salima who emigrated from it, in the past and the present. These are people we failed to mention in the previous chapter on emigration where we talked about their departure. We discussed the individual expatriates or told the story about each family.

Here let us say that the people of Salima were just like all the Lebanese families. The majority lived in that holy mountain, content and satisfied. If one of them gets upset over his situation, whether a tradesman, or professional, servant to a Princes or Sheikhs, or working for the government of his village; if he gets upset, he quits. But shortly afterwards he goes back to it.

As for those whose life situation causes them to emigrate from their village and family, the longer they are away, the more their ties to their land and relations are severed, bit by bit. But fortunately, many sons of this village were always suffering homesickness. This happens so often to those who have moved away. That is the reason why we think it will be nice to talk about them here, just as we previously did for others. This will be a nice memento for both the expatriates and our homeland residents.

In The Countryside

The people of Salima, both Christians and Druzes, frequently went to the countryside for their agricultural businesses, especially in the lands belonging to the Princes of Salima, the Lam's. Some of their jobs took them even further away, to the regions of Baalbek. They worked there as employees or partners of the Princes and others. They ploughed the fields and planted; in summer, they collected the harvest. Then they returned home to spend the rest of the year with their families. The relationship of the Salima people and the countryside was very close. It seemed beautiful and unlimited. Then the tithes and taxes were imposed by the governors of the countryside under the Sham (Syria) State. Such impositions meant that the Lebanese farmers hard work was practically for free.

But the patriotic Lebanese was convinced that he could not eliminate the countryside work because it was the source of his livelihood. So, he was obliged to go back there, no matter the tithes and taxes. He faced his daily economic crisis in the mountains. It was becoming harder and harder to make a living. Day by day, some started to leave the mountain and settle in the countryside. That is what happened with the people of Salima. At the beginning of the last century they started to leave and become the partners of the Princes and other owners. Then, the majority were able to buy the large properties in Makse, Taalabaya, Chtaura, and el Mraijat which became the colonies of Salima people. They lived there with the rest of the expatriates from the mountain's villages. They established mutual patriotic and social relationships with each other. Hereafter, we will briefly talk about each of those villages:

Chtaura. It is one of the oldest villages which has been colonized by the Bachaalany folks. They did so because of its abundant water, fertile soil, and good crops. Our grandfather, the late Tanous, bought grapevines there and in the village of Jdita. Then he was forced to sell them because of the tithes and taxes. The Abou 'Oql House, the old Nader Gad'oun House and other families belonging to the Bachaalany House, possessed lands in Chtaura then left them. Now, the only one remaining there, from Salima, is Elias Ghaleb Mar'ei Ghaleb Bachaalany. He is known for his courage, sense of honour, and generosity. He succeeded his father in the management of the properties of the famous Salma Bou Ouled Mohsena. He is now living there with his son, Nasef and his son's family.

363

Makse.   This second village where the people of Salima have lived for a long time, is Makse. In this village, many of the families that originated in Salima grew up. As a matter of fact, they are the majority of its inhabitants today. In El Mraijat, the inhabitants are both Christians and Druzes. In Makse, the Church of Saint Michael, which has existed for a long time, is still there with its source of mineral water. The citizens were working on the plain during the day, coming home at night. Some of them lived, for a while, in a place on the plain called "Mandara", but lately, they left it to live in Makse, Qaabb Elias, and El Mraijat. Now, a small group from Salima are still there, while all the rest went to El Mraijat.

El Mraijat. It is a nice village, with a nice climate and abundant water. It is located on a sloping mountain side looking over the plain. In the past it was a plantation belonging to the Salima Sheikhdom and its lands were those of the Lam's Princes. It remained that way until the year 1926. Then it became an independent Sheikhdom following the Zahle province. It was populated thanks to the people of Salima. They own the largest part of the lands. The first one to settle there was Asaad Youssef Ghaleb Bachaalany and his brothers. Asaad De'ebess Saada and Habib Fares Anton built houses for people, and they were done perfectly. Thus, people came there to live. They came from Salima, Mairouba, Ain Dara, Jouar El Haouz, and many other places. Thus, it became populated and became an important center for agriculture.

In this village, Asaad Ghaleb built a house and a storehouse for cereals beside it. His business grew and spread over the villages of the Metn where he had branches and representatives for his store. This business growth was due to his straight forwardness and honesty in dealing with people. Especially so, when dealing with the great grain dealers of the Sham. His piety and zeal drove him to build the Church of Saint George in Mraijat. His brother-in-law, Qablan Bin Asaad De'ebess, worked with him in that effort. Selim Beik Ayoub Thabet donated the necessary land to build it. He owned a large amount of real estate in the region. In general, Asaad Ghaleb was very well known in el Mraijat and in other places. He was a strong support for his family and country.

His elder son, Qablan, has followed his principles in fame and commerce. He took over the Reconciliation Sheikhdom of El Mraijat after it was seperated from the Salima Sheikhdom in 1920. He remained its Sheikh for about ten years. Then he migrated to Africa and came back after gaining considerable wealth. He took care to educate his children in the schools of Beirut. His son, Edmon, was a genius and has finished high school at the Hekma Institute. Now, he is in his third year at The School of Law in France and he works as a clerk in the Ministery of Education. Also, he is a writer and a musician. As for George, the brother of Sheikh Qablan, he is a rich expatriate in Brazil. His third brother, Francis, has his own commercial mall. He is an important person among our expatriates in San Louis in Africa.

Asaad Ghaleb had four brothers: Khatar, Mikhail, Mansour, and Elias. They worked with their children at the Railway Company. Some also worked on the mechanical maintenance. Others opened important stores in Beirut and Bkirki. Some of them were specializd workers, like Elias Ghaleb who became a distinguished engineer, because he was courageous, bold, and an experienced knight. When he was driving the train, he imagined himself riding a horse!

Also among them were master mechanics, like Ibrahim Bin Mikhail, Boutros Bin Khatar, and Caesar Bin Elias. Caesar had some inventions in this field, as did his brothers. Boutros Bin Mansour built a workshop for carpentry and wood working. His brother Boulos built a workshop for reversed wood working with equipment that he manufactured himself, as if he were the inventor.

Among those who lived in El Mraijat, were the sons of Khatar Saloum: Abdou, Fares, and Hanna. Abdou and his sons worked in carpentry. Fares was working in the insurance business, mainly real estate, and he was the manager of the properties of the Thabet family in Makse. Hanna worked in commerce.

The children of Fares are educated: Habib and Ghatas are expatriates in Mexico. Michel lives with his family in Makse. Elie continued his studies at the Hekma Institute and now he is in Paris. Last year, and this year too, he was first among thousands of students in the School of Medicine. But we are saddened because he is calling himself "Elie Machaalany" and neglecting his original surname "Bachaalany" which is the proof of his clear and honorable origins. Those who were educated, like Youssef Bin Elias Neama Bachaalany, whose father was keen on educating him, worked as a teacher in El Mraijat for a while.

Noaman Maalouf bought the grinding mill (using European equipment on water) from the Frenchman, Mr. Fré. Above the mill he had a house where he lived with some of his chidlren and grandchildren. They renovated it beautifully and modernized it. Beside it, they built a chocolate factory which is today under the supervision of his older child, our friend, Caesar Beik Maalouf, the talented writer and innovative poet. Our patriotic Youssef Daher Matar Masry, the owner of many real estate holdings, has followed in his footsteps. He, too, has built a factory for chocolate making. The same was done by Tawfik Melhem Saada, and, all three have succeeded in their plants.

Thanks to the efforts of its inhabitants, and its location, El Mraijat has become populated, developed its own municipality, with its own chief, who is from our village, Mr. Emil Habib Fares, and, its Mayor, Beshir Mikhail, who is one of "the Bachaalany" not "the Machaalany". The previous Mayor was Michel Jemeyel Nader Bachaalany.

Habib Fares bought a large piece of land in El Mraijat, and built a beautiful home in the middle of it. Then, beside it, he built another house and connected abundant water to both of them. He has planted gardens all around. Also, he built a pottery workshop for different kinds of earthenware and baked bricks. Habib Fares died, then, his son Felix died too. They are both buried in El Mraijat. His two sons, Philip and Emil, with their children, still spend their summer there. Their mother, Lady Louise, is still living and with a clear mind.

We previously mentioned that Asaad De'ebess was among the first inhabitants of El Mraijat. His father, De'ebess Bin Fadel Saada, moved from Maaroub in Kisrawan and went first to Bouarej, then he moved to El Mraijat with his brother Sasin. They lived there with their offspring.

Asaad was a wise and understanding man. Because of his honesty, he left good memories. His children followed his good footsteps: Qablan, who was, for a long time, the trustee for the Church of Saint George; Melhem, and Eskandar. Eskandar begot Girgis, Jemeyel, Josef, and Tanious. As for Qablan, he begot Khalil, Abdou, and Asaad. Khalil begot Edward, John, and Elie. Melhem begot Tawfik.

Sasin Mansour Saada begot Mansour and Elias. Elias begot Habib and Girgis. Mansour Sasin begot Abdou and Sasin. Sasin begot Girgis, Elias, and …. Concerning Abdo, he begot George.

The Saada House had marital ties to the people of Salima. Qablan married Henna, the daughter of Daher Bou Saqr. And, his two sons married girls from the Bachaalany family: Khalil married Alice, the daughter of Andrea Girgis; and, his brother, Abdou, married her sister, Malaka. Eskandar got married to the daughter of Abdou Malakoun, and there were many other such marriages. The same happened when many young people from our family got married to girls from the Saada House.

Among the inhabitants of El Mraijat, there is Youssef Azar who moved there in his childhood from Qaabb Elias. With his hard work and ability, he found a high position for himself. He built a big house there, very well constructed, in a modern style, costing thousands of liras. His family is one of the noble Maronite Jezzine families that we talked about in our detailed book <u>The History Of The Maronite Families.</u>

365

Najib Beshir S'eid from Salima bought all the properties of the Shaqeer House in El Mraijat through the mediation of his uncle, Qassem Ali. He lived there. After his death, his widow, Lady Badi'a, managed the house and the family.

There is also Youssef Abdulallah Abou Nasar. He moved from Bahr Safa and went to El Mraijat in 1880. He married a girl from the Bachaalany family and lived in Salima for a while. He begot Khalil and Hanna and both have children. There is also Elias Fares Bou Younes, who moved from Bitbiyat and went to El Mraijat. He married the daughter of Mansour Ghaleb Bachaalany. He is originally from the Abou Younes House in Hammana and begot ....

Taalabaya. It is one of the countryside villages to which the folks of Sowan Bachaalany went since the beginning of the last century. We previously talked about them and mentioned their offspring. They became related to the inhabitants of Taalabaya not only by moving there from the mountian but also by marriage and patriotic matters. Sowan folks were known for vitality, chivalry and strong ethics. They participated in agricultural and cultural jobs. A group of them migrated to America and other places.

The Expatriate Young People Of Salima.

Immigration has gradually influenced many of the Lebanese expatriates, their ethics, traditions, principles, and beliefs. So much so, that for some, even their religious beliefs have been changed, something that was once as firm and deep rooted as the rocks of their mountains.

However, that change didn't take long. As their life improved in their new places of settlement, their social and religious characteristics changed. The wise among them, especially the older ones, started to make reforms to re-establish the traditional values. They established denominational and national organizations. They built churches which were serviced by zealous and generous priests. They guided the expatriates back to the ways of goodness. Thus, they were actively performing their religious duties after having neglected them while trying to improve their lives. Now they are keeping their strong ethics and preserving their good Lebanese traditions. They are helping their relatives and their mother country, financially and culturally. The emigrants who left Lebanon seeking wealth and a better way to earn a living, or who fled from the oppression and injustice, or who sought freedom and the opportunity to fulfill their ideals, they have been faithful to this country. They have kept their nationality, their Lebanese character. They aimed to return to it despite all the political changes, disasters, and injustice that have overwhelmed it. They have presented their fair share to defend it with the necessary help. They have done this, even if the guardians here denied their constitutional rights and their Lebanese nationality.

Evolution and Regression

It would be nice if we had the opportunity to discuss in detail the situations that our expatriates have encountered, epochs of degredation and evolution. In Egypt, Marseilles, America, and, Africa, they have created a record of history worthy to be added to the history of the Lebanese migration. The social life in Salima had its share of the periods of evolution and degradation of people and groups. We want to say, in brief, what will complete our interest in this matter: The expatriates from Salima lived a golden era in Egypt, before the Revolution of Orabi Pasha. Their trade evolved, so they were able to accumulate wealth and its corresponding way of living. The children of 'Oql Genid built a modern house, which was and still is, one of the most modern and beautiful houses. But it is still second to the houses of the Lam's Princes. The same for Melhem and Selim Azar Khashan who built modern houses. The situation of those who went to Egypt saw life improve considerably.

In Brazil, the expatriates from Salima lived in a golden era. Abdulallah Habib Saloum, for example, gained a high degree of prestige and succeeded in his trading for a wide area. He was a great support and refuge for the sons of Salima, rather, to all Lebanese and Syrian emigrants. His business developed and his capital reached 200 000.00 golden lira by the end of the 19th century.

However, this young man was unforunate. His business declined until he lost everything, dying a poor man. After him, some of the families succeeded and gained wealth. Their commerce and fame expanded. An example is Youssef Mikhail Abdou and his brothers, Abdou and Moussa. They acquired a huge fortune and were men of privilege in the field of commerce. They were also held in high ethical regard for their honesty and good management. Their elder, Youssef, was especially known for his ethics, intelligence, zeal, and patriotism. This is what made him a leader of the community and the President of the Maronite organization in Rio de Janeiro.

The same holds true for the children of Girgis Anton, particularly Shokry, the owner of "Al Adl" newspaper. He had a great influence on the French Embassy because he was the main assistant to the emigrants. The same also applies to the sons of Youssef Wakim, the sons of Metri A Zaghloul, the sons of Nasef Haddad, and the sons of Samaan Khoury. They have all succeeded in the world of business.

Because times change and people are creatures of habit, success is often followed by failure. The specific reasons are many. Some expatriates liked to take great risks in business and stock trading; others immersed themselves in amusements and excessive life styles. General business crises sometime occur, such as the decline in the value of the Lira which affected all of Salima's people. Changes in money values caused some expatriates to watch their wealth crumble.

That is why many of our emigrants' lives became worse and worse. After being rich, they became poor. Their parents in Lebanon were asking for money, but no replies came. However, if the emigrant did reply, he often used the line that the expatriates in Brazil were saying: "The health is good and the money is expensive."

There are some very touching and sad memories that are recalled, dating from the end of the last century. We remember the days when the mail would arrive in Salima. The people would eagerly await the arrival of the postman. Among them would be invalid old men and women, badly in need of the money sent from their children abroad. When the postman finished reading the names of those who had letters, those missing a letter, especially the old people, went back to their homes in desperation.

In Marseilles

We previously mentioned how Anton Fares traveled to Marseille and how he issued his newspaper "Al Mersad" and brought his wife and children to live with him. He was responsible for arranging the travel of the expatriates from Lebanon and Syria to the United States. The emigrants considered him as their supporter who treated them with kindness, arranged their matters, and solved their problems. He made things easier. Whoever has read the novel Alas ! Ze'eitar , What A Pity, written by Shoulry Khoury, the famous journalist and the owner of "Abou Al Hol" (The Sphinx)" in San Paolo, will notice the deeds done by Anton for those emigrants. He faced many problems and disasters in Marseilles.

Hanna Girgis Anton, his paternal cousin, travelled to him at the beginning of this century. At first, he worked with him. Then, he opened an office to arrange the travel of emigrants like himself. Thanks to his hard work and the activity of his wife, he could soon afford to buy an extensive piece of land in the suburbs of Marseilles. He built a hotel there, with a travel agency, and his home. He was highly successful. He took care of educating his children who live in Marseilles. He was known, together with his wife, for helping the sons of the homeland as if they were their own brothers. In addition, he made significant donations to the churches in Salima, mostly in gifts of pictures and vestments.

List of the Immigrants in Brazil, from Salima.   With the year of their departure and their death.

Abdulallah Saloum emigrated in 1888 and died in 1904; Youssef Mikhail Abdou 1895 – 1912; his brother Abdou, 1895; his brother Moussa, 1903; Wakim Youssef Wakim, 1892; his brother Selim, 1892; his brother Tawfik, 1909; his brother Najib, 1910; Asaad Girgis Maroun, 1892 – 1910; his brother Abdou, 1893 – 1912; Assaf Girgis Hatem, 1892 – 1941; his brother Youssef, 1895 – 1943; his brother Boutros 1905; Boutros Abdou Freha, 1893 – 1896; S'eid Mikhail Maroun, 1893 -   ; his brother Daher, 1892 - 1926; his brother Shaker, 1901; Youssef Hanna Nasef, 1893 - ; his brother Nasef, 1898 -   ; Assaf Girgis Ghanatious, 1893 – 1920; his brother, 1900; Mansour Hanna Freha, 1896; Moussa Metri, 1896 – 1930; his brother Hanna, 1895 – 1947; Saada Asaad Khalil, 1891 no news about him; his brother Qablan, 1893; Shaker Amin, 1893; Moussa Tanious Nasef, 1903; his brother Girgi, 1910; Hanna Boutros Wakim, 1891; Hanna Metri Zaghloul, 1893; his brother Elias, 1893; his brother Mikhail, 1893; Rashid Nasef Zaghloul, 1908; Mansour Hanna Ghanatious, 1896 – 1947; Abdou Hanna Youssef, 1893 – 1941; Anton Girgis Abdou, 1893; his brother Hanna, 1898; Hanna Abdou, 1896; his son Abdou, 1896; Ibrahim Salem, 1896 – 1926; Moussa Bou Assly, 1893 – 1917; his brother Youssef, 1893 – 1913; Nasrallah Hanna Nasrallah, 1895; Hanna Saab, 1893 – 1925; Mansour Hanna Mansour Daham, 1893; Daoud Boutros Youssef Nejm, 1910; Nasef Bou'oun, 1910; Habib Freha Bachaalany, 1901 (This list was written by Habib Freha). Elias Youssef Wakim, 1911-1934; Nejm Daher Nejm Andrea, 1896 – 1943; Anton Youssef Saadallah; Shaia Hanna Abdou, 1926 – 1943; George Asaad Ghaleb, 1919; Girgi Nasef Zaghloul, 1923; Girgis Hanna Freha, 1921; Mansour Hanna Girgis, 1912; his brother Girgis, 1920; Khalil Freha, 1920.

Nejm Daher Andrea

He is Nejm, the son of Daher Nejm Andrea Bachaalany, born in Salima, on January 3rd, 1868. He was raised upon the same Christian principals and high ethics which his father and grandfather followed. He migrated to Brazil at the end of the last century. He lived in Oliveira with his wife and children until he died. Throughout his entire life, he displayed a strong sense of self esteem, a hatred for evil, and straight forwardness in his behaviour with others. He was honest in his words and work. He did not gain material wealth , but accumulated intellectual wealth and a sterling reputation. His children were his greatest wealth. He died in 1943 and left four sons: Daher, Elias, François, and Emil. The older one, Daher, is like his father in ethics and ability. He is acquainted with a broad range of important individuals including politicians and Presidents. He married Eugenie, the daughter of the late George Khoury Karam from Hadath, Beirut. He was the famous orator and poet. He died in Brazil. The brother of his wife, Fouad, married his sister Alice, so the two families were related by a dual marriage relationship.

Mansour Ghanatious

He was born in 1868 and his father died in 1872. He was raised by his mother Mahaba. He was the security of his maternal uncle, Daher Nejm Andrea, and his brother-in-law, Abdou Tanous Freha. He learned how to read and write at the school of the Capuchin Fathers. As he grew older he worked in a variety of jobs. In 1896, he travelled to Brazil and faced many problems in the early days of his emigration.   Events did not unfold in his favor. He moved from place to place until he stopped at Oliveira, one of the villages of Minas. He lived there until he died on November

368

25, 1947. He was buried in the presence of the Lebanese community from Salima and others. Mansour Ghanatious was eloquent. He was argumentative in debate and dignified in gatherings. He was good looking, and had a melodious voice. We have preserved among the papers of our archive, a great collection of his letters which he sent to us after migrating to Brazil. They continued right up to the days just before his death. They contain a vast amount of information about the emigration and the emigrants. He shared opinions about the country, the governors, and the rulers. It shows the true picture, the rightness, the zeal, etc which was worth recording. We are publishing two letters below. The first one, he received from some of his close friends in Brazil before he himself emigrated from Salima. The second is a letter he sent from Brazil to Habib Bachaalany, the son of his sister, when he was still in Salima.

From Daher Mikhail Asaad and Saada Asaad Khalil to Mansour Hanna Ghanatious.

" In San Juan De Lary (Brazil), February 28th, 1893.

My dear respected brother – With a strong emotion, I imagine that I am kissing your shoulders. With great sadness, we ask about your health. We long to hear some good news that you are being successful, so, please, keep no secrets from us. Reading good things about you in our correspondence is the only thing that can console us in our life of emigration, so far away from our family and country. Even if some people may forget us because we are away, still we think of you all. We thank God that we are in good health, successful and that we lack for nothing other than to see you and all our relatives. We hope that you will tell us about them and how things are going in our home. Whether good or bad, please keep us informed. Of our work in Brazil, we can only say that we are constantly on the go and tired. If one is intelligent and quick to think, that is enough to be successful. ...and good bye.
-- Daher

1. We sailed and the boat was our transport. Our tears were running like water in the waterwheel. When you leave Ain el Sawaqee , breathe the air that remembers us.
2. When I arrived by boat with the birds flying about, I remembered my family and sent my regards on their flighted wings. Daher's heart is so sad, longing to welcome you.

Saada writes:
1. You brought grief to my dear heart, you came and planted regret in my heart. My Heart! Be patient about the missing one. I am patient, having faith.
2. The evil flowers of neglect surround the face that appears before my sparkling eyes. Do you think that I will go back and hear a voice chanting: 'Yallah!' Dahr El Shir, shrouded with Ataba (songs of blame)."

Mansour replied to that letter and sent the attached reproaching verses:

"1. I received your letter and understood your sentences. We admired your style to convey the meaning and the sentences. I am weeping for all those many days of absence. They left my heart full of agony.
2. My tears ran down my cheeks and still have not dried. My partially healed wound has been re-opened.
They brought the doctor who said that I had not grown accustomed to the seperation.
3. My tears run down my cheeks because of the seperation, like the bird that mourns its lost companion.
Oh God, when will you reunite us, to once again live our lives in joy and happiness.
4. My tears run down my cheeks at the thought of those coming back. Your letter brought the fragrance that stirred my vision of you returning.... Oh God, when we will be united and return to those remembered days of satisfaction."

The above letters show the kind of relationship that existed between the brothers and in-laws; the love and sense of fraternity. How they were longing for their family and their countryside of Salima. They remembered its beautiful plains and the beloved walking paths, like Ein Al Sawaqee, and Dahr El Sheir where they used to hold meetings in the summertime. They would chant the popular songs "Al Ataba" and "Al Baghdady" along with other old and new songs. In those days, America was never a thing to think about. The contentment they had was their provision in their emigration. In their emigration, they were longing for the songs of their uncle Mansour who was the best of the youth at that time. He was the same age as they were. There was no entertainment gathering that took place unless he joined in. And no entertainment show began until he started it.

This was his concern in Salima before he emigrated. However, in America, the place of his emigration, he could only wish for those days, with their rules and procedures, to come again.

From Mansour Ghanatious Bachaalany to Habib Freha Bachaalany. Oliveira, May 13, 1904.

"My dear nephew (sister's son), May God keep you safe. I received the first issue of your newspaper (manuscript), in which there is local news and many other subjects. As to your request that I critique it, I would like to tell you that I am unable to do so. I never learned how to write properly. I never learned the rules of grammar. So, how could I criticize you, an editor? We also read the second issue and found many interesting things and some great principles. It shows that you have great, independent ideas. I wish you were emigrating because a person like you, with such a range of ideas, would be free in this country of freedom. The is a country that gives people rights. In this country, the writer is not afraid of anything when he is asleep.

Hold on to your ideas and come with me to this country. Have a look at the new world. Journalism and oration rule it. You will see that the public, the governors, and the whole country are all journalists! The judge and the accused, the governor and the governed, even the father in his house, all are afraid of them. If any kind of accident happens during the night, you read about it in the morning. They honor the people of the press. They like having knowledge spread throughout their country. If they discover some minor mistake, they manifest it in the streets, shouting "Viva freedom and death to oppression, governor so-and-so must die!" Just imagine. The governor hears these shouts about himself! When will something like that happen in our country. When will the trumpet of freedom sound in that sad land. When they shout "death to the governor, let justice live" they say that Brazil is a mean country. That is not true. If one looks at it as a critical analyzer, he will see that in less than half a century Brazil will be one of the greatest countries in the world. If only European capitalists and everyday people will come here, it will happen. In each town, no, in each plantation, like "Hasbaiya" and "Al Zahriye", the government has established a school. And in villages like ours, may God keep it safe, there are three schools, and both girls and boys learn. So, look at this mean country, for God sake, and look at its government which is working hard to improve the lot of its people situation and to spread knowledge throughout the country. Remember the famous cities of Syria and her large and fertile countryside. In the past, that region developed into a center for the holy prophets, a country of science, knowledge, and industry. Look at its schools, what its government is doing. So it can be for Brazil.

Now we feel that we are free, living in the country of freedom. We say whatever we want to say and do whatever we want to do, with no fear. We travel from one country to another. We safely carry our money with us, as if we were in the bossom of our mother. We don't even think about the possibility of being attacked by highway robbers like those in the Qarn Valley, or the Kurd horsemen in Qalaa. We give no thought to being robbed as often happens with the gangsters and rabble of Beirut, or the thieves who plunder our money and belongings at her ports.

Remembering these things hurt me alot. I admit that I have not gained great wealth as others have done. But I feel a sense of relief at no longer being subject to the dangers that I was living with in that holy land where I was born.

In all, the many years I have spent here, I have never asked someone to lend me money. To the contrary, in any village I have gone to, thousands of liras are given to me by its tradesmen. Nobody asks me to write out a promissory note as a guarantee. My body shakes when I think about such things. But it is a matter of luck. Thank God, my business is getting better this year and my health is good.... I think that the Sheikhdom of Salima is worried about what the district commissioner, the members of the government, and the press have complained about. It seems as if the Lord has ordained that our town should suffer from fanaticism and separations. Oh, Bachaalany, Nakouzy, Masry, and S'eid, couldn't you find enough wise men to solve your puzzle and get rid of the calamity. Hardship brings hardship, and happiness brings happiness. May God guide us to what will be to our benefit.

Andrea (our maternal cousin) is trying to persuade Nejm, (another maternal cousin) to come to this country but I think this might take a long time. We have mastered the language of this country so we can go out and collect debts. And, we have established relationships with the citizens. We have grown accustomed to their traditions and forgotten many of ours. We had started to hate the way we were living at home. And, having been away for such a long time, we have started to forget the longing that we felt for our homeland and her people. Moreover, the difficulties of our homeland, the hard living, the unemployment, the various disputes, and the fanaticism. Add to that the poverty and it was all too much to bear. Still, we ask God to unify us. Don't be afraid, my nephew (son of my sister). You know our situation. Don't think that we have forgotten our country, where we were born. This is impossible. However, the circumstances of our country oblige even the greatest of men to abandon his country to make living for himself..."

Mansour Freha

He is Mansour Bin Hanna Gibrail Freha Bachaalany. He was born in Salima on April 15th, and was baptised on April 23rd, 1882. He studied at the Capuchin Fathers' School. On May 8th, 1896, he emigrated to Brazil. He wrote letters to his father from Marseilles, Rio, and San Paulo on June 4th. He settled in Lamas, worked with some of his relatives on a salary basis, and, after five months, worked alone. His only intention was to help his father who needed money for his medical treatments, first for his bad leg, and later, for the other ills of his family. In the end, he went to Buizos de Cladess (Buzios?) and studied Law. He mastered the Portugues language. He married in 1910. His writings at that time showed the maturity of his ideas, acknowledging his duties for his parents, especially his mother. He always talked about the pain she endured for the sake of the family. Also, he took great care to see that his brothers and sisters received an education, learning the sciences and literature.

In our archives, we preserve some of his letters addressed to his parents. They provide much information about him. He bought a plantation in Buizos De Cladess, where there is mineral water for only 5 piasters, a service for the people. The following letter is about that:

"Rio De Janeiro, March 4, 1948. Lebanon Embassy legation.

Dear Mr. Tanous Freha,

By coincidence, when I was thinking about writing to you, I received your beauticul greeting card for the new year with your comments and you wish for a prosperous and successful year. Concerning the occasion you mention, I was seizing an opportunity. Let me explain. A long time ago, I went to one of the Brazil's summer resorts. It is a place which is in Buzios De Cladess (Buzios). It's a space of about 1200 meters. From San Paulo, it takes 45 minutes by plane to get there. In that resort, there is a place of mineral waters to which vacationers go. It is called "Ain Freha". So I told my wife: "I want to meet that man. We went to the water's source which, by car, took about half an hour from the hotel. A man about seventy years old welcomed us. After we talked with him, I learned that his name is Mansour Freha, the son of Hanna Gibrail Freha. He emigrated to Brazil 51 years ago. His maternal uncle, Youssef Ibrahim Salama Melki from Baabdat, preceded him here. His wife is the daughter of Tanious Abdulallah from Tripoli. Her mother is from Jbail from the Bared House. Mansour has nine children, four sons and five daughters. 1. Shafik Freha, a tradesman in Buzios De Clades; 2. Dr. Rezk Freha, an engineer and the chairman of the Metal Materials Department in the government Ministery (Rio De Janeiro), and, in 1946, he was the mayor of Buizos De Clades region. 3. Anouar Freha, who has a refrigeration company; and, 4. Selim Freha, who is studying engineering.

Mansour started his life by being a traveling pedlar and selling in the San Paulo State for five years. Then, he came to Buzios De Clades to trade. Twenty-five five years ago, he bought a large farm. On the farm he found the best mineral waters in the town. Thus, he called it "Ain Freha". Vacationers came to drink the water. Many of them would fill big bottles and take them to the hotels. His son Rezk was, at one time, elected mayor of the town. Even with all this, Mansour still maintains his Lebanese simplicity, like a true, first class highlander. The thing that has made me the happiest is that he is proud of how he started and how he ended. He is proud of how he educated his children and accomplished his duty toward them. Each has become an important person. I asked him about you, and he said that he knows a little about you. I remember that he talked about your grandfather and said that your grandfather, Tanous Freha, is the brother of his grandfather, Gibrail Freha. He said that there are thousands of people called Mansour Freha. Wherever you go, you find men, women, and children with the name. Many of them have changed their original names, so that now, you can't recognize them.

A few days ago, someone by the road asked me to stop. He asked: "Are you the Ambassador of Lebanon? I am a Lebanese." I asked: "What's your name?" So, he answered: "Miguel Araogo". I said: "How is Araogo a Lebanese name?" He said: "My father, Mikhail Selim El 'Akary, wrote Araogo instead of Arkary, and the name stayed!" And, in Buzios De Clades, there is a baker who is Lebanese. His name is Miguel Felix De Silfa (its translation is Mikhail Asaad Al Salebe).

And, do you know, this Mansour, one of your relatives, and what I mentioned about his children, all of this will be lost if we don't record it. If we don't record these thousands of Lebanese and keep track of them, their children and grandchildren, within a few years, will not be able to find any trace of these expatriate Lebanese.

I ask God to grant you good health and success. It will make me very happy if you keep corresponding with me. Keep me informed of your good news and that of your country. May God prolong your life for the sake of your brother, - Youssef El Sawda"

Nasef Mikhail Haddad

He was one of the first Lebanese emigrants in Brazil. He was an intelligent and judicious man. In judging matters, he showed wisdom and freedom from error. He was dignified, yet with a sense of humor. He was honest and always ready with an anecdote. He was one of the masters of popular poetry. He gave his poems thoughts of wisdom and ethics.

He composed verses in his popular poems which are as eloquent and fine as Arabic poems. Native people and expatriates would both read and copy his poems because of their perfect composition and wonderful meanings. He went to the capital, and, then to Oliveira, in the State of Minas. He gained material and literary wealth. He was highly respected among his people. He died in Oliveira, leaving behind a hugh estate and memories of a good old age.

In Mexico

In Mexico, there are a remarkable number of expatriates from Salima. In the field of commerce, Shokry Freha Bachaalany was a genius, in both the capital and Paopla, where he established a comb business. He lost his wife, the best of women. But, his unique daughter, Victoria, consoled him. She surpassed even her mother in her intelligence, attractive features, and good manners. She married Elias Far'oun, one of the expatriates originating from Deir Al Qamar, who was on a ship that went down and he died. Thus, Shokry had to bring his daughter back home and help her to forget her sorrows. He renewed his trading business with his daughter and things returned to their previous condition.

Also among the big expatriate tradesmen was Ibrahim Shiban Bachaalany. He died young, full of courage and bravery. Others, include his paternal cousins, the sons of his uncle Tanous Shiban. The oldest, Louis, died and left a large estate. Before him, his brother, Amin, died. He was known for his piety and his hobby of buying rare books in the languages that he was learning. Their brother Shiban remained with his family as did their paternal cousin, Youssef Shiban and his wife.

Also, in Mexico, is a large group of expatriates from the S'eid folks. The first ones were Amin and Najib Qassem Ali. There was also Girgis Anton Boutros, surnamed by himself as Girgis Khoury, which is wrong. Others include the children of Ibrahim Khoury Bashwar, the children of Elias Shebli, the children of Abdou Saadallah, Mansour Gad'oun, Youssef Bou 'Oun, and Mary Youssef El Ghaziri.

THE FAMILIES EMERGING FROM BCHAALEH

Section 5

Early in the book, we mentioned that researchers are of the opinion that the Lebanese families, especially the Maronites, are Aramaic Phoenicians and that their ties to the Ghassanid and the Syriac Yaakoubians (Jacobian) is untrue. As we pointed out, the stories about the origins being connected to the Ghassanid and Yaakoubians are all just rumor, not history. There are no documents, reliable stories, or logic to prove the claims.

We have proven with documents and trusted historians that the Maronites were in Bchaaleh, in the upper Batroun district during the sixteenth and seventeenth centuries. That is when the Bachaalany people left there with other families who also left. This is what was reported by Douaihy and other researchers. It is also possible, we said, that they are the remanants of the old Maradahs (Mardaites).

We have dismissed the claim that the Bachaalany families originated from the Ghassanid. We proved that it is based on only unsubstantiated stories. And once we had determined the origins of the stories and the person responsible, we became certain that the there was no documentation and no merit to it. There are even contradictions in the story when compared to the reliable and trusted historians of the past.

Furthermore, the material recently published by Count Philip Terazy, the Syriac Catholic, claiming Syriac Yaakoubians ties, we have disproven in this book as well as in our article in the "Al Bairak" Newspaper, issue 4795, dated July 26, 1948. Count Terazi relied his claim totally on a single paragraph in the book of Bishop Youssef Dagher <u>Lebanon—A General View of Her History</u> on page 137 dealing with vestiges and families. The paragraph says: "It was said that Yaakoubian monks lived at the monastery of Mar Domt in Bchaaleh during the 8th century." The thoughtless statement of the Bishop has been used by the Conte for personal reasons. He treated it as if the sentence were an actual proven, historical fact. He conveniently removed the words "It was said" with no thought as to who might challenge it or to the merit of his source. He will be severely judged for his unsubstantiated story. He thought that he could single handedly decide on historical truths that even the greatest historians were unable to prove. The Count wrote:

"The Syriac people lived in Bchaaleh from the beginning of Christianity. They multiplied there and in the surrounding regions. Their monks built a monastery there in the 8th century and named it The Syriac Mar Dimt. Its ruins can still be seen there today.

In Bchaaleh there are many old churches, which make us believe that their builders were the Syriac people, not people of other Lebanese Christian doctrines. Furthermore, what draws us to that conclusion is that they have the names of Syriac saints, not Lebanese. They lived and were famous in the towns between the two rivers .... Honouring them from the Lebanese were the Syriac people who built the churches and monasteries in the mountains heights and along its coasts .

In Bchaaleh came the Bachaalany family who begot a great number of virtuous and chivalrous people, like Bishop Boutros Bachaalany in the 17ᵗʰ century (He may have been referring to Bishop Girgis Habqouq Bachaalany, the Bishop of Aaqoura) *and Abi Rezq Al Bachaalany who was martyred in Qonieh in 1654.*

As in most cases, the above mentioned family was one of the deviated Syriac families who left their original doctrine and over time, joined the Maronite doctrine. From the offshoots of the Bachaalany family or their kin have come many famous Lebanese families like: The Sheikhs of the Khoury folks in Rechmaya.... ...then the Saad folks in Ain Trez...."

Here the Count noted a reference in the margin saying: "Lebanon and Youssef Beik Karam written by Father Stephen Bachaalany, page 77" which insinuates that the Count took the passage from our book. But the truth is that he just extracted the names of some of the Bachaalany family members.

With all that has been said, and all that has been plagiarized, it still remains that it has been proven, after lengthy research, that the families who have emerged from Bchaaleh, come from noble Maronite families who had lived in that village for a very long time. They were there before the Arab era began. We must emphasize, too, that there are no vestiges, no documents, or any other evidence proving that Arabs or Yaakoubians ever lived in this village. Also, we lived in Bchaaleh for a long time and we never heard anyone speak of such stories. And we have thoroughly read the books of our great historians, like Douaihy, Mosaad, Shebli, Debs, Hathouni, Harfoush, Manss, and others. None of them, whenever they have mentioned Bchaaleh, its vestiges, or its families, have ever said anything contrary to what we have written of its history and the history of its families.

As for the families who emerged in the past from Bchaaleh, excluding the Bachaalany family, who were previously mentioned, they are:

1. the Moubarak House
2. the Khoury House
3. the Saad House
4. the Habqouq House
5. the Harfoush House
6. the Abi Rashed House
7. the Gibran House
8. the Qash'amy and Abi Nakd House
9. the Abi Eissa and Meshleb House, and,
10. the Jabour, Mel'eb, Shahwan House.

The kinds of relationships that existed between those families cannot be known. Nor can we determine how far back their association goes. Nor can we determine the date when they left Bchaaleh. All these things happened a very long ago. We have no documents or evidence that shed any light on those days of antiquity. All we can say, at this point, is, simply this: all of these Houses came from Bchaaleh. This is according to the stories and oral traditions that we have.

Hereafter, we will talk about the history of each family in brief. We hope to talk about them in much more detail in our book The History of the Maronite Families, God willing.

THE MOUBARAK HOUSE

Chapter 1

Their Origin

There are many contradictions about the origin of this family, when they left for Kisrawan, and the emigration of Father Beshara to Rechmaya. Father Beshara was the son of Moubarak and the grandfather of the Khoury family.

Some of the Khoury folks have claimed that they originated from Ethiopia, their forefather having emigrated to the village of Menie near Tripoli. Then, his children moved to Ghousta. After that Father Beshara Moubarak, the grandfather of the Khoury House emigrated to Rechmaya in 1582 and lived there. (Ref. Daerat Al Maaref -Al Bostany, term: Al Khoury; The Orient 8: 346).

Some others among them have claimed that the Khoury House who are in Rechmaya are derived from the Moubarak House of Ghousta. Their forefather, called Sahyoun, came to Bchaaleh from Kfar Tabou Akar in 1300 AD. He was originally one of the Ghasan Folks, the kings of Al Sham, and the Christianized Arabians. The grand-child of Sahyoun, the so-called Moubarak left for Ghousta. Among his offspring was Father Saleh who moved to Rechmaya in 1700 AD. He is the grandfather of the Khoury House. Among the children of Father Saleh is Subdeacon Ghandour who begot Saad, the grandfather of the Saad family in Ain Trez. (Taken from Father Youssef Saada Hasarate, known as the Zanaty).

What has been determined by us, after reviewing all that has been said and written about this subject is that: the Moubarak folks originate from Bchaaleh village situated in the upper Batroun district. That they are the descendants of their forefather, Moubarak, who moved from Bchaaleh around the year 1600 going to the Kisrawan district. He lived with his offspring in Batha and Ghousta, neighbouring villages. After that, his children spread throughout Kisrawan and the Chouf.

Those who have agreed that these developments are most likely true, include Patriarch Boulos Mosaad and Father Mansour Hatouni (Kisrawan Province, page 72), Father Ibrahim Harfoush (The Orient 8: 68). And, the same story was told to us by the late Najib Beik and the late Habib Pasha Saad, passed down from their father, Ghandour Beik. We also heard it from other families originating from Bchaaleh.

As for the offspring of this family, they are :

1- the Moubarak House in Batha, Ghousta, Raifoun and Aintoura
2- the Moubarak House in Bqatouta, Dbaiye, Kanaan, Kfar Tai, and Beskinta.
3- the Khoury House in Rechmaya.
4- the Moubarak House in Rechmaya besides the Khoury House
5- the Saad House in Ain Trez.
6- the Moubarak House in Bdadoun and Aabadiye.

It seems that all of them are derived from the same origin, the Moubarak who originates from Bchaaleh. However, it is impossible to know the exact parental relationships of those offspring.

Their Lineage

Moubarak moved from Bchaaleh around the year 1600 going to Batha, a village in Kisrawan. He begot, or it was known that from one of his offspring are, the Subdeacon Samaan and Father Beshara who moved to Rechmaya around the year 1648. The Subdeacon Samaan begot Soliman and Hanna, or Elias, the father of Hanna.

We found among the vestiges of Patriarch Mosaad, a paper in his handwriting saying: "The purchase made by Father Soliman Moubarak and his brother, Hanna from Batha, in the year 1083 Hegira, 1673AD …. " There is another handwritten document by Douaihy that was passed down from Father Harfoush and from Bishop Shebli, saying: "Hanna Ibn Elias from the Moubarak House in Batha was sent to the Great School in Rome in 1639 to study …and his son, Elias, joined the same school in 1664, and graduated from it in 1671. Then he went to Macedonia where his parents were living and he was ordained a priest. He was assigned there to the Sisters Convent, where he died." (The Orient 8 : 68). However, we don't know what happened to the offspring of Hanna Moubarak in Macedonia.

Pastor Soliman, son of Subdeacon Samaan, begot six sons and one daughter. They are: 1- Bishop Youssef Moubarak. 2- Bishop Gibrail the first. 3- The Jesuite Father Boutros. 4- Pastor Serkis. 5- Abdulallah. 6- An anonymous son who was the father of the priest, Rezk Moubarak, and his offspring lived in Aintoura. 7- The nun, Henna, who died in 1738.

The Offspring of Abdulallah

Abdulallah is the son of Pastor Soliman, the son of the Subdeacon Samaan Moubarak.

He begot: Pastor Moubarak who became a bishop named Gibrail The Second, and, Sham'oun who begot three sons.

The three sons of Sham'oun are: Bishop Boutros Moubarak, surnamed Francis, Ghasebe who had no offspring, and, Serkis who had four sons.

The four sons of Serkis are: Father Gibrail, surnamed Girgis, Pastor Francis, Father Saleh, and Gibrail.

As for Father Gibrail, he begot: Father Francis and Bakhous. Bakhous had Father Yohanna Moubarak, Father Youssef (the General Deputy of the Lebanese mission), Mansour, Doctor Youssef, and Serkis.

Gibrail Bin Serkis Bin Sham'oun Bin Abdulallah, the son of Pastor Soliman Moubarak, begot Father Boutros. Father Boutros, in turn, had: Father Francis, the Badriot Gibrail Moubarak, Abdou, Beshara, and Selim.

Abdou had: Philip, Boutros, Alfred, and George. Boutros Bin Abdou had Tawfiq. Alfred begot Kamil.

Selim, the son of Father Boutros, had six sons: Edward, Anton, Moris, Henry, Charles, and Robert. Beshara, the son of father Boutros begot: Youssef, Wadie', Albert, Moubarak, and…. All of them are in Raifoun.

As for Father Rezk Moubarak who lived with his offspring in Aintoura in Kisrawan, he died in 1728. One of his sons was Father Ibrahim who served the Church of the Lady of Jiita and died in 1829. Another son was Moussa who begot: Eissa (died a virgin), Soliman (who had no offspring), Moussa (who begot Pastor Girgis and Hanna), and Saloum (who had Boutros and Tanous). Tanous begot Mansour, Eissa, and Francis. Francis had Fares, the father of Mansour and Anton.

As for Hanna Bin Moussa, he begot Father Youssef who begot: Hanna and Moussa. This latter Moussa begot Melhem and Hanna. Hanna had Youssef, Selim, Gibrail, and Emil, the plantation poet. Melhem begot Moussa who had Melhem and ….(Passed down from Father Ibrahim Harfoush and Abdou Moubarak).

About Them

First and foremost in importance is the fact that Soliman Ibn Al Shediak Samaan Moubarak (Soliman the son of the teacher Samaan Moubarak) from Batha, neighboring Ghousta in Kisrawan, was born in the year 1623. He married a girl from the Najim Family. They had seven children. After the death of his wife, he abandoned worldly affairs together with four of his sons and his daughter, Henna. They first went to live at the Mar Sheleta Maqbas Monastery. After a while, Soliman sold what he owned in Ghousta and bought land at the Raifoun Monastery on which he constructed a new monastery. He named it Mar Serkis. And, it was purchased "with his money, for himself and for his children after his death".

They started the construction in 1655. Pastor 'Oun Kamel Najim, the son of Soliman's brother–in–law, was with them. They completed the building in 1674.

After many years, Soliman Moubarak was ordained a priest and was given the name Pastor Soliman. This virtuous and vigorous man died on March 28, 1713, when he was almost 90 years old. In completing his life's work, he purchased for his monastery many pieces of property, gaining for himself an eternal remembrance.

Youssef Moubarak

He is Youssef, the son of Pastor Soliman Moubarak. He grew up in a house of virtue, piety and asceticism. Thus, from his childhood days, he wanted to be a part of the monasticism that surrounded him. He followed in the footsteps of his father in going to the Monastery and becoming a monk. Then, after being ordained a priest, he became the Abbot of Mar Serkis. All this happened during his father's lifetime.

Because of his great virtue, Patriarch Estephan El Douaihy promoted him to be a Bishop. He was appointed the Bishop of Sayda on June 6, 1648. The ceremony for this was held in Ghousta at the chapel of the Castle of Sheikh Abi Qansowah Khazen. The Sheikh had helped the Moubarak family in constructing the Raifoun Monastery.

Bishop Girgis Habqouq Bachaalany and two other bishops assisted in the ceremony which fifteen priests and a huge crowd attended.

Thanks to his endeavor and hard work, the monastery's income increased as he bought more properties. In addition, he constructed annexes to the monastery for the residence of its monks.

In 1710, there was a period of disruption and confusion at the Maronite Patriarchy. It ended with the removal of Patriarch Yaakoub Awad. He was replaced by Bishop Youssef Moubarak. However, the Holy Synod voted to restore Patriarch Yaakoub claiming that his forced resignation was invalid.

Bishop Youssef Moubarak died on September 18, 1713, just a few months after the death of his father. This information is from the inscription carved on a marble stone over his grave in the old Church of Our Lady which is kept in Mar Serkis Church. The text reads:

"In the name of our Ever Living, Eternal God. Here lies the trice ordained Patriarch Youssef Bin Moubarak from Ghousta. From the days of his childhood, he walked on the path of monasticism with his father and brothers. He established the Raifoun Monastery and wrote many books about it. He was a Bishop for 28 years, serving the Qannubin See, with bravery, honesty, and courage.... ...Then he was ordained the Patriarch, and only lived for three more years. He was full of zeal for his Maronite religion, and extremely merciful to his priests and monks. Then, as God wished, he was laid to rest in his Monastery, in the presence of bishops, Sheikhs of the Abi Noufal House, the children of Abi Qansowah, and the children of Abi Nasef (the Khazen) on September 18, 1713."

The Savant Boutros Moubarak

He is Boutros, the son of Father Soliman who was the son of the Subdeacon Samaan Ibn Moubarak, originating from Bchaaleh. He was born in Batha, near Ghousta in June, 1663. He performed his advanced studies at the Maronite School in Rome (1672–1685). He mastered seven languages: Arabic, Syriac, Hebrew, Greek, Latin, Italian, and French.

When he came back to Lebanon, Patriarch Douaihy ordained him on June 29, 1687. He was assigned to the chapel of Qannubin and charged him caring for the Ghousta congregation. In 1691, he sent him to perform some affairs for the Patriarchal See in Rome. He accomplished his mission there and left for Florence. There, he achieved a position of great privilege because the Prince and his daughter took a strong liking to him. The Princess was probably the most famous Princess of the day, well known for her liberal ideas and great intelligence. The Prince charged Boutros Moubarak with the management of the Medici Library. Due to his abundant knowledge and intellectual abilities he was able to fulfill his assignment perfectly.

In 1700, the Prince appointed him, with the Pope's permission, as a teacher of Oriental Languages in Pisa. He was given the job of translating and explaining the Holy Bible. This gave him a considerable amount of fame and social standing. So much so, that kings and princes, as well as the savants, were talking about his knowledge and showing off their friendship with him .

With his own money, he built a school for Maronites in Aintoura, Lebanon, which he allowed the Jesuit priests to administer. It remained under their control until their activities were temporarily suspended in 1773. Then, the Maronites ran it themselves.

The Lebanese Convention held a meeting in 1737, where they said, on page 548 of their report:

"We extend our deepest praise to the man of great piety and good intentions who is so deserving of it. This devout man is our dear son, the Maronite Jesuit, Father Boutros Moubarak.

Although he gained fame for his knowledge and piety, he didn't forget his people or his father's House. Seeking to benefit his people, he built a school for them in Aintoura in Lebanon, and paid for it himself. He designated the administration of the school to the Jesuit missionaries according to certain conditions which guarantee the right of the Maronites in the future."

On November 3, 1707, he joined the Jesuit monastery.

After that, the Pope appointed him to be an editor and reviewer of some books printed in Greek. The Pope relied on his words and points of view. In the monastery he taught the Holy Bible, preaching and offering guidance in monasteries. In addition, he was practicing works of charity. He was the first one to translate the book of Saint Avram from Syriac to Latin from the original, which was unknown to Europeans (1730). He published the first and second volumes and started the third. He translated the book <u>Al Manaer</u> (The Holy Lighthouse) and the book <u>Al Mohama</u> (The Law) written by El Douaihy in Syriac but never published. He translated some Greek books on rituals to Latin, and, he wrote some critiques on some authors.

He continued his works for religion and science until he became seriously ill from an incurable disease. He died on September 8, 1742. He was a gentle and robust man of deep perception. He was loved by everyone who made his acquaintance.. Most of all, he was devouted to serving God.

The Raifoun Monastery

In 1702, the Abbot of this monastery was Pastor Gibrail, the son of Soliman Moubarak. This was when his brother, Bishop Youssef, was alive. Pastor Gibrail had been admitted as a monk and he remained the Abbot until he died in 1733. He was virtuous and zealous. After him, Pastor Moubarak, the son of Abdulallah Soliman Moubarak, became the Abbot. In 1763, Patriarch Tobia Khazen promoted him to be Bishop of Baalbek and he was given the name Bishop Gibrail II. He is the maternal uncle of Saad Al Khoury, the grandfather of the Saad House (Al Manara 8:11). He went to Rome in 1767 at the request of Patriarch Youssef Estephan in a mission for the Patriarchal See. This Bishop died in 1788 and was succeeded by Father Francis Moubarak as the next Abbot of the Monastery. This latter is the son of Sham'oun Bin Abdullah, son of Pastor Soliman. He was ordained by Patriarch Youssef Estephan as a Bishop and was surnamed Bishop Boutros Moubarak. In his days the Monastery was successful. He died in 1808. Then, Pastor Girgis Abi Moussa, one of the grandchildren of Father Rezk, became Abbot on orders of Patriarch Youssef Tiyan. He was followed in 1811 by Pastor Francis Serkis Sham'oun Moubarak, known for his intelligence and many acquaintances. Both Patriarchs Al Tiyan and Al Helow appointed him as a clerk in the Patriarchal Office. During his term of leadership in 1816, The Nuns of Raifoun Monastery were separated from the monks as ordered by the Society for the Propagation of the Faith. This was what had been done at other monasteries.

In 1818, legal action was initiated between the sheikhs of the Khazen House and the Moubarak House. It involved the position of the Abbot of Raifoun Monastery. At first, the Louisa Assembly Court judged that the right to occupy the position of Abbot should go to the Khazen House. However, the Moubarak House brought a legal action to the Apostolic See. They reviewed the case and made their ruling in 1826 in favor the Moubaraks. Then, the case was appealed before the Patriarchs, the Apostolic Delegates, the Bishops and Church judges. Finally, the Apostolic See approved and gave its final judgment in favor of the Moubarak House on June 9, 1832.

Then, the Moubarak folks asked the Apostolic See to transform the Raifoun Monastery to an Ecclesiastic School which would graduate qualified youth to positions in the Maronite Rite. The Holy Assembly approved that proposal and put the school under the supervision of the Patriarch. Thus, Pastor Francis enlarged the buildings and renovated existing ones. After his death in 1840, his brother, Father Saleh, succeeded him.

In Father Saleh's era, the Eccelsiastical students from all the bishoprics gathered there. In 1859, his nephew, the son of Father Francis, took his place. So, he again renovated the buildings of the school. He died in 1872. He was succeeded by Father Nimatallah Safir and Father Francis Khoury from Shahtoul because no one of the Moubarak house was a celibate priest. Many virtuous priests graduated from that school due to the efforts of their teachers, like Father Yohanna Deeb, Father Youssef Moubarak, Father Yohanna Maroun Sabaaly, and Father Boulos Aqoury. All three of them are Lebanese missionaries. Then, the Bardiot Gibrail Moubarak became the headmaster of the school for a while, and, then, later, of the Maronite School in Rome (1893–1897). He was one of the great Maronite geniuses who ever studied in Rome. At that time, his paternal cousin, Yohanna Moubarak, was the headmaster of the Raifoun school.

Father Youssef Moubarak

He was knowledgeable and virtuous. He was in charge of the General Council of the Organization of Lebanese Missionaries before its current president. In addition to that, he was a glorious poet of his time.

Among his literary vestiges is a poem eulogizing Youssef Beik Karam, 1889, which the late Moussa Safir gave to us. Hereafter we present some selected verses which we published in our book Lebanon and Youssef Beik Karam , page 623.

Gallant people of Lebanon! Weep at dawn, and make of your hearts, rivers of blood.
Oh mountains, made so famous in time, melt, leaving no traces of that which happened.
What happened to the honorable one has filled our hearts with sorrow right to the core!
Where is the road when the sun of glory has set. Have you seen that the crescent above, at the horizon, has eclipsed.
You who ask about the deceased one for whom we wail. You do not understand what you you are asking to know.
The unique one has died. No one could be like him even if they lived for ages.
You, Oh Lebanon, who has existed for so long, have you ever seen one similar to the one we speak of.
He sold his life to buy, with his benevolence, a country so high. Thus he has become an elite.
He cast politics behind him and exchanged it for fasting and praying, day and night.
My dear "Karam", mourning demolished every soul. The famous, as well as all free people, have nothing to talk about but you.
You, the Saad, are not the only ones who have lost, whole regions suffer your loss.
We must bear this with patience because the one who has passed has gone to paradise above.
Time, itself, shows its pride in him and eulogizes him. God has never immortalized another so worthy.

The Moubarak House In Bqatoute.

Their Origin And Lineage.

Their forefather is Father Serkis Farah. He comes from the Moubarak House in Ghousta and Raifoun. Around the year 1760, he first came and lived on a plantation called Jomaa's Hole, near the village of Bqatoute in Kisrawan. That farm belonged to the Monastery of Our Lady of Lamentation of the Roman Catholic Church. It was built around the year 1767. And after a long time, his offspring moved to Bqatoute. Father Serkis begot two sons: Farah and Andrea. Farah begot two sons: Tanious and Anton who both died and had no offspring. The remaining one of this familly was Andrea, thus, the family of the Moubarak in Bqatoute was surnamed "the Andrea House" after his name. Andrea had Youssef who gained a position of privilege and consideration among the people of the Monastery. This was because of his honesty, loyalty, and extreme care about the donations that were made.

For this reason, the priests of that Monastery, and its nuns, insisted on burying him at the Monastery as one of their own.

This Youssef begot a son called Elias who had four sons: Nasef, Hanna, Youssef, and 'Oql. 'Oql had Abdou and this Abdou later begot Anton, Moubarak, Sasin, George, and Josef.

As for Naseef, he had no sons. Hanna had Mansour who begot Andrea, a professor at the Education Department, and Jan. Youssef Bin Elias had Rashid and Elias. Rashid had Josef, Wadie', and Nabih. Those two brothers were known for their intelligence. They had culture and knew science. They also both had a nice calligraphy. Elias studied at the Marist Brothers' School in Jounie. Then he taught at the schools of the Education Department for a number of years. Now he is a clerk for the Municipality of Beirut. He is a glorious writer and a talented poet. Below are just a couple of his poems, chosen from the many he has written:

Oh, mountain! Leave the heights of Glory. Be proud. Attain the depths of yourself without fear or hesitation.
You are still teaching the generations just beginning. You are a glory whose supporters are few.
You rejected the earth's leaders traveling in caravans. They have not realised their hopes.
How many kings and soldiers have totally vanished, and still, your men have not been approached even by deceptions.
There you smashed a head full of greediness, so it was said "is it the head of a goat?"
Lebanon is a land taking a view of the whole earth. It has the most generous soil. How glorious it is!

How many heros devoted to God have grown up in our Lebanon. How many men, but even they were few, but they represented a country.
How many times has the flag fluttered for the sword, the guest, and the pen; in this, our fair climate for which the expatriates long.
How many men, coming and going, on the other side of the sea are a pride of this land!

And, another selection:

I can't imagine a summer more wonderful than the one of my country, under the shade of a humble fig tree.
Though I might have a very long life, still, I would not choose another land, or another sea.
In Sannine, there is the voice of the river, the magical languid eyes....
...the source of light, the cradle of the universe, the beam of humanity's religion.
Here is the source of light, the cradle of poetry, the mine of magic, and the quarry of ideas.
...How many crowns were taken off and gone, and Lebanon stayed in its place and has never gone.
She wears the charity of God as a scarf and sits comfortably in her place.

The Moubarak House In Bkhochtai, Kfartai, Chiyah, and Beskinta

Their Lineage And About Them

They are one of the offsprings of the Moubarak House who came from Ghousta and Raifoun going to Bkhochtai Kanaan in Kisrawan. Five Houses are known to be derived from them: The House of the two brothers, Younes and Francis, the House of the two brothers, Massoud and Moussa, the Lahoud House, the Nejm House, and the Abi Khaddaj House (we have no information about the Abi Khaddah House).

1. The House of the Two Brothers, Younes and Francis.

The ones we know of from the Younes offspring are: Asaad, who begot Younes, and this Younes begot Nasr, Heikal, and Younes. This latter Younes had Asaad, Elias, and Father Youssef. As for Asaad, he emigrated to Cali in Colombia. He acquired a huge fortune there. He was known as Josef Copo. He begot Alexi and Edmond. Alexi is an engineer in the United States, and Edmond one of the big lawyers in Cali, Colombia. Asaad came back to his country after 40 years and gave a ceramic chancel to the Mar Abda Church in Bkhochtai. Engraved on it is his name, "Josef Copo Moubarak". His brother. Elias, emigrated to Porto Alegre in Brazil. He died there, leaving a large family. Father Youssef who resides in Bkhochtai, begot: Tanious and Henry. Tanious emigrated to Colombia and married his paternal cousin, the daughter of the mentioned Asaad and had children.

As for Nasr Bin Younes, he begot: Fares and Boutros who emigrated to Brazil. Fares begot: Nasr, Youssef, and Moris. Heikal Bin Younes emigrated to Porto Alegre and begot Youssef who had Girgis, who begot Victor, Albert, and Emil.

Francis, the brother of Younes, begot Girgis who begot Tanious. Tanious had Elias and Beshara who had Michel and Youssef. And Elias begot Farid and Jamil.

2. Now, For The Two Brothers, Massoud and Moussa: Massoud begot Salebe and Saleh. Saleh had Abdou.
Salebe had Moussa who begot Said the expatriate. As for Moussa, he begot Abdulallah who had Souma who begot Abdulallah and Abdou.

3. **The Lahoud House:** Lahoud begot Shahin and Abdou. Abdou moved to Beskinta and begot Fares who begot Aboud and Josef. Meanwhile, Shahin begot Lahoud who begot Milad who had Nassib and Gibrail. Gibrail had Antoin. Nassib had Elias.

4. **The Nejm House:** Nejm begot: Father Youssef, Moussa, Gharious, and Elias. Elias begot Yaakoub who had Haidar and Hanna. Heidar had Abdou, Elias, and Yaakoub. Hanna is an expatriate in Colombia and had Doctor Yaakoub, a member in the Council of the Cali Government in Colombia. Gharious begot Salem who begot Rashid and Metri. Rashid begot Fouad, Farid, and Boulos. Metri begot Shayboub.

Moussa had Tanous who begot Eskandar who had Rokz and Youssef. Father Youssef Nejm went to the Archbishopric of Beirut and lived in Chiyah. He was appointed a representative Bishop by Bishop Tobia 'Oun at Beirut Coast and the examiner of priesthood candidates (1851–1885). He was married and his offspring still live in Chiyah. His brother's offspring live in Kfartai.

Something that caught our attention is that the name "Andrea" is mentioned twice in the lineage chain of the Moubarak offspring in Bqatoute, as well as in the offspring of the Neama Bachaalany House in Salima. Since it is mentioned three times that made them come to be known as the Andrea House. The same applied to the name "Nejm". It is mentioned in the Neama offspring in Salima and in the Moubarak offspring in Baqaata many times. It tends to prove that there is surely a relationship between them. There is also the name of Serkis mentioned among the lineage of the Moubarak House in Kisrawan. They even built their monastery in Raifoun and named it Mar Serkis. Moreover, it is repeated among the names of the Bchaaleh people and of the mediator of one of their houses.

The Poet of the plantation

Emil Moubarak surnamed as "the poet of the plantation" was famous for popular poetry and his most famous poem is this popular Arab song:

I am longing so much to return to the plantation,
I desire ardently to eat a little of the figs and hunted birds.
I am longing to shepherd the goats with playing flute,
And to defoliating leaves and feeding silkworms.

And among his popular hymns with the feelings of an expatriate:

I was a child and became an adult through the moving train.
I don't think about anything else than the holy House.

He is the greatest propagandist advocating a return to the country living. So, he called far and near to the expatriates saying:

The plantation is calling you, come back my children.
Come back, the land which raised you misses you.

The Moubarak House In Rechmaya.

Their Origin And Lineage.

The present family known as the Moubarak House in Rechmaya has no relationship with the sheikhs of the Khoury House who will be mentioned afterwards. This Moubarak House is the offspring of Moubarak Men'em Abi Men'em. Even with all of the research we did, we could not determine their links with the offspring of the Moubarak House.

Perhaps they are the offspring of Father Moussa Moubarak who came to Rechmaya with his paternal cousin Father Beshara Moubarak, the grandfather of the Khoury House. He was also ordained the Bardiot of the Mar Qeryaqous Church in Rechmaya by Douaihy on March 26, 1684.

Father Moussa Moubarak begot Mikhail who begot Girgis and Daher. Girgis had Shahin who begot Girgis. Daher begot Youssef who had Daher and this Daher begot Youssef. Hereafter is the lineage tree of the Moubarak Bou Men'em House: Abou Men'em begot Men'em and Moubarak. Moubarak had Elias who begot Abdou, Moubarak, and Qaryaqous. Abdou begot Elias, Fares, and Girgis.

Meanwhile, Men'em Abou Men'em begot Ghantous and Hanna. Hanna had Girgis and Nasef. Nasef begot eleven sons among them Men'em and Hanna. All of them are in Brazil.

As for Ghantous Abi Men'em, he begot Youssef who begot Rashid and Men'em (who is Father Nimatallah Moubarak, the head of the Lebanese missionaries), Mansour, and Nimatallah (the regulator Tobia of the Lebanese monasticism), Ghantous (who is Bishop Eghnatious, the Archbishop of Beirut), Father Shoukr Allah (the Lebanese missionary), and Shoukry. Shoukry begot Youssef. Rashid died and had no children. Mansour begot Michel, Wadie', and Boutros.

The Moubarak House In Nasra (Nasriye?) and Egypt

They say that their origins are the Moubarak House in Rechmaya. They came down from Nasra (Nasriye) a long time ago. Some of them joined the Aintoura School on August 1, 1820. This included Ayoub, son of Anton Francis, who was 14 years old. When he left the school, he rejoined his parents, then he went to Egypt. In Egypt he joined his brother Yaakoub. He opened a school for boys. He married a woman from Sayda and begot a daughter. (This information was passed on to us from the registry of Ain Warka, from Estephan Moubarak of Nasera, and Father Ibrahim Harfoush, The Orient 8:70).

The Moubarak House In Bdadoun And Aabboudiye.

In Bdadoun.

The Moubarak folks say that they came from Rechmaya around the year 1700. Either they came from Rechmaya or Kisrawan. Their relationship is fixed by tradition and succession. Moreover, we have found a new proof of this relationship. In the archives of the Patriarchal See is a letter from Father Hanna Moubarak, the attendant of Bdadoun, dated June 15, 1762, sent to the Patriarch and saying:

"We have ordered our paternal cousin, Abou Fares Saad (priest) to mediate between the good Prince Youssef (Shehab, the governor of Lebanon) and Bishop Youssef (Estephan) who told us: Prince Youssef was so angry with him and he thought that he would kill him, but with mediation and begging, the Prince was calmed. This is what we know and so inform your highness ...."

From that vestige we can learn that Father Hanna, one of the forfathers of the Moubarak House in Bdadoun was officially calling Father Saad, the grandfather of the Saad House, his paternal cousin.

Bishop Boutros Moubarak

A famous person from the offspring of Bdadoun is the Bishop, Boutros Moubarak who was named Beshara. He took his advanced studies in France in the charge of some noblemen during the era of Bishop Youssef Debs. He was the headmaster of the Bishopric Divan (Bureau) of the Hekma School. Then he was in charge of the Mar Girgis Cathedral in Beirut. And last, he was appointed one of the Secretaries of the Maronite Patriarchical See. He mastered the Arabic and French languages. He wrote a brief biography of Saint Therésa. The Orient Magazine published his Theological and Philosophical lectures. Also, he translated the book titled The Life of Jesus.

In Aabboudiye

The ones who were in Aabboudiye are the offspring of Father Abdulallah Moubarak who came from Bdadoun in the beginning of last century and served the village of Aabboudiye. He died in 1862.

During the era of Bishop Toubia 'Oun (1847–1855) and among the names that were recorded, we find the name of Beshara, the son of Father Abdulallah Moubarak. We learned this from his offspring, his grandson, Father Abdullah, who died and left children and grandchildren many years ago.

The Moubarak House In Kfar Dhabian And Batroun

There is a group of the Moubarak House in the plantation of Kafr Dhabian. We could not determine their exact relationship with that family nor their lineage tree. The same is true for the Moubarak folks in the town of Batroun. We could not determine their exact relationship with the Moubarak family. For that reason, we have postponed any discussion of those matters until we publish our book The History of the Maronite Families. We want to thoroughly and accurately research the matter.

THE KHOURY HOUSE

Chapter 2

About Them And Their Origin

The Khoury House in Rechmaya is a noble family. They are mainly the descendants of its forefather, Father Beshara Moubarak, originating from Bchaaleh. The handwritten notation in a prayer book, found in the Mar Qaryaqous Church in Rechmaya is proof of that. It says:

"With the help of God, may He be exalted, these people have completed the prayers through Bishop Elias Hada-nany, in the year (Asmah) 1648 AD, in the month of July. The keeper of that book was Father Beshara from Batha, Kisrawan, He moved to the Shahar district (El Gerd). With his efforts and donations, a church was built.

Surely, Father Beshara had come to Rechmaya a few years before the date written in the book. Moussa, his paternal cousin, was accompanying him. Moussa was an ordained priest who succeeded him in servicing the congregation after his death.

"on March 26, 1684, Patriarch Estephan Douaihy ordained Father Moussa as Bardiot of the Chancel of the Mar Qaryaqous Church in the village of Rechmaya."

"In 1685, on May 6, that Patriarch ordained the Deacon Abdulallah, son of Father Beshara Moubarak, the priest of that already mentioned church."

Prince Haidar Shehabi, the Lebanon Governor, put Father Abdulallah in charge of the village of Rechmaya, so he was in charge of governing its matters. This is a practise that the other Sheikhs of the other districts and fiefs in Lebanon were putting into action.

On June 3, 1714, Father Abdulallah died. His son Father Saleh succeeded him.

We surmise that he frequently used to go to Kisrawan, his forefathers' homeland. He married the daughter of his relative there. His son, the Subdeacon Ghandour, married the daughter of his kin, Abdulallah, the son of Father Soliman Moubarak.

It seems that Father Saleh came back to Rechmaya in 1700, for the last time. He settled there. Some historians thought that he was the first one of his family who came to Rechmaya, and, that he was the forefather of Khoury family there. However, this intrepid priest was so famous for his courage, good opinions, and trusted word, that he surpassed all those who preceeded him. Because of this, I think that those historians just imagined that he was the forefather of the Khoury House. After all, it was their own families in Rechmaya that they were attributing to him. But we have this information:

"In 1718. Bishop Abdulallah Qaraly, the Bishop of Beirut and the Sham, went to Damascus to take over the Maro-nite Church there from the European missionaries. Father Saleh Bin Moubarak was accompanying him and he was one of those who wanted to get the Church back. He wanted the return of the Church because he had been there twice before to collect the tithe and he observed that there were problems between the Maronite parishioners and the European priests. Father Saleh was a wise man, of noble birth, and able to discern problems and their soluti-ons.

So, the keys were turned over, in the presence of Father Saleh and the noble Maronites.... As the Badriot Yaakoub accepted the keys, he knelt down before Bishop Abdulallah and presented them to him, in public." (This is a summary of those events written by Bishop Germanos Farahat and Bishop Boulos Qaraly, copied from the original in his book: The Pearls of Bishop Abdulallah Qaraly , 2:243.)

In that book, on page 325, to be exact, it mentions the efforts made by Father Saleh of Rechmaya, in the year 1722, to reconciliate a dispute between Patriarch Yaakoub Ghawad and Bishop Abdulallah Qaraly.

The following selection is from the margins of a religious book entitled Balance of Time which is preserved in the library of the Halabian Maronite Priests in Rome. Father Boulos Mosaad Halaby put it in the biography he wrote: The Memory of Bishop Farahat, page 47:

"In the year 1714, Father Abdulallah, the son of Moubarak, from the village of Rechmaya, passed away to the mercy of God. It was on Sunday morning, the third day of June. May God have mercy upon him, and make his home in the paradise for those who pleased God. Whoever reads these words should ask God to have mercy upon the soul of Father Abdulallah and call on him, as written: his son, the priest Saleh."

"In the year 1730, we went to Europe in the blessed month of July. A groomman, Hadj Youssef Ibn Al Gamaty and his son Deacon 'Ebss, were accompanying us. We left from Sayda, asking God to bring us back safely. Our paternal cousin, Moubarak, was accompanying us. Written: Father Saleh Ibn Moubarak."

"This book was read by Father Saleh Ibn Moubarak from Rechmaya village, He was in the Mar Boutros and Mar Shelin monasteries in Rome during the presidencial period of Father Mikhail Eskandar, the headmaster, and Pastor Youwasaf, the headmaster of the mentioned monastery at that time (He is the Bishop Youwasaf from Beskinta). Written in 1740."

Their Lineage

We had intended to publish a correct lineage tree of the Sheikhs of the Khoury folks in Rechmaya, however, we encountered some complications. We found differences in the lineage series written by Sheikh Tanous Shediak in his printed book About the Notables, on page 103, and the series sent by Ghandour Beik Saad to Patriarch Boulos Mosaad.

We took a copy of the Saad version and consulted with his son, Najib Beik Al Saad, who made some corrections in it. Then, we had three different copies!

For that reason, we have postponed its publishing date until we start the puiblishing process for our detailed book The History of the Maronite Families in the near future. For the moment we will be content with the corrected version of the lineage of the forefathers of this family that is according to other documents and vestiges.

Sheikh Beshara

He is Beshara, the son of Father Anton, the son of Abdulallah II, the son of Father Saleh, the son of Father Abdulallah I, and the son of Father Beshar Moubarak. His father, Anton the priest, died in 1836 and left five sons. The most intelligent one was Beshara who studied in the Ain Waraka School, which graduated the best men of our society, for the advancement of our religion, and the life of the congregation, and betterment of our country.

After his graduation he was sent with his school mate, Habib Al Khoury Al Batadiny (Bishop Yohanna Habib) to Beirut, and, then, to Tripoli to study Jurisprudence through one of the Muslim savant sheikhs. According to the archives of the Maronite Patriarchal See, that was on the orders of Prince Shehab II, the governor of Lebanon, and on the charge of the masters and notables of the Maronite congregation.

The following is the text of one of those documents, written by Habib Al Khoury Al Batadiny:

"It is brought to your attention, say we, the undersigned names, that we have applied for admission to the program for the study of jurisprudence, under the care of Mr. Mare Youssef (Hebeish). This is done on the charge of the most Holy Patriarch, and, of the nobles of our Maronite congregation. And the fees covering the complete course of studies, our personal expenses during that time, and the cost of our books, are all being paid for by the congregation. Accordingly, we shall be faithful to this praiseworthy purpose and to fulfill the rights of the congregation stemming from our obligation. We have promised the holy Patriarch, that after we finish our studies, we will fufill any request for help which may be asked for the benefit of the congregation. And when both of us, or, just one, is demanded by his highness to teach jurisprudence to the youth of the congregation, we will teach this knowledge, whether one or more. Our annual fees will not be more than one thousand piasters plus our pocket money, covering only food, beverage, and accommodation. Even if we have not been appointed judges.

However, if it will not include pocket money, then, the salary will be 1500 piasters for each per year. The holy patriarch is the one who will determine if there will be an amount for pocket money or won't. And he will determine the place of the lessons. And as long as we are tied by our obedience to his highness at School, so accordingly, we promise that we will not teach jurisprudence to anyone out of our congregation unless it is permitted by his highness.

If it should happen and we violate our promise, either both of us or just one of us does not fulfill the order of his highness which has been written above, we owe his honor a full refund all that he has paid to us and what the notables of the congregation have paid for us to study the Jurisprudence. In recognition of that, we wrote that act and have delivered it by hand it to his highness. Written on March 27, 1838, certifying what has been written: Habib Al Khoury Al Batabiny."

"The salary of the Efendi (Teacher)who is Sheikh Aarabi Al Zeilaa from Tripoli, has been fixed at five thousand piasters with a pocket money allowance at five thousand. This amount is allocated to be paid by the following individuals named below, by order and will of his highness. (Prince Beshir)."

The following is the list of the money paid for that purpose :

"From the Bishop Anton Al Khazen 400 piasters; from the Bishop Abdulallah Blibel 400; from the Bishop Boutros Karam 400; from the Abbot of the Lebanese monks 1000; from the Abbot of the Antonian monks 500; from the Abbot of the Halabian monks 300; from the Bishop Abdulallah Al Boustany 400; from the Bishop Youssef Al Khazen 300; from the Roman school as instructed by the late Prince Haidar Ahmed Shehab's charity 200; from his highness Prince Amin Beshir Shehab Al Afkham 2700, from his kindness to the Rifoun Monastery 430; from his felicity on behalf of the Ain Waraka School from the charity of Prince Haidar Ahmed Shehab 500; from his felicity on behalf of the Mar Abda Harharia School from the charity of prince Haidar 500; from his felicity from the income of the Eintoura School 2000; from the felicity, the balance of the requested amount, 234. The total, 10,264 piasters. The whole amount has been spent for the salary of the teacher and the two students' expenses."

And it seems that Sheikh Beshara and Subdeacon Habib were bound by the Maronite Patriarchy's orders after they completed their studies at the Ain Waraka School, at the request of the congregation. Ghandour Beik Al Saad wrote a letter to the Patriarch on February 8, 1837, asking his permission for his in-law, Sheikh Beshara, to teach him Grammar. Also, that Sheikh Beshara would reside in his house and that he, Ghandour, would pay him the requested salary. (The Archives of Bekerky, Jarour Al Hebeshi, and Al Samt of Sabaaly. 5:184).

In the year 1840, Sheikh Beshara became the judge of Bteddine during the era of Prince Beshir II and Prince Beshir III in 1841. From 1844 to 1860, he was appointed the judge of the Maronites at the Council's Office, which was organized by Shakib Effendi for the Druze governorate in El Choueifat.

In our archives, we have a valuable document mentioning that the Council issued an order concerning the suit activated by the Sheikhs of the Amin El Dine House against the people of Silfaya, their partners in the gardens of that village. It was issued on the order of the field-marshal of Al Ayala (Aalali?). The president and the members of the council signed the order, all, except for Sheikh Beshara, the Judge of the Maronites, and Sajaan 'Oun, the Maronite member of the council. Therefore, the governor asked in writing why they refused to sign. Sheikh Beshara replied in writing. It was an elaborate letter, written with boldness, intelligence, and knowledge of the law. He explained that the reason why he could not sign the judgment was because it was contrary to considered traditions, the rules, the laws, and it would harm the rights of the Lebanese farmers, who the Sheikhs wanted to take advantage of.

We have told the story as it was described in the original document. Some people, however, have told versions that differ.

Sheikh Beshara died and left two sons: Father Louis and Khalil Beik. Father Louis spent his life tending to the congregation in the Mar Elias Church in Ras Beirut. Khalil Beik spent a long time as the director of The Arabic Department in the district office of Lebanon. He died leaving six sons: Sheikh Behsara, the President of the Republic of Lebanon, Sheikhs Fouad, Selim, Nadim, Sami, and Caesar.

From the Khoury house, there came many men of religion, law, journalism, and fame, like the Sheikhs Beshir, Amin Rashed, Nadim Effendi, Melhem, and Selim Khattar (silk tradesman in Falougha). The list also includes the kin of Father Al Dhabet. We must also add Habib Saab, a Doctor in Science and Language, as well as an educator, and a journalist, both here and in Brazil. Also, there is Selim Ibn Boulos, Amin Bin ....and others.

THE SAAD HOUSE
Chapter 3

This House is one of the great noble Lebanese houses. Their forefather, Father Beshara Moubarak, originating form Bchaaleh, moved from Ghousta around the year 1648 to Rechmaya in the Chouf where the number of Maronites increased.

At the beginning of 1710, his grandson, Youssef, and his strong men participated in the famous battle of Ain Dara. They fought courageously and captured two princes from the Yamanites. Thus, Prince Haidar Shehabi, the governor, rewarded him by giving him Rechmaya. Accordingly, he and his offspring gained a position of privilege among the Shehabis. The Shehabis made them their counselors and they became famous for their policies. Their role also was of great interest to their Maronite congregation as well as the whole country. The size of their fief grew as neighboring villages were drawn into Rechmaya.

Then, Youssef was ordained a priest and was known as Father Saleh. His grandson, Saad Bin Ghandour Al Khoury Saleh, grew up and became one of the trustees for Prince Melhem Shehaby, the great governor. Before his death, the Prince appointed him to be the guardian of his children. So Saad worked at having Prince Youssef invested as the governor of Lebanon in 1771. Saad remained his counselor for his whole life.

He worked on cutting off the Matawlians' violence which ravaged the country. In addition, his actions for supporting his congregation and all the Christian congregations during their hard times, are so famous we need not state them, and, they are more numerous than we can count.

As proof of just how famous he was for his generosity to Chistianity, the Apostolic See, under Pope Pius, honored him in a letter which began: *"To my beloved son and nobleman, our salutation and apostolic blessing…"*.

When he died, the Pope wrote to the Patriarch of the Maronites, presenting his condolences to him and to the congregation, consoling them for their grave loss. He also indicated his preference that his son be his successor.

Sheikh Saad Al Khoury was the owner of Rechmaya and the counselor of Jbeil Lebnan (Mount Lebanon) under the government of Prince Youssef Al Shehabi. He worked on elevating the country. He served the concerns of his congregation, being a firm believer, and preserving the dignity of his principles. He was courageous, of good opinion, and practicing sound management. He was a man respected for his holiness. And, he was a man who had influence over governors, chiefs, and the people. He became a great concern in the country because his decisions and imposed measures determined the state of political and religious matters.

There were negotiations between him and the Apostolic See. They relied on him to solve the congregation's problems and to implement reforms. There are letters from the Holy Pontiff and the Synod addressed successively to Sheikh Saad.

When the inevitable destiny came, around the year 1785, his son, Sheikh Ghandour, succeeded him. He administered affairs with wisdom, zeal, and intelligence, just as his father had. He was growing in wisdom and his followers were increasing. Then, King Louis XVI appointed him as the French Consul in Beirut in 1787. This was done on orders from the Patriarch, Youssef Estephan, through his delegate, Father Anton Al Qayala, originating from Beirut. Prince Youssef Shehab, the Governor of Lebanon, also ordered the same.

So it was that the King of France bestowed this high position on Sheikh Ghandour who became the Consul of France, the Prime Minister of the Lebanese government, and the Chief of the Maronite Congregation.

At the Cathedral of Mar Girgis in Beirut, he recited the royal vows while wearing his royal costume. It was a celebrated event full of elegance.

Sadly, Sheikh Ghandour was the victim of injustice and died for the sake of his country in 1790. He left a testament which he wrote before his death, showing how pious he was. Our friend, Father Aghnatious Tanous, published it in Al Bashir, issue #6617.

"Sheikh Ghandour begot Habib who begot Ghandour. Ghandour Beik begot Najib, Habib, Fouad, and Mourad. Najib Beik and Mourad Beik didn't get married. Habib Pasha had only girls, while Fouad Beik begot Raji, Amin, and Ghandour (who died young and unmarried). Raji Beik begot Fouad, Najib, and Habib. Amin Beik begot ...."

Below is a poetic history of Ghandour Beik Al Saad's birth, which Nicholas Al Turk composed. We are presenting it from our archives:

"In the month of April came the most honorable appearance which covered the year with light.
The suns of humans rose with this son in whom full happiness was realised.
A lion cub, humanity's beloved, he grew up upon the generosity of his fathers.
When his full moon revealed itself ... etc."
"Ghandour be one of the long-lived people". (1818)

Habib Pasha Al Saad

He was born around the year 1866 in Ain Trez and studied the sciences and languages at the schools of Beirut: the Patriachate, the Jesuites', and the Hekma. He worked in different jobs and occupied different positions in the Lebanese government. He received titles and decorations from the spiritual and civil authorities.

During the era of the District Governors and the Parliament, he presided over the Board. He was the Prime Minister, then, the President of the Republic of Lebanon in 1934. He died on May 5, 1942. His funeral was crowded, something rarely seen before in this country.

We decided that we must publish some extracts of the elegy composed by Amin Beik Naser El Dine, the great poet and writer:

"Today, Lebanon is weeping for the great one with his knowledge, and having the two ornaments; nobility and generosity.
Loyal and independent, he did not use the law to blame like some who used it for interdiction.
He was one of acute mind. In hardship, he was undismayed, If he spoke, he invaded.
In influencing, he was clement if he ever surprised, never violent in his reaction or seeking revenge.
He was the brother of reverence for whom eyes would be cast down if he was looking to people.
He was the keeper of cordiality, as the heart keeps itself, the keeper of the soul from wrong thinking.
He was complete, abstinent, like money controls those who worshiped it as an idol.
He was the master composer, paper and pen were so pleased with his phraseology.
Nobles didn't know that a new noble was born. People didn't know that others were in attendance besides themselves.
The highest presidents gave him leadership but it did not add anything to him. He was already a noble born.

And the height of his positions did not tempt him, showing that modesty is the ethics of the free one, if he is great.
... When I announced his death to the loyal people, they cried. They were almost weeping tears of blood.
What happened is a catastrophe that touched nobility, ethics, and nature.
I was the support for those who have chosen you. For they were used to seeing you honor those who served.
You, the Son of the Saads, created in this people what you talked about. And, if the conceited weep for you, it shows their meanness.
I salute the soil in which you are buried. It embraces the man whose nature was the most generous ever."

THE HABQOUQ HOUSE
Chapter 4

About Them And Their Origin

The Habqouq folks are a highborn family who grew up in Bchaaleh. Many of its people were famous and have been mentioned in history. A group of them moved to Bikfaya; another group lived in Aarabet Qizhaiya where their off-spring are still living, and in the nearby Ban village. From those who remained in Bikfaya, a family arose still known today with that name. From it, the Shantiry and the Aassy folks in Bikfaya are derived, as are the Tobia folks in Beit Shabab and Mer'eb folks in Beirut.

As for those who moved to Aarabet Qizhaiya, they purchased the properties of the Qizhaiya Monastery from the Samarany family for the price of 12 bags which is equal to 6000 piasters, a compensation for their work in the Monastery and its income.

Then, they started to construct and build, and they continued to do so for years. Among them, two monks have been ordained in that Monastery: Bishop Abdulallah and Bishop Hanna. When the Lebanese monasticism came to be, they turned over the Monastery and its properties. Also, they did the same with the Monastery of Mar Boutros Karim Ennin.

The greatest one who grew up from that family is Bishop Girgis Habqouq Bachaalany, the Bishop of Aaqoura. He was an example of generosity and honesty. He was a monk, then Patriarch Youssef Halib from Aaqoura elevated him to be a Bishop in 1648 and he lived in Qannubin.

After the death of Patriarch Yohanna Safrawi, the chiefs and notables elected him to succeed the Patriarch Yohanna, but, out of modesty, he completely refused. He hid when the people strongly insisted. He stayed in hiding until they chose another person.

He was the one who presided at the Bishop's convention that elected Patriarch Douaihy, and he exerted a strong influence in his election (1670). He helped him in the ordination of Bishop Boutros Makhlouf, in the presence of the Ambassador of King Louis XVII (1674). He also assisted in the ordination of Bishop Youssef Sham'oun Hasarouni (1675).

According to the letter written by Douaihy to him, we know the standing of the Pontiff among the governors and chiefs. Also, he was the one giving Patriarch Douaihy the most support and loyalty. Bishop Habqouq lived long and was a cunning man in politics. He was pious and honest. He loved learning, especially history. He collected many rare and precious books. To every monastery he visited, or in every history book he read, he made notations about the events with comments about its benefits.

Their Vestiges

The following is a vestige of Bishop Habqouq, one of his many, transferred from the original written in the prayer book kept at the Qods Al Sharif. We publish it with its original text:

"The Humble Girgis Ibn Habqouq Bachaalany, the Bishop of Al Aaqoura. At the beginning of the Christian year 1692, I, Humble among the chiefs, Bishop Girgis Ibn Habqouq Bachaalany, came and visited the tomb and the holy places. We attended the Shenena and Eastern, may God support every believer. I was accompanied by Father Yohanna Qarm, the attendant of the village of Zouk Mesbah, Pastor Yohanna, the monk from the Raifoun Monastery, Sheikh Abou Shedid Dhaher Ibn Al Roz, Sheikh Salhoub, and his mother and paternal cousin, Sheikh Youness Ibn Salhab from Haqel. Sheikh Sorour from the capital, Halab, was present with us as well as he who wrote these letters, Deacon Samaan, the Deacon of the Bishop." (Transferred from the Lebanese Father Aghnatious Tanous, as per the archives of the Maronite Monasticism of Tripoli.)

THE HARFOUSH HOUSE

Chapter 5

About Them And Their Origin

What has been proven by tradition and through readings, is that the Harfoush folks are a family that has been related by marriage with the family of Abi Rezk Bachaalany, but this relationship is not asserted. However, what has been learned from the children of that family, is that they are relatives of Abi Rezk whose offspring moved to Salima.

Their great-grandfather is Harfoush. After the catastrophe that befell the Bachaalany folks in Tripoli, he went to Prince Ahmed Ma'n, the last Ma'n Prince. He died in 1697. They first went to Niha, in the Chouf, seeking protection at the houses of the Sheikh Assaf Druz who welcomed them. They were generous and sympathised with them. So it was that Rashed came to manage the properties of the Assaf House. The Sheikhs of the Hamdan folks living in Bater granted Harfoush and Elias, Ein Al Romany, a plantation in the Jezzine province.

It just so happened that Prince Ahmed Al Ma'n passed by Bater near Niha, but the Hamdan folks paid no attention him. Then he passed by Niha, where Sheikh Assaf honored him and kindly received his delegation. So, Rashed seized the occasion and became acquainted with him. He spoke to him about himself, saying that he wanted to align himself and his two brothers with the Prince. So Prince Ahmed gave him a land grant to construct a building for him. The Prince gave him and his Christian brothers protection and money to support themselves.

Prince Ahmed met his brothers, Harfoush and Elias, at the plantation of Al Romana and they were ploughing the soil. They invited him to their home and he accepted. They told him about what had happened with the Assaf El Dine House and that inflamed him. He was filled with rage against him. Therefore, he called his secretary, and he wrote an endowment deed for them, covering the plantation of Ain Al Romana and an additional large amount of money, not more than 25 piasters, and he gave them a part of Niha's prairie.

Then, Harfoush married a girl from Bkassine and moved there. He built a house near the Church and there are still a number of his offspring living there in the same place. His son, Saleh, built a quarter at the west side of the village. Today, it is still known as Saleh's Quarter (Haret Saleh).

As for Rashed, the brother of Harfoush, he remained in Niha and his offspring are still living there today. The properties were divided between the offspring of Harfoush and those of Rashed. However, some properties remained shared between them at the plantation of Al Romana and Niha until recently.

The first one who started to research about this family was Father Ethnasious Harfoush, the Lebanese monk (1819–1882). He was very generous and intelligent. Some of his papers were dispersed and Soliman Harfoush, the father of Doctor Abdulallah and Mr. Nadim, have collected some information about the family. Some material was taken from Father Ethnasious and some from others. Lately, one of the virtuous Harfoush children wrote a biography of the Harfoush family. He is Father Ibrahim Harfoush, the famous Lebanese missionary. He is one of the famous Maronite genius', so we have taken some of his information.

Their Famous People.

Many of them are famous:

1. The savant Antonious, one of the Lebanese monasticism experts.

2. The teacher, Youssef Harfoush, who studied in Versaille and taught on the Saint Josef Faculty and wrote his famous books in French.

3. His brother, George Harfoush, worked in different jobs for the Ottoman government, gaining various titles and ranks. He was also a member of the Mail and Telegraph Council in Istanbul. He accompanied Najib Pasha Melhema as his Chancellor.

4. Shaker 'Oun, he was named with his mother's first name, but he is from the Harfoush House. He studied in France and taught the French language in Beirut Schools. He assisted the teacher Abdulallah Al Boustany in the translation of The General History by Boissier, and, established a magazine entitled Al Nadeem with Mr. Elias Tanous Howeik who was a philosopher.

THE ABI RASHED HOUSE

Chapter 6

Their Origin And Homes.

From what has we have previously mentioned about the Harfoush House, it is clear that the family of Abi Rashed is one of the families belonging to Bachaalany's. That relationship is established through Abou Rashed, their great-grandfather who was the brother or the paternal cousin of Abi Harfoush. Also, from the history of the two families, their forefathers moved from the Kisrawan fief where they were hiding after the catastrophe of their kin, Abi Rezk Bachaalany and his children in Tripoli. They went to the regions of the Chouf which were under the protection of Prince Ahmed Ma'n, the Governor of Lebanon (1658–1697). This Prince brought them nearer and put in their possession the plantation of Al Romana in the Jezzine District, and a part of the Niha land at the Chouf.

After the Ma'ns perished, the Shehabi Princes governed Lebanon. The Abi Rashed folks remained and the Harfoush folks left Niha and lived in Bekasin. Meanwhile, the offspring of Abi Rashed remained in Niha and are still there today.

A group of them moved to the Charoun Valley and the forefather of the Nahra folks moved to Kfar Chima. From them came Selim Beik Shaker who resides in Egypt. It is most probable that they are from the offspring of Nahra Abi Rashed in Niha, not from the offspring of Nahra Abi Gouda in the Herf Monastery as some have claimed.

At the Charoun Valley

There was a migration of a group of the Abi Rashed House from Niha to the Charoun Valley around 1750. Thus, they were living there when it was part of the fief of Prince Ali, the first Shehabi Prince who became a Christian…. The house of Abi Rashed in the valley is divided into offshoots: the Mansour House, the Abi Rezk House, and others. Some of their names were mentioned among those recorded in 1849 by Bishop Toubia 'Oun. They are: Girgis and Lotfallah Mansour Abi Rashed; Francis Yohanna Abi Rashed Tanous Tadrous; Elias and Daher Khatar; Khalil Mikhail Abi Rashed; Asaad Abi Rashed; Elias Bin Aboud Abi Rezk Abi Rashed. This latter Elias begot Youssef, Naoum, Nasry, Aboud, Hani, and Gibran. As for Youssef, he begot Michel, Ghibrail, Farid, and Henry. Naoum begot Fouad, Emil, Elias, and John.

Their Famous People.

In the past, just like today, there have been some members of this family who were noted for their generosity, fame, patriotism, and courage. Some of them excelled in the sciences, literature, commerce, and industry. The one who we personally remember of those and whose news has reached us is Abou Rashed, the forefather, who was known in his time for his sound judgment and management skills.

Those who were famous for their courage and patriotism include: Moubarak, Nahra, and Nemr Abi Rashed. Sheikh Elias Aboud Abi Rezk, the Sheikh of Reconciliation for the valley, was famous for his patriotism. His children followed in this after his death: Aboud Beik, the bold journalist and author who established a political newspapers called <u>Al Naseer.</u> He also translated into Arabic the book titled <u>Dante</u> about the great Italian poet. He also occupied high positions in the Italian consuls. His brother, Naoum, is a master at commerce.

In the valley, there was also the late Father Youssef Abi Rashed who studied at the school of the Jesuites Fathers in Beirut. He was ordained a priest at the chancel of Mar Yohanna in the valley. The whole congregation attended with zeal and various activities. In addition to that, he taught the young people of his village, emphasizing true religion and other knowledge.

Among them also is our friend, Aziz Abi Rashed, one of our intellectual youth. He spent years in the French delegation. From this family there was the in-law of Abi Rashed, the Sheikh of Reconciliation of Niha, known for his patriotism. His sons inherited that characteristic from him. They are: Wadie', Elias, and…. This family formed a family organization, taking care of its affairs and unifying their opinions. It was established in 1945.

THE GIBRAN HOUSE

Chapter 7

Their Origins.

According to the stories told by the Gibran folks *"they originate from the Sham (Syria). At the beginning of the 16th century, their forefather moved to Baalbek. Finally, his children migrated to the village of Bchaaleh, at the upper Batroun, and they lived there. Then in the year 1672, five of them, all brothers, left Bchaaleh after the horrible events that occurred. Thus, Youssef Gibran and his two brothers, Moussa and Mikhail, lived in Bcharre. The fourth brother went to the Sayda region. The fifth one lived in Salima."*

This story was taken from Hanna Abou Rashed in his book <u>The General Dictionary</u> when he wrote the biography of Gibran. The historian George Baz adopted this kinship story in his biography of Gibran. He added to it that *"the family of Gibran is one of the Bachaalany families ... ...and it is a Ghasanian one, according to what narrators say".* While the writer, Edmond Wahba, one of Gibran's friends said: *"The Gibrans are a Caldanian family, their name was Jabroun and they migrated from Sham to dwell in Bcharre."*

From our research, we acertained that the Gibran House is like the other families originating from Bchaaleh, they migrated from there to the town of the Lieutnant Colonels in the 17th century. Among the documents kept by Patriarch Boulos at the Maronite Patriarchal See, is a paper in his handwriting about the origins of the families of Bcharre. In brief, he says: *"the Gibran House originates from Bchaaleh".* He didn't say any more than that. And we can't add anything to this original text no matter what stories are told about the families of Bchaaleh. There is no evident reference that we can trust. All that we can say is: Gibran, the great-grandfather of this family, moved from Bchaaleh to Bcharre for the same reasons that caused the other old grandfathers to leave. The tale was inherited by the children of this family and the rest of the sister families, namely, that: the Gibran House is originally from Bchaaleh and they are the descendants of their forefather, Gibran, the first one who resided in Bcharre (also spelled Bsharri).

About Them.

Gibran folks had a special rank among the families of Bcharre (also spelled Bsharri). The men among them were famous for their generosity, courage, and knowledge, notably, Monsignor Boulos Bin Nicholas Youssef Gibran, the priest of Bcharre.

In a precious document we published in our book <u>Lebanon and Youssef Beik Karam</u> it tells about a delegation from the people of Bcharre going to Karam to defend their patriotic interests in 1861. And at the top of the signatures of the Bcharre people, there are three seals of this family, who are: Tanous Gibran, Saad Gibran, and Eissa Ibrahim Gibran.

Tanous Gibran is one of the hero fighters who was with Karam at the Einata battle with Habib Saad. Tanous Gibran visited the hero of Lebanon in Naples when he was on his way back to his homeland from Brazil in 1887. With Tanous was his son Colonel Selim Tanous Saad Gibran, one of the great expatriates in Paranagua in Brazil.

He told our brother, Habib Bachaalany, in Brazil, about the conversation of that visit of Youssef Beik which Karam wrote of in his diary.

He talked about *"the visit of Sheikh Tanous Gibran with his friends, in their journey by sea from Naples to Lebanon, and how they escaped from danger thanks to the intercession of the Saint Youssef.* (see <u>Lebanon and Youssef Beik</u>: 45, 577, 644).

Gibran Khalil Gibran

Gibran Khalil Gibran, is the genius Lebanese and international author. He is one of the members of this Gibran family. He is Gibran, the son of Khalil Bin Mikhail Bin Saad, related to the family of the Maronite Youssef Gibran from Bchaaleh. He was born in Bcharre on December 6, 1883, and grew up there. His father was brave and died in 1894. His mother is Camela, the daughter of Father Estephan Rahma from Bcharre. She died in 1903. Gibran had a brother, Boutros, who died young in 1903. He also had two sisters: Soltana, who died in 1902, and Mariana.

Gibran emigrated at the age of twelve to the United States. He was travelling between New York and Paris to study and work as a painter. That is how he became a master in art and writing. His art is unprecedented. His drawings and wonderful pictures surpassed the masters of art and ideology. His most famous paintings are: Ibn Sina, the greatest Arab doctor, a Persian, and a philosophers; Abi Al Alaa Al Me'ary, one of the greatest ideologist of the Orient; Al Ghazaly; Mohamed; and the fount of Leila. Each picture clearly reveals the person, their ethics, and their character, not to mention they are accurate representations of the person's actual appearance and clothing.

Moreover, during that period, he was writing articles and stories in the Arabic newspapers like <u>Al Hoda</u> and others. Then, he published his books, written in Arabic, in which he perfectly phrased and composed poems. His writings were in great demand because of their spirit and new ideas. He was a philisopher, a writer, a creator, and a renovator of the highest class. However, what made him internationally famous, are his writings in English. Once he published his writings in English, people adopted the human principles and emancipated ideas he presented. They lifted the human spirit above materialism and took him to the spiritual world. People were coming to read them with longing and admiration. The books of Gibran have been translated into the European languages, especially, his book titled <u>The Prophet.</u> This book gained for him the surname of "Gibran the prophet" because he preached to people with high human principles. He urged them to practise wellness, affection, and virtue. He also warned of the consequences of wickedness and rancour. Thus, he was, in the age of materialism, a voice in the wilderness, a prophet of his age.

THE QASH'AMY AND ABI NAKD HOUSE

Chapter 8

The two great-grandfathers are brothers. The Qash'amy folks have lived in Bikfaya and the Abi Nakd folks lived near it, in El Mhaidse. The first ones are Roman Catholics and the others are Orthodox. And, of course, they are originally Maronites because only the Maronites lived in Bchaaleh. They married people from the Roman Church and over time, became one of them. So, the Qash'amy folks embraced Catholicism, while the Abi Nakd folks remained Orthodox.

The common tales passed down say that their great-grandfather is one of the Bachaalany who escaped from Tripoli to Zouk Al Kharab and to the Balana district in Kisrawan after the catastrophe of Abi Rezk Bachaalany with his children and his brother Abi Saab.

Our friend Sheikh Edmond Blibel found among some old documents at the home of Massoud 'Afish, in El Mhaidse, papers that confirm that relationship. And in our archives are documents of Prince Haidar Al Lam', the Christians' Governor, which show that the name of Al Qash'amy is mentioned often in both family offshoots.

Also, it seems that this family has not increased, especially pertaining to the offspring of Abi Nakd from which we knew Khalil and Asaad Abi Nakd in the last century. We also knew Ghantous Al Qash'amy who was one of the famous silk tradesmen of his time and had his own plant in Bikfaya.

And one of our classmates at the Mar Youssef School in Qornet Chahouane, was Youssef, the son of Asaad Abi Nakd. He was studying vocabulary with Sheikh Ibrahim Al Mondher and phrasing with Father Nimatallah Dagher in the year 1890.

He became a teacher of Phrasing and Oratory at the National School for Na'eem Baik Sawaya in Baabdat. Then, he migrated to Egypt and worked as a writer for a while. After that he worked in commerce and became rich.

He has moved to Bikfaya with his family where he bought a house and properties. Youssef Abi Nakd was a writer, an orator, and a poet. He has taken care to educate his children and enrolled them in outstanding schools. They are: the writer Na'eem, the pharmacist Adeeb, and the Dentist Labib.

As for the Qash'amy folks, from them came men of generosity and knowledge in Bikfaya and Egypt. Among them the two lawyers, Selim and Emil, Doctor Demitri, and the writer William, who invented chemical products known by his name, as the brand name "Wicor".

THE ABI EISSA AND MESHLEB HOUSE

Chapter 9

About Them And Their Origin.

This is a family belonging to Bchaaleh and its folks say that their great-grandfather came first to Majdel Meouch then Ramliye where he bought a land which was known as the Ramliyean, not far from that mentioned village. After that it was known by Bashweit. It is a village of agriculture with fertile soil. The ambition of its people caused it to be even more productive. They are people known for their strength, courage, and health.

This family was divided in two offshoots: Abou Eissa and Meshleb, who were either brothers or paternal cousins. The number of their offspring reached three hundred people. Half of them are expatriates and the other half are still living in the homeland. The majority of those who migrated are in Brazil. The others are in Argentina and Australia. Many of them are rich and have educated children.

During the era of Prince Beshir the Great, Father Youssef Abou Eissa grew up. He is the one who gained influence over governors and chiefs. He was a Bishop representative and the agent of the Saint Toqla endowment in Rechmaya.

He had ardor and was wise. One of his grand-children was named after him, Father Youssef Bou Eissa. He is the one who was assigned to different congregations in the Beirut diocese.

Among them also were Father Tanious Meshleb who lived to be about a hundred years old, his son, Father Boulos, who died around 1914, and, Father Tanious Ayoub Meshleb who named himself using his grandfather's name. Today he is serving the congregation of his village.

Their Vestiges.

In our archives are old documents and contracts which we present in brief:

"In 1184 (1770) Hegira, Meshleb, the son of Saady from Shoreit village ... has bought the 'Ardan field known in Yaghy ...."

"In 1193 (1779) Hegira, Meshleb bought from his brother Bou Youssef Ghanem from Shoreit, the two cinnamon bark and their places are known in Al 'Ardan at Ein Fikh ...."

" ...In 1242 (1826), Fares Meshleb from Shoreit has bought from Bou Samra ... the apiary of Bou Nofal in Al Ramliya at the neighrbourhood of Al Majnouna..."

"In 1230 Hegira (1814), the sons of Meshleb from Soreit: Qaryaqous, his sons, their paternal uncle Fares, and his nephew (brother's son) Marei from ... ...from the Assaf House (the Druzes of Al Ramliye originating from Aindara) for the price of 4600 piasters."

THE JABOUR, MEL'EB
AND SHAHWAN HOUSE
Chapter 10

Jabour House

They say that the forefather of this House is from the Bachaalany folks of Salima. He left there and went to Abiah and they are wrongly known as the Machaalany.

There is Fares who moved to Beirut. His children attended the American University and became: Dr. Najib, the famous surgeon in Egypt and in Brazil. He was oustanding. His surgeries were highly successful, like the one he performed on our Habib Bachaalany. Another son, George Beik, served in the Egyptian Army and has established the Dobress of Beirut and the Souk Al Gharb. He died in 1947 and left a son called Henry. His brother, Philip, is now a professor of the American University, and we will provide you with more details on him in our new book on the history of the families.

Mel'eb House

The Mel'eb family in Kfar Chima is one of the families belonging to the Bachaalany folks. According to the narration of the late Bishop Mikhail Howeish and the Badriot Youssef Sader, they both agree that this Mel'eb house comes from the Bachaalany family. The known forefathers of them are: Tanous Mel'eb and Abdel Ahad Mel'eb. In the registery of the people who have been recorded, the Register of 1848, the mentioned names are: Abdou Bin Mel'eb, and, Lodia and Berjoute, the daughters of Mel'eb Bachaalany. Their offspring still live there today.

Shahwan House

The Shahwan folks in Baabda say that they are from the Bachaalany in Salima. And according to what Youssef Wakim and others told us: The well-known Youssef Shahwan, great-grandfather of this family, around 1870, invited the Bachaalany family to attend his wedding. A group of our youth went to Baabda in response to the invitation. Youssef was very happy and proud that they did this because he had no family support in Baabda. What we can mention about him, is that he sold one of his gardens to pay the expenses for those invitations and the wedding celebratons.

Youssef Shahwan begot Asaad and Elias who lived with the Bedouins and begot Shehab. Abou Shehab had a melodious voice and used to chant the Mijana and Ataba folk songs in his special way. He also played the "rebeck" which added an additional touch of beauty to his chants. He composed his own chants and folksongs which are printed in a notebook. He was a popular Arabic poet. As for his brother Asaad, he begot two sons who are married.

407

THE PRESENT FAMILIES OF BCHAALEH

Section 6

We have talked in detail in this book about Bchaaleh and the families who were born and raised there. It remains, now, to mention, in brief, the history of the existing families, whether old or new, family by family.

When mentioning the kinships, we will be limited to the names of the males unless the contrary is necessary. We are basing much of our information on material left to us by our relations and our praiseworthy professor, the late Father Estephan Shedid, may God have mercy upon him. He told of relationships of the families of his village up to the time he died, around 1930. We also used information provided by the knowledgeable, trustee Sheikhs of Bchaaleh, especially Youssef Tadros Saqr, known as Youssef Al Gar. He always tells genuine stories and he has a good memory. Plus, we also used the documents and information we preserve.

Before we get into that information, we will publish some documents relating to the history of the Bchaaleh families. Some of them were taken from the documents preserved by the late Anton Soliman Shedid left by his maternal grandfather, Rameh Tanous Nasr Shediak.

And it is thanks to his son, the author, Fouad Anton Shedid, because he is the one who kept that valuable material. From it, we can learn about the religious and social life in the past. Not to mention we can re-live and enjoy many interesting memories told in them. Others items were found in the congregation's Church.

The following are the names of the people who died in Bchaaleh, as it was noted in the margins attached to the books of Syriac prayers, the "Shahim Books" and the "Rishqaryan", both of them preserved in Mar Estaphan Church (Saint Stephen Church):

*"**Year 1789:** Anton Ibn Shedid, on April 15.*

* **Year 1795:** Father Abdulallah Geagea (or Al Geagea Al Shalfoun), on January 25, and, his son on February 8, and, Yaakoub Wahba on April 19 (mentioned in another reference) that Father Abdullah died on November 18, 1796.*

***Year 1797:** Moussa Mansour on October 1, Oum Youssef Soliman on September 25, Youssef Hanna on October 25, Dhiba (daughter of Youssef Soliman) on January 11, Henna (daughter of Bou Yazbak) in February, Mikhail Boutros from Kfifane in January, the wife of Girgis Hanna, Ghalia (daughter of Bou Rezk Gabour, the wife of Moussa Younes), Hanna the son of Al Shediak (the Subdeacon) Nasr Hanna on February 3, the wife of Anton Ibn Shedid, Nassar Barakat (the grandfather of the Nassar House).*

***Year 1798:** Youssef Hanna in January, Nasr Saqr.*

***Year 1800:** The mother of Younes (the son of Bou Shedid).*

409

Year 1801: *Moussa Wahba on February 1.*

Year 1806: *Boutros Al Hamsh on April 8, Youssef, the wife of Moussa Wahba on July 3, Girgis Al Gizini.*

Year 1807: *the wife of Rezk Al Khoury, Domt Al Soht on June 10 (He was a brave hero).* **Year 1822:** *Serkis Al Hamsh, Lahoud, Bou Yazbak..., Girgis Shedid (the father of the priest Estaphan I), Qoronfela (daughter of Anton Shedid), Tanous Bin Maroun from Bchaaleh who was killed at Lahfad Sheir on September 8, the farm boys transported him and burried him in Bchaaleh in 1822, also, Youssef Moussa Wahba and Tadros Qazah were killed at Lahfad Battle and Youssef Moussa Wahba so they transported them to Bchaaleh, Tanous Bou Mansour from Bchaaleh was killed in Al Yamouna in Baalbek on the 23rd of the month of ...and they took his head to the Beshri Well at Prince Beshir's (and the Prince was impressed for the killing of Tanous Bou Mansour because such a man had to be arrested).*

Year 1828: *The mother of Tarbia on June 14, Domt Al Baalbeki on June 15.*

Year 1830: *Daher (Perhaps he is the grandfather of the Areef House) on February 4, Father Youssef Mourad (from Tanoureen) on February 24, (Nasr Al Halal from Beskinta has two daughters: the wife of Youssef Qazah and the wife of Anton Wahba), Anton Bin Youssef Al Shediak (from the house of Deacon or Subdeacon Faysal originating from Aaqoura), Tanous son of Moussa Wahba on October 24, Elias Rezk on October 25.*

Year 1831: *Estephan Bou Mikhail (Maroun) on September 13, Father Tanious (Nasrallah Mehana Al 'Aqoury) on April 3 during the Great Feast, the wife of Aboud Bou Nasar on November 3, Ghalia the wife of Moussa Wahba on November 21.*

Year 1834: *Moussa son of Youssef Hanna on January 10.*

Year 1835: *Mosleh Al Zoghby on March 10 (He left only two daughters, one was the wife of Anton Wahba and the other one married in Asia).*

Year 1842: *Father Girgis Wahba on February 12.*

Year 1844: *Moussa Youssef Hanna in January.*

Year 1849: *Ghariba the wife of Moussa Wahba on January 30.*

- - - - -

"The register of the Mayor of Bchaaleh for the year 1237 Hegira (1821): Anton Youssef, Father Natanios, Rezk Wahba, Tanous Maroun, Estephan Bou Mikhail, Tanous Bou Manssour. Domt Mikhail. Nasr Hanna. Tanous bou Youssef. Rezk Al Waqf, Milan Nassar. Boutros Saqr, Gibarail Al Hamsh, Hanna Assaf, Eissa Bou Shedid, Barakat Bou Shedid, Aboud Bou Nasar, Eissa Wahba and his brother Hanna Wahba, (there is a blank space where there should be a woman's name)... and her brother Wahba, Moussa Wahba, the wife of Yaakoub, Hanna Moussa, Mikhail Bou Yazbak, Nasrallah Al Aaqrab, Nasar Youssef, Anton Boutros, Rezk Gabour and his brother Mikhail, the sons of Al Samrah, Katoul, Tanous Al Baalbeky, Mikhail Gibran, Mikhail Deeb, Aboud Meslem, the sons of Abou Daher: Three and a half and five silver coin (the total due is 733 piasters)".

- - - - -

Hereafter is the history of those families:

1. The Families Of Abi Rezk, Al Sheidak and Abi Marq

The family of Abi Rezk is a noble Maronite family. From the days when Maronites first existed in Bchaaleh, this family was there. Over the years they grew in number.

A good number of them still remain in the village today despite the events and catastophes they have faced. You already know what happened to the head of this family, Sheikh Abi Rezk Bachaalany, and his brother and sons. You know how they were granted glory and power in Tripoli and Bcharre Well. How their offspring have been separated and spread all over the country after their catastrophe in Tripoli. In particular, this applies to the Bachaalany family who lived in Salima in the Metn district. The remnants of this family have been in Bchaaleh and Salima for ages, and they are still there. Here are its three offshoot in Bchaaleh:

The Rezk Family.

The grandfather, Abou Rezk, begot Rezk and Nakhoul. Nakhoul begot Deeb and Hanna surnamed "Moqdous". Deeb had Tanous who begot Youssef, Nasr, and Deeb, while Hanna begot Estephan and Girgis who lived in the city of Tripoli. Estephan begot Hanna and Anton. Anton had Estephan and Hanna. As for Hanna Bin Estephan, he is in America with his children.

Rezk Bin Abi Rezk begot Youssef anf Gabour. Gabour had no children. Youssef Rezk begot Tanous, Risha, and Rezk (who died and had no children). Risha had Khalil and Youssef. Youssef begot Tanios, the expatriate. Khalil Bin Risha had Anis, Tanios (deceased), and Nabih.

The Shediak "Subdeacon" Family.

Hanna Bin Abi Rezk begot Subdeacon Nasr, and Girgis. Girgis had Tanous. Tanous had Nasr, Hanna, and Youssef. Youssef begot Tamer and Anton who was surnamed Al Zir and who dwelled with his family in Egypt. Tamer had Youssef, Anton, Soliman, and Girgis. Girgis begot Youssef and Estephan. Anton Tamer begot Tanious. While Hanna Bin Tanous had Tanous who had Molhem and Hanna. Molhem had Nasr and Domt. Hanna had Youssef and Massoud. As for Nasr Bin Tanous, he begot Tanous who had Nasr, Rameh, Mansour, and Khalil. Mansour had Tanous and Nasr. Rameh and Nasr are in America. And the Subdeacon Nasr begot Tanous who had Rameh, the father of Maania, the wife of Soliman Youssef.

About Tanous Shediak.

He was one of the country's famous people. He was an experienced knight and the Sheikh of Reconciliation in Bchaaleh. That information appeared in the list of the fiscal taxes which we previously mentioned when we showed the text relating to his vestiges.

Then, "Al Amia" happened. A revolt was started by a group of people against Prince Beshir the Great. They refused to pay the taxes he was obliged to impose on them. He had to raise money to meet the requirments of the tyrant, Ahmed Al Gazar and the people like him, the agents of the Ottoman empire.

The Prince sent an expedition to stop them. At that time, the people of Bchaaleh delegated Tanous Al Shediak to defend them and to participate in the negotiations between the citizens and the Government. They gave him their permission to do anything in relation to "Al Amia" that he thought proper, as is mentioned in the authorization contract which was among his preserved papers. The sheikhs said that Tanous Shediak had fallen down from a lofty height in the Lahfad Battle (1821). They said that he and his horse both fell but that, by a miracle, he landed safely.

"The reason for writing and editing this, is that we, whose names appear below, citizens of Bchaaleh, all of us, the old and the young, have completely accepted and have devoted ourselves and our matters, to whatever we are asked to do for the benefit of Al Amia in general and in part, to our compatriot, Tanous Al Shediak Nasr. He will have full authority over our costs and losses. And, when requested, we will be at his disposal, as long as it is to our benefit and the benefit of the public of Al Amia. And there will be neither opposition nor laziness from our side. Should anyone not perform as obligated, even acknowledging that we have the freedom to do so, all of us will utmostly stand against him. Therefore, this is what we agreed upon, and he will do what his conscience dictates and he won't discriminate between any parties. ...He won't delay our matters. And whatever he arranges for us we accept. ... dispute won't happened from our side nor from his about anything, no matter what it is. God is our witness.

If there is a loss, we all will bear it and divide it among ourselves. We will be like brothers of one soul, one interest, one word, and one aim. Whoever does not respect this, or who may humiliate us, or play the hypocrite, may God and Saint Elias be his enemy in life and after. We edit this act between us for our benefit .... Edited on August 15, in the Christian year 1821. Written by Youssef Al Shediak Mikhail from Bchaaleh. The Bchaaleh people in general have accepted it." (Copy of the preserved origin).

Their Vestiges

"It was written that we have sold to our brother, the subdeacon Nasr from Bchaaleh, the garden in Sama Al Darabla and Al Tawila as well as an olive terraced land beside the said land in Shlalah village. Ten reefs which we took from the sons of Geageaa (Hamada), the sheikhs, in Kafr Helda for the price of 997 piastres ... as per the assessor Youssef Eissy from Ahmag. The taxes are paid to the sheikhs, the sons of Geahgeah, only 25 piasters. The deal is done. Written and valid in 1199 (1784). Yazbak Kheirallah and his brother from Ghobali have accepted this. Witnessed by Rayess Mar Yohanna Doma Aftimious and Moussa Eissa, the son of the assessor, Father Abdulallah, the pastor of Bchaaleh. and Mansour Zakhya from Bchaaleh. Written by Subdeacon Soliman Al Khoury from Ahmaj ..."

- - - - -

"...We sold to our brother, subdeacon Nasr, our share of the olives, the mulberry, the vines, the land, water, fresh air and Al Ain Road for the price of ...170 piasters and a half ... and the tax and fees according to the place. The assessor of the olive trees is Nassar Barakat, the land and its annexes estimated by Rezk Al Khoury... in the year 1206 Hegira (1791). Accepted by Girgis Ibn Hanna from Bchaaleh. Written by Qablan from Tanoureen. The witnesses of the act are: Rezk Wahba, Nassar Youssef. Mansour Zakhia. And Maroun Youssef."

- - - - -

"This is true as the witnessing is valid and was legally implemented. The humble Germanous Tabet, the Bishop of Jbail and Batroun (Stamp).

- - - - -

"Tanous, the son of the seller, came, and, his paternal cousin, Tanous, the son of the buyer, and they asked for verification of the validity of the sale. We called on our son, Father Youssef Rashwan, and he testified that the act was written by him in his handwriting. ...Therefore, since then, we have proved the sale and that there were no liens or claims about it any more. Written on September 18, 1818. The humble Patriarch Youssef Tiyan. (stamp)"

- - - - -

"The reason for writing this is that we possess and we owe our paternal cousin, Tanous Shediak, the amount of twelve piasters. Its half would be six piasters which we take upon ourselves to pay from our money on the next crop season on the Feast of the Crucifixion. There will be no excuses. We wrote this legal act in our handwriting as a declaration and as a necessity. Acknowledged by Mikhail Abou Rezk on November 2, 1825. Written by Khairallah Khairallah from Bazaoun. Witnessed by Anton Shedid in the attendance of Father Youssef, the attendant of Bchaaleh."

- - - - -

"This is an estimation report of our share, which is half of the property that we are sharing with our nephew, the son of our brother: Our land in Al Karnish 250, in Al Mahrouma 150, in Al Zaeqa 150, ... vine supports 100, Apple Carriage 200, ...the mulberries and the pit of mulberry trees 150, the Valley of the citrus fruits 20, at the same place, six loads of mulberry leaves 600, ...Old Mulberry trees 100, Isaac's home 199, Mulberry square and vegetable garden in front of the cave 400, Small fig sun dryer 50, vines at an attic of the apple trees except a small water well that we endowed to our sister Henna 200, Olive trees 12, arrack 250, a home with a loft, vegetable garden and the surrounding area 400, houses in Sahyoun's vines and the mulberries beside the trellis and fields of mulberries in Al Marga 700, aliment (the furniture) of the house and the silk tools, boxes and vats, 6 porcelains, a wall and agriculture tools: colter 2, pickaxes 4, hatchets 2, scythe 3, The total 50, our equipment for tissue and gridles 300, two head of cow, a riding animal with his fellow 400. Copper: caldron and pans 2, frying pans and pail 60, thresher and wooden and utensils and grinding utensils in the house 50, beds 60, a field of land in Ain Al Fouqa Valley beside the property of the sons of Bou Soliman Shedid 47. The total 5987 piasters.

- - - - -

"It is correct, I, Anton, and I, Antonia, take out from the value of our share of the above mentioned revenue, for requiems when we die. I, Anton, authorize for my nephew (brother's son) the amount of fifteen hundred piasters for ten requiems every year. And we took off a quarter of the rest for our wife, as written above, for subsistence.

It is correct, I, Antonia, authorize for my nephew (brother's son) on my behalf, five hundred piasters, and endow my sister, Henna, after my death, one hundred piasters from the value of my share. The remaining amount, to be disposed as written above. ...Except for a third of my share, I, Anton, of the Karam Sahyoun House, ... Those I gave to my wife as her own properties, to release my conscience with her. The remaining of those properties we sold to our nephew, Tanous, son of our late brother, Moussa, a correct and legal sale ...at the price of 3300 piasters, of the lioned piasters and Sultanic exchange which are used in these days. We endowed that amount ... an irrefutable endowment .... And we relied on our nephew for our living, as long as we are alive, and for all we need to keep our body ... written on Sptember 15, 1838, and we accepted it by ourselves, we declare what was written, we: Anton, and his sister, children of Youssef Hanna in Bchaaleh. Witnesses: Tabiya Zakhya, Mikhail Al Ashy, Youssef Soliman, Moussa Wahba. In the attendance of our priests: Father Girgis and Father Maroun. Written by Youssef Al Shediak."

- - - - -

"Anton and his sister Antonia, the children of Youssef Hanna, came before us and recognized what is in the donation contract to the favour of their nephew, the son of their brother. They donated properties and crops to Tanous, the son of their brother, and the mentioned Tanous, will provide them with their necessities of clothing, provisions and all else that is necessary. The mentioned localities remain the property of Tanous, except the localities of the quarter share of the wife. That happened with the consent and acceptance of both parties. We are witness to this. The humble Bishop Samaan (Zouin), agent of the Patriarch. (stamp)."

413

The Abi Moroq House

Abou Yazbak Abdulallah Bin Abi Rezk begot Yazbak and Mikhail known as Abi Moroq. Yazbak had no children. Abou Moroq begot Tanous, Abdulallah, and Yazbak. Yazbak had Daoud, Eid, and Abdulallah and they are in Egypt. Abdulallah Abi Moroq had Elias, and Boutros who died young and unmarried.

Elias Abdullah had Nessim who died and had no children. What remained from the offshoot of Abdulallah Abi Moroq is only Nadhira (the wife of Said Anton Al Ashy), and Salma (the wife of a man from Akar, they are now at Montevidio). Tanous Bin Abi Moroq had Hanna, Abdullah, and Nakhla. Nakhla begot Francis who begot Adeed and Josef. Abdulallah died young and unmarried. Hanna begot Hafez, Mansour, and Fayez . Fayez had George. Mansour died young. Hafez had Selim. All of them are in Egypt.

About The Abi Moroq House.

Mikhail, the son of Tanous Abi Rezk was surnamed Abi Moroq because of an incident that happened to him with Prince Beshir the Great. Mikhail demonstrated a rare boldness.

He met the great governor of Lebanon and begged him, on behalf of the citizens of Bchaaleh, to order a cessation to the oppression they were enduring, to stop cutting down the trees of their forests. So, the Prince answered him with his famous saying: "Omroq", which means pass and go away. Then, Abou Moroq said: "To where, Sir? To Istambul? I don't have the money to go there. Above to the sky? I can't. So what should I do?" So, the prince repeated it, twice, three times, the same word. And Abou Moroq kept repeating the same answer, too. Finally, the prince calmed down and heard his complaint. Then he stop the oppression of his village.

Abou Moroq was known for his sound logic and good opinions. The people of his village went to him about their matters and took his sincere advise.

His grandson, Hanna, the son of Tanous Abi Moroq was a genius and emigrated around 1890 to Egypt where his talents flourished. He gained considerable wealth and fame due to his alertness, intelligence, and bravery. His son Hafez was a brave writer who studied at the Mar Youssef, the Maronite School in Cairo. His Arabic teacher at that time was Rashid Al Shartouni. His paternal cousin, Yassy Yazbak, was known for his intelligence and sense of humor.

Elias, the son of Abdulallah Abi Moroq, went to Egypt at that time and worked in the contracting field in the town of Menia. He came back home in 1900. His son Nessim, grew up in Bchaaleh where he completed his elementary grades in the re-opened school (1893–1898). When his father came back from Egypt, he traveled with him to Montevideo in Uruguay where his father died. Then, his mother and two sisters joined him. Nessim started to work as the Lebanese expatriates were doing. He reached a high intellectual position, something rarely accomplished by others, thanks to the gifts that God gave him, his intelligence, good manners, and pride. In addition to that, he had acquired knowledge in many areas, mastered the language of the country, and took part in the political, economic and social events.

He married a girl whose family was from Zahle but who was born in Uruguay. She was highly cultured, however, they had no sons, as God destined. Then, Nesim died before being 60 years old, and his two daughters were the remaining offshoot of Elias Abdulallah Abi Rezk Abi Moroq: Nadhira (the wife of Said Anton Al Ashy) and Salma (who married a young expatriate originating from 'Akkar).

The Abu Rezk Story

When we were in Bchaaleh teaching its youth, on the night preceeding the feast of Mar Domt, on August 17, 1894, a group of its students performed a play reliving the story of the murder of the great-grandfather, Abu Rezk Al Bachaalany. It is a poetic play composed by our poet Youssef Al Khoury Al Bachaalany.

The people of Bchaaleh, some in the audiences from Doma, some from the neighouring villages, and, some from Tripoli saw the play. The actors performed perfectly even though they were new to acting. The audience was so impressed. The most important performers were: our brother, Habib Bachaalany, who was living in Bchaaleh at that time, Nessim Elias Abdulallah Abou Moroq (both of them are Abu Rezk offspring), Risha Girgis Khoury Shedid, Hanoun (Father Hanna) Maroun, Youssef Soliman Geagea, Youssef Domt Barakat who played the role of Abu Rezk Bachaalany, the star of the story.

They also performed the play The Tiller written by Khalil Bakhous, as well as the story of Ester which they performed before Patriarch Howeik in 1897 when he was a bishop. And, they were perfect, especially Nadhira, the sister of Nessim Elias Abdulallah. She successfully played the role of the queen.

Those were some of the memories I have of my excellent students. I am proud of them and of their success in this country and in the lands to which they migrated.

2- The House of Maroun.

Their Origin And About Them.

The Maroun family is the oldest Maronite family that has lived in Bchaaleh. Many great priests have grown up from it, faithfully serving the Church. Just one of them that I personally know, Father Khairallah, was distinguished for his melodious voice. He died at the end of the last century. Today, among them, is the honourable Sheikh, the Archpriest Boulos Maroun who studied at the Mar Yohanna Maroun School in Kafrhay. He taught the Arabic and Syriac languges there, as well as theology for a long time. Then, he became the administrator of that school. Now he stays at his home in Bchaaleh .

His nephew, Father Youssef Maroun, has excelled. He took his advanced studies in Paris and was a teacher in many Lebanese institutions. Then he left for Egypt where his talents flourished. He wrote valuable books about the Arabic language, such as Al Ma'een which talks about the history of Arabic Literature and he took great care to include illustrated maps in which he gathered the names of the famous Arabian writers and their pictures. It was presented in a remarkable historic and artistic style which had never been done before. He is still teaching Arabic in Cairo schools and is considered of one of the famous genius' of this language and its writers.

We must also mention his brother, Professor Soliman Maroun, who studied sciences in Lebanon, Egypt, and Paris, receiving advanced degrees. He taught Mathematics in the Hekma Institute, and, Engineering in the Aintoura School. Today, he is working in contracting in Lebanon.

Among them, also, is Father Hanna Maroun, one of my old students in Bchaaleh. He completed his studies at the Kfarhay School. Also, there are Anton, Tanios, and Eid, the sons of Rameh Youssef Maroun. The first two worked in Commerce in Beirut and they bought estates and homes there. Their brother Eid lives in Bchaaleh and works in various jobs and, today, is the mayor of the village.

And from Abi Hanna, an offshoot of the Maroun House is Father Tanious, one of the students of the Mar Yohanna Maroun School. Also, Anton, son of Hanna Abi Hanna, who studied in that school and was the only child of his parents. His father was one of the village's distinguished men.

Anton, then, joined his children Josef, Elias, and Hanna for their schooling. Josef finished his studies in Aintoura and Beirut. After that, he emigrated with his family to Argentina where he is now in charge of the direction of Jean Mc Krazel Stores. He is one of our great Lebanese expatriates in the commercial and industrial fields. From that family, Hanna Youssef Abi Hanna, is one of the renowned expatriates of Bchaaleh and is in Los Angeles. He has done many favors for fellow expatriates. He was one of the founders of the Bachaalany Organization in 1918 and he has participated in the construction of the Maronite Church in Los Angeles where his son Badi' Hanna resides. Badi' Hanna is one of the supporters of that organization as well as one of the expatriate authors in that city.

Their Kinships.

Maroun begot Mikhail who had Father Hanna and Rezk. Rezk had no children. Father Hanna begot Mikhail and Rezk. Mikhail had Tanous, Maroun, and Youssef. Youssef had no chidlren. Tanous had Estephan and Mikhail. Mikhail had no children. Estephan begot Tanous and Father Tanous. Tanous begot girls and Father Maroun had Pastor Boutros, Father Maroun, and Risha. Risha begot Hanna and Tanous, the father of Risha who had Tanous.

As for Maroun Bin Mikhail, he had three sons: Tanous, Father Youssef, and Moussa. Moussa begot Tanous and he had four sons: Asaad, Ze'itar, Youssef, and Moussa. Moussa is the Archpriest Boulos. Asaad did not get married. Ze'itar had Tanous who had no children. As for Youssef, he begot Father Youssef, Anton, and Soliman. Anton had Youssef.

Concerning Father Youssef, the son of Maroun Bin Mikhail, he begot five sons: Father Hanna, Mikhail, Maroun, Tanous, and Soliman. Soliman had no children. Father Hanna begot Youssef (who died) and Soliman who had Girgis. Father Mikhail had Anton and Youssef. Youssef had Mikhail and Girgis. Anton Bin Mikahil had Youssef. And Maroun Al Khoury had Soliman who begot three sons: Youssef, Hanna, and Mansour. Meanwhile, Tanous, the son of Father Youssef Bin Maroun, begot Youssef who had Hanna, but he died, leaving only Barbara as the only one remaining of his offspring. Soliman Al Khoury Youssef had no children.

As for Anton, the son of Maroun Mikhail Al Khoury Hanna, he begot Youssef known as "Al Mir" and who had Anton and Rameh. Anton begot Youssef who died. Rameh had three sons: Anton, Tanious, and Eid. Anton had Youssef, Raymond, and Pierre. Tanious had Josef.

Tanous, the son of Maroun Mikhail Al Khoury Hanna begot Estephan and Hanna. Hanna had Moussa and Anton. Anton begot Hanna and Tanous. Tanous had no children.

Moussa had three sons: Anton (who had no children), Father Hanna Batoul, and Youssef who had four sons, all living in America: Moussa, Anton, Nessim, and Hanna.

Meanwhile, Estephan Bin Tanous begot Tanous who had Estephan (he died unmarried) and Khalil surnamed as Zaarour. Zaarour had two daughters.

Rezk Al Khoury Hanna Mikhail Maroun had Mikahil who begot Moussa and Domt who had Youssef and Rezk. Rezk is Father Khairallah and his children are: Mata, Daoud, Domt, and Anton. Anton had no children. Mata begot Anton and Youssef, both of them emigrated. Daoud had Youssef and Rezkallah, the expatriate who has a boy. Youssef had Rashid. Domt begot Anton who had two sons.

Youssef, the son of Domt Mikhail, begot Hanna who had Anton. Anton had: Josef, Elias, and Hanna. Josef had Anton, Elias had Youssef, and Hanna had Anton. While the children of Moussa, the son of Mikhail Rezk are: Hanna Anton, Mikhail, and Tanous. Tanous had Hanna and Youssef (surnamed "Dino") and had girls. Hanna begot Anton who died unmarried and Father Tanious.

Mikhail Bin Moussa had Moussa and Youssef. Youssef had Hanna and lived in Hamat. While Moussa begot Mikhail who had Johnny. And Anton Moussa had girls. Hanna, the son of Moussa Mikhail, begot Youssef, Anton, Moussa, Tanous, and Mikhail. Youssef had Anton and Hanna. Anton Hanna had Youssef, Caesar, Emil, and Alfred. Ceasar had four boys, and Hanna Youssef had Badie'. The brothers of Youssef, the son of Hanna Bin Moussa, had no children and died without any remaining offspring.

Youssef, the son of Tanous Al Khoury Youssef Maroun was brave and one of the generous members of this family. He was known for his courage and generous hospitality. He was one of the brilliant hunters of the Bchaaleh village.

3- Shedid House.

Their Origin.

The Shedid family is one of the noble Maronite families who has lived in Bchaaleh from long ago. From it grew up heros like Eissa Abi Shadid who was famous with his fights against the Matawela who were spreading corruption all over the country. Thus, the Maronites were revolting against them, trying to cut off their influence and expel them from the country. Other members of this family were people of knowledge and virtue, both priests and laymen. Some of them, in the past as well as in the present, were distinguished in the field of commerce and industry, both in Lebanon and in the lands to which they migrated.

Their Kinships.

Moussa Shedid Ebeid had six sons: Shedid, Anton, Eissa, Younes, Barakat, and Youssef. Youssef had no children. Shedid had Soliman, Girgis, and Youssef. Two of them died and Girgis remained. Girgis had Anton, Risha, and Youssef. Youssef had Soliman who had Anton, Ze'itar, and Rameh. Rameh had Soliman. This latter had Victor. As for Anton, he begot Fouad who had Anton and George. While Ze'itar died in Argentina and left Soliman, Farid, Edward, Anton, and Frederic. Youssef had Soliman and Estephan.

Concerning Anton Girgis Shedid, he had Elias, Daoud, Beshir, Youssef, and Risha. Risha became a priest with the name Father Estephan I and he had Girgis, Tanous, and Anton. Anton only had daughters: Shama, Maania, Jamila, Katoul, and Milada.

Girgis Al Khoury had Soliman, Risha, Tanous, and Estephan. Estephan begot Tanous, Girgis, Soliman, ... Soliman and Tanous died and Girgis remained. Risha had Anton. The children of Anton Girgis Shedid are Daoud, Beshir, and Youssef. They died young. Elias Anton begot Anton and Soliman who had Anton. And Anton Elias had Elias, Rashwan, and Estephan. The first two died leaving just Estephan surviving.

The Domt House.

As for Anton and Youssef, the sons of Moussa Shedid, they had no offspring. Eissa had Domt, Eissa, and Youssef. Eissa and Youssef died unmarried. Domt had five sons: Anton, Mikhail, Tanous, Hanna, and Khairallah. Khairallah begot Shaiban who had Khairallah and Raymond. Anton Domt had two daughters. Mikhail Domt begot Anton, Tanous, Nimatallah, and Hanna. Hanna had Estaphan and Anton. Anton Mikhail died in Los Angles unmarried.

417

Tanous had Mike and Nabih, while Nimatallah had Shamel and Mikhail. Tanous Domt begot Youssef, Domt, Habib, and Boutros. Boutros died young and unmarried. Habib had a son who died when he was a child.

The Younes House.

Younes, the son of Moussa Shedid had Moussa, Youssef, and Anton. Anton had no offspring. Moussa begot Anton and Gabour. Gabour had Anton and Tanous. Both died during the War in 1914. Anton, the son of Moussa Younes, begot Shedid, Moussa, and Eid.

Shedid died at War and Moussa had a daughter. Youssef Bin Younes begot Shedid who died young, and his sister Set El Beit remained. She married Father Estephan Shedid II.

Barakat Bin Moussa Shedid had Tanous and Badawy who had no offspring, while Tanous had Youssef and Badawy. This Badawy had Youssef and Tanous. This latter emigrated with his father to the Sudan. Youssef, the son of Tanous Barakat died unmarried.

About Them.

Father Estephan Shedid I was a notable and virtuous man. He was born at the end of the 18th century. According to the documents kept in his house, it is proven that the chiefs trusted his honesty and zeal, so they charged him to carry out the affairs of Bchaaleh and of other places. He was good looking, of tall stature, venerable, respectable, and beloved. He took care of enrolling his son Tanous in the Mar Yohanna Maroun School in Kfarhay. That school produced many priests known for their knowledge and apostolic zealouness. When Father Tanous finished his studies, he was ordained to the priesthood in 1870 and was named after his father, Father Estephan.

Father Estephan II was born around the year 1844. He was one of the schoolmates of Patriarch Elias Al Howeik in the Kfarhay School when Father Youssef Al Dess (the famous savant archbishop of Beirut) was in charge of teaching. Father Estephan was one of the brilliant students.

In our archives, there are certificates proving that he was awarded the first prizes in his studies in 1861, especialy in the Syriac language. He could speak and write in Syriac. He wrote poems showing how well versed he was in that language. He got married to Set El Beit, the daughter of Youssef Shedid, who was his kin. She was an only child after her brother, Shedid, died. Thus, she inherited a considerable estate.

Father Estephan took his father's place in the service of the congregation in Bchaaleh for about sixty years. His opinion was respected. He was noted for his holiness. So much so that his religious superiors often put him in charge of studying and resolving legal suits. He accomplished this perfectly due to his gifted eloquence, mental agility, quick thinking, and vast experience.

Like his father, he had some knowledge about traditional medicine that he acquired through practice. He felt obliged to do so because of the lack of doctors and the poverty of the people.

In general, the majority of the Bchaaleh people and the people of the neighbouring villages, would go to Father Estephan for help in dealing with their spiritual and temporal matters.

Thus, he was treating patients who has body pains and anguished souls. He was caring for the miserable and the oppressed. So it was that he became the lieutnant colonel and chief of his village people. In his personal life at home, he was hospitable and generous. May God have mercy upon him.

He used to tell stories of events and news in such a way that the audience was delighted to hear him. Droll stories and anecdotes were included in his speeches. He would tell of some of the memorable things that happened to him, and it would also show his unusual capability of reacting properly in critical situations.

He was fond of and brilliant in hunting. There were very few who could compete with him. He possessed the same brilliance in horse back riding. He was one of the best.

He was of tall stature, round face, olive complexion, and erect stature. He also had full and wide shoulders. He was a nice talker, robust, courageous and intrepid.

He showed great favor and kindness to the author of this historical book. It was the sort of favor a parent shows their own child. Through him, I learned Syriac and theology. Also, I lived at his house for five years (1893–1898) during which time I was treated as a son.

He attended my ordination ceremony in the Qarn Shahwan See. And, he attended my first Mass in Salima. And our kin, Youssoufeya Najl Andrea, the wife of Najl Bin Youssef, sent him an eloquent expression saying: "May God prolong your life, because you built us this monument". Then, he died around 1930. May god have mercy on him and grant him a generous reward in heaven.

To this family belongs Soliman Youssef Shedid who was well known and took care to educate his four sons. Anton Soliman studied at the Kafhay School then in the Hekma Institute where he studied advanced sciences, and then, Jurisprudence under Sheikh Youssef Assir. He was appointed to the Batroun Court as a Clerk, then took charge of the Endowment Department along with his father for a long time. He died in Beirut and was transported to Bchaaleh where he was buried in the Mar Estephan Church in 1914.

His brother, Ze'itar emigrated to Argentina and died there. His family stayed there. Rameh Soliman is one of Bchaaleh notables and intellectual people. Something to mention, is that Maania, the wife of Soliman Youssef, inherited from her father, Rameh Tanous Nasr Al Shediak, a significant estate which enriched her husband's wealth.

When reviewing the vestiges of the Shediak House, the value and importance of their properties are known.

The Domt House.

In treating of the offspring of the Shedid House, we mentioned Domt Eissa had five sons: Anton, Mikhail, Tanous, Hanna, and Khairallah. They were intellectuals and industrious. They were known for their sincerity and good behavior. They were famous in the construction field. The cupola on the roof of the Saint Estephan Church in their village of Bchaaleh is one of the evidences of their capabilities and accuracy. Some people told us that they constructed it like the cupola of the Church of Our Lady of Deliverance in Zahle. Then, their sons followed in their footsteps, so they, too, became successful through hard work. This was particularly true for the sons of Tanous Domt: Youssef, Domt (known as Antonio Domt), and Boutros. They were very successful in the place to which they migrated, namely, Los Angeles and Mexico.

The factory of Domt is still today, the greatest industrial factory in that capital. In Mexico, it was called "the King of Shoes".

Bchaaleh has the right to be proud of its pious youth. We are so proud of the Lebanese expatriates. And we should mention, with great sorrow, that this House has lost one of its main leaders, the recently deceased Boutros. He was a shining example of vitality, sincerity, and high ardor. He had just decided and was preparing to return back to Lebanon when he died suddenly, and still in his prime. Surely, he has joined his saintly mother who preceeded him in Heaven.

Bchaaleh And Youssef Beik Karam.

When talking about Bchaaleh, we failed to mention what we discussed in our Book <u>Lebanon and Youssef Beik Karam,</u> on pages 458-460, about what happened between "the hero of Lebanon" and the people of Bchaaleh in his revolution against Daoud Pasha, the Provincial Governor of lebanon. Karam was defending the people's rights.

To put it briefly, after the Battle of Itou in 1866, Youssef Beik started to travel all over the country and people were welcoming him. Until he arrived at the Mar Yaakoub Monastery situated between Doma and Bchaaleh. He was lodging at the nearby Al Hesn Fortress. From its highest part, he was looking over the whole town. Soldiers never dared to approach him because, behind him, there were three invincible fortresses: his dignity, Bchaaleh village, and its fortress!

Karam was calling Bchaaleh "Little Ehden". He liked its people because they were brave and courageous. Strong bonds of loyalty and kinship existed between them and him. Also, this was because the folks of the Al 'Ashy Sheikhs from the Bchaaleh families were the sons-in-law of the Karam House. Among his men, there were those who came from Bchaaleh, like Tanous Abou Elwan who witnessed the Al Hadath battle.

After the famous battle of Bansha'ie, the people of Bchaaleh sent an abundant supply of wheat, barley, butter, and honey with 15 young men, among them, Father Youssef Hanna Maroun known as Al Mesholah, Youssef Hanna Al Khoury Mehna, Youssef Al Shediak, Anton Gibrail Al Hany, Qablan Hanna Wahba, Mikhail Youssef Nakhoul, Risha Bou Haidar, Youssef Fares Ibrahim, Elias Nasef Al Helow, Al Badaway Barakat Shedid, Girgis Sarkis Wahba, Anton Hanna Maroun, Youssef Moussa Tarbeiyah, Boutros Soliman Wahba, and Domt Barakat Nasar.

When those men arrived at Kassba, they were attacked by 30 knights and 200 soldiers of Daoud Pasha. They arrested them and drove them to Tripoli. They sold their mules with the supplies on them. So, the famous hero, Boutros Toma, hurried with his men to rescue them. But couldn't reach them. However, two of them escaped and the rest were taken to a boat at sea. There, they were tortured to force them to admit their relation with Karam.

Then, Tanous Fares Abou Mansour, the Reconciliation Sheikh of Bchaaleh, and the famous Tanous Maroun of Bchaaleh went to ask for forgivness and to get them released. But they, too, were arrested and put with the others. They were accused of being spies for Youssef Beik Karam and his partisans. After that they were sent to Beit ed Dine.

4. The Abi Mansour House.

Their Origin And About Them.

One of the oldest families in Bchaaleh is the family of Abi Mansour. Intellectuals, geniuses, and distinguished men of merit have come from this family.

There are three offspring: the Abi Mansour House, the Abi Tarbeiyah House, and the Abi Haidar House. Tanous Abi Mansour was well known and was one of the high ranking people of the Batroun district. He was also one of the decision makers determining Lebanon's wealth and policy, especially during the era of Prince Beshir the Great. The Prince was opposed by a group of Bchaaleh people because of the heavy taxes. That revolution was known as "Al

Amia". It resulted in the Lahfed battle in which a number of previously mentioned Bchaaleh men were killed. They were Tanous Bin Maroun, Youssef Moussa Wahba, Tadros Qazah, and Tanious Abi Mansour. Tanous Abi Mansour was one of the revolution's leaders and a supporter of Al Amia. The Prince's men killed him on September 23, 1822, in Al Maymouna at Baalbek. They took his head to Prince Beshir who was at Beshri Well. The Prince was upset at that and said that he should not have been killed. It would have been enough to have arrested him and put him in prison. His body was taken to Bchaaleh and was buried like a hero and a nobleman of his country. He was buried as a defender of the rights of his people. His son Fares followed him in being a distinguished individual, then, so did his grandson, Tanous Fares. I was privileged to know him when I was in Bchaaleh. He was the Reconciliation Sheikh there and one of its generous renowned citizens. His son Mansour, was the first to emigrate from Bchaaleh to Brazil. He studied at the Kfarhay School, gained a broad education and was an intellectual man and author. Because of his knowledge and generosity, he was elected the President of the Maronite Organization in Rio De Janeiro, where he died at the end of the last century in the spring of life.

We also got acquainted with Fares Mansour who was known for being straightforward, pious, and of sound ethics. His brother, Girgis, emigrated to Montevideo, and his sons Alfredo, José, and Felix grew up in that capital. There they studied the new sciences. The government of Uruguay had appointed one of them, José, as its consul for one of its districts in 1946. He was known for his varied capabilities, especially for his knowledge of Spanish and Spanish literature. He had some important writings.

We became acquainted with Youssef Tanous Youssef Tarbeihyah, a sincere and honest man. For that reason he was chosen by the citizens to be the assessor of their properties. They trusted his conscience and experience. He died in 1946.

There are many other young people from this family, both here in Lebanon and in various other lands, who are known for their generosity and patriotism.

Their Kinship.

Abou Mansour Zakhia had Mansour, Tanous, Tarbiea, and Louis. Mansour Zakhia had no children. Tanous Abou Mansour had Fares and Habib. Habib died and had no children. Fares begot Mansour and Tanous. Tanous had Mansour and Habib who died with their father in Brazil and had not married. Mansour Fares had Fares and Girgis. Girgis had Alfred, José (the Consul), and Felix in Uruguay. Fares Mansour had Mansour, Tanous, Hanna, Abdulallah, and Mikhail.

As for Tarbeia Bou Mansour, he had Moussa, Tanous, and Youssef. Youssef had Tanous and he had Youssef who begot Anton (who died), Noaman, and Tanous. Moussa Tarbeia had Youssef and Tarbeia. Tarbeia had Tanous and Youssef. Youssef Bin Moussa had: Saada, the wife of Youssef Tadros (the neighbor), Sara, the wife of Youssef Wahba. Tanous Bin Moussa had De'ebess, Mansour, and Youssef. Youssef had Anton, the expatriate, with his children, Eid, and Tanous who had Fayez, Farid, and Anton. Mansour did not get married. De'ebess had Tanous, the expatriate who lives in Los Angeles with his children. Eid had Hanna. Youssef and Anton.

As for Louis Abou Mansour, surnamed Abi Haidar, he had Haidar and Latouf. Latouf had Youssef, Tanous, and Hanna. Hanna begot Youssef and Ragi with whom his offspring stopped.. Tanous Latouf was known as Al Zagheer and he had Shehada who had Estephan, Youssef, and Anton. Youssef was surnamed 'Aazrail and had no offspring.

Concering Haidar Abi Haidar, he begot Hanna, Moussa, and Nasr. Nasr had Tanous who had Mansour. This latter had Tanious who died young in 1940.

Hanna Abi Haidar had Youssef and Risha. Risha had Selim and Youssef who both emigrated to the Gokatana (in Cuba ?). While Youssef Bin Hanna begot Hanna who had the expatriate Fahim. Moussa Abi Haidar had Anton who had only Saada, the wife of Fadlallah Al Geageaa.

5. The Nasar House.

Their Origin And About Them.

It was said that they originated from Al 'Aaqoura, which we were not able to prove. What we do know is that they are one of the oldest families in Bchaaleh. The family flourished, and, from it, strong and healthy men grew up. The ones who emigrated from this family reached high social positions and high rank in commerce. A group of them were our students. We are very proud of their excellence and brilliance. This includes people like Rashid Anton Risha Nasar living in Los Angeles. He is one of the most important supporters of the Bachaalany's in that city. He is a man of good manners and ethics.

His brother Domt is one of the revolutionaries who is the headmaster of the University branch in that town. The children of his paternal uncle Tanous are Said, Anton , Risha and others.

Their Kinships.

Nasar begot Hanna, Abou Lahoud, Milan, and Girgis. Hanna Nasar surnamed "Al Alloush" begot Moussa and Risha. Risha had Anton and Tanous. Anton begot three sons: Rashid, Domt, and Beshara. Beshara had Anton, Youssef, Rashid, and Baie'.

Rashid Bin Anton went to Los Angeles and has five daughters: Annie, Badie, Marie, Engy, and Katherine. Domt had Rashid, Anton, and Fuad. While Tanous Bin Risha had Said, Anton, and Risha. Said had Tanous,…. While Anton had: Fayez, Tanous, Samir, Hamid, and Said. As for Moussa Al Alloush, he begot Hanna and Elias. Elias had Mikhail who had Estephan. Hanna had Anton who had Mariam, a nun in the Crucifix Monastery.

Concerning Abou Lahoud Aboud Nasar, he begot Barakat and Tanous. Tanous begot Nicholas. Nicholas had Amin, Tanous, and Soliman. Solimanis an emigramt in Uruguay and has a son. Amin had Soliman who had Nicholas and …. Tanous Nicholas begot Wadie' (who died unmarried). While Barakat Abi Lahoud begot Youssef, Hanna, Domt, and Lahoud (who died). Youssef Barakat had Tanous and Anton. Anton had Youssef who emigrated in Buenos Aires. Abdullah Tanous had no children. As for Hanna Barakat, he has Habib (Assa) who had Youssef. Youssef is an expatriate in Montevideo and had a son. Domt Barakat had Youssef and Mar'ei (who died young). Youssef had Nessim who lived in Beirut and had children among them, Barakat.

Concerning Milan Nasar, he had Tanous and Youssef known as Al Khawaja and who had Tanous. Tanous had Youssef and Anton. Anton had Mejid. Mejid had Tanous, Youssef, and ….

Youssef Bin Tanous begot Rashid who had Youssef and Fuad. While Tanous Milan had: Milan and Youssef (who died unmarried). Milan had Eskandar who had Henna, the wife of Elias Lahd.

Girgis Nasar begot Abou Khalil Anton who had Khalil and Zeitar who had Khalil, Said, and Seada (a nun of Al Wardia). Said is in Los Angeles. Khalil Ze'itar had Anton, while Khalil Abou Khalil had Anton who had Badie' and … in Los Angeles.

6. The Ashy House.

The Ashy House is a Maronite family raised in the plain of Safra, to the eastern side of Panias. A group of them are still to be found there today. The most famous one of this House is Sheikh Selim Al Ashy and his children. It was said that this family originated from Ehden and that there were still a good number of them remaining there. Some of them were the in-laws of the Karam House. Some of them are in Tripoli. Sheikh Mikhail is from Tripoli and went to Bchaaleh around the year 1800.

At the Bchaaleh Church, there is a book, in its margins was written "Mikhail Al Ashy bought the loft of Domt Mikhail Al Khoury on 1827". In Bchaaleh there are five houses of Mikhail's children: Elias, Boutros, Abdulallah, Sirkis, and Anton.

Elias died in 1886 and left Mikhail who had Neama, Elias, Girgis, Youssef, and Assad. Neama and Assad died young. Elias had no children and Girgis went to Ecuador where he had Mikhail, Josef, and Elias. Youssef begot Karam.

Boutros Al Ashy begot Asaad, Khalil (Father Mikhail), Habib, Eskandar, and Youssef. As for Asaad, he had Boutros. Habib had Khalil and Boulos. The three of them live in Montevideo. Khalil had Mikhail, Boulos, and Youssef. While Eskandar had Al Badawy (who died), Mikhail, and Lotfallah who had Estephan. Mikhail had Rashid, while Youssef Al Ashy begot Shehada who has had no children so far.

Concerning Abdulallah Ashy, he had Amin who didn't get married, and Berber who had Abdulallah.

Sirkis Ashy had Selim who had Shahin (living in Montevideo), Wahib (who died unmarried), and Youssef (who had Selim, Philip, and Tanious).

Anton Ashy's children are: Najib, Rashid, Said, Wadie', Nessim, and Girgis. Najib had Anton, Said, and Girgis. Rashid had Adeeb, Nazih, Anton, and Wadie' (who died young). Adeeb had Robert. Anton had Rashid. Said Bin Anton Ashy is in Montevideo and had children, but the only one we know of is Wadie'. Nessim is in Brazil and had children. One of them is called Nessimito.

About Them.

Father Mikhail Al Ashy studied the Sciences at the Mar Yohanna Maroun (Saint John Maron) School, then travelled to Brazil around the year of 1888. He met its Emperor Don Pedro II. After that he went to Mexico and returned back home. He died in 1911.

Amin Abdulallah Al Ashy studied at the same school and in Beirut. Then he emigrated to Havana, Cuba, and gained literary rank. He died unmarried.

Shehada Al Ashy reached a high position among the expatriates in Cordoba in Argentina. The sons of Anton Ashy were also famous in their country of emigration, thanks to their courage and bravery. One of them called Wadie' is educated. Sheikh Elias Bin Mikhail Ashy died in 1947. His death was a loss for the country because of his high ethical standards. He left no son to succeed him. However, his widow, Mrs. Hayfa Khazen, and his sister, Mrs. Minoush, the widow of Najib Neama Gharfin, were ladies with wisdom and virtue, and they preserved the dignity of that House.

7. The Wahba House.

Their Origin And About Them.

It was said that they are originally from Sabaal. A document mentions: *"Neama Ibn Farah from the village of Maad was ordained by the Metropolitan Aghnatious Sharabieh and was surnamed Wahba, for the village of Bchaaleh, in mid March, 1734."*

Thus, it is obvious that this priest is the grandfather of the Wahba House. The virtuous Father Youssef was among those of this House who were raised in Bchaaleh. The same is true for Soliman and Hanna, the sons of his brother. Soliman went to Egypt where he gave the Khediv one of his products, a water pipe "Narghila", to be smoked by three people at the same time. He liked it a lot.

In Beirut, at the square of the tower on the northern road to Sham (Syria), he built a hotel for people of the Mountain. He died unmarried.

Also, there was Soliman Anton Shediak. We were personally acquainted with him and his melodious voice. He was a collector of anecdotes. He came back from Egypt where he emigrated, and died in his village. His brother, Youssef Wahba and his children, Fayez, Anton, and Wadie are living with their children in Egypt and where they have achieved financial and intellectual status.

There were also other prominent people who belonged to Wahba House: Daoud Yaakoub and his brother, Abdulallah with his children: Father Louis Bachaalany, the Lebanese monk, and his brothers who have emigrated and those staying here. Also, Moussa Tanous Hanna Youssef Wahba and his children: Shoukry, Rezkallah, and Neama, and their paternal cousin, Father Mikhail.

Their Kinships.

Wahba had Yaakoub and Youssef. Yaakoub had no boys but had daughters. Youssef had six sons: Wahba, Moussa, Eissa, Father Girgis, Hanna, and Nakhoul (who died). Wahba had Anton and Samaan had only girls. Anton Wahba begot Wahba who had Anton, Youssef, and Daoud. Daoud emigrated with his brother Youssef to Montevideo. Anton, had five sons: Girgis, Wahba, Toma, Fares, and Saadallah.

As for Moussa Bin Youssef Wahba, he had Youssef and Soliman. Soliman begot Father Youssef, Aboud, and Boutros (who had no) children. And Aboud had Soliman and Hanna. Soliman didn't get married and Hanna had Soliman and Youssef who had Emil and … . Soliman had Shehada and Hanna.

Youssef, the son of Moussa Youssef Wahba had Hanna (who died) and Moussa who begot Nasef. Nasef had Moussa who begot Youssef (in America) and Nasef. This latter Nasef begot Moussa and Youssef.

As for Eissa Bin Youssef Wahba, he begot Wahba and Yaakoub. Yaakoub begot Daoud and Abdulallah. Abdulallah had Youssef and Aziz (in America), Fares (Pastor Louis, the Lebanese monk), and Tanious who begot Abdulallah and… . Concerning Daoud and Yaakoub, they had only girls: Bahga (the wife of Rameh Soliman), Saeda (the wife of Hanna Youssef Hanna), and Meroun (the wife of Youssef Anton Mehana).

Father Girgis had Serkis and Samaan. Samaan had Tanous, Boutros, and Youssef. Serkis begot Girgis who had Assaf and Serkis.

As for Hanna Bin Youssef Wahba, he begot Tanous, Anton, Qablan, and Domt (who died). Tanous begot Hanna and Moussa. Moussa had Shoukry, Rezkallah, and Neama. Shoukry is with his children in Montevideo. Hanna had Tanous, Khalil (Father Mikhail), and Youssef. Youssef had Jamil and Hanna. Tanous begot Hanna and Khairallah.

Concerning Anton, the son of Hanna Youssef Wahba, known Al Shediak, he had Soliman, Eskandar, Khalil, and Youssef who emigrated with his brothers to Egypt and had Fayez, Anton, Wadie', Wadie'a, Fayqa, Asma, Edward, Edmon, Anissa, Aida, and Anis.

Fayez begot three sons. Anton had Audette, Loris, Josef, and Liliane. Wadie' had Suzan, Diana, and Leila. Edward had Robert and Leila. Edmon begot Teraz.

As for Soliman Shediak, he begot Youssef, Khalil (who died), Said (who died), and Eskandar Shediak, an expatriate in the United States who had one boy and six girls.

Khalil Shediak died unmarried. Qablan Bin Hanna had Tanous and Rameh. Rameh had Said (in Baalbek) and Tanous who had Rameh and Khairallah.

Tanous Qablan begot Qablan, Domt, and Rameh (they died), and Qablan who went to Los Angeles. He has a big store there. His four children are with him there. They are married and have children of their own.

8. Abi 'Elwan House.

This is one of the old families in Bchaaleh. Their grandfather is Abou Youssef, surnamed Abi 'Elwan. He had Tanous who had Youssef, Moussa, and Estephan (who died). And Youssef had Tanous, Boutros, Moussa, Hanna, and Nohra. Nohra begot Youssef, Tanous and Girgis.

As for Youssef Nohra, he was one of Bchaaleh's distinguished intellectuals. He had Henry, Girgis, and …. His brothers, Tanous and Girgis, emigrated and had children. Hanna and Boutros are in America with their children. Moussa had Youssef and Selim. Youssef didn't get married and Selim had only two daughters. Some members of this family have emigrated to Uruguay and other places.

9. The Hany House.

They are originally from Ehden. A group of them left for Ghazir and Zouq el Mkayel and from them, some went on to Beirut. Among those who were famous are: Beshara Hany who were one of the Maronite famous rich people. He was famous for his generosity, his virtue, and his piety. Also, there is Rezk Youssef (the patriotic martyr), Najib and Anis, Habib and Jean. Some of them are in Batroun, Beskinta, and Ain Al Qabou. While those who lived in Bchaaleh are Boutros, known as Al Hamsh. He had Gibrail and Serkis (who has a daughter). Gibrail had Anton, Hanna, Moussa, and Girgis. Moussa had Eskandar and Youssef. Youssef had Wahid, Michel, Eskandar, Shafik, and … .

Eskandar Bin Moussa had the expatriate Elias. Concerning Girgis, we ignore his offspring. Anton Gibrail Hany was one of the intellectuals and men of ardor. With his intelligence and his generous ethics, he married Raheel Al Rezi, from one of the most important Maronite families who was the best of the intelligent and virtuous women. They begot Gibrail and Rofael who died young and unmarried. As for Gibrail Hany, he is one of Lebanon genius's. Hereafter is his biography, copied from a document written by Father Estephan Shedid. It was written as a testimony to himself, read on the day he married a French girl. It says:

"The Khawaja (the foreigner), Gibrail Al Hany was born of two Maronite parents in our village of Bchaaleh of Jibel Lebnan (Mount Lebanon) on October 20, 1862. On April 6, 1863, he was baptized by Father Anton, the pastor for the village of Qanat Village, with the permission of our priest, Estephan Shedid I, the pastor of Bchaaleh. His godfather was Asaad Boutros and his godmother was Sabat, the daughter of Father Estephan.

He was raised in Bchaaleh where he learned the rules of his religion, and both Arabic and Syriac. On October 1, 1872, he joined the Jesuit Fathers' School and stayed there in Ghazeer for two years. Then he spent five years in Beirut.

In May, 1880, he was appointed a French teacher for three years at the Mar Yohanna Maroun School in Kfarhay, and four years at the Aintoura School.

On Novemeber 1, 1886, he traveled to Marseilles. During all that time, he lived a Christian life, satisfying God, and praised by people. He continued performing his religious duties. From what we know, he was free from any ecclesiastic or civil bond.

Because a testimony is a religious virtue to be given when properly requested, so it is that we present our testimony here. This is a testimony to our son, Anton Al Hany, the father of Gibrail. It is given in May, 1888. Written by Father Estephan Shedid, Pastor of Bchaaleh (Stamp)."

This was confirmed by Sheikh Shedid Al 'Azar, the chief of the Batroun district.

Gibrail Hany got married and had only two daughters: Mary, the wife of a French man, and Rachel, the wife of our friend Pierre Shlalah. He travelled from France to Brazil, where he was appointed a translator for the French Ambassador in the capital. He stayed there for many years. Then, he came back to Lebanon with his family around the year 1910. He was appointed the translator of the Brazilian Counsul in Beirut. He held that position until he died.

Even in the short space we have, we must publish some of his pen's writings from the French, the language he mastered. There is a card which has a drawing on it, showing Patriarch Howeik, General Ghourou, and the logo's for France and Lebanon. The verses were written in his own hand:

> *Great Old Man, Lebanon, you have been a martyr for so long.*
> *Through your voice, you have made a call for an end to the suffering.*
> *Gouraud, the great Soldier, came on behalf of France.*
> *So our dearest wishes have been realised.*
> *September 1, 1920   G. A. Hani*

He also wrote an elegy for his grandson, the son of his daughter Rachel, "Edmond Pierre Shelala", (1932), entitled "An Angel Is Buried".

> *A charming Angel, wandering the earth.*
> *One day, he found his way to the skies.*
> *Without hesitation, he left father and mother,*
> *To join the quite enjoyable journey.*
> *Dear Mother, farewell, dry your tears.*
> *I am in the sky so cry no more for me.*
> *My days on earth were not as charming.*
> *I can care for you better from Heaven.*
> *Before I forget, take care of my sisters, my brothers.*
> *Teach them the virtues of honor.*
> *Without virtue, all is misery.*
> *Happiness is found in the virtue!*
> *If I passed near you like a dream,*
> *Don't keep it as a sad souvenir.*

Keep your sight always lifted towards God.
He is the only One Who can soothe your sorrows!

Behind the name of Edmond, this angel was hiding.
He lived on earth, so much among us.
But we sometimes found him strange,
His clear expression, so dreamy and so sweet!
                    --G. A. H

10. The Helow House.

Mikhail Al Helow, surnamed Dasher, had three sons: Nasef, Youssef, and Moussa. Nasef begot Heikal, Elias, and Al Helow. Al Helow had Youssef. Youssef had Daoud, Mikhail, and Nohra. Daoud had Beshara and Youssef who are immigrants. Mikhail had only Ranja who married Anton Areef, and Mariam who was the wife of Selim Hanna Al Shediak. Nohra begot Minoush (the wife of Yassy Yazbak), Saada (the wife of Beshara Daoud Al Helow), and Rowanda (the wife of Anton Gibrail Harb).

As for Heikal Bin Nasef, he begot Nakhla who died in America. And Elias Bin Nasef had Nasef who emigrated to America. Moussa Bin Mikhail begot Mikhail (who is unmarried) and Tanous who emigrated to Jokatana (Cuba?).

11. The Mehana House.

Nasrallah Mehana, originating from Al 'Aaqoura, had a son who became a priest and was named Father Tanious. Father Tanious begot: Youssef and Hanna. Youssef had three sons: Anton, Tanous, and Ze'itar. Anton begot Youssef who begot Anton. While Tanous had Selim (who died young) and two daughters who are the remnants of his off-spring. Ze'itar begot Anton who had no children and still alive. As for Hanna, the son of Father Tanious, he had Youssef (known as Al 'Akary) and Heikal. Heikal had the expatriate Hanna (who died in 1942). Al 'Akary died unmarried.

12. The House of Faysal Al Shediak.

They are originally from Al 'Aaqoura. They left for Bchaaleh around the year 1750 and were known in the past as the House of Faisal Al Shediak, then as the Shamas House. Today, they have gone back to their original surname. Their grandfather, Mikhail, had two sons, Youssef, and, Father Anton who was celebate and served the congregation of Tripoli where he died. Among his vestiges which I saw at the home of Hanna, the son of his brother Youssef, was a copy of the history of El Douaihy. It is a manuscript dating from the era of the writer. It was one of the copies which Professor Rashid Shartouni, the publisher of that history, relied on.

Youssef Mikhail Shediak begot Mikhail and Hanna. Hanna was known as Shamas (Deacon) and begot Youssef and Selim. Youssef had Anton who had Nimatallah, Domt, Saad, and Mikhail. Selim had Hanna and Tanious. Hanna Bin Selim had Tanious and Fayez. While Mikhail, the son of Youssef Mikhail, he is the grandfather of the House of the Subdeacon Abou Francis, and, he had Francis and Anton. Anton had Selim and his brothers, all of them are in Montevideo. Francis had Mikhail and Youssef. Youssef had Selim and … .

There was also the House of Anton which originated from Aaqoura. They lived in Bchaaleh but they are now extinct.

13. The Abi Barakat House.

Their grandfather is Rezk Wahba Raad, of Al Aaqoura origin. He had Tanous who was surnamed Abi Barakat. From the memories of the Patriarch Boulos Mosaad, it was mentioned that the children of Barakat Raad in Bchaaleh are the offspring of Fodoul, the son of Deacon Toma Al Aqoury. As for Tanous Abou Barakat, in Bchaaleh, he had Hanna who had Shehada and Boutros. Hanna Abou Barakat was known as a very religious person.

14. The House Of The Geagea Al Shalfoun

Their grandfather is Abdulallah Al Shalfoun who was ordained a priest of Bchaaleh. The people of Bchaaleh built a house for him next to the Church. They also allocated part of a public farm for him.

Father Abdulallah came to Bchaaleh from the village of Sahel Alma. Then his paternal cousin Anton, who escaped from there because of a murder, joined him.

The house of Al Shalfoun is one of the oldest Maronite families and it was said that they came from Dahr Safra to Lebanon. So, they lived in Ghousta and Sahel Alma and Beirut, where, from them, the House of the Arabs of Al Shalfoun were raised.

Father Abdulallah died around the year 1795 after tending to the congregation of Bchaaleh for a long time. He begot Domt who had Tanous. This latter begot Abdulallah who died with no offspring. While Anton, the paternal cousin of Father Abdulallah, was the husband of Raja, the daughter of the mentioned Father Abdulallah. And they had Soliman, Youssef, and Hanna. The two first died unmarried and Hanna, surnamed as Al Geagea, had Soliman, Anton, and Abdel Ahad.

Soliman was a talkative person, eloquent like his father Hanna, a valuable narrator with a charming feature showing his gifted intelligence and eloquence.

Soliman had two sons Hanna and Youssef who died in America, young and unmarried. While Hanna begot Tanious, Youssef, Soliman, and Rashid. Tanious had Hanna and Soliman had Albert and Josef. Rashid had Hanna and Raymond.

As for Anton, the son of Hanna Anton Al Shalfoun, he begot Soliman and Hanna (who died unmarried). Soliman had Anton who had Soliman.

Abdel Ahad had Anton, Al Shalfoun, Elias, Soliman, Hanna and Fadl Allah.

Anton Abdel Ahad had Abdel Ahad. Al Shalfoun had Abdel Ahad. Elias begot Anton and Etien. Anton Bin Elias died in World War II when he was hit by a bomb when he was in the train of Jounie with his father. Soliman Abdel Ahad had Shehada and Milad. Hana Abdel Ahad had Soliman and Shahid. Fadl Allah begot Anton, Abdou, Al Shalfoun and Habib.

This family was known by their liveliness, intelligence, and their approach to different industries. Tanious the son of Hanna Soliman Al Geagea was distinguished by their alertness, eloquence, and merging their speech with popular arabic poems which he inherited from his grandfather Soliman. He practiced it in the days when popular poetry had been revived.

15. The Areef House.

This family was known as Abi Daher Hanna, who had Daher (deceased) and Moussa who had Tanous. So, Tanous, the son of Moussa Hanna, was surnamed "Areef" (Sergeant) and he had Anton, Hanna, and Youssef. Hanna and Youssef Areef emigrated in 1888 to Uruguay and died abroad unmarried.

Members of that family were peace loving. They lived a satisfactory life from the past like all Lebanese. As the proverb says "Self sufficient farmer, has a hidden power". Their properties are the best properties in Bchaaleh because they are the most fertile and profitable. The wife of Areef, called Henna, the daughter of Father Estepahan Shedid I, was one of the virtuous women. Anton had Tanous and Youssef. Tanous had Anton, Hanna, and Youssef.

16. The Saqr House.

Their origins are from Bejje in Jbail. They moved to Bchaaleh around the year 1755 because of a paternal aunt who married Bazkhia Abi Mansour in Bchaaleh. The Saqr folks are from the old Maronite families in Jbail, and from others.

The members who emigrated to Bchaaleh were four brothers: Nasr, Boutros, Tadrous, and Girgis (who died unmarried). Boutros had only two daughters, and they both went back to Bejje. Nasr married a girl from Bejje and had Youssef and Hanna (who died unmarried). Youssef begot Anton who was a famous popular poet and had only Almas, the wife of Ze'itar Tanous Moussa Maroun.

As for Tadrous Saqr, he was killed at "Amia Lahfd" in 1822. He had Tanous who begot Youssef who gave us a huge amount of information about the kinships of the Bchaaleh families. Today, he is over 85 years old but still of sound mind and body, and, he has a strong memory. His children are: Tanous, Anton, Boutros, and Soliman. Tanous is in the United States and had Youssef. Anton had Youssef. Boutros had Tanous, Anton, Ze'itar, and Youssef. Soliman had Antoin.

In the past, they were known as the House of Saqr Al Bejjeni. They are surnamed the Qazah House (the house of the rainbow), the Nasr House (the name of one of their grandfathers), and the Tadros House, (from the name of their grandfather), and by mistake, the Al Jar (neighbour) House as per the surname of Tegar, the wife of Tadros.

17. The Chabtiney (Shabatini) House.

Around the year 1850, two young men from the village of Chabtine came to Bchaaleh. Their names were Tanous and Serkis, the sons of Youssef Rezk and the well known Saada family in Chabtine, Bejje, and other Lebanese villages. It is said that this family is of Ehden origin.

After a while, Tanous and Serkis got married in Bchaaleh and lived there. They had a third brother called Beshara who stayed in Chabtine. The only person remaining from his offspring today is one son called Youssef Beshara Rezk who emigrated to Egypt and had a son called Tawfik.

As for Tanous Rezk Chabtiney, he had Amin and Selim (who died young) in Bchaaleh. Amin had Tanous and Selim. Tanous Bin Amin had Youssef. Meanwhile, Serkis Chabtiney had Hanna and Youssef (who emigrated to Montevideo). Hanna had Tanious, Anton, Serkis, Youssef, Said, and Amin. The first four sons got married.

18. The Father Boutros House.

Originally, they are from Kfifane in Al Batroun. Their grandfather, Mikhail Boutros, came and lived in Bchaaleh. He died in 1797.

In Kfifane, his family was known as the Romanos family or Zahra family. It is said that their origins go back to Aaquora (review the Aaqoura history).

From the family of Mikhail Boutros came Father Boutros who was born in 1820 and died in 1893. He had paternal uncles who had no offspring. Father Boutros married Loulia, the sister of Monsignor Arsanios Moussa from Mehmarch, Batroun. They had Youssef who had Soliman, Elias, and Boutros. Soliman, the son of Father Youssef died unmarried in Jokatana in Havana. Elias was one of our students in Bchaaleh and was ordained a priest keeping his own name. He begot Victor, one of the Ain Waraka School students. As for Boutros, he begot Soliman, Youssef and … .

19. The House of Fares Ibrahim.

It is said that their origin is from Daraoun in Kisrawan. Their grandfather, Fares Ibrahim, came to Bchaaleh around the year 1800. He joined the service of Tanous Nasr Shediak. He married a girl from the 'Aqrab Family and has been surnamed with their family name. Thus, Fares 'Aqrab begot Ibrahim who had Fares. This Fares had Youssef and Ibrahim. Ibrahim had Jean and Abdulallah. Abdulallah emigrated to Montevideo.

20. The Dagher House.

They are originally from Tannourine in the North of the Batroun town. There, the family of Dagher raised their offspring and they spread all over the villages of Lebanese.

Monsignor Youssef Dagher wrote the history of his family in his printed book Lebanon, General Views On Its History, Vestiges and Families. It is based on a manuscript containing the origins of Tannourine families.

The most we can say about this information is that most of it is not based on a document or a trusted narration. The Dagher folks are like the other families who come from ancient Maronite families. All the stories about their arrival in Lebanon is based on unsubstantiated tales and oral traditions.

The Dagher folks emigrated from Tannourine to Bchaaleh around the year 1930 when Hanna Dagher got married to the daughter of Youssef Ashy from Bchaaleh. His brother, Monsignor Youssef, bought properties in that village and lived there. Hanna begot two educated sons: Emil and Anton.

ANNEX

In the early part of the book, we talked about Sheikh Younes Bachaalany and his brother, Sheikh Abou Youssef. We also saw what the French traveler, De La Roque, wrote about them. We showed what we found in the archives of the French Government, the writings of Patriarch Estephan El Douaihy, and the Arabic translation of what the two Jesuit priests, Fathers Ghodar and Rabat, wrote about it.

At this point, we would like to present the text of some of the original documents we used as sources. We think some readers will find it interesting to read the material on their own, and, perhaps, more importantly, we want to preserve these prescious vestiges and treasures. Some of them are rarely found, like the book of De La Roque, and others, like the documents from the French Archives are difficult to access.

(Editor's Note: Today some of these rare books can be found, for free, in their entirety, on Google Books. It is also rather easy, in thie modern high tech era, to be able to translate foreign languages, again, with free services like Google Translate. What wonderful research Father Stephen Bachaalany could have conducted with all of the resources of the internet, not to mention all of the advances of DNA research! Fortunately for us, Father's distant relatives, he has laid a firm foundation for us to build on.)

The following, then, is the original text of those treasures:

The History Of Prince Younes, The Maronite

He died for the sake of his religion during this time.

From : <u>A Journey In Syria</u> by De La Roque.

Paris, André, Cailleau. 1722, Volume II, Page 263

"Prince Younes was raised in a family that was well known throughout the whole Mount Lebanon area (Jibel Lebnan). He is the next of kin and ally of the Prince and Chief of the Maronite governorate. He was the owner of several good pieces of land, on the slope of Mount Lebanon, as well as in the suburbs of Tripoli and Jbail. From them, he was collecting an income of approximately a hundred thousand Liras.

In addition, Younes had a good personality, an easy going spirit, ingratiating, and he had various outstanding talents in handling the business affairs of the nobles. And because his qualifications were joined to a sense of caution, he was held in high esteem by the ministries of the Sublime Porte. Many Pashas in Syria charged him with the most important jobs relating to their governments. So much so, that, slowly, he practically became equal in power to the governors.

Wealth made the people around him envious. Some general officials, some significant Turks, and even people in his own ministry joined together to get rid of him.

To that end, they used the miserly and cruel man, Kablan Ibn Al Matargi. He was a new pasha of Tripoli, from Syria, a rich man who was born in the same country (Latakia). Before him, they presented several acusations against Younes, especially pertaining to his properties and some new acquisitions.

The Pasha lent them a sympathetic ear. He started things off by giving the order to arrest Prince Younes. But not just Younes, also arrested were Prince Josef, his brother, the women, the children of all ages and sexes of the two families, and, even many of their relatives and acquaintances. More than fifty people were put in jail.

Then, they told poor Prince Younes that his case was a critical matter for him and his entire family. The said that the only thing he could do to save himself from a cruel and humiliating death was to deny his Christianity and become a Muslim.

At first, Prince Younes resisted them as a Prince and a true Christian. He resisted the threats and all the plots arranged to sway him to their side. But his family was most important to him. They took priority. He was afraid of what might happen to his family if they changed their religion, especially if he should die first. But then he thought of a temporary but dangerous solution that would allow them all to escape.

The solution was simple. He decided to declare that he would become a Muslim, but only on condition that his family be allowed to remain Christian. The Pasha did not want to lose such a valuable administrator as Younes, and could see no problems if he accepted Younes' offer. Younes, then, pretended to become a Muslim. The Pasha was fooled by Younes' exterior display of being a Muslim and he freed the family as agreed.

Younes said that he condemned this plot from the moment the idea came to him because it was unlawful. But he remarked that it was also praiseworthy, in some ways, because by doing this, he could save several souls from falling to the Muslims. Also, by doing this, he could avoid having his daughters and neices married off to some rich Turkish Lords.

Younes remained there at the court of the Pasha, for another forty days to make certain that his deception was working. Then he implemented his real plan. He sent his wife, his children, and his whole family, to the high mountains of Kisrawan, a safe haven. Then, after the forty days, he joined them.

The first thing Younes did was to go to the Patriarch of the Maronites. He wept bitterly at his feet and confessed his weakness. He loudly declared that he has never been anything other than a Christian. He renewed his profession of Christianity. With humility he accepted the penance imposed on him. He was absolved and reconciled with the church by the Patriarch. It was an impressive scene. All of Mount Lebanon was full of edification.

After having fulfilled his religion obligations, Younes felt he had to explain himself to the people. He appealed everything that the Pasha of Tripoli had done to him. Furthermore, he appealed the accusations that had been brought against him and related how violently he had been treated. He had considerable influence with some of the ministers so he was able to get his case brought before the Grand-Seigneur.

The Pasha sent arguments to defend himself and to call upon friends for support. However, because the case has been reported to the Divan, the Grand Seigneur realised that a matter of religion and doctrine was involved. Accordingly, he assigned the final decision to the Grand Mufti of Constantinople.

The Mufti thoroughly examined the case and his judgment was solemn, and, in favour of Prince Younes. He declared that his profession to become a Muslim was null and void because it was the result of violence inflicted on him by the Pasha of Tripoli. The Mufti has prohibited the use of violence in such matters in the future.

Many people were astonished at the judgment, but the most enlightened people were expecting that the Ottoman court would remember his services and the favours of Younes once they saw who he was.

Still, the Prince was not completely satisfied. He felt such a deep and secret pain because of the shame he had caused to the Christians of such a large city.

His feelings compeled him to go to Tripoli. One day, in the presence of the Pasha and his entire court, Younes loudly confessed his faith. Then, he did the same thing throughout the village, with unexpected boldness. People were astonished.

The Turks had to disguise what he was doing, even if it was a delicate procedure. Younes was so happy. He was even called by the new Pasha, who had taken charge a little while later. This new Pasha called him to manage his main affairs. He put into his hands the administration of the whole Tripoli countryside. It was an area so large and diverse that it was not completely safe. Younes held an order from the Pasha from Tripoli which strengthened and enforced the ruling of the Mufti. Younes and his whole family was allowed to practice their religion with specific orders not to be hindered or disturbed in the future.

For five years, Younes lived in peace with his whole family in Tripoli. He carried out his governmental functions with great honor and fidelity. However, at the end of that period, which was at the beginning of the year 1695, the Pasha of Tripoli was changed. The friends of Younes who had worked for the Subleme Porte died or were dismissed. Therefore, Younes' enemies took that opportunity to eliminate him permanently. Before the new Pasha, they again accused him of many crimes. They accused him of having insulted and offended their Muslim religion. Therefore the first thing that the Pasha did was to put him in irons. Then, for more than two years, in prison, he was subject to threats, torture, plots and deceits, all designed to weaken the Prince's religious faith. They promised him that he would be able to keep his properties and would be able to continue his rule over the Province, and even that he would be the successor of the General Government in Tripoli.

Younes remained firm and unmoved. His speeches showed so much Chistianity and were so impressive. He even testified that this last persecution was a gift from the Lord to clear his first fault. He said that he would pay with his blood and shed his life in the defence of the real religion.

The Pasha even went in person to ask Younes to reconsider. But Younes answered that he was not willing to exchange "the precious stone of the Christian Faith for the stinking filth of the faith of Mohammed". Infuriated by this statement as a horrible blasphemy, the Pasha tore his robe (an ancient oriental custom). He called Younes an unfaithful dog and condemned him to be impaled on the field.

During the era of the Ottoman Empire, the province's governors had the power to kill or not to kill people of the Grand Seigneur. Their irrevocable judgment was immidiately applicable. However, the Pasha made two other attempts to save Younes. In the first one, he sent his friends to try to convince him to change his mind. But it was in vain. It only strengthened his refusal. Finally, he was taken out of prison, a pale face on his shoulders. He was followed by a huge crowd who were hurling insults at him. He walked across the whole village like that. He was driven to a hill in the neighbourhood. There he would meet his punishment, his death.

For the last time the Pasha sent someone with a proposal for him. He could remain alive, get back his properties, and return to his family. The Pasha did his utmost to get him out of that fateful situation, but, all his efforts were in vain. Younes said loudly, as a christian hero, and repeated over and over again: "I put myself into the hands of God. He will take care of my family and my properties." By constantly resisting with all the strength at his disposal, with his great Christian faith, he suffered the harshest punishments. In front of the whole village, a huge crowd gathered from many places in the neighborhood to see that scene. Some were regretting it, others were scoffing. Some were complaining about it, all were admiring him. From the time that they started to lift that pointed wooden stake, until the last second of his life, he never stopped to thank God. He was continually glorifying and praying to the Lord. He had recourse to the Holy Virgin and the Saints. He repeated his profession of faith and he died after many acts of love and contrition. He died the death of a martyr in May, 1697.

His body remained impaled for five days. Two companies of soldiers were stationed there because they were afraid that the Maronites would take his body. Trusted witnesses have testified under oath, that on the first night of the execution, a fiery crown appeared over his head. It so frightened the guards that they ran away. Then, rumors spread that it was hell fire which came to burn that apostate of the Muslim faith. Because of that, some of the resident Turks explained to the Pasha the inconviniences of leaving the body any longer. They said, too, that it might incite the people to revolt. Accordingly, the Pasha allowed one of Prince Younes' cousins to take the body. He put the body in a well near the Maronite cemetery. Two days later he transported it, secretly, to a sepulcher located directly behind the tribune of the Saint John's Church in Tripoli.

It was astonishing and unreal, but the body of the Prince remained smooth and fresh, even after eight days. And, there was no bad smell.

After the death of Prince Younes, it was the turn of his brother, Prince Youssef, to suffer persecution. He, too, would have been killed but for the intercession of his friends. They convinced the Pasha to spare of the lives of the Prince, his family, and his brother's family if they turned over all of their remaining properties.

After escaping, that poor Prince travelled all over Europe stirring the compassion of the Christian rulers to his favor. I met him in Paris a few months ago. He had the look of a modest man resigned to his circumstances.

The King was very kind to him and recommended him to his ambassador in Constantinople and to the chancellors of the Levant (Eastern Mediterranean countries). Moreover, His Majesty gave him an honor by writing to the Patriarch of the Maronites concerning that subject. It was a letter expressing kindness and words of comfort.

It was from Prince Youssef that I learned the details of the life and death of his brother, Prince Younes. From that information, I wrote this short account. It also came from the text of various documents including the letters that the Maronite Patriarch wrote to the Pope and the King about these events. They were signed by all the bishops of Mount Lebanon, the Proces-verbale of the French Consul in Syria (which was his testimony in Tripoli), as well as by distinguished, religious French and Spanish men from the Holy Land."

The British Minister, Henry Maundrell, who printed the events of his journey from the Alps to Jerusalem, said that on May 8, 1697, the Consul of England drove him to visit the castle of Tripoli, where the poor Younes was a prisoner. He was there because he had embraced the doctrine of Mohammed and then repented.

Hereafter, we reproduce the exact text written by Maudrelle:

"Saturday, May 8. After Dinner: The Consul Hastings drove us to see the Castle of Tripoli. It is greatly situated on a Mountain that overlooks the whole village. When we were there, there was a poor Maronite Christian prisoner called Younes. That man had in the past apostatized. He had embraced the religion of Mohammed. But he repented in his later days and was condemned to death because of that. He was impaled two days after our departure, by the order of the Pasha of Tripoli. That was the punishment of the Turks. It was the way they punished those found guilty of the most serious crimes. It was certainly the most odiouis and barbarous sort of punishment done by humans. The execution happened as follows. They take a log as thick as a leg and about eight or nine feet long.

Its end is very well sharpened. They oblige the poor criminal to hold it on his back and walk with it up to the place of execution. This is how the Romans treated their criminals with their crucifix. Once they arrived at the final place, they drive that log into the backside of that miserable person and with harshness, they pull the legs until the log appears from the shoulders. Then they dig a hole in the ground to insert the log. The poor criminal remains alive on that stand. The executioners and witnesses are at ease. They smoke, drink, and talk in good humor. Some of them live for twenty four hours, suffering that horrible misery. Sometimes it happens that after one or two hours, living in such a pitiful and disgraceful position, they permit one of the audience to be kind. They let them pierce his heart to terminate his miserable life".

(Henry Maundrell, <u>Journey From The Alps to Jerusalem</u>, on Easter in the Year 1697. Transalted from English, Printed in the Year M. D . CCV. Autrech).

- - - - -

D . O . M

(The portion below was originally in Latin.)

STEPHANUS PERTUS,

The Humble Patriarch of Antioch.

These words are for those who would like to read or listen to our wishes of good health and God's blessings.

We inform you that our favorite son, Abu Yusef Rezk, is an Orthodox believer, a citizen of the city of Maronites, our subject, and of our highest estate. That Shcikh Younes, who was expelled by force and tyranny by the Ottomans, had to violate his own will and deny his faith in word to free his little sons. With the help of the true God, he escaped after about the fourtieth day. He brought away his sons at night, and ran to the Kisrawan district, where he confessed his guilt and accepted his punishment. He did so of his own accord, laid upon himself, from all his heart. He managed the documents for his appeal to the Great Leader of the Ottomans himself. The decision was successful. In a decision that was favorable to him, the court declared his renunciation of faith as being invalid because it was forcibly wrung out of him. He then went to Tripolis (Three Cities) and openly proclaimed his Christian faith. After five years, those in power seized him, imprisoned and mocked him. They killed him by impaling him. During this method of torment he still courageously confessed his faith in the Lord Jesus. For this same reason, his brother Rezk, was caught and put in jail. He suffered, losing a large amount of money. He sold all the good furnishings and household items, including the house itself.   But with all that, he would still not be able to lead the same normal life. He could not support his family which includes his sons and the sons of his brother Younes, ten and five in number. Having no means of making a living or paying their many debts, each of them pleaded with us often, and in a very humble manner. They asked that we compose a letter to inform readers that Sheikh Rezk is a father and an uncle, in his father's line, to the above mentioned children. We do hope that in your sincere love for the Lord Jesus and his purest Mother, that you may also feel compassion and kindness toward his sons and the sons of his brother.   In doing so, I am sure you will deservedly obtain great mercy from God.   Great was the glory and praise to the One Who in His Holy Gospel said and promised: "What you do to these, the little ones, you do, also, to Me."   Both you and we strive diligently for the Greatest, Most Worthy God, knowing that the goodness done will return a hundredfold in this time and in the coming ages of eternal life.

Given in Qannubin, at our residence, on October 5, 1699, from the Incarnation of the Word."

The names of the Bishops followed.

- - - - -

"August 10, 1701. in Marly

Mr. De Fériol

The sheikh Abou Youssef Rezk, the Roman Catholic Maronite, said that his brother, the Sheikh Younes and himself were of the notables of the town, property holders and Catholic. He said that they have always been so, and this caused jealousy and hatred from the Turks. His brother was a victim of their revenge, being impaled, while he had to escape to save his life, the lives of his children and those of his brother, who are 13 (or 14?). After having checked his properties, he found that they had been plundered and confiscated. The Patriarch of Antioch assures us that all that he says is true. He also recommends him to be under my protection. Confirming that he is one of the country's leading people, it would be necessary and useful for the Catholic religion if he were to be once again restored after that collapse. I am writing this letter to you, asking you to help him with your care and your divine services in all the forthcoming occasions. I ask you to provide him with the exact and reasonable things that he might request and to see that he endures no more troubles in the future about his religion. Thus…"

- - - - -

"August 7, 1701. A receipt for 300 lira, the extraordinary gratification for the Sheikh Abou Youssef Rezk, the Roman Catholic Maronite"

- - - - -

"August 7, 1701.   In Versailles.

(Keep) Pay cash to the Sheikh Abou Youssef, the Roman Catholic Maronite, the amount of 300, three hundred pounds, which I ordered by extraordinary gratification."

- - - - -

"August 20, 1701. To the attention of M. de Férriole, to the favor of Sheikh Abou Youssef, the Roman Catholic Maronite."

"August 20, 1701.   In Marly.

Sir: In the attached letter of the King, you will know of the intentions of his majesty about the persecution that the Sheikh Abou Youssef has suffered. I just wanted to add that, if we want to do something for him in the East, on the occasion of his travel, do so as a compensation for what he did for this country. You must use your care and divine services to help him as much as you can. The passport of this sheikh is an ordinary one and is 138…"

- - - - -

A List Of The Attached Pictures

There are many pictures of people and places in our archives. Because of the cost and other reasons, we simply could not publish them. However, we found that we could publish what we could fit into the following pages attached to the book. The following is a list of the pictures. We have inserted three dots (…) in the places of the people we didn't know.

Picture 1: 1. Bchaaleh. 1928, painted by Badie' Hanna Bchaaleh. 2. Salima. 3. The Castles of the Princes after it became a school, painted by Felix Fares, 1916.

Picture 2: 1. The castles of the Lam' Princes in the past, 1861, painted by Bonfis. 2. Prince Haidar Abi Al Lam', the Prince of Salima and the Governor of the Christians of Lebanon.

Picture 3: The students outside of the Capuchin Fathers' school, standing beside their monastery, in Salima, 1881. (appearing from right to left, first row up): Ibrahim Shiban; Mansour Girgis Kassab; Nejm Melhem; Rashid Fares Khatar Maroun; Abdulallah Maroun; Abdou Kassab; Shaker Hanna Khatar; Habib Shiban; Moussa Bou Assly. (Second Row) Youssef Habib Al Hanoud; Shahin Girgis Shahin; Ibrahim Zein; Youssef Asaad Sabra; Youssef Girgis Anton; Assaf Girgis Saad; Daoud Boutros Shahin. (Third Row) Hatem Girgis Hatem; Anton Abdel Hay; Shokry Anton; Hanna Al Zaghloul; Youssef Shahin Ghaleb; Hanna Boutros Wakim; Aboud Asaad Aboud; Mansour Hanna Tanious; Nichola Al Haddad; Maroun Fares Ghatas. (Fourth row) Nejm Assaf; Anton Girgis Abdou; Girgis Youssef Nasef; (…); Elias Girgis Saad; Zein Girgis Zein; Mansour Hanna Daham: (...); (...); Girgis Hanna Mansour; Elias Al Hanoud; Moussa Hanna Moussa; Youssef Al Khoury Hanna; Youssef Melhem Nahra; (Fifth row) Amin Girgis Al Mazmouk; Rashid Ghaleb; Wakim Youssef Wakim; (...); (…); Youssef Abdou Freha (the author); Assaf Hanna Girgis Al Khoury; Daoud Bou Heriz; Mansour Daher; (...); Abdou Girgis Asaad; (Sixth Row) (…); Melhem Ibrahim Mar'ei; Shaker Mikhail Asaad; Ibrahim Rabib Al Khoury; Boutros Rashed (Rashid); Asaad Abdou; Youssef Al Zaghloul; Elias Al Zaghloul; Nasef Wakim; (…); The headmaster, the teachers, and some people from Salima: right (sitting) The Capuchin Father Andraos Lawensa, the Headmaster of Mar Boutros Monastery. Father Hanna Bachaalany; Sabra (Father Youssef); Asaad Sabra; Father Boutros Bachaalany; Girgis Zein; Anton Fares; Melhem Nahra; Anton Wakim; Youssef Wakim; Asaad Samaan Al Mazmouk.

Picture 4: The teachers and students of School of Our Lady of Lourdes, in Salima, during the Presidency of Father Anton Al Asmar (1906). Picture by Ghatas Fares Salima. (First Upper Row) Nasry Hanna Anton; Ibrahim Guargora; Moussa Sahyoun; Girgis Hanna Khatar; Amin Hanna Mansour; Tawfik Bou Do; Asaad Azar; Habib Fares Ghatas; Melhem Ibrahim Bashwar; Mikhail Elias Shebli; Selim Daoud Al Asmar; Bou Hatem Hamana; S'eid El Nagar; Shokry El Baaqaliny. (Second Row) Nejm Teama; (...); Na'eim Khoury Baaqaliny; Soliman Nichola Al Asmar; Nessib Abou Shaqra; Soliman Heriz; Nekhla El Tafkajy; Gibrail El Jermani; Tanious Daoud; Anton Boutros Al Asmar; (…); (…); Youssef Ghazal; Wadie' Ahmed Al Awar. (Third row) (…); (…); Noaman Abou Shaqra; (…); Elia Abou Radi; Jemeyel Noweihed; (…); (...); Soliman Daoud; Elias Bou Hatem; Hussein Al Masry; Qassem Asaad Shebli; Rashid Shequir; Shahin Mohamed Masry; Najib Wakim; Nader Beshara Nader; (…). (Fourth Row) Najib Mohamed Sabra; Mourad Fares Zein (…); Mohamed S'eid Bou Ali; Tawfik Girgis Tanous; Farid Laoun Khoury; Najib Asmar; Samaan Bou Farah; Boutros Nahra; Nimatallah Al Khoury; Jemeyel Salha; George Bachaalany; Tanious Al Asmar. (Fifth Row – the teachers) Tamer Al Asmar; Asaad Baaqaliny; Youssef Shahin Ghaleb; Father Youssef Khoury Bazbadeen; Father Anton Asmar; Father Youssef El Hayek; Youssef Al Khoury Al Bachaalany; Hamad Heriz. (Sixth Row) Anis Bou Hatem; Fouad Laoun Khoury; Samaan Elias Shebli; Elias Daoud Khoury; Jemeyel Shiban.

Picture 5: A community residing in Oliveira, Brazil, its majority being from Salima. Around the year 1900: (from the right up, First Row) Daoud Boutros Younes; Rashid Naser Eddine S'eid; Youssef Bou Assly; Selim Wakim; Assaf Hatem; Ayoub Kanaan Bermana; (…); Mikhail Al Zaghloul; Nejm Daher Andrea; Shaker Samaan.

(Second Row) Youssef Al Zaghloul; Moussa Mikhail Abdou; Rashid Al Zaghloul; Khalil Nasef Al Haddad; Girgis Freha Ras Al Metn; Halim Freha; Rashid Abdou Arsoun; Hassan S'eid; Assad Girgis Maroun; Mansour Hanna Ghanatious; (the maternal uncle of the writer); Eskandar Al Khoury Al Haddad. (Second Row) Hanna Zaghloul; Lotfallah Yazbak Beirut; Andraos Samaan; Nasef Al Haddad; Najib Hemya Majdeliya; Girgis Kanaan Bermana; S'eid Hemya; Mikhail Nasef Al Haddad; Daoud Kenaan Bermana.

Picture 6: The girls of the brotherhood (sitting) the widow of Boutros Wakim; Nada the widow of Hanna Nasef; Saady the wife of Youssef Shahin; Nejma the widow of Al Khoury Hanna; Jamila the widow of Tanious Nasef; the headmistress Sofia Abou Assly; Mariam the wife of Faragallah Freha; Eida the widow of Fares Shiban; Mariam the widow of Abdou Freha (the mother of the author), Mahaba the widow of Hanna Boulos; Zahra the wife of Youssef Saadallah. (Second Row) Fadoua Ghanatious; Jamila Faragallah; Malaka Freha; Eugenia the wife of NejmAssaf; Mariam the wife of Salebe Zein; Rashida the wife of Youssef Al Qasouf; Soltana Abdou Saadallah; Mariam Tanious Elias: Najiba Teama; Mariam Daoud Bou Assla; Toqla Boutros Sowan; Mariam the wife of Youssef Bou Heriz. (Third Row) Rose Watwat, Alice Andrea, Anisa Freha; Labiba Hanna Freha; Shafika Hanna Abdou; Olina Bou Assly; Nemnem the wife of Nasef Bou 'Oun; Hanna Abnou Assly; Saady Hanna Girgis; Rahil Abou Assly; Ester Youssef Nejm; Abla Tanious Nasef; Hana Girgis Asaad; Anisa the widow of Youssef Abou Assla; Khalil Freha.

Picture 7: A group of the Bachaalany folks and those from the Bachaalany family from Salima on the day they visited Salima, 1931.

Picture 8: The musical group of the Bachaalany Mar Girgis organization. 1931.

Picture 9: His excellency the Bishop Aghnatious Moubarak visiting Bchaaleh, the homeland of the forefathers. 1935.

Picture 10: The author in the beginning of his preisthood and his teacher Father Estephan Shedid.

Picture 11: The author with his family. The author in the middle with his brother Tanous and his son, Youssef Freha.

Picture 12: Habib Bachaalany, the brother of the author, with his daughter.

Picture 13: The mother of the author, his maternal uncle, and his brother Khalil.

Picture 14: Shokry Freha.

Picture 15: The House of Girgis Zein and his family.

Picture 16: The Wedding of Jemeyel Zein.

Events In The Author's Life During The Publication Process.

During the publishing of this book, we have experienced some events which we found essential to mention. They hold lessons for us as well as historical memories. They are the witnesses to the end of life. They are the days moving between happiness and sadness, with only God, the generous Lord, being the only constant. After his death, a human being leaves his good things behind. In the after life, his good deeds will be of benefit for him because it will provide him with eternal happiness, no more sorrow or pain. The events are : 1. The Golden Jubilee of our ordaination to the priesthood (1898 – 1948) 2. The Graduation in Law of our son and nephew, Youssef, the son of our brother, Tanous Freha Bachaalany. 3. The death of our maternal uncle, Mansour Ghanatious Bachaalany in Brazil. 4. The death of our brother, Khalil Freha Bachaalany on October 15, 1948.

We were organizing and getting ready to modestly celebrate the two first occasions with the parents, relatives, and various people, thanking God for this undescribed blessing. Then, we suffered the loss of our maternal uncle who was a tender father for us. We faced this incident with patience, recognizing God's plans, especially since he was eighty years old. However, the second event was a tragedy and a terrible loss. The beloved fellow was still a young man, one of the supports of the House. He was the father of a family which is badly in need of him. Thus, losing him came as a real shock which disturbed our peaceful life. It was almost enough to weaken our resolve, demoralize us, and prevent us from continuing this work. Nevertheless, our generous and almighty God helped us and consoled us with his mercy. He renewed within us, faith and hope. Our dear brother died and took with him the holy secrets of the resurrection. He sought the vestiges of the fathers and forefathers. He has called his three sons after the name of the sons of our great-grandfather, Abi Rezk Bachaalany: Abdou (Abdulallah), Rezk, and Younes.

I remained beside him during his illness and stood up beside his bed during the last hours. I was a priest in his death as well as a brother and a father in life. I encourage him, and so he died. He died while talking as he used to when he was powerful during his life. He noticed the interest of his brother, Tanous, and said to the doctor that he was spending everything he had, money and estate for the recovery of his brother. Then he turned around to those who were surrouding him and said: "Pity on anyone who doesn't have a brother Tanous Freha." After that he said to Youssef, his nephew: "Be courageous and a man. Take care and pay attention to your paternal cousins." The relatives, the people around us, and our generous friends have greatly expressed their condolences by sharing our tragedy.

Before that, they were gently visiting our brother during his illness. Then overcame the hard travel and came to the funeral in our village, Salima. That was a medicine for our grief and a sedative for our anguish. Therefore, they deserve to be greatly thanked and have a record of their honest sympathy and distinguished feelings. Also, we thank those friends in the country and abroad who sent their condolence letters, asking God to help them overcome the loss of a dear one.

My Assistants And Helpers

Finally, we thank God, may He be exalted, because he has provided us the means to accomplish this book. And we think that we should mention the people who helped us in the expenses of printing and publishing the book. Without their help, no one would have read it. They are: 1. Brother Habib Bachaalany, the expatriate journalist in Brazil. 2. Tanous Freha Bachaalany, the lawyer living in this country. 3. Our paternal cousin, Shokry Freha Bachaalany, the expatriate tradesman in Mexico City. 4. The generous citizens, the Zein brothers, great businessmen in Charleston, in the United States. 5. The Bachaalany organization of Los Angeles, in the United States, holding the expatriates together.

The History of the Maronite Families

We ask the Great Lord to be with us and give us the power and help to accomplish our historical project which we constantly mentioned in this book. It is a historical encyclopedia or dictionary of all the Maronite families, classified alphabetically. His Excellency, the Patriarch Mar Anton Areida, has said about it: "It is a big project". We hope that the generous Maronite families will help us publish this work. It will be an important event in the history of the families.   Beirut.   December 31, 1948.

- - - - -

Lebanon And Youssef Beik Karam

He is the superb hero we mentioned in the introduction of this book. We printed this book in 1924 and only ten copies remain. It has become rare. It contains important information about the history of Lebanon, the Lebanese issue. It has detailed informations about the hero of Lebanon. It contains original documents as well as corrected texts and current issues. Thus, whoever would like to buy a well bound copy, send the order with 25 lebanese Lira if it is inside Lebanon, and 10 dollars for outside the country. Send it to: Al Khoury Estephan Al Bachaalany – Salima – Al Metn – Lebanon.

- - - - -

The following addition to the original book is a letter which sadly speaks for itself, describing the destruction of Salima from the Syrian invasion.

"Dear loving cousin Paul;

After greeting you and asking about your health, I'd rather tell you that on the 29th of March, 1988, I received your letter which included the 150 dollar check and it had been opened because it had been sent by mistake to the city of Baalbeck to a person whose name is similar to mine. Fortunately, you have written my account number at the bank, so he returned the letter being not able to benefit out of the check. I'll delay putting it at the bank till my letter reaches you so that you may allow paying it. (i.e. because I had informed you previously to stop it.)

I'll tell you in details about what happened to us in Salima. When the Syrian Forces entered Lebanon, some of the military Christian forces helped them to enter Salima in 1976. They burned the Drouz's houses, stole them and killed seventy of them. With their help, we stayed in our houses and used to give them money and gifts and invite their officers to meals to keep us safe. My brothers and I, didn't hold weapons against anyone, but instead we were very helpful and saved not less than a hundred of the Drouz from death. When the Israel army entered Lebanon in 1982, specially to mountains inhabited by the Maronite and Drouz, the katash sent their militaryforces to the mountain regions. Then troubles began; they killed the Drouz who in their turn revenged and killed Christians. When the agreement of the 17th of May between Israel and Lebanon failed, Israel as well as Syrian began to help the Drouz openly. When Israel left the Lebanese mountain in 5 September 1983, strong battles began. So the Jews, Syrians and Palestinians united together to help the Drouz to force all Christians to abondon their houses and villages. There only remained the city of "Deir Al Kamar". After the slaughter of "Bmariam" (a small village near Salima) (40 Christians were murdered) (p.t.o.) occurred, I left Salima with my family on the 12th of August 1983 and came to Baabdat. My brothers Edward and Najib kept going to Salima from time to time. Later things were worse…till the 24th of September 1983 when my two brothers paid a large amount of money to save not less than 150 Christians from being slaughtered by the Drouz with the help of the Syrian Army and very few of the good Drouz. Since that time, they began to rob and burn houses or ruin them by exploding dynamites. My brothers couldn't take anything out of their richly furnished houses. With the help of Edward and one Syrian officer, only I could take some important things out of my house.

They like all others, left everything there, to go to Baabdat having only the clothes they wore. Later by God's will, they could rent a house and furnish it when the dollar cost 7 Lebanese pounds only.

With respect to me, as you know, my family is big, I sold an Iranian carpet which I could move secretly from Salima. This helped me a lot to face the lack of money and the loss of all our belongings and wide lands. You know what difficulty I faced from the letters I wrote to you specially when the dollar reached 600 Lebanese pounds.

Now Salima has all become ruined. There are only 8 of the criminals of the Drouz damaging the roofs of houses to sell their iron bars and share the money among them and the Syrian Army. Also the entrances of houses decorated with valuable stones were sold. They also cut the trees so that Salima has become a pile of stones. We now live eleven kilometers far from it and keep watching it without daring to go there. I'll seize any opportunity to send you some photographs of the ruined houses there, if I can take them. I don't know (p.t.o.) English, but there is a friendly, kind teacher who translates my letters. I'll also send you two books about our family written in Arabic with some English and French. My sons are learning English but they cannot write letters yet. I'm encouraging them to perfect it. Then they can tell you about everything. By this I wish you a very happy Easter with Christ who arose from death. I ask Him as well to keep you and your little son in good health. My mother, wife and brothers send you their warm kisses.

I kindly ask you to send me a copy of the photographs you took, in Salima when you visited Lebanon.
                    Sincerely your faithful cousin,   Michel Bachaalany"

This old photo is from the Editor's collection. This is Anthony Bishallany, referred to as the first immigrant from Lebanon to the United States.

*****

(Editor's Note: As a modern update about Bcheale, you might be interested in reading about the famous ancient olive trees of Bcheale. Just google **The Sisters** or **The Sisters Olive Trees of Noah**. They are a grove of sixteen olilve trees that date back thousands of years.)

*****

#1. The Castles of the Princes. Bche'le, 1928, and Salima.

Picture #2. The Castle of the Lam' Princes at Salima. 1861.   Prince Haidar Abi Al Lam'.

Picture 8: The musical group of the Bachaalany Gar Girgis organization. 1931.

Picture 3: The students of the Capuchin Fathers' school, at the monastery, in Salima, 1881.

Picture 4: The teachers and students of the School of Our Lady of Lourdes, in Salima, during the era of Father Anton Al Asmar (1906).

Picture 5: A community residing in Oliveira, Brazil. c. 1900.

Picture 6: The girls of the sisterhood, in front of the Blessed Virgin Church. 1914.

Picture 7. A group of the Bachaalany folks and those from the Bachaalany family from Salima on the day they visited Salima. 1931.

Picture 9: Bishop Aghnatous Moubarak visiting Bchaaleh, 1935.

Picture 10: The author in the beginning of his priesthood & Fr. Estephan Shedid.

Picture 11: The author with his family.

Picture 12: Habib Bachaalany, the brother of the author, with his daughter.

Picture 13: The author's mother, maternal uncle, and brother Khalil.

Picture 14: Shokry Freha.

Picture 15: The House of Girgis Zein and his family.

Picture 16: The Wedding of Jemeyel Zein

The Knieser Genealogy
(from page 240-241)

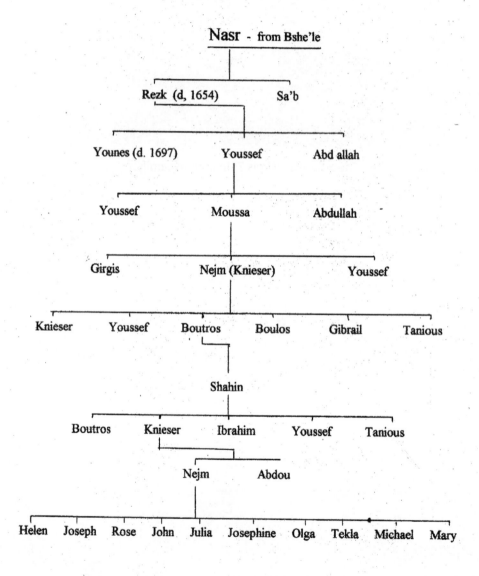

Milton Keynes UK
Ingram Content Group UK Ltd.
UKHW031811041223
433765UK00014B/1265

9 783732 388622